Towards a Neutral Formulary Apportionment System in Regional Integration

EUCOTAX Series on European Taxation

VOLUME 71

Series Editors

Introduction

EUCOTAX (European Universities Cooperating on Taxes) is a network of tax institutes currently consisting of eleven universities: WU (Vienna University of Economics and Business) in Austria, Katholieke Universiteit Leuven in Belgium, Corvinus University of Budapest, Hungary, Université Paris-I Panthéon-Sorbonne in France, Universität Osnabrück in Germany, Libera, Università Internazionale di Studi Sociali in Rome (and Università degli Studi di Bologna for the research part), in Italy, Fiscaal Instituut Tilburg at Tilburg University in the Netherlands, Universidad de Barcelona in Spain, Uppsala University in Sweden, Queen Mary and Westfield College at the University of London in the United Kingdom, and Georgetown University in Washington DC, United States of America. The network aims at initiating and coordinating both comparative education in taxation, through the organization of activities such as winter courses and guest lectures, and comparative research in the field, by means of joint research projects, international conferences and exchange of researchers between various countries.

Contents/Subjects

The EUCOTAX series covers a wide range of topics in European tax law. For example tax treaties, EC case law, tax planning, exchange of information and VAT. The series is well-known for its high-quality research and practical solutions.

Objective

The series aims to provide insights on new developments in European taxation.

Readership

Practitioners and academics dealing with European tax law.

Frequency of Publication

2-3 new volumes published each year.

The titles published in this series are listed at the end of this volume.

Towards a Neutral Formulary Apportionment System in Regional Integration

Shu-Chien Chen

Wolters Kluwer

Published by:
Kluwer Law International B.V.
PO Box 316
2400 AH Alphen aan den Rijn
The Netherlands
E-mail: lrs-sales@wolterskluwer.com
Website: www.wolterskluwer.com/en/solutions/kluwerlawinternational

Sold and distributed by:
Wolters Kluwer Legal & Regulatory U.S.
920 Links Avenue
Landisville, PA 17538
United States of America
E-mail: customer.service@wolterskluwer.com

ISBN 978-94-035-3276-9

e-Book: ISBN 978-94-035-3296-7
web-PDF: ISBN 978-94-035-3306-3

Table of Contents

List of Figures

List of Tables

List of Abbreviations

ALP	Arm's Length Principle
AOA	Authorised OECD Approach
APA	Advance Pricing Agreement
ATAD	Anti-Tax Avoidance Directive
B2B	Business-to-Business
B2C	Business-to-Consumer
BEFIT	Business in Europe: Framework for Income Taxation
BEPS	Base Erosion and Profit Shifting
CCCTB	Common Consolidated Corporate Tax Base
CCTB	Common Corporate Tax Base
CEN	Capital Export Neutrality
CEO	Chief Executive Officer
CFC	Controlled Foreign Corporation
CFO	Chief Financial Officer
CIN	Capital Import Neutrality
CIT	Corporate Income Tax
CJEU (ECJ)	Court of Justice of the European Union (European Court of Justice)
CMU	Capital Market Union
CON	Capital Ownership Neutrality
COO	Chief Operating Officer
COP	Cost of Performance
DBCFT	Destination-Based Cash Flow Tax
DCF	Discounted Cash Flow
DEMPE	Development, Enhancement, Maintenance, Protection, and Exploration
DST	Digital Services Tax

DTC	Double Taxation Convention
DWL	Deadweight Loss
E&P	Exploration and Production
EEA	European Economic Area
EU	European Union
FA	Formulary Apportionment
FDI	Foreign Direct Investment
FICA	Federal Insurance Contributions Act
FTB	Franchise Tax Board
FTE	Full Time Equivalent
FUTA	Federal Unemployment Tax Act
GAAR	General Anti-Avoidance Rule
GATT	General Agreement on Tariffs and Trade
GDP	Gross Domestic Product
GST	Goods and Services Tax
HTVI	Hard-to-Value Intangibles
IaaS	Infrastructure as a Service
IAS	International Accounting Standard
IFRS	International Financial Reporting Standards
IHC	Intangible Holding Companies
ILO	International Labour Organization
IRC	Internal Revenue Code
IRS	Internal Revenue Service
KERT	Key Entrepreneurial Risk-Taking
KPI	Kmart Properties, Incorporated
KPL	Kensai Pipeline
MAP	Mutual Agreement Procedure
MLE	Multiple Location Entities
MLI	Multilateral Instrument Treaty
MN	Market Neutrality
MNE	Multinational Enterprise
MTC	Multistate Tax Commission
NAFTA	North American Free Trade Agreement
OCS	Outer Continental Shelf
OECD	Organiszation for Economic Co-operation and Development
PaaS	Platform as a Service
PE	Permanent Establishment
PEO	Professional Employer Organization
POEM	Place of Effective Management
PPT	Principal Purpose Test

R&D	Research and Development
REIT	Real Estate Investment Trust
RPS	Regulated Profit Splitting
SA	Separate Accounting
SAAR	Specific Anti-Avoidance Rules
SaaS	Software as a Service
SDP	Significant Digital Presence
SES	Single European Sky
SINAA	Solicitation, Investigation, Negotiation, Approval, and Administration
SLE	Single Location Entities
SPE	Special Purpose Entity
SPF	significant people functions
TEC	Treaty Establishing the European Community
TFEU	Treaty on the Functioning of the European Union
TP	Transfer Pricing
TPSM	Transactional Profit Split Method
TRADE	Trabajador Autonomo Dependiente Economicamente (economically dependent self-employee)
TRIPS	Agreement on Trade-Related Aspects of Intellectual Property Rights
UDITPA	Uniform Division of Income for Tax Purposes Act
UPS	United Parcel Service
UN	United Nations
VAT	Value Added Tax
VCA	Value Chain Analysis

Preface

Formulary Apportionment (FA) has been a less-accepted perspective on dividing taxing rights on cross-border economic activities in the international tax regime, although there are already a few subnational level FA systems. However, the latest development of the international tax reform efforts, including the Organisation for Economic Co-operation and Development's (OECD's) Pillar One Proposal and the European Union's (EU's) tax reform project 'Business in Europe: Framework for Income Taxation' (BEFIT), demonstrates that FA as a possible option to address the problem of Base Erosion and Profit Shifting (BEPS) is gaining increasing acceptance and attention. The core puzzle remains: when FA becomes a feasible option, what will be important for a good FA system? This book focuses specifically on the EU.

This book revisits existing principles and theories in the international tax regime. The aim of this research is to rebuild the normative framework for the EU's tax reform. Here the key findings are to build a reformed tax neutrality framework for the EU's FA regime. First, corporate tax should be analysed not merely from the perspective of deadweight loss (DWL) but also from the conceptual measurement of public benefits. Public benefits are justification to tax. In this way, the meaning of 'tax neutrality' is combined with the benefit principle. Taxpayers' economic activities are indicators and evidence of the corresponding public benefits being used and mobilized. Second, the government's public benefits are not unlimited, and therefore taxation should not exceed the public benefits provided. Only when tax exceeds the public benefits is the part in excess DWL.

The normative framework for the EU's FA incorporates two elements: the public benefit principle and market neutrality (MN). Based on this benefit-based MN framework, taxpayers' input and output activities justify the selection of factors for the EU's FA regime. Therefore, the sales factor, the labour factor, and the asset factor are all necessary for EU formula and should be weighted equally. The sales factor represents the public benefits of maintaining the customers' market; the labour factor represents the public benefits of maintaining the labour market; and the asset factor represents the public benefits of providing local non-human resources. Following the same rationale, the sales factor should follow the sales-by-destination rationale; the labour factor should follow the workforce by function-performing rationale; and the asset factor should follow the utilization rationale. This three-factor FA regime would also be consistent with the goal of aligning value creation and taxation because each weighting factor represents the value-creation chain. Accordingly, the taxable nexus for the EU's FA should use 'factor presence nexus' instead of traditional permanent establishment (PE).

By adopting this three-factor structure as the standard formula, the special industry formulas should be designed based on the three-factor structure as the embodiment of the three-factor standard formula with modifications in each weighting factor when there is a special corresponding public interest. Namely, managing the monetary capital for the financial industry; addressing the potential resource in the case of the extractive industry; and managing the departure and the arrival for the international transportation industry.

When the EU's FA regime is designed according to the benefit-based MN framework, the need to invoke the safeguard clause to adjust unfair apportionment results ad hoc would be largely reduced.

Acknowledgement

It takes a village to raise a kid, and this rule applies to obtaining a PhD degree. This book is based on my PhD thesis at Erasmus University Rotterdam, the Netherlands. I could not have completed this book without the generous support and continuing encouragement from my family and friends, in Taiwan and the Netherlands. Thank you all for being patient and having confidence in me, even when I had doubts about myself. My husband and my best friend, Andrew, is the most important support in this project, as well as the support of our household for taking care of our beloved daughter Elisabeth. My parents and parents-in-law are always supportive of my academic dreams.

I would like to thank my PhD mentors Professor Maarten de Wilde and Professor Reinout Kok for guiding my research while giving me complete academic freedom. Thank you for being open-minded and believing in me in the summer of 2017 and during the chaotic COVID-19 pandemic period from 2020 to 2021. It is unforgettable. I also want to thank Wilma Puper and colleagues for their administrative assistance.

I would like to thank my examination committee: Professor Sigrid Hemels, Professor Peter Kavelaars, and Professor Daniel Smit. Thanks for all the constructive suggestions that make the manuscript more comprehensive. I would like to thank members of the plenary doctoral committee: Professor Irma Mosquera Valderrama, Professor Hans van den Hurk, and Professor Henk Vording.

Because of conducting this research, I have had precious opportunities to travel to different places, meet many excellent people, and receive their help. Please allow me to mention them separately.

I would like to thank Dr Carel Smith for organizing the Talent Programme at Leiden Law School where I have started to prepare my PhD research. I would also like to thank Professor Frans Pennings, Professor Ashley Terlouw, Professor Janneke Gerards, Professor Piet Hein van Kempen, Professor Reuven S. Avi-Yonah, Professor Walter Hellerstein, Professor David Gamage, Professor Darien Shanske, Professor Steve Shay, Professor Sol Picciotto, Professor Sunita Jogarajan, and Professor Madeleine Merkx for making time to discuss my research with me.

My PhD research has compared EU and US FA systems, and I am very lucky to have experiences in the US and in Brussels. I would like to express my gratitude to the University of Amsterdam for supporting me, so I could take the summer course on state taxation in California. Professor William Byrnes from Texas A&M University School of Law introduced me to several US tax experts in person, and thus I am so privileged to discuss US state taxation with experts: Benjamin Miller and Professor Richard Pomp. I would also like to thank Dr Adam Zalasinski for being my supervisor in my traineeship at DG Taxud at the European Commission where I learned firsthand knowledge about EU tax law.

I would like to thank those who gave me teaching opportunities: Professor Maarten de Wilde from Erasmus University Rotterdam, Dr Kati Cseres from the University of Amsterdam, Professor Haile Gebreselassie and Ioana Bratu from Vrije University Amsterdam, and Professor Yingfeng Long from Lixin University. Teaching has been the most rewarding experience during this journey.

I would like to also thank my friends for their encouragement: Brigitte Spiegeler, Jos Hellebrekers, Germaine Gekwest, Elise Okhuizen, Yu-Wen Chen, Ying Cui, Yu Chen, Yu-Ching Chen, Jung-Chin Chang, Jingye Li, Candice Lin, Po-Liang Lin, Huei Chen, Ashley Wu, Lawrence Hu, Mandy Huang, Margret Amirkhan, Leijie Wei, Duoqi Xu, Penny Peng, Sarah Yuan, Shaomei Chen, Shu Li, Wei Xiong, Jie Wang, Emma Zhang, Ran Chang, Shengnan Jia, Haiyang Yu, Katarzyna Fras, Roland Pierik, Iris Bergwerff, Irene Koster, Cecilia Liu, Rinze van Minnen, and Franco Roccatagliata.

Last but not least, I sincerely thank Stephen Machon and Erasmus Fiscal Studies (EFS) BV for supporting me in completing the final stages of my PhD.

CHAPTER 1
Introduction

we had everything before us, we had nothing before us, we were all going direct to Heaven, we were all going direct the other way...

A Tale of Two Cities[1]

1.1 THE STARTING POINT OF THE RESEARCH

1.1.1 The Background: The EU's Efforts to Conduct Its Own International Tax Reform

The background of this research is the ongoing debate of a revolutionary reform of the traditional international tax regime. Formulary Apportionment (FA) is one possible option, even though it is also a politically controversial option and shrouded in doubt. This book revisits the debates and theories around an FA system in order to clarify some theoretical foundations.

This book further focuses on the Common Consolidated Corporate Tax Base (CCCTB) Directive Proposal,[2] the EU's corporate tax reform project of adopting FA,

1. Charles Dickens, *A Tale of Two Cities* (Dover Publications 1999).
2. The European Commission on their official website has published the development and legislative record of the CCCTB and CCTB: https://ec.europa.eu/taxation_customs/business/company-tax/common-consolidated-corporate-tax-base-ccctb_en.

   The European Commission has tried twice to release the CCCTB Directive Proposal in 2011 and 2016, respectively: the CCCTB Directive Proposal (2011), European Commission, 'Proposal for a Council Directive on a Common Consolidated Corporate Tax Base (CCCTB) {SEC(2011) 315} {SEC(2011) 316}' and the CCCTB Directive Proposal (2016), European Commission, 'Proposal for a COUNCIL DIRECTIVE on a Common Consolidated Corporate Tax Base (CCCTB) {SWD(2016) 341 Final} {SWD(2016) 342 Final}'.

which dates back to the late twentieth century and early 2000s[3] and has continued to evolve up to 2021.[4]

Moreover, this book rebuilds the normative framework and further assesses existing CCCTB proposal(s) from the normative framework of 'benefit-based market neutrality', which is elaborated in Chapter 2.

To understand and analyse the current CCCTB Directive Proposal and its development,[5] it is necessary to understand the CCCTB Directive Proposal in a broad

3. The origin of the CCCTB project can be traced to the European Commission's Ruding Report on identifying the company taxation problems in the EU in 1992, Commission of the European Communities (eds), *Report of the Committee of Independent Experts on Company Taxation* (Ruding Report) (Office for Official Publications of the European Communities 1992).

   Regarding comments about the Ruding Report: Michael Devereux, The Ruding Committee Report: An Economic Assessment, 13 Fiscal Studies 96 (1992); Malcolm Gammie, *The Ruding Committee Report: An Initial Response* (Institute for Fiscal Studies London 1992); Brigitte Knobbe-Keuk, Ruding Committee Report – An Impressive Vision of European Company Taxation for the Year 2000, 1 EC Tax Review 22 (1992); Charles E McLure Jr, Coordinating Business Taxation in the Single European Market: The Ruding Committee Report 1 EC Tax Review 13 (1992); Frans Vanistendael, The Ruding Committee Report: A Personal View 13 Fiscal Studies 85 (1992); Frans Vanistendael, Comments on the Ruding Committee Report, 1 EC Tax Review 3 (1992).

   Regarding the company taxation problem in the late twentieth century, *see* the European Commission's staff working paper: Office for Official Publications of the European Communities (ed.), *Company Taxation in the Internal Market* (European Commission 2002).
4. In May 2021, the European Commission issued its new tax reform package (BEFIT) in the context of the post-COVID-19 outbreak. The European Commission aims to adopt the improved EU-wide FA system as a new proposal in 2023, which will continue the goal of pursuing FA but will replace and withdraw the pending reform projects, i.e., the Common Consolidated Corporate Tax Base (CCCTB) Directive Proposal. European Commission, Communication from the Commission to the European Parliament and the Council: Business Taxation for the 21st Century, COM(2021) 251 final, 11.

   Although the current CCCTB will be eventually withdrawn, the new reform package of BEFIT has the same character as CCCTB: they both aim to create an EU-level FA system for allocating the taxing rights between the Member States. In short, BEFIT continues but aims to upgrade and improve the work done while preparing the current CCCTB Directive Proposal.
5. Discussions on the CCCTB project before the 2011 version of CCCTB Directive Proposal being released: Antony Ting, Multilateral Formulary Apportionment Model-A Reality Check, Australian Tax Forum (2010); Joann Martens Weiner, Practical Aspects of Implementing Formulary Apportionment in the European Union, 8 Florida Tax Review 629 (2006); Norbert Herzig, Manuel Teschke & Christian Joisten, Between Extremes: Merging the Advantages of Separate Accounting and Unitary Taxation, 38 Intertax 334 (2010); HTPM Van den Hurk, The Common Consolidated Corporate Tax Base: A Desirable Alternative to a Flat EU Corporate Income Tax? 4 Bulletin for International Fiscal Documentation 260 (2011); Joann Martens Weiner, Formula One – The Race to Find a Common Formula to Apportion the EU Tax Base, 17 EC Tax Review 100 (2008); Michael Lang & others, *Common Consolidated Corporate Tax Base* (Linde 2008); Lilian V Faulhaber, Sovereignty, Integration and Tax Avoidance in the European Union: Striking the Proper Balance, 48 Columbia Journal of Transnational Law 177 (2009); Nerissa Haskic, The Arm's Length Principle and the CCCTB (Common Consolidated Corporate Tax Base): Solutions to Transfer Pricing Issues for Individual Countries and the European Union?, 19 Revenue Law Journal 71 (2009); Ioanna Mitroyanni, *Integration Approaches to Group Taxation in the European Internal Market* (Wolters Kluwer Law & Business 2008), at Chapter 8; Ioanna Mitroyanni & Chiara Putzolu, CCCTB and Business Reorganizations: The Common Consolidated Corporate Tax Base and Business Reorganizations, 37 Intertax 436 (2009).

   For the comments of scholars from different Member States after the 2011 version of CCCTB Directive proposal was released: Pierre-Jean Douvier & Mathieu Daudé, France-Common Consolidated Corporate Tax Base, 18 International Transfer Pricing Journal (2011); Danny

context. The context involves: failures of the current international tax regime in the general level, problems of 'Base Erosion and Profit Shifting (BEPS)'[6] recognized by the OECD, as well as establishment of the EU internal market.[7] The CCCTB is also the EU's tax reform response[8] to addressing the failures of the current international tax regime and the BEPS campaign since 2013. The consensus to address BEPS problems has become one of the goals of the current CCCTB Directive Proposal.[9]

The necessity to conduct an international tax reform is obvious. The current international tax regimes and practices, developed since the early twentieth century,[10] are now heavily criticized for failing to fairly levy corporate tax on giant multinational taxpayers in the current globalized and digitalized world.[11] Such failure is systematic, due to a lack of coordination, complexity, and various mismatches of the current national law systems and due to the rapid development of technology and the digital economy. Since 2013, OECD has been working on the BEPS project, i.e., the tax reform

---

Oosterhoff & Bo Wingerter, Netherlands – The Dutch View on the Common Consolidated Corporate Tax Base, 18 International Transfer Pricing Journal 352 (2011); Monica Erasmus-Koen, International-Common Consolidated Corporate Tax Base: A 'Fair Share' of the Tax Base?, 18 International Transfer Pricing Journal 237 (2011).

For economic analysis after the 2011 version of CCCTB Directive proposal was released, *see* Christoph Spengel & York Zöllkau (eds), *Common Corporate Tax Base (CC(C)TB) and Determination of Taxable Income: An International Comparison* (Springer 2012). Collection of conference essays on CCCTB, *see* DM Weber & Amsterdam Centre for Tax Law (eds), *CCCTB: Selected Issues* (Kluwer Law International 2012); D Weber & Jan van de Streek (eds), *The EU Common Consolidated Corporate Tax Base: Critical Analysis* (Kluwer Law International BV 2018); Ana Paula Dourado (ed.), *Movement of Persons and Tax Mobility in the EU: Changing Winds* (IBFD 2013); Michael Lang & others (eds), *Corporate Income Taxation in Europe: The Common Consolidated Corporate Tax Base (CCCTB) and Third Countries* (Edward Elgar 2013).

As to the UK's discussions about CCCTB, before and after Brexit, *see* Christiana HJI Panayi, *The Common Consolidated Corporate Tax Base and the UK Tax System* (Institute for Fiscal Studies 2011); Peter Cussons & Andrew Casley, United Kingdom – Reactions to the Common Consolidated Corporate Tax Base Proposals of the European Commission, 18 International Transfer Pricing Journal 358 (2011); Joann Weiner & others, *The CCCTB, Brexit, and Unitary Taxation, Proceedings. Annual Conference on Taxation and Minutes of the Annual Meeting of the National Tax Association* (National Tax Association 2016); Judith Freedman, Tax and Brexit, 33 Oxford Review of Economic Policy S79 (2017).

6. The OECD's BEPS project covers the most controversial issues of the international tax regime. The official website for the BEPS is https://www.oecd.org/tax/aggressive/beps-actions.htm; for a review of the existing literature on BEPS, until 2018, *see* Nadine Riedel, Quantifying International Tax Avoidance: A Review of the Academic Literature, 69 Review of Economics 169 (2018).
7. The problem of Base Erosion and Profit Shifting is detrimental to EU Member States. Empirical data estimated that 40% of foreign profits are shifted to tax havens, and non-tax haven EU Member States are the 'losers' of BEPS scenarios. *See* Thomas R Tørsløv, Ludvig S Wier & Gabriel Zucman, The Missing Profits of Nations, National Bureau of Economic Research Working Papers No. 24701 (2018).
8. For a short overview of the EU's responses to the BEPS until 2018, *see* Arnaud de Graaf & Klaas-Jan Visser, BEPS: Will the Current Commitments and Peer Review Model Prove Effective?, 27 EC Tax Review 36 (2018).
9. *See* the preamble of the 2016 CCCTB Directive Proposal.
10. For the early history of the international tax regime and critical remarks, *see* Michael J Graetz, The David R. Tillinghast Lecture Taxing International Income: Inadequate Principles, Outdated Concepts, and Unsatisfactory Policies, 54 Tax Law Review 261 (2000).
11. Steven A Bank, The Globalization of Corporate Tax Reform, 40 Pepperdine Law Review 1307 (2012).

campaign especially on multinational enterprise (MNE) taxpayers to address the systematic failures of the international tax regime.

The failures of the current international tax law regime trigger rigorous discussions on enhancing taxation on the digital economy, especially addressed in BEPS Action 1. There are legislative proposals concerning the digital economy under EU law[12] as well as national tax laws.[13] These proposals all demonstrate the consensus of sovereign states and the general public that taxation of new rising Internet giants, such as Google,[14] Facebook,[15] Apple,[16] and Uber/Airbnb[17] is not sufficient.

Moreover, the current transfer pricing (TP) practices, including the arm's length principle (ALP), are accused of becoming the source of tax avoidance and complexities.[18] ALP is criticized for being unrealistic because comparable transactions could not

---

12. Georg Kofler & Julia Sinnig, Equalization Taxes and the EU's 'Digital Services Tax' 47 Intertax 176 (2019).

    See also Chapter 3.5 of this book. The relationship between EU's Digital Service Tax (DST) and the CCCTB is questioned. DST as such is criticized as infringing EU fundamental freedoms, *see* Christina Dimitropoulou, The Digital Services Tax and Fundamental Freedoms: Appraisal under the Doctrine of Measures Having Equivalent Effect to Quantitative Restrictions, 47 Intertax 201 (2019).
13. For example, in March 2019, France followed the European Commission's Digital Service Tax Proposal to consider its national digital service tax (the 'GAFA' tax, referring to Google, Apple, Facebook, Amazon), *see* https://taxinsights.ey.com/archive/archive-news/french-government-submits-draft-bill-on-digital-services.aspx.
14. To address the issue of internet-based MNE taxpayers such as 'Google', several jurisdictions have even started to levy 'Google tax', *see* Reuven S Avi-Yonah, Three Steps Forward, One Step Back? Reflections on 'Google Taxes' and the Destination-Based Corporate Tax, 2016 Nordic Tax Journal 69 (2016).
15. Scholars also notice 'free usage' of this digital service, such as Facebook and Google, *see* Michael P Devereux & John Vella, Debate: Implications of Digitalization for International Corporate Tax Reform, 46 Intertax 550 (2018).
16. Antony Ting, ITax-Apple's International Tax Structure and the Double Non-Taxation Issue, British Tax Review 40 (2014); John Sokatch, Transfer-Pricing with Software Allows for Effective Circumvention of Subpart F Income: Google's 'Sandwich' Costs Taxpayers Millions, The International Lawyer 725 (2011).
17. Regarding taxing the sharing economy such as Uber or Airbnb, *see* Carrie Brandon Elliot, Taxation of the Sharing Economy: Recurring Issues, 72 Bulletin for International Taxation (2018); Stephen R Miller, First Principles for Regulating the Sharing Economy, 53 Harvard Journal on Legislation 147 (2016); Devereux & Vella, *supra* n. 15.

    In Europe, the difficulty of regulating and taxing sharing economy is obvious. *See* Katerina Pantazatou, Taxation of the Sharing Economy in the European Union, in Nestor M Davidson, John Infranca & Michèle Finck (eds), *The Cambridge Handbook of Law and Regulation of the Sharing Economy* (Cambridge University Press 2018); Vassilis Hatzopoulos & Sofia Roma, Caring for Sharing? The Collaborative Economy under EU Law, 54 Common Market Law Review 81 (2017).
18. Such criticisms against the transfer pricing practice are enormous. Here I name a few as examples, though this book does not completely agree with the approach of blaming the only black sheep. Some critics result in advocating the unitary taxation/FA, such as Sol Picciotto, *Towards Unitary Taxation of Transnational Corporations* (Tax Justice Network London 2012).

    Other critics claim that transfer pricing rules are already manipulated by MNE taxpayers to conduct tax avoidance, especially regarding intangibles. Prem Sikka & Hugh Willmott, The Dark Side of Transfer Pricing: Its Role in Tax Avoidance and Wealth Retentiveness, 21 Critical Perspectives on Accounting 342 (2010); Raymond W Baker, *Capitalism's Achilles Heel: Dirty Money and How to Renew the Free-Market System* (John Wiley & Sons 2005); Joel Barker, Kwadwo Asare & Sharon Brickman, Transfer Pricing as a Vehicle in Corporate Tax Avoidance, 33 Journal of Applied Business Research (JABR) 9 (2017); In a developing country, tax

be found.[19] So BEPS Actions 8, 9, and 10 especially deal with the hard cases in the TP guidelines: intangibles, capital and risks.[20] The pre-BEPS TP practices have created problems and disputes and need to be reformed.[21]

The current international tax reform project led by OECD/G20 includes various subjects on corporate tax of 'giant' multinational taxpayers, so the BEPS project has 15 action plans, but there does not yet seem to be a coherent underlying guiding principle for sovereign states, except for the strong consensus on 'taxing a fair share'. In addition, the reforms of the BEPS action plans are still based on several concepts from the traditional framework and try to fix the problems. Therefore, the BEPS reform attempts do not fully deliver the original promises to improve TP[22] or the digital economy.[23] For many critics, the BEPS action plans do not deal with the systematic failures but preclude effective coordination.[24]

This book (re)builds the normative framework that can select good practices and prevent problematic experiences from different law regimes and tax reforms in the past, especially for the EU. The present is the best time to reform the international tax regime because of the consensus; though it still could be the worst time because there

avoidance via transfer pricing also exists, *see* Olatunde Julius Otusanya, The Role of Multinational Companies in Tax Evasion and Tax Avoidance: The Case of Nigeria, 22 Critical Perspectives on Accounting 316 (2011).

19. Reuven S Avi-Yonah, Kimberly A Clausing & Michael C Durst, Allocating Business Profits for Tax Purposes: A Proposal to Adopt a Formulary Profit Split, 5 Florida Tax Review 9 (2009).
20. *See* the OECD BEPS Project Action 8-10 and the general view, Michael Lang & Alfred Storck, *Transfer Pricing in a Post-BEPS World* (Kluwer Law International 2016).
21. There are also transfer pricing researchers arguing that transfer pricing rules can still address the challenges in the digital economy, as long as they are correctly applied, *see* Raffaele Petruzzi & Svitlana Buriak, Addressing the Tax Challenges of the Digitalization of the Economy – A Possible Answer in the Proper Application of the Transfer Pricing Rules, 72 Bulletin for International Taxation (2018). Petruzzi and Buriak argue that a proper functional analysis in combination with a new PE concept would be a feasible solution. As to the functional analysis, *see* Chapter 6 of this book. In my view, transfer pricing practices provide various perspectives to provide how business activities are performed and how value is created. Taking away the artificiality, transfer pricing practices are not the enemy of an FA system, and vice versa.
22. For example, Brauner criticized that BEPS actions on transfer pricing are not quite successful but create confusion. *See* Yariv Brauner, Changes? BEPS, Transfer Pricing for Intangibles, and CCAS, in Global Transfer Pricing Conference-WU-Proceedings (2016). Other criticism, Mindy Herzfeld, The Case Against BEPS: Lessons for Tax Coordination, 21 Florida Tax Review 1 (2017), at 52.
23. Piergiorgio Valente, Digital Revolution-Tax Revolution, 72 Bulletin for International Taxation (2018); Marcel Olbert & Christoph Spengel, International Taxation in the Digital Economy: Challenge Accepted, 9 World Tax Journal 3 (2017).
24. Mindy Herzfeld, The Case Against BEPS: Lessons for Tax Coordination, 21 Florida Tax Review 1 (2017); Tsilly Dagan, *International Tax Policy: Between Competition and Cooperation* (CUP 2018); some other criticism of the BEPS project, Eva Escribano, Is the OECD/G20 BEPS Initiative Heading in the Right Direction? Some Forgotten (and Uncomfortable) Questions, 71 Bulletin for International Taxation (2017); Observations on the BEPS policy options on tax authorities, arguing that non-tax haven authorities focus on each other instead of tax haven jurisdictions, *see* Tørsløv, Wier & Zucman, *supra* n. 7.

    Reflections on and criticism of the BEPS project's conservative actions, *see* Arthur J Cockfield, Shaping International Tax Law and Policy in Challenging Times, 54 Stanford Journal of International Law 223 (2018). Cockfield argued that for addressing BEPS problems in addition to enhanced tax administration, substantial tax laws should be amended, though he does not support adopting an FA system as an alternative.

are still rigid practices and assumptions of international tax law, and it is difficult to let go of outdated practices and select those good alternatives to keep.[25]

The starting point of this book, however, is from the perspective of identifying the systematic failures of the international tax regime and the conservative feature of the BEPS reform, not from claiming and blaming (or even naming and shaming) MNE taxpayers or tax haven jurisdictions[26] for abusing international tax law. Instead, this book aims to indicate that the current failures are systematic problems resulting from rapid developments in the economy and technology. A systematic solution is necessary to address systematic problems. Therefore, accepting an alternative assumption of considering dividing taxing rights is necessary.

1.1.2 The Problem Statement: Understanding the CCCTB in the Context of the Failures of the International Tax Regime and Its Reform

There has been an inherent dilemma of the international tax regime from the very beginning: double taxation and double non-taxation. For MNE taxpayers, they have concerns of 'double taxation' levied on the same income by different jurisdictions. For tax authorities, they have concerns about 'double non-taxation'[27] or 'stateless income'[28] created by taxpayers' aggressive tax planning scenarios or simply due to disparities of national laws.

The concern about double taxation has always been the main focus. In the early twentieth century, the League of Nations tried to address the first concern about 'double taxation'.[29] Later, the expert groups of the OECD and the United Nations (UN) have developed model conventions as solutions to mitigate the problem of double taxation. States usually start their bilateral tax treaty negotiations using the OECD or UN model conventions as the starting point. The OECD model convention (updated regularly every 5-10 years) and the OECD's experts' opinion have become the *lingua franca* of international tax scholars and practitioners. The model convention for

25. For example, in response to the BEPS project, there are several policy options discussed, including FA, such as International Monetary Fund, *Corporate Taxation in the Global Economy* (IMF 2019). The discussions about FA by IMF are negative.
26. Tax havens refer to some jurisdictions which do not exchange information with tax authorities and are claimed to be the source of tax avoidance or tax evasion. The EU has published a tax haven blacklist since 2017 https://ec.europa.eu/taxation_customs/tax-common-eu-list_en.
27. Avi-Yonah's work analysed the historical development of international tax law and policy in US and demonstrates that, double taxation and non-double taxation are actually both the core concern since the early twentieth century when the international tax law was initiated and developed. Reuven S Avi-Yonah, All of a Piece Throughout: The Four Ages of US International Taxation, 25 Virginia Tax Review 313 (2005).
28. Kleinbard's work has explored the idea of 'stateless income' extensively especially from the perspective of US multinationals. Edward D Kleinbard, Stateless Income, 11 Florida Tax Review 699 (2011); Edward D Kleinbard, The Lessons of Stateless Income, 65 Tax Law Review 99 (2011); Edward D Kleinbard, Stateless Income and Its Remedies, USC CLASS Research Papers Series No. CLASS14-12 (2014).
29. On League of Nations' work on eliminating double taxation, *see* Sunita Jogarajan, *Double Taxation and the League of Nations* (Cambridge University Press 2018).

eliminating double taxation and relevant soft laws represent the efforts expended to solve the concern about 'double taxation'.

The concern of non-double taxation was relatively obscure at first, but now it is also under the spotlights and discussed in the context of 'combating tax avoidance'. The OECD's BEPS project and Multilateral Instrument Treaty (MLI)[30] have tried to address the concern about 'double non-taxation' and stateless income planned by MNE taxpayers.[31] The whole BEPS project attempted to address various multinational taxpayers' tax avoidance scenarios that have existed for decades. Briefly speaking, the BEPS project claims that traditional international tax law is too outdated and that there should be a global tax reform.

To cover the concepts of both double taxation and double non-taxation, some scholars argue that the 'single tax principle'[32] in international tax law should apply; while some other scholars cast doubts as to the existence of the single tax principle for being too obscure and not really explaining the superiority of a 'single tax'.[33] On the one hand, the advocates of the single tax principle argue that being subject to 'single taxation' means that income earned from a cross-border transaction involving two jurisdictions should not be less or more favourable than the domestic income. On the other hand, the critics of the single tax principle argue that recognizing this principle would go beyond a nation's capacity,[34] oversimplifying the different concepts around the concept of a single tax,[35] thus mixing the different questions of 'how much tax' and 'how many times'.[36] Even in the context of a single internal market like the EU, it is also

30. For the history of a multilateral tax treaty, *see* DM Broekhuijsen, *A Multilateral Tax Treaty: Designing an Instrument to Modernise International Tax Law* (Kluwer Law International 2018); criticism of the MLI for being complex and uncertain, *see* David Kleist, The Multilateral Convention to Implement Tax Treaty Related Measures to Prevent BEPS - Some Thoughts on Complexity and Uncertainty, 2018 Nordic Tax Journal 31 (2018).

    The official website of MLI is https://www.oecd.org/tax/treaties/multilateral-convention-to-implement-tax-treaty-related-measures-to-prevent-beps.htm. The number of signing states are continuously increasing.

31. Jogarajan, *supra* n. 29. According to Jogarajan's research, experts in 1920 were aware of this issue: 'The possibility of profit-shifting and double non-taxation had already been recognized by the 1925 Experts almost 90 years ago.'

32. Reuven S Avi-Yonah, Who Invented the Single Tax Principle?: An Essay on the History of US Treaty Policy, New York Law School Law Review 59, no. 2 (2015); Reuven S Avi-Yonah, Full Circle? The Single Tax Principle, BEPS, and the New US Model, U of Michigan Public Law Research Paper 1 (2015).

33. For criticism of the single tax principle, *see* Daniel Shaviro, The Two Faces of the Single Tax Principle, 41 Brook. J. Int'l L. (2016); Julie Roin, Taxation Without Coordination, 31 Journal of Legal Studies S61 (2002); Mitchell A Kane, Strategy and Cooperation in National Responses to International Tax Arbitrage, 53 Emory Law Journal 89 (2004); Adam H Rosenzweig, Harnessing the Costs of International Tax Arbitrage, 26 Virginia Tax Review 555 (2006). Most contributors from J Wheeler (ed.), *Single Taxation?* (IBFD 2018) are critics too.

34. Luís Eduardo Schoueri & Guilherme Galdino, Single Taxation as a Policy Goal: Controversial Meaning, Lack of Justification and Unfeasibility, in J Wheeler (ed.), *Single Taxation?* (IBFD 2018).

35. Francesco De Lillo, In Search of Single Taxation, in J Wheeler (ed.), *Single Taxation?* (IBFD 2018).

36. Shaviro, *supra* n. 33.

hard to establish the 'single tax principle'.[37] These unresolved disputes are not merely academic but demonstrate the lack of a coherent guiding principle in international tax law, even in the post-BEPS era,[38] except for the acceptance of 'full taxation'.[39]

In my view, in the current international tax law regime and its reform, there are two overarching questions that have not been fully solved: (1) where is the value created (value creation),[40] i.e., where the profits are generated?;[41] and (2) what is the relationship between tax levied (from the levy side) and corresponding public benefits (from the expenditure) that is sufficient and conceptually logical to fulfil factual needs and government services of a specific country? These two questions lack a clear consensus of opinion, whether in a digitalized economy or in a traditional economy. These questions do not only need empirical answers but also new perspectives to analyse the failures.

The BEPS project has produced various fragmented mandates and policy reform options, but it does not address these unanswered questions comprehensively enough from a theoretical view.[42] It would be meaningful to analyse these issues also from some new perspectives, such as FA.

37. Frans Vanistendael, Single Taxation in a Single Market?, in J Wheeler (ed.), *Single Taxation?* (IBFD 2018).
38. For similar criticism, *see* Elizabeth Gil García, The Single Tax Principle: Fiction or Reality in a Non-Comprehensive International Tax Regime?, 11 World Tax Journal 497 (2019).
39. Mason argues that 'full-taxation' is the widely accepted new norm due to the BEPS project and thus still endorses the achievement by the OECD. *See* Leopoldo Parada, Full Taxation: The Single Tax Emperor's New Clothes, 24 Florida Tax Review 729 (2021).
40. Value creation is a key goal in the BEPS Action, but it is not a traditional international tax law concept. *See* Johannes Becker & Joachim Englisch, Taxing Where Value Is Created: What's 'User Involvement' Got to Do with It?, 47 Intertax 161 (2019); SC Morse, Value Creation: A Standard in Search of a Process, 72 Bulletin for International Taxation 196 (2018); Aleksandra Bal, (Mis)Guided by the Value Creation Principle – Can New Concepts Solve Old Problems?, 72 Bulletin for International Taxation (2018); Olbert & Spengel, Taxation in the Digital Economy – Recent Policy Developments and the Question of Value Creation, ZEW – Centre for European Economic Research Discussion Paper (2019); Analysis regarding value creation in the digital economy, Devereux & Vella, *supra* n. 15.

    We will still need proxies to decide value creation, and it is still difficult in the digital economy, 'when the user is not necessarily a consumer'.

    From developing countries' perspective, value creation could be accepted as a consensus for taxing multinationals, *see* Michael Lennard, Act of Creation: The OECD/G20 Test of 'Value Creation' as a Basis for Taxing Rights and Its Relevance to Developing Countries, 25 Transnational Corporations 55 (2018).
41. Luca Cerioni, The Quest for a New Corporate Taxation Model and for an Effective Fight Against International Tax Avoidance Within the EU, 44 Intertax 463 (2016). Where profits are generated is unsolved even though there are discussions about international tax avoidance; in this book, I distinguish between these two questions of 'where the value creation takes place' and 'where profits are generated'; as I see the value creation as the whole process from production to market; profits are the result of the MNE's market activities.
42. Herzfeld, *supra* n. 24. Claiming value creation as a 'pseudo-principle' and giving critical remarks especially on Action 1 Digital Economy, *see* Olbert & Spengel, *supra* n. 40. Readers might be wondering if the question of 'how much tax is levied to correspond to the public benefits' can be a scientific question to answer; my answer is affirmative: in the field of the discipline of tax and development, scholars argue that there must be enough tax to support the infrastructure in a country, and scholars use tax revenue/GDP ratio but still no universal consensus on the specific ratio. *See* Chapter 2.

FA is an often-discussed but not-so-preferred alternative option[43] in the current international tax regime, and the OECD TP guidelines have expressly rejected an FA system.[44] It seems that FA has the original sin of being rough, diverse[45] and thus implies arbitrariness, even though there have been quite a few academic articles and books advocating an FA system and clarifying misunderstandings about it.[46]

The EU's attempt to provide a harmonized corporate tax along with a supranational level sharing formula to replace the current bilateral tax treaties between EU Member States is extraordinarily ambitious because the current FA experiences are only implemented between subnational regimes, such as the US, Canada,[47] Germany, Switzerland,[48] Australia,[49] and France[50] (in the nineteenth century). The EU's FA regime, once adopted, would be the first supranational/regional level FA system in the world.

The FA system is not problem-free or perfect, just like other policy options. One observation[51] on the FA is remarkable: adopting an FA system would need new normative and theoretical content because it is indeed a relatively less-developed option in the international tax law regime. Although being less often adopted, an FA system does provide some new insights into dividing taxing rights between sovereign states. Therefore, in addition to advocating a global FA[52] or the single-sales global

---

In my view, regarding how much tax levied is fair and corresponding to different jurisdictions in the international tax context, the old debate of source versus residence jurisdiction demonstrates the scientific/theoretical attempt.

43. For discussions on FA as the US's reform alternative, *see* David C Engel, Would Formula Apportionment for International Transactions Be a More Efficient Approach, 24 International Tax Journal 23 (1998). This paper illustrates several criticisms of the FA, including the difficulty to define 'unitary business' and arbitrarily defining 'permanent establishment', etc. Many arguments are still invoked repeatedly against FA.
44. *OECD Transfer Pricing Guidelines for Multinational Enterprises and Tax Administrations*, Chapter I, section C.1, paragraph 1.17 (OECD 2010); It was clearly rejected in the early version of OECD, *Transfer Pricing and Multinational Enterprises – Report of the OECD Committee on Fiscal Affairs* (OECD 1979), paragraph 14; Cansu Bagran Ilhan, The Use of Value Chain Analysis in a Profit Split, 25 International Transfer Pricing Journal (2018).
45. The concern of inconsistency in FA has become the semi-consensus for business communities when discussing international tax reform, even in a non-FA discussion context, *see*, for example, comments in Guglielmo Maisto (ed.), *Taxation of Shipping and Air Transport in Domestic Law, EU Law and Tax Treaties* (IBFD 2017).
46. Reuven S Avi-Yonah & Ilan Benshalom, Formulary Apportionment: Myths and Prospects, 3 World Tax Journal (2011); Yariv Brauner, Between Arm's Length and Formulary Apportionment, in Richard E Krever & François Vaillancourt, *The Allocation of Multinational Business Income: Reassessing the Formulary Apportionment Option* (Kluwer Law International 2020).
47. As to US's and Canada's experiences, *see* Joanna Weiner, Formulary Apportionment and Group Taxation in the European Union: Insights from the United States and Canada, European Commission Taxation Papers, 2005; Michael Smart & François Vaillancourt, Formulary Apportionment in Canada and Taxation of Corporate Income in 2019: Current Practice, Origins and Evaluation in Krever & Vaillancourt, *supra* n. 46.
48. As to Germany and Switzerland, *see* Stefan Mayer, *Formulary Apportionment for the Internal Market* (IBFD 2009), at 3.4 and 3.5.
49. Richard E Krever & Peter Mellor, *History and Theory of Formulary Apportionment*, in Krever & Vaillancourt, *supra* n. 46.
50. *Ibid.*
51. International Monetary Fund, *supra* n. 25.
52. Such as Susan C Morse, Revisiting Global Formulary Apportionment, 29 Virginia Tax Review 593 (2009).

formula,[53] there is more and more academic discussion trying to seek a middle path, such as adopting an FA system specifically for financial income,[54] or only for residual profits[55] that are not easily sourced, etc.

The existing FA systems have demonstrated some weaknesses. Criticisms of an FA system especially refer to 'arbitrariness'[56] and creating factor-shifting behaviours.[57] From the experiences of US state taxation, these criticisms are not pointless. Among 47 states in the US which levy corporate tax, there are enormous differences between the types of standard formulas and special industry formulas. In the US, as long as states do not violate constitutional requirements,[58] states have quite wide discretion to decide on a formula for the needs of their own policy. This is also the reason why there is clearly a current trend that most states in the US are starting to adopt the single sales factor.[59] A state's own policy is not inherently arbitrary: but what the current FA system discussions really lack is a coherent rationale behind the design of the formula, to accommodate each weighting factor, including composition, attribution, and even any deviation[60] from the standard formula.

In my view, FA and TP/separate accounting (SA) are neither enemies nor mutually exclusive. Instead, even FA advocates admit that incorporating a formula in a TP rule could be feasible.[61] What FA practices and TP practices have in common is that they both seek non-rigid and logical rules which reflect economic realities (in the current popular terminology, 'value creation' and 'profit creation') of MNE taxpayers and the involved state's economic policy. In my view, there is no superior status

53. Maarten de Wilde, Sharing the Pie: Taxing Multinationals in a Global Market, 43 Intertax 438 (2015). His approach is often cited as 'corporate tax 2.0'.
54. Ilan Benshalom, Taxing the Financial Income of Multinational Enterprises by Employing a Hybrid Formulary and Arm's Length Allocation Method, 28 Virginia Tax Review 619 (2008); Ilan Benshalom, The Quest to Tax Financial Income in a Global Economy: Emerging to an Allocation Phase, 28 VirginiaTax Review 165 (2008); Lindsay Marie France Clement Célestin, Formulary Approach to the Taxation of Transnational Corporations A Realistic Alternative? (University of Sydney PhD thesis 2000), at Chapter 8: Formulary Apportionment Applied to the Global Financial Industry; *see also* Chapter 7.2 of this book.
55. Jaap Bellingwout, Blueprint for a New Common Corporate Tax Base, 55 European Taxation 3 (2015).
56. Criticism examples, *see* Avi-Yonah & Benshalom, *supra* n. 46; Julie Roin, Can the Income Tax Be Saved – The Promise and Pitfalls of Adopting Worldwide Formulary Apportionment, 61 Tax Law Review 169 (2007).
57. J Clifton Fleming Jr, Robert J Peroni & Stephen E Shay, Formulary Apportionment in the US International Income Tax System: Putting Lipstick on a Pig?, Michigan Journal of International Law (2015); Rosanne Altshuler & Harry Grubert, Formula Apportionment: Is It Better than the Current System and Are There Better Alternatives?, 63 National Tax Journal (2010).
58. *See* Chapter 3.2.3 of this book.
59. Kimberly A Clausing, Lessons for International Tax Reform from the US State Experience under Formulary Apportionment, in Tax Analysts & Mindy Herzfeld (eds), *U.S. State Tax Considerations for International Tax Reform* (Tax Analysts 2014), available at SSRN 2359724.
60. Here, I refer to formulas applying to specific industries. *See* Chapter 7. Regarding industry formulas, especially the formula for the digital sector, *see also* Kerrie Sadiq, A Framework for Assessing Business Sector Formulary Apportionment, in Krever & Vaillancourt, *supra* n. 46.
61. The same opinion, Paul A Blay, Reviving Transfer Pricing Enforcement Through Formulary Apportionment, 7 Tax Development Journal (2017); Reuven S Avi-Yonah, *Advanced Introduction to International Tax Law* (Edward Elgar 2019).

between an FA[62] or an SA approach,[63] and it would be practical and feasible to seek a compromise involving the best of two worlds when designing a new FA system for the EU.

1.1.3 The Research Purpose: Redesigning a Normative Theoretical Framework to Evaluate and Provide Suggestions on the EU's Corporate Tax Reform

This book aims to build a normative framework for the FA regime for the EU. By critically evaluating the existing CCCTB Directive Proposal against this normative framework, this book would like to redesign a tax-neutral FA framework for the EU.

Although the starting point as well as the final purpose of this research is to design a tax-neutral FA regime for the EU, the result is expected to have some universal applicability or reference to some certain extent.[64] The existing CCCTB Directive Proposal, though it will be withdrawn, is the starting point and the cumulation of the development of the FA regime in the EU context. To critically revisit the current CCCTB Directive Proposal is the first step towards the reformed EU FA regime.

By a metaphor of 'a pie and a knife' to describe the CCCTB system, a MNE group active in different EU Member States can file their harmonized consolidated tax base from all qualifying group members from different EU Member States, and such consolidated tax base is like a big pie, jointly contributed by all group members; and the formula is like a knife to decide the share/a piece of the pie which is apportioned to each group member.

Therefore, each group member's apportioned share of the taxable pie of the whole group would be calculated as follows:

$$\text{the consolidated tax base} \times \left(\frac{1}{3} \times \frac{\textit{the member's sales}}{\textit{group sales}} + \frac{1}{3} \times \frac{\textit{the member's assets}}{\textit{group assets}} + \frac{1}{3} \times \frac{\textit{the member's labour}}{\textit{group labour}}\right)$$

The overview of the CCCTB is illustrated in Figure 1.

62. Formulary apportionment is neither perfect nor a panacea, *see* David Spencer, Transfer Pricing: Formulary Apportionment Is Not a Panacea, Part 1, Journal of International Taxation (2014).
63. The same opinion, Herzig, Teschke & Joisten, *supra* n. 5.
64. CCCTB could be a good reference for the rest of the world regarding international tax reform, Alexander Ezenagu, Faltering Blocks in the Arguments Against Unitary Taxation and the Formulary Apportionment Approach to Income Allocation, 17 Asper Review of International Business and Trade Law 131 (2017).

Figure 1 Overview of the Common Consolidated Corporate Tax Base Directive Proposal

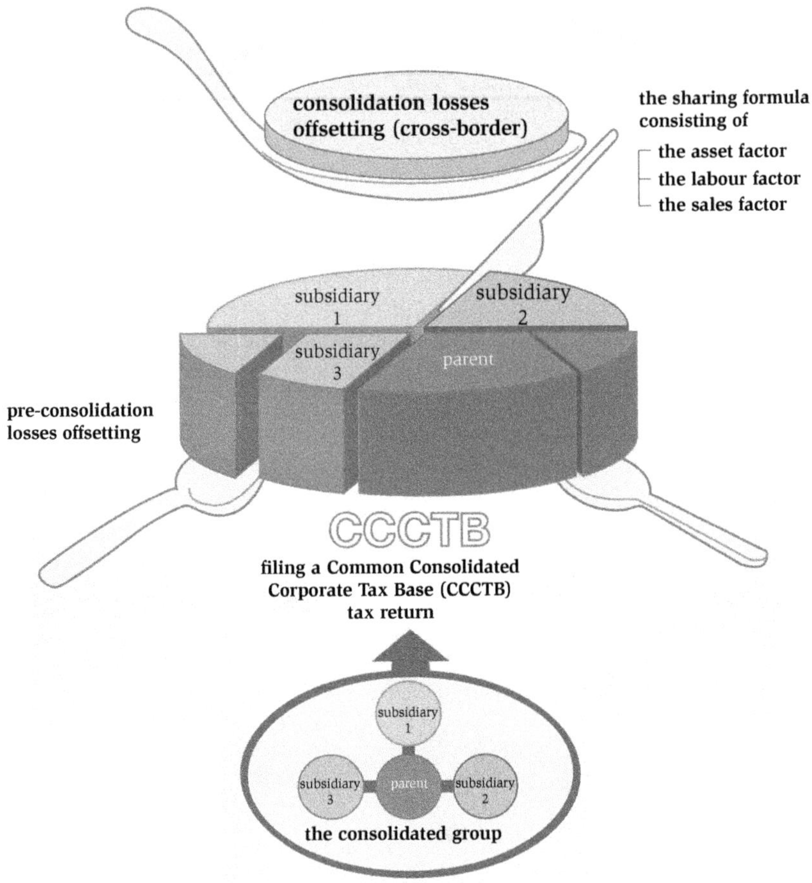

Source: The author.

This CCCTB Directive proposal uses a predetermined formula to apportion taxable income of MNE taxpayers. This legislative proposal is a tax reform effort at the EU level to provide all EU Member States a uniform consolidated (i.e., group) corporate tax base and a formula to divide their taxing powers on MNEs' income.

In this regard, the EU's FA regime of the 2021 BEFIT package has the same features as the current CCCTB Directive Proposal: It would replace the bilateral tax treaties between these EU Member States when adopted. Corporate taxation matters are still rarely harmonized by EU legislation. Therefore, when the EU's formulary apportioned regime is adopted by EU Member States, it would be a milestone also for the development of EU law.

To build a normative framework, this book raises a more fundamental question: what is a proper way of dividing taxing powers on MNE group taxpayers' cross-border economic activities in the EU context? A consensus of opinion on an answer to this question has never been achieved, even in the post-BEPS era.

1.1.4 EU Tax Law Harmonization Has a Multidimensional Policy Goal

As part of the development of its internal market, the EU has also attempted to eliminate obstacles arising from tax law disparities. In the twentieth century, EU tax law slowly developed its own tax law system[65] in parallel with the development of international tax law that is mainly driven by OECD.

Being different from the OECD model convention's main goal of eliminating double taxation, the development of EU tax legislation is based on a broader purpose of building an internal market. With such broad purpose, a piece of EU tax legislation would need to consider (potential) interests of three different stakeholders: taxpayers, Member States, and the EU. Since the mid-1980s, there have been continuous efforts to harmonize company taxation law in the EU.[66] The current CCCTB Directive Proposal is one of the attempts to eliminate fiscal obstacles and to provide a more business-friendly regime at the EU level.

Formally being independent of the OECD, the EU has always closely cooperated with working groups of the OECD, and thus the CCCTB Directive Proposal has also become an important policy in response to the BEPS project.[67] The EU has clearly indicated that the CCCTB should become a useful measure to address the emerging BEPS problems because the CCCTB would regulate MNE taxpayers' pan-EU taxable income.

The CCCTB, relaunched in 2015, is part of the EU's response to the BEPS problem and failures of the international tax regime.[68] In the policy statement in the 2015 Corporate Tax Action Plan, the European Commission referred to five key areas and corresponding measures: (1) relaunching the CCCTB project; (2) ensuring effective taxation where profits are generated; (3) achieving a better tax environment for businesses; (4) ensuring tax transparency; and (5) improving EU cooperation. Although the CCCTB is only one area among these five, these areas are all interrelated.

---

65. Bank observes that cooperate taxation law harmonization (and harmonization attempts) in the EU also represents the global convergence of corporate tax law to tackle the various manipulations, *see* Steven A Bank, *Anglo-American Corporate Taxation: Tracing the Common Roots of Divergent Approaches* (Cambridge University Press 2011), at Chapter 7.
66. For a brief history of EU direct tax harmonization legislation, *see* Christiana HJI Panayi, *European Union Corporate Tax Law* (Cambridge University Press 2013), at Chapter 2.
67. *See* Explanatory Memorandum of the 2016 CCCTB Directive Proposal, at 3 and Explanatory Memorandum of the 2016 CCTB Directive Proposal, at 4, 9, 10. Cerioni, *supra* n. 41.
68. Another example is that the EU published the Pillar 2 Directive Proposal in 2021 in response to the OECD's Pillar 2 project, *see* European Commission, Proposal for a Council Directive on ensuring a global minimum level of taxation for multinational groups in the Union {SWD(2021) 580 final}.

The European Commission's tax reform package in 2015 reflects the phenomenon of 'competing paradigms'[69] in the field of economic integration of the EU internal market. There are two parallel paradigms in EU law integration: one is 'promoting harmonization'[70] and the other is 'ensuring tax competition'.[71] These two competing paradigms make it difficult to establish a consistent normative framework. On the one hand, EU harmonization reduces national law disparities and creates an EU level internal market. On the other hand, EU harmonization wishes to create a level playing field for individuals as well as Member States to conduct free and healthy competition and still maintain diversity. Such two different parallel paradigms[72] could lead to a paradox in policy in a tax law reform.

In the 2021 BEFIT tax reform package, the European Commission reiterated that the EU pursues multiple policy goals in parallel:

> Business taxation should ensure the tax burden is fairly shared across businesses and that taxable revenue is fairly shared between different jurisdictions. The overall system should be simple, in order to reduce compliance costs, and should facilitate investment and growth, thus reinforcing the Single Market.[73]

Therefore, the theoretical framework for assessing the supranational FA regime for the EU needs to be multidimensional and combine different traditional international tax law principles selectively and consistently, so it would be able to pursue the imperatives of the EU internal market. In order to clarify and establish the normative framework, it is necessary to revisit tax neutrality, which is widely used in the public economy literature but conveys diverse and sometimes conflicting meanings. It is also necessary to take a flexible approach to embrace valuable lessons not only from corporate tax law but also from VAT, labour law, and TP practices.

1.2 THE RESEARCH QUESTIONS, SUB-QUESTIONS, AND THE RESEARCH SCOPE

1.2.1 The Core Research Question and Assumptions: What Does a Benefit-Based Market-Neutral Formula Look Like?

This book assumes that there would be an optimal corporate tax rate and such corporate tax rate neither would be 0%, nor would it be so high that it exceeded the margin (the 'prohibitive range') and became a disincentive for taxpayers' economic

69. Alexandre Saydé, *Abuse of EU Law and Regulation of the Internal Market* (Bloomsbury 2014), at Chapter 6 'the competing paradigms of economic integration'.
70. In Saydé's term, it is 'regulatory neutrality', *ibid.*
71. In Saydé's term, it is 'regulatory competition', *ibid.*
72. For another observation on CCCTB's different paradigm developments, *see* Shafi U Khan Niazi, Re-Launch of the Proposal for a Common Consolidated Corporate Tax Base (CCCTB) in the EU: A Shift in Paradigm, 44 Legal Issues of Economic Integration 293 (2017).
73. *See* https://eur-lex.europa.eu/legal-content/EN/TXT/PDF/?uri=CELEX:52021DC0251&rid=3.

activities.[74] Since the public benefits are not unlimited, an overly high tax rate or overly heavy tax burden is not justified.

The core research question of this book is then: how should an EU-level FA system be designed? The theoretical framework of this book is the 'benefit-based market neutrality framework'. This book argues that the EU-level formula should be in line with MNE taxpayers' input and output activities as well as respecting Member States' fiscal autonomy and maintaining healthy tax competition.[75]

As the metaphor indicated above, we can see MNE taxpayers' tax base across EU Member States as a 'taxable pie',[76] the formula is the 'knife' to divide the pie. The whole BEPS project also addresses the problem of failing to 'divide the pie' properly. With this background of the global tax reform campaign, this book seeks the answer to how an FA system in a regional integration (EU) should be designed.

The current CCCTB Directive Proposal's 'knife' to apportion the tax base has three different weighting factors: the sales, the assets, and the labour factors. Therefore, the sub-questions of this book are: what should benefit-based MN mean in the context of the EU's FA? (Chapter 2); How should the sales factor, the assets factor, and the labour factor in the formula be designed? (from Chapter 3 to Chapter 7); What procedures could adjust the unreasonable FA result? (Chapter 8). These sub-questions all try to contribute to the knowledge gap of the theoretical design of FA, especially as to the composition and attribution of each weighting factor.

1.2.2 Topics Not Directly Addressed in the Book

Although this book explores the fair tax share question as the BEPS project does, this book has a quite specific scope: it focuses on the FA design issue, not some typical

74. According to Arthur Laffer's theory about deciding tax rate, when the tax rate becomes too high, taxpayers lose the incentives to conduct economic activities, and it turned out that the tax revenue would decrease. *See* Arthur B Laffer, The Laffer Curve: Past, Present, and Future, 1765 Backgrounder 1 (2004).

    My book is based on the assumption that the tax rate is already within the accepted range, not the prohibitive range. Tax in the prohibited range is deadweight loss (DWL). Taxation should be sufficient but not exceeding the reasonable margin that becomes a deterrent to economic activities.

    For similar remarks, *see* Cathal Long & Mark Miller, Taxation and the Sustainable Development Goals: Do Good Things Come to Those Who Tax More?, Overseas Development Institute (ODI) Briefing Note 1 (2017).

75. These objectives are clearly mentioned in the European Commission's CCCTB Directive Proposal Preamble. As to allowing the tax rate competition, *see* the explanatory memorandum of the 2016 CCCTB Directive Proposal, 5 and 2011 CCCTB Directive Proposal, 4. The 2016 CCCTB Directive Proposal emphasizes combating tax avoidance.

76. The metaphor of sharing a taxable pie is also used by other scholars, such as Maarten de Wilde, *Sharing the Pie: Taxing Multinationals in a Global Market* (IBFD 2017). Andreas Wagener, Evolutionary Tax Competition with Formulary Apportionment, WU International Taxation Research Paper Series (2017).

corporate taxation issues related to the consolidated tax base.[77] In addition, this book focuses on the EU context and thus will not focus on the OECD's latest proposals,[78] though the OECD's Pillar One Project mentions formula-related approaches.[79] I would see such developments as the background of the post-BEPS era that FAs have gradually been gaining recognition and acceptance as tax reform options.

This book also does not directly address academic discussions and debates of the following issues: the PE threshold issue,[80] the definition and scope of a group,[81]

77. As to the economic effects and comparison of the 2011 CCCTB and 2016 CCTB Directive Proposals, *see* Christoph Spengel & others, *The Impact of the CCTB on the Effective Tax Burden of Corporations: Results from the Tax Analyzer Model-Final Report*, Vol. 75 (Publications Office of the European Union 2019).

    According to this assessment and stimulation, 'Upon the introduction of the CCTB, the effective tax burden decreases in all Member States except for Cyprus and Malta (average decrease: 5.1%)', at 10.

    As to the estimated impact of introducing the 2016 CCTB Directive proposal, *see* Danuše Nerudová & Veronika Solilová, The Impact of the Introduction of a CCCTB in the EU, 54 Intereconomics 160 (2019). They distinguish three sets of data: MNEs obliged under CCCTB (above the threshold), MNEs voluntarily opting in CCCTB, SMEs voluntarily opting in CCCTB. They concluded that the tax base of the groups of MNEs voluntarily opting in CCCTB and SMEs voluntarily opting in CCCTB will increase, and the tax base of the group of MNEs obliged under CCCTB will decrease. Overall, CCCTB is evaluated as a positive policy.

    For an assessment of the 2011 CCCTB Directive Proposal, *see* Christoph Spengel & others, A Common Corporate Tax Base for Europe: An Impact Assessment of the Draft Council Directive on a CC (C) TB, 4 World Tax Journal (2012). Regarding the effective tax burden, 'While effective tax burdens would considerably increase in Portugal, Romania and Switzerland, the largest reductions are determined for Cyprus, Ireland and Italy.'

    It should be noted that there are some research results showing that adopting a formula including immobile factors could increase tax revenue, *see* Marco Runkel & Guttorm Schjelderup, The Choice of Apportionment Factors under Formula Apportionment, 52 International Economic Review 913 (2011). Runkel and Schjelderup argue that as long as immobile factors such as employees are used in the formula, the result would never be optimal, and comparing it to the SA system, adopting an FA system would lead to an increase in revenue.
78. OECD, Tax Challenges Arising from Digitalisation – Interim Report 2018, Inclusive Framework on BEPS, OECD/G20 Base Erosion and Profit Shifting Project (OECD 16 March 2018).
79. It is worth noting that the FA feature of Pillar One is also recognized by the FA experts of the MTC in the US. The MTC provides the OECD with a concise description of FA practice in state taxation in the US. *See* Multistate Tax Commission, Response of the Multistate Tax Commission Public Consultation Document on the Report on the Tax Challenges Arising from Digitalisation Report on Pillar One Blueprint – Items III and IV (Multistate Tax Commission 2020), which can be requested at http://www.mtc.gov.
80. As to PE and criticism, Antonio Carlos dos Santos & Cidália Mota Lopes, Tax Sovereignty, Tax Competition and the Base Erosion and Profit Shifting Concept of Permanent Establishment, 25 EC Tax Review 296 (2016); Maarten Floris de Wilde, Lowering the Permanent Establishment Threshold via the Anti-BEPS Convention: Much Ado About Nothing? 45 Intertax 556 (2017); Carlo Garbarino, Permanent Establishments and BEPS Action 7: Perspectives in Evolution, 47 Intertax 365 (2019); There is still a clear trend of lowering the PE threshold, an example of Japan, Adam Becker, Japanese Tax Reforms Square Up to BEPS Action 1 to Tackle Tax Challenges of the Growing Digital Economy, 72 Bulletin for International Taxation (2018).

    Some early reflections on the PE, Mary C Bennett & Carol A Dunahoo, Attribution of Profits to a Permanent Establishment: Issues and Recommendations, 33 Intertax 51 (2005); Michael Kobetsky, *International Taxation of Permanent Establishments: Principles and Policy* (Cambridge University Press 2011).
81. As to the group concept under the CCCTB, *see* TA Pereira, *International Aspects of the CCCTB in Europe* (Maastricht University 2014); Bruno Da Silva, *The Impact of Tax Treaties and EU Law on Group Taxation Regimes* (Kluwer Law International 2016); Guglielmo Maisto, Taxation of

loss-offsetting,[82] interest deduction,[83] etc. In other words, this book does not discuss 'the size of a taxable pie'[84] but how the taxable pie should be divided across EU Member States. Since this book does not address 'the size of a taxable pie', this book also does not address precisely how much the tax rate should be for a corporate tax system; this would be an empirical fact. The book assumes such optimal corporate tax rate exists and explores only how cross-border taxing rights are shared.

This book does not address well-known hybrid-mismatch examples either[85] for two reasons. First, since hybrid mismatch problems occur due to national tax law disparities applicable to different subsidiaries, the EU's FA regime would eliminate disparities and form a 'group taxation', and a harmonized group taxation as such could eliminate mismatches to a large extent. Therefore, it is no longer needed to design specific solutions. Second, this book does not focus on specific tax avoidance scenarios but the underlying rationale. This book expects that, when the design of the EU's FA regime is designed in a market-neutral way, mismatches and tax avoidance scenarios would be naturally reduced.

Groups and CCCTB, in Dourado (ed.), *supra* n. 5; Jan van de Streek, The CCCTB Concept of Consolidation and the Rules on Entering a Group, 40 Intertax 24 (2012).

82. I have published previously regarding the income shifting incentive from the loss-offsetting mechanism under the CCCTB by shifting weighting factors. *See* Shu-Chien Chen, The Strategy of Shifting-To-Losses: The Case of Common Consolidated Corporate Tax Base (CCCTB) in the European Union, 2 UCPH Fiscal Relations Law Journal (2019); for a similar observation, Jeanette Calleja Borg, Tax Treatment of Losses under the Proposed Common Consolidated Corporate Tax Base Directive, 41 Intertax 581 (2013). For another general introduction to loss-offsetting under the CCCTB, Pereira, *supra* n. 81, Chapter 6. As to some technical comments on the 2016 CCCTB Directive Proposal, B da Silva, Cross-Border Loss Relief under the Proposed CCTB Directive, in Weber & Streek (eds), *supra* n. 5. For earlier comments regarding losses, *see* Saturnina Moreno González & José Alberto Sanz Diaz-Palacios, The Common Consolidated Corporate Tax Base: Treatment of Losses, in Lang & others, *supra* n. 5; Antony Ting, *The Taxation of Corporate Groups under Consolidation: An International Comparison* (Cambridge University Press 2013), at Chapter 6.

83. There are works regarding excessive interest deduction, *see* Edoardo Traversa, Interest Deductibility and the BEPS Action Plan: Nihil Novi Sub Sole? 5 British Tax Review 607 (2013); In the context of CCCTB, *see* Ana Paula Dourado & Rita de la Feria, Thin Capitalization Rules in the Context of the CCCTB, 804 Working Papers from Oxford University Centre for Business Taxation (2008).

84. Since this book does not cover the tax base issue, this book will not directly deal with the question of whether hidden reserve should be taxed under the CCCTB. For relevant discussions on hidden reserves under the CCCTB, *see* Ulrich Schreiber, The Taxation of Hidden Reserves under the Common Consolidated Corporate Tax Base, 49 European Taxation 84 (2009).

85. In the literature, there are discussions about the 'Double Irish scheme' or the 'CV-BV structure'. The Double Irish scheme makes use of the low Irish corporate tax rate in combination with a Dutch subsidiary (like a sandwich); the CV-BC structure makes use of a Dutch partnership, and both arrangements are used to reduce MNE taxpayers' tax burden of US taxation.

For a description of the Double Irish Sandwich, *see* Joseph Darby & Kelsey Lemaster, Double Irish More than Doubles the Tax Saving: Hybrid Structure Reduces Irish, US and Worldwide Taxation. Practical US, 11 International Tax Strategies 2 (2007); Kleinbard, Stateless Income, *supra* n. 28; Stephen C Loomis, The Double Irish Sandwich: Reforming Overseas Tax Havens, 43 Mary's Law Journal 825 (2011). For a description of the CV-BV structure under the Dutch law, *see* De Lillo, *supra* n. 35, at 1.3.

Furthermore, this book does not directly address the general anti-avoidance rule (GAAR)[86] or specific anti-avoidance rule (SAAR)[87] either because this book concerns the rationale behind the design, not any detailed tax avoidance scenarios or how a GAAR-like rule should be designed. Therefore, the discussions of the principal purpose test (PPT)[88] from the BEPS project are also not directly addressed in this book. In my view, when evaluating the policy design related to a tax reform, the perspective should go beyond the tax avoidance and tax evasion concerns.[89]

In short, this book does not comprehensively address academic discussions about GAAR, PE, hybrid-mismatches, and the OECD's Pillar One, but focuses on the case of the EU. Only when the discussions are related to EU-level FA, will they be covered.

1.3 THE RESEARCH METHOD: THE METHODOLOGY AND METHODOLOGICAL LIMITATIONS

1.3.1 The Challenge of the Comparative Legal Research Method for Analysing a Tax Reform Project

As to methodology, this book uses a hybrid approach, comparing it to the traditional comparative legal research discipline. There are several innovative attempts in the methodology used in this book. Traditional comparative legal research aims to find

86. Regarding the issue of GAAR, for example, different contributions on national GAARs based on the standard questionnaire are collected and published at Michael Lang & others, *GAARs: A Key Element of Tax Systems in the Post-BEPS World* (IBFD 2016); Markus Seiler, *GAARs and Judicial Anti-Avoidance in Germany, the UK and the EU: Schriftenreihe IStR Band 98* (Linde Verlag GmbH 2016). The ultimate academic dispute between the advocates and the opponents of a GAAR is on legal certainty. Opponents of a GAAR usually argue that a GAAR infringes legal certainty, whereas the advocates would analyse applicable conditions in a GAAR to justify the existence of such general rule and predict some pattern in a GAAR. For some pre-BEPS literature on the abuse of law, *see* Rita De La Feria, Prohibition of Abuse of (Community) Law: The Creation of a New General Principle of EC Law Through Tax, 45 Common Market Law Review 395 (2008).

    For new discussions after the EU's ATAD, *see* Rita de la Feria, *EU General Anti-(Tax) Avoidance Mechanisms: From GAAP to GAAR, The Dynamics of Taxation* (Hart 2020); Frederik Zimmer, In Defence of General Anti-Avoidance Rules, 73 Bulletin for International Taxation (2019).

87. Regarding the SAARs of the CCCTB, *see* Pereira, *supra* n. 81, at Chapter 6. Rønfeldt also mentions that the CCCTB itself cannot really provide a comprehensive anti-avoidance framework at the EU level. *See* Thomas Rønfeldt, Anti-Abuse Clause or Harmonization?, 39 Intertax 12 (2011).

88. As to discussions on the PPT, *see* Andrés Báez Moreno, GAARs and Treaties: From the Guiding Principle to the Principal Purpose Test: What Have We Gained from BEPS Action 6?, 45 Intertax 432 (2017); Craig Elliffe, The Meaning of the Principal Purpose Test: One Ring to Bind Them All?, 11 World Tax Journal (2019); Blazej Kuzniacki, The Principal Purpose Test (PPT) in BEPS Action 6 and the MLI: Exploring Challenges Arising from Its Legal Implementation and Practical Application, 10 World Tax Journal 233 (2018). The possible status of PPT as a type of customary international law, *see* Irma Johanna Mosquera Valderrama, BEPS Principal Purpose Test and Customary International Law, Leiden Journal of International Law 1 (2020).

89. For a similar opinion, *see* Allison Christians & Laurens van Apeldoorn, Taxing Income Where Value Is Created, 22 Florida Tax Review 1 (2018).

'solutions' and insights to solve a well-identified problem. This book conducts comparative legal research for not only finding answers but also identifying problems that can arise from an FA system. Therefore, a traditional comparative law research approach needs adjustments.

First, this book uses the comparative legal research method to discuss FA examples in a critical way. In addition to the US, Canada, Germany, and Switzerland are also popular targets to be compared with the current CCCTB Directive Proposal.[90] However, since traditional comparative legal research methods focus on the similarities and differences in the laws, comparative law researchers often aim to provide solutions for a specific legal question, either by the problem-solving approach or by the functional approach. This book goes beyond that.

To build a theoretical normative framework for a tax law reform project for the EU's FA regime, the aim of conducting comparative legal research is not only to discuss a specific legal problem or a specific function of a piece of law, but to dig into the question 'what underlying rationale' should be the guidance of a cross-border tax law reform. In section 1.3.5, I elaborate on the traditional justifications to conduct comparative legal research for this book.

In this regard, the most serious risk to conduct comparative legal research to learn some 'lessons' is 'being lost in translation' and 'implementing a wrong legal transplantation' because any norm taken out of its original context can be easily misunderstood and misinterpreted. It is more important to extract the underlying rationale instead of copying the contents.

Extracting the underlying rationale is especially important for analysing a tax law reform project because tax law often involves more complex technicalities than other fields of law. The existing comparative law research on FA systems between different jurisdictions seems to focus on the details more than deciphering the underlying rationale and overly replying to the conclusions proposed by economy scholars. There are quite a few discussions in the existing literature on the examples of US FA experiences, but there are not sufficient discussions on what lessons/insights EU could take to develop its own FA framework. This book fills this gap.

1.3.2 Lessons from Other Relevant Fields of Law

Furthermore, this book breaks down the conceptual (and also conventional) boundary between tax law and other fields of law as well as the boundary between corporate income tax (CIT) law and other types of tax law, such as Value Added Tax (VAT) and TP. The research breaks down the presumption that FA and TP practices are mutually exclusive. Instead, this book discusses each weighting factor in the formula in separate chapters not only by referring to different fields of tax law (such as VAT or TP) but also by referring to other fields of law, which could reflect the public benefits provided, including human resources of the labour market, the customers' market, and resources contributed to production.

90. Mayer, *supra* n. 48.

Therefore, when discussing the 'destination' of the sales factor, not only the examples of the US's FA are compared, but also the destination concept in the field of VAT. When discussing the function and location of an asset, including intangible assets, I also use the functional and factual analysis developed by TP practices as a reference. This is unlike the traditional FA literature which excludes the intangibles simply due to administrative complexity. As to the discussions on the labour/payroll factor, in addition to the US's experiences, I also use discussions in labour law and social security law to explore the definition and the attribution of employee. As to the assets factor, I also revisit discussions about attribution and evaluation of intangibles in the context of TP context.

1.3.3 Adopting New Perspectives to Analyse the Benefit Principle and Market Neutrality

Moreover, this research broadens the discussions of the benefit principle in the context of corporate taxation. Although the benefit principle has been accepted for long in the field of international tax law to justify that both the residence state's and the source state's taxing powers, such classical dichotomy itself is ironically inconsistent with public benefits used by multinationals in a globalized world. Therefore, it is necessary to revisit the benefit principle in an international tax regime.

In addition, the benefit principle is not thoroughly discussed and accepted in the context of corporate tax. This is because a corporation is a separate legal person, so it is not so clear 'who' actually bears the benefits and burdens related to corporate tax. This book analyses this topic from another perspective: when we interpret public benefits in the broad sense, including 'providing a market environment', it is logical that the benefit principle should also apply to corporate tax. How can MN be embedded with the benefit principle? These discussions also enrich the arguments on the relationship between the benefit principle and the FA.

1.3.4 Methodological Limitations

Although this book has addressed the underlying theory that is suitable for evaluating corporate tax levied on MNE taxpayers' cross-border activities, it is necessary to mention that this book may have two inherent limitations. First, implementing a supranational FA system would require a supranational institution, such as the tax authority, to coordinate with national tax authorities. It could be difficult or time-consuming to convince different countries to support and create this system, even under current EU law. Many scholars have expressed their concerns too. Second, the theory developed by this book is based on a regional integration with a longer history; the aim of the benefit-based MN normative framework is to ensure that the EU's FA regime would be consistent with the taxpayers' real economic activities and reduce distortions due to an un-neutral tax law. Therefore, the book focuses on the EU and the US and is inevitably EU-centred.

The EU and the US are both classified as economically developed countries. There have been academic discussions on unitary business and FA in developing countries, such as African countries and China,[91] and they are not within the scope of this book because the regional integration is relatively new in relation to the EU and the US. Since this book focuses predominantly on the EU, these research outputs on application FA/Unitary Taxation in the context of developing countries are unfortunately not included for discussion.

Moreover, this book focuses on the question of law and thus this research is still mainly within the law discipline. The economic literature and empirical data are presumed to be reliable and used as facts to analyse possible options for law reform. Therefore, this book would presume that economists' data are correct, for example, the existence of BEPS phenomenon.[92] Yet, I also present empirical data from economists who have the opposite findings and arguments, when available, to elaborate on the policy options that I assess as consistent with the benefit-based market-neutral framework.

1.3.5 The Justifications of Using the Comparative Legal Research Method: A Hybrid Approach

1.3.5.1 The Functional Approach

While embracing a modified and innovative methodology where I can seek useful lessons from other fields of law, the research method used in this book is still justified by its traditional comparative legal research methods. Briefly speaking, this book intentionally mixes the functional and problem-solving approaches developed in the discipline of comparative law. This mixture is justified because I seek answers for the EU tax reform project which does not have a specific case or dispute yet.

In order to uncover the problems and seek the solutions for the current CCCTB Directive Proposal, I have chosen the comparative legal research method to gain inspiration and useful lessons from other jurisdictions, especially the US.

91. For example, for Nigeria, Alexander Ezenagu, Unitary Taxation of Multinational Enterprises for a Just Allocation of Income: Nigeria as a Case Study of Africa's Largest Economies' (PhD Thesis, McGill University 2019); for China, Fei Gao & Antony Ting, Is Arm's Length Profit Split Methodology Morphing into a Formulary Apportionment Hybrid: The Chinese Example, in Krever & Vaillancourt (eds), *supra* n. 46; from the perspective of developing countries, Michael C Durst, The Tax Policy Outlook for Developing Countries: Reflections on International Formulary Apportionment, ICTD Working Paper 32 (2015); According to Titus, Kenya and South Africa are considering creating a bilateral formula to allocate taxing rights. Afton Titus, *The Promise of Non-Arm's Length Practices: Is the Destination-Based Cash Flow Tax or Unitary Taxation the Panacea of Which Developing Countries Are in Search?*, in Irma JohannaMosquera Valderrama, Dries Lesage, Wouter Lips (eds), Taxation, International Cooperation and the 2030 Sustainable Development Agenda (Springer 2021).

92. For example, Maria Alvarez-Martinez & others, How Large Is the Corporate Tax Base Erosion and Profit Shifting? A General Equilibrium Approach, 34 Economic Systems Research (2022).

The functional approach[93] seeks the comparable function of a norm or institution in a different legal system.[94] Since its inception, drafters and experts of the current CCCTB Directive Proposal in the European Commission have relied on this functional approach, while they discussed and designed the current CCCTB Directive Proposal.[95] Although there have been doubts about applying the functional approach to compare issues in public law and tax law,[96] arguing that the function of each provision in public law/tax law might be multiple or hybrid or even unclear, this book still makes use of the functional approach as one of the perspectives. By seeking the underlying rationale of each provision compared, not limited to the technical 'function', such comparison can still contribute to a tax reform project.

1.3.5.2 The Problem Solving Approach

Another typical comparative law method is 'the problem-solving approach'. By this approach, the specific legal problem is identified, and the comparative research analyses how this specific legal problem is solved in different jurisdictions. Therefore, to seek tax reform solutions that can solve the problems occurring in the current international tax regime is consistent with the research aim of this book.

1.3.5.3 The Mixture of These Two Traditional Comparative Legal Research Methods

The functional approach and the problem-solving approach are separate approaches in the comparative legal research methodology but are often regarded as two perspectives of the same method.[97] In this research, I also adopt both perspectives. Since the research aim of this book is to find out the problems in the current CCCTB Directive Proposal and suggest a better design for the EU FA regime, I identify the existing problems of the CCCTB Directive Proposal that are not consistent with the normative framework and compare the solutions from the current CCCTB Directive Proposal with the US system.

After identifying these problems, I further conduct the problem-solving approach to seek a better solution. In each chapter, I adopt two different comparative law methods. The ultimate aim is to design a benefit-based market-neutral EU-level FA

93. Reuven S Avi-Yonah, Nicola Sartori & Omri Marian, *Global Perspectives on Income Taxation Law* (Oxford University Press 2011), at 4.
94. *Ibid.*
95. Carlo Garbarino, An Evolutionary Approach to Comparative Taxation: Theory, Methods and Agenda for Research, Bocconi Legal Studies Research Paper (2008). Garbarino mentions the CCCTB as an example that the CCCTB Directive extracted the common function of the group taxation systems of different Member States, i.e., the result of 'offsetting of profits and losses of different companies belonging to the same group'.
96. The limitation of comparative law approach to the public law regime, Anthony C Infanti, *Our Selfish Tax Laws: Toward Tax Reform That Mirrors Our Better Selves* (MIT Press 2018), at Chapter 2.
97. Esin Örücü, *The Enigma of Comparative Law: Variations on a Theme for the Twenty-First Century* (Springer 2013), at 34 and 62.

regime. Examples being compared are for ease of reference. When examples in the US or other fields of law are also not tax neutral, I propose a tax-neutral option for the EU, so as not to repeat the same mistakes.

1.3.5.4 *The Comparability of the Legal System(s) Selected*

To conduct comparative legal research and to achieve a meaningful comparison and evaluation, the comparability of the legal systems selected must be established.[98] Selecting the US FA rules is justified because the current CCCTB Directive Proposal, especially the formulary sharing mechanism, is a legal transplantation project mainly from, but not limited to, the US. This is repeatedly shown in the legislative history documents.[99]

Therefore, it is meaningful to analyse and compare the origin of the legal transplantation because the origin of the legal transplantation can reflect some inherent weakness of the system. Since the aim of this research is to find loopholes and consequent solutions, it is justified to choose the US as the main comparison object.

However, I am fully aware that FA experience developed in US state taxation has its own constitutional context[100] and cannot (and should not) always easily apply to the EU or an international context. I indicate this in the discussions when appropriate.

1.4 THE RELEVANT LITERATURE AND ACADEMIC DISCUSSIONS

This book involves three main discussion lines of the existing literature: corporate taxation, different tax neutrality principles and their interaction with the benefit principle, and FA.

1.4.1 Corporate Taxation: Justification and Failures

This book analyses the corporate taxation related literature, including the existence of corporate taxation, the actual burden of corporate taxation, and tax avoidance of corporate taxation, such as the impact of the digital economy and the international tax avoidance problem of BEPS. Although there are different theoretical justifications for the existing corporate tax system as such, there is a consensus that nowadays at the international level, MNEs' corporate tax bases are seriously eroded in various aggressive ways. The existing literature regarding corporate taxation heavily focuses on tax avoidance phenomena and proposes 'practical' solutions. However, it seems that the comprehensive theoretical framework to build the alternative to the failing international tax regime is still missing. This research can contribute to filling this gap.

98. *Ibid.*, 33.
99. *See* European Commission CCCTB Working Paper No. 47 (17 November 2006) and No. 60 (13 November 2007).
100. Walter Hellerstein, The Application of Formulary Apportionment to Related Entities: Lessons from the US Experience, in Krever & Vaillancourt (eds), *supra* n. 46, at 5.04.

1.4.2 Interactions Between the Benefit Principle and Market Neutrality

The normative framework developed by the book involves two principles: the benefit principle and market neutrality (MN). This research revisits the literature related to the benefit principle and different concepts of tax neutrality. In Chapter 2, I establish how MN is consistent with the benefit principle and how they can be intertwined.

As to the first element in the normative framework, the benefit principle mandates that a tax system is justified when there are relevant public benefits. The normative framework of this research consists of both the benefit principle and MN. It is also an attempt to reconcile the efficiency (represented by MN) and equity (represented by the benefit principle) in the corporate tax system.[101]

While relying on the benefit principle, there are still some theoretical puzzles which need resolution. As to how the benefit principle is formulated, this book explores the academic arguments at both international and national tax levels. It should be noted that, even though being quoted often, the benefit principle is not yet thoroughly discussed consistently in the field of international tax law either.

According to Avi-Yonah's early work, the (traditional) benefit principle of international tax law justifies the residence state's taxing powers on 'active income' and the source state's taxing powers on 'passive income' such as interest and dividend income.[102] But since the distinction of passive/active income or residence/source state taxation is also reconsidered for not being able any longer to reflect MNE taxpayers' economic activities in the current digital economy, Avi-Yonah, together with Xu[103] even changed his early proposal on the benefit principle. Some other scholars like Fleming, Peroni, and Shay[104] negate the benefit principle in the international tax regime and claim that the benefit principle has failed and the ability to pay principle is the right theory for the US's international tax policy. The meaning of the benefit principle is still evolving. I further elaborate on this in Chapter 2.1 and Chapter 2.2.

Unlike Fleming, Robert, and Shay, this book does not include 'the-ability-to-pay principle' in the normative framework; however, when refining and improving the benefit principle by using a general formulation of public benefits, taking away the specific link between the benefit and the individual taxpayer and making economic activities as the criterion to establish existence of public benefits, the ability to pay principle is consistent with the revised benefit principle. Moreover, legal systems that perform the redistribution function are also classified as a type of public benefit. The redistribution function of the ability to pay principle can be fulfilled by the benefit principle too.

---

101. To reconcile the two seemingly conflicting tax law principles 'efficiency' and 'equity' and make a comprehensive theory, *see* James R Repetti, The Appropriate Roles for Equity and Efficiency in a Progressive Income Tax, 23 Florida Tax Review 522 (2020). Repetti's paper does not touch upon CIT. This book expands this effort to the field of CIT of multinational taxpayers.
102. Reuven S Avi-Yonah, International Taxation of Electronic Commerce, 52 Tax Law Review 507 (1996).
103. Reuven S Avi-Yonah & Haiyan Xu, Evaluating BEPS: A Reconsideration of the Benefits Principle and Proposal for UN Oversight, 6 Harvard Business Law Review 185 (2016).
104. J Clifton Fleming Jr, Robert J Peroni & Stephen E Shay, Fairness in International Taxation: The Ability-to-Pay Case for Taxing Worldwide Income, 5 Florida Tax Review 299 (2001).

In addition to Klaus Vogel and David Hasen's discussions on the relationship between tax neutrality and the benefit principle, this research also refers to Liam Murphy and Thomas Nagel's work on 'tax justice'[105] in the context of national taxation. According to Murphy and Nagel's analysis, when public benefits are interpreted as 'providing a free market economy' or 'the precondition of property right', such as relevant legal and economic systems, the benefit principle is indeed the justification for levying tax. This book has advanced the understanding of the benefit principle in the context of a cross-border situation and tested the tax justice concept developed in the context of national taxation.

As to the second element in the normative framework: the tax neutrality principle (regardless of which one) requires that a tax system not distort taxpayers' economic decisions, and typical examples include capital import neutrality (CIN), capital export neutrality (CEN), capital ownership neutrality (CON), and MN. These tax neutrality principles widely cited in the field of the international tax law regime can be traced back to the 1960s. This book's analysis ranges from Peggy Musgrave's early work to recent work from Mihir Desai and James Hines, Michael Devereux. Musgrave[106] was the first to distinguish CEN and CIN which represent different tax policies regarding capital export or capital import. In Musgrave's work, neutrality means, 'not negatively influenced'. Peggy Musgrave has her own preference for CEN because she emphasizes that states should not hinder outbound investments to another state and outbound investment is good for the global economy. Different from Musgrave, Mihir Desai and James Hines develop the concept of CON to emphasize that a taxation system should not distort capital ownership and asset transfer.[107] Michael Devereux[108] uses the MN concept to emphasize that taxation should not distort market competition, in general. Each of these tax neutrality principles involve a specific policy, and thus David Weisbach argues that there is no hierarchy between these tax neutrality principles.[109]

This book argues that by combining with the benefit principle, MN would be suitable for examining the EU's FA system. By including the benefit principle, the concept of MN can be enriched and become able to cover the other tax neutrality concepts. For example, legal scholars, such as Klaus Vogel[110] and David Hasen,[111] argue that tax neutrality could be formulated differently and take into account that providing public benefits rely on levying tax.

105. Liam Murphy & Thomas Nagel, *The Myth of Ownership: Taxes and Justice* (Oxford University Press 2002).
106. Peggy B Musgrave, *Taxation of Foreign Investment Income: An Economic Analysis* (Johns Hopkins Press 1963).
107. Mihir A Desai & James R Hines Jr, Evaluating International Tax Reform, National Tax Journal 487 (2003).
108. Michael P Devereux, Taxation of Outbound Direct Investment: Economic Principles and Tax Policy Considerations, 24 Oxford Review of Economic Policy 698 (2008).
109. David A Weisbach, The Use of Neutralities in International Tax Policy, 68 National Tax Journal 635 (2015).
110. Klaus Vogel & Johan Brands, *Taxation of Cross-Border Income, Harmonization, and Tax Neutrality under European Community Law: An Institutional Approach* (Kluwer Law International 1994).
111. David Hasen, Tax Neutrality and Tax Amenities, 12 Florida Tax Review 57 (2012).

1.4.3 Formulary Apportionment Experiences and Implications for the EU's Tax Reform

As to the third type of literature, this book explores the literature related to FA, including state taxation experiences in the US and discussions on the development of the CCCTB Directive Proposal of the EU. The discussions focus on the selection of the weighting factors. Currently there is a popular view to adopt the single sales factor, such as Avi-Yonah and Clausing.[112] It should be noted that the most cited work by Avi-Yonah and Clausing that supports the single sales factor is especially in the context of the US tax reform project in 2007. Conversely, Joanna Weiner[113] and Stefan Mayer[114] both favour a multiple-factor formula. The existing literature that supports the single-sales-factor formula argues that a single-sales-factor formula is more neutral than other types of formulas. It is because the single-sales-factor formula does not distort the production side (the asset and the labour) at all. In Chapter 3, I revisit the arguments regarding the selection of weighting factors.

This book has discussed other more recent developments of FA in the US as well as the results of empirical research to show the complete view and criticize some weaknesses in the early research. This research has updated the information and academic discussions in the US to facilitate more thorough debates. Last but not least, scholars from North America have been exploring the question how and if an FA system would also be applicable to allocating corporate tax on MNE taxpayers' cross-border activities in the regime of the North American Free Trade Agreement (NAFTA).[115] If we see the US as a mature internal market, NAFTA or some similar recent project could be an extension for this mature market. Moreover, it would be meaningful to investigate how the most well-known FA system in the US[116] evolves and deals with challenges.

---

112. Reuven Avi-Yonah & Kimberly A Clausing, *Reforming Corporate Taxation in a Global Economy: A Proposal to Adopt Formulary Apportionment* (Brookings Institution Washington, DC 2007).
113. Joann M Weiner, CCCTB and Formulary Apportionment: The European Commission Finds the Right Formula, in Weber & Amsterdam Centre for Tax Law (eds), *supra* n. 5. For another supportive view on the three-factor formula in the early US literature, *see* Benjamin N Henszey & Ronald S Koot, Is a Three Factor Apportionment Formula Fair, 35 Tax Executive 141 (1982).
114. Mayer, *supra* n. 48.
115. The following contributions discuss FA in the context of NFTA: Paul R McDaniel, Formulary Taxation in the North American Free Trade Zone, 49 Tax Law Review 691 (1993); John S Brown, Formulary Taxation and NAFTA, 49 Tax Law Review 759 (1993); Michael J McIntyre, The Design of Tax Rules for the North American Free Trade Alliance, 49 Tax Law Review 769 (1993); Richard D Pomp, Issues in the Design of Formulary Apportionment in the Context of NAFTA, 49 Tax Law Review 795 (1993).
116. Reform projects in US state taxation since the 1980s can be found in the archives of the MTC's website, http://www.mtc.gov. While preparing this manuscript in 2014, I had also consulted the MTC's counsel to scan some non-uploaded/unavailable files in 1990s, to study and understand the legislative history and record. The general inquiry was sent to mtc@mtc.gov.

1.5 RESULTS, INNOVATION STEPS, AND SOCIETAL RELEVANCE

1.5.1 The Benefit-Based Market Neutrality Framework in a Nutshell

In each chapter, this book applies the benefit-based MN principle to possible options for the current CCCTB Directive Proposal and shows how the rules should be designed for the EU FA regime. The benefit-based market (tax) neutrality principle can be illustrated as shown in Figure 2.

The baseline of the tax neutrality framework should not be a hypothetical 'no tax' situation but the optimal public benefits provided in each jurisdiction involved. The optimal taxation is presumed as the actual empirical fact in this book, so we do not calculate how much that amount of tax is in this book. The economic activities each taxpayer conducts within a jurisdiction are presumed to be the public benefits being enjoyed.

Figure 2 Tax Neutrality Baseline for the Common Consolidated Corporate Tax Base

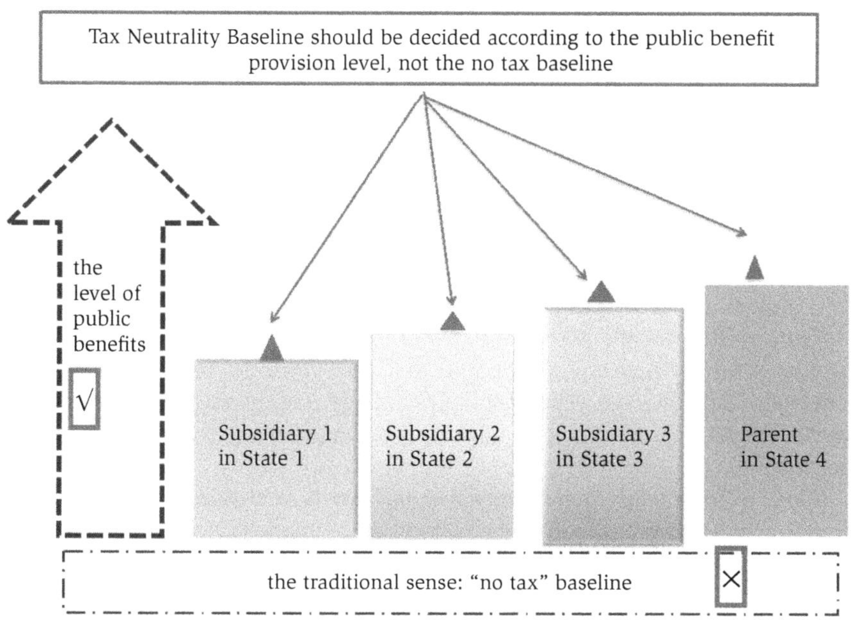

Source: The author.

As the general design, harmonizing the tax base and formula but leaving the tax rate unharmonized is consistent with this normative framework. Tax rate competition between EU Member States is still acceptable because they have discretion to decide how much it costs (which is from taxes levied) to provide the comparable level of public benefits. Furthermore, a formula consisting of both the input side and the output side of economic activities is consistent with the normative framework: a single-sales-factor formula is not enough because a single-sales-factor formula cannot reflect the public benefits related to the input side of economic activities. Chapter 3 provides detailed discussions.

The results derived from this book could be useful for policy makers of EU for the future EU FA regime reform. The effort of this book is to provide not only a comprehensive but also a critical understanding of the classic dilemma of the international tax regime of double taxation and double non-taxation. Such understanding would not only be limited to the EU but could be useful for international tax policy makers that need to deal with the issue of dividing the taxing powers in any jurisdiction. Even for the current bilateral tax treaty negotiations, the rationale of 'benefit-based market neutrality formulary apportionment' could serve as a potential element in a specific provision related to corporate taxation when needed.

1.5.2 Chapter Summaries and Main Findings

Chapter 2

The tax reform under EU law aims to pursue not only 'efficiency', i.e., reducing compliance costs, but also 'fairness', i.e., less vulnerable to tax avoidance or aggressive tax planning. This reform has several related but different mandates. Therefore, evaluating a tax reform project should take several different perspectives into account.

Chapter 2 analyses the different meanings of the benefit principle, while taking the development of different tax neutrality concepts into account, especially MN, in the context of EU law. 'Pursuing the benefit principle to achieve market neutrality' is the normative framework. In a nutshell, the revised benefit principle is the foundation and justification for (1) levying corporate tax, (2) conducting an international tax reform, and (3) designing and adopting a FA regime.

The benefit principle is reformulated as 'ensuring a taxation system which can faithfully reflect the taxpayers' economic activities from the production side to the demand side of the market'. The benefit principle is also consistent with the objective of the OECD's BEPS Project, i.e., 're-aligning the economic activity and the tax law' and value creation.

MN is consequently achieved, when tax law is designed to reflect taxpayers' economic activities faithfully from production to the market.

Chapter 3

Chapter 3 assesses key policy options of a typical FA system against benefit-based MN. These options include: FA as a genre, taxable nexus, formula factor selection, apportionment rules (including the sales factor by destination, the assets factor, the labour factor), implications of the digital economy, and tax rate competition.

Chapter 3 first clarifies the claimed inherent distortions caused by FA in the existing literature. An FA tax system is not distortive per se. Instead, FA examples and experiences in the international tax regime and US state taxation both demonstrate that the guiding principle to allocate taxing rights is the public benefits provided. On the contrary, the all-or-nothing approach of allocating taxing right in the traditional bilateral treaty is not in line with the benefit principle.

As to the nexus, the PE as the taxable nexus is not in line with the benefit principle (even though the older literature claims it is). Factor-presence nexus is the more reasonable option because factors represent the public benefits. As to the selection of weighting factors, adopting a three-factor formula: the sales, the assets, and the labour factors, is in line with the benefit principle instead of adopting a single-factor formula. Moreover, EU Member States should be allowed to decide the statutory corporate tax rate because EU Member States are better positioned to decide how much tax should be levied to sustain the public benefits of their part of the EU internal market. A minimum tax rate harmonization for the EU is justified[117] because minimum public benefits are needed to have a well-functioning market environment.

Chapter 4

From Chapter 4 onwards, this book discusses each factor of the formula used in the current CCCTB Directive Proposal. Chapter 4 explores 'the sales factor in action' from existing tax law including US state taxation and EU VAT regimes, showing deviations from the sales-by-destination rationale. The deviation from the sales-by-destination principle is due to political and administrative concerns: when the destination is not desirable, not convenient, or not ascertainable. These deviations often go beyond what is necessary and cause complexities.

There are two aspects of the sales factor discussed: the scope of the sales (definition) and the attribution of the sales. Chapter 4 demonstrates the disputes of defining the sales and deciding the scope. In the US, the definition of sales closely resembles the 'unitary business' concept, and thus the 'transactional test' and 'functional test' to determine a unitary business are also used to define sales, especially regarding intangibles. In practice, the definition of sales in legislation is also formulated negatively: providing an exclusion list of 'non-sales', or a throw-out rule for intangible income the location of which is uncertain.

The current CCCTB Directive Proposal's sales factor followed the US's interpretation and used the criterion 'earned in the ordinary course of trade and business', which is a similar term in the international tax law. It might look reasonable, but when the sales are still understood as receipts earned 'in the ordinary business course', and not understood as a 'response to the clients/customers' market', the 'non-sales' exclusion list still can lack items that economically are not responsive to the market,

117. In response to the OECD's Pillar Two proposal and the need to support recovery from the COVID-19 crisis, the minimum corporate tax rate was proposed in the European Commission's 2021 Tax Policy Agenda, *see* European Commission, Communication From the Commission to the European Parliament and the Council: Business Taxation for the 21st Century, COM(2021) 251 final, 9.

Besides endorsing the minimum tax rate under the CCCTB, *see* European Parliament, Committee on Economic and Monetary Affairs (Rapporteur A. Lamassoure), Report on the Proposal for a Council Directive on a Common Consolidated Corporate Tax Base (CCCTB), A8-0051/2018 44 (1 March 2018); comments by Martti Nieminen, Debate on the CCCTB: Destination-with-Credit Formula: A Simple Add-On That Would Make the CCCTB More Resilient in the Face of Tax Competition and Tax Planning, 47 Intertax 490 (2019).

especially for receipts earned in the form of purchase/sale transactions. The typical examples are short-term marketable securities and hedging transactions, which are indeed generated in the course of trade business, but they are not taxpayers' responses to clients or customers.

Further in Chapter 4, I also demonstrate that the sales-by-destination rationale is not fully implemented in VAT regimes or FA reforms in the US, even when the attribution rules are designed 'in the name of the destination principle'. There are three types of approaches to attribution among these various attribution rules: the origin-based, the destination-based, and the hybrid attribution approach. When the destination is not convenient (for example, VAT) and when the destination is not desirable (for example, the US's throw-back rule for 'no-where sales') are the two main occasions where attribution rules deviate from the sales-by-destination principle. The real purposes are pursuing tax administration convenience and fear of losing revenue, respectively. These purposes are unfortunately merely a compromise and cannot guarantee efficiency or simplicity either. Most importantly, these rules of 'deemed' destination are not market neutral because the deemed destinations deviate from the customers' market.

Chapter 5

Chapter 5 deals with the labour factor. The labour factor under the current CCCTB Directive Proposal is one of the three weighting factors of the formula, which is designed to reflect how MNE taxpayers make use of the labour market.

Although the definition of employees is the most essential question, there is still no uniform definition of employee across EU Member States or at the EU level, either in labour law or in social security law. So, it is impossible to transplant any consensus because such consensus does not exist.

There are two common features regarding indicators that are used to decide the employee status across the US and the EU, though. First, the key to deciding employee status represents the power imbalance in the employment relationship. Second, the binary distinction between employee versus self/employee/entrepreneur is still widely used but being challenged. In order to enhance protection of employees, there is also a common trend to explore the grey area between these two categories, either by accepting the third category or by extending the scope of employee.

For designing the labour factor, it should take this trend into account. This trend shows that human resources in the labour market nowadays can be provided in so many different flexible forms, and even in the form of 'gig economy/platform economy', like Uber drivers or platform freelancers. The new technology has made the labour market more flexible for employers to make use of and enjoy benefits.

Therefore, the labour factor should exclude purely independent contractors based on commercial relationships. By using the 'ABC test' developed in the US, the scope of purely independent contractors would be quite limited. As to attributing employees, they should be attributed to where they physically and actually perform tasks because the location represents the labour market being utilized. When an employee works for different group members or companies or in different jurisdictions, that employee's attribution should be calculated pro rata according to the time actually spent. Such approach is also suitable for attributing workers in the digital economy.

Chapter 6

The assets factor (or the term 'the property factor' used in the US) represents taxpayers' input side production activities too. The public benefit justifies the assets factor as the environment providing non-human resources. The assets factor had been used in many early state formulas in the US, whereas Canada abandoned the assets factor from its FA system. The design of the assets factor has been confronted with two difficult issues: the treatment of intangibles and valuation.

Chapter 6 asks: what is a market-neutral design assets factor to reflect taxpayers' economic activities from the production side? In traditional FA systems, intangibles are excluded from the assets factor because of being mobile, easy to manipulate, and hard to value. The current CCCTB Directive Proposal has followed this rationale of excluding intangibles. However, such exclusion ignores the fact that IP rights are the main driver of value creation. Where innovation activities take place is closely linked to the environment encouraging and promoting innovation. Such environment is a public benefit justifying the inclusion of intangibles. Therefore, it is legitimate and necessary to include intellectual property (IP) rights: the traditional idea of excluding intangibles is not market neutral because such exclusion ignores the public benefits provided for encouraging a 'knowledge economy'. The EU's new tax reform package BEFIT also expressly announces that it will include intangibles in the assets factor. This approach is on the right track.

Chapter 6 concludes that, in addition to tangible assets, the assets factor should include IP rights that are contributed for taxpayers' production activities. The evaluation method of assets should be based on the historical price, not on the market price. The attribution rules should be based on where such assets are actually used, not which group member has economic or legal ownership over the asset. Therefore, fixed assets should be attributed to the physical location's utilization. As to intangibles that can be included, where development, enhancement, maintenance, protection, and exploration (DEMPE) activities take place is the attribution criterion for attributing intangibles (which can be attributed to multiple places); the costs of DEMPE activities are the valuation method.

Chapter 7

The design of the standard three-factor formula is based on the manufacturing/merchandising industry model. Therefore, a few special industry formulas are necessary to reflect more closely the economic reality of non-manufacturing industries. This chapter discusses three special industry formulas other than the standard formula: the financial industry, the transportation industry, and the extractive (oil and gas) industry under the current CCCTB Directive Proposal.

In my view, there are two common features of these three 'special' industries: mobility and their (positive and negative) externality. Mobility means the mobile features of the economic activities, such as transportation and financial transactions; positive externality means some industries are key to flourish over other industries: the oil and gas industry provides energy resources; the transportation industry facilitates the flow of goods; the financial industry facilitates the flow of monetary capital. From an economic development perspective, these industries are key facilitators; but from the environmental and societal perspective, the practices of these three industries are also responsible for negative possibilities caused to society, such as environmental impact, climate change, or financial crisis. These two features also justify adoption of an FA system for these industries because these industries involve different relationships with the public benefits provided in specific jurisdictions. These jurisdictions have higher regulatory needs to address these industries.

Although referring to these industry formulas as 'special', FA experiences in these industries are in fact traced back to the late nineteenth century in the US. Therefore, to design benefit-based MN industry formulas is to rediscover the root and the fundamental purpose of adopting an FA to levy corporate tax: to reflect MNE taxpayers' cross-border activities that make use of different public benefits in different jurisdictions. To adopt special industry formulas does not imply the failures or incompetence of the standard formula or an FA system as such. Therefore, the relationship between the standard formula and special industry formulas are not the principle and exceptions nor do they derogate from the norm. Instead, the standard formula and special industry formulas both pursue the benefit principle-based tax neutrality, and special industry formulas implement the standard formula nuancedly.

Chapter 8

The final chapter discusses the procedure of adjusting unfair apportionment results, the 'safeguard clause' and 'equitable apportionment' in the US. In my view, such procedure will correct any unfair results in a specific case but should be used sparingly. The equitable apportionment clause is not the same as a GAAR, although their functions sometimes overlap.

From the substantive design to the procedural action, benefit-based MN should be fully implemented comprehensively so that MNE taxpayers' economic activities and tax base apportionment would be consistent with each other. By implementing the benefit-based MN framework for the EU's FA regime in the first place, the need to adjust unfair results would be reduced. The EU's FA regime should be selective based on the US's experiences with equitable apportionment and not allow too many ad hoc adjustments in the name of pursuing fair apportionment.

CHAPTER 2

The Normative Framework: Implementing the Benefit(s) Principle to Achieve Market Neutrality

if there is to be a limitation on the taxing power of each of these States, that limitation surely cannot be on a first-come-first-tax basis.

Justice Goldberg[118]

2.1 THE BENEFIT PRINCIPLE AS JUSTIFICATION FOR TAXATION

2.1.1 Two Elements of the Normative Framework: The Benefit Principle and Market Neutrality

An ideal EU FA regime is expected to achieve different objectives simultaneously: mitigating the BEPS problems and creating an obstacle-free business environment, which can be seen in the preamble of the 2016 CCCTB Directive Proposal. To achieve such a multidimension objective simultaneously, a supranational tax system needs a more inclusive guiding principle as the framework to balance the interests of the different stakeholders involved: the EU, Member States, and MNE taxpayers.

Therefore, the normative framework of this book consists of two interconnected elements: (1) implementing the benefit principle and (2) achieving MN.

The basis of the normative framework is: while causing inevitable DWL, taxation provides the preconditions of public benefits. Public benefits are understood broadly, not narrowly in reference to specific individuals or companies, but as sustaining a free and healthy market. In other words, 'benefits' should not be understood as specific

118. US Supreme Court, *General Motors Corp. v. Washington*, 377 U.S. 436 (1964), Mr Justice Goldberg, with whom Mr Justice Stewart and Mr Justice White join, dissenting., at 377 U.S. 458.

benefits offered or received but should be understood as 'all relevant public goods maintaining a market'.[119]

Economic activities are the indicators of using a market as public benefits. To be more precise, when there are economic activities, it is presumed that taxpayers utilize public benefits. MN is a status in which tax is levied according to economic activities. In this status, public benefits are sufficient (but not wasting public expenditure) to support economic activities. MN status exists when optimal taxation is levied. As governments should provide sufficient public benefits to maintain the free-market economy, a tax levied to sustain the market is justified. However, governments are not almighty, and public benefits are not unlimited. Therefore, no tax and excessive tax are both contrary to the benefit principle. When taxes exceed the public benefits provided, such excessive tax increases unnecessary DWL.

Here another fundamental question arises: why do I not simply use the 'inter-nation equity' as the framework? Putting it differently, is it still logical to design the normative framework as MN and the benefit principle instead of as one? My affirmative answer is that it is still logical and necessary to start from the benefit principle and MN and extend the borderline to 'inter-nation equity' or fairness,[120] but not the other way around.

The reason is that the EU's FA regime is an effort at harmonization from the EU's internal market perspective, whereas inter-nation equity, as developed by Peggy Musgrave and other economists, is the norm of pursuing fairness between 'fully' sovereign states. Even though they are still sovereign with fiscal autonomy, EU Member States have the obligation not to hinder the functioning of the internal market but to facilitate the internal market. Therefore, inter-nation equity is not self-implementing. Therefore, while acknowledging that the benefit-based MN framework might in part overlap with inter-nation equity, these two concepts are neither conceptually identical nor interchangeable.

To have a complete picture of the theoretical tension, section 2.1 briefly discusses the feature of taxation and the relevance of the benefit principle. Section 2.2 revisits the development of the benefit principle. I demonstrate how the revised benefit principle is suitable for levying CIT and dividing taxing rights by an FA system in the cross-border context. When implementing the benefit principle to design a cross-border tax regime, the status of MN (elaborated in section 2.3) will be achieved accordingly.

119. The 'new' benefit principle is analysed by Joseph M Dodge, Theories of Tax Justice: Ruminations on the Benefit, Partnership, and Ability-to-Pay Principles, 58 Tax Law Review 399 (2004).
120. There are quite a few studies analysing the idea of the 'fairness' principle in the context of international tax law. *See* Nancy H Kaufman, Fairness and the Taxation of International Income, 29 Law and Policy in International Business 145 (1997); Fleming, Peroni & Shay, *supra* n. 104.

2.1.2 The Benefit Principle Is Justification for Optimal Taxation: Weighting Tax-Caused Deadweight Loss Versus Conceptual Measurement Units of Public Benefits

In the public economics literature, taxation is formulated as causing 'deadweight loss' (DWL),[121] which creates inefficiency and hinders the optimal welfare maximum.[122] This DWL concept, followed and elaborated on by many tax scholars,[123] is primarily influenced by the work of the well-known economist Arnold Harberger in the mid-twentieth century.[124]

According to Harberger, levying tax on companies would cause a price increase of goods or services provided by a company. Harberger used the classic economic supply-and-demand curve to show that levying tax could 'distort' the optimal outcome. The famous 'Harberger's triangle' describes the DWL caused by taxation in the supply-and-demand curve. If there were no tax levied, the outcome would be completely undistorted. Based on this DWL concept, some research further argues that corporate taxation is distortive per se at both the national and international levels,[125] and corporate taxation should be eliminated.[126] For some economists, taxation,

121. 'Tax as deadweight loss' has been used in many basic textbooks, for example, Pasquale Pistone & others, *Fundamentals of Taxation: An Introduction to Tax Policy, Tax Law and Tax Administration* (IBFD 2019). DWL caused by taxation is also widely used in mainstream public finance textbooks, such as Jonathan Gruber, *Public Finance and Public Policy* (6th ed., Macmillan International Higher Education 2019), at 51, and at 619 to discuss the relationship between taxation and economic efficiency.
122. A quite prevailing view of economic theory of optimal taxation is that, in the long term, there should 'not' be any tax levied on capital or labour because such tax would hinder accumulation of capital or workers. *See* the remarks and overview, Anton Korinek, Taxation and the Vanishing Labor Market in the Age of AI, 16 The Ohio State Technology Law Journal (2020): 'One of the most surprising, and simultaneously most instructive, theorems in the economics of optimal taxation is that it is optimal not to impose any taxes on capital in the long-run, no matter if we care mostly about efficiency or mostly about inequality.'
123. For example, Shoven estimated the size of the DWL of capital income originating from the 'corporate' sector to be 40%, which is more significant than Harberger's original estimate. Feldstein estimated it at 30%, *see* Martin Feldstein, Tax Avoidance and the Deadweight Loss of the Income Tax, 81 Review of Economics and Statistics 674 (1999). Goolsbee's estimate is around 5%-10%. *See* Austan Goolsbee, Taxes, Organizational Form, and the Deadweight Loss of the Corporate Income Tax, 69 Journal of Public Economics 143 (1998).
    Harberger's theory on DWL is influential worldwide, including in Europe. For research data from North Europe, *see* Peter Birch Sørensen, Measuring the Deadweight Loss from Taxation in a Small Open Economy: A General Method with an Application to Sweden, 117 Journal of Public Economics 115 (2014). Sørensen tests data from Sweden and also argues the existence of DWL of corporate tax and the burden on wages. Numerous studies accept Harberger's assumption and theory.
124. AC Harberger, *The Corporation Income Tax: An Empirical Appraisal. Tax Revision Compendium* 1 (House Committee on Ways and Means, 86th Congress, First Session) (1959), at 231-240; comments, James R Hines, Three Sides of Harberger Triangles, 13 Journal of Economic Perspectives 167 (1999). The DWL size of corporate tax, Harberger estimated, is around 2.5%.
125. For example, Gaetan Nicodeme, Corporate Income Tax and Economic Distortions, Taxation Papers from Directorate General Taxation and Customs Union, European Commission (2009).
126. Walt Schubert, A Note on Eliminating the Corporate Income Tax, 17 Journal of Accounting and Finance (2017).

including corporate tax, is suspected of being an inherent distortion and thus an enemy of economic efficiency.[127]

In contrast to focusing on DWL, some other economists formulate taxation as a reflection of public benefits enjoyed or provided. This is the concept that the benefit principle is based on. Welfare economists also accept that discussions about (in)efficiency of taxation should focus not only on DWL (i.e., costs) but also on the benefit perspective that taxation can bring.[128] For example, Manski especially criticizes that many scholarly works overemphasize taxation as DWL, as distortion, and as 'inefficiency' and neglect taxation's function to support public spending.[129] Instead, Manski embraces the reality of 'ambiguity'[130] on the income tax-financed public expenditure and thus he does not feel uncomfortable with taxation, nor does he classify taxation as inherent distortion or inherent inefficiency.

It is also worth noting that even though Harberger is the pioneer of advancing the 'taxation as deadweight loss' argument and is sceptical of the economic justification of corporate tax,[131] he does not hold a completely identical opinion as many economists who emphasize (thus condemn) taxation as DWL.[132] In a recent extensive interview in

127. It should be noted that, there are other economists who redefine the DWL effect of a tax that 'prevents an economic behavior from happening' as a type of benefit 'real option value', i.e., 'the ability to wait' for 'the possibility that the economic activity will take place in the future under better conditions.' *See* Adi Libson, Is the Deadweight Actually Dead-Real Option Value and Taxation of Oil and Gas, 45 Seton Hall Law Review 833 (2015).

Libson discussed the real option value for taxation of oil and gas and cited the work of Avinash K Dixit & Robert S Pindyck, *Investment under Uncertainty* (Princeton University Press 1994), at 8. Dixit and Pindyck's theory is not discussed here, but the concept of 'uncertainty' or 'ambiguity' will also be presumed.

128. Charles F Manski, Choosing Size of Government under Ambiguity: Infrastructure Spending and Income Taxation, 124 Economic Journal 359 (2014).

James A Mirrlees, An Exploration in the Theory of Optimum Income Taxation, 38 Review of Economic Studies 175 (1971).

129. Charles Manski, Removing Deadweight Loss from Economic Discourse on Income Taxation and Public Spending, VoxEU (2013).

It seems that the 'efficiency' argument in the field of taxation has prevailed over 'equity' by many economic scholars.

For example, in Agúndez-García's analysis, efficiency and equity are opposite benchmarks: neutrality belongs to efficiency whereas benefit belongs to equity. *See* Ana Agúndez-García, The Delineation and Apportionment of an EU Consolidated Tax Base for Multi-Jurisdictional Corporate Income Taxation: A Review of Issues and Options, Taxation Papers from Directorate General Taxation and Customs Union, European Commission (2006) at 43.

In the different context of progressive personal income tax, James Repetti has sharp remarks: even though there is no theoretical or empirical data showing that progressive personal income tax would lead to a decrease in labour supply, many economists still firmly assume so. *See* Repetti, *supra* n. 101. Repetti's paper does not touch upon CIT.

In my view, such belief is due to overgeneralizing the terms 'inefficiency', 'distortions' and 'deadweight losses' caused from levying tax and overemphasizing the possible negative or hindering effect due to a specific type of tax. In Chapter 3 of this book, I explain the term 'distortions' in the context of FA and emerging confusions.

130. Manski, *supra* n. 128.

131. Arnold C Harberger, *Taxation and Welfare* (Little Brown 1974), at Chapter 6, Corporate Income Taxes, at 123. Harberger argues that CIT is mainly out of 'administrative feasibility' and 'political popularity'.

132. In Harberger's interview in 2012, he commented that: 'That's why I say that most people who talk about Harberger triangles are talking about Dupuit triangles, Marshall triangles, Hicks

2012,[133] Harberger reaffirmed that he defines taxation and subsidies as his main distortions to the supply-demand line.[134] Harberger advocates that imposing taxation and granting subsidies would create 'distortions'. However, he also expresses that it is not necessary to eliminate every single distortion. Distortion is a descriptive term, not a normative term that always requires action to be taken. Harberger does not negate taxation as such. Rather, Harberger still endorses conducting a cost-benefit analysis as well as a benefit-cost analysis to any policy, including taxation. He also endorses the importance of providing public infrastructure financed by taxation.[135] That is to say, even Harberger, the economist who created the term 'deadweight loss', also acknowledges the benefit principle to justify levying tax.

In my view, there is acceptable ambiguity, as Manski describes, to assume there could be an optimal taxation that the public benefits provided can outweigh the DWL provided. Taxation is neither purely DWL nor purely public-benefit measurement units. In this regard, there is only a rough relationship, not a precise equation between (corporate) taxation and public expenditure to provide public goods. But we can say that only when levying a tax which does not represent a corresponding public benefit, i.e., by levying far too much tax to support a healthy market, is such tax DWL.

---

triangles – anybody's triangles but Harberger's.' His remarks replied to the definition of 'demand'. He clarified that he sees 'my demand curve is the end point with the tax', and his general equilibrium theory actually takes into account all types of tax levied into a 'reduced form', as a tax rate. Therefore, when scholars use Harberger's triangles in a special equilibrium discussion, i.e., calculating the relation of the effect of levying a specific tax on one substitute and the reaction of another substitute, it might deviate from Harberger's original intention of his triangle. *See* Arnold Harberger & Richard Just, A Conversation with Arnold Harberger, 4 Annual Review of Resource Economics 1 (2012).

133. *Ibid.*, 7. Here is the quote from Arnold Harberger:

> I believe that we have a sensible alternative, which I call basic-needs externalities. The big key to basic-needs externalities is that it is not a weighting of the utility of the recipients; it is a weighting of their welfare as judged by others – others being the government, others being the taxpayers, others being the voting citizens, however you want to make it. My example is that, whereas anybody concerned with the utility of the recipient basically must say giving them money is the best you can do, why is it, then, that when we provide for public education, we say the kid has to go to school? We don't give the parent the money and say, 'You can have a party or send your kid to school.' That would be a utility approach. We say, 'Send your kid to school or else he doesn't get anything.' Medical care: 'Send him to the doctor or he doesn't get anything.' Housing: 'You occupy these public housing facilities, or you won't get anything.'

134. *Ibid.*, 14-15:

> Richard Just: The supply and demand curves that you're talking about typically depend on what the allocation of resources is, right? When you define a distortion, is that with respect to the status quo allocation of resources and endowments, and is that something economists should be a little bit more up front about?
>
> Arnold Harberger: No. My main distortions are taxes and subsidies, and they depend on what the law was. The allocations of resources and the economy are changing all the time, and these damned taxes are there. Of course, as the allocations change the demands change, and the resulting efficiency-cost triangle would change. But that means only that your underlying givens of the situation are changing through time, and we simply have to live with that.

135. Harberger & Just, *supra* n. 132, at 14-15.

Governments still have limitations, so the public benefits are not unlimited. Therefore, there would be a maximum cap on levying tax.

While accepting taxation causes DWL, my perspective on corporate tax reform would never lean towards 'abolishing corporate tax'[136] or eliminating corporate tax as much as possible. Corporations, especially multinationals, conduct enormous cross-border activities. Therefore, they make use of public benefits from different jurisdictions. As long as there are public benefits being provided, represented by economic activities, taxes should be levied.

To sum up, this book emphasizes that taxation is not merely inherent DWL and focuses on taxation being a measurement unit of public benefits with externality, or 'public goods'.[137] When there is a need to establish public benefits, levying taxes is justified. Part of levying taxes could inevitably be DWL (cost), but the DWL is merely marginal, and the main part of levying taxes would contribute to public benefits with positive externalities. In other words, ideal corporate tax would correspond to the public benefits enjoyed by MNE taxpayers, and these public benefits would be represented by MNE taxpayers' economic activities, including production and response to their customers in the market.

2.1.3 The Benefit Principle Is Justification for Conducting International Corporate Tax Reform

'Aligning value creation with taxation' is the core element of the OECD's BEPS project. It is consistent with the benefit principle too. When a jurisdiction provides its market for a corporation to conduct its economic activities, it is justified to have taxing rights. In other words, the rationale of the international tax reform led by the OECD/G20 is consistent with the benefit principle.

It should be noted that the literature, such as Avi-Yonah's work (*see* section 2.2.2), demonstrates that the traditional tax regime is or claims to be based on the benefit principle from the very beginning. It might feel confusing to argue the benefit principle as the rationale for the reform if the existing system is already based on it.

136. There are long-standing economic arguments of 'for and against the corporate income tax,' review and criticisms, *see* Richard J Vann, Policy Forum: The Policy Underpinnings of the BEPS Project – Preserving the International Corporate Income Tax?, 62 Canadian Tax Journal 433 (2014).

137. Discussions regarding the origin of the benefit theory, *see* Graeme S Cooper, The Benefit Theory of Taxation, 11 Australian Tax Forum 397 (1994). For a more recent discussion, *see* Miranda Stewart, The Tax State, Benefit and Legitimacy, TTPI – Working Paper 1 (2015); James R Hines, What Is Benefit Taxation?, 75 Journal of Public Economics 483 (2000).

In the field of political science, scholars use the term 'the Capture Principle' to describe justifications of taxing rights used in the international tax regime, broken down as 'the Principle of Fair Play,' 'a Compensatory Principle,' 'a Principle of Contribution.'

These are benefit principle arguments in the broad sense. *See* Adam Kern, Illusions of Justice in International Taxation, 48 Philosophy & Public Affairs 151 (2020). Kern casts doubts on these justifications, but his research has not yet reached an alternative. The philosophical discussions would go beyond the scope of this book, but these arguments do show some weakness of the benefit principle in the international tax regime.

However, although the approach of using residence versus source taxation to allocate taxing right is also claimed to be based on the benefit principle, in reality, it is not. The approach of deciding only one jurisdiction has the primary taxing right is a compromise to achieve the purpose of relieving double taxation. Both source and residence jurisdictions provide some public benefits but only one jurisdiction can have this primary taxing right. To decide a jurisdiction, source, or residence, that agrees to give up a taxing right while economic activities are being conducted in its territory already deviates from the benefit principle, and it is based on administrative practicality and political compromise. This compromise can be demonstrated in a typical bilateral tax treaty: some type of income is attributed to the residence jurisdiction, some to the source jurisdiction, even when both jurisdictions provide part of public benefits for a cross-border activity to generate a specific income.

Therefore, aligning value creation with taxation is an effort to realign taxing rights with the public benefits provided. This approach is also endorsed by Eva Escribano's latest theory of Presumptive Benefit Principle (elaborated in section 2.2.2).[138]

2.1.4 The Benefit Principle Is Justification for Adopting a Formula of Multiple Factors

In the academic discussions on the FA in the EU internal market context, Mayer has endorsed the benefit principle for adopting the three-factor formula because each factor is a proxy for public benefits.[139] Although Mayer's work does not elaborate further on what benefits exactly are reflected by these 'proxies', we can still see the sales factor, the assets factor, and the labour factor representing different stages of the value-creation chain from producers to customers. Since the benefit principle is suitable to describe the relationship with the jurisdiction involved, it would also be suitable to evaluate the weighting factor in the formula, including selection, composition, and attribution of each weighting factor.[140]

138. Eva Escribano, *Jurisdiction to Tax Corporate Income Pursuant to the Presumptive Benefit Principle: A Critical Analysis of Structural Paradigms Underlying Corporate Income Taxation and Proposals for Reform* (Kluwer Law International 2019).

139. Mayer, *supra* n. 48, at 2.3.1.7.-2.3.1.8; same opinion, Giammarco Cottani, Formulary Apportionment: A Revamp in the Post-Base Erosion and Profit Shifting Era?, 44 Intertax 755 (2016).

140. *See* Chapter 4, Chapter 5 and Chapter 6 of this book.

It might also be interesting to see the negative opinion on the benefit principle and value creation, *see* Koukoulioti's argument. Koukoulioti's argument is mainly based on 'disagreements on how we define benefits and the difficulty of ascribing physical location to income.' But if we can presume an acceptable degree of ambiguity on tax incidence and accept that income could just have multiple sources, the benefit principle and a chain of value creation might not be that incompatible with each other. Koukoulioti's understanding of the benefit principle seems to be still based on the all-or-nothing approach that distinguishes the residence versus source mutually exclusively.

V. Koukoulioti, User Contribution to Value Creation: The Benefit Principle in the Spotlight, in Pasquale Pistone & DM Weber (eds), *Taxing the Digital Economy: The EU Proposals and Other Insights* (IBFD 2019).

Moreover, since it is uncertain who bears the corporate tax incidence and whether or not the actual tax incidence of a formula lies on weighting factors,[141] it would not be wise to exclude any specific weighting factor or adopt a single-factor formula.

Weighting factors (assets, employees, sales) of the FA system are already the direct indicators of public benefits presumptively enjoyed by taxpayers. When making use of assets, it represents taxpayers' capacity to utilize the resources in that jurisdiction; when hiring employees, it represents making use of the labour market and enjoying the well-maintained healthy labour market and industrial relations; when conducting sales, it represents access to the customers' market. These three factors represent taxpayers' input and output activities, and thus these three are the most suitable factors. There might be other factors, such as 'departure ratio' or 'mileage ratio' in the existing formulas, but these 'special formulas' are just the embodiment of these three factors. As to the selection of the factors, section 3.4 of this book explains these factors in detail.

2.2 THE DEVELOPMENT OF THE BENEFIT PRINCIPLE IN DIFFERENT CONTEXTS

2.2.1 The Link Between Levying Taxation and Public Benefits Are Presumed When There Are Economic Activities

2.2.1.1 The Development of the Benefit Principle Revisited: From Specific Service to General Presumption

To further illustrate the role that the benefit principle[142] plays, I would like to revisit the meaning and the implications of the benefit principle. In the literature, the benefit principle in the context of domestic taxation and the benefit principle in the context of international tax have slightly different meanings.

In the field of (domestic) taxation, the benefit principle is an essential fundamental principle, just like the ability to pay principle. According to the benefit principle, a tax levied on taxpayers should be proportional to the benefits/public goods/public services received by taxpayers.[143] Levying tax is to finance the public goods provided by the government. Thus, the benefit principle justifies the government's taxing powers. Such principle can be traced far back to economic theories in the eighteenth

141. McLure supports the argument that tax incidence of a formula lies in weighting factors, *see* Charles E McLure, *State Corporate Income Tax: Lambs in Wolves' Clothing?* (Office of Tax Analysis, US Treasury Department 1977). Weiner argues the opposite. Joann M Weiner, An Economist's View of Income Allocation Under the Arm's Length Standard and Under Formulary Apportionment, *The State and Local Tax Lawyer. Symposium Edition* (American Bar Association 2009).
142. It seems that the 'benefits principle' in the plural form, and the 'benefit principle' are both accepted in the literature.
143. For analysis of the origin of the benefit principle, *see* Cooper, *supra* n. 137.

and nineteenth centuries, such as Adam Smith.[144] In the twentieth century, the famous philosopher Rawls's writing also reflects this perspective. Many economists also endorse the rationale of 'benefit-based' taxation.[145] Benefit-based taxation seems to reconcile seamlessly the ability to pay principle when we assume that the best measurement of tax is a taxpayer's income-generating ability. Such ability is the result of both endowed ability and public goods.[146]

It should also be noted that taxation still has its general features under the benefits principle. The definition of 'benefits' does not refer to the direct cost or charge of 'a specific service' but the general costs for bundled public goods that the government maintains and orders the market economy.[147] Therefore, in the context of the digital economy, even without direct physical contact, such public benefits can include 'providing a customers' market' for a foreign/non-resident business by conducting e-commerce.[148] Even the function of redistribution can be seen as a type of public benefit.[149] Therefore, when we describe taxation's functions of 'the ability to pay principle' and 'the benefit principle,' these two functions are not mutually exclusive. Instead, when we accept the benefit principle as including more types of public benefits/public goods, including 'a level playing field' or 'a re-distribution mechanism,' the benefit principle could even include 'implementing the ability to pay principle'. Therefore, I do not use the ability to pay principle in the normative framework.

The applicability of the benefit principle to CIT is nevertheless arguable. Peggy Musgrave, for example, has expressed that[150] corporate taxation is NOT a benefit-based taxation. Thus, even when the benefit principle is well-funded, it is not applicable to the state's entitlement to 'corporate income tax' in her view. Moreover, the difficulty in making the benefit principle apply to corporate income taxation is to establish the specific amount and causal link between the benefits and the taxpayers' actual enjoyment.[151]

Although some scholars argue that[152] the original benefit principle has already collapsed, even the 'revised'/'new' benefit principle still failed to measure the benefits

144. The origin of the benefit theory can be traced back to Adam Smith, *see* Cooper's analysis, *ibid.*
145. Matthew Weinzierl, Revisiting the Classical View of Benefit-Based Taxation, 128 Economic Journal F37 (2018).
146. *Ibid.*, 61.
147. Analysing the origin of the benefit theory, *see* Cooper, *supra* n. 137; Fleming, Peroni & Shay, *supra* n. 104, at 334.
148. Gianluigi Bizioliin, Fairness of the Taxation of the Digital Economy, in Werner C Haslehner & others (eds), *Tax and the Digital Economy: Challenges and Proposals for Reform* (Kluwer Law International 2019).
149. For how Stewart elaborates the ideas of benefits broadly, *see* Murphy & Nagel, *supra* n. 105, at 81.
150. Peggy B Musgrave, Principles for Dividing the State Corporate Tax Base, in *The State Corporation Income Tax: Issues in Worldwide Unitary Combination* (Stanford 1984); Peggy B Musgrave, Economic Criteria, Principles and Policies of the Taxation of Foreign Investment Income, in Musgrave, *supra* n. 106, at 6.
151. This is also a well-accepted theory in the field of the welfare economy, *see* Arnold C Harberger, Three Basic Postulates for Applied Welfare Economics: An Interpretive Essay, 9 Journal of Economic Literature 785 (1971).
152. Fleming, Peroni & Shay, *supra* n. 104.

provided for corporates by levying CIT, so the benefit principle cannot replace the ability to pay principle. I can partially agree with this argument. While seeing economic activities as indicators of enjoying public benefits, the ability to pay principle can be transcribed as the ability to make use of benefit principles: these two principles can exist in parallel and be consistent with each other.[153]

Moreover, the benefit principle provides justification to corporate tax law when we look at the special status corporations enjoy in the modern economy. As Brooks analyses, corporations enjoy two sets of benefits that justify levying CIT: the first type of benefit, for shareholders, is the legal personality and limited liability of a corporation.[154] Such legal privilege would enable shareholders to invest more freely via a corporation. The second type of benefit is various 'legal, social, and economic infrastructure to earn profits' that a corporation receives from the state, including a healthy and qualified workforce, transportation and communication infrastructures, etc. Despite theoretical objections, it is undeniable that these two types of benefits are enjoyed and provided to corporations in the modern market economy.

Liam Murphy and Thomas Nagel[155] have provided another interpretation of the benefit principle to argue that the public benefit is the condition of 'pre-tax income'. Murphy and Nagel provocatively argue that the natural right to pre-tax income is a myth because taxation is essential for the state to provide public goods, and earning income is based on an environment with sufficient public goods. In other words, without taxation or such public goods, earning any pre-tax income is simply impossible. Therefore, instead of regarding that pre-tax income should be owned by taxpayers, Murphy and Nagel argue that in any case taxpayers cannot claim 100% of the pre-tax income, and the state has the legitimacy to levy tax.

Murphy and Nagel still endorse the outcome of the 'free' market and competition because such an outcome reflects personal choices and responsibilities.[156] But a well-functioning market is not a free gift from God. Murphy and Nagel argue that a well-functioning market requires comprehensive legislation and government services from all aspects, such as anti-trust legislation, monetary policy, transportation policy, etc.,[157] and taxation needs to pay for these infrastructures.[158] Therefore, taxation and government are essential to establish a market.

2.2.1.2 The Uncertain Tax Incidence of CIT Does Not Negate the Benefit Principle or an FA System

When discussing the corporate tax design, there has been a dispute as to 'who' actually bears the burden of corporate tax because corporate tax is levied on corporations. Still,

153. The same opinion, De Wilde, *supra* n. 76, at 2.2.2.2.
154. Kim Brooks, Learning to Live with an Imperfect Tax: A Defence of the Corporate Tax, 36 U. Brit. Colum. Law Review 621 (2003).
155. Murphy & Nagel, *supra* n. 105.
156. *Ibid.*, 66.
157. *Ibid.*, 32-33.
158. The same remarks, Escribano, *supra* n. 138, at 2.02.

the tax burden of corporate tax will be borne by natural persons, such as shareholders, employees, or consumers. There has been no consensus until now.[159]

Traditionally, it is believed that the shareholders of corporations will bear the corporate tax.[160] More recently, scholars have started to argue that employees[161] of companies will be the people who ultimately bear the corporate tax incidence.[162] But recent studies also show that the corporate tax incidence is not necessarily the employees' burden.[163] The actual incidence of corporate tax could also be influenced over time, not in a single tax year. Thus, current shareholders and future shareholders both bear some part of tax incidence.[164] It is not clear where CIT incidence actually falls.

In the context of an FA system, the issue of CIT incidence would also play a role regarding 'weighting factor selection'. Some economists, like McLure, argue that the factors of the formula will also bear tax incidence of CIT, so customers, employees, and immobile capital (asset) owners will de facto bear the corporate tax incidence.[165] There is an undesirable implication that selecting the payroll factor or the asset factor in the formula would put the CIT burden on the employees or asset owners. However, according to Weiner, an FA corporate tax is not equivalent to different types of excise tax and simply creates a set of factors that bear tax incidence.[166] Such tax incidence effect does not cause economic double taxation either.[167]

159. Milanez's literature review shows that the existing empirical research on CIT economic incidence (shifted to labour or customers) has a wide range of estimated results, *see* Anne Milanez, Legal Tax Liability, Legal Remittance Responsibility and Tax Incidence: Three Dimensions of Business Taxation, OECD Taxation Working Papers 32 (2017), at 34-37.
160. The view is supported by the data and research from Arnold C Harberger, The Incidence of the Corporation Income Tax, 70 Journal of Political economy 215 (1962); Jennifer Gravelle, Corporate Tax Incidence: Review of General Equilibrium Estimates and Analysis, 66 National Tax Journal 185 (2013); Jane G Gravelle & Kent A Smetters, Does the Open Economy Assumption Really Mean That Labor Bears the Burden of a Capital Income Tax?, 6 The BE Journal of Economic Analysis & Policy (2006).
161. This seems to be the mainstream view currently. For the academic literature's review on tax incidence, *see* Clemens Fuest, Who Bears the Burden of Corporate Income Taxation, ETPF Policy Paper (2015); Other works argue the corporate tax incidence is borne on employees/wages, *see* Wiji Arulampalam, Michael P Devereux & Giorgia Maffini, The Direct Incidence of Corporate Income Tax on Wages, 56 European Economic Review 1038 (2012).
162. The economic incidence of corporate tax law is a difficult issue without a consensus. *See* Brooks, *supra* n. 154, at 632. Brooks cited an early academic discussion that demonstrates the difficulty for lawyers; *see* William A Klein, The Incidence of the Corporation Income Tax: A Lawyer's View of a Problem in Economics, Wisconsin Law Review 576 (1965).
163. For the new empirical data showing the opposite conclusion to the mainstream theory of corporate tax incidence, *see* Kimberly A Clausing, Who Pays the Corporate Tax in a Global Economy?, 66 National Tax Journal 151 (2013).
164. Alan J Auerbach, Who Bears the Corporate Tax? A Review of What We Know, 20 Tax Policy and the Economy 1 (2006).
165. Charles E McLure Jr, The Elusive Incidence of the Corporate Income Tax: The State Case, 9 Public Finance Quarterly 395 (1981).
166. Weiner, *supra* n. 141.
167. Johanna Hey, EU Common Consolidated Corporate Tax Base: Guided Variety versus Strict Uniformity-Lessons from the US States' Tax Chaos (Jean Monnet Chair 2008), at 49.

Moreover, until now, no precise data can demonstrate the actual amount of corporate tax incidence.[168] It is likely that shareholders, employees, investors, and customers all bear part of corporate tax incidence, but we are not sure exactly to what extent.[169] This tax incidence of the issue of corporate tax is an unresolved scholarly debate. Some American economists argue that corporate tax cuts would also favour employees, but others show that the historical data does not always demonstrate the link between 'wage rise' and 'corporate tax cut'.[170] Therefore, it would be oversimplified to abolish or even refuse to increase corporate tax, purely based on the tax incidence concerns, because there is not yet a solid scholarly consensus.

In addition, from the sociopolitical perspective of ensuring equality and combating inequality,[171] accepting tax incidence on natural persons is not a reason to completely abolish corporate tax income. The way of levying corporate taxation or cutting it[172] should not create obvious inequality in society.[173] Therefore, to negate CIT completely, by arguing that the actual corporate tax burden/tax incidence being borne by customers and employees, seems to overlook the redistribution function of corporate tax.[174]

All in all, recognizing the effect of corporate tax incidence on natural persons, whether on shareholders, customers, or employees, should not negate corporate tax or

168. The data showing different stakeholders all bearing the corporate tax incidence, especially employees, *see* Terry Shevlin & others, Who Bears the Costs of the Corporate Income Tax? Evidence from State Tax Changes and Accounting Data, Hawai'i Accounting Research Conference (HARC) paper (2019), at http://hdl.handle.net/10125/59340.

    Shevlin's work is quite insightful because he also researched the situation between the (state) corporate tax cut and wage variation. He found out that, a 'large tax cut' could result in a wage increase. Consequently, Shevlin argued that employees do bear part of the corporate tax incidence and can also enjoy the benefits of large tax cuts, at least partially.

169. For example, Clausing also indicates the complexity to model corporate tax and thus it is not definitive yet to draw conclusions on corporate tax incidence. Kimberly A Clausing, 'In Search of Corporate Tax Incidence, 65 Tax Law Review 433 (2011). Moreover, there is also data showing that corporate tax incidence is on customers. *See* James M Sallee, The Surprising Incidence of Tax Credits for the Toyota Prius, 3 American Economic Journal: Economic Policy 189 (2011).

170. For example, Cline is quite sceptical of the argument that 'large tax cuts cause a Large Increase in Wages' by demonstrating the historical data of the federal statutory tax rate. *See* William R Cline, Will Corporate Tax Cuts Cause a Large Increase in Wages?, Policy Briefs PB17-30 (2017), Peterson Institute for International Economics.

171. Robert Couzin, Policy Forum: The End of Transfer Pricing, 61 Canadian Tax Journal 159 (2013), 174.

172. Empirical research shows that cutting corporate tax could lead to inequalities between top earners and bottom earners. *See* Suresh Nallareddy, Ethan Rouen & Juan Carlos Suárez Serrato, *Do Corporate Tax Cuts Increase Income Inequality?* (National Bureau of Economic Research 2018). In my view, the recognized aggressive tax planning scenarios arising from corporate taxation have created inequalities from two aspects: (i) creating inequality to other market competitors who do not conduct such tax planning, and (ii) creating inequality to individuals who do not invest as corporate shareholders.

173. The phenomenon of 'paying merely small amount of tax' has been recognized as the evidence of inequalities caused by the various planning scenarios embedded in the current (international) corporate tax systems, *see* Thomas Piketty, *Capital in the Twenty-First Century* (Arthur Goldhammer tr, Harvard University Press 2017).

174. It might be accepted that due to the possible tax incidence effects, corporate taxation should not be the 'only measure' to pursue re-distribution, but the tax incidence effects should not be the main reason to negate corporate taxation completely either.

the justification of each weighting factor. At the end of the day, there is no consensus on who/what groups of natural persons bear corporate tax incidence. Even if CIT incidence ultimately is on natural persons, the public benefits should still justify levying CIT and adopting an FA system.

2.2.2 The Wrong Application of the Benefit Principle to the Traditional International Taxation Regime: The Residence Versus Source Distinction Needs to Be Reconsidered

There are also discussions about implementation of the benefit principle in the field of international taxation. The benefit principle was believed to be the starting point of international tax law in 1923, when tax economics reached a compromise between source and residence taxation.[175]

Prior to the compromise of the source and residence principle in the early twentieth century, Von Schanz, in the late nineteenth century, argued that, based on 'the economic allegiance theory'[176] and the benefit theory, where a cross-border income arises, the source jurisdiction should levy 75% of the income whereas the residence jurisdiction should levy 25%.[177] Von Schanz's ratio seems a little bit random, but it is vital that he realized quite early that to generate a cross-border income, both the source and the residence jurisdiction contribute to it.[178]

It is widely accepted that the two fundamental international tax law principles, i.e., the residence principle and the source principle, are also subject to and mandated by the benefit principle. In Avi-Yonah's analysis,[179] the benefit principle and the single taxation principle are the cornerstones of international taxation. Following these two principles, taxation will be levied according to the public services provided for taxpayers' generating the income, and the income should only be taxed once. International tax law is presumed to achieve efficiency and fairness when two principles are implemented.

According to Avi-Yonah, in the classical international tax system, passive investment income should be taxed in the residence country. The active business

175. Avi-Yonah, *supra* n. 61, at Chapter 1.
176. The economic allegiance principle and the benefit theory are synonyms. For some critical views on the economic allegiance principle, *see* Laurens Van Apeldoorn, BEPS, Tax Sovereignty and Global Justice, 21 Critical Review of International Social and Political Philosophy 478 (2018). Van Apeldoorn argued that the economic allegiance principle is still vulnerable when we examine it from the perspective of global re-distribution justice and the tax competition between sovereign states can just make winners stronger and losers weaker. 'Assuming that being allocated a greater share of the tax base increases one's fiscal self-determination, the principle of economic allegiance does not reliably give priority to increasing the fiscal self-determination of low-income countries.'
177. Klaus Vogel, Worldwide vs. Source Taxation of Income: A Review and Re-Evaluation of Arguments (Part I), 16 Intertax 216 (1988).
178. Jinyan Li, Global Profit Split: An Evolutionary Approach to International Income Allocation, 50 Canadian Tax Journal 823 (2002).
179. Avi-Yonah, Who Invented the Single Tax Principle? *supra* n. 32.

income should be taxed at the source country, based on the benefit principle.[180] The residence country justifies its right to tax passive investment income earned abroad because the residence country provides the capital. Ideally, under coordination between residence and source countries, one income will be only taxed once, and such a result will also be consistent with the single tax principle.

It should be noted, although the distinction between residence and source has existed for a long time, the concept of 'source' is not self-evident.[181] Source has been described as the opposite of 'residence': tax not being levied based on residence is categorized as 'source' taxation.[182] Furthermore, even when discussing source taxation, scholars cannot reach a consensus on whether 'origin-based taxation' or 'destination-based taxation' is more efficient and desirable.[183] The benefit principle can justify both 'origin-based taxation' and 'destination-based taxation' because origin jurisdiction and destination jurisdiction both provide public benefits in different aspects.[184]

In the international tax regime, using the benefits principle to justify the residence and source jurisdictions to have taxing rights on active income and passive income is mainly based on a rule of thumb and practices rather than being close to the original idea of benefit principle. As Avi-Yonah discussed in his influential essay,[185] active business incomes are primarily earned by companies, and passive investment incomes are earned by individuals in the early twentieth century when the international tax regime was initiated. Residence is a more proper nexus for taxing individuals because individuals usually belong to one society, and residence can function better to serve the purpose of redistribution. On the contrary, residence of multinational companies is less relevant for their active business incomes. Furthermore, the source country provides significant benefits to the corporations that carry out business activities within the source jurisdiction, including various local infrastructures.

Using the benefit principle to justify the dichotomy of passive versus active income and the residence versus source principle is also challenged.[186] For example, Avi-Yonah and Xu argue that the benefit principle applied in international tax law has

180. It is the origin of the international tax regime since 1920. Avi-Yonah & Xu, *supra* n. 103; Reuven S Avi-Yonah, Tax Competition, Tax Arbitrage, and the International Tax Regime, U of Michigan Law & Economics, Olin Working Paper (2007).
181. Vogel, *supra* n. 177.
182. Such historical distinction has been discussed as meriting reconsideration, *see* Bret Wells & Cym H Lowell, Income Tax Treaty in the 21st Century: Residence vs. Source, 5 Columbia Journal Tax Law 1 (2013); Bret Wells & Cym Lowell, Tax Base Erosion and Homeless Income: Collection at Source Is the Linchpin, 65 Tax Law Review 535 (2011).
183. Michael Devereux & Rita de la Feria, Designing and Implementing a Destination-Based Corporate Tax, University of Oxford Centre of Business Taxation Working Papers (2014); ECCM Kemmeren, Source of Income in Globalizing Economies: Overview of the Issues and a Plea for an Origin-Based Approach, 60 Bulletin for International Taxation 438 (2006).
184. Similar formulations, Keen and Hellerstein introduce the basic economic arguments: the origin-based taxation achieves 'consumption efficiency' whereas the destination-based taxation achieves 'production efficiency'. *See* Michael Keen & Walter Hellerstein, Interjurisdictional Issues in the Design of a VAT, 63 Tax Law Review 359 (2009), 363-364. (The second part of this paper focuses on VAT design).
185. Avi-Yonah, *supra* n. 102, at 520.
186. Avi-Yonah & Xu, *supra* n. 103.

failed to allocate the taxing powers of sovereign states properly, and problems that OECD BEPS reports have revealed cannot be solved by the application of the existing benefit principle: i.e., passive income being allocated to the residence state and active income being allocated to the source state. Avi-Yonah and Xu argue that the existing benefit principle previously developed in the international tax regime should apply 'reversely' to the residence state and the source state. In other words, they argue that the 'old' benefit principle will not solve the problems of BEPS.

It is quite interesting that Avi-Yonah and Xu already saw the inevitable weakness of the BEPS Project and argued for a reverse application of the benefit principle to active and passive income. I especially agree with their observation regarding the weakness of the BEPS Project. However, I am still doubtful of a simple reverse application of the residence and source state because such reverse application is still based on (a new) rule of thumb.

The broad concept of 'benefit' for justifying jurisdiction to levy corporate tax in the international tax regime has become increasingly popular. For example, Peter Hongler also observed that the benefit principle has its normative value, especially for jurisdiction to tax and limitation to tax claim.[187] As for more recent work, Eva Escribano uses 'the presumptive benefit principle' to describe that an MNE can make use of various public infrastructures of a jurisdiction, and the indications of such enjoyment include 'physical performance in the jurisdiction or 'accessing the market even remotely'.[188]

The discussions of the concept of PE[189] are also part of the benefit principle in the international tax regime. In response to BEPS Project Action 7, some argue that it is necessary to lower the traditional concept of PE in order to comply with the benefit principle.[190] For example, Hongler and Pistone argue that in the era of the digital economy, a new type of 'virtual PE' should be accepted because doing business in a jurisdiction by e-commerce no longer requires a fixed place. An enterprise or MNE can enjoy various public benefits and pubic services provided by a jurisdiction without involving a PE in the traditional sense. These public benefits include various infrastructures, such as energy supply, waste recycling, enforcement of customers' payment maintenance of the digital environment, the legal system in general, etc.[191] Escribano proposed a similar idea as 'remote-sales PE' based on the presumptive benefit principle.[192]

Hongler and Pistone believe that recognizing a virtual PE in the OECD Model Convention can solve the problem and thus they propose a quantitative minimum threshold for a virtual PE involving access to online environment/

187. Peter Hongler, *Justice in International Tax Law: A Normative Review of the International Tax Regime* (IBFD 2019).
188. Escribano, *supra* n. 138, at 2.02.
189. Regarding the nexus, the weakness of PE in the FA will be discussed in Chapter 3.3 of this book.
190. Peter Hongler & Pasquale Pistone, Blueprints for a New PE Nexus to Tax Business Income in the Era of the Digital Economy, available at SSRN 2586196 (2015).
191. Dale Pinto, The Need to Reconceptualize the Permanent Establishment Threshold, 60 Bulletin for International Taxation 266 (2006).
192. Escribano, *supra* n. 138, at 4.02 [c].

application/database, users of applications/websites, certain time threshold, and amount of revenue earned. In other words, they are still the proponents of the PE concept based on the benefit principle. Some criticism indicates that even lowering the PE threshold by admitting commissionaire arrangements or auxiliary activities as PE in the MLI could not fundamentally solve the problem of the traditional international tax regime because more legal uncertainties are very likely to be created.[193]

It should be noted that Escribano's presumptive benefit principle overlaps with the normative framework of benefit-based MN of this book, but with a difference: Escribano uses 'physical indicia' and 'market indicia' that presume infrastructures and legal systems being used, and Escribano would like to improve the traditional proxies, such as PE or residence to be included with these indicia. Escribano also proposes to improve the residence concept to be more in line with the presumptive public benefit: the residence state cannot purely rely on a weak formal connection to be allocated a taxing right.

In other words, Escribano proposes to fix the problems of the current double taxation model convention by reforming the residence and the PE concepts and negating the FA because an FA like CCCTB is still a political utopia in her opinion.[194] The key difference between Escribano's theory and this book is that I argue that economic activities are already indicators of public benefits, and therefore the approach of dividing taxing rights can directly include these activities as weighting factors in the formula. It is unnecessary to rely on old concepts like PE or residence as the proxies for allocating taxing rights. Economic activities themselves qualify as proxies in a formula. What Escribano and this book have in common is we both presume the existence and utilization of the public benefits without establishing the quantity and causal link.

In my view, the distinction between source and residence and the concept of PE in international tax law should be completely abandoned in an FA system. A multinational taxpayer, who generates cross-border income, enjoys benefits from both source state and residence state to a different extent. Nowadays, it is extremely hard to imagine that a multinational taxpayer who does NOT involve e-commerce. E-commerce in a digital economy is the mainstream instead of the exception. The old international tax law concepts are no longer suitable for the modern digital economy.

Allocating taxing powers according to the clear distinction between source state and residence state or active income versus passive income, regardless of being based on the old benefit principle or Avi-Yonah and Xu's reverse benefit principle, still embrace the 'all-or-nothing' approach: residence states have the primary rights to tax some types of income and source states have the others. In fact, the traditional distinction between passive and active income seems also outdated as well as the distinction between residence and source principle.

It is extremely difficult to decide where the value is generated for an MNE taxpayer's activities involving more than two jurisdictions: an income can be derived from multiple jurisdictions and thus multiple 'sources'. Simply reversing the source

193. Similar opinion, De Wilde, *supra* n. 76.
194. Escribano, *supra* n. 138, at 5.

and residence principle might miss the point. So, in this book, I argue that we should go back to the activities that lead to income generation and embrace a broader idea of 'source', which should not be limited to the geographical location.[195]

The benefit principle in the context of the international tax regime is to establish a reasonable 'relationship' between a jurisdiction and the economic activity in order to justify the jurisdiction's taxing rights. However, the traditional benefit principle has also been limited as an all-or-nothing viewpoint and ignores that a cross-border economic activity's origin and destination can both qualify as a type of 'source' of the income. The rigid dichotomy of 'residence versus source' and 'passive versus active' has the same problem.

So, the classical distinction between residence and source – as well as the all-or-nothing attribution rule developed in international tax law – might be not only reversed but also completely reconsidered. Therefore, the benefit principle in the international tax law regime should not only be reversed but could also be reformulated so as to replace the traditional all-or-nothing rationale.

As indicated in section 2.1.3, the BEPS Project's 'value creation' concept also indicates a reformed benefit principle, which is no longer purely based on the 'origin'.[196] Value creation also reaffirms that the benefit principle has constantly been influencing international tax law.[197] In my view, the distinctions of 'residence versus source', 'passive versus active', or 'origin versus destination' should all be set aside when we formulate the benefit principle under a new international tax law reform.

2.2.3 A Well-Functioning Internal Market Requires Sufficient Public Benefits and Taxation

Richard Musgrave has written that taxation has three functions: macro-economy stabilization, redistribution, and resource allocation.[198] These three functions are public benefits in the broad sense and the necessary conditions of a well-functioning market.

When we discuss the benefit principle in the context of the internal market of the EU, we are confronted with a question: is there a minimum public benefit requirement

195. Kemmeren refers to 'origin' (in his other term: 'economic location', which is more precise), *supra* n. 183.
196. Morse observes the link but argues that value creation still lacks a solid theory; *see* Morse, *supra* n. 40.
197. Jinyan Li, Nathan Jin Bao & Huaning Christina Li, Value Creation: A Constant Principle in a Changing World of International Taxation, 67 Canadian Tax Journal 1107 (2019).
198. Scholars have elaborated on this based on Richard Musgrave's early work on these three functions. *See* Charles McLure & Jorge Martinez-Vazquez, *The Assignment of Revenues and Expenditures in Intergovernmental Fiscal Relations, Core Course on Intergovernmental Relations and Local Financial Management* (World Bank Institute, Washington, DC: World Bank 2000). Available at https://gsdrc.org/document-library/the-assignment-of-revenues-and-expenditures-in-intergovernmental-fiscal-relations/.

    Peggy Musgrave explains again that this three-branch model is the normative idea but does not necessarily match the reality since the reality is far more complex. *See* Peggy B Musgrave, Comments on Two Musgravian Concepts, 32 Journal of Economics and Finance 340 (2008).

for every Member State to maintain their jurisdiction as a part of the well-functioning internal market? Put differently, should EU Member States' fiscal autonomy/taxing rights still be subject to constitutional restrictions, so they should not reduce public benefits to an unreasonable degree?

The answer is affirmative: EU Member States do have their own fiscal autonomy and their own competence. It is legitimate to compete to provide the best and cost-efficient public benefits. Since Member States have different socioeconomic situations, Member States would need to implement their own approaches, even pursuing the same goal of establishing the 'internal market'. Therefore, the subsidiarity principle is a fundamental principle of EU law.

However, Member States' fiscal autonomy is still subject to EU law, including fundamental freedoms and state aid rules.[199] Illegal fiscal state aid is state aid in the form of state tax legislation. Member States may not give up their taxing rights or grant tax advantages to the extent that results in illegal state aid and hinders competition between Member States.

In addition, the Council in 1997 issued the code of conduct for business taxation[200] which requires Member States to refrain from harmful tax competition. Although the code of conduct for business taxation is soft law, the rationale of fighting harmful tax competition has also been applied by the Court of Justice of the European Union (CJEU) in state aid cases.[201] One reason to fight harmful tax competition in the EU is to prevent a 'race to the bottom'[202] of tax which would hinder the welfare of EU Member States, though it is still arguable whether or not there has been a 'race to the bottom'.[203]

Furthermore, maintaining a well-functioning competitive market needs sufficient public benefits and thus sufficient taxation. The EU is not only a monetary union but also 'a social union'[204] and the Charter of Fundamental Rights of the EU is primary EU

199. The CJEU's analysis of fundamental freedoms and state aid rule has been converging. *See* Rita Szudoczky, Convergence of the Analysis of National Tax Measures under the EU State Aid Rules and the Fundamental Freedoms, 15 European State Aid Law Quarterly 357 (2016).
200. For the early literature, Wolfgang Schön, Tax Competition in Europe – General Report (2003); Carlo Pinto, EU and OECD to Fight Harmful Tax Competition: Has the Right Path Been Undertaken, 26 Intertax 386 (1998); For post-BEPS, *see* Antonio Carlos dos Santos, What Is Substantial Economic Activity for Tax Purposes in the Context of the European Union and the OECD Initiatives Against Harmful Tax Competition, 24 EC Tax Review 166 (2015).
201. Edoardo Traversa & Alessandra Flamini, Fighting Harmful Tax Competition Through EU State Aid Law, 14 European State Aid Law Quarterly 323 (2015).
202. *See* Gerard Meussen, The EU-Fight Against Harmful Tax Competition; Future Developments, 11 EC Tax Review 157 (2002); Jan AM Klaver & Ad JM Timmermans, EU Taxation: Policy Competition or Policy Coordination, 8 EC Tax Review 185 (1999); Ben J Kiekebeld, *Harmful Tax Competition in the European Union: Code of Conduct, Countermeasures and EU Law* (Kluwer 2004).
203. Enrique G Mendoza & Linda L Tesar, Why Hasn't Tax Competition Triggered a Race to the Bottom? Some Quantitative Lessons from the EU, 52 Journal of Monetary Economics 163 (2005).
204. Frank Vandenbroucke, Why We Need a European Social Union, 52 Reflets et perspectives de la vie économique 97 (2013); FIG Vandenbroucke, The Idea of a European Social Union: A Normative Introduction, in Frank Vandenbroucke, Catherine Barnard & G de Baere (eds), *A European Social Union after the Crisis* (Cambridge University Press 2017).

law.[205] All relevant public infrastructures and social policies which make the EU an internal market and a social union are not free of charge.

EU Member States do have the autonomy to decide how much tax they need to levy to provide a well-functioning market, in the most cost-efficient way, but they are not completely free to do any type of tax competition. This implies that to keep a well-functioning internal market requires minimum/sufficient public benefits and taxation. As to when the amount of public benefits and taxation is 'sufficient', it is a political question that needs to be decided democratically.[206]

2.2.4 The Benefit Principle of Taxation in the EU Internal Market: Hidden under Other Names

The benefit principle as justification of levying taxation can also be found in the development of EU tax law. The CJEU, in its jurisprudence, does not directly express its opinion regarding the benefit principle. In the field of personal direct taxation, for example, it seems that the Court does not view personal direct tax as the price for a bundle of public goods, as expressed in the *Schumacker* decision.[207]

However, the doctrine from *Schumacker* does not preclude the benefit principle from applying to CIT. Instead, the CJEU seems implicitly to decide its cases regarding Member States' tax treaty laws in line with the benefit principle:[208] the Court rejects the most favourable treatment principle applicable in tax law and recognizes the disparity of withholding tax rates of different Member States. In other words, EU Member States have no obligation to adopt the minimum withholding tax rate among all Member

205. The legal status of the EU Charter, Koen Lenaerts, Exploring the Limits of the EU Charter of Fundamental Rights, 8 European Constitutional Law Review 375 (2012); Juliane Kokott & Christoph Sobotta, The Charter of Fundamental Rights of the European Union after Lisbon, Working Paper, EUI AEL, 2010/06, Distinguished Lectures of the Academy (2010).

206. In the literature discussing the relationship between tax revenue and economic development, it is popular to use the tax revenue-GDP ratio as a benchmark to evaluate if a state collects sufficient revenue to provide public infrastructures for conducting economic activities. If the ratio is too low (for example, the tax revenue-GDP ratio below 15% for developing countries), it means that the state fails to collect enough tax to maintain the public revenue and it is a problem for many developing or low-income countries. Since it is an empirical question, so this book will not cover this part. *See* Vitor Gaspar, Laura Jaramillo & Mr Philippe Wingender, *Tax Capacity and Growth: Is There a Tipping Point?* (IMF 2016).

207. Wolfgang Schön, Playing Different Games? Regulatory Competition in Tax and Company Law Compared, 42 Common Market Law Review 331 (2005), at 340; For a different opinion, *see* Barbara Hagen, Schumacker Comparability – the Conditions of the Schumacker Doctrine, in Kasper Dziurdz & Christoph Marchgraber (eds), *Non-Discrimination in European and Tax Treaty Law* (Linde 2015).

For comments on the Schumacker case and the Schumacker doctrine, *see* Peter J Wattel, Red Herrings in Direct Tax Cases Before the ECJ, 31 Legal Issues of Economic Integration 81 (2004); Carl Otto Lenz, The Jurisprudence of the European Court of Justice in Tax Matters, 6 EC Tax Review 80 (1997); Hannelore Niesten, Growing Impetus for Harmonization of Personal and Family Allowances: Current State of Affairs of the Schumacker-Doctrine after Imfeld and Garcet, 24 EC Tax Review 185 (2015); Hannelore Niesten, Personal and Family Tax Benefits in the EU Internal Market: From Schumacker to Fractional Tax Treatment, 55 Common Market Law Review 819 (2018).

208. J. Englisch, Tax Coordination Between Member States in the EU – Role of the ECJ in M. Lang et al. (eds), *Horizontal Tax Coordination* (IBFD 2012).

States. As Englisch's analysis[209] of case law demonstrates, the benefit principle is the cornerstone supporting Member States' fiscal autonomy and thus this principle is indirectly reflected in the CJEU's jurisprudence.

It should be noted that in the CJEU's fiscal state aid decisions, the benefit principle being applicable is implied by giving a new interpretation of the 'arm's length principle'. In fiscal state aid cases since 2015, CJEU has been making use of the 'arm's length principle' to assess if a national advance TP ruling (advance pricing agreement, APA) grants a selective and distortive tax advantage to specific multinational taxpayers.[210] The meaning of the ALP in these CJEU judgments is not identical to the OECD's TP guidelines and functions more like a new type of anti-avoidance rule.[211] EU state aid law has the ultimate aim of ensuring market competition and prevent EU Member States from distorting trade and competition in the internal market. There is quite some criticism of the CJEU's approach, but the CJEU's approach to fiscal state aid is consistent with the benefit-based MN framework of this book. In my view, granting selective and distortive fiscal advantage to a taxpayer (ruling applicant) is contrary to the benefit principle too. Unlawful fiscal aid in the form of an advance TP tax ruling results in some taxpayers paying less tax than other comparable taxpayers not having a ruling. These comparable taxpayers all make use of the same market (enjoying the same public benefit) but the tax ruling holders paid less than others.[212] In addition, as Smit observes,[213] the CJEU's new ALP can go beyond an anti-avoidance rule to reaffirm the economic alliance theory as justification for establishing the taxing right for the EU's FA regime. I agree with Smit's interpretation.

The benefit principle has long existed in EU tax policy objectives. In 1992, the Ruding Report mentioned the benefits principle. In addition to identifying distortions in corporate taxation, the Ruding Report refers to the benefits principle in the context of 'intra-community fairness'.[214] Intra-community fairness in the Ruding Report involves three principles: (1) source-country entitlement; (2) non-discrimination; and (3) reciprocity. The Ruding Report interprets 'source-country entitlement' in line with the benefit principle:

> According to the first principle (i.e., the source-country-entitlement principle), the source country has the prior right to tax business income from direct investment earned within its jurisdiction. This principle can be justified on the grounds that the source country has to finance the infrastructure and public services from which the business benefits.

209. *Ibid.*
210. Case law development, *see* Svitlana Buriak & Ivan Lazarov, Between State Aid and the Fundamental Freedoms: The Arm's Length Principle and EU Law, 56 Common Market Law Review (2019).
211. Peter J Wattel, Stateless Income, State Aid and the (Which?) Arm's Length Principle, 44 Intertax (2016); Ruth Mason, Tax Rulings as State Aid – Part 4: Whose Arm's-Length Standard?, 155 Tax Notes (2017).
212. Similar remarks by Smit on the European Commissions' argument in the Apple state aid case, *see* DS Smit, *International Income Allocation under EU Tax Law: Tinker, Tailor, Soldier, Sailor* (Kluwer Law International 2016), at 23.
213. DS Smit, The Arm's Length Standard: A Blind Spot in the CC(C)TB Proposal, in Weber & Streek (eds), *supra* n. 5, at 109.
214. Commission of the European Communities (eds), *supra* n. 3, at 198.

In other words, a state is entitled or justified to levy tax because that state has provided public services from which businesses benefit. The Ruding Report reiterates that the source-country entitlement principle is as important as the other two principles in order to pursue 'intra-community fairness', which is synonymous with intra-nation equity within the EU.

Therefore, when it comes to analysing taxation of the EU's internal market, the benefit principle is intertwined with efficiency, i.e., tax neutrality (elaborated further in section 2.3). For example, Vogel uses the 'net administrative output' concept,[215] i.e., Member States' public administration efficiency, to establish the principle of cross-border neutrality/inter-nation neutrality as the new paradigm to examine the development of EU tax law harmonization. The administrative output is exactly a type of public benefit. In my view, Vogel's 'inter-nation neutrality' and Musgrave's 'inter-nation equity'[216] converge here. Musgrave also affirms that inter-nation equity under the benefit principle is self-implementing.[217] In other words, the distinction between inter-nation neutrality and inter-nation equity is somewhat blurred when the benefit principle is also considered.

2.2.5 The Public Benefit as the Baseline of the Normative Framework

As I indicated in Chapter 1 and the thesis statement in section 2.1.1, public benefits are not unlimited because governments are not almighty. Taxation should not be higher than the necessary level of providing public benefits to maintain a well-functioning market; otherwise it is also not neutral and becomes waste. It is imperative to levy taxation cautiously and with justification. But when taxation is reduced to zero or to the degree of being less than the public benefits provided, it is not neutral either.

There are some scholars who no longer use the no-tax baseline as the analysis baseline when discussing tax neutrality. For example, Hasen reconsiders[218] the presumption of a no-tax baseline for the neutrality principle but opts for the baseline which takes taxation covering public revenues into account.[219] Knoll also questions using a no-tax baseline to examine a potential tax reform.[220]

215. Klaus Vogel, Worldwide vs. Source Taxation of Income: A Review and Re-Evaluation of Arguments (Part II), 16 Intertax 310 (1988), at 314.
216. Richard A Musgrave & Peggy B Musgrave, Inter-nation Equity in *Modern Fiscal Issues: Essays in Honour of Carl S. Shoup* (1972), at 63-85; Peggy B. Musgrave, Sovereignty, Entitlement, and Cooperation in International Taxation, 26 *Brooklyn Journal of International Law* (2001), at 1335, 1336.
217. Musgrave & Musgrave, *ibid.*, 74. It should be noted that Peggy Musgrave does not see corporate tax as taxation based on the benefit principle, though she still accepts residence taxation as a justification of tax from a benefit term.
218. The following paragraphs are partially derived from Shu-Chien Chen, Neutrality as Tax Justice: The Case of Common Consolidated Corporate Tax Base under EU Law, 5 European Studies – the Review of European Law, Economics and Politics 33 (2018); as to linking tax neutrality and the benefit principle, *see also* Hasen, *supra* n. 111.
219. *Ibid.* Hasen redefines taxation that can enhance taxpayers' production ability as 'Tax Amenities'.
220. Michael S Knoll, Reconsidering International Tax Neutrality, 64 Tax Law Review 99 (2010).

Before I proceed to discuss MN as the second element of the normative framework, here I illustrate the following metaphor in Figure 3 below to explain why tax neutrality and the benefit principle are both necessary in the framework and not just using the benefit principle to replace the tax neutrality.

It is because these two principles represent different statuses. In my view, the well-functional market or the level playing field is not pre-existing; instead, the 'field' is full of market failure holes and gaps that need to be filled by providing public benefits. After providing proper public benefits and levying tax to finance such benefits, the level playing field (the black line in the figure) is achieved, and it is the tax neutrality. The EU internal market as a whole needs different Member States to provide public benefits to achieve the status of a well-functioning market. So, when a tax system is designed based on the public benefits provided, it is market neutral in this scenario.

Figure 3 The Benefit-Based Market Neutrality Framework

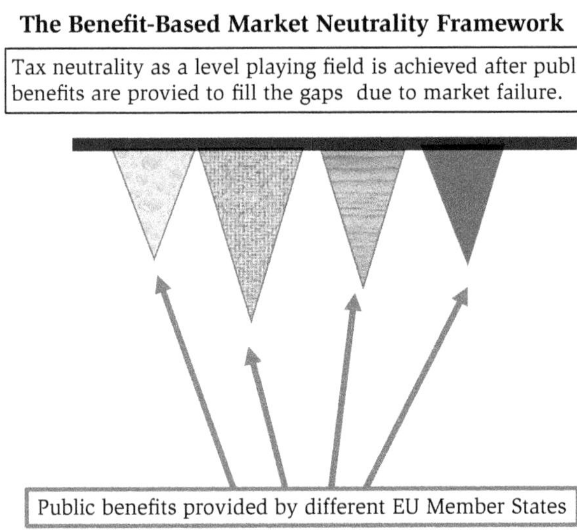

Source: The author.

Moreover, it is legitimate to reserve the diversity between Member States: diversity in providing public services and thus diversity in taxation would also be acceptable, and the benefit principle would be a justification to accommodate such diversity. The relationship between MN and the benefit principle would no longer be a trade-off if we define neutrality as the baseline that necessary public services relate to in maintaining the market.[221]

221. In early 2000, McLure and Weiner used a similar approach of combining different principles to evaluate the possibility to adopt the EU's FA for corporate tax, *see* Charles E McLure & Joann M Weiner, Deciding Whether the European Union Should Adopt Formula Apportionment of Company Income, in Sijbren Cnossen (ed.), *Taxing Capital Income in the European Union:*

2.3 TOWARDS MARKET NEUTRALITY AND ITS CONSISTENCY WITH THE BENEFIT PRINCIPLE

The second element of the normative framework is 'market neutrality', a concept proposed by Michael Devereux and which is derived from discussions of international tax neutrality.

To understand MN, it is necessary to revisit the principles of tax neutrality. The term 'tax neutrality' conveys different meanings in different contexts,[222] even in a domestic tax situation. Some scholars, such as Harberger, also noticed that different economists use 'neutrality' for their own definition.[223]

When it comes to 'international tax neutrality', Weisbach observes that the formulation of tax neutrality is diverse in the economic literature and develops over time. The concept of international tax neutrality refers to different sets of trade-offs, and these concepts of neutrality do not have a specific, inherent hierarchy.[224] To discuss an international tax regime reform, it is necessary to revisit how the concept of tax neutrality is formulated in different contexts.

Although some scholars reject the existence of neutral tax and assert that taxation can never be neutral, just like money cannot be neutral. I respectfully disagree with such assertion. Taxation or tax reform policy aims to achieve some effects and can result in side effects. Implementing the neutrality principle in a new proposed tax system like CCCTB not only ensures the effectiveness of the reform but also prevents possible future distortions. In other words, to pursue a neutral tax system, one needs to seek an ideal and optimal status and try to remain close to that status.

Kahn observes from the US tax law literature that the concept of neutrality in fact has two faces.[225] Neutrality can mean 'an ideal tax system,' in a broad sense, but neutrality can also mean 'not creating a bias for taxpayers to choose an instrument/a legal form over another'. While most economics literature refers to every tax neutrality principle in combination with a specific 'ground'.

Issues and Options for Reform (Oxford University Press 2000); the difference between this book and McLure & Weiner's work is that this chapter has tried to establish the tax neutrality principle in the broad sense so that it can be based on the benefit principle. McLure & Weiner's work analyses different principles as they are separate from different perspectives.

222. Similar remarks on diversity of the neutrality concepts have appeared in Moyal's work revisiting principles of international tax law. Shay Shimon Moyal, Back to Basics: Rethinking Normative Principles in International Tax, 73 Tax Lawyer (2019).
223. Arnold C Harberger, Tax Neutrality in Investment Incentives, The Economics of Taxation 299 (1980).

    Harberger observes that 'Samuelson Neutrality' and 'Musgrave Neutrality' refer to different benchmarks to evaluate a 'neutral incentive scheme.' Samuelson Neutrality is based on Paul Samuelson's work in 1964 and Musgrave Neutrality is based on Richard A. Musgrave's work in 1959. Briefly speaking, Musgrave Neutrality sees 'zero' tax as neutral; Samuelson Neutrality simply holds that 'after-tax rate of discount of 10% and a tax rate of 50%'. For the relevance of this book, these different sets of neutrality concepts demonstrate that 'tax neutrality' is not a simple norm that we can take for granted. Instead, it is necessary to define it clearly before proceeding with discussions.
224. Weisbach, *supra* n. 109.
225. Douglas A Kahn, The Two Faces of Tax Neutrality: Do They Interact or Are They Mutually Exclusive, 18 Northern Kentucky Law Review 1 (1990).

In the EU context, Freeman and Macdonald[226] observe that tax neutrality has two dimensions. First, tax neutrality refers to the non-discrimination principle: all transactions within the tax base should be taxed equally; otherwise choices between transactions will be distorted and cause economic efficiency. Second, when a tax system aims to encourage or discourage some behaviour, that specific rule might be explicitly 'non-neutral'. Therefore, the criterion of neutrality should depend on the policy objective. Freeman and Macdonald's two dimensions of tax neutrality both use a specific benchmark of a policy or a type of transaction as a comparison. Freeman and Macdonald's opinion on neutrality is closer to Khan's neutrality in the narrow sense.

The following sections demonstrate varieties of the 'tax neutrality principle', especially in a cross-border setting. In most cases, tax neutrality is formulated in combination with a specific 'ground', i.e., the narrow sense as Kahn observes. After revisiting all these variations, I explain why MN is more appropriate for the EU's FA regime than other concepts of neutrality when it is combined with the benefit principle.

2.3.1 Tax Neutrality in the Traditional Sense: Capital Import Neutrality and Capital Export Neutrality

The concepts of international tax law are the starting point for harmonizing EU Member States' tax law at the EU law level.[227] Just as EU law has evolved from public international law and has developed its own concept of supra-nationality,[228] EU tax law integration has evolved from international tax law to develop its own normative parameters and fundamental principles.

In the traditional (international) tax law regime, there have been two opposite concepts to describe how tax should be 'neutral', i.e., not interfering with an economic operator's decision and activities. The main traditional concepts are CIN and CEN.[229] These two concepts are widely accepted as common knowledge in the field of international tax law and policy.

Originally, the concepts of CEN and CIN were developed and discussed by welfare economists in the 1960s to evaluate the US's national taxation of foreign investment outside the US. Richard Musgrave[230] argued that a taxation system pursuing 'capital export neutrality' will maximize global welfare and thus CEN is a

226. Judith Freedman & Graeme Macdonald, The Tax Base for CCCTB: The Role of Principles, Working Papers 0807, Oxford University Centre for Business Taxation, 7-8 (2008).
227. Sjoerd CW Douma, *Legal Research in International and EU Tax Law: Rede in Verkorte Vorm* (Kluwer 2014).
228. Magdalena Ličková, European Exceptionalism in International Law, 19 European Journal of International Law 463 (2008).
229. For observations on the ambiguity of these two concepts and mixed terminology, *see* Knoll, *supra* n. 220.
230. Further on two aspects of neutrality, *see* Richard A Musgrave, Criteria for Foreign Tax Credit, *Taxation of Operation Abroad* (The Tax Institute 1959), at 83-93.
    Later Peggy Musgrave also further writes about the distinction of CEN and CIN. *See* Musgrave, *supra* n. 106. Reprinted in Peggy B Musgrave, *Tax Policy in the Global Economy* (Edward Elgar 2002).

more desirable tax policy. Later on, these two concepts were also used to evaluate international taxation.

Briefly speaking, a tax system consistent with CIN means that levying that tax does not negatively influence 'import' activities, including inbound investments. Conversely, a tax system consistent with CEN means that levying that tax does not negatively influence 'export' activities, including outbound investments. It should be noted that CIN and CEN both use the 'no tax world' as the baseline[231] to examine whether a tax system influences inbound or outbound investments. If inbound or outbound investments are hindered by the tax system, then CIN or CEN are not achieved. Such system is then 'not tax neutral'.

Based on CEN, a neutral tax system is very often (but not necessarily always) designed as residence taxation:[232] a country will have the taxing powers to the residence taxpayer's worldwide income. The location of outbound investment will be tax neutral in any case because the taxpayer is subject to tax based on its residence. CEN is sometimes described as 'locational neutrality'.[233]

Based on CIN, on the contrary, a neutral tax system is designed as a source tax system. Inbound investments will only be taxed at the source country, therefore imported capital to the residence country will not be subject to the tax of the residence country.

To implement these neutrality concepts as international tax policies, CIN has been used as a synonym for 'source taxation/source principle' or 'territorial system',[234] and CEN has been used as a synonym for 'residence principle' and 'worldwide system'.[235] However, we can only describe a system as 'consistent with' CIN or CEN and should be careful with using them as synonyms, and we always have to indicate clearly what 'neutrality' in the context means.

It should also be noted that these 'neutrality' concepts themselves are not neutral.[236] Each neutrality principle deals with only one aspect. We should read the word 'neutrality' in the economics literature as 'not negatively influenced'. However, when a tax is specially designed to be 'neutral' to something, i.e., having no negative effect on a specific issue/activity, it does not automatically mean that it has no other negative effect on another activity.

Many economists argue that CIN and CEN cannot be achieved simultaneously unless every sovereign state has 'the same tax rate'.[237] When the tax rate is the same, tax no longer matters to import/export or domestic transactions. In a wider context, this is also because economists usually comment that using the baseline to evaluate CIN/CEN is to compare a hypothetical no-tax world to observe the tax system involved.

231. Fadi Shaheen, International Tax Neutrality: Reconsiderations, 27 Virginia Tax Review 203 (2007); Fadi Shaheen, International Tax Neutrality: Revisited, 64 Tax Law Review 131 (2010).
232. Shaheen (2007), *supra* n. 231.
233. *Ibid.*
234. For example, Dale Pinto, *E-Commerce and Source-Based Income Taxation* (IBFD 2003), at 2.2.2.
235. For example, an IMF Working Paper uses this expression. *See* Peter Mullins, Moving to Territoriality? Implications for the United States and the Rest of the World, IMF Working Papers 1 (2006).
236. De Wilde, *supra* n. 76, at 116; Vogel & Brands, *supra* n. 110.
237. McLure & Weiner, *supra* n. 221.

As to the conflict between CEN and CIN, Vogel even argued that the concept of neutrality is a 'non-concept' because the term neutrality is only used in combination with a specific ground. In Vogel's view, a proper concept for the neutrality principle under EU law seems to be 'cross-border neutrality' or 'inter-nation neutrality'. It should no longer distinguish 'CEN' or 'CIN'.[238]

In the context of building an internal market, the distinction between CEN and CIN should disappear. Vogel's statement is consistent with the CCCTB Working Document No. 1: CCCTB has the general principle of 'neutrality,' and it will pursue both CEN and CIN at the same time. To pursue CEN and CIN simultaneously, in my observation, the real objective of tax neutrality of the CCCTB Directive will cover more than one neutrality/non-discrimination ground.

2.3.2 Tax Neutrality in the Broad Sense: Not Focusing on Only One Aspect But Transactions

Since the 1980s, other 'neutrality' concepts have developed in the economics literature, including CON and MN.

CON means a system 'where the "transfer of an investment" to a new investor is not distorted by tax wedge'.[239] Desai and Hines[240] in 2003 introduced this concept which requires that taxation does not influence those who own assets, and Desai and Hines hold that ownership of assets will affect taxpayers' productivity. In other words, CON mandates an undistorted ownership decision (including investment and ownership transfer). By integrating the cross-border element, CON can include both CEN and CIN.

Supporters of CON, such as Shaheen, argue that CON is a better criterion than CEN and CIN. Unlike the long-accepted argument regarding the impossibility of achieving CIN and CEN at the same time without harmonizing the tax rate, Shaheen argued that both CEN and CIN can be achieved simultaneously without harmonizing the tax rate of different states if all sovereign states universally adopt source taxation.[241] Shaheen's empirical data show that the real tax burden from the source taxation system is borne by immobile factors, such as labour and land, and thus a source-based taxation system would be 'neutral' (read: create no burden) to mobile factors, such as capital.

Knoll partially disagrees with Shaheen's support of 'CON'[242] and is sceptical about Shaheen's presumption as well as using the baseline of 'no-tax world' for the

238. De Wilde casts doubt and criticism on Volgal's concept of 'inter-nation neutrality', and argues that CIN, CEN and even inter-nation neutrality all will result in 'unequal treatments on equal circumstances'. De Wilde argues that inter-nation neutrality purely based on the benefit principle neglects the ability to pay principle, so inter-nation neutrality itself is just similar to CIN. *See* De Wilde, *supra* n. 76, at 3.3.
239. Weisbach, *supra* n. 109.
240. Desai & Hines Jr, *supra* n. 107.
241. Shaheen, *supra* n. 231 Virginia Tax Review.
242. Knoll observed the phenomenon of inconsistent use of the term 'CIN' by different economists, and argued that there are two normative meanings of CIN: savings neutrality and CON. According to Knoll's criticism against Saheen's work, since Saheen seems to interpret CIN as

neutrality principle. Shaheen replies[243] to Knoll's criticism that a no-tax baseline is the most accepted way to evaluate the neutrality of a specific measure, and it would be well-accepted by most economists.

Being also critical of the concept of CON, Kleinbard further argues that CON has the presumption that source country taxation is fully capitalized into a company's price of operating in that source country,[244] but the existence of 'stateless income', which is subject to tax only in a jurisdiction that is not the location of the company's customers or the factors of production through which the income was derived, and is not the domicile of the group's parent company',[245] negates this presumption. Even when being consistent with CON, states still do not solve the difficulty of taxing 'stateless income', which is a typical BEPS problem.[246] In other words, even when accepting every jurisdiction could be the source country, a system that fails to levy tax on stateless income would be consistent with CON because such system does not negatively hinder taxpayers' investment. However, BEPS problems as such are already the evidence of distorted investment decisions.

Devereux created a more generalized term, 'market neutrality', in 2008.[247] Devereux defines MN as taxation that does not distort competition between taxpayers. Therefore, sometimes MN is also formulated as 'competitiveness neutrality'. The problem with MN is that it is not always clear what it means because it is a general expression.

Although Devereux was seemingly the first to use this term, 'market neutrality', another scholar used Vogel's earlier formulation of neutrality in 1988 but which also required neutrality between market participants.[248] Vogel refers to this requirement as 'inter-nation neutrality'. Vogel had always argued that international neutrality is derived from equity and efficiency, and that equity and efficiency should not be distinguished when evaluating international tax law. Except for being general, the concept of 'market neutrality' or 'competitiveness neutrality' seems convincing in the context of establishing an internal market. In the context of evaluating the constitutionality of state taxation in the US, 'competition neutrality' has also been understood as the theoretical and economic foundation of the dormant commerce clause.[249] Therefore, MN seems a suitable norm for the internal market.

The concept of tax neutrality changes over time because economic theories regarding neutrality have also evolved in three waves since the late 1890s.[250] The first wave of neutrality can be traced back to Goerg von Schanz's writings in 1892. The

savings neutrality, Shaheen can derive the conclusion that a universal source system without uniform tax rates will satisfy both CEN and CIN. *See* Knoll, *supra* n. 220.

243. Fadi Shaheen (2010), *supra* n. 231.
244. Kleinbard, The Lessons of Stateless Income, *supra* n. 28.
245. Kleinbard, Stateless Income, *supra* n. 28. Kleinbard used this term first in Edward D Kleinbard, Throw Territorial Taxation from the Train, 46 Tax Notes International 63 (2007).
246. Yariv Brauner, What the BEPS?, 16 Florida Tax Review (2014).
247. Devereux, *supra* n. 108.
248. Peters' analysis, Cees Peters, *On the Legitimacy of International Tax Law* (IBFD 2014).
249. Michael S Knoll & Ruth Mason, The Economic Foundation of the Dormant Commerce Clause, Virginia Law Review 309 (2017). *See* further in Chapter 3 of this book.
250. Peters, *supra* n. 248, at 4.4.2.

essence of Von Schanz's theory is that he refers to economic allegiance as the foundation for justifying states' taxation.[251] Economic allegiance describes the sufficient economic relationship between the state and the taxpayer, and economic allegiance can be based on various factors. Von Schanz's doctrine has been linked with the benefit principle and is regarded as one of the origins of the benefit principle.[252]

Musgrave's CEN and CIN theory discussed earlier is the second wave. The main discussions derived from CEN and CIN are still prevalent nowadays. The third wave refers to works in the 1990s and the early 2000s.[253] According to Peters' analysis, the third wave of the neutrality discussion is greatly influenced by the first wave. The first wave used 'economic allegiance' to justify the allocating taxing powers to the source state and the residence state and thus influenced the third wave: the benefits that a state provides will influence the baseline of evaluating 'neutrality'. According to Vogel, public services provided in different states are not identical, and thus taxation levied differently by different states is the real 'neutrality'. Therefore, neutrality under EU tax law should mean 'being absent from company tax distortions and business decisions are based on economic conditions, not on tax law conditions'.[254] As Smit correctly indicates,[255] a neutral tax system does not adversely influence the relationship between tax and public goods.

From the discussions above, we can conclude that the concept of 'international tax neutrality' is a living instrument in the field of the development of international/EU tax law. Different formulations represent different policy considerations, and they are based on different presumptions.[256] EU law has been regarded as the 'economic constitution' to develop the EU internal market. It seems that the third wave of economic scholarship has greatly influenced EU tax law.[257]

Therefore, MN is the right option for establishing the framework of assessing EU tax law reform like CCCTB. When combining MN with the benefit principle, it coincides with the third wave of neutrality discussions.

I further demonstrate the variety as follows to support the view that tax neutrality for designing the EU FA regime should be referred to as a broader sense of MN because one single neutrality concept might not fulfil the underlying rationale of the EU internal market.

---

251. Kemmeren, *supra* n. 183.
252. *Ibid.*
253. Peters, *supra* n. 248, Chapter 4.
254. DS Smit, *EU Freedoms, Non-EU Countries and Company Taxation* (Kluwer Law International 2012).

     Smit also rejects the 'no-tax world' as the baseline, by criticizing works from Ture and endorsing Vogel. *See* Klaus Vogel, Which Method Should the European Community Adopt for the Avoidance of Double Taxation?, 56 Bulletin for International Fiscal Documentation 4 (2002).

     Smit writes: 'when neutrality means the absence of (nearly) all external influences, distinguishing between different types of neutrality is self-contradictory.'
255. Smit, *ibid.*, Chapter 2.4.
256. Weisbach, *supra* n. 109.
257. Peters, *supra* n. 248, at 4.4.2.2.

2.3.3 Tax Neutrality in EU Primary Law and Case Law: Development Towards Market Neutrality

The notion of 'tax neutrality' has been a key concept in the development of EU internal market law as well as EU tax law.[258] Tax neutrality is also a relative concept. The opposite of neutrality is 'distortions', which imply inefficiency, thus are not desirable for the internal market. Also, distortions also include failures of the current international tax system, such as being vulnerable to tax planning, requiring too many compliance costs, and overly complicated TP rules. These existing distortions are harmful to the internal market. The pursuit of neutrality is expected to eliminate these distortions.

However, the concept of tax neutrality is not consistently used in different contexts in EU law.[259] In some contexts, the term 'neutrality' is not explicitly mentioned, but it refers to eliminating specific obstacles such as the form of neutralizing pre-existing distortions. In some contexts, neutrality is a synonym for non-discrimination. Even the CJEU's approach to examining tax neutrality issues has been criticized as 'murky'[260] because, in different cases, the Court seems to accept both CEN and CIN, which are actually pursuing different goals.

2.3.3.1 Tax Neutrality in EU Primary Law: From Preventing Double Taxation to Fostering a Fiscal Obstacle-Free Internal Market

The objective of pursuing neutrality can be found in EU primary law, based on 'economic efficiency'. As Schön analyses,[261] neutrality is a fundamental EU law principle for the internal market and is embedded in several articles of the Treaty on the Functioning of the European Union (TFEU). Article 26 of TFEU provides the imperative of ensuring four free movement freedoms, and Article 120 of TFEU[262] also refers to the EU as '*the Member States shall act in accordance with the principle of an open market economy with free competition, favoring an efficient allocation of resources*'. The objective of efficiency is the underlying rationale of tax neutrality. The aim of pursing tax neutrality is to allocate resources via the power of the market better and more efficiently, i.e., ensuring free competition between economic operators in the EU.

---

258. Wolfgang Schön, Neutrality and Territoriality – Competing or Converging Concepts in European Tax Law, 69 Bulletin for International Taxation (IBFD Bulletin) 271 (2015).
259. The variety of tax neutrality concept under EU tax law has been widely recognized. *See* Mark Bowler Smith, *The Taxing Road to Sustainable Growth: Resource Productivity and Corporate Taxation* (IBFD 2013), at 3.2.3.1.
O'Shea argued that the current state of fiscal neutrality does not have a consistent normative content, and thus it is not a general principle of EU law. *See* Tom O'Shea, European Tax Controversies: Fiscal Neutrality and EU Law, in Servaas van Thiel, Piergiorgio Valente & Stella Raventós Calvo (eds), *CFE Tax Advisors Europe: 60th Anniversary – Liber Amicorum* (IBFD 2019).
260. De Wilde, *supra* n. 76, at 3.2.4.3.
261. Schön, *supra* n. 258.
262. Article 98 of the TEC.

Prior to the Lisbon Treaty implementing the TFEU, the second indent of Article 293 of the Treaty establishing the European Community (TEC) used to provide that:

> Member States shall, so far as is necessary, enter into negotiations with each other with a view to securing for the benefit of their nationals: (…)
>
> – the abolition of double taxation within the Community.

When the Lisbon Treaty was ratified, Article 293 of TEC had already been repealed.[263] The status of Article 293 was also disputed. It seems that Article 293 does not have direct effect or create an obligation per se for Member States to eliminate double taxation.[264] Article 293 does not preclude the EU from taking Union actions to eliminate double taxation.[265] Although Article 293 of TEC is now repealed,[266] it is clear that double taxation has been recognized as a distortion to the internal market, and eliminating such distortion has also reflected the objective of pursuing neutrality. It is also expected that the Court will be free to adjudicate and decide if double taxation infringes the internal market.

Comparing the second indent of Article 293 of TEC and Article 120 of TFEU, Article 293 has a more restrictive scope than Article 120 of TFEU. Article 293 focuses on neutralizing one specific distortion, 'double taxation,' whereas Article 120 of TFEU embraces a broader sense of 'neutrality,' derived from the objective of pursuing efficiency. Being formulated differently, both provisions are going in the same direction: an internal market allowing free competition and free movement.

263. *See* the table of equivalence of TFEU and TEC, Official Journal of the European Union C326/363 at https://eur-lex.europa.eu/resource.html?uri=cellar:c382f65d-618a-4c72-9135-1e68087499fa.0006.02/DOC_7&format=PDF.

264. For the history and development of Article 293 of TEC, *see* Jérôme Monsenego, *Taxation of Foreign Business Income within the European Internal Market: An Analysis of the Conflict between the Objective of Achievement of the European Internal Market and the Principles of Territoriality and Worldwide Taxation*, Vol. 22 (IBFD 2012) at 6.2.2.

For a similar opinion that Member States do not have obligation to eliminate double taxation, *see* Marjaana Helminen, The Principle of Elimination of Double Taxation under EU Law – Does It Exist?, in Cécile Brokelind & Group for Research on European International Taxation (eds), *Principles of Law: Function, Status and Impact in EU Tax Law* (IBFD 2014).

265. Michael Lang & others, Double Taxation and EC Law, in RS Avi-Yonah, JR Hines, & M Lang (eds), *Comparative Fiscal Federalism: Comparing the European Court of Justice and the US Supreme Court's Tax Jurisprudence* (Kluwer Law International 2007).

266. On the consequence of repealing Article 293 of TEC, Jérôme Monsenego also argued two possibilities of why Member States repeal Article 293 of TEC: 'By repealing article 293 TEC in the Treaty of Lisbon, Member States may no longer be willing to have elimination of double taxation as an objective or a field of competence of the Union. Alternatively, they perhaps considered that the objective of elimination of double taxation was reached.' *See* Jérôme Monsenego, Taxation of Foreign Business Income Within the European Internal Market: An Analysis of the Conflict Between the Objective of Achievement of the European Internal Market and the Principles of Territoriality and Worldwide Taxation, Vol. 22 (IBFD 2012).

I disagree with both speculations. In my view, it can be argued that the function Article 293 has been replaced with other provisions in TFEU.

Deleting Article 293 of TEC also implies that[267] EU direct tax law has gradually developed its own autonomous approach and does not need to rely heavily on international tax law. Therefore, the traditional goal of 'eliminating double taxation'[268] embedded in international tax treaties, while still being meaningful, would not be the most fundamental goal in the harmonization of EU tax law. Other relevant requirements to build an obstacle-free internal market should also be considered.

2.3.3.2 Neutrality in the Jurisprudence of the Court of Justice of the European Union

The tension between pursuing tax neutrality under the internal market while preserving Member States' fiscal autonomy on direct taxation has been addressed by the CJEU. However, the CJEU has not truly developed a consistent approach to dealing with cases involving CIN and CEN.[269] In other words, the CJEU has not yet decided to choose one of these two concepts of neutrality.[270] Therefore, in some ad hoc cases, the CJEU seems to support CIN or CEN on an ad hoc basis.[271] Since in direct tax cases, the CJEU mainly examines non-discrimination issues, thus eliminating restrictions to/in the market in relation to free movements,[272] the CJEU is not able to really choose directly what kind of tax neutrality (CIN/CEN) it endorses. This leaves room for academic discussions.

One might argue that the CJEU wants to support 'both' CIN and CEN, whereas the concept of neutrality under EU harmonization has to be understood differently and not be restricted by or limited to one single specific neutrality principle developed by

267. Shafi U Niazi & Richard Krever, Romance and Divorce Between International Law and EU Law: Implications for European Competence on Direct Taxes, 53 Stanford Journal of International Law 129 (2017).
268. It is also interesting that in the international tax law academic discussions, the goal of eliminating double taxation is also under reflection and might not necessarily be the paramount goal anymore. Cui argues that the conceptual overlapping between the residence concept and the source concept are the consequences of 'inadequate normative criteria for the design of international income taxation.' Cui argues that 'the inadequacy of the principle of avoiding double taxation: by ignoring the economic incidence of tax, devices purportedly mitigating double taxation in fact produce double non-taxation.'

    Wei Cui, Minimalism about Residence and Source, 38 Michigan Journal of International Law 245 (2017).
269. De Wilde, *supra* n. 76, at 3.2.4.3. Luca Cerioni, *The European Union and Direct Taxation: A Solution for a Difficult Relationship* (Routledge 2015).
270. The same remarks and endorsement, Peters, *supra* n. 248, at 9.2.2 and 9.2.3.
271. The same opinion, Walter Hellerstein, Georg W Kofler & Ruth Mason, Constitutional Restraints on Corporate Tax Integration, 62 Tax Law Review 1 (2008).

    Some scholars use 'capital movement neutrality' to describe the CJEU's ruling, *see* Jacques Malherbe, The Impact of the Rulings of the European Court of Justice in the Area of Direct Taxation (2008), http://www.europarl.europa.eu/RegData/etudes/etudes/join/2008/404888/IPOL-ECON_ET(2008)404888_EN.pdf.

    This study was updated in 2010, available at paragraph 208, *see* Jacques Malherbe, The Impact of the Rulings of the European Court of Justice in the Area of Direct Taxation (2010), http://www.europarl.europa.eu/document/activities/cont/201203/20120313ATT40640/20120313ATT40640EN.pdf.
272. For these two sets of case law, *see* Adam Zalasinski, 35 Years of ECJ Direct Tax Case Law: An Historical Overview on the Occasion of the 60th Anniversary of European Taxation, 61 European Taxation (2021).

economists. In my view, the CJEU's market restrictions criterion in the field of direct tax cases is compatible with MN.

2.3.4 Tax Neutrality in the Development of EU Secondary Law: VAT, the Ruding Report, CCCTB

2.3.4.1 Fiscal Neutrality of VAT: Non-discrimination and Competition Neutrality

In indirect taxation/VAT, the neutrality principle is also cited repeatedly. In the field of EU VAT law, 'fiscal neutrality' of VAT has been directly mentioned in VAT legislation. Fiscal neutrality in the context of EU VAT rules is a principle derived from the non-discrimination principle or the equal treatment principle from the Charter of Fundamental Rights of the European Union.[273] However, when we read the Charter, fiscal neutrality means more than 'non-discrimination'.

The normative content of the fiscal neutrality of EU VAT refers to two subconcepts:[274] (1) VAT should be neutral for competition of similar goods and services, and (2) VAT levied upon similar goods and similar services should not be different whatever the length of the production and distribution chain.[275] Fiscal neutrality in VAT especially focuses on ensuring non-discrimination between similar goods and similar services to achieve the status of 'neutrality in competition'.

From the formulation of the fiscal neutrality of VAT, the two dimensions of fiscal neutrality, i.e., non-discrimination and competition neutrality, are intertwined. The basis for implementing the non-discrimination principle is the similarity of goods/services. Such similarity derives from the perspective of economic reality: when two items are similar and are in competition with each other. It seems that VAT fiscal neutrality equates ensuring non-discrimination to ensuring competition by conducting the similarity test in VAT.

Fiscal neutrality of VAT has also been used by the CJEU to extend the scope of the VAT exemption.[276] De La Feria analysed that VAT is a general consumption tax, and thus the VAT exemption and reduced tax rate are traditionally interpreted restrictively (the strict interpretation method) as exceptions; however, the CJEU has used the fiscal neutrality principle to take the perspective from 'customers' to decide whether two

273. Ben JM Terra & Julie Kajus, *A Guide to the European VAT Directives* (IBFD 2015), at section 2.5.
274. *See* the preamble of the Sixth VAT Directive Council Directive 2006/112/EC of 28 November 2006, Recital 7 '(7) The common system of VAT should, even if rates and exemptions are not fully harmonised, result in neutrality in competition, such that within the territory of each Member State similar goods and services bear the same tax burden, whatever the length of the production and distribution chain.' *See* Article 2 and Article 4 of First VAT Directive.
275. For discussions of two dimensions of VAT fiscal neutrality, *see* Saydé, *supra* n. 69, at 187-188.
276. Rita de la Feria, *EU VAT Principles as Interpretative Aids to EU VAT Rules: The Inherent Paradox*, Oxford University Centre for Business Taxation (2016); Emma Linklater, Neutrality of VAT Rates under European Law: All books Are Created Equal, But Some Are More Equal Than Others?, 30 Publishing Research Quarterly (2014), 300-312.

items should be subject to the same VAT tax burden.[277] De La Feria argued that using the fiscal neutrality principle in the analysis instead of the strict interpretation approach can result in a less distortive tax system.

To sum up, fiscal neutrality in the field of VAT has been formulated in the form of non-discrimination and equal treatment; however, we can also see that the economic reality analysis has influenced the criterion of 'similarity' of goods or services, such as taking customers' preferences and substitutes into account.[278] In my view, the fiscal neutrality principle in VAT has been expanded in a broader sense and as performing different functions, though there is also criticism of VAT neutrality in EU law as lacking a historical or economic foundation and creating logical inconsistencies.[279]

2.3.4.2 A Historical View: Tax Neutrality from the Ruding Report

The concept of neutrality is developed and formulated differently in the field of corporate taxation. After the signing of the Maastricht Treaty, pursing the internal market was reaffirmed by establishing the EU.[280] As to corporate taxation, the Ruding Committee was established in 1992 to conduct research into directing corporate tax law harmonization for the EU. The Ruding Committee's report[281] mentions neutrality in several contexts, including:[282]

- between different legal structures (incorporated and non-incorporated businesses);[283]
- between different methods of financing (debt versus equity finance);[284]
- between distributed and undistributed profits; and
- between investment in domestic shares and investment in the shares of companies of other Member States.

277. For example, Rank Group Case (ECJ Case C-259/10), *see* Christian Amand, VAT Neutrality: A Principle of EU Law or a Principle of the VAT system?, 2 World Journal of VAT/GST Law (2013), 163-181.
278. A famous but very disputed and difficult example is whether printed books and e-books should be treated as the same for the purpose of VAT. The CJEU has repeatedly ruled that the reduced VAT tax rate applicable to printed books cannot be extended to e-books because such a reduced VAT tax rate is listed in the Annex of the VAT Directive. Such a ruling has triggered the amendment proposal from the European Commission. We can see that developments in technology can greatly influence the economy and produce some legal problems that legislators cannot even imagine. For comments, *see* Linklater, *supra* n. 276.
279. Amand, *supra* n. 277.
280. Regarding the development of EU tax law, *see* Panayi, *supra* n. 66, at Chapter 1.
281. Commission of the European Communities (eds), *supra* n. 3. Panayi's introduction on the Ruding Report, *ibid.*, Panayi, at 18.
282. The Ruding Report, *ibid.*, 441.
283. The Ruding Report also refers to this as 'neutrality of legal form', to require equal treatment between subsidiaries and PE.
284. This neutrality has been adopted in CC(C)TB. In the 2016 CCTB & CCCTB Proposals, the relaunch of CCCTB is to be implemented in two stages: the first step is to implement CCTB and the second step is to implement CCCTB. The 2016 CCTB Proposal aims to pursue 'neutrality between debt and equity financing'. It does not directly refer to FA but refers to a specific distinction for company financing, *see* the preamble of the 2016 CCCTB Directive. This topic is outside the scope of the book.

Each of the concepts of 'neutrality' in the Ruding Report represents one type of distortion that the Ruding Report has identified, and the notion of neutrality in each concept is also understood in the strict sense: i.e., the non-legitimate distinction or non-discrimination.

These concepts of neutrality from the Ruding Report have been partially implemented in later legislative developments. For example, since the Parent-Subsidiary Directive does not distinguish PE and subsidiaries regarding profits distribution, the Parent-Subsidiary Directive achieves neutrality between different legal structures.[285] The Merger Directive eliminates the immediate tax burden for cross-border mergers and thus achieves neutrality between investment in domestic shares and investment in the shares of companies of other Member States.

There are only a few directives in the field of direct taxation regarding corporate tax law. Tax neutrality in these directives is understood as eliminating economic double taxation or immediate tax burden.[286] For example, the Parent-Subsidiary Directive and the Interest and Royalty Directive both have a very clear objective to eliminate the distortion arising from economic double taxation.[287] The Merger Directive defers the tax burden which would have been triggered immediately in the case of a cross-border merger.

De Wilde opines that these EU secondary laws in the field of corporate tax are quite ambiguous. According to his observation,[288] the Parent-Subsidiary Directive seems to accept both CEN and CIN, whereas the Interest and Royalty Directive embraces CEN. The Merger Directive seems to embrace the idea of 'cross-border neutrality', and it even provides a more favourable treatment to cross-border mergers and thus creates a 'reverse discrimination' for a purely internal merger.[289] In any case, neither pure CEN nor pure CIN is inappropriate for describing a tax-neutral internal market.

2.3.4.3 *Tax Neutrality in the CCCTB: Prior to the 2011 CCCTB Directive Proposal*

Formulation of tax neutrality from the CCCTB Directive Proposal seems wider than the concepts of neutrality in the Ruding Report. The objective of 'neutrality' is mentioned as a general principle in the CCCTB Working Document No. 1 from the very beginning.[290] In the original thinking of the Commission,[291] the CCCTB Directive, as

285. Article 1 of the Parent-Subsidiary Directive.
286. For analysis of the benchmarks against Directives of Direct taxation, *see* Cerioni, *supra* n. 269. Cerioni uses various benchmarks including elimination of double taxation and non-double taxation, legal certainty, countering aggressive tax planning, and he seems to use them as the combination as the normative framework.
287. *Ibid.*, 2.4.5.1.
288. *De Wilde, supra* n. 76, at 3.2.2.4.
289. *See* Article 1 of the Merger Directive requires a cross-border element.
290. The European Commission, CCCTB Working Document, No.1 General Tax Principles, CCCTB/WP\001Rev1\doc\en, published at https://ec.europa.eu/taxation_customs/sites/taxation/files/docs/body/cctbwp1finalrev1_en.pdf.
291. *Ibid.*, paragraph 15.

harmonization for all EU Member States, will naturally insure both CEN and CIN within the EU. The European Commission does not see differential tax rates as an obstacle to pursuing CEN and CIN at the same time. Such a proposal differs from that of many economists,[292] who clearly distinguish between CEN and CIN and argue that it is impossible to pursue both unless the tax rates of different countries are all equal.

Prior to the initial release of the 2011 CCCTB Directive Proposal, there had been academic discussions on what the neutrality principle really means in the CCCTB. From their discussions, we already see quite a few disparities but still pointing in the same direction: taxation should reflect economic reality. In the case of the CCCTB Directive, Freeman and Macdonald argue[293] that CIN, CEN, and CON should all be taken into account and be balanced, but they do not explain why these three principles especially matter to the CCCTB or how these principles are achieved for the CCCTB.

Andersson[294] interprets the CCCTB Directive as being based on the CIN principle because CCCTB will be attractive to bring in inbound investments from third countries. This formulation is not completely correct but forms only part of the story. I agree with Andersson's argument that CIN is important for the CCCTB Directive, but CIN is not the only or the most dominant principle for CCCTB.

Schön discussed the neutrality principle under the CCCTB and argued that the CCCTB Directive reflects 'capital ownership neutrality'.[295] Schön also interpreted the neutrality principle under the CCCTB Directive as broad. Schön's starting point seems to be that a decision within the group is regarded as an internal activity, which the CCCTB considers a group taxation, and that transferring the investment from one subsidiary to another will be regarded as non-consistent for tax purposes. Schön further indicates that the CCCTB should be consistent with 'group neutrality' and 'decision neutrality'. According to Schön, 'the decision neutrality' is the same idea of efficiency under Article 120 of TFEU: taxpayers' decisions should not be distorted by taxation. 'Group neutrality' means that the definition of group should be based on a material criterion, such as a unitary business, instead of a formal criterion like shareholding. As long as sister subsidiaries are under joint control and constitute a unitary business, they also form part of the same group. This concept of 'group neutrality' is also from a perspective of economic reality.

Agúndez-García[296] uses neutrality as a parameter to evaluate the possible options for designing the CCCTB. Neutrality is defined as a part of the efficiency criterion to examine the policy. Agúndez-García describes neutrality as:

> the apportioning method should be neutral to economic agents' behaviour and influence economic decisions as little as possible: ideally, economic agents should

292. For example, Charles E McLure Jr, International Aspects of Tax Policy for the 21st Century, 8 American Journal of Tax Policy 167 (1989).
293. Freedman & Macdonald, *supra* n. 226.
294. Krister Andersson, An Optional Common Consolidated Corporate Tax Base in the European Union, in National Tax Policy in Europe (Springer 2007).
295. Wolfgang Schön, International Tax Coordination for a Second-Best World (Part I), 1 World Tax Journal 67 (2009), 81; Wolfgang Schön, Group Taxation and the CCCTB, 48 Tax Notes International 1063 (2007).
296. Agundez-Garcia, *supra* n. 129, at 37, 42-43.

> behave after the introduction of the tax regime just as they would have behaved in a no-tax scenario.

It should be noted that Agúndez-García uses 'no-tax world' as an ideal status and the baseline for examining 'neutrality', and it seems that taxation per se creates some distortion. Here we can see that the no-tax world as an ideal status was adopted by some 'classical' economists as the starting point, and this influences their analysis of tax neutrality.

2.3.4.4 Tax Neutrality in the CCCTB: The 2011 CCCTB Proposal and the 2016 CCCTB Proposal

The concept of neutrality is implicitly mentioned in the text of the CCCTB Directive Proposal. 2011 CCCTB Directive mentions:

> allowing the immediate consolidation of profits and losses for computing the EU-wide taxable bases is a step towards reducing over-taxation in cross-border situations and thereby towards improving the tax neutrality conditions between domestic and cross-border activities to better exploit the potential of the Internal Market.

The neutrality here refers to non-discrimination between domestic and cross-border activities, and it focuses on the distortion arising from not allowing cross-border loss-offsetting.

With regard to the FA system under the CCCTB, there is no specific term 'neutrality' in either the 2011 or the 2016 CCCTB Directive Proposal. But the current CCCTB Directive Proposal also aims to eliminate various types of efficiencies due to national law disparities or tax avoidance phenomena, such as OECD's BEPS Project, later revealed in 2013, and mentions neutrality as its fundamental objective.[297]

The CCCTB Directive Proposal is expected to solve various kinds of distortions and thus scholars have proposed neutrality requirements from different dimensions. The neutrality principle that the FA of the CCCTB Directive Proposal should pursue is in the broad sense, i.e., creating a taxation system that will faithfully reflect, not distort, the economic activities in the Member States. Such a design of taxation would be

297. Neutrality has been mentioned in different formations even in the CCCTB Directive Proposal legislation documents, *see* CCCTB Directive Working Document No.1, Common Consolidated Corporate Tax Base Working Group (CCCTB WG) General Tax Principles, Meeting to be held on Tuesday 23 November 2004, at 4: 'Both Capital Export Neutrality (CEN) and Capital Import Neutrality (CIN) are concepts which aim to ensure neutrality', available and archived at https://ec.europa.eu/taxation_customs/sites/taxation/files/docs/body/cctbwp1finalrev1_en.pdf; European Commission, 'Impact Assessment Accompanying Document to the Proposal for a COUNCIL DIRECTIVE on a Common Consolidated Corporate Tax Base (CCCTB) {COM(2011) 121 Final} {SEC(2011) 316 Final}' (2011), at 16 'revenue neutrality'; at 26 'cross-investment neutrality', as a synonym of 'improving efficiency'; available at https://ec.europa.eu/taxation_customs/sites/taxation/files/docs/body/com_sec_2011_315_impact_assesment_en.pdf; European Commission, Impact Assessment Accompanying the Document Proposals for a Council Directive on a Common Corporate Tax Base and a Common Consolidated Corporate Tax Base (CCCTB) {COM(2016) 683 Final} {SWD(2016) 342 Final} (2016), at 13, available at https://ec.europa.eu/taxation_customs/sites/taxation/files/swd_2016_341_en.pdf.

neutral because it is consistent with economic reality and does not cause further distortion.

2.3.5 Final Remarks: Market Neutrality Is Suitable for the EU Because It Is Consistent with the Benefit Principle

As demonstrated earlier, the concept of neutrality in EU law means different things in different contexts. In EU primary law, the neutrality principle is closer to the broader idea of 'an ideal system': neutrality is understood as efficiency. In various direct taxation directives, nevertheless, the concept of neutrality seems to be formulated in the strict sense: to eliminate double taxation. The effect of eliminating double taxation due to different national tax laws is to implement non-discrimination between domestic and cross-border (intra-EU) arrangements. It seems that EU secondary law and the CJEU do not have a consistent approach to neutrality yet. It is not yet crystal clear whether CIN or CEN is preferred.

Kolozs argues that in the context of VAT, the concept of neutrality for direct taxation and indirect taxation is the same and should not be understood differently.[298] In my view, MN, i.e., competition neutrality, is applicable to both direct tax and VAT.

Also in my view, achieving both CEN and CIN at the same time is necessary under EU law, and it is both a positive and a negative integration process. Just as Panayi described,[299] freedom of establishment has inbound and outbound dimensions. Therefore, aspects of CEN and CIN are both relevant and must be achieved simultaneously. In this regard, the CJEU's case law that uses market restrictions to assess infringement of free movement has developed in the direction of the broader concept of MN.[300]

When MN is combined with the benefit principle, it becomes a better and more practical paradigm to explain the relationship between the EU and Member States' fiscal autonomy[301] and the relationship between the Member States. Most importantly, the benefit principle will change the analytical baseline of the 'classical' neutrality principle: no-tax should not be presumed as perfect but merely 'utopia,' a 'nowhere'.[302]

---

298. Borbála Kolozs, Neutrality in VAT, in Michael Lang & others (eds), *Value Added Tax and Direct Taxation: Similarities and Differences* (IBFD 2009).
299. Panayi, *supra* n. 66, at 175.
300. Saydé has a different view. According to Saydé, when there are no EU positive integration measures provided, the CJEU might inevitably choose between two conflicting norms, i.e., CEN and CIN. *See* Saydé, *supra* n. 69, at 273-274. Saydé uses 'home equality' and 'host equality' as synonyms for CIN and CEN, respectively.
301. The optimal boundary between the EU's harmonization/free movements/the internal market versus Member States' fiscal autonomy has been also described as 'two-fold neutrality' by Advocate General Maduro in his opinion on the *Marks& Spencer* case, *see* further discussion, Sjoerd Douma, *Optimization of Tax Sovereignty and Free Movement* (IBFD 2011), at 125.
302. Vogel & Brands, *supra* n. 110, at 28.

2.4 CHAPTER CONCLUSIONS: THE BENEFIT-BASED MARKET NEUTRALITY FRAMEWORK

I have explained the benefit-based MN framework in this chapter. This framework has two necessary elements: the benefit principle and MN. These elements are intertwined.[303] The baseline of MN should be the baseline where Member States provide their public services/benefits to maintain the EU internal market. When the benefits are provided optimally, the status will be MN and where taxation does not hinder competition but sustains a healthy market. The following Chapter 3 assess the typical policy options available for designing an FA regime by benefit-based MN framework to explore how the EU's FA regime should be designed.

303. It is intriguing that other scholars also observe that to build a normative framework for international tax, it often involves multiple guiding principles, no matter what principles are mentioned, among which there is an internal logic. *See* Edoardo Traversa, Commentary on Chapter 13: The Magic Triangle of Sovereignty, Cooperation and Transparency in International Taxation, in Pasquale Pistone (ed.), *European Tax Integration: Law, Policy and Politics* (IBFD 2018). Traversa refers to 'Sovereignty, Cooperation and Transparency' as the three guiding principles.
Another example: Moyal, *supra* n. 222. Moyal refers 'Benefits, Single Tax, and Neutrality' as the three guiding principles.

CHAPTER 3

An Overview of Policy Options Towards a Benefit-Based Market-Neutral Formula: Putting Old Wine in a New Bottle

allocating income among various taxing jurisdictions bears some resemblance... to slicing a shadow.

Container, Container Corp. of America v. Franchise Tax Board[304]

3.1 INTRODUCTION

I concluded in Chapter 2 that essential aspects in a FA tax system should all be consistent with the benefit-based MN framework. In this chapter, the sub-research question is: how the taxable nexus, factor selection, and factor weighting should be designed according to the normative framework.

By glancing at the benefit-based MN framework, we can look for the proper design for the main rules of the CCCTB Directive Proposal. Such tax neutrality should reflect CCCTB taxpayers' economic activities from the production and supply side to the customers' market and demand side.

This chapter is structured as follows. Section 3.2 reviews the trend that an FA approach is used in different contexts. I revisit the debates on the FA in the international tax regime and experiences of state taxation in the US. Section 3.3 discusses the nexus criterion and tests it against the tax neutrality based on the benefit theory. For the EU's FA regime, the PE criterion from international tax law should be reconsidered, and EU should adopt the factor presence nexus instead. Section 3.4 discusses how the weighting factor selection, factor scope, and attribution should be assessed and their justification. I examine the relationship between value creation and weighting factors

304. *Container, Container Corp. of America v. Franchise Tax Board*, 463 U.S. 159 (1983), at 192. This statement vividly illustrates the difficulty of multijurisdictional taxing rights.

in a formula. Section 3.5 further discusses the impact of the 'digital economy' under the EU's FA regime, and how the appearance of a 'significant digital nexus' or 'personal data factor' shows the need for new rules for the digital economy. Section 3.6 reviews some discussions regarding tax competition and endorses a tax rate competition under the EU's FA regime.

3.2 FORMULARY APPORTIONMENT AS A BENEFIT-BASED APPROACH

3.2.1 No 'inherent' Distortion Caused by Formulary Apportionment

Before I proceed with an analysis of FA, it is important to first clarify some arguments and concerns regarding inherent distortion. In the literature, there are arguments about 'inherent distortions' when adopting an FA, especially in regard to new investments, as Weiner in 2002 argued.[305] According to Weiner,[306] FA as such has caused inherent distortions to business as well as state tax policy makers because selecting specific weighting factors will influence business investments and employment decisions; state policy makers will also be influenced because state policy makers would choose the weighting factors that can function as tax incentives to attract inbound investments from business.[307]

Weiner's arguments need to be clarified for two reasons. First, Weiner's main argument of reducing the weight on the payroll factor and the assets factor/increasing the weight of the sales factor can induce 'new' cross-border business investments is based on the early research by Goolsbee and Maydew published in 2001. The same empirical data from Goolsbee and Maydew's has already been replicated, corrected, retested, challenged, and turned down by more recent empirical research by David Merriman in 2015.[308] Since the factual ground of such argument is no longer solid due to new findings, the corresponding argument should also be reconsidered.

---

305. Joann Weiner, Formulary Apportionment and the Future of Company Taxation in the European Union: Company Taxation and the Internal Market, *CESifo Forum* (München: ifo Institut für Wirtschaftsforschung an der Universität München 2002). For similar arguments, *see*, Jack Mintz & Joann Martens Weiner, Exploring Formula Allocation for the European Union, 10 International Tax and Public Finance 695 (2003), at 3.1., under the subtitle 'Regarding old and new investment distortions'

    IMF's research report still has similar formulations, *see* Thornton Matheson & others, Formulary Apportionment in Theory and Practice, *Corporate Income Taxes under Pressure: Why Reform Is Needed and How It Could Be Designed* (IMF 2021).
306. Weiner's argument is based on her own PhD research in the mid-1990s as well as eminent economics scholars' empirical data between 1980 and 2000, such as Goolsbee and Maydew. *See* Weiner, *ibid.* Austan Goolsbee & Edward L Maydew, Coveting Thy Neighbor's Manufacturing: The Dilemma of State Income Apportionment, 75 Journal of Public Economics 125 (2000).
307. For similar formulations, *see* Mintz & Weiner, *supra* n. 305, at 3.1; Charles E McLure Jr, Implementing State Corporate Income Taxes in the Digital Age, 53 National Tax Journal 1287 (2000).
308. David Merriman, A Replication of 'Coveting Thy Neighbor's Manufacturing: The Dilemma of State Income Apportionment (Journal of Public Economics 2000)', 43 Public Finance Review 185 (2015). I explore this topic further in section 3.4.2.1 of this book.

Second, based on Goolsbee and Maydew's data, Weiner presented[309] that when the corporate tax rate is reduced, or when the weight of the sales factor is increased, taxpayers respond to a reduced corporate rate or a tax credit to increase investments (so the capital and employment in that jurisdiction increase), at least temporarily. This is not a specific problem due to adopting FA, but a common phenomenon when different tax rates in different jurisdictions are involved.[310] In addition, Merriman has negated the investment-incentive effect of increasing the weight of the sales factor, and therefore the belief of the sales factor being superior to other factors is ungrounded.

In my view, Weiner's language of 'distortion' caused by an FA has led to a normative implication and confusion. A response to (either reduced or increased) tax rate is inherently problematic. In her 2002 paper, Weiner describes 'distortions' as a behavioural response caused by a tax or a subsidy.[311] Weiner's usage is normal usage by economists in a specific context, but it should not be misunderstood as 'being inherently contrary to market neutrality'.

Moreover, the attraction to a relatively low-tax-rate jurisdiction for taxpayers does exist for business investment. While choosing this low-tax-rate jurisdiction also means choosing the public benefits provided by that jurisdiction. Assuming this does not involve tax avoidance or abuse, I do not see this as problematic. In fact, each state has different capacities to provide public services, including providing bail-out programs when taxpayers are facing natural disasters or a global pandemic crisis. When placing economic activities in a low-tax-rate jurisdiction, taxpayers may choose fewer public services or more cost-efficient services, and this is also a business risk to take.

To sum up, the term 'distortion' in Weiner's early literature on FA is a descriptive term, not a normative term implying we need to take actions to. Taxpayers' different responses due to different tax rates or different tax policies are not problematic either, though in some economics literature it is referred to as 'distortion'.

309. Weiner, *supra* n. 305.

310. We can also see this assumption of tax as DWL and assertion of a 'response' being as distortion in other examples criticizing a FA. For example, when Vella argued that 'value creation' is not an appropriate norm for evaluating taxation, *see* John Vella, Value Creation and the Allocation of Profits under a Formulary Apportionment System, in Krever & Vaillancourt, *supra* n. 46.

Mueller even argued that FA could 'always' be subject to tax planning because taxpayers have incentives to shift weighting factors to reduce tax burden. Also *see* Peter Mueller, Formula Apportionment - Approaches to Reduce Tax Planning Incentives, available at SSRN 1730178 (2010). These arguments are not entirely correct.

311. Harberger has also expressed that economists use 'distortions' loosely, and it does not have a normative implication. *See* section 2.1.3 above, Harberger & Just, *supra* n. 132, at 14-15, worth citing again: 'My main distortions are taxes and subsidies, and they depend on what the law was. The allocations of resources and the economy are changing all the time, and these damned taxes are there.'

'Arnold Harberger: My natural statement of a distortion is a gap between a supply price and a demand price, or a gap between some activity's marginal social benefit and its marginal social cost. That's what I would call a distortion.'

In Harberger's definition, distortion is just an objective difference and does not immediately have a normative implication.

3.2.2 Formulary Apportionment in the International Tax Law Regime

3.2.2.1 A Convergence Between Formulary Apportionment and Transfer Pricing Techniques

Traditionally, there are two opposite options for conducting an international tax reform: opting for the FA approach,[312] or reforming the TP regimes based on SA but keeping the ALP.[313]

However, these two approaches are no longer mutually exclusive in academic discussions.[314] There is a trend towards a convergence between these two. Scholars who endorse FA also admit that FA might be problematic to exclude intangibles that still are subject to ALP.[315] Supporters of TP regimes are also gradually open to including an FA element or as one TP method, such as Scheriber[316] and Bauner.[317] Sadiq also acknowledges that[318] TP methods adopted by US tax authorities (Internal Revenue Service (IRS)) also uses the risk factor[319] in its APA of multinational financial institutions' global trading.

Although OECD TP guidelines in the past rejected FA as a separate approach, the underlying theory of FA has already influenced the TP practices and discussions of the digital economy.[320] For example, Sadiq emphasizes that FA is quite suitable for the

---

312. For example, advocates of FA over SA/ALP, *see* Marco Runkel, In Favor of Formulary Apportionment A Comment on Kroppen/Dawid/Schmidtke: Profit Split, the Future of Transfer Pricing? Arm's Length Principle and Formulary Apportionment Revisited from a Theoretical and a Practical Perspective, in W Schön & KA Konrad (eds), *Fundamentals of International Transfer Pricing in Law and Economics* (Springer 2012).
    Advocates of applying FA to allocating profits of PEs, *see*, for example, Kobetsky, *supra* n. 80, at Chapter 14.
313. Advocates of SA, *see,* for example, Heinz-Klaus Kroppen, Roman Dawid & Richard Schmidtke, Profit Split, the Future of Transfer Pricing? Arm's Length Principle and Formulary Apportionment Revisited from a Theoretical and a Practical Perspective, in W. Schön & K.A. Konrad (eds), *supra* n. 312, at 267-293.
314. Reuven S Avi-Yonah, The Rise and Fall of Arm's Length: A Study in the Evolution of US International Taxation, 15 Virginia Tax Review 89 (1995). In fact, since early many authors are very practical and willing to accept a compromise or hybrid between an FA and a transfer pricing system. Monica Brown Gianni, Transfer Pricing and Formulary Apportionment, 74 Taxes169 (1996).
315. Avi-Yonah & Benshalom, *supra* n. 46.
316. Ulrich Schreiber, Sales-Based Apportionment of Profits, 72 Bulletin for International Taxation 1 (2018).
317. Yariv Brauner, Formula Based Transfer Pricing, 42 Intertax 615 (2014).
318. Kerrie Sadiq, Unitary Taxation of the Financial Sector, ICTD Working Paper 25 (2014); Kerrie Sadiq, The Case for Unitary Taxation with Formulary Apportionment in the Finance Sector and the Effect on Developing Nations, 44 Australian Tax Review 75 (2015).
319. Notice 94-40, Global Trading Advance Pricing Agreements; Advocates of FA applying to global trading, *see* Kelvin K Leung, Taxing Global Trading: An Appropriate Testing Ground for Formula Apportionment, 1 Minn. J. Global Trade 201(1992).
320. It has been observed that in the context of the digital economy, the OECD is starting to admit that using a fraction/ratio/'metric' of revenue or employee could be a feasible solution, *see* Public Consultation Document, paragraphs 77-78. For comments, *see* Maarten Floris de Wilde & Ciska Wisman, OECD Consultations on the Digital Economy: 'Tax Base Reallocation' and 'I'll Tax If You Don't'?, available at SSRN 3349078 (2019).

digital economy.[321] FA as such is not completely incompatible with the existing TP practices,[322] otherwise it would not be used in domestic laws, such as the US. All these arguments and observations above support a compromise as a way to a tax reform between FA and traditional TP developments.[323]

It should be noted that the OECD's latest development also demonstrates the gradual acceptance of FA. The OECD's Pillar One Project also plans to use various 'allocation keys', such as a 'Global Allocation Key',[324] to source income. These allocation keys are ratios to estimate the proportion of the market share.

There is another evident trend towards a reconciliation between FA and TP practices:[325] Even for the most rigid traditional supporters of the ALP, it is clear that, with the same name, the ALP will be adapted and become more 'flexible' in order to survive.[326] A formula embodies such flexibility. In the current academic discussions, a new TP approach 'Formulary Profit Split' has been developed.[327] FA as a tax legislation technique has been utilized in some specific contexts, such as an APA or global trading, allocating profits to PEs, etc.[328] Therefore, the distinction between FA and TP is not absolute, but it can be extracted to create a new compromise system.[329] For example, the rationale of the sales factor, i.e., the profits and outputs of taxpayers, has been also applied in the TP regime, such as the transactional profit split method (TPSM)[330] and evaluation approach of hard-to-value intangibles (HTVI). Taxpayers' ex post output[331] or performance in the market have been recognized by the OECD guidelines as an important indicator to pursue the reform's purpose of 'aligning transfer pricing

321. Sadiq, *supra* n. 60.
322. Their relationship is neither binary nor mutually exclusive, *see* Brauner, *supra* n. 46.
323. A theory of a mixture of a FA and a transfer pricing developed by Brauner, *see* Brauner, *ibid.*
324. *See* the OECD, the draft rules for nexus and revenue sourcing under Pillar One Amount A, 4 February 2022, https://www.oecd.org/tax/beps/oecd-invites-public-input-on-the-draft-rules-for-nexus-and-revenue-sourcing-under-pillar-one-amount-a.htm.
325. For similar observations, *see* Robert Robillard, BEPS: Is the OECD Now at the Gates of Global Formulary Apportionment?, 43 Intertax 447 (2015). Robillard is critical of this trend of introducing FA in the BEPS. René Offermans & others, European Union – Bridging the CCCTB and the Arm's Length Principle – A Value Chain Analysis Approach, 57 European Taxation 466 (2017). The same remark, *see* International Fiscal Association Proceeding Summary Report 2019, 'Arm's length Principle 2.0'.
326. John Neighbour & Jeffrey Owens, Transfer Pricing in the New Millennium: Will the Arm's Length Principle Survive, 10 George Mason Law Review 951 (2001).
327. *See* MJ Keen & others, *Spillovers in International Corporate Taxation* (IMF 2014), paragraphs 72–73; *see* Reuven S Avi-Yonah, Between Formulary Apportionment and the OECD Guidelines: A Proposal for Reconciliation, World Tax Journal (2010).
328. Li, *supra* n. 178, at 861-866. Li has given several examples from transfer pricing to domestic tax law usage of the FA technique.
329. *Ibid.* In Li's term, it could be the result of 'developing an international consensus'.
330. Cottani also observes the similarities between FA and transfer pricing; *see* Cottani, *supra* n. 139.
331. Marta Pankiv, Post-BEPS Application of the Arm's Length Principle to Intangibles Structures, 23 International Transfer Pricing Journal 463 (2016), footnote 32: 'Actual (or ex post) remuneration refers to the income actually earned by a member of the group through the exploitation of the intangible.' Such remuneration can be included in the sales factor of a formula. Similar opinion, Stefan Greil, The Dealing at Arm's Length Fallacy: A Way Forward to a Formula-Based Transactional Profit Split?, 45 Intertax 624 (2017).

outcomes with value creation'. The indicators "development, enhancement, maintenance, protection, exploitation" (DEMPE functions) for deciding ownership of intangibles are also seen as a type of formulistic approach.[332] These new TP adjustment techniques can provide inspiration to designing a formula.

Since the value-creation process has involved taxpayers' input and output, a formula that is based on the presumption that the business is integrated, would not per se be incompatible with the OECD's TP suggestions or BEPS actions, though the term FA is not the officially authorized OECD approach nor is it mentioned in Pillar One Project.

Therefore, FA accepts the inherent difficulty of deciding the source and attribution of a multinational taxpayer's income by embracing a more flexible approach. As long as the rationale of the design of each factor has its own consistency, a formula is justified. TP practices can also provide insights. FA and TP practices are no longer mutually exclusive; rather, they both are the efforts to answer the big question of how to allocate the taxing powers on MNE taxpayers' taxable income, which involves different jurisdictions in a globalized world.

This book thus embraces any insightful ideas that are compatible with the formula design from existing international tax law or cross-border taxation practices. To sum up, neither FA nor TP/SA methods can claim to be perfect, and each of them has its own economic rationale as well as weakness.[333] By comparing FA experiences and relevant TP practices, and seeking useful lessons from both sides,[334] we could still make an effort to design a CCCTB Directive that is consistent with the benefit principle and achieves MN status.[335]

3.2.2.2 Formulary Apportionment Represents Public Benefits Utilization

Compared to the residence-source dichotomy of the international tax regime, a modernized FA system is actually more closely aligned with the evolution of the globalized economy and the corresponding public benefits involved in the twenty-first century. Also, the EU's FA regime should not be categorized as 'source' taxation in the traditional context of international tax law because the residence-source distinction is not meaningful for an FA.[336] An FA actually embraces the flexible idea of 'everywhere

332. *See*, Mirna Solange Screpante, The Arm's Length Principle Evolves Towards a 'Value Creation Functional (Ie DEMPE) Formula Standard': A Barrier or a Gateway to Locational Business Planning?, 48 Intertax (2020), especially at 2.3 and 4.2. Screpante observes that the post-BEPD DEMPE analysis is a functional formula-based standard. *See also* Chapter 6 of this book.
333. Weiner, *supra* n. 141, at 25-56.
334. My approach is also inspired by Grinberg's work to use principles and experience from FA as a benchmark to evaluate international reform options, *see* Itai Grinberg, Formulating the International Tax Debate: Where Does Formulary Apportionment Fit?, in Krever & Vaillancourt (eds), *supra* n. 46.
335. McLure & Weiner, *supra* n. 221.
336. For different formulations, asserting corporate taxation should be source taxation, *see* Christian Jaag & Tobias F Rohner, Why Corporate Taxation Should Mean Source Taxation: A Response to the OECD's Actions Against Base Erosion and Profit Shifting, 9 World Tax Journal 352 (2017). They assert a 'source-based corporate income tax' and argue that corporate tax should

could be source',[337] so FA does not divide taxing rights via an all-or-nothing approach based on the source-residence dichotomy in the traditional international tax regime.

The all-or-nothing thinking based on the source-residence dichotomy in the traditional international tax regime is a historical fact due to administrative convenience and former practice. As indicated in Chapter 2, the distinction between the residence versus source principle is empty,[338] and 'source' does not have a clear definition. We can even argue that the residence state of a corporation is also a type of source when active business activities take place in the jurisdiction of a corporation's seat. The distinction of residence versus source is merely a historical and outdated choice of the early twentieth century. This is why the distinction lacks substantial meaning[339] and cannot be mutually exclusive.[340]

It is true that residence was a useful tool in the past. As Jogaraja analyses:[341] 'Residence-taxation was justified as a better measure of ability to pay and because the residence-country provided protection. As a solution for international double taxation, exclusive residence-taxation was considered simple and more complex methods unnecessary'. Residence taxation was also justified from the perspective of 'social contract'[342] because non-residents are not a party to the social contract of the jurisdiction whereas residents are.

But nowadays, the residence state of corporations no longer plays the key role for conducting business activities and providing 'protection' as in the past. To determine a corporate's residence, there are two sets of approach: a formal one, i.e., 'the incorporation test' and a less formal one, i.e., 'the control and management test'.[343] Even when adopting a 'less formal' approach to decide a corporate's residence, it is quite easy to choose the location of 'control and management' strategically and still conduct a globalized business, thanks to the development of communication technology. In the past, due to the different approaches to decide residence, corporations could be a no-where resident; nowadays, corporations can even smartly choose a residence jurisdiction to minimize their tax burden or maximize their tax advantages. MNE

---

not be understood as a tax of residence (the status quo, depending on the company registration) but source taxation. They argue that residence taxation is no longer appropriate for current MNE taxpayers because corporate business activities have an input side and an output side. I agree with their argument and observation. However, from the perspective of the traditional sense of 'source' taxation, only the input side qualifies as 'source', so this book would still avoid using this disputed term of 'source' to classify an FA system such as CCCTB.

337. John A Swain & Walter Hellerstein, State Jurisdiction to Tax Nowhere Activity, 33 Virginia Tax Review 209 (2013), 267.
338. Vogel, *supra* n. 177.
339. *See* Cui, *supra* n. 268.
340. Todd A Lard, Domicile Versus Source Based Taxation: Must One Define the Other?, *The State and Local Tax Lawyer. Symposium Edition* (American Bar Association 2009).
341. Jogarajan, *supra* n. 29, at 178. In the early twentieth century when the international tax regime was just started, the residence principle for the market economy at that period still means a lot. This is why in that period, international tax law experts from the UK embraced the residence principle and the British government strongly supported exclusive residence taxation.
342. Moyal, *supra* n. 222.
343. Avi-Yonah, *supra* n. 61, Chapter 2.2.

taxpayers' strategy might be facilitated because of the imperfect tax competition between states.[344]

Therefore, in my view, the residence of a corporation no longer reflects the taxpayer's economic activities and corresponding public benefits but becomes an easy tool for the tax planning or maximizing tax benefits, such as tax incentives. For designing a tax-neutral FA, the concept of residence is no longer useful and should be abandoned. Since the concept of residence is not useful, its counterpart 'source' in the traditional tax regime should also be reconsidered. In other words, if a resident company has only very few economic activities, such as some paper work or incorporation registration, it is not justified for the residence jurisdiction to claim a large portion of the tax base. By using an FA approach, the weighting factors can solve the issue of 'empty residence'.

3.2.3 Formulary Apportionment in the US

In addition to the international tax regime, FA is much more widely used in the subnational context, such as the US. It is especially important to analyse developments in US state taxation experience and constitutional requirements, including the Commerce Clause and the Due Process Clause. This is because the US is a mature internal market and its constitutional requirements to regulate FA at the state level actually sheds light on and corresponds to the tax neutrality framework of this book. There are quite a few similarities between US constitutional requirements and EU internal market concepts.

Moreover, the legal concept developed in US Supreme Court case law on state taxation, including the unitary business (the apportionability of the taxable income), the internal and external consistency, reaffirm and coincide with the benefit-based MN framework established in Chapter 2. Here I demonstrate how developments in US FA fit in the normative framework below.

3.2.3.1 *Formulary Apportionment Is Considered as the Most Logical Method in the US*

The US levies CIT both at the federal level and at the state level.[345] A taxpayer that has a tax nexus in a state is subject to that state's taxation. A group that conducts interstate economic activities might be subject to several states' tax laws.[346] Therefore, states

344. Dagan, *supra* n. 24.
345. For the general overview of corporate taxation in the US, *see* Wooje Choi & John G Rienstra, *United States – Corporate Taxation, in Country Tax Guides* (IBFD 2020); Richard D Pomp, *State & Local Taxation* (RD Pomp 2015), at Chapter 10; Walter Hellerstein & others, *State and Local Taxation: Cases and Materials* (10th ed. West Academic 2014), at Chapter 1.
346. A comparative perspective to understand the US's state taxation, *see* Charles E McLure, The Long Shadow of History: Sovereignty, Tax Assignment, Legislation and Judicial Decisions on Corporate Income Taxes in the US and the EU, in Avi-Yonah, Hines, & Lang (eds), *supra* n. 265.

have developed their own methods of taxing a multistate group's activities in order to reduce double taxation[347] or excessive taxation.

There are three different methods[348] for states to divide the tax base generated from multistate activities: separate geographic accounting, specific allocation, and FA.

The first method, separate geographic accounting, divides the taxable income according to the geographic territory. This method is out of favour[349] now because the separate geographic accounting method has theoretical and practical problems:[350] theoretically, the separate geographical accounting method assumes that the profits earned from a group can be clearly allocated to each group member, but this is inconsistent with the economic reality of a group; practically, the separate geographical accounting method adopts the TP rules to estimate the profits attribution, and it is difficult to find a comparable indicator. Now the separate geographic accounting method is out of favour and only functions as an alternative method when FA leads to obviously unfair results.[351]

The second method is the 'specific allocation' approach. The 'specific allocation' approach applies to specific types of income directly allocated to a single state. By Pomp's metaphor, the allocable taxable income is a ball of ice cream allocated to a scoop. In practice, business income earned from a unitary business is divided by FA; non-business income is divided according to the specific allocation rule. Specific allocation was used often to decide the taxing rights on allocable income earned from intangibles, such as interest and royalties, since the early twentieth century. However, it was also a result of history when income earned from intangibles was not related to business income.[352] This approach is now outdated.

347. It is important to re-emphasize here that the term double taxation in this context refers to being subject to multiple states of the US and not to be understood as international double taxation.
348. Pomp, *supra* n. 345, at 10-14.
349. Jerome R Hellerstein, Walter Hellerstein & John A Swain, *State Taxation* (3rd ed. Thomson Reuters/Tax & Accounting 2015), at 8.06[1].
350. Pomp, *supra* n. 345, at 10-15.
351. I discuss the application of the alternative method in Chapter 8 of this book.
352. Walter Hellerstein, State Taxation of Corporate Income from Intangibles: Allied-Signal and Beyond, 48 Tax Law Review 739 (1992), 777-778, at footnote 201. Hellerstein cited the report of 1922; also *see* Carl S Lamb & others, *Report of Committee on the Apportionment Between States of Taxes on Mercantile and Manufacturing Business, Proceedings of the Annual Conference on Taxation under the Auspices of the National Tax Association* (National Tax Association 1922).

Hellerstein discussed the historical development of allocating income earned from intangibles. According to Hellerstein's analysis on the academic and policy discussions in 1922: 'In 1922, the National Tax Association's influential Committee on the Apportionment Between the States of Taxes on Mercantile and Manufacturing Business recommended a Model Business Income Tax that required the deduction from "business income" of a taxpayer's interest, dividends, royalties, and gains not received in the connection with the business. Any remaining intangible "business income" was allocated to the particular state in which it was "received in connection with business"'.

FA[353] is the method most often used for dividing the multistate tax base.[354] As Pomp and other scholars describe it,[355] the FA method regards a taxpayer's apportionable multistate activities as a taxable 'pie', as a 'unitary business',[356] and a US state can be entitled to a share of the pie to the extent that the taxpayer has a taxable nexus.

Conceptually speaking, apportionability, i.e., the unitary business principle, should be separated from the discussion of nexus.[357] The operationality/unitary business refers to the size of the pie, while the nexus refers to the minimum threshold and condition to really start to apportion. The state will get a piece of 'pie' by applying the FA when there is sufficient in-state nexus. The apportionability is the first step of the analysis and the nexus is the second step. However, since unitary business and nexus both deal with the tax base issue, the discussions of both are inevitably intertwined sometimes. In this book, I also clearly separate them in two different sections.

3.2.3.2 States' Collective Efforts to Reduce Formulary Apportionment Disparities

To pursue uniformity regarding levying tax on multistate business income, the Uniform Division of Income for Tax Purposes Act (UDITPA) was adopted in 1957. UDITPA

353. In this book, I focus my discussions only on state taxation of the US because I would like to extract lessons for EU dividing taxing rights between EU Member States. However, apportionment and allocation are also legislative techniques used in the tax laws and regulations at the federal level in the US for deciding foreign companies' US source income. These discussions on 'apportionment' are outside the scope of this research but the international tax regime of the US is not.

    For the sake of completeness, works from Robert Feinschreiber are mentioned here. *See* Robert Feinschreiber, Final Regulations for Allocating and Apportioning Deductions, 3 International Tax Journal 278 (1976); Robert Feinschreiber, Treaty Provisions for Allocating and Apportioning Deductions, 4 International Tax Journal 995 (1977); Robert Feinscheiber, Analysis of the Allocation and Apportionment Cases: The Early Years, 4 International Tax Journal 745 (1977); Robert Feinschreiber, Analysis of the Allocation and Apportionment Examples – Part II, 5 International Tax Journal 45 (1978); Robert Feinschreiber, Analysis of the Allocation and Apportionment Cases: 1934 to Present, 4 International Tax Journal 769 (1977); Robert Feinschreiber, Allocation and Apportionment of Miscellaneous Deductions, 4 International Tax Journal 653 (1977); Robert Feinscheiber, Analysis of the Allocation and Apportionment Examples – Part I, 4 International Tax Journal 1027 (1977).
354. A FA approach has been widely (though not identically) adopted in the US for many advantages. *See* Michael J McIntyre, *Design of a National Formulary Apportionment Tax System, Proceedings of the Annual Conference on Taxation Held under the Auspices of the National Tax Association-Tax Institute of America* (National Tax Association 1991).
355. Pomp, *supra* n. 345, at 10-23.
356. For an overview, *ibid.*, 10-63. By applying the unitary business principle, it can justify a state's taxing right on out-of-state capital gains, *see* Clark Milner, Taxation – State Tax Apportionment of Out-of-State Business Income – Constitutionality and Propriety of a State's Apportionment and Taxation of Capital Gains as Business Earnings: *Blue Bell Creameries, LP v. Roberts*, 79 Tenn. Law Review 437 (2012); as to out-of-state IHCs, *see* Hellerstein, Hellerstein & Swain, *supra* n. 349: Nexus Over Out-of-State Intangible Holding Companies Based on In-State Presence of Parent or Affiliate.
357. Hellerstein, Hellerstein & Swain, *supra* n. 349, at 6.14[2]. Concerning the inapplicability of the unitary business concept in establishing nexus for income tax purposes, Hellerstein rightly concludes that the unitary business principle is the linchpin of apportionability, not the linchpin of taxable nexus.

apportions the 'business income' according to a three-equal-weighted factor: property, payroll, and sales.[358] UDITPA is a uniform act in the US that states can voluntarily join[359] for the purpose of pursuing uniformity.[360] In addition to UDITPA, other stakeholders also work on pursuing uniformity in the division of multistate taxable income. In 1967, a group of state tax administrators presented states with the 'Multistate Tax Compact', which copies UDITPA and establishes an interstate agency, the 'Multistate Tax Commission' (MTC).[361]

For European readers, it is easier to understand the MTC as a type of intergovernmental organization like the OECD. It is not a supranational organization like the EU. Just like the OECD, the MTC does have great de facto influence in US states. The MTC, as an intergovernmental state tax agency based on the Multistate Tax Compact,[362] issues soft laws for these states. Regarding the sharing formulas, the MTC has recommended formulas for general corporations and corporations from specific industries. These recommendations are soft law but are developed by state tax experts sent from all states. Therefore, states' legislators and tax authorities quite often follow these recommendations. A lower court in California even admitted the priority of the Multistate Tax Compact as a legal source, even being higher than the states' enacted tax law, though this opinion was not upheld by the higher court.[363] The strong influence from the MTC on states in the US is undeniable.

The MTC has laid down various detailed recommendations in the form of model regulations or model statutes on issues in state taxation. It is expected that states will

358. Such three-factor formula is also known as the 'Massachusetts formula', *see* Joann M Weiner, Using the Experience in the US States to Evaluate Issues in Implementing Formula Apportionment at the International Level, 83 OTA paper (1999), 10.
359. The states joining the UDITPA can be found on the Uniform Law Commission's website. The enacting states are Alabama, Alaska, Arizona, Arkansas, California, Colorado, District of Columbia, Hawaii, Idaho, Kansas, Kentucky, Maine, Michigan, Minnesota, Missouri, Montana, New Mexico, North Dakota, Oregon, Pennsylvania, South Dakota, Texas, Utah, and Washington. For more information, *see* the official website https://www.uniformlaws.org/home.
360. For the history and reform process of UDITPA, *see* Joe B Huddleston & Shirley K Sicilian, Should UDITPA Be Revisited?, *The State and Local Tax Lawyer. Symposium Edition* (American Bar Association 2009).
361. *See* the official website of the MTC: http://www.mtc.gov. Not only public servants but also practitioners from the American Bar Association (ABA) actively engage in the MTC's work, *see* Philip M Tatarowicz, A History of the State and Local Taxes Committee and Its Most Recent Quarter Century of Work, 68 Tax Law, 595 (2014).
362. As to the constitutional status of the Multistate Tax Compact, *see* Robert M White, The Constitutionality of the Multistate Tax Compact, 29 Vanderbilt Law Review, 453 (1976); Natasha N Varyani, A Contract among States: Capturing Income of the World's Multijurisdictional Taxpayers, 1 University of Bologna Law Review 219 (2016).
363. The California case, *Gillette Co. v. Franchise Tax Board* 62 Cal. 4th 468 (2015), the Court of Appeal reversed the trial court and ruled that California may not unilaterally change or repudiate mandatory terms of the Compact. The California Supreme Court reversed again the Court of Appeal's ruling and ruled that the Multistate Tax Compact is not reciprocally binding on states and the MTC's regulations are advisory only, California legislation can preclude the Multistate Tax Compact's specific rule.

   Michigan Court of Appeals adjudicated the same issue and concluded that the Multistate Tax Compact is not binding on Michigan state legislation, *see* John A Biek, Alternative Formulary Apportionment under the Multistate Tax Compact, 16 J. Passthrough Entities (2013), 41.

adopt the MTC's recommendations voluntarily and the phenomenon of path dependency will happen, and thus the states' taxation will gradually converge and achieve uniformity. Since the UDITPA/Multistate Tax Compact are soft law[364] and are not self-executing, there is a great variety of states' FA rules.[365] The Multistate Tax Compact and UDITPA are model laws, i.e., soft law, and states are free to enact them in their state tax legislation. Therefore, as to the state income tax apportionment, not every state enacts UDITPA or Multistate Tax Compact, and some states may have similar but different provisions that have the same functions.

In addition to laying down regulations, the MTC also continues to reform the Multistate Tax Compact. In 2014 and 2015, amendments were made to the Multistate Tax Compact regarding the definition of sales (gross receipts),[366] the attribution rule of the sales factor,[367] and the equitable apportionment (alternative apportionment method) clause.[368] Although the Multistate Tax Compact and the MTC's regulations are not compulsory, the amendments are discussed widely by various stakeholders, including the state taxation administration representatives, experts, practitioners, and scholars; and thus they are quite influential for the future development of state taxation.

To sum up, the MTC reforms of the FAs rules also reflect an important fact that the original UDITPA/MTC designed in the mid-twentieth century needs new rules to fulfil the new needs in the digital era. When EU legislators are seeking to learn lessons about taxation, the experiences of ongoing tax reforms should also be considered.[369]

364. Although it has been accepted that the Multistate Tax Compact is only the model law for the participating member states, taxpayers have started to claim their rights to choose the formula provided by the Multistate Tax Compact, even if such a formula is not provided by state law. Therefore, it is disputed whether the Multistate Tax Compact is also a valid legal source for taxpayers. In California, the *Gillette* case deals with this issue. The California Court of Appeal affirmed the taxpayer's right to elect the Multistate Tax Compact, even if California law does not, but the California Supreme Court rejected the Multistate Tax Compact as a reciprocally binding agreement between states, so taxpayers cannot claim rights based on it. For the California Supreme Court ruling, *see The Gillette Company, et. al. v. California Franchise Tax Board*, Case No. S206587 (Cal. 2015).
365. For the history and problems of adopting UDITPA, *see* James Smith, UDITPA Turns 50, 25 Journal of State Taxation 13 (2006). Smith mentions the serious problem of nowhere sales in combination with a heavily weighted/single-sales-factor formula and the importance that states adopt a uniform rule.
366. In July 2014, the MTC amended the definition of 'gross receipts' for the sales factor in Article IV, section 1(g) of the Multistate Tax Compact. For further discussion, *see* Chapter 4 of this book.
367. In July 2014, the MTC amended the attribution rule for the sales factor in Article IV, section 17 of the Multistate Tax Compact, to adopt 'market sourcing' to attribute the sales for the sales factor of the formula. For further discussion, *see* Chapter 4 of this book.
368. In July 2015, the MTC amended the alternative apportionment in Article IV, section 18 of the Multistate Tax Compact. For further discussion, *see* Chapter 8 of this book.
369. I especially include the discussions about the MTC's recent reforms in Chapter 4 about the definition of sales and the attribution rule of the sales factor, and in Chapter 8 about the alternative apportionment method.

3.2.3.3 *'Unitary Business' as the Linchpin of Formulary Apportionment*

According to established case law[370] in the US, the 'linchpin'[371] or the precondition to exercising FA is 'the unitary business'.[372] It means that different business affiliates form a 'unity'. For European readers, we can understand the unitary business concept as to address the question of what (type of) income the consolidated group tax base should include. Unlike the CCCTB's formalistic approach of using shareholding as the criterion, the 'unitary business' concept focuses on the actual relationship between group members. This precondition also justifies a consolidated tax base consisting of income earned outside the state[373] as long as such income is earned from a part of the unitary business.

On a side note, the unitary business principle should not be confused with the 'combined reporting method' in the literature and practice. These two concepts sometimes look very similar and sometimes appear in related discussions about corporate tax reform,[374] but they do not address the same issue. The combined reporting method is merely one method to filing a tax return for a unitary business.[375] There are different methods of filing the income earned from a unitary business adopted in US states, even including 'separate entity reporting'.[376] By the separate entity reporting method, each company must file its own state tax return for the unitary business income which is attributable to the state and calculate their own FA result. By the combined reporting method or the consolidated tax method, in contrast, a group of companies file a combined reporting for their unitary business income, even if part of

370. For some early discussions in the mid-1980s on case law in the US on the unitary business, *see* Lloyd V Crawford, Alternatives to Worldwide Unitary Apportionment – An Analysis, 36 U. Florida Law Review 1051 (1984).
371. This term is from US Supreme Court case law: *Mobil Oil Corp. v. Commissioner of Taxes*, 445 U.S. 425, 439 (1980).
372. Hellerstein, *supra* n. 352, at 74-75; Hellerstein, Hellerstein & Swain, *supra* n. 349, at 8.07[2]; Charles E McLure Jr, *Defining a Unitary Business: An Economist's View* (National Bureau of Economic Research 1983).
373. *See* Mayer, *supra* n. 48, at 3.2.2.3.
374. The combined reporting method has an inherent advantage that combined reporting can increase transparency to transactions and scenarios between the group members. This is why combined reporting is a useful anti-avoidance measure, especially against tax avoidance scenarios arising from IHCs, *see* Pomp, *supra* n. 345, at 10-91. As to addressing tax avoidance scenarios of real estate investment trusts (REITs) or other captive companies by adopting combined reporting, *see* Michael Mazerov, State Corporate Tax Shelters and the Need for 'Combined Reporting', 46 State Tax Notes 621(2007).
375. Joe Huddleston & Shirley Sicilian, History and Considerations for Combined Reporting: Will States Adopt a Model Combined Reporting Statute?, *The State and Local Tax Lawyer. Symposium Edition* (American Bar Association 2008); for some counter arguments against the combined reporting, *see* Ann Holley & Mariann Evans, The Pros and Cons of Combined Reporting: A Compendium of Arguments for and Against Combined Reporting, *The State and Local Tax Lawyer. Symposium Edition* (American Bar Association 2008). Opponents argue that adopting combined reporting can still introduce complexities and extra administrative burdens regarding audits and cannot always reduce tax planning.
376. The separate entity reporting should not be confused with the 'separate (geographic) accounting' indicated above.

the unitary business income is earned geographically from another state.[377] As Pomp[378] correctly mentions, the combined reporting will be the 'logical extension' of FA. I fully agree. The current CCCTB Directive Proposal also follows the same rationale to adopt the element of consolidation. However, the unitary business principle is still a separate concept that describes the economic relationship between group members but does not refer to any filing method in practice.

In my view, this unitary business concept is consistent with the normative framework established in Chapter 2 because the unitary feature describes the deep integration of MNE taxpayers' economic activities; the unitary business feature also implies that MNE taxpayers function as a group, and they enjoy mixed public benefits from multiple jurisdictions. In other words, the integration of the business structure also leads to integration and intertwined enjoyment of corresponding public benefits. Therefore, even though the current CCCTB Directive Proposal does not copy the unitary business concept to decide the scope of the consolidated tax base, the unitary business concept is still the logical option for FA.

The US Supreme Court in the *Mobil* case formulated the criterion of a unitary business:[379] a unitary business is characterized by 'functional integration', 'centralization of management', and 'economies of scale' that business activities operate as a whole or have substantial mutual interdependence.

Major shareholding is a strong indicator of a unitary business but neither the only indicator nor the most decisive one. Unitary business still emphasizes the interactions and economic activities between the affiliates. For example, in a case regarding income earned intangibles (dividends, interests, capital gains) paid by out-of-state subsidiary, the Supreme Court used a 'factor representation' concept to decide if an income earned can be included as business income by assessing the relationship between payor and payee; if there are no indicators of a unitary relationship, i.e., 'functional integration', 'centralization of management', and 'economies of scale', such income earned from intangibles should not be included in the apportionable tax base.[380] In other words, the 'factor representation' means that there should be factors in the unitary business that can represent the generation of the intangible income.[381]

377. It should be noted that, like different formulas adopted by states, 'combined reporting' also refers to different designs in different states, though being roughly similar. For a comprehensive survey, *see* Charlotte Noel & Carolyn Joy Lee, Would States Adopt a Uniform Model Combined Reporting Statute in a New Wave of Combined Reporting?, *The State and Local Tax Lawyer. Symposium Edition* (American Bar Association 2008). According to Noel and Lee's work, it seems unlikely that states would adopt uniform combined reporting due to political reasons.
378. Pomp, *supra* n. 345, at 10-85.
379. Hellerstein, Hellerstein & Swain, *supra* n. 349, at 8.07[3][a] General Principles; extracted from *Mobil Oil Corp. v. Commissioner of Taxes*, 445 US 425, 100 S. Ct. 1223 (1980).
380. Hellerstein, *supra* n. 100. Walter Hellerstein, State Income Taxation of Multijurisdictional Corporations, Part II: Reflections on ASARCO and Woolworth, 81Michigan Law Review 157 (1982); Marissa R Arrache, Factor Representation in the Apportionment of Income from Intangibles, 36 Santa Clara Law Review 485 (1995).
381. The factor representation requirement is discussed at the level of tax base. 'Factor presentation might be misunderstood with the question of whether 'a formula is fair', but it is not the same question.

The concept of unitary business is also codified in section 1(b) of the MTC Regulation IV:

> A unitary business is a single economic enterprise that is made up either of separate parts of a single business entity or of a commonly controlled group of business entities that are sufficiently interdependent, integrated and interrelated through their activities so as to provide a synergy and mutual benefit that produces a sharing or exchange of value among them and a significant flow of value to the separate parts.

Sections 1(b), (2), (3), and (4) of the MTC Regulation IV further provide several tests which embody the factors in *Mobil* and also indicate that 'common controlled companies',[382] i.e., sister companies, can also form a unitary business.

MTC Regulation IV also codifies the case law[383] of the unitary business income (now the term 'business income' is amended as 'apportionable income') and mentions that there are two tests to decide the unitary business income: 'the transactional test' and 'the functional test',[384] from the different perspectives of involving a 'typical transaction' with their trade partners or just involving a 'function'.[385] According to MTC Regulation IV, the transactional test requires that 'Apportionable income includes income arising from transactions and activity in the regular course of the taxpayer's trade or business'. In contrast, the functional test requires that 'Apportionable income also includes income from tangible and intangible property, if the acquisition, management, employment, development, or disposition of the property is or was related to the operation of[386] the taxpayer's trade or business. "Property" includes any direct or indirect interest in, control over, or use of real property, tangible personal property and intangible property by the taxpayer'.

The functional test is easier to fulfil than the transactional test, and more and more states are starting to adopt a functional test in order to extend the scope of the unitary business and their taxing rights. As long as one test is fulfilled, the unitary business relationship is established.

382. As to the advantages of the common control test, *see* Michael Aikins, Common Control and the Delineation of the Taxable Entity, 121 Yale Law Journal 624 (2011). Aikins argues that the common control test is easier to apply and less manipulative than the unitary business concept.
383. For information on the interpretation and application of the functional test and the transactional test in state courts, *see* Hellerstein, Hellerstein & Swain, *supra* n. 349, at 9.05; Hellerstein, *supra* n. 100.
384. *See* Model General Allocation & Apportionment Regulations with Amendments Submitted for Adoption by the Commission February 24, 2017 (i.e., MTC Regulations IV), Reg. IV.1.(a)(4) and Reg. IV.1.(a)(5).
385. MTC Regulation IV also uses the transactional test and the functional test to decide if a receipt should be included in the sales factor, but this application is not theoretically convincing. I explain this in Chapter 4 of this book. *See* the Prefatory Notes of the Model General Allocation & Apportionment Regulations with Amendments Submitted for Adoption by the Commission February 24, 2017, 5.
386. In the former version of MTC Regulations IV, the functional test uses the term 'constitute integral parts of the taxpayer's regular trade or business operations', not 'related to'. So in the case law, when we read 'integral parts' in the court's analysis, it refers to the functional test. The MTC's amendment takes Professor Michael J. McIntyre's suggestion into account, *see* the presentation 'Introduction to Business Income' in 2009, archived at the MTC website.

As Sicilian and Huddleston summarize,[387] these indicators developed from cases include: 'same general line of business, vertical integration, strong central management, functional integration (transfer of asset or value; pooling of asset of value)'.[388]

Here another question arises: should CCCTB still adopt the unitary business principle in the group definition and use the unitary business principle to exclude some items from the tax base? In my view, the answer should be conditionally in the affirmative but not a complete transplantation.

Whether a specific activity constitutes 'unitary business' is one of the most controversial issues in US state taxation cases.[389] Some scholars, such as Hellerstein, are a bit sceptical about following the US experience of 'unitary business' to conduct a tax reform because it is easier to adopt a more formalistic approach when designing a new FA system.[390] The European Commission has adopted this formalistic approach because the current 2016 Common Corporate Tax Base (CCTB) Directive Proposal already adopted a quite formal requirement for the group membership by 75% shareholding or 50% voting rights,[391] and this already reduces the number of many possible disputes. I think the European Commission has chosen a practical solution in the 2016 CCTB Directive Proposal but could have made use of the unitary business concept for the CCCTB selectively.

In my view, although it is not necessary to copy the whole saga of the unitary business principle, it is still a very useful interpretation tool for the CJEU to address future disputes concerning the CCCTB, especially on borderline cases where there are no major shareholdings or voting rights, but there is effective control between the group members.

The unitary business principle has a strong and convincing theoretical foundation and describes the economic reality that the MNE groups' economic activities of each of the group members are deeply integrated. Such deep integration, or 'unitary business', also implies that all corresponding public benefits that an MNE group enjoy

---

387. Shirley Sicilian & JB Huddleston, The US States' Experience with Formulary Apportionment, in Krever & Vaillancourt (eds), *supra* n. 46. *See* their summary in Table 2.1 about indicators of a unitary business.
388. *Ibid.*
389. Weiner, *supra* n. 113.
390. Hellerstein, *supra* n. 100.
391. Article 3 of the 2016 Common Corporate Tax Base Directive Proposal.

    Article 3 Parent company and qualifying subsidiaries
    1. A qualifying subsidiary means every immediate and lower-tier subsidiary in which the parent company holds the following rights:
        (a) it has a right to exercise more than 50% of the voting rights; and
        (b) it has an ownership right amounting to more than 75% of the subsidiary's capital or owns more than 75% of the rights giving entitlement to profit.
    2. For the purpose of calculating the thresholds referred to in paragraph 1 in relation to lower-tier subsidiaries, the following rules shall be applied:
        (a) once the voting-right threshold is reached in respect of a subsidiary, the parent company shall be considered to hold 100% of these rights;
        (b) entitlement to profit and ownership of capital shall be calculated by multiplying the interests held, directly and indirectly, in subsidiaries at each tier. Ownership rights amounting to 75% or less held directly or indirectly by the parent company, including rights in companies resident in a third country, shall also be taken into account in the calculation.

are also integrated. The unitary business principle describes a fluid and organic feature of the MNE group's economic activities as well as public benefits provided by different EU Member States. Therefore, it is consistent with the benefit-based MN framework in Chapter 2. In this regard, the unitary business principle can assist in interpretating, understanding, and assessing the relationship between group members in practice.

3.2.3.4 Constitutional Requirements in the US Concern the Benefit Principle and Market Neutrality

3.2.3.4.1 The Commerce Clause Is Consistent with the Benefit Principle

It should also be noted that any state formula of state taxation legislation in the US should be subject to the requirements of the US Constitution: the Commerce Clause, especially the Dormant Commerce Clause[392] and the Interstate Commerce Clause.[393] For European readers, the Commerce Clause is comparable to the concept of the internal market mandate under EU law.[394] The ultimate aim of the Dormant Commerce Clause in the US Constitution is to ensure cross-border and domestic commerce have the same opportunities to flourish.[395] The Commerce Clause is also understood as

392. Jerome R Hellerstein, Foreword: State Taxation under the Commerce Clause: An Historical Perspective, 29 Vanderbilt Law Review 335 (1976); for criticism of the inconsistent case law of the Dormant Commerce Clause developed by the Supreme Court, *see* Ryan Lirette & Alan D Viard, Putting the Commerce Back in the Dormant Commerce Clause: State Taxes, State Subsidies, and Commerce Neutrality, 24 Journal of Law and Policy 467 (2016). They argue that pursuing equal treatment between 'in-state' and 'out-of-state' commerce is a misunderstanding, but equal treatment should be made between 'intra-state' and 'interstate'.

    For an analysis of the case law on the development of the dormant commerce clause, *see* Craig B Fields & Michael W McLoughlin, An Analysis of the Historical Development of the Dormant Commerce Clause in State Tax Cases, *The State and Local Tax Lawyer. Symposium Edition* (American Bar Association 2007).

393. Hellerstein, Hellerstein & Swain, *supra* n. 349, at 4.01 and 4.03. Hellerstein has following remarks: 'The interstate commerce clause of the Constitution does not give immunity to movable property from local taxation which is not discriminative, unless it is in actual continuous transit in interstate commerce. When it is shipped by a common carrier from one State to another, in the course of such an uninterrupted journey it is clearly immune. In *Minnesota v. Blasius*, 290 US 1, 9, 54 S. Ct. 34 (1933), the Court likewise stated: Thus, the States cannot tax interstate commerce, either by laying the tax upon the business which constitutes such commerce or the privilege of engaging in it, or upon the receipts, as such, derived from it. Similarly, the States may not tax property in transit in interstate commerce.'

    There are other types of commerce clause in the constitution, including the foreign commerce clause and the Indian commerce clause, and these are not within the scope of this book. *See* Hellerstein, Hellerstein & Swain, *supra* n. 349, at 4. 01.

394. Scholars have seen the comparable function of the internal market mandate in EU law and the commerce clause in the US. *See*, for example, Georg Haibach, The Interpretation of Article 30 of the EC Treaty and the 'Dormant' Commerce Clause by the European Court of Justice and the US Supreme Court, 48 International & Comparative Law Quarterly 155 (1999); Although the internal market is the European counterpart of the commerce clause, there are still differences, *see* Klaudia Galka, Borderless Market Legislation Practice in EU and USA: Competence of Central Authorities in the Federal Model, 4 MaRBLe Research Papers (2013).

395. *See* the commentary, Knoll & Mason, *supra* n. 249. The dormant commerce clause does not address the double taxation issue but has the mandate to ensure that cross-border activities are not discriminated against by protectionist state legislation.

prohibiting multiple taxation that can hinder commerce among states.[396] This is the same goal pursued by the EU internal market. The US Supreme Court and CJEU have used them as a similar approach to striking down unconstitutional state legislation.[397]

There is another constitutional requirement, the 'Due Process Clause', which can be roughly understood by European readers as a prohibition on extraterritorial taxation.[398] The difference[399] between the Commerce Clause and the Due Process Clause is not the topic of this book, but a state tax can be declared unconstitutional due to it infringing a constitutional clause.[400] Although the Supreme Court often discusses these two clauses together, the Due Process Clause deals more with the taxable nexus threshold, and the Commerce Clause is used more to address whether apportionment is 'fair'. In many cases, the analysis is mixed.

The key ruling from the Supreme Court about state taxation being consistent with the Commerce Clause is *Complete Auto Transit*[401] where the Court established a four-prong test, including:

(1) The tax must be applied to an activity that has a substantial nexus with the state.
(2) The tax must be fairly apportioned to activities carried on by the taxpayer in the state.
(3) The tax must not discriminate against interstate commerce.
(4) The tax must be fairly related to services provided by the state.[402]

The first prong and the second prong refer to a substantial nexus and fair apportionment, which I discuss in the following sections.

The third prong of this test is the Commerce Clause,[403] which focuses on the 'cross-border' nature of the activity, and it clearly prohibits discrimination against cross-border activity, i.e., 'interstate commerce'. The non-discrimination requirement of the third prong is the same as the CJEU's case law about free movement. Also, since the third prong emphasizes 'cross-border' activities, it is closely related to levying tax on some industries that are inherently mobile and function as 'instrumentalities of

396. Mayer, *supra* n. 48, at 3.2.1.3.
397. The US Supreme Court, however, seems more lenient to states than the CJEU when invoking the Commerce Clause; *see* Reuven S Avi-Yonah, Federalism and the Commerce Clause: A Comparative Perspective, *The State and Local Tax Lawyer. Symposium Edition* (American Bar Association 2007).
398. Mayer, *supra* n. 48, at 3.2.1.3. Constitutional limitations on state taxation and apportionment.
399. *Ibid.*, footnote 401.
400. For the relationship between the Commerce Clause and the Dormant Commerce Clause, *see* Hayes R Holderness, Taking Tax Due Process Seriously: The Give and Take of State Taxation, 20 Florida Tax Review 371(2016). Holderness also criticized the physical presence nexus as a hurdle to effectively using the Dormant Commerce Clause. There is indeed a trend that the Dormant Commerce Clause has been declining since the 1970s. *See* Daniel Francis, The Decline of the Dormant Commerce Clause, 94 Denver Law Review 255 (2016).
401. Complete Auto Transit, 430 US 274, 277–279, 287, 97 S. Ct. 1076 (1977).
402. For comments about *Complete Auto Transit*, *see* Hellerstein, Hellerstein & Swain, *Supra* n. 349, at 4.12.
403. Hellerstein, Hellerstein & Swain, *supra* n. 349, at 4.13 and 4.14. For the implications for special industry formulas, *see* Chapter 7.1.2 of this book.

interstate commerce',[404] including land transportation, maritime transportation, aviation transportation, telecommunication and broadcasting. These types of industries can facilitate cross-border/interstate commerce, and thus they should not be discriminated against by state taxation.

Last but not least, it is especially clear that the fourth prong actually embodies the benefit principle: the fourth prong of this test exactly corresponds to the benefit principle[405] because it emphasized that levying tax should be fairly related to states' 'services'. In this regard, the Court ruled in *Commonwealth Edison* that[406] the fourth prong does not compare 'the amount of the tax or the value of the benefits allegedly bestowed as measured by the costs the State incurs on account of the taxpayer's activities', but it examines 'whether the measure of tax is reasonably related to the extent of the contact, since it is the activities or presence of the taxpayer in the State that may properly be made to bear a "just" share of State tax burden'.[407]

In my view, the Court's ruling on 'fairly related to services provided by the state' test, also correspond to the 'acceptable ambiguity' discussed in Chapter 2 above: to assume tax as a benefit does not require an exact causal link between the tax paid and the exact value of public services enjoyed; instead, the benefit principle sees taxation as the conceptual measurement of the public benefits, which sometimes cannot be easily measured and have positive externalities.

3.2.3.4.2 Fair Apportionment Is Consistent with MN

When apportionability is established, the next question is: what does it mean by 'fair apportionment'? This question was answered by the US Supreme Court in *Container* by introducing the 'internal consistency test' and 'external consistency test'.[408] When we read closely, it is especially clear that the internal consistency test perfectly coincides with benefit-based MN established in Chapter 2. Here I explain why.

The US Supreme Court recognized the difficulty of dividing the multistate tax base in the *Container* case and describes it as 'slicing a shadow'.[409] In this case, the Court established two tests to examine whether the state taxation's apportionment method was 'fair' under the Commerce Clause and the Due Process Clause:[410] the internal consistency test and the external consistency test. The internal consistency

404. Hellerstein, Hellerstein & Swain, *supra* n. 349, at 4.13[2].
405. For elaboration, *see* Walter Hellerstein, State Taxation in the Federal System: Perspectives on Louisiana's First Use Tax on Natural Gas, 55 Tulane Law Review 601 (1980).
406. Hellerstein, Hellerstein & Swain, *supra* n. 349, at 4.18: Severance and Other Taxes on Natural Resources Sold Largely Out-Of-State, at 4.18[2][c].
407. Commonwealth Edison, 453 US 609, 626, 101 S. Ct. 2946 (1981).
408. Container, *Container Corp. of America v. Franchise Tax Board*, 463 U.S. 159 (1983); for commentary on the case, *see* Cathy M Rudisill, Container Corporation of America v. Franchise Tax Board: California's Three-Factor Apportionment Formula for Taxing US Corporations' Foreign Subsidiaries Held Constitutional, 9 North Carolina Journal of International Law & Commercial Regulation 337 (1983).
409. The vivid description is from the Supreme Court's ruling in Container, *Container Corp. of America v. Franchise Tax Board*, 463 U.S. 159, 192 (1983).
410. Bradley W Joondeph, The Meaning of Fair Apportionment and the Prohibition on Extraterritorial State Taxation, 71 Fordham Law Review 149 (2002).

test[411] first hypotheses that the state tax formula at issue was adopted by all 50 states identically and asked: would interstate commerce (i.e., commerce among states) be taxed more heavily than in-state commerce in this case? If the answer is affirmative, the formula fails the internal consistency test and is unconstitutional. The external consistency test[412] examines 'whether the State has taxed only that portion of the revenues from the interstate activity which reasonably reflects the in-state component of the activity being taxed'. As long as the state taxation formula passes the two tests, it is fair and legitimate. The internal consistency test supplements the four-prong analysis of the *Complete Auto Transit* case discussed above.[413]

For European readers, we can roughly understand the internal consistency test as a hybrid combination of 'non-discrimination' test and restriction/hindrance to the market access test used by the CJEU[414] because this internal consistency test hypothesizes that all states are equal (to adopt the same taxation formula) and then looks into the effect of implementing a specific tax.[415]

More importantly, the internal consistency test reaffirms the tax neutrality framework in Chapter 2. The first step of the hypothesis, that 'every state adopts the same formula', implies that the formula is accepted by all 50 states, and CEN and CIN are achieved simultaneously. The internal consistency test's second step has achieved cross-border neutrality because it makes sure that cross-border commerce is not disadvantaged due to a heavier tax burden.

---

411. Hellerstein, Hellerstein & Swain, *supra* n. 349, at 4.16[1]. Regarding the meaning and criticism of the internal consistency test, *see* Ruth Mason, Made in America for European Tax: The Internal Consistency Test, 49 Boston College Law Review 1277 (2008); Walter Hellerstein, Is 'Internal Consistency' Foolish?: Reflections on an Emerging Commerce Clause Restraint on State Taxation, 87 Michigan Law Review 138 (1988); Walter Hellerstein, Is Internal Consistency Dead: Reflections on an Evolving Commerce Clause Restraint on State Taxation, 61 Tax Law Review 1 (2007); Mackenzie Catherine Schott, Inconsistency with the Internal Consistency Test, 77 Lancaster Law Review 947 (2016); Alexander G Andrews, Lessons from Wynne: Why New York City's Internally Consistent Income Tax Nonetheless Violates the Dormant Commerce Clause, 50 Connecticut Law Review 1077 (2018).

412. For further discussion, *see* Hellerstein, Hellerstein & Swain, *supra* n. 349, at 4.16[2].

413. Schott, *supra* n. 411, footnote 50. Schott has created a table showing that the history of the court using Complete Auto test and the internal consistency test.

414. Regarding the CJEU, two types (two generations) of approach applied in the freedom of establishment, *see* Catherine Barnard, *The Substantive Law of the EU: The Four Freedoms* (4th ed. Oxford University Press 2013), at Chapter 10.

On the tax law cases, *see* Adam Zalasinski, Limits of the EC Concept of Direct Tax Restriction on Free Movement Rights, the Principles of Equality and Ability to Pay, and the Interstate Fiscal Equity, 37 Intertax 282 (2009).

Scholars observe these two approaches shift back and forth, Marcel Guido Herwig Schaper, *The Structure and Organization of EU Law in the Field of Direct Taxes* (IBFD 2013), at 3.6.2.2.

415. Some works argue that the CJEU's approach to direct taxation is similar to the internal consistency test, such as Mason, *supra* n. 411. For the different opinion, Werner Haslehner, 'Consistency' and Fundamental Freedoms: The Case of Direct Taxation, 50 Common Market Law Review 737 (2013). Haslehner argues that the CJEU does not analyse from 'inbound' and 'outbound' perspectives.

As to the external consistency test, it is quite similar to the territory principle[416] in the tax law.[417] It reiterates the Due Process Clause that state taxation should not unreasonably be imposed on exterritorial activities. The external consistency test is also consistent with the benefit-based MN framework: the essence of the external consistency requires that states should not have taxing rights to completely purely exterritorial activities that have neither unitary relationship nor nexus with the in-state business activities.

In other words, the accepted goal of the external consistency test is also consistent with the benefit-based MN framework: tax represents the public benefits provided by the government and thus tax can only be imposed on economic activities that are reasonably related to corresponding public benefits. Therefore, taxation does not hinder MN.

In my view, the formulation of an external consistency nexus links the taxing rights and the in-state activities, and this embodies the benefit principle. The formulation of an internal consistency nexus embodies the CIN, CEN, and cross-border neutrality by its two-step analysis (assuming every state adopts the same formula and examines the consequences on cross-border activities). In short, the fair apportionment in the US Constitution cases can also be explained by the benefit-based MN framework in Chapter 2.

To sum up, after analysing the constitutional requirements for the US's FA, it is clear that the unitary business concept explains the integration of an MNE's economic activities and a mixture of corresponding public benefits in different jurisdictions. The Commerce Clause and the Due Process Clause under the US Constitution are comparable to the internal market provision under EU law. Also, case law of the US Supreme Court is consistent with the tax neutrality framework in Chapter 2. Although in practice, there are still some examples that are not consistent with the tax neutrality framework of this book, I demonstrate in Chapters 4 to 6 that such deviation is mainly due to reasons of administrative convenience or history and not the Constitution.

3.3 SEEKING A BENEFIT-BASED MARKET-NEUTRAL NEXUS FOR FORMULARY APPORTIONMENT FOR THE EU

3.3.1 A Permanent Establishment as the Nexus Is Not Neutral

According to the current CCCTB Directive Proposal, the minimum threshold for constituting a CCTB group is a PE.[418] The definition of a PE is 'harmonized' by Article 5 of the CCTB Directive, which copies verbatim Article 5 of the OECD Model

416. For an explanation of the principle of territoriality, *see* Otto Marres, The Principle of Territoriality and Cross-Border Loss Compensation, 39 Intertax 112 (2011).
417. While we rely on the analogy to understand these tests, we should still bear in mind that these two tests are developed in a different context in the US. As to the procedural consequence of adjusting unfair apportionment, I further discuss this in Chapter 8.
418. Canada also adopted the PE as taxable nexus for its FA, *see* Weiner, *supra* n. 47. Weiner, *supra* n. 5.

Convention. Unfortunately, it is not a wise option to borrow the controversial concept of PE for the EU's FA regime.

Although the concept of PE can also be traced to the benefit principle in the international tax regime, the traditional concept of PE in the OECD Model Convention has been criticized for being inconsistent.[419] Since different items in Article 5 of the OECD Model Convention actually represent different levels of being fixed or being dependent, the concept of 'permanent establishment' in Article 5 is fragmented and outdated. Such PE concept in Article 5 of the OECD Model Convention cannot reflect e-commerce business activities in a today's digital economy,[420] which no longer needs a fixed place or continuity to access customers. The PE threshold no longer reflects the public benefits of the customers' market enjoyed by MNE taxpayers. So, the concept of PE, in particular, needs reforming for the e-commerce and digital economy.[421]

Avoiding PE status has been a prevalent worldwide problem in the international tax regime, recognized by BEPS Action 7. In other words, purely adopting a PE of the current standard as a nexus is no longer an appropriate criterion for the EU's FA system.[422] After the BEPS actions project started, the argument of lowering the traditional PE threshold has become more popular. In the digital economy, the PE threshold will inevitably need to be lowered. Scholars even argue that[423] 'a virtual PE' in the digitalized world is needed.[424]

Lowering the PE criteria demonstrates the attempts to pursue the benefit principle or 'economic allegiance' in the literature.[425] When we accept that customers' market actually also involve public benefits maintained and provided by the jurisdiction where sales take place, economic operators of a digital economy can still access the customers' market and enjoy such public benefit without maintaining a PE in the traditional sense (or even a lowered-threshold PE). However, when we do not accept that customers' market jurisdiction can also be a substantial source of income, the effort to lower the PE threshold by accepting commissionaire arrangements or auxiliary activities as a deemed PE might still be in vain[426] because it is possible to access and make use of the customers' market without any fixed contacts with the jurisdiction.

Unfortunately, lowering the PE criterion still cannot solve the fundamental problem that the PE concept is already outdated. Since a neutral corporate tax system should reflect the taxpayer's economic activities and corresponding public benefits, the

419. For the general criticism against a PE, *see* section 1.2.2 of this book and the accompanying footnote.
420. Y Brauner & P Pistone, Some Comments on the Attribution of Profits to the Digital Permanent Establishment, 72 Bulletin for International Taxation (2018).
421. Arthur J Cockfield, Reforming the Permanent Establishment Principle Through a Quantitative Economic Presence Test, 38 Canadian Business Law Journal 400 (2003). Cockfield also argues that a PE concept should be replaced by a quantitative economic presence test, which is similar to the factor presence nexus; *see* section 3.3.3 of this book.
422. Schön, *supra* n. 295, at 99; for the same opinion, *see* Joann Martens Weiner, *Company Tax Reform in the European Union: Guidance from the United States and Canada on Implementing Formulary Apportionment in the EU* (Springer Science & Business Media 2006), at 64.
423. Hongler & Pistone, *supra* n. 190.
424. De Wilde, *supra* n. 80.
425. For a similar opinion, *see* Hongler & Pistone, *supra* n. 190.
426. De Wilde, *supra* n. 80.

legitimate criterion of establishing a taxable nexus for cross-border income earned by multinational taxpayers should focus on the activities, not a formal PE threshold, that was developed in the early twentieth century when e-commerce did not even exist. Lowering the PE threshold, such as a virtual PE or proposals in BEPS Project Action 7, is still embracing the old structure, but ignoring the essence of the PE concept has been eroded and has changed over time. Just like Skaar's argument cited by Dale,[427] 'A [permanent establishment] is merely a piece of evidence of economic allegiance, not the reason for source state taxation, ... that requires all enterprises which obtain such benefits from a country to render a corresponding contribution to this society, whether or not they have a [permanent establishment]'. I fully agree.

Supporters of adopting PE for the EU's FA regime, like the CCCTB Directive, may have still two supporting arguments: first, PE is a familiar concept of international tax law, and therefore it is easier to use under the EU's FA regime. Second, an FA system, such as in Canada,[428] also adopts the PE as its taxable nexus. The example of Canada gives us a feeling that adopting a PE in the FA is completely fine, and whether or not adopting PE as the nexus is purely a political choice.

Arguments that adopting PE as the nexus are well-accepted both in the international tax regime and in Canada, are actually ill-funded. As to the status of PE in the international tax regime because the concept of PE has been criticized so much, it would be not wise to embrace such an old concept to advance tax reform at the EU level. Second, although Canada's FA system indeed uses 'PE' as the nexus, Canada's PE threshold is extremely low[429] and the concept of PE under Canadian law is not

427. Pinto, *supra* n. 191.
428. Weiner, *supra* n. 47.
429. For information about the FA system in Canada in general, *see also* Smart & Vaillancourt, *supra* n. 47. The threshold to qualify as a PE used for provincial and territorial corporation tax in Canada is actually really low. https://www.canada.ca/en/revenue-agency/services/tax/businesses/topics/corporations/provincial-territorial-corporation-tax.html.

See Regulation 400(2) of the Income Tax Regulations,

> 400(2) For the purposes of this Part, *permanent establishment* in respect of a corporation means a fixed place of business of the corporation, including an office, a branch, a mine, an oil well, a farm, a timberland, a factory, a workshop or a warehouse, and
>
> (a) where the corporation does not have any fixed place of business it means the principal place in which the corporation's business is conducted;
> (b) where a corporation carries on business through an employee or agent, established in a particular place, who has general authority to contract for his employer or principal or who has a stock of merchandise owned by his employer or principal from which he regularly fills orders which he receives, the corporation shall be deemed to have a permanent establishment in that place;
> (c) an insurance corporation is deemed to have a permanent establishment in each province and country in which the corporation is registered or licensed to do business;
> (d) where a corporation, otherwise having a permanent establishment in Canada, owns land in a province, such land shall be deemed to be a permanent establishment;
> (e) where a corporation uses substantial machinery or equipment in a particular place at any time in a taxation year it shall be deemed to have a permanent establishment in that place;
> (e.1) if, but for this paragraph, a corporation would not have a permanent establishment, the corporation is deemed to have a permanent establishment at the place designated in its incorporating documents or bylaws as its head office or registered office;

exactly the same concept as under the OECD Model Convention. Even when the activity is not fixed or continuous, a PE can be deemed as existing in Canada for its local and provincial taxation. Therefore, since the concept of PE in the international tax regime is now also under reform and Canada's FA regime actually adopts a very low threshold PE, the EU's FA regime should reconsider its dependence on the concept of PE as its nexus threshold.

To sum up, a PE threshold developed in international tax law is not appropriate for attributing MNE taxpayers' cross-border income. Even a lowered PE threshold is not appropriate because BEPS Project Action 7 just tries to solve the problem within the old framework. In my view, the current CCCTB Directive Proposal should have taken a more revolutionary approach to choosing a different criterion as nexus for FA. The fundamental spirit of BEPS is to 'better align rights to tax with economic activity', and the PE threshold is unfortunately too outdated and too rigid to align economic activity with tax law. For a new tax reform of adopting the EU-level FA regime, it is more desirable to seek another threshold as nexus to catch economic activities in a digitalized global world.

3.3.2 Keeping Permanent Establishment as the Nexus Does Not Avoid Complexities

Although the concept of PE is an old and widely accepted concept from the international tax regime, using it in the current CCCTB Directive Proposal does not reduce any complexities. Besides, the Commission clearly indicated[430] that the PE definition in the current CCCTB Directive Proposal is only applicable to PEs situated in the EU; as to a PE (of an EU parent company) situated outside the EU, it is the Member States' responsibility to renegotiate with third countries.[431] Therefore, even from a tax administration perspective, adopting a PE is no longer a good option.

(f) the fact that a corporation has business dealings through a commission agent, broker or other independent agent or maintains an office solely for the purchase of merchandise shall not of itself be held to mean that the corporation has a permanent establishment; and

(g) the fact that a corporation has a subsidiary controlled corporation in a place or a subsidiary controlled corporation engaged in trade or business in a place shall not of itself be held to mean that the corporation is operating a permanent establishment in that place.

NOTE: Application provisions are not included in the consolidated text; *see* relevant amending Acts and regulations. SOR/78-772, s. 1; SOR/81-267, s. 1; SOR/86-390, s. 1; SOR/94-140, s. 1; SOR/94-686, ss. 4(F), 57(F), 79(F); 2009, c. 2, s. 91; SOR/2010-93, s. 8(F); 2013, c. 33, s. 32.

430. The 2016 CCTB Directive, 'Detailed Explanation of the Specific Provisions of the Proposal' (2016), 9.

431. The preamble of the CCTB Directive Proposal, at 9. 'Definition of a permanent establishment: the concept of a permanent establishment in this Directive is defined closely to the post-BEPS recommended definition of permanent establishment in the OECD Model Tax Convention. Different from the proposal of 2011, the revised definition covers only permanent establishments situated within the Union and belonging to a taxpayer who is resident for tax purposes within the Union. The aim would be to ensure that all concerned taxpayers share a common understanding and to exclude the possibility of a mismatch due to divergent definitions. It was

In the current CCCTB Directive Proposal, a PE fulfils two functions: First, a PE of a company in one EU Member State is a group member, and thus the consolidated corporate tax base can be apportioned to the PE. This is a nexus for the purpose of FA. Second, a PE of a non-resident company from a third country (the EU-based PE), is also eligible according to the CCCTB Directive when the PE's parent company fulfils some conditions.[432] In the second context, a PE also functions as a minimum threshold that the CCCTB Directive may exercise the taxing power on a 'non-resident taxpayer'. An 'EU-based PE' of a third-country parent company would be eligible as a taxpayer, a group member, and even 'a principal taxpayer'[433] under the current CCCTB Directive Proposal. So, it can file its consolidated corporate tax return for its third-country parent company.

As indicated in the international tax regime context, I clearly reject the first function of PE, i.e., how to share the consolidated taxable base between Member States. In my view, neither can the fragmented PE threshold or the lowered PE threshold any longer faithfully reflect taxpayers' economic activities and corresponding public, nor is the PE threshold a suitable nexus for the EU's FA regime.

As to the second function of the concept of PE, an EU-based PE from a third-country parent company is also not a wise option. Adopting a PE as a group member causes an ironic dilemma:[434] First, recognizing a PE, even a single PE from a third-country parent as a CCCTB 'group member' might make tax planning of a double-dip of a tax loss possible (in an EU Member State and in the third-country parent) because that PE is subject to the current CCCTB Directive Proposal. And second, creating the PE concept under the current CCCTB Directive Proposal could cause a burdensome obligation for Member States to renegotiate all their double tax conventions with third countries. This is why Pereira further argues that PEs from third-country parents should be excluded from the scope of the CCCTB because such exclusion will not infringe the freedom of establishment under EU law (because freedom of establishment does not have an external effect on third countries), and such exclusion will not infringe the non-discrimination clause under Double Taxation Conventions (DTCs).[435] The Commission's approach to a PE in the 2016 CCCTB

not seen as essential to put forward a common definition of permanent establishments situated in a third country, or in the Union but belonging to a taxpayer who is resident for tax purposes in a third country. The third-country dimension is thus left to be dealt with in bilateral tax treaties and national law.'

432. Eric CCM Kemmeren & Daniël S Smit, *Taxation of EU-Non-Resident Companies under the CCCTB System: Analysis and Suggestions for Improvement, Corporate Income Taxation in Europe* (Edward Elgar 2013).

433. There might be a loophole under the CCCTB for a PE of a third-country parent company because a non-resident company's single PE in an EU Member State might not be qualified as a taxpayer or a principal taxpayer if there is no other subsidiary or PE doing business within the EU according to the text of the definition of 'taxpayer' and 'principal taxpayer' under the CCTB and the CCCTB Directive. *See* arguments by Kemmeren & Smit, *ibid*.

Pereira also argues that, in combination of the definition of 'taxpayer' and 'non-resident taxpayer', we still can conclude that a single EU-PE should be eligible as a taxpayer, a group member and a principal taxpayer under the CCCTB regime if a systematic interpretation method is used. *See* Pereira, *supra* n. 81, at 180.

434. Pereira, *supra* n. 81, at 192.

435. *Ibid*.

Directive Proposal is consistent with Pereira's suggestion. In the 2016 CCCTB Proposal, the Commission clearly mentions that the definition of PE in the Directive Proposal as the nexus does not apply to EU-based PEs that belong to third-country parent companies.[436] But in my view such exclusion is still not enough to eliminate complexities.

Due to the lack of EU competence, the Commission refuses to provide a harmonized definition of PE for an EU-based PE of third-country parent companies in the 2016 CCTB Directive Proposal. DTCs signed between EU Member States and third countries are not within the EU's competence.[437] Unlike the trade-related treaties signed with third countries, which fall within the Common Commercial Policy competence,[438] the EU does not have the comprehensive competence to sign a DTC together with EU Member States, though after adopting the EU's Anti-Tax Avoidance Directives (ATADs) 1 and 2, the EU seems to have acquired some external competence of regulating 'branch mismatch'.[439] The EU does not have the external competence to regulate a harmonized and uniform PE of all third countries, even if the current CCCTB Directive Proposal could be adopted.

Therefore, to keep the outdated PE in the current CCCTB Directive Proposal simply causes more complexities. The result is that a Member State has two sets of definitions for PE: one is the PE under the current CCCTB Directive Proposal, being applicable to EU Member States with each other; the other is the PE in their own DTCs with other third countries. The immediate problem is potential conflict of qualifications. Another obvious problem of still allowing two sets of the concept of PE for the current CCCTB Directive Proposal is treaty shopping. When an EU Member State has a higher threshold for PE, it is possible that a third-country parent's non-PE entity/non-PE activities within that Member State might have constituted a PE in another EU Member State. This creates an opportunity for treaty shopping for a third-country MNE taxpayer, to pick and choose an EU Member State's DTC which has the highest threshold for PE, as its 'gate' to enter the EU internal market to make strategic use of the current CCCTB Directive Proposal.

To sum up, since the EU's FA regime is a tax reform which aims to revolutionarily create a theoretically sound and practicable, feasible new system, it should realistically

436. The explanation of the 2016 CCTB Directive Proposal:

> Different from the proposal of 2011, the revised definition covers only permanent establishments situated within the Union and belonging to a taxpayer who is resident for tax purposes within the Union. The aim would be to ensure that all concerned taxpayers share a common understanding and to exclude the possibility of a mismatch due to divergent definitions. It was not seen as essential to put forward a common definition of permanent establishments situated in a third country, or in the Union but belonging to a taxpayer who is resident for tax purposes in a third country.

437. Pasquale Pistone, The Impact of European Law on the Relations with Third Countries in the Field of Direct Taxation, 34 Intertax 234 (2006), 243.

438. *Ibid.*

439. Cécile Brokelind, Coordination of Negotiation of Member States' Double Tax Treaties with Third States in a Post-BEPS and Post-ATAD Era: The Case of Hybrid Mismatches, in Adolfo J. Martín Jiménez (ed.), *The External Tax Strategy of the EU in a Post-BEPS Environment* (IBFD 2019).

give up the problematic PE concept as its nexus threshold and seek an alternative. No matter how much effort to revise the PE concept and lower the PE threshold (such as a virtual PE), it is still too difficult to cultivate the PE concept of the international tax regime into a new workable solution. When keeping the PE concept in the EU's FA regime, the problems arising from the PE concept will cause more inconsistencies.

3.3.3 The PE Nexus Artificially Distinguishes Freedom of Establishment and Free Movement of Services

Furthermore, adopting a PE as the nexus for the purpose of FA under the EU's FA regime will distinguish the freedom of establishment and the free movement of services in an artificial way. Corporations, which exercise free movement of services, might face a different tax burden in an EU Member State, compared to corporations which exercise their freedom of establishment because the former might not necessarily constitute a PE under applicable tax law. Such distinction does not have a real meaning in the sense of economic reality but does offer an invitation to circumvent the PE threshold or make use of an artificial threshold to create a nexus in order to shift profits.[440]

Under EU law, freedom of establishment and free movement of services are under the same level of protection and are subject to the same derogations. Although freedom of establishment is applicable to 'continuous' activities whereas free movement of services is applicable to non-'continuous' activities, from a theoretical perspective, these two freedoms actually refer to the same level of EU internal market access. When the EU's FA regime uses the PE as the minimum threshold for FA, the Member State where there is a PE will have taxing powers but the Member State where there is no PE will not. Taxpayers who exercise their freedom of establishment will be subject to the tax jurisdiction but taxpayers who exercise free movement of services will not. Such distinction is not legitimate.

One might want to invoke the benefit principle to justify the concept of PE and argue that taxpayers' PE/continuous activities will enjoy more public services than the service provider taxpayers without a PE. Such benefit principle-based argument is not precise. From the perspective of access to a market of consumers, a service provider can be both on a continuous basis and on a non-continuous basis and enjoy the same access to customers. Both are genuine enough to be protected under EU law. Member States will have to maintain a market of customers at the same level, regardless of whether the service provider from another Member State is continuous or not. Member States make the market of customers available, and such availability (i.e., benefits) is not less for cross-border service providers or more for a PE under tax law.

The distinction between freedom of establishment and free movement of services is merely dogmatic rather than realistic in internal market law. Another significant example is the 'Services Directive',[441] which aims to liberalize and promote providing

440. De Wilde, *supra* n. 76, at 6.3.3.2.4.
441. Directive 2006/123/EC; contrary to its name, the Services Directive treats the free movement of services and freedom of establishment equally. *See* Timm Rentrop, The Services Directive: What Is Actually New?, 2007 EIPAScope 1 (2007).

services freely within the EU internal market, has clearly included both freedom of establishment and freedom of service.[442] Taking into account the development of EU internal market law, it is illogical to insist on the distinction between freedom of establishment and freedom of services by adopting the PE status in the EU's FA regime.

3.3.4 Inspiration from the Factor Presence Nexus Discussions from the US

Since the PE threshold is not suitable for the EU's FA regime, an alternative is needed. In order to seek alternatives to replace the concept of PE, US state taxation experiences regarding physical presence nexus/the economic nexus and factor presence nexus are discussed. In the end, I conclude that factor presence nexus is the most suitable alternative, and I also explain how other examples of nexus can provide some insights for designing the factor presence nexus.

3.3.4.1 The Physical Presence Nexus Has a Long History in US State Taxation

In US state taxation, the nexus issue has also been litigated in the context of constitutional disputes.[443] The taxing power of a specific state can only be based on the acceptable nexus, and the state taxation nexus should be consistent with the constitutional requirement in the Commerce Clause[444] and the Due Process Clause in the US Constitution. Just like the apportionability issue discussed in the previous section, when assessing the state taxation nexus under Constitutional requirements, the Commerce Clause and the Due Process Clause address different issues.[445]

As to the Due Process Clause, it concerns 'the fundamental fairness of governmental activity,' so the Due Process Clause nexus requires that an individual's connections with a State are 'substantial enough to legitimate the State's exercise of

In addition, the CJEU's case law shows a trend of convergence of market freedoms, *see* Alina Tryfonidou, Further Steps on the Road to Convergence among the Market Freedoms, 35 European Law Review 36 (2010).

In specific cases, the Court of Justice did not examine separately the free movement of services as an unavoidable consequence of any restriction on freedom of establishment: 'If, as submitted by the applicants in the main proceedings and Ireland, that legislation has restrictive effects on the free movement of services and the free movement of capital, such effects are an unavoidable consequence of any restriction on freedom of establishment and do not justify, in any event, an independent examination of that legislation in the light of Articles 49 EC and 56 EC (*see*, to that effect, Case C-36/02 Omega [2004] ECR I-9609, paragraph 27).'

442. Preamble (1) of the Services Directive.
443. For a short overview of the nexus of state taxation, *see* Walter Hellerstein, A Primer on State Tax Nexus: Law, Power, and Policy, Testimony of Walter Hellerstein Francis Shackelford Professor of Taxation University of Georgia Law School Before the Subcommittee on Commercial and Administrative Law of the Committee on the Judiciary United States House of Representatives Hearing on State Taxation: The Role of Congress in Defining Nexus (2010), https://cost.org/globalassets/cost/state-tax-resources-pdf-pages/other-state-tax-studies-articles-reports/hellerstein-testimony-on-nexus.pdf.
444. Hellerstein, Hellerstein & Swain, *supra* n. 349, at 4.24-26.
445. *Ibid.*, 4.24-26 and 6.03.

power over him'.[446] According to the Supreme Court in *Quill*,[447] the Due Process Clause requires that the taxpayer 'purposefully avail itself of the benefits of an economic market' in the state, 'irrespective of ... [its] physical presence in the taxing State'. Although the physical presence nexus is no longer the main criterion of nexus after 2018 (*see* the *Wayfair* case below), how the Supreme Court interprets the Due Process Clause is still meaningful. 'The Due Process Clause Nexus' is another example that US Constitutional requirements on state taxation embody the benefit principle because the 'taxpayer purposefully avail itself of the benefits of an economic market' is a typical example of recognizing the economic market as a type of public benefit.

As to the nexus under the Commerce Clause,[448] it requires that any state taxation should not disadvantage 'interstate commerce', which means commerce among states,[449] by imposing heavier tax burdens on interstate commerce because the Commerce Clause concerns 'national economic unity and the effects of state regulation on the national economy'. Therefore, the Commerce Clause nexus has long been also constructed as 'substantial nexus' which has a 'substantial' link with the jurisdiction and very often referred to as 'physical presence nexus',[450] until recently (*see* discussion at 3.3.4.2 and 3.3.4.3 below).

Moreover, in the US, there are also limitations to a state taxation nexus under federal legislation. According to Public Law 86-272,[451] the Congress prohibits 'states from imposing a tax on net income derived by a person from interstate commerce if the person's activities in the state do not exceed solicitation'.[452] In other words, mere 'solicitation' does not qualify as a sufficient nexus. Public Law 86-272 is a federal statutory limitation on state tax jurisdiction, which aims to prevent any state legislation from hindering interstate commerce by levying tax on solicitation activities because such tax would discourage foreign economic operators from trying to access the

446. *Ibid.*, 6.03[1].
447. Supreme Court 26 May 1992, 504 U.S. 298, *Quill Corp. v. North Dakota*. There has been criticism of the case law Quill and similar legislative proposals on the physical presence nexus, *see*, for example, Edward A Zelinsky, Rethinking Tax Nexus and Apportionment: Voice, Exit, and the Dormant Commerce Clause, 28 Virginia Tax Review 1 (2008).
448. For the development and history of the Commerce Clause, *see* Pomp, *supra* n. 345, Chapter 1. There are several commerce clauses in the Constitution, and in the state taxation context, we are discussing 'the dormant/negative commerce clause'. For a recent comment on the dormant commerce clause, *see* Brian Galle, Kill Quill, Keep the Dormant Commerce Clause: History's Lessons on Congressional Control of State Taxation, 70 Stanford Law Review Online 158 (2017). As Galle observes, the dormant commerce clause has been 'a kind of judge-made free-trade zone'.
449. Hellerstein, Hellerstein & Swain, *supra* n. 349, at 4.02.
450. *Ibid.*, 6.03[2]; for the definition of physical presence, *see* the note by Richard D Pomp, Revisiting Miller Brothers, Bellas Hess, and Quill, 65 American University Law Review 1115 (2015). Pomp argues that the physical presence nexus, which can be justified for individual taxation, is actually not appropriate for corporate taxation since a corporation is an entity based on 'law'.
451. Public Law 86-272, 15 U.S.C. §§ 381-84.
See Hellerstein, *supra* n. 443, footnote 9; Bradley W Joondeph, Exploring the Myth of Parity in State Taxation: State Court Decisions Interpreting Public Law 86-272, 13 Washington University Journal of Law & Policy 205 (2003).
452. Hellerstein, Hellerstein & Swain, *supra* n. 349, at 6.17-6.29.

in-state market. In my view, the rationale of Public Law 86-272 is similar to the Commerce Clause and can also be interpreted to support the physical presence nexus.

3.3.4.2 The Economic Nexus Is Gradually Being Accepted in the Digital Economy

Among the constitutional cases about nexus, the main discussions are developed around the 'physical presence nexus' and the 'economic nexus'.[453] The 'physical presence nexus' requires physical and substantial contact within the state to establish taxing powers[454] and the physical presence nexus test has been supported by the US Supreme Court (the 'Quill test'),[455] whereas the economic nexus only requires economic activities, even including doing business via 'intangibles' such as using a trademark for a fee within the state. In other words, the economic nexus is usually easier to fulfil than the physical presence nexus.[456]

As indicated above, the physical presence nexus has long been affirmed by the Supreme Court, but it is also under severe challenges. The physical presence nexus is outdated for e-commerce and the digital economy. Since 1957 (when the US's UDITPA finally was successfully passed), there have been a lot of changes regarding technology as well as MNE taxpayers' activities. Nowadays, sales of goods can be conducted without the traditional physical nexus; services can be provided via the Internet and telecommunications; employees can also be supervised and perform their work from a geographical location other than their office's location. The physical presence nexus is no longer the only indicator of public benefits used by taxpayers.

453. For discussion of the economic nexus, *see* Craig J Langstraat & Emily S Lemmon, Economic Nexus: Legislative Presumption or Legitimate Proposition, 14 Akron Tax J. 1 (1999); Christina Berger, Nexus and the Need for Clarification: The Rise of Economic and Attributional Nexus, J. S'. Tax'n 26 (2008), 29; Adam B Thimmesch, The Illusory Promise of Economic Nexus, Florida Tax Review 13 (2012), 157. The economic nexus does address the traditional weakness of the physical presence nexus, especially for e-commerce arising since the late 1990s, but these authors are also aware that the economic nexus is not precise and formulated in an ad hoc way by different states. This creates uncertainties.

454. Hellerstein, Hellerstein & Swain, *supra* n. 349, at 6.03.

455. The key leading case law in the US to confirm the physical presence nexus is U.S. Supreme Court, 26 May 1992, 504 U.S. 298, *Quill Corp. v. North Dakota*.

456. States might want to collect more tax, so they adopt the lower nexus standard. However, the economic effect of adopting the economic nexus does not necessarily make adopting states collect more CIT, *see* Ann Davis & Amy M Hageman, An Exploration of the Antecedents and Consequences of State Income Tax Nexus: Does Economic Nexus Really Benefit States?, 2012 AAA Annual Meeting-Tax Concurrent Sessions (2012). Ann Davis and Amy M Hageman analyse the economic effects on the states which adopt the economic nexus and the factor presence nexus. According to Davis and Hageman, 'states that adopt economic nexus standards have lower levels of corporate taxation revenue than those that follow a physical presence standard', even though the economic presence nexus is broader than the physical presence nexus and easier to fulfil. However, other scholars suggest the opposite: adopting a lower threshold nexus can increase corporate income collection. *See* Giles Sutton, Jamie C Yesnowitz & Chuck Jones, Breaking State and Local Developments: 2010 Nexus Developments, 29 Journal of State Taxation 37 (2010).

In 2018, the US Supreme Court in *Wayfair, Inc.*[457] overruled its opinion about the physical presence nexus test developed since the *Quill* in 1992. The *Wayfair* case is a typical difficulty of the digital economy for levying sales tax on out-of-state remote sellers who use the online webshops and have no physical presence in the market jurisdiction. The Supreme Court decided that a state where customers are situated may still levy tax, constitutionally, on a remote seller on sales, even though there is no physical presence within the state. Briefly speaking, in a digitalized economy, the rationale of the physical nexus is already outdated and has been manipulated for the advantage of MNE taxpayers.[458]

Some scholars also correctly observe that Public Law 86-272 would not provide protection to MNE taxpayers' cloud computing services income from reaching the nexus threshold after *Wayfair* because Public Law 86-272 does not apply to business models other than delivering tangible goods.[459] In any event, *Wayfair* has already changed current practice concerning the nexus in the US.[460]

After *Wayfair*, although the physical presence nexus can still be an option for states, many states have passed 'Wayfair legislation' to collect sales tax from out-of-state remote sellers. So, in practice, in addition to the physical presence nexus, states are allowed to adopt other types of economic nexus, since *Wayfair* affirms the constitutionality of economic nexus other than the physical presence nexus. In practice, two types of nexus exist in parallel.

457. U.S. Supreme Court 21 June 2018, No. 17-494, *South Dakota v. Wayfair, Inc.;* Alex Brill & others, Amicus Brief in Wayfair v. South Dakota, South Dakota (5 March 2018); Ruth Mason, Case Law Note: Implications of Wayfair, 46 Intertax 810 (2018). For the implications for international tax, *see* Reuven S Avi-Yonah, Designing a 21st Century Taxing Threshold: Some International Implications of South Dakota vs. Wayfair, U of Michigan Public Law Research Paper (2018). He vividly describes the new powers struggles in the twenty-first century regarding international tax, also elaborated in *Wayfair*: 'For the reasons eloquently set forth by Justice Kennedy in *Wayfair*, the large market jurisdictions cannot tolerate the ability of remote enterprises to exploit their market without paying a penny in tax because of a physical presence rule stemming from nineteenth century realities and imported into twentieth century model tax treaties because of a desire to protect businesses from taxation.'

458. Richard D. Pomp, Wayfair and the Myth of Substantial Nexus, J. St. Tax (2018). According to Pomp, the reasoning on the case Wayfair does not solve the problem completely and could still lead to future disputes. Further comments on the case Wayfair from the perspective of non-compliance by foreign remote vendors, *see* Richard D Pomp, Foreign Remote Vendors and the Possibility of Non-Compliance: Is the Only Thing We Have to Fear Is the Fear Itself?, 37 Journal of Taxation 39 (2019). Pomp argues that non-compliance issues by MNE taxpayers of the digital economy are exaggerated.

Richard D Pomp, Wayfair: Its Implications and Missed Opportunities, 58 Washington University Journal of Law & Policy 1 (2019).

459. Richard L Cram, No Shade for Cloud Computing Income Under P.L. 86-272, State Tax Notes (2018); the opposite opinion argues that Public Law 86-272 will still apply even in a cloud computing service, *see* Martin I Eisenstein & Nathaniel A Bessey, Public Law 86-272: Sunlight for a Cloud Service, State Tax Notes 769 (2019); Metisse Lutz & Jamie Yesnowitz, Wayfair: Practical Implications for the Business World, Tax Executive (2018).

460. For responses to *Wayfair* and the development of nexus of the remote and internet sales tax, *see* Joseph Bishop-Henchman, The History of Internet Sales Taxes from 1789 to the Present Day: *South Dakota v. Wayfair*, Cato Supreme Court Review (2018).

3.3.4.3 *The Factor Presence Nexus Is Market Neutral*

There is another hybrid type of nexus of physical nexus and economic nexus directly based on weighting factors in the formula, the 'factor presence nexus'. A typical example is from the MTC's recommendation on nexus in 2002.[461] The MTC proposed the factor presence nexus criterion for states to establish their taxable nexus: it provides that a nexus is established when a taxpayer's sales factor reaches USD 500,000, property factor or payroll factor reaches USD 50,000, or 25% of the taxpayer's total sales or property or payroll. As long as one-factor presence test is fulfilled, then the nexus is established. A factor presence nexus is a quantitative threshold.

The rationale of the factor presence test is simple: the presence of weighting factors above a threshold can establish the nexus because these weighting factors represent the taxpayer's economic activities within the state. The nexus rule and the apportionment rule should be closely related.[462] Under the normative framework of benefit-based MN, the factor presence nexus is market neutral because these weighting factors are the direct indicators of corresponding public benefits in the jurisdictions.

More and more states are adopting the economic nexus or the factor presence nexus to establish their taxing powers on out-of-state enterprises (mainly online remote sellers) that make use of their in-state market. There is no consensus yet on what the factor presence nexus should be among states. Despite the MTC's recommendation, there is no federal criterion for factor presence nexus yet, and states adopt different thresholds for their factor presence nexus.[463] Up to 2017, for example, there were already 13 states in the US that had adopted the factor presence nexus standard for their state corporate tax. Some of these states follow the MTC's recommendation and some adopt even lower thresholds than the MTC's factor presence nexus recommendation.[464] Although the MTC's factor presence nexus recommendation is not adopted widely by states, setting a quantitative threshold like the factor presence nexus indeed has the advantage of legal certainty.

In my view, 'factor presence nexus' is a logical and suitable criterion for FA because the factor presence reconnects tax and economic activities. As indicated above, the PE is no longer an appropriate nexus to align economic activity and tax law,

---

461. Factor Presence Nexus Standard for Business Activity Taxes, Approved by the MTC, 17 October 2002.
462. McLure, *supra* n. 307, at 5.
463. Thimmesch, *supra* n. 453.
464. *See* 2017 Survey of State Tax Departments, Bloomberg BNA. P. S-17 to S-22.
The factor presence nexus of Virginia is quite low. As long as one of the apportionment factors is positive, the nexus is presumed to be established. *See* the tax ruling on Date Issued 05-11-2016 from the Virginia tax authorities: 'Virginia Code § 58.1-400 imposes an income tax on the Virginia taxable income for each taxable year of every corporation organized under the laws of the Commonwealth and every foreign corporation having income from Virginia sources.' Generally, a corporation will have income from Virginia sources if there is sufficient business activity within Virginia to make any one or more of the applicable apportionment factors positive. 'The existence of positive Virginia apportionment factors clearly establishes income from Virginia sources.'

nor is the physical presence nexus is appropriate either. Instead, factor presence seems a more logical nexus for aligning economic activities with tax under FA.[465]

However, what threshold is appropriate for the factor nexus is still a hard question. It is in the end a political question of how much the factor presence nexus threshold should be. Also, the market situation in different states might need different consideration. As Thimmesch gives vivid examples for big states and small states: '$250,000 of sales into Wyoming is very different than $250,000 of sales into New York'.[466] Such criterion cannot be left to EU Member States but should be coordinated at the EU level. Therefore, I recommend that the Council should decide this nexus when the EU's FA regime is discussed.

In current EU law, there are already examples of 'quantitative threshold'. In the EU VAT context, De Wilde also suggests that[467] a quantitative turnover threshold,[468] like the VAT threshold for distance sales in EU VAT law, would be feasible. The VAT threshold for distance sales varies depending on each EU Member State, ranging between EUR 35,000 and EUR 100,000. Another example of quantitative threshold is the Significant Digital Presence (SDP) Directive Proposal.[469] In short, such policy option is familiar to the EU legislators and already exist. The EU's FA regime can follow these existing examples.

3.3.4.4 *Addressing the Weakness of the Factor Presence Nexus*

Although it is clear that there is a uniform criterion for factor presence nexus, the factor presence nexus still faces some tax planning opportunities to avoid establishing the nexus threshold. It is an inevitable weakness when adopting a blue-line quantitative factor presence nexus: When planning carefully below the threshold, it is still possible to avoid establishing the nexus. All quantitative threshold criteria will face the manipulation at margin; it is the Achilles' heel that can happen to any type of quantitative threshold.

As to addressing the weakness of 'avoiding' the factor nexus presence threshold, there should be a catch-all clause in the factor presence nexus threshold: when a taxpayer's factor presence is all only slightly under the threshold, there must be an adjustment to establish a taxable nexus in that situation. In this catch-all clause, the discussions of the economic nexus/substantial nexus can be supplementary to the blue-line factor presence nexus. When a taxpayer's factors do exist and there is sufficient link to the Member State, the catch-all clause should intervene to adjust and establish the nexus. Such adjustment should be cautiously applied.

---

465. For the same opinion, *see* Luzius U Cavelti, Christian Jaag & Tobias Rohner, Why Corporate Taxation Should Mean Source Taxation: A Response to the OECD's Actions Against Base Erosion and Profit Shifting, 9 World Tax Journal 352 (2017), at 3.3.1.2-3.3.1.3.
466. *See* Thimmesch, *supra* n. 453.
467. De Wilde, *supra* n. 76, at 6.4.4.2.2.
468. *Ibid.*
469. *See section* 3.5.1 of this book.

Procedurally, the current CCCTB Directive Proposal already confers powers on the European Commission to establish delegated acts;[470] and via such delegated acts, the European Commission may have discretion to adjust the threshold and announce the new threshold for every period. Such measures can provide legal certainty and therefore the EU's new tax reform package BEFIT should keep these procedures. However, there might be democratic concerns in the form of delegated acts because nexus is the core condition of CIT. It might be feasible to make a separate provision in the new BEFIT Directive Proposal.

The discretion of adjusting the factor presence nexus exists in California and Alabama, where tax authorities can adjust and update their factor presence nexus which is indexed for inflation.[471] Such discretion in California is regulated by legislation so that democratic legitimacy is fulfilled. Keeping a flexible margin when setting a quantitative threshold for the factor presence nexus is also feasible for the EU's FA regime.

3.4 SEEKING BENEFIT-BASED MARKET-NEUTRAL APPORTIONMENT RULES FROM BOTH THE INPUT SIDE AND OUTPUT SIDE

3.4.1 'Value Creation' Coincides with the Benefit-Based Market Neutrality Framework

Some early literature regarding FA in the US asserted that 'choosing weighting factors' of UDITPA in 1957 was not based on any specific economic theory.[472] The assertion of a 'no theory' for a formula should be reconsidered nowadays. It is true that existing formulas in the US are based on states' own policies, but these policies are subject to US Constitutional requirements that maintain and protect an internal market. And as indicated above, the Constitutional requirements in the US also embody the benefit principle.

In my view, the benefit-based MN principle also coincides with the new concept of 'value creation', as developed by the OECD's BEPS Project, although the concept of 'value creation' is used in the context of reforming old TP practices.[473] 'Value creation' is not a traditional concept from the drafting and development of the OECD Model Convention,[474] but it has become the guiding principle of the post-BEPS era. 'Aligning taxation with value creation' is the new paradigm to address the existing BEPS

470. Article 75 of the 2016 CCCTB Directive Proposal.
471. Section 23101 of the Revenue and Taxation Code (R&TC) in California; The amount of the threshold is indexed annually and is published on Franchise Tax Board's website.
472. Office for Official Publications of the European Communities (ed.), *supra* n. 3, cited in Hellerstein, Hellerstein & Swain, *supra* n. 349, at 9.20.
473. Johanna Hey is sceptical that this is further a vague and uncertain concept and a political consensus on the formula for the EU seems unrealistic. *See* Johanna Hey, Taxation Where Value Is Created and the OECD/G20 Base Erosion and Profit Shifting Initiative, 72 Bulletin for International Taxation (2018).
474. Becker & Englisch, *supra* n. 40. Schön is also quite critical about the benefit principle being over simplified, *see* Wolfgang Schön, *Value Creation, the Benefit Principle and Efficiency-Related*

problems. While the value-creation concept seeks 'value', it also seeks the precondition of creating value, and thus its formulation is actually the same as the benefit principle embedded in the tax neutrality framework.

In other words, under the benefit-based MN framework, taxing economic activities is justified because these activities represent public benefits that create the precondition for these economic activities; the reason to align taxation and value creation is to faithfully demonstrate the degree of public benefits being provided to create value for taxpayers.

3.4.1.1 Adopting a Formula Consisting of Multiple Factors from Both the Input and Output Sides Is Consistent with Benefit-Based Market Neutrality

According to benefit-based MN, taxpayers' economic activities are the key criterion for assigning taxing powers. Taxpayers' economic activities can be observed from two different perspectives: from the input side and the output side.[475]

Moreover, FA assumes that the profit-generating ability of every weighting factor is the same.[476] A multiple-factor formula thus also recognizes that both the 'supply side and demand side' of economic activities are contributing to 'value creation'. Selecting weighting factors from both the supply side and the demand side for a sharing formula is in line with the idea of 'aligning taxation with value creation'.[477] All the weighting factors represent taxpayers' economic activities and the corresponding public benefits. Since the source of cross-border income earned by MNE taxpayers refers to 'all'

Allocation of Taxing Rights (May 19, 2021). EATLP 2020 Congress Report (EATLP International Tax Series 19, available at SSRN: https://ssrn.com/abstract=3849322 or http://dx.doi.org/10.2139/ssrn.3849322.

475. This book does not discuss the possibility of selecting 'macro-based' factors in the formula, such as population or GDP or VAT of each country involved. It is because these macro-based factors represent less the corresponding public benefits for economic activities than the presence of economic activities themselves. The CCCTB's working paper has the same opinion: such approach 'presents the fundamental drawback of disconnecting the real economic activity performed by a company in a country with its tax liability in that country, which conflicts with the very idea of a "fair" distribution of the tax base', according to the expert's opinion in the European Commission's CCCTB working meetings. *See* CCCTB Working Document No. 52 para 8-10 and CCCTB Working Document No. 47 paras 8-9. For research on options for selecting macro-based factors in the formula, *see* Office for Official Publications of the European Communities (ed.), *supra* n. 3.

476. This is a well-accepted assumption for FA supporters; *see* McLure & Weiner, *supra* n. 221, at 258; Mintz & Weiner, *supra* n. 305, at 698.

For sceptics of FA, they do not accept this assumption. *See*, for example, Erik Röder, Proposal for an Enhanced CCTB as Alternative to a CCCTB with Formulary Apportionment, 4 World Tax Journal 125 (2012).

477. For a similar idea in the context of residual profits, *see* Li, Bao & Li, *supra* n. 197, at 1133: 'Allocation of residual profit on the basis of a single factor or on the basis of the market jurisdiction alone does not reflect either business realities or the value-creation principle.' In this book, I do not discuss the distinction between residual profits and routine profits.

jurisdictions involved jurisdictions,[478] a multiple-factor formula is consistent with the idea of 'value creation' and also market neutral.

3.4.1.2 Seeing Labour/Manufacturing as Lower Value Is Not Market Neutral

There are doubts about value creation being a normative framework for assessing corporate taxation, but these are misunderstandings. For example, Vella asserts that FA itself does not fulfil the criterion of 'value creation' because weighting factors are items which 'decrease' the profits generated.[479] Vella argues that labour costs 'reduce MNE taxpayers' profits'.[480] This is a traditional view about value creation that contributions from the labour side are lower than the market side.

The traditional view of the supply chain valuation model assumes that most value is mainly created in high-income jurisdictions.[481] It is usually low-income jurisdictions that have production activities and more working employees, whereas less value is regarded as created there; so, the value creation is usually illustrated as a 'smile curve'. This smile curve will always attribute value to the wealthiest countries, but this result is directly contrary to the benefit principle and not neutral; the smile curve view of value creation also negates the goal of the BEPS project.[482]

I have copied the smile curve from van Apeldoorn's article as follows:

Figure 4 The Smile Curve of Supply Chain Valuation

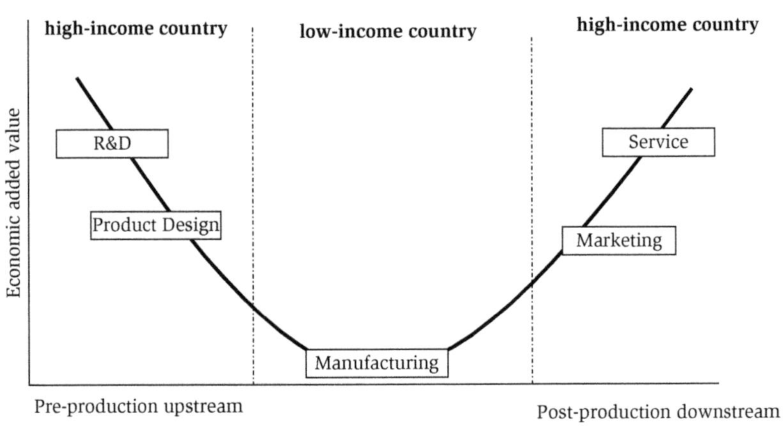

Source: Laurens van Apeldoorn.

478. Swain & Hellerstein, *supra* n. 337.
479. Vella, *supra* n. 310.
480. *Ibid.*, 271.
481. Laurens van Apeldoorn, Exploitation, International Taxation, and Global Justice, 77 Review of Social Economy 163 (2019), at 7; Gary Gereffi & Karina Fernandez-Stark, Global Value Chain Analysis: A Primer, Center on Globalization, Governance & Competitiveness (CGGC) (2011), Duke University, North Carolina, USA, at 14.
482. Allison Christians, Taxing According to Value Creation, 90 Tax Notes International (2018).

Without the labour factor in the sharing formula that recognizes the value created in the low-income country, the public goods in the jurisdiction where manufacturing activities take place would be completely ignored.[483] A formula without the labour factor is therefore not market neutral because it simply ignores the input side of the economic activities. In contrast, including a labour factor in the formula reflects value creation in these relatively low-income yet labour-intensive jurisdictions and thus corrects the old view of the smile curve supply chain. This is especially true when a formula evaluates the labour factor not only from the perspective of 'payroll/remuneration' but also headcounts the 'labour market distortion' problem could be mitigated.[484] In this regard, the labour factor under the current CCCTB Directive Proposal has provided a good example, as I demonstrate in Chapter 5.

3.4.1.3 'Sales by Destination' and 'Production by Functions' for Attribution Rules

In addition to choice of weighting factors, the attribution rules are also important. Roughly speaking, the sales factor follows the 'sales by destination' rationale, and it aims to reflect taxpayers' response to taxpayers' clients' market. The factors from the production side should reflect taxpayers' production-related activities, and the attribution rule should reflect how taxpayers make use of their human resources and assets. Some scholars would describe the production side as 'origin', in contrast to 'sales by destination', but the term 'origin' is not precise enough to describe the input side.

It is worth emphasizing that in the chain of value creation, the 'origin' and 'destination' are in fact closely linked and not always easy to distinguish.[485] This is especially obvious regarding services provided by an intermediary. An economic activity has double functions in the origin and in the destination. For example, a taxpayer (presumably a company) hires employees to conduct production activities, and these employees are included in the taxpayer's labour factor. But when the taxpayer hires these employees via a human resources agency as an intermediary (which is another company), these employees are hired from another 'labour market' where job agencies provide their services; in this labour market, the first taxpayer, being an employer who pays renumeration, is the customer/services recipient of this labour market. For the intermediary/a human resources agency, they should include the service fees (which may include the renumeration) received, in their sales factor.

483. For the same arguments, *see* Peter Dietsch, *Catching Capital: The Ethics of Tax Competition* (Oxford University Press 2015), at 75-76; Li, Bao & Li, *supra* n. 197.

484. Christians and Laurens argue that the labour market value is distorted due to labour exploration, and thus the norm of 'value creation' is inherently problematic. I agree in this regard, but I would argue that we should also see production activities by workers also as 'value creation' and give such value creation a proper status. Therefore the number of employees could also be justified as an evaluation parameter. *See also* Christians & Van Apeldoorn, *supra* n. 89.

485. As a side note, VAT scholars observe the same phenomenon that in the consumption timeline, it is possible that the origin and destination 'overlap', but they do not truly overlap, but that is a result of the different observation perspectives. *See* Rebecca Millar, Echoes of Source and Residence in VAT Jurisdictional Rules, in Lang & others (eds), *supra* n. 298, Diagram 5.

As long as we are clear about what we are observing, the destination and the origin are not mixed, even though they are closely linked.

The destination is a relative concept, as is the concept of origin. Therefore, when we design the attribution rule for every weighting factor, the underlying rationale and function of this factor should be taken into account. When a factor aims to represent taxpayers' supply or taxpayers' customers' demand, then the attribution rule should be consistent with the specific activity according to the activity's function in the specific market. A factor which represents the production side should reflect the production process: the origin means where production activities perform their function.

In the following sections, I further analyse what options we should choose for the sales factor, the assets factor, and the labour factor in order to comply with benefit-based MN. I seek the proper 'economic location'[486] that the attribution rules attribute sales/labour/assets to. The attribution rules are vital when the factor presence nexus is adopted. As analysed in the previous section at 3.3, since the attribution rules decide the 'presence' of each factor, they play an important role alongside the factor presence nexus.

3.4.2 The Output Side: The Sales Factor Represents the Public Benefits of Maintaining the Customers' Market

3.4.2.1 The Single Sales Factor Formula Is Not Inherently More Neutral

3.4.2.1.1 The Sales Factor Is Widely Used

The sales factor is a factor widely accepted by both FA supporters and SA/ALP tax scholars. As Schreiber observed,[487] a sales factor can be applied to 'sales-based transactional profit split' and 'sales-based group profit split'. The sales factor seems to be the common ground that FA and SA/ALP supporters both recognize. Therefore, for designing the EU's FA regime, selecting the sales factor in the formula is indeed a reasonable option.

The classical fundamental rationale of the sales factor is to represent MNE taxpayers' output side activities, or the response to 'clients' market',[488] but actual implementation of the sales factor is not always consistent with this fundamental rationale. The deviation is not necessarily due to a specific purpose but, in most cases,

486. Kemmeren uses the terminology 'origin'. In order not to be confused with the sales-by-destination principle, I use 'economic location'. Kemmeren, *supra* n. 183.

487. Schreiber, *supra* n. 316; Ulrich Schreiber & Lisa Maria Fell, International Profit Allocation, Intangibles and Sales-Based Transactional Profit Split, 9 World Tax Journal (2017).

488. Many scholars use 'buyers' market' to represent the rationale of the sales factor. In some early literature, there are also arguments that the sales factor is not justified by the economic analysis because in a buyers' market, the buyer does not create extra income and buyers just 'use' their income. *See* C Lowell Harriss, Economic Aspects of Interstate Apportionment of Business Income, 37 Taxes 327 (1959). From such disclosure, what we need to notice is that any 'economic analysis' sometimes has some traditional perspectives, and we should not treat it as an undisputable fact, so the same applies to the interpretation of 'empirical' data.

due to historical or convenience reasons.[489] From the early days prior to UDITPA (1957), there was no uniform definition of the sales factor among states which adopted the sales factor.[490]

The built-in incentive of the single-sales-factor formula is struck down by more recent research.

In the US, increasing the weight of the sales factor in the formula not only focuses on reflecting the taxpayer's output side of economic activities but is also expected to promote economic growth. Since the 1980s, there has been a clear trend that states in the US have started to adopt the single-sales-factor formula[491] to apportion state taxation rights on cross-border business income.[492] In addition to the administrative convenience claimed, most state taxation policy makers have relied on Goolsbee and Maydew's empirical research,[493] in combination with McLure's factor incidence theory,[494] to adopt 'the single sales factor formula' in order to encourage investments in production activities such as payroll and properties. But we should note that McLure himself is not convinced by the single-sales-factor formula:

> it is obvious that sales-only apportionment generally does not reflect where income is earned; it would be an unusual economic activity in which neither payroll nor property played a significant role in the creation of income. Indeed, I believe that any weight on sales greater than 50 percent is likely to be too great.[495]

The underlying belief of adopting the single-sales-factor formula or double-weighted sales factor in the formula is that the single-sales-factor formula will result in the effect of making the tax incidence on the sales/customers and lifting the corporate tax incidence away from employees or property owners. Therefore, for single-sales-factor formula advocates adopting a single-sales-factor formula would have the same effect as subsidizing the companies investing in production activities in the state

489. Similar phenomenon of deviation also takes place in the field of VAT in EU law, the destination principle is not fully implemented regarding services. Such deviation is being criticized. *See* further discussions in Chapter 4.
490. For example, in 1945, among 34 states adopting franchise tax, 22 states adopted the sales factor, but disparities have led to great uncertainties. *See* Edward Roesken, The Sales Factor in State Franchise Tax Allocation, 23 Taxes 157 (1945).
491. Mark L Nachbar & Brian L Browdy, The Single Sales Factor Apportionment Method Origins and Development, 27 Journal of State Taxation 31 (2008).
492. The overview of states adopting the single-sales-factor formula, *see* Pereira, *supra* n. 81; Mayer, *supra* n. 48, at 3.2.5.1.; a survey Federal Tax Administration, until 2018/01/01 https://www.taxadmin.org/assets/docs/Research/Rates/apport.pdf; Hellerstein, Hellerstein & Swain, *supra* n. 349, at 9.2.
493. Most supporters of the single-sales factor cited the empirical data and interpretation from Goolsbee & Maydew, *supra* n. 306; Austan Goolsbee & Edward L Maydew, The Economic Impact of Single Factor Sales Apportionment for the State of New York (The Public Policy Institute of New York State, Inc 2000).
494. Charles E McLure Jr, The State Corporation Income Tax: Lambs in Wolves Clothing, in *The Economics of Taxation* (Brookings Institution 1980); McLure, *supra* n. 165, at 395-413.
495. Charles E McLure Jr, A Comprehensive and Sensible UDITPA, 37 State Tax Notes 929 (2005); McLure later describes the policy of adopting the single-sales-factor formula as 'Often convergence will be the result of beggar-thy-neighbor policies, in which case the result is not likely to be desirable.' *See* Charles E McLure Jr, Understanding Uniformity and Diversity in State Corporate Income Taxes, National Tax Journal 141 (2008).

because their payroll and property are not bearing any tax incidence. The rationale why the states of the US are adopting the single-sales-factor formula or the double-weighted sales-factor formula is to 'encourage' inbound investment and to create more employment. The single-sales-factor formula or a double-weighted sales-factor formula is regarded as having a 'built-in' incentive.[496]

Some scholars assert[497] that sales are less manipulative and more useful against profit- shifting than the labour and assets factors because economic operators can control the production factors, but they cannot control the consumers and the market.[498] For the supporters of the single-sales-factor formula, adopting a single-sales-factor formula seems to be more consistent with the neutrality principle.[499] Therefore, there are also advocates for adopting the single-sales-factor formula for the EU.[500] However, such argument is not correct.

The latest empirical data also show that the correlation between an increase in employment and adopting the single-sales factor is not significant in every state.[501] In the early 2000s, Mazerov critically argued that the effect of encouraging economic growth or promoting employment claimed by the advocates of the single-sales-factor formula is actually weak.[502] The data that was used for supporting the single-sales-factor formula has also been proven to be mistaken. According to replication and correction by David Merriman in 2015, there is no significant correlation between adopting the single-sales factor and the increase in employment activities for most states.[503] Even in some states in the US, there seems to be a correlation between

496. For example, De Wilde, *supra* n. 76, at 6.4.5.2.
497. For example, Avi-Yonah & Clausing, *supra* n. 112.
498. However, there is also opposing data showing that corporates still could manage to decrease their sales factor ratio when they are in jurisdictions which adopt 'throw-back rules for out-of-state sales'. *See* Kenneth J Klassen & Douglas A Shackelford, State and Provincial Corporate Tax Planning: Income Shifting and Sales Apportionment Factor Management, 25 Journal of Accounting and Economics 385 (1998).
499. For example, Estefanía López Llopis, Formulary Apportionment in the European Union, 45 Intertax 631 (2017).
500. Maarten Floris de Wilde, On the Future of Business Income Taxation in Europe (2019) https://www.ssrn.com/abstract=3424681; Maarten de Wilde, The CCCTB Relaunch: A Critical Assessment and Some Suggestions for Modification, in Pistone (ed.), *supra* n. 303. For criticism, *see* Lluís M Fargas Mas, Commentary on Chapter 2: CCCTB Relaunch: Why a Destination-Based Model Would Not Work, in Pistone (ed.), *supra* n. 303.
501. For example, Wisconsin data show that there is no significant relationship between adopting the single-sales-factor formula and increasing manufacturing employments, *see* Jamie Bernthal & others, Single Sales-Factor Corporate Income Tax Apportionment: Evaluating the Impact in Wisconsin, Workshop in Public Affairs May (2012).

    California data show that shifting the sales-factor formula does not increase California's corporate tax income tax capacity, *see* Darien Shanske, A New Theory of the State Corporate Income Tax: The State Corporate Income Tax as Retail Sales Tax Complement, 66 Tax Law Review 305 (2012). Shanske still supports US states adopting the single-sales-factor formula for levying state taxation but based on a different rationale: according to Shanske, the single-sales-factor formula will make state corporate income taxation a complementary tax to retail sales tax. Such 'tax complement' is small but stable.
502. Michael Mazerov, *The 'Single Sales Factor' Formula for State Corporate Taxes* (Washington, DC: Center on Budget and Policy Priorities 2005). Mazerov assessed the data of states adopting the single-sales-factor formula since 1995 to 2005 and concluded that the claimed effects do not really exist, *see* p. 48 of the report, table 2 and table 3.
503. For the replication and criticism of Goolsbee and Maydew's work, *see* Merriman, *supra* n. 308.

increased employment and adoption of the single-sales-factor formula; any increased employment is from existing in-state enterprises, not from enterprises outside the state.[504] In addition, the states which adopted the single-sales-factor formula early might benefit more than the states which followed the trend later. The 'early' states already won the tax competition and the follower states, though they adopt the single-sales factor now, cannot achieve the same result as the early states.[505]

In short, the 'built-in incentive' argument, i.e., encouraging manufacturing, employment, inbound investments, that the single-sales-factor formula is based on has been challenged and struck down by other new empirical research data. Even previous built-in incentive supporters, such as Clausing,[506] admit that the evidence of built-in incentive is not enough. Also, the effect of encouraging economic growth by 'destination-based taxation' is not significant in the services sector.[507] It would be too risky to reply to such a controversial argument whose empirical data is challenged by later data. Therefore, the 'built-in incentive' should not be the supporting rationale for adopting the single-sales-factor formula for the EU's FA regime.

For the EU, we need to be realistic to decide if the effect of adopting the single-sales-factor formula is still consistent with the goals of the internal market under EU law. The assertion that the built-in incentive of the single-sales-factor formula has been largely influenced by the US literature discussed above[508] is not a well-founded economic consequence.

Furthermore, the single-sales-factor formula seems to ignore the fact that even the demand side of the market can be heavily regulated and restricted for some industries. Adopting a single-sales-factor formula, which only reflects the demand side of economic activities, no longer seems market neutral because it does not reflect the whole economic activity chain. Focusing on one factor is not neutral and can create extra distortions, especially when the demand side market is a regulated market, such as the tobacco market, and the taxpayer cannot exercise its marketing activities freely to stimulate the demands from customers.[509]

504. Clausing, *supra* n. 59.
For a similar conclusion, *see* Charles Swenson, On the Effectiveness of Single Sales Factors for State Taxation (Working Paper, The University of Southern California 2011). Swenson's data show that the single-sales-factor formula 'does in fact increase overall employment in these states after adoption. However, this net employment increase was comprised of an employment increase for locally-based firms, and a decrease for out of state-based firms.'

505. Swenson, *ibid.*

506. Clausing, *supra* n. 59. According to Clausing, 'However, in the period of this study, 1986 to 2012, there is scant evidence that state employment, investment, or sales are sensitive to corporate tax policy parameters, once an adequate set of control variables are included in the analysis.'

507. *See* William F Fox & Zhou Yang, Destination Taxation: Road to Economic Success?, 69 National Tax Journal 285 (2016).

508. Arguments from De Wilde, *supra* n. 76, at 6.4.5.1.

509. This is the new argument in a pending petition case before the California tax authorities in 2017, by Phillip Morris, a tobacco company, the case taxpayer's brief in support of section 25137 petition In the Matter of Philip Morris USA Inc. ('PM USA') and its unitary affiliates, EIN: 13-1607658: 'Because Phillip Morris USA is so capital intensive, the economically appropriate apportionment formula, and the apportionment formula that accurately and fairly reflects PM

3.4.2.1.2 *The Single Sales Factor Formula Is Not Simpler for Administration*

Last but not least, interpreting the trend of adopting the single-factor formula in the US should also be done cautiously. Until January 2019,[510] there was a clear trend in US states to adopt the single-sales-factor formula or double-weighted sales-factor formula, and some scholars argue that adopting the single-sales-factor formula could also make administration simpler and naturally develop towards harmonization by competition. US states have been shifting towards a single-sales-factor formula or heavily-weighted sales-factor formula via path dependence, and it was expected that other sovereign states would also follow this trend, if the US adopted a single-sales-factor formula first. Therefore, the single-sales-factor formula is advocated by academics as the 'future of European taxation'.[511]

Such arguments for the single-sales-factor formula are not completely true. It is a little too naïve to claim 'a single-sales-factor formula could make administration simple'. It should be noted that in the US, the equitable apportionment/the alternative apportionment provision[512] that could be invoked to challenge a formula by taxpayers or tax authorities. The definition of sales and various throw-back and throw-out rules[513] have been disputed, also via the channel of the equitable apportionment/the alternative apportionment provision. This is also why the sales factor has been the most controversial factor in US state taxation practice and already involves many complicated tax administration rules. When we observe the trend of adopting the single-sales factor, we should also be aware that the far side of the moon, or the other side of the coin, has involved more complications. So, we have to be very cautious not to 'get lost in translation' while trying to learn lessons from the sales factor saga from US state taxation experiences. Therefore, I would not support an argument for simplification for adopting a single-sales-factor formula.

To sum up, in the context of the EU's FA regime, a single-sales-factor formula is not in line with benefit-based MN. The 'build-in incentive' empirical evidence being used to support the single-sales-factor formula is still disputable. Adopting the single-factor formula is not suitable for the EU's FA regime. The European Commission has chosen the right formula for the current CCCTB Directive Proposal.[514]

USA's economic activity in California, is a four-factor formula consisting of double-weighted property, payroll, and sales.' In the end, the California tax authorities (FTB) still rejected Phillip Morris petition on 15 June 2017 on this case, but in a rare manner FTB opened the oral sessions later on, *See* FTB notice 2017-05 and FTB Notice 2018-02, published at https://www.ftb.ca.gov/tax-pros/law/ftb-notices/index.html.

510. The survey of states' formulas in the US until January 2019, *see* https://www.taxadmin.org/assets/docs/Research/Rates/apport.pdf.
511. Avi-Yonah, Clausing & Durst, *supra* n. 19; De Wilde (2019), *supra* n. 500; Maarten de Wilde, Om de Toekomst van de Belastingheffing van Ondernemingswinsten in Europa (Oratie), 13 TPE Digitaal 60 (2019).
512. This is discussed in Chapter 8 of this book. *See also* Carolyn Joy Lee & Charlotte Noel, Per Se Versus 'As Applied' Challenges and the Use of Alternative Apportionment Provisions, *The State and Local Tax Lawyer. Symposium Edition* (American Bar Association 2009).
513. *See* section 4.4 of this book, regarding the throw-back rule and the complex dispute in combination with combined reporting.
514. For a similar opinion, *see* Weiner, *supra* n. 113. *See also*, Weiner, *supra* n. 5.

3.4.2.2 *The Sales Factor Should Reflect Taxpayers' Response to the Customers' Market*[515]

The sales factor represents the public benefit of maintaining a healthy customers' market, so its design should represent the taxpayer's economic activities in response to the customers' demand in the market. Maintaining a healthy customers' market requires various forms of legislation and enforcement, for example, regulations regarding quality of goods, consumer protection, qualification for service providers, competition law, etc. These market-maintaining laws and policies belong to a market infrastructure in the broad sense and justify as a public benefit enjoyed by corporate taxpayers to make profits from their customers in a well-functioning market.

It is consistent with benefit-based MN when the design of the sales factor reflects the customers' market. Theoretically speaking, a logical sales factor can only be 'sales by destination' because only 'destination' faithfully refers to the customers' market. A formulation of 'sales by origin' is an oxymoron. Since the labour factor and the assets factor already have the element of origin, the sales factor should follow the destination rule and seek the customers' location.

With the same rationale, the scope and definition of sales should include all monetary renumeration earned via providing services or goods to the taxpayers' customers/clients. The rationale of the sales-by-destination rule will also be helpful to distinguish what items should 'not' be included in the sales factor, even though these items involve the form of a sales-purchase transaction. The sales factor should not include monetary receipts from activities not related to providing customers with services or goods.

The attribution rule for the sales factor should indicate where the taxpayers' consumers, i.e., the demand side, use the market. It is usually the physical location of the consumers. The physical location of a customer is not necessarily where consumption or enjoyment exactly takes place but the physical location of the market that the customer constitutes and participates in. The physical location of the market may refer to where the customers' purchase takes place, or the IP scope where the digital services/goods are available or the customers' permanent residence. These are indicators of where the market is formed but not the destinations per se.

In many cases, the sales-by-destination rule for an FA system coincides with the VAT rules.[516] For example, if a Dutch traveller buys a hardcopy book in a multilateral retailer shop at an airport in France and takes the book to Italy and reads it there, the destination of the purchase of the book for VAT purposes is France. From the perspective of CIT, the destination of sales of the retailer shop is attributed to France too because it is where the transferring customers physically buy the hardcopy book. It is a sale of a book in the French market.

When it involves a digitalized product, such as a digital book, the answer is different from attributing a hardcopy book in the transfer airport because there is no

515. In Chapter 4, I further elaborate and demonstrate the development of the sales factor. In this section, we focus on the fundamental rationale of adopting the sales factor.
516. I elaborate on the destination concept in the field of VAT in Chapter 4.

one specific physical location of a travelling consumer. Presume a French digital book is sold by a French publisher to a Dutch traveller's smartphone on a flight to Italy, and the Dutch traveller continues to read the book in Italy. In the sales-by-destination rationale for the sales factor, the digital book publisher sells the digital product to the Dutch customers market digitally, unless such digital books are only accessible within the IP scope of France. If the digital book is only accessible in France, and even if the Dutch traveller paid VAT for the digital book according to EU VAT rules, the sales should still be attributed to France for the purpose of attributing the sales factor because France, in this transaction, is where the market is formed.

Presuming the publishers do not set any IP restrictions to geographical regime of selling such French digital books, it means that the sellers are open to global customers; such transactions are actually done towards the Dutch market, where the Dutch traveller takes part in and makes use of the Dutch online payment system.[517]

3.4.2.2.1 The Current CCCTB Proposal Adopts the Sales by Destination Principle, But with Illogical Deviations

The current CCCTB Directive Proposal text seems to follow the destination principle for the sales factor but not completely. In its preamble and the article headings, it has expressly mentioned the rationale of 'sales by destination', not 'sales by origin', for the sales of goods.[518] In the CCCTB Working Group meetings, experts agreed that the attribution rule of the sales factor should follow the 'sales by destination rule', instead of 'sales by origin rule'. Since the sales factor is designed to reflect the demand side of the market, i.e., taxpayers' response to the consumers' market, the sales-by-destination rule would be consistent with the MN principle because attributing sales to the destination would coincide with the consumption side of the market. In contrast, 'the sales by origin rationale' seems illogical in this regard. Although in theory 'the sales by origin rationale' might still be used by a state of the goods origin when these states want to increase the sales factor attributed to the state, it is more out of a political concern and deviates from the MN norm.

The sales-by-destination rationale is indeed market neutral; however, in the current CCCTB Directive Proposal, the destination principle is not completely implemented for receipts earned from providing services[519] and receipts earned from

517. In the EU VAT context after 2015, for this case, 'the customer is a consumer (non-taxable person) so the location is the country where they are registered, have their permanent address or usually live'. *See* European Commission, *The Basic EU VAT Rules for Electronically Supplied Services Explained for Micro Businesses*, available at https://ec.europa.eu/taxation_customs/business/vat/telecommunications-broadcasting-electronic-services/sites/default/files/taxud-2016-00734-01-00-en.pdf.

518. Article 38(1) of the 2016 CCCTB Directive Proposal; CCCTB Working Document No. 52, paragraph 41; No. 60, paragraph 59.

It is clearly indicated as the title of Article 38, especially the sales of goods: sales of goods are attributed to the destination: 'Sales of goods shall be included in the sales factor of the group member located in the Member State where the dispatch or transport of the goods to the person acquiring them ends.'

519. Article 38(2) of the 2016 CCCTB Directive Proposal.

intangibles,[520] even under the heading of 'sales by destination' in the same article. In other words, the current sales factor attribution rule under the current CCCTB Directive Proposal is in fact spilt into two conflicting rationales.[521]

To be more precise, the sales of services are attributed to the location of the service being 'carried out and supplied' according to the current CCCTB Directive Proposal. When the service is performed via telecommunications, it will be attributed to the service provider's (i.e., taxpayer's) location, not the 'destination' (the customers' location) because being carried out and supplied is not equal to 'being received'. This is actually an origin-based rule, and thus it is not market neutral for the sales factor. Similarly, receipts earned from interest/dividends/royalties/proceeds of the disposal of fixed assets are attributed to the 'beneficiary' of those receipts.[522] Attributing to the beneficiary might look simple, but it is contrary to the rationale of sales by destination and perfectly negates the purpose of the sales factor to represent the demand side of the market. This is thus not market neutral.

3.4.2.2.2 *CCCTB's Legal Transplantation Mistakenly Ignores the US's Paradigm Shift*

It is worth emphasizing that the attribution rules for providing services under the current CCCTB Directive Proposal are transplanted from the old formula from the UDITPA/old section 17 MTC in the US. UDITPA/old section 17 MTC has been long criticized and officially under reform since early 2014.[523] Unfortunately, the European Commission does not incorporate the reforms into the CCCTB Directive Proposal.

In the past, the UDITPA/old MTC adopted the location of service performance as the key attribution criterion for attribution. It is also formulated as the 'costs of performance'[524] approach: the single state where most of the costs of the income-generating activity of a specific cross-border service take place will result in all of the receipts earned from that service in the sales factor. It is an all-or-nothing approach and creates an unfair result for cross-border services involving plural states.

Since December 2014, MTC has been reforming the attribution rules for providing services in the sales factor, and there has been a paradigm shift. In 2015, Article IV section 17 of the Multistate Tax Compact was amended, and in 2017, the corresponding

520. Article 38(3) of the 2016 CCCTB Directive Proposal.
521. In the CCCTB Working Group meetings, experts have agreed that the attribution rule of the sales factor should follow the 'sales by destination rule', instead of 'sales by origin rule'. Since the sales factor is designed to reflect the demand side of the market, i.e., taxpayers' response to the consumers' market, the sales-by-destination rule would be consistent with the neutrality principle because attributing the sales to the destination would coincide with the consumption side of the market. In contrast, 'the sales by origin rationale' seems illogical in this regard. Although in theory 'the sales by origin rationale' might still be used by a state of the goods origin when these states want to increase the sales factor attributed to the state, it is more out of a political concern and deviate from the tax neutrality norm.
522. Article 38(3) of the 2016 CCCTB Directive Proposal.
523. The reform project is available and can be requested at the MTC official website http://www.mtc.gov/.
524. *See* section 17 UDITPA, Article IV section 17 Multistate Tax Compact, Article 17(4)(B)(c) MTC Regulation IV (prior to 2014).

implementation regulation was also approved.[525] The new attribution rules of the MTC adopt 'the market sourcing' approach to attribute the receipts from providing services and abandon the cost-of-performance (COP) approach. It is clear that there is already a paradigm shift regarding the sales factor in the FA: the market-sourcing approach represents the importance of the demand side of the market. The sales factor will embrace this rationale more thoroughly and aim to reflect the business activities from the demand side and consumer side of the market, not from the perspective of the origin state.

The paradigm of the sales factor in the sharing formula has been revolutionarily changed in US state taxation, which can be reflected in the development of the MTC's reform of the sales factor attribution rules. The CCCTB Working Group chose the right direction when it adopted the sales-by-destination rationale, though not implemented completely. This is a logical rationale for attributing sales and is also consistent with the neutrality framework discussed above.

It is still problematic that the attribution rules for providing services and receipts earned from intangibles deviate from this rationale under the current CCCTB Directive Proposal.[526] In Chapter 4, I further elaborate on the cases on the definition of sales and demonstrate the current CCCTB Directive Proposal's weakness and non-neutral consequences. Such weakness is not what the European Commission intended to cause but comes from the mistake in the legal transplantation process. For the new tax reform package BEFIT, the European Commission should take the opportunity to correct it.

3.4.2.3 Elimination of Intra-group Sales Does Not Create Distortion

Due to the consolidation, the current CCCTB Directive Proposal also provides that intra-group sales are (regarded as) eliminated.[527] In other words, intra-group sales will not be included in the sales factor of the seller group member either.

A question arises here: since the sales factor does not include the transaction with another group member but includes the transaction with a third party, does the CCCTB Directive Proposal create a heavier tax burden to taxpayers conducting more transactions with a third party than with a group member? Put differently, does the current

---

525. *See section* 4.4.2 of this book about the MTC's new market-sourcing rules.
526. *See* further discussions in Chapter 4 of this book.
527. Article 9 of the 2016 CCCTB Directive Proposal:
Article 9

Elimination of intra-group transactions

1. With the exception of the cases referred to in subparagraph 2 of Article 42 and Article 43, profits and losses arising from intra-group transactions shall be ignored when calculating the consolidated tax base.
2. Groups shall apply a consistent and adequately documented method for recording intra-group transactions. Groups may change the method only for valid commercial reasons and only at the beginning of a tax year.
3. The method for recording intra-group transactions shall enable all intra-group transfers and sales to be identified at the lowest cost for assets not subject to depreciation or the value for tax purposes for depreciable assets.
4. Intra-group transfers shall not change the status of self-generated intangible assets.

CCCTB Directive Proposal discriminate against companies that do not form a CCCTB group?

The answer is negative for two reasons. First, a consolidated group aggregates all group members' economic activities as a whole. A group can be regarded as an economic operator which can mobilize more resources and control the value-creation chain by vertically or horizontally integrating the market. Therefore, even when intra-group sales are not calculated in the sales factor of the group and each member, it does not mean a more favourable treatment because the consolidated tax base could be larger and the nexus threshold is easier to qualify. Besides, the consolidated group will also include all of the assets factor and the labour factor into the sharing formula, and thus the final ratio would not necessarily be smaller when intra-group sales are regarded as non-existent.

Second, the fundamental rationale of the sales factor is to reflect the taxpayer's response to its clients' market, i.e., the destination. Transactions between group members do not qualify the fundamental rationale of the sales factor because such transactions have not reached their 'destination' because intra-group transactions are not responses to their clients' market.

Lastly, concerns about manipulating or circumventing the group membership criterion or generating sales in a low-tax jurisdiction are irrelevant here. For tax avoidance scenarios, there are other types of anti-avoidance rules to address the problem, such as GAAR or Controlled Foreign Corporation (CFC) rules.[528] A consolidated group acts like an economic operator as a whole, and since the sales factor should represent this economic operator's output activity and response to its clients' demand, it would be logical to eliminate the intra-group sales from the tax base as well as the formula.

3.4.3 The Input Side: The Labour and Assets Factors Represent Material and Human Resources

3.4.3.1 The Assets Factor Should Include Tangibles and Intellectual Property

3.4.3.1.1 The Assets Factor Represents a Direct Link to Resources in the Jurisdiction

The assets factor in the formula represents the beginning of the production process. Taxpayers first own or make use of assets in order to start the production process. Historically, the assets factor was a quite widely used factor in FA in most states in the US from the nineteenth century to the late 1970s.[529] Assets, especially from the

528. Panayi observed that the CFC rule under the CCCTB might not be able to apply to low-tax rate EU Member States, *see* Christiana HJI Panayi, CFC Rules Within the CCCTB, in Michael Lang & others (eds), Corporate Income Taxation in Europe: The Common Consolidated Corporate Tax Base (CCCTB) and Third Countries (Edward Elgar 2013).

529. Hellerstein, Hellerstein & Swain, *supra* n. 349, at 9.16.

perspective of the benefit principle, tangible assets and real estate create a clear link with the states that provide relevant public services for taxpayers to make use of the assets in the production process.[530]

There has been criticism that the assets factor is too mobile and easier to control than the sales factor. Some scholars argue for abolishing the assets factor from the sharing formula.[531] Canada, for example, does not use the assets factor in its formula.[532] However, such criticism ignores the important public benefit involved in the production process: material resources. The assets factor is also the key criterion for nexus and justified by the benefit principle because the tangible/real assets do create a link to the public service of the jurisdiction. Therefore, in my view, a formula should include the assets factor.

When we see the assets factor as one necessary prong in the 'production process', it is logical to include only assets having a production function. These assets can include fixed assets[533] but are not limited to tangible assets. But inventories that do not need to be further worked are already the end results of production and thus should be excluded from the assets factor because these assets no longer represent the production process: inventories are ready to be sold immediately.[534]

3.4.3.1.2 Intellectual Property Contributing to the Production Process Should Be in the Assets Factor

Here another question arises: should intangibles be excluded from the assets factor? In the traditional FA regime, the assets factor only includes tangible assets, mainly for the purpose of preventing manipulation. Exclusion of intangibles is nevertheless also criticized because many MNE taxpayers do rely on intangibles to generate profits. Even though there are some exceptions,[535] it seems that the assets factor in existing formulas does not embrace the possibility of including intangibles. I think this outdated approach should be reconsidered. Intangibles should be included when certain conditions are fulfilled.

It is undeniable that, in the production process, an intangible, for example, key know-how or a key patent, can play an essential role. IP, as a type of intangible, has

530. Mayer, *supra* n. 349.
531. De Wilde, *supra* n. 76, at 6.4.4.2.2.
532. Weiner, *supra* n. 47, at 2.3; *De Wilde, supra* n. 76, at 6.4.4.2.2.
533. For example, the current CCCTB Directive Proposal includes fixed assets, not current assets in the assets factor.
534. Although it sounds convincing that the concern about anti-abuse that locations of inventories are easier to manipulate by setting up a warehouse in a preferred jurisdiction, such concern is not the main reason to exclude inventories, *see* the comparison between the CCCTB and the US regarding treating inventories in Chapter 6 of this book.
535. For example, intangibles are, in principle, excluded under the CCCTB. Article 34 (2) of 2016 CCCTB Directive Proposal further provides a special type of 'intangible' which is calculated via the proxy: costs of research, development, marketing, advertising spent in six-years prior to joining, and these amount can stay at the asset factor for five years. So briefly speaking, the CCCTB already accepts intangibles in the assets factor but under strict conditions. I explain this further in Chapter 6.5.

become an essential value-creation driver for MNEs.[536] In this regard, excluding such intangible from the assets factor would be contrary to the fundamental rationale of the assets factor. The concerns about manipulation and difficult evaluation do not seem to justify unconditional complete exclusion. The current CCCTB Directive Proposal has provided the exception that a special type of intangible valued as the costs of research and development (R&D) can be included. This is consistent with the production function rationale because the result of R&D has been part of the production process; even failed R&D activities can result in know-how regarding what is 'not' useful.

Whether the assets factor should include intangibles might influence whether the EU's FA regime is ultimately accepted. Some relatively smaller EU Member States, such as the Netherlands[537] and Ireland,[538] are really critical of the current CCCTB Directive Proposal because intangibles are regarded as the important component of their 'smart economy'.[539] This argument of ensuring the taxing rights of the smart economy is not completely convincing because these countries have been conducting tax reduction by setting either a low-tax-rate or a special tax regime, especially for attracting R&D activities and patent registrations. It would be conflicting to argue that establishing the taxing rights on the intangibles and at the same time voluntarily reducing taxing rights on the same issue.

To be included in the assets factor, intangibles should be related to innovation. Self-created intangibles, such as copyrighted know-how, or patents, or even the result of data mining,[540] can be regarded as efficiencies that taxpayers create themselves, and these efficiencies can make their production process faster in the future. The possible future profits arising from the intangibles, such as royalties, will be reflected in the sales factor. By licensing to other economic operators, the royalties can be included in the sales factor of the licensor. The amount of royalties should not be included for the value of the intangible in the assets factor of the licensor because royalties do not represent the taxpayer's production side of activities regarding this intangible.

Some might argue that self-created intangibles, such as know-how or self-created R&D and patent portfolios, are already reflected in the labour factor, so it is not necessary to include these in the assets factor again. This argument is not quite convincing because two factors represent different types of public benefits. To recognize intangibles in the assets factor, in addition to the payroll factor, is to represent the public benefits that provide the environment encouraging innovation and taking risks

536. OECD, *supra* n. 78; Anuschka Bakker & others, Increasing Importance of IP Rights, in Isabel Verlinden & Anuschka Bakker (eds), *Mastering the IP Life Cycle from a Legal, Tax and Accounting Perspective* (IBFD 2018), at 1.1.3 and 1.1.4.
537. National Parliament Reasoned Opinion on Subsidiarity, Reasoned Opinion by the House of Representatives of the Kingdom of the Netherlands on the Proposal for a Council Directive on a Common Consolidated Corporate Tax Base (CCCTB) (Com(2016)0683 – C8-0471/2016 – 2016/0336(CNS)).
538. National Parliament Reasoned Opinion on Subsidiarity of Ireland, Reasoned opinion of Seanad éireann on the proposal for a Council Directive on a Common Consolidated Corporate Tax Base (CCCTB)(COM(2016)683 – C8-0471/2016 – 2016/0336(CNS)).
539. J van de Streek, Some Introductory Remarks on the Re-launched CCTB/CCCTB Proposals from a Policy Perspective, 2017, in Weber & Streek (eds), *supra* n. 5.
540. The business model of data mining, *see* Olbert & Spengel, *supra* n. 40.

to innovate. Innovation is crucial in the production process, and the jurisdiction where the environment for R&Ds take place is justified in dividing part of the taxable pie. In other words, including the intangibles in the assets factor is justified because it represents an extra type of public benefit, i.e., promotion of innovation. In Chapter 6, I explain the issue of intangibles in the FA in detail.

As to the actual design of the factor, part of R&D costs might seem to conceptually overlap with the calculation of the labour factor because salaries of researchers would also be included in the labour factor.[541] It might not be that surprising because both the labour factor and the assets factor represent the production side. However, there is still a meaningful distinction, including R&D activities in the assets factor as well as in the labour factor. In the assets factor, R&D costs are the proxy of intangibles and focus on IP. That is to say, such intangible from R&D could contribute to the production process in a way of making the production process more efficient and effective. Therefore, as to non-self-generated intangibles, i.e., purchased or licensed intangibles from third parties outside the group, including patents or various production methods, as long as these intangibles are also used and contribute to the production process, it would be justified to include these non-self-generated intangibles in the assets factor.[542]

Also, the 2016 CCCTB Directive Proposal's sales factor provides a very broad scope for including the receipts earned from intangibles, such as royalties and interest, in the sales factor. It is logical to include intangibles both in the sales factor and in the assets factor, provided that the scope and evaluation are consistent with the rationale of 'the response to the customers' market' and the 'production process', respectively. Therefore, there is also no 'overlapping' concern or mistake in logic to include receipts earned from intangibles in the sales factor and to include the intangibles used for production in the assets factor.

3.4.3.1.3 The Rationale of Excluding Intangibles from the Assets Factor in the US Is Outdated

It should be noted that the taxability of the income earned from intangibles, the treatment of intangibles in the assets factor, and the treatment of receipts earned from intangibles in the sales factor are issues from separate levels, but they are closely related. In fact, the taxable income earned from intangible income also constitutes the consolidated tax base.

Regarding the US FA experience on the treatment of intangibles, the apportionability (tax base) and the assets factor are often discussed together. It is also because, historically, income earned from intangibles was classified as non-business income

541. Similar arguments discussed at the European Commission, *see* CCCTB Working Document No. 60.

542. Although the Commission's document on the CCCTB focused only on 'self-generated intangibles', from the perspective of the assets factor, there is no reason to exclude purchased intangibles as long as these intangibles are indeed used for the production process. There might be a concern regarding the traditional tax avoidance scenario of setting up a purely intangible holding company to manipulate the assets factor. However, when the attribution rule is based on utilization, not ownership, such manipulation concern would be eliminated.

and thus not subject to apportionment at all.[543] Therefore, these discussions have sometimes caused confusion and given an impression that intangibles per se should not be subject to the apportionment or should also not be included in the sales factor or in the assets factor. But exclusion of intangibles is merely due to administrative concerns and comes from historical reasons. Nowadays, it would be practical and reasonable to reconsider the presumption of intangibles in the digital economy.

For example, the typical three-factor formula which is based on the manufacturing industry and the automotive industry is quite often described as an ideal model example that can show the formula from the production side to the customers' market. At first, such three-factor formula did not include intangibles in the assets factor.[544] However, since the Supreme Court has clearly affirmed the unitary business, i.e., the apportionability of income earned from intangibles for state taxation, in the leading case of *Allied-Signal* in the early 1990s, which also involved the automotive industry, the function of intangibles for taxpayers' income-generating activities is well established. In fact, in the twenty-first century, it is even clearer that the automotive industry undoubtedly has involved intangibles intensively. For example, in the MNE Tesla, producing and designing autonomous vehicles/self-driving vehicles would involve enormous intangibles. Intangibles are not only embedded in the end products but also used in the production process. It is naïve to refuse to accept the great influence of intangibles in every aspect of taxpayers' economic activities. The design of any tax law should not deviate from economic reality.

It is true that Hellerstein argued in 1992 that purchased intangibles and internally developed intangibles should be treated equally, so both are excluded from the assets factor.[545] I have the opposite view. Hellerstein's argument of 1992 needs to be reconsidered in the current context of the digital economy. It is undeniable that IP rights have contributed to the production process; innovation that results in IP rights is the key driver for the value creation of a business. As to the intangibles, I discuss these further in section 6.5.

3.4.3.1.4 The Rationale of Attributing Assets to Functional Utilization

And now the third question arises: what attribution rule for the assets factor is consistent with the principle of tax neutrality? To answer this question, we need to reflect on the function of the assets factor in the sharing formula.

As to the rationale of attribution, De Wilde argues that the 'functional utilization' of an asset should be a criterion of the attribution rule.[546] From the role that the asset plays in the production process, this approach is convincing and neutral. The asset will

543. For some history regarding the unitary business and intangibles, *see* Hellerstein, *supra* n. 352; for comments on the Allied-Signal case and a survey of state law, *see* James H Peters & Benjamin F Miller, Apportionability in State Income Taxation: The Uniform Division of Income for Tax Purposes Act and Allied-Signal, 60 Tax Lawyer 57 (2006).
544. For example, McIntyre uses an example based on the automotive industry, McIntyre, *supra* n. 354, at 119.
545. Hellerstein, *supra* n. 352, at 869.
546. De Wilde, *supra* n. 76, at 6.4.4.2.3, under the subtitle 'Location'.

be attributed to a location where such asset is utilized in the production process. When assets are mobile or in transit, we can use a pro-rata method based on the actual amount of time of utilization being spent.

3.4.3.1.5 The Valuation Method for Assets Should Be Cost-Based

There is a particularly difficult issue in the assets factor: the valuation of an asset and the inclusion/exclusion of intangible assets. According to De Wilde, assets should be valuated according to the historical costs when the asset was purchased by taxpayers, not the asset's 'market fair value'.[547] The difficulty of valuation is sometimes used as an argument to exclude intangibles, asserting that intangibles cannot be valuated objectively.[548] This is not correct.

Some scholars argue that the asset valuation method should be based on 'fair market value'.[549] I do not agree with this market value approach from the benefit-based MN framework. Adopting the market value evaluation in the asset factor will deviate from the rationale of 'the production process'. As long as an asset can represent taxpayers' production process and non-human resources (i.e., 'material' resources in the broad sense), whether tangible or intangible, it is necessary to include it in the asset factor.

To sum up, the attribution rule for the assets factor should be based on the production process, attributing to the jurisdiction where the assets are functionally utilized. The valuation of these assets should be based on historical costs.[550] Furthermore, based on the rationale of reflecting the production process, completely excluding intangibles is illogical. In Chapter 6, I discuss and compare the assets factor from US state taxation experiences and the legislative records of the CCCTB, to further demonstrate why and how the assets factor should reflect MNE taxpayers' input from non-human resources (including tangible and intangible assets) as well as represent MNE taxpayers' ability to control and make use of 'assets'. Regarding the financial assets, they do not contribute to production, so they are not in the assets factor. But for the financial industry, financial assets would need some special treatment, which I explain in section 7.2.

3.4.3.2 The Labour Factor Attribution Represents the Labour Market

3.4.3.2.1 The Public Benefit of Maintaining a Healthy Labour Market

The labour factor represents taxpayers' production side activities conducted by human efforts. In other words, the labour factor represents MNE taxpayers' ability to mobilize,

547. *Ibid.*
548. *Ibid.*
549. For some discussion on these debates, *see* Walter Hellerstein, *Tax Planning under the CCCTB's Formulary Apportionment Provisions: The Good, the Bad and the Ugly, CCCTB; Selected Issues* (Kluwer Law International 2012), at 221.
550. It should be noted that depreciation rules are provided in Articles 30 to 40 of Chapter 5 of the 2016 CCTB Directive Proposal.

control, and make use of human resources. The public benefit of maintaining a healthy labour market justifies including the labour factor in the formula. The nature of a 'labour market' is different from a capitalist market for products[551] because it has an inherent imbalance of powers between employers and employees. The government must pay additional attention to maintaining a healthy labour market, such as providing rules and public policies, for coordinating and maintaining smooth industrial relations.

The public benefit of maintaining a healthy labour market also justifies a harmonized and broad definition of employees. Adopting a broad and harmonized definition of employee for the labour factor under the CCCTB would eliminate the artificial (also controversial) distinction between typical employees and atypical employees, and this would be more consistent with the benefit principle because such definition could reflect more faithfully the human resources mobilized. When the distinction between typical employees and atypical employees disappears, there is less incentive for employers to hire atypical employees.[552]

There has been another argument that adopting the labour factor would lead to a disadvantaged situation for enterprises that hire more employees. This argument is not true. This incorrect argument is similar to advocates of a single-sales-factor formula, believing that taking the labour factor out of the formula would increase the attractiveness of the jurisdiction, and enterprises would be encouraged to have stronger incentives to invest in employment.[553] Such assertions of 'tax hindering employment' are not new and have already appeared in the literature regarding the relation between tax competition and boosting employment.[554] But from the benefit-principle perspective, hiring many employees means making use of many human resources, and the consequent increased labour factor is still justified.

The labour attribution rule should be consistent with the economic reality. Since employees are human beings, they would need a physical location to work, and such location is actually controlled by the employers when employees are performing their tasks. When an employee works from long-distance in a jurisdiction other than the jurisdiction where his or her actual employer has its main office, the long-distance employee should be attributed to the jurisdiction of the physical location. This rule is also applicable to employees who physically work from a non-EU/third country.

The attribution rule of the labour factor is similar to the rationale of the assets factor, but the labour factor should reflect the work performed by employees. In most

551. Ruth Dukes, From the Labour Constitution to an Economic Sociology of Labour Law, 9 Jurisprudence 418 (2018).
552. Michael Bowen, Slicing the Pie: A Call for Congress to Enact Single-Factor Payroll Apportionment of Interstate Business Revenue, 4 Belmont Law Review 187 (2017). Bowen argued that a single payroll factor would be a most straightforward solution and trigger the least compliance costs.
553. This is also one of the reasons for many states in the US to adopt the single-sales-factor formula presuming that taxpayers who hire more employees will be subject to less state corporate taxation. *See* section 3.4.2 of this book. Goolsbee & Maydew, *supra* n. 306; Goolsbee & Maydew, *supra* n. 493.
554. Hikaru Ogawa, Yasuhiro Sato & Toshiki Tamai, A Note on Unemployment and Capital Tax Competition, 60 Journal of Urban Economics 350 (2006).

cases, employees will perform their work and receive control and supervision in the same jurisdiction where the taxpayer is located. In other words, the employer and employees are in the same jurisdiction, physically, as the traditional form.

However, in a digitalized era, hiring a workforce from another jurisdiction and giving instructions via telecommunication are much more convenient than in the past. Even for work that does not need a traditional physical working space, such as web designers or platform freelancers, these human beings can work anywhere, and they still perform their work in a location.

When the employee is performing tasks in a jurisdiction other than the physical location of the employer, that employee's payroll/headcount should be attributed to the jurisdiction where the work has been done. That is to say, when an employee works from 'home', that home jurisdiction provides the labour market to the employer, and it is justified to attribute the work-from-home employee to the home jurisdiction.

The employer exercises its capacity to mobilize the human resources at the employee's working location; in this time of a pandemic, it is quite a common arrangement. In my view, this is the destination of the employee's work being delivered, also the employer's production.

In Chapter 5, I further explore state taxation experiences from the US to design the labour factor, including a definition of employee in labour law and attributing cross-border employees in social security law. Chapter 5 demonstrates that a labour factor based on the input from human resources controlled by MNE taxpayers would be helpful in clarifying conceptual complexities and choose between conflicting arguments.

3.4.3.2.2 Solving the Paradox Between the Labour Factor and Tax Competition in Economic Growth

Some scholars predict that, since the current CCCTB Directive Proposal does hot harmonize the definition of employee, EU Members States would compete to adopt a narrow definition of employee to reduce the apportioned share from the labour factor,[555] since states would compete for attracting more foreign investment and increasing domestic employment. This is a type of tax competition and can result in harming the labour market.

The temptation of reducing the labour factor for 'encouraging employment' presumes that economic growth and social policies are opposite: this results in a vicious circle between tax competition and local economic development. A tax law reform project (both at the international level and at the EU level) also aims to pursue

555. Eva Eberhartinger & Matthias Petutschnig, CCCTB: The Employment Factor Game, 43 European Journal of Law and Economics 333 (2017).

'sustainable' growth.[556] A tax reform project should prevent the vicious circle of tax and development[557] but encourage the 'virtuous circle' between EU Member States.

There is a vicious circle of race to the bottom to attract Foreign Direct Investment (FDI) in the international tax regime. The vicious circle demonstrates that states' competition for mobile capital and employment growth involves various types of 'race to the bottom,'[558] not only regarding tax rate but also the collective labour law standard.[559] The lowered tax revenue and lowered labour law standards result in a reduction of public benefits and make the labour market more imbalanced. In other words, states unwisely harm the national labour market to attract more FDI via tax competition. When the labour market is harmed, economic growth and welfare will not be satisfactory for states, and then those states will again need to reduce taxation or attract FDI and expect economic growth.

The current CCCTB Directive Proposal's labour factor has an important meaning for the EU internal market to break the vicious circle and myth. Including the labour factor in the formula with the harmonized but broad definition of employees would mitigate Member States' regulatory competition to narrow the definition of employee in their national law. Having no possibility to compete to narrow the definition of employee, Member States could normally compete in different aspects. Member States would not compete to boost imaginary employment, whereas in reality such competition of narrowing the definition of employee may just attract 'exploitation'.[560] When taking the perspective to see the internal market as an economic union as well as a social union,[561] the attitude towards the labour factor is no longer negative or worrying about hindering growth.[562] Instead, the EU should take this opportunity to design the

556. *See* Christiana HJI Panayi, The Globalisation of Tax Good Governance, Singapore Management University School of Accountancy Research Paper 74 (2018).
557. This term 'vicious circle' is borrowed from the blogpost of Allison Christians, The Virtuous and Vicious Cycles of Tax Law and Development, 30 April 2019, http://taxpol.blogspot.com/2019/04/the-virtuous-and-vicious-cycles-of-tax.html.
558. Ronald B Davies & Krishna Chaitanya Vadlamannati, A Race to the Bottom in Labor Standards? An Empirical Investigation, 103 Journal of Development Economics 1 (2013).
559. Layna Mosley & Saika Uno, Racing to the Bottom or Climbing to the Top? Economic Globalization and Collective Labor Rights, 40 Comparative Political Studies 923 (2007). Their data suggest that globalization has a mixed impact on labour standards: 'As "climb to the top" accounts suggest, FDI inflows are positively and significantly related to the rights of workers. But at the same time, trade competition generates downward 'race to the bottom' pressures on collective labor rights.'
560. The argument inspired by Apeldoorn, *supra* n. 481.
561. The view is also implemented by EU's another project: The European Pillar of Social Rights, to comprehensively improve the labour law standard. Sacha Garben, The European Pillar of Social Rights: Effectively Addressing Displacement?, 14 European Constitutional Law Review 210 (2018).
562. Adopting a harmonized and broad definition of employee in the labour factor is also not a punishment to enterprises that mobilize more human resources. This type of concern comes from the traditional presumption in the contracting purpose of economy policies (aiming to boost economic growth) and social policies (aiming to protection employees as a weaker party), and it is also based on the presumption that levying taxation would discourage employment. It can be traced to the assumption of taxation as DWL. But such concern is an illusion, not theoretically sounded to negate the labour factor in the sharing formula.

labour factor to reflect 'human capital' and 'human resources' utilized in EU Member States.

3.4.4 The Sales Factor, the Assets Factor, and the Labour Factor Should Be Equally Important

Under the benefit-based MN framework, three factors (the sales factor, the assets factor, and the labour factor) are equally important. So, they should be weighted equally, i.e., one-third of each factor. It should be emphasized that this weighting ratio is based on the conclusion that intangibles are included in the assets factor when they represent the production process; monetary receipts earned from licensing or selling intangibles are included in the sales factor when they represent taxpayers' response to their customers. Therefore, although the weighting ratio is the same as the classical Massachusetts formula, the rationale is not the same.

As discussed above, it is contrary to the benefit principle to adopt 100% weight for the sales factor and to ignore other factors. The effect of encouraging investment of the single-sales-factor formula is not guaranteed.

Now we might be wondering, how about 50% weighting on the sales factor, as the demand side, 50% weighing in total on the supply side, i.e., 25% payroll factor and 25% tangible assets factor.[563] This is the 'double-weighted sales formula'.[564] The short answer: it is also not tax neutral to adopt a formula consisting of the double-weighted sales factor with one-fourth weighted payroll factor as well as assets factor.

The double-weighted sales-factor formula is based on the following model of value creation: The input side and the output side are symmetric, and therefore, they are both weighted as 50% because they contributed equally to the tax base. Since the input side is weighted at 50%, the labour factor and the assets factor are 25%, respectively. It can be illustrated as follows.

563. The Canadian system has a similar approach of equally weighting the demand side and the supply side, but it does not have the asset factor, so the formula becomes 50% sales factor and 50% payroll factor. *See* Weiner, *supra* n. 47; reflections and discussions, De Wilde, *supra* n. 76, at 6.4.1.

564. For the supporting argument of a double-weighted sales factor, three factor formula as the good compromise between the single-sales-factor formula and three equally weighted factor formula for CCCTB, *see* Michael K Mahoney, Recommending an Apportionment Formula for the European Union's Common Consolidated Corporate Tax Base, 34 Seton Hall Legislative Journal 313 (2009).

Figure 5 The Rationale of a Double-Weighted Sales-Factor Formula

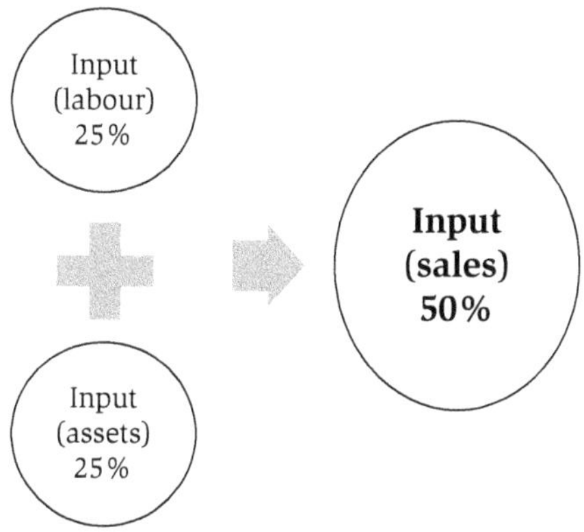

Source: The author.

However, the value-creation model should not be based purely on the clear-cut distinction between 'input' and 'output'. The input side and the output side are closely linked. There is a production 'process' that links all the inputs from the labour and tangible assets, and at the same time creates various types of intangibles in the production process. The output side is the result of production, which is the response to the market and the demand side.

Intangibles will represent all aspects[565] from the sales factor, the labour factor, and the assets factor. Taxpayers can make use of their self-generated intangibles or purchased/licensed intangibles to conduct production processes or further development. So, these intangibles can be included in the assets factor. As to royalties or receipts earned from licensing or assigning to clients/users, these will be included in the sales factor. Most importantly, intangibles are created by individual workers' intellectual activities in the process of research and knowledge generation.

Therefore, when we take intangibles into consideration, three equally weighted factors would be the most logical option to comply with the tax neutrality principle. More precisely, if we regard 'intangible' in the production process as 'three' extra conceptually separate factors that are linked to each of the three traditional weighting factors respectively, the weighting of the sales factor, the labour factor, and the assets factor would be $\frac{2}{6}$ (So, it is equal to $\frac{1}{3}$).

My understanding of the relationship between the input and the output is illustrated in Figure 5. To sum up, the value creation is a dynamic value-creation chain, so it is logical to adopt a formula consisting of the input side and the output side. The input side and the output side are linked, and there is a production process embedded in the value-creation chain. Intangibles involved in this production process also create

565. It is worth noting that there are similar remarks from CCCTB Working Document No. 60, paragraph 34, but which lead to justifying complete exclusion of intangibles from the assets factor.

value,[566] and these intangibles' contribution will be reflected in weighting factors. Therefore, it would be logical to equalize the weighting as $\frac{1}{3}$.

Figure 6 The Value-Creation Process and the Equally Weighted Three-Factor Formula

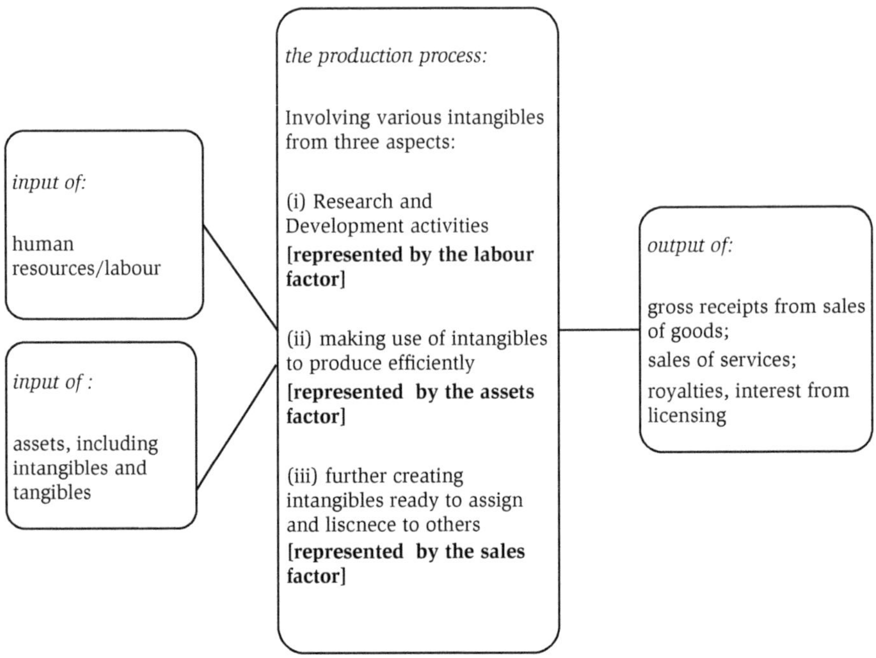

Source: The author.

3.4.5 The Formula Should Be Three Factors: The Sales Factor, the Assets Factor, and the Labour Factor

As to selecting weighting factors, there is a final remark and clarification about the necessity of the structure of the sales factor, the assets factor, and the labour factor. The puzzle is: 'should these three factors be the only factors selected, and no other factors?'

The answer to this puzzle is affirmative: the formula should consist of these three factors only. Such puzzle seems understandable because one might argue that other factors represent taxpayers' 'value creation' and the corresponding public benefits better. Such argument also appears when arguing for a special industry formula (*See* Chapter 7), but it is not correct.

Also, the European Commission's CCCTB Working Group has explored using the 'macro-based factor' in the formula, such as EU Member States' gross domestic product

566. Interesting to see that Vella also admits this, *see* Vella, *supra* n. 310.

(GDP) or national VAT base.[567] The experts concluded that macro-based factors do not reflect closely enough each MNE group's economic activities, and thus they endorse micro-based factors, including sales, assets, and labour.

The three-factor structure formula is consistent with the basic concepts of modern economics on value creation. These three factors represent the output side and the input side. It is undoubted that the sales factor represents value being created from the customers' market, as taxpayers' output side. For example, in the early 2000s, Amit and Zott[568] established that customers are one of the important sources of value creation for e-business (together with a company's suppliers and partners). Such idea is also accepted by other economists, such as Olbert and Spengel, in a digital economy context, and they extend to accept 'user participation' as part of value creation.[569]

But the sales factor is not the only aspect that represents value creation. As to the remaining two factors, the labour factor and the assets factor of the formula, they coincide with the concept of 'factors of production', which can be traced back to Adam Smith.[570] Adam Smith's concept of factors of production is still influential and widely accepted by modern growth economists and the economics of companies.[571]

According to Adam Smith, the factors of production are 'land, labour, capital'; the concept of 'capital' in Adam Smith's sense does not mean monetary capital but refers to 'property bought for the purpose of production' (as Adam Smith also uses the term 'capital stock' to describe this).[572] Therefore, the assets factor of a formula coincides with Adam Smith's factors of production of 'land and capital stock', and the labour factor of a formula coincides with Adam Smith's concept of labour. In other words, the labour factor and the assets factor are both necessary for the input side of economic activities.

In other words, the sales factor, the labour factor, and the assets factor are the ultimate basic elements to create value and contribute to production. It is true that the global economy of the twenty-first century is different from the eighteenth century when Adam Smith was alive, but the basic starting points of economics are still valid and stand. In the following chapters, I demonstrate the specific contents of these three factors which might need some adjustment, such as treatment of intangibles, financial assets, or costs of R&D, but these special rules are still within the scope of the three-factor structure.

567. CCCTB Working Document No. 47 and No. 52.
568. Raphael Amit & Christoph Zott, Value Creation in E-Business, 22 Strategic Management Journal 493 (2001).
569. Olbert & Spengel, *supra* n. 40.
570. Adam Smith, *An Inquiry into the Nature and Causes of the Wealth of Nations* (Librito Mondi 1791), at Chapter 6.
571. Mary M Cleveland, A Classical Model of Distribution, Productivity and Growth: Adam Smith Was Right (2003); Adam Smith, From Wealth of the Nations, collected in Randy Kroszner & Louis G Putterman (eds), *The Economic Nature of the Firm: A Reader* (3rd ed. Cambridge University Press 2009).
572. KH Hennings, Capital as a Factor of Production, in J Eatwell, M Milgate, P Newman (eds) *Capital Theory* (The New Palgrave. Palgrave Macmillan 1990).

3.5 RETHINKING DIGITALIZATION: THE DIGITAL NEXUS AND THE DIGITAL FACTOR

3.5.1 Digital Nexus for the Digital Economy Can Be Justifiable, But Still Redundant

The digital economy is one of the most influential elements in the BEPS Actions. BEPS Action 1 clearly indicates that the digital economy has caused and accelerated base erosion and the phenomenon of profit shifting, and thus sovereign states should take action. The EU has made a lot of effort[573] in response to BEPS Action 1. Among these efforts, the current CCCTB Directive Proposal is expected to play an active role in addressing part of the BEPS problems, also in the field of the digital economy. There are several ongoing tax reform projects in parallel with the current CCCTB Directive Proposal, and in the following sections, I discuss the relationships between them because it is the same question that the future EU's FA regime will face.

The first one is about the nexus in the digital economy. There has been a lot of discussion on lowering the nexus threshold for taxing the digital economy, such as 'virtual permanent establishment (PE)',[574] also discussed in section 3.3. In response to the difficulty of taxing the digital economy, the European Commission released a proposal of 'corporate taxation on Significant Digital Presence' in 2018 as the ultimate solution to the interim solution of a digital services tax (DST). This proposal supplements the current CCCTB Directive Proposal. The SDP Directive Proposal aims to solve the problem that the traditional concept of PE cannot catch the economic activities in the digital economy. At the same time, the European Commission has also proposed the DST proposal[575] as an interim solution and the 'significant digital presence' SDP Directive Proposal[576] which aims to establish a more flexible and appropriate nexus threshold for the digital economy.[577] These two proposals also acknowledge the taxing

573. Ana Paula Dourado, Debate: Digital Taxation Opens the Pandora Box: The OECD Interim Report and the European Commission Proposals, 46 Intertax 565 (2018).
574. Hongler & Pistone, *supra* n. 190.
575. Proposal for a Council Directive Laying down Rules relating to the Corporate Taxation of a Significant Digital Presence, EUR COMM'N COM (2018) 147 final (21 March 2018).
576. Proposal for a Council Directive on the Common System of a Digital Services Tax on Revenues Resulting from the Provision of Certain Digital Services, EUR COMM'N COM(2018) 148 final (21 March2018).
577. For commentaries on these two directive proposals, *see* Yariv Brauner & Pasquale Pistone, Adapting Current International Taxation to New Business Models: Two Proposals for the European Union, 71 Bulletin for International Taxation 681(2017); Georg Kofler, Gunter Mayr & Christoph Schlager, European Union – Taxation of the Digital Economy: 'Quick Fixes' or Long-Term Solution?, 57 European Taxation 523 (2017); Georg Kofler, Gunter Mayr & Christoph Schlager, International-Taxation of the Digital Economy: A Pragmatic Approach to Short-Term Measures, 58 European Taxation 123 (2018); Wolfgang Schön, Ten Questions about Why and How to Tax the Digitalized Economy, 72 Bulletin for International Taxation (IBFD-Bulletin) 278 (2018); Peter Bräumann, *Digital Permanent Establishments on Its Way to Becoming a Reality? The EU Commission's Proposal on Taxing 'Significant Digital Presence'* (Kluwer Law International 2019) in Haslehner & others (eds), *supra* n. 148.

rights of the 'users' jurisdiction'.[578] According to the European Commission, DST would be an interim measure as 'equalization tax',[579] and the 'significant digital presence' would be the long-term solution. As part of the fair tax package proposed by the European Commission, CCCTB would have to follow the same SDP nexus rule.

According to the SDP criterion proposed by the European Commission in Article 4 of the Council Directive laying down rules relating to the corporate taxation of an SDP:

> A 'significant digital presence' shall be considered to exist in a Member State in a tax period if the business carried on through it consists wholly or partly of the supply of digital services through a digital interface and one or more of the following conditions is met with respect to the supply of those services by the entity carrying on that business, taken together with the supply of any such services through a digital interface by each of that entity's associated enterprises in aggregate:
>
> (a) the proportion of total revenues obtained in that tax period and resulting from the supply of those digital services to users located in that Member State in that tax period exceeds EUR 7,000,000;
> (b) the number of users of one or more of those digital services who are located in that Member State in that tax period exceeds 100,000;
> (c) the number of business contracts for the supply of any such digital service that are concluded in that tax period by users located in that Member State exceeds 3,000.

The criterion of the significant digital nexus is quantitative, and thus it is a blue-light criterion similar to a 'virtual PE'. Its structure is also similar to the MTC's factor presence nexus discussed in section 3.3.

There is criticism[580] of DST and SDP to challenge their justification. The main theme of the criticism of SDP is that the current design does not seem to achieve the policy goal, especially criticism of 'the users criterion', arguing that 'the fact that a fee is paid for a service does not generate value per se'.[581] There is also empirical data indicating that digital companies do not pay less than other companies,[582] so levying a

578. Louise Fjord Kjærsgaard & Peter Koerver Schmidt, Allocation of the Right to Tax Income from Digital Intermediary Platforms: Challenges and Possibilities for Taxation in the Jurisdiction of the User, Nordic Journal of Commercial Law 27 (2018), 158. They see 'free usage of digital service' of Internet platforms and search engines, such as Facebook or Google as 'non-monetary transactions' or 'barter transaction' to justify the taxing rights of jurisdictions where users are located.
579. Kofler & Sinnig, *supra* n. 12.
580. Eva Escribano, A Preliminary Assessment of the EU Proposal on Significant Digital Presence: A Brave Attempt Requires and Deserves Further Analysis, in José Manuel Almudí Cid, Jorge A. Ferreras Gutiérrez, & Pablo A. Hernández González-Barreda (eds), *Combating Tax Avoidance in the EU: Harmonization and Cooperation in Direct Taxation* (Kluwer Law International 2019). Daniel Bunn, *A Summary of Criticisms of the EU Digital Tax* (Tax Foundation 2018).
581. Escribano, *ibid.*
582. Bauer indicates that the European Commission's research seems to focus only on 'big' digital companies, and ignores the fact that there are also SME digital companies. *See* Matthias Bauer, Digital Companies and Their Fair Share of Taxes: Myths and Misconceptions (ECIPE Occasional Paper 2018). 'Real world data also demonstrate that traditional sectors have a great number of highly profitable traditional corporations. At the same time, it is digital companies

separate digital tax might rely on some myths and misunderstandings. Some others are concerned that the DST and SDP Directive Proposals are discriminatory.[583]

Although DST is designed as the short-term solution to mitigate the distortion and unfairness between digital services and non-digital services, there are also conceptual defences for DST.[584] Cui argues that DST is justified because it can represent the 'localized rent' in the jurisdiction where a digital service is served to the customers. In other words, DST is designed for taxing location-specific rent earned by digital platforms. The argument of location-specific rent is quite similar to the line of reasoning to affirm the concept of 'virtual' PEs.[585]

Cui's 'location-specific rent' argument is precisely consistent with the rationale of the benefit principle discussed in this book. Although Cui only uses the location-specific rent argument in the discussion of the DST, in my view, this argument is also suitable for justifying the SDP proposal.

From the perspective of the EU's FA regime, adopting the SDP is not necessary any longer when we adopt the factor presence as taxable nexus because they follow the same rationale. The mandate of DST and SDP also clearly shows the important role of users from the market side in the digital economy because users are not only clients who enjoy and receive services but also a driver to give feedback of enormous data to taxpayers to understand and respond to the market situation more precisely. In other words, DST/SDP proposals could have the same justification as the sales factor of a sharing formula when we acknowledge sales factor presence as taxable nexus.

It is worth emphasizing that the Factor Presence Nexus (*see* section 3.3) has another advantage that the SDP proposal does not have: The Factor Presence Nexus can address the production side of the digital economy, whereas SDP cannot. The

---

that show the highest effective corporate tax rates – not traditional companies. Moreover, real-world data for effective corporate tax rates suggest that there is no systematic difference in income taxes paid by digital corporations compared to their traditional peers.'

583. Ruth Mason & Leopoldo Parada, The Legality of Digital Taxes in Europe, 40 Virginia Tax Review 1 (2020), 175.

584. Wei Cui, The Digital Services Tax: A Conceptual Defense, 73 Tax Law Review 69 (2019).

585. Anandapadmanabhan Unnikrishnan and Meyyappan Nagappan, Virtual Permanent Establishments: Indian Law and Practice, 46 Intertax 520 (2018). In this contribution at section 4.3.1, the authors cite one Indian ruling on a cargo network which has especially convincing reasoning:

> The portal designed by the applicant is hosted on its server in Singapore with Internet accessibility on one side to cargo agents and on the other side to different airways. The portal which is a complex, commercial, Internet site provides a gateway for processing requests for cargo booking to different airlines, and obtaining their acceptance. The use of portal is not possible without the use of server that provides Internet access to the cargo agents/subscribers on the one hand and to different airlines on the other hand for to and from communication. Therefore, the portal and the server together constitute integrated commercial-cum-scientific equipment and for obtaining Internet access to airlines the use of portal without server is unthinkable.

The use of a portal by clients (two sides: cargo agents and airlines) is integrated with the server via the internet. The cargo agents who use the portal are in India and cannot be separated from the use of the server. For the efforts of the US Congress to adopt a virtual PE, *see* Reuven S Avi-Yonah, Virtual PE: International Taxation and the Fairness Act, U of Michigan Public Law Research Paper (2013).

'Significant Digital Presence' proposal demonstrates an emphasis on 'users of digitalized services or digitalized intangibles', which refers to the market jurisdiction. The DST and SDP focus on the market side, i.e., customers or digital services/good users, but we should also be aware that in a digitalized economy environment, not only the customers and clients are influenced but also the workforce. With the help of the internet and algorithm platforms, it is now easier to mobilize human resources globally than ever before. Since the labour factor still plays an important role in the process of the value-creation chain, the attribution of workforce in the context of FA should take it into account.[586]

To sum up, the SDP Directive Proposal would have an overlapping function with the Factor Presence Nexus, since the users in market jurisdictions can be included in the sales factor. The SDP is justifiable by the benefit principle, but it would be redundant for the EU's FA regime when the above-mentioned factor presence nexus is adopted.

3.5.2 The Data Factor Is Not Needed as a Separate Factor Either

Around the same time when the European Commission issued the DST and SDP Directive Proposals, the European Parliament issued its amendment to the CCCTB Directive Proposal regarding FA. It is quite clear that the European Parliament is also quite aware of the difficulty of levying tax on the digital economy, so it proposed the fourth weighting factor, 'data factor', in the CCCTB Directive Proposal.[587] In response to the difficulty, the European Parliament proposed a fourth factor for the CCCTB formula, the 'data factor'.

Although the European Parliament's intention is benign, the 'data factor' is not needed for the EU's FA. I explain this below.

According to the European Parliament's report,[588] the data factor means 'the collection and exploitation for commercial purposes of personal data of online platforms and services users in one or more Member States'.[589] The consolidated tax base is to be shared between the group members in each tax year on the basis of a formula for apportionment. In determining the apportioned share of a group member A, the formula will take the following form, giving equal weight to the factors of sales, labour, assets *'and the data factor'* (emphasis added).

The question then arises: is it necessary to have a separate weighting factor to reflect the benefit of the jurisdiction where personal data is collected? Adopting a separate data factor in the formula is also a type of 'ring-fence' rationale to demonstrate the importance of 'data' by adding a separate factor.

586. As to platform workers in the digital economy in the labour factor, *see* the discussion in section 5.5 of this book.
587. 1 March 2018, on the proposal for a Council Directive on a Common Consolidated Corporate Tax Base (CCCTB) (COM(2016)0683 - C8-0471/2016 - 2016/0336(CNS)).
588. *See* the European Parliament's legislation website: http://www.europarl.europa.eu/sides/getDoc.do?type=REPORT&reference=A8-2018-0051&language=EN.
589. *See* the European Parliament's legislation website: http://www.europarl.europa.eu/sides/getDoc.do?type=REPORT&reference=A8-2018-0051&language=EN (28a).

From the perspective of the benefit theory, the answer is negative because the data factor proposed by the European Parliament for the CCCTB is just reaffirming the destination principle of the sales factor in the context of the digital economy to reflect the market of the service users of the online platforms. If the sales factor has an attribution rule which can reflect the jurisdiction where customers enjoy the service via the internet technology, the data factor seems redundant as a separate weighting factor.

Although the data factor might already overlap with the sales factor, it is insightful that the European Parliament acknowledges the important role that 'data' plays in the digital economy, and such acknowledgement should influence the design and interpretation of two other weighting factors from MNE taxpayers' input side. As to the assets factor, the personal data of customers are pooled with other relevant data (as big data) has become a type of valuable intangible, which could be analysed and redesigned as an advertisement package in the market or just be used internally for production or marketing.

Therefore, EU legislators should change the traditional design of the assets factor in the FA experiences that completely excludes 'intangibles' mainly due to administrative or tax abuse concerns.[590] As to designing the labour factor, from the perspective of the digital economy and the high value of 'personal data', input from human beings to analyse the big/personal data collected actually plays a more important role. Without being analysed by intellectual workforce, pure data has no value for the production process/input side. However, after the collected data is well analysed and studied, data can be very useful and valuable. Therefore, recognizing the power of big data reaffirms the justification to adopt the labour factor in a sharing formula. Human capital/human resources are still an essential element in the digital economy.[591] Fortunately, the European Commission will address intangibles in the assets factor in the tax reform package BEFIT, and this move is in the right direction.

To sum up, the data factor itself might not necessarily be a separate weighting factor, but the importance and value of personal data are reflected in MNE taxpayers' input side and output side in the current digital economy. This is because the digital economy has become the normality for MNE taxpayers. It would be native if we believe it is possible to 'ring fence' the digital economy.[592] The European Parliament's proposed 'data factor' indicates the right direction for designing other weighting factors in line with 'value creation' in the digital economy. Personal data is indeed an important feature of the digital economy, but personal data is merely mirroring the input and the output side of economic activities; it does not add an extra perspective to the input and the output side. When the sales factor, the assets factor, and the labour factor are designed according to economic activities to include intangibles and customers, the contribution from personal data in the digital economy would be embodied in the formula.

590. Olbert & Spengel, *supra* n. 40.
591. The same opinion, Eric CCM Kemmeren, Should the Taxation of the Digital Economy Really Be Different?, 27 EC Tax Review 72 (2018).
592. Devereux & Vella, *supra* n. 15.

3.6 UNHARMONIZED TAX RATE IN THE EU'S FA SYSTEM CAN STILL BE CONSISTENT WITH BENEFIT-BASED MARKET NEUTRALITY

3.6.1 International Tax Rate Competition Exists

In the current international tax environment based on SA, the phenomenon of corporate tax rate competition is already detected.[593] Tax competition is implemented in different forms to attract different types of FDI projects.[594] Tax rate competition is one example of attracting FDI.[595] Setting differential national tax rates means that countries have the freedom and incentives to compete for the taxable base by strategically altering their tax rates in order to attract economic operators' activities to their jurisdiction.

When sovereign states engage in tax competition, the extent of 'harmful tax competition'[596] or turning into a 'tax haven' which adopts a zero or extremely low-tax rate already harms other sovereign states' fiscal interests.

Harmful tax competition is contrary to the benefit principle because it will lead to a clear asymmetry between taxation paid and the public benefits enjoyed by taxpayers. MNE taxpayers pay too low an amount of tax to enjoy public benefits, and they directly profit from harmful tax competition. As Dagan observes,[597] the current tax competition between sovereign states has become a vicious circle of tax competition because states compete for FDIs by giving up their taxing rights. As discussed in Chapter 2, a well-functioning internal market is not free of charge but requires sufficient public benefits to maintain it. This is also why harmful tax competition that gives up taxing rights discriminatorily and unlimitedly could also hinder a well-functioning, competitive healthy market.

It is difficult to draw the line between sound tax competition and harmful tax competition, but Avi-Yonah's distinction criterion seems reasonable:[598] sound tax competition reflects policy preferences with democratic legitimacy, whereas harmful

593. Philipp Genschel & Peter Schwarz, Tax Competition: A Literature Review, 9 Socio-Economic Review 339 (2011).
594. Arjan Reurink & Javier Garcia-Bernardo, Competing for Capitals: The Great Fragmentation of the Firm and Varieties of FDI Attraction Profiles in the European Union, 28 Review of International Political Economy 5 (2020).
595. *See* Joeri Gorter & Ashok Parikh, How Sensitive Is FDI to Differences in Corporate Income Taxation Within the EU?, 151 De Economist 193 (2003). The data showed that there is a 4% increase in FDI in the jurisdiction if it is expected to be subject to lower income tax rate later. Different industry sectors have different responses to tax rate competition. *See* Sven Stöwhase, Tax-Rate Differentials and Sector-Specific Foreign Direct Investment: Empirical Evidence from the EU, 61 FinanzArchiv: Public Finance Analysis 535 (2005).
596. On the introduction of harmful tax competition in the EU context, *see* Kiekebeld, *supra* n. 202; for a survey of tax competition situations of EU Member States, *see* Schön, *supra* n. 200.
597. Dagan, *supra* n. 24; Reviews: Yariv Brauner, International Tax Policy: Between Competition and Cooperation, 22 Florida Tax Review 571 (2019); Laurens van Apeldoorn, A Sceptic's Guide to Justice in International Tax Policy, 32 Canadian Journal of Law & Jurisprudence 499 (2019).
598. Reuven S Avi-Yonah, Globalization, Tax Competition, and the Fiscal Crisis of the Welfare State, Harvard Law Review (2000), at 1626.

tax competition aims 'solely' to attract foreign investors and even adopts a zero or low-tax rate as a tax haven.

When there is sound tax competition, it is possible to have tax competition to be consistent with the benefit principle. Allowing sound tax competition between local governments will encourage local governments to provide the most cost-efficient public services to attract the most economic operators to move to the jurisdiction.[599] MNE enterprises might be even more sensitive to the tax system than individuals because they have stronger capacities than individuals to move to another jurisdiction.

Under sound tax competition, EU Member States would be able to learn from each other and agree on the best practice among their diversities. They would compete to provide better or more efficient public benefits and not surrender to over-competing just for some short-term FDI capital inflow.[600]

3.6.2 Race to the Bottom, Race to the Top, and Race to the Optimal Are All Possible in an FA System

Prior to the COVID-19 crisis in 2020, there was a trend of racing to the bottom of CIT rates, according to the empirical data.[601] According to empirical data, it seems that the intensity of tax competition between EU Members States is stronger[602] than between states in other regions and even stronger than competition between regions. Being/Becoming an EU Member State can even cause more intense tax competition,[603] especially between the new EU Member States.[604] However, Nicodème argued that the decline in tax rates as such does not lead to revenue deduction.[605] In any case, the EU's FA system would need to address the tax rate competition issue.

599. Charles M Tiebout, A Pure Theory of Local Expenditures, 64 Journal of Political Economy 416 (1956); Robin Boadway & Jean-François Tremblay, Reassessment of the Tiebout Model, 96 Journal of Public Economics 1063 (2012).
600. This argument is also the Commission's goal. *See* A ŠEMETA, EU Commissioner for Taxation and Customs Union, Audit and Anti-Fraud Competitive Tax Policy and Tax Competition in the EU '2nd Taxation Forum of Diario Economico/OTOC' (SPEECH/11/712 2011).
601. Empirical research by Michael Overesch & Johannes Rincke, What Drives Corporate Tax Rates down? A Reassessment of Globalization, Tax Competition, and Dynamic Adjustment to Shocks, 113 Scandinavian Journal of Economics 579 (2011).
602. Philipp Genschel, Achim Kemmerling & Eric Seils, Accelerating Downhill: How the EU Shapes Corporate Tax Competition in the Single Market, 49 Journal of Common Market Studies 585 (2011).
603. After enlargement in 2004, new EU Member States have intensified their tax competition. *See* Arjan Vliegenthart & Henk Overbeek, Corporate Tax Reform in Neoliberal Europe: Central and Eastern Europe as a Template for Deepening the Neoliberal European Integration Project?, in Bastiaan van Apeldoorn, Jan Drahokoupil & Laura Horn, *Contradictions and Limits of Neoliberal European Governance From Lisbon to Lisbon* (Palgrave Macmillan 2009), at 159: 'Enlargement has not in itself caused tax competition to emerge: it already existed well before accession. However, enlargement has in fact intensified the competitive pressures towards the lowering of corporate and income taxes.'
604. Dorothee Bohle, *Race to the Bottom? Transnational Companies and Reinforced Competition in the Enlarged European Union, Contradictions and Limits of Neoliberal European Governance* (Springer 2009).
605. Gaëtan Nicodème, Corporate Tax Competition and Coordination in the European Union: What Do We Know? Where Do We Stand, International Taxation Handbook 171 (2007).

There have also been concerns that adopting the harmonized tax base and FA under the –EU like CCCTB – would not deter tax competition.[606] Economists have created models to evaluate the consequences of possible tax rate competition in a harmonized EU FA system. Sørensen's model and data show that adopting a harmonized FA while still allowing differentiated tax rates would change the nature of the pre-existing tax competition. An FA in the EU might result in sharper tax competition but would lead to the result of a 'race to the top'.[607] The possible response of Member States' 'race to the top', i.e., creating inefficiently high rates of CIT, is also not desirable for the EU.

Pethig and Wagener[608] have concluded that race-to-the-bottom and race-to-the-top are both possible under an EU FA. Pethig and Wagener's model predicts that the different formulas would have different forms of tax competition. The property-based formula would tend to result in 'race to the bottom' tax competition, i.e., too low-tax rates; the sales-based formula and the payroll-based formula would tend to result in 'race to the top' tax competition, i.e., too high tax rates. Pethig and Wagener indicate that even after adopting FA, harmful tax competition would not be mitigated. Different formulas would just lead to different types of tax competition.

However, the existence of tax rate competition is still not a justification for harmonizing the tax rate for the EU's FA system. EU Member States are more competent in deciding their tax rate to sustain public service/benefits to maintain and implement the internal market, according to the EU's subsidiarity principle.[609] Implementing the subsidiarity principle does not mean providing unlimited fiscal autonomy; the subsidiarity principle should be exercised in line with the objective of pursing a well-functioning internal market and should not create new distortions. Empirically, some Member States have decided to increase their corporate tax rate after the COVID-19 crisis. For example, the Netherlands has increased its corporate tax rate from 25% to 25.8% in the financial year 2022[610] in order to levy more taxes; the UK also

606. Maarten De Wilde, Tax Competition within the European Union: Is the CCCTB Directive a Solution, 7 Erasmus Law Review 24 (2014); Maarten Floris de Wilde, Tax Competition Within the European Union Revisited – Is the Relaunched CCCTB a Solution?, in Weber & Streek (eds), *supra* n. 5.

607. Peter Birch Sørensen, Company Tax Reform in the European Union, 11 International Tax and Public Finance 91 (2004).

608. Rüdiger Pethig & Andreas Wagener, Profit Tax Competition and Formula Apportionment, 14 International Tax and Public Finance 631 (2007).

609. For discussions of the subsidiarity principle in the CCCTB, *see* Rita Szudoczky, Is the CCCTB Proposal in Line with the Principle of Subsidiarity?: Negative Opinions Submitted by National Parliaments in the 'Yellow Card Procedure', in Weber & the Amsterdam Centre for Tax Law (eds), *supra* n. 5. As Szudoczky analyses, the 13 negative reasoned opinions submitted by parliaments of the Member States have a common feature: these reasoned opinions are formulated as being more similar to discuss the proportionality of the element of consolidation of the CCCTB Directive Proposal, instead of arguing the two tests indicated in the impact assessment. Member States argue the same objectives, including that eliminating compliance costs from national tax law disparities and lowering high transfer-pricing costs should be achieved in a less intrusive way for Member States.

610. *See* the Dutch Tax Plan 2022, Wet van 22 December 2021 tot wijziging van enkele belastingwetten en enige andere wetten (Belastingplan 2022), at https://zoek.officielebekendmakingen.nl/stb-2021-651.html. It was decided in the budget plan in September 2021, *see* commentary in English by IBFD: Netherlands – Tax Plan 2022 – Netherlands Confirms Corporate Income

increased its CIT from April 2023.[611] These examples embody the necessity for EU Member States to keep the freedom to decide their own tax rate.

Therefore, a compromise solution to prevent distortions or tax havens is to coordinate tax competition. Member States are free to compete within a coordinated range which has been discussed and agreed by the Member States in advance.[612]

In addition, adopting a uniform tax rate for Member States is not consistent with the benefit principle. EU Member States are all different, and thus they tax differently to achieve the optimal status that sufficient public benefits are provided for the EU internal market.

In this regard, if the tax rate is not fully harmonized but coordinated in advance, there is a proper balance between the EU and Member States, and such balance would be a 'new source of legitimacy'[613] of tax harmonization of the internal market. In this regard, the Commission has made the right decision for the current CCCTB Directive Proposal. It is projected that the corporate tax rate will not be fully harmonized in the EU's BEFIT project.

In short, both 'race to the bottom' and 'race to the top' create inefficiencies and are not desirable. But tax competition under proper coordination can mitigate such inefficiencies and preserve the diversity of Member States and comply with the subsidiarity principle. Coordinated-tax competition is necessary.

3.6.3 Towards Tax Rate Coordination Based on Minimum Public Benefits to Achieve Market Neutrality: Adopting Multiple Factors

The scope of tax competition under the current CCCTB Directive Proposal is limited to tax rate. The tax rate is easier to observe and monitor if tax rate competition between Member States has turned into harmful tax competition.

The next question is what kind of coordination for tax rate competition is necessary. In this regard, the EU has followed the latest development by the OECD/G7

Tax Rates Will Remain Unchanged in 2022 (22 September 2021), News IBFD (accessed 13 February 2022), at https://research.ibfd.org/#/doc?url=/document/tns_2021-09-22_nl_3.

611. Corporation Tax charge and rates from 1 April 2022 and Small Profits Rate and Marginal Relief from 1 April 2023 at https://www.gov.uk/government/publications/corporation-tax-charge-and-rates-from-1-april-2022-and-small-profits-rate-and-marginal-relief-from-1-april-2023/corporation-tax-charge-and-rates-from-1-april-2022-and-small-profits-rate-and-marginal-relief-from-1-april-2023.

612. This would also be consistent with the value-creation principle in the BEPS Project, *see* Paolo Piantavigna, Tax Competition and Tax Coordination in Aggressive Tax Planning: A False Dichotomy, 9 World Tax Journal 477 (2017). Piantavigna uses the term 'a fair but fierce tax competition' to describe tax competition under proper coordination in the EU context.

613. Ricardo Garcia Anton, The Limits of Tax Sovereignty Imposed by the Interpretation of Supranational Law, in Pistone (ed.), *supra* n. 303. García Antón correctly indicates that the concept of the internal market under the EU law has diverse meaning, even from the case law of CJEU. The lack of an univocal definition of the internal market would require a new source of legitimacy that mutual trust can be built upon.

on a minimum global corporate tax rate[614] to adopt the Pillar Two Directive Proposal[615] to set a minimum corporate tax rate. The Pillar Two Directive Proposal is expected to be applicable to the new EU FA system when adopted. The minimum tax rate can ensure the provision of a minimum level of public benefits.

Moreover, empirical data show that EU Member States have used different tax measures to compete for different types of FDI, not only by reducing tax rates.[616] Member States can enact regulatory competition measures in other fields other than the CIT rate to attract foreign economic activities to their jurisdictions.[617]

In other words, while competing on the tax rate, the real target of tax competition between sovereign states is that they want to attract more 'tax base'. A harmonized FA system, especially a multiple-factor formula, can be an option to mitigate tax rate competition.[618] Member States have their own different strengths and need to attract different types of economic activities. Under the EU's FA system with equally weighted three factors, like the current CCCTB Directive Proposal, it would not be a zero-sum competition because the three-factor formula already represents sales, assets, and labour with which EU Member States can compete with their own strength.

To sum up, since minimum public benefits are necessary for the EU internal market, a minimum CIT rate[619] for Member States could be established to prevent any Member State from playing a 'race to the bottom' game. It is also consistent with the development of the international tax regime such as the OECD's Pillar Two Project.

3.7 CONCLUSIONS: BENEFIT-BASED MARKET NEUTRALITY POLICY OPTIONS

FA experiences in the international tax regime and US state taxation show that FA is an alternative way of allocating taxing rights to replace an all-or-nothing rationale. FA can represent the public benefits provided in the jurisdiction better than the traditional international tax regime.

The taxable nexus threshold of a PE is neither market neutral nor consistent with the benefit principle. I propose to use an activities-based, quantitative nexus threshold, i.e., the factor presence nexus, for the purpose of FA.

---

614. On 5 June 2021, G7 agreed the tax deal of a minimum corporate tax rate. *See* comments from the IMF https://blogs.imf.org/2021/06/09/the-benefits-of-setting-a-lower-limit-on-corporate-taxation/.
615. European Commission, *supra* n. 68.
616. Reurink & Garcia-Bernardo, *supra* n. 594.
617. Claudio M Radaelli, The Puzzle of Regulatory Competition, 24 Journal of Public Policy 1 (2004).
618. Dietsch, *supra* n. 483. While endorsing FA, Dietsch is quite critical of the single-sales-factor formula.
619. European Parliament, *supra* n. 117; comments by Nieminen, *supra* n. 117. For some supporting arguments for the minimum tax rate, *see* Ruud A De Mooij, A Minimum Corporate Tax Rate in the EU Combines the Best of Two Worlds, 39 Intereconomics 180 (2004). The opposite view, Clemens Fuest & Winfried Fuest, A Minimum Corporate Tax Rate Would Be Harmful for Both High and Low Tax Countries, 39 Intereconomics 183 (2004).

Due to the diversity of EU Member States' economic situations, adopting a multi-factor formula for the EU's FA regime is necessary and legitimate. The equally weighted three-factor formula could be designed to align value creation and economic activities, which would also be suitable in the context of the digital economy. The sales factor represents the output side; the assets factor and the labour factor represent the input side of taxpayers' activities.

With the same rationale of benefit-based MN, coordinated tax rate competition in combination with a minimum tax rate would be allowed under the EU FA system.

CHAPTER 4

Towards the Market-Neutral Sales Factor: A Customer-Centred Destination-Based Sales Factor

The weather was so stormy that the sailors said they saw the Flying Dutchman. The common story is that this Dutchman came to the Cape in distress of weather and wanted to get into harbour but could not get a pilot to conduct her [the ship St. Helen] and was lost and that ever since in very bad weather her vision appears.

Travels in Various Parts of Europe, Asia and Africa[620]

4.1 INTRODUCTION

4.1.1 The Sales Factor as the Most Controversial Factor in Formulary Apportionment

The main policy options of a typical FA were discussed in Chapter 3, including the justification for selecting factors in a formula and the debates on whether the EU FA regime should adopt the single-sales-factor formula like many US states. I concluded in Chapter 3 that it is justified to include the sales factor in a formula, but it is not justified to adopt a 'single sales factor formula' for the EU because the single-sales-factor formula ignores the production side, and it does not have the claimed built-in effect of encouraging growth according to new empirical data.[621] The formula should include the sales factor and be designed according to the sales-by-destination rationale, to reflect the taxpayer's response to its customers' demand in the market.

620. John Macdonald, Travels in Various Parts of Europe, Asia and Africa (1790), 276.
621. *See* Chapter 3.4.1 of this book.

The sales factor has always been the most controversial factor in the FA literature.[622] The controversy is not only about its claimed economic effect of attracting out-of-state investments by adopting the single-sales-factor formula but also about the nature of the sales factor that involves a 'flow of value' between group members in a unitary group.[623] So how to measure the unit of sales factor of each group member and how to decide the 'destination' of such flow would be crucial. Even prior to all the disputes regarding e-commerce or the digital economy, the sales factor had been complex when it came to services. Comparing it to the assets factor and the labour factor which usually involve physical items, the sales factor is based on 'receipts of remuneration', i.e., payment flows. Defining and attributing this flow is not easy. Besides, it is even more difficult to trace the 'flow of value' of cross-border services or intangibles than sales of tangible goods. This is why the sales factor is harder to attribute in its nature and causes more disputes.

The 'sales by destination' rationale is the underlying rationale of a benefit-based and market-neutral sales factor because it represents access to the customers' market. But what and where the sales by destination is, has been a difficult question. The sub-research questions in this chapter are: under benefit-based MN, what is the proper definition of 'sales' under the sales–by-destination rationale? And where is the 'destination' for the neutral sales factor that reflects the customers' market side?

The sales-by-destination principle might seem trivial and obvious, but the reality is the opposite. The chapter especially focuses on the situations that do not fully follow the destination rule: when sales are attributed not according to the destination rule based on the customers' physical location but by using proxies that are either 'origin' or a hybrid criterion. Even though these 'deemed' destinations are claimed in the name of the destination principle, they are not tax neutral for the sales. This chapter analyses practical examples in different (national/ regional) tax law systems, including VAT and the sales factor development in US state taxation that directly deviate from the 'sales by destination' rationale or indirectly deviate by using proxies other than the ultimate customers' physical location.

4.1.2 The Structure of This Chapter

From the literature on FA, the heated controversy about the sales factor arises from following aspects: (1) the definition of sales or 'gross receipts', (2) the throw-back rule for the no-taxed sales, (3) the attribution rule for gross receipts earned from services, which involves the illogical 'cost-of-performance' rule and complicated and diverse 'market-sourcing'. This chapter discusses each of these aspects in turn. By analysing the rules and practices of the sales factor under the current CCCTB Directive Proposal

622. Similar remarks, Charles E McLure Jr, How Should the UDITPA Sales Factor Treat Receipts from Transactions Involving Financial Instruments?, *The State and Local Tax Lawyer. Symposium Edition* (American Bar Association 2009).

623. This value of flow test is widely used in state taxation cases in USA to examine if there is a unitary business, *see* Weiner, *supra* n. 47.

and US state taxation, this chapter aims to provide recommendations for the EU's future FA of the new tax reform agenda.

This chapter is structured as follows: in section 4.2, I revisit the theoretical foundation to design the sales factor for the EU's FA regime. Although the destination principle seems dominant now, in the beginning in the US, attributing services for the sales factor did not follow the destination rationale. Only the attribution rules of sales of 'goods' followed the destination rationale in the US. Section 4.2 reiterates how the sales–by-destination rule has become the current paradigm, and such paradigm applies not only to sales of goods but also to services and all transactions in both the Business-to-Business (B2B) and Business-to-Consumer (B2C) contexts. Section 4.2 also clarifies that, when it is not convenient or not desirable to use customers' physical locations as the criterion of destination, the deviation to use other proxies is not consistent with the normative framework in Chapter 2.

In section 4.3, I analyse the different definitions of 'sales' and 'non-sales' under the current CCCTB Directive Proposal and US state taxation legislation and cases.[624] Since drafting of the current CCCTB Directive Proposal is greatly influenced by US state taxation, I especially delve into the development of and disputes about the definition of 'sales' in the US and how US experiences are transplanted into the current CCCTB Directive Proposal.

In section 4.4, I discuss further the attribution rule of sales in the US that deviate from the sales-by-destination rationale and explain why they are not tax neutral, even in the name of the destination principle. I discuss the throw-back rule to address the 'no-where sales' problem. These throw-back rules in the US have good intentions, but they make the sales attribution rules more complicated and make the results arbitrary. I also critically review the latest development of the MTC's regulations on 'market-sourcing' for services in the US.

In addition to the US, I also discuss the attribution rules of the EU VAT regime and the OECD VAT/Goods and Services Tax (GST) guidelines to demonstrate that the destination principle can be implemented in various ways but already deviates from the economic reality, so that it no longer reflects customers and the market. I especially analyse 'deemed destinations', which deviate from the locations of customers and demonstrate why these existing examples are not consistent with the benefit-based MN framework. These deviations might have good intentions, but they create undesirable results.

Section 4.5 focuses on the attribution of the sales factor in the digital economy because the digital economy has become the new reality and the most pressing challenge. I discuss the new emerging difficulties of attributing sales in the digitalized

624. As to the question of 'what the sales is', I will not discuss the definition of 'sales' in the context of VAT because VAT regimes do not really provide insights to the definition of 'sales', since VAT regimes usually just define taxable transactions broadly and are based on 'turnover' or 'consideration', calculated according to the price of each stage of a chain of transactions. *See* BJM Terra & Julie Kajus, A Guide to the European VAT Directives: Volumes 1&2 (2019), at Chapter 7.

J. Kollmann, *The European Value Added Tax System in Taxable Supplies and Their Consideration in European VAT: With Selected Examples of the Digital Economy* (IBFD 2019).

era. It is even more difficult to trace the value flow from a digitalized business activity, and the digitalized business is actually the new normal in a globalized world. Nowadays, no MNE would conduct business activities in a 'non-digitalized' way.[625]

Under the current CCCTB Directive Proposal, which is largely based on the traditional international tax law prototype, to attribute the sales factor from these digitalized industries might be difficult. Even when we uphold the sales-by-destination principle, we will need to clarify what and where the customers' market is to design a market-neutral attribution rule for the sales factor. Such difficulty is not only a special problem for the regional FA systems like the current CCCTB Directive Proposal or state taxation in the US but also a prevalent problem for the current VAT regimes.

4.2 DECIPHERING THE THEORY OF THE SALES-BY-DESTINATION RATIONALE: 'THE CUSTOMERS' MARKET'

4.2.1 'Sales by Destination': Representing Taxpayers' Response to Their Customers

The fundamental theory to uphold the sales factor in a sharing formula is to represent the output side, so that the sales factor also counterbalances the input side (the assets and the labour factor of the sharing formula).[626] The sales factor, just like the labour factor and the assets factor, would create a taxable nexus, as discussed in Chapter 3.[627] The rationale of representing the market side is also embodied in the valuation method of the sales, and 'market value' is the ultimate key.[628]

The sales factor reflects the taxpayers' customers' market which means the 'sales by destination' idea is the only logical and tax-neutral option because the sales factor

---

625. As De la Feria describes, '*The digital economy is no longer just a part of the economy but is becoming the actual economy itself.*' *See* Rita De La Feria, EU Tax Rules Are Not Currently Prepared for the Digital Economy (European Economic and Social Committee official website, 5 August 2017), https://www.eesc.europa.eu/en/news-media/press-releases/eu-tax-rules-are-not-currently-prepared-digital-economy.
626. Hellerstein, Hellerstein & Swain, *supra* n. 349, 8.06[3] Receipts or Sales Factor.
627. *See* Chapter 3 of this book.
628. The valuation of sales under the 2016 CCCTB Directive proposal refers to Article 20 of 2016 CCTB Directive Proposal.
   Article 20 of 2016 Common Corporate Tax Base (emphasis added):

   1. The tax base shall be calculated on the basis of the following elements:
      (a) the monetary consideration for the transaction, such as the price of the goods sold or the services provided;
      (b) the market value, where the consideration for the transaction is wholly or partly non-monetary;
      (c) the market value, in the case of a non-monetary gift;
      (d) the market value of financial assets and liabilities held for trading.
   2. The tax base, including revenues and expenses, shall be expressed in EUR during the tax year or on the last day of the tax year, at the annual average exchange rate for the calendar year issued by the European Central Bank or, if the tax year does not coincide with the calendar year, at the average of daily observations issued by the European Central Bank through the tax year.
   3. Paragraph 2 shall not apply to a taxpayer in a Member State that has not adopted the EUR.

has to reflect the demand side of the market, not the production side.[629] 'Customers' and their physical location are the core elements for deciding the neutral sales factor. In short, maintaining the customers' market is the public benefit provided by the state, and this justifies the sales factor in the formula; thus, for attributing the sales factor, the destination of the customers' market is where the customers enjoy the goods or service or intangibles, i.e., the physical location(s) of customers.

To design the definition and the destination of the sales factor, it is essential to establish 'what' and 'where' the customers' market is that the taxpayer is responding to. This question is not always easy to answer. To define the scope of the sales factor, it is essential to decide what the relevant customers' market really is. It is necessary to check if the amount of money received from a specific transaction is the result of its MNE taxpayers' response to its customers. Only when the answer is in the affirmative can such item be defined and included in the sales factor. When the amount of money received is the result of non-economic activities or the result that the MNE taxpayer itself 'being' the customer, such item should not be defined as sales, even where the amount of money received looks like it was earned in the form of a sales-purchase transaction.

4.2.1.1 In-State Market Jurisdiction as Destination: VAT and DBCFT

The concept of 'destination' has been widely used in different fields of tax law. A typical example is VAT and other types of consumption tax. VAT is a broad-based consumption tax and (at least theoretically) the tax base is 'consumption'. In the consumption tax context, destination is a synonym for 'market', i.e., where consumption takes place. In the general sense of indirect taxation, sales tax and VAT as such both follow the destination principle. The meaning of the destination principle in VAT is: only in-state consumption or sales is subject to such tax, and export (i.e., the destination is in another foreign jurisdiction) is not subject to such tax or subject to

629. This is because the single-sales-factor formula is not the option; if we adopt the single-sales-factor formula, it will need the sales factor to represent both destination and origin.

See discussions about the definition of gross receipts, Shirley Sicilian, Multistate Tax Commission Report of Multistate Tax Compact Article IV Recommended Amendments, 3 May 2012, at 16:

It's generally agreed that the purpose of the sales factor is to reflect the taxpayer's market activity, not its production activity. If that is the case, then the type of receipts that are included in the sales factor should be those that reflect the contribution of the taxpayer's market to the earning of income. It is unnecessary, and maybe counter-productive, to include receipts from transactions involving the taxpayer's production property – such as plant, machinery, and equipment – in the sales factor. Including receipts from these types of assets would not reflect the market for the taxpayer's product and could essentially double count the property factor. In a three-factor apportionment formula, the sales factor is intended to balance the property and payroll factors, and it should be defined to offset rather than amplify the contributions of the production states. If the Executive Committee were to adopt a single sales factor, then this analysis may be different. In that case, it may be reasonable to provide for some reflection of the contributions of production states, even if that is accomplished through the sales factor.

The report is archived online and can be requested at the MTC official website http://www.mtc.gov/.

zero-rating.[630] The OECD VAT guidelines also reiterate the fundamental role of 'the destination principle' in the field of VAT.[631] The EU VAT system has also expressly followed the destination principle in two senses: first, levying tax on consumption in the market; second, adopting zero-rated VAT on exports.[632] The OECD and the EU VAT regimes influence the developments of each other,[633] and the destination principle is the consensus in the OECD VAT guidelines and the EU VAT regime, at least in theory.

Besides being inspired by VAT, there are emerging academic discussions and a proposal on a new type of tax, 'Destination Based Cash Flow Tax' (DBCFT).[634] For this book, DBCFT itself does not provide any additional valuable insights into the concept of 'destination'. In the DBCFT context, the destination concept is extremely simple and merely means 'only levying tax based on imported cash flow and exempting the export cash flow'. In other words, DBCFT follows the general idea of VAT regarding 'exempting export', but it does not copy any considerations regarding proxies of seeking consumption from VAT. The destination of DBCFT just refers to the cashflow 'imported' destination.

DBCFT is an example reaffirming that 'destination' is a relative concept that can be formulated differently for different purposes. Therefore, even though the DBCFT proposal was expected to solve the problem of the current international tax system, the destination principle concept proposed by DBCFT does not provide further instructions for an FA system. Therefore, DBCFT will not play an important role in this chapter in the discussion of sales destination for the EU's FA regime.

4.2.1.2 The Destination of the Sales of Goods, Services, and Intangibles Should Be the Same

In the literature, the attribution rules of the sales factor are broken down into two categories: sales of goods and services, and sometimes there is a third category of licensing or assigning intangibles. For example, a typical VAT regime has only two categories: sales of goods and services; intangibles-related issues are within the scope of 'services'. Adopting three categories (sales of goods, services, and intangibles) is

630. OECD International VAT/GST Guidelines, 2017, at 1.9, hereafter OECD VAT/GST Guidelines.
631. Hereafter OECD VAT/GST Guidelines, at 1.8.
632. Alan Schenk, Victor Thuronyi & Wei Cui, *Value Added Tax: A Comparative Approach* (2nd ed., Cambridge University Press 2015), 48-49.
633. The close relation is mainly because EU takes part in the work of OECD. It is quite common for EU VAT scholars to compare EU VAT and OECD VAT guidelines, such as Lamensch, European Commission's New Package of Proposals on E-Commerce: A Critical Assessment, 28 International VAT Monitor (2017).
634. Introduction of DBCFT, *see* Johannes Becker & Joachim Englisch, A European Perspective on the US Plans for a Destination Based Cash Flow Tax, University of Oxford Centre of Business Taxation Working Papers (2017); Alan Auerbach & others, Destination-Based Cash Flow Taxation WP 17/01, University of Oxford Centre of Business Taxation Working Papers (2017); Wei Cui, Destination-Based Cash-Flow Taxation: A Critical Appraisal, 67 University of Toronto Law Journal 301 (2017); David S Miller, Tax Planning Under the Destination Based Cash Flow Tax: A Guide for Policymakers and Practitioners, 8 Columbia Journal of Tax Law 295 (2017).

especially popular in the discussions of state taxation practice in the US[635] and international trade law that the World Trade Organization agreements are based on: General Agreement on Tariffs and Trade (GATT) and Agreement on Trade-Related Aspects of Intellectual Property Rights (TRIPS).

Conceptually, goods, services, and intangibles are provided and delivered in a different manner, so the attribution rules of them are different. Sales of goods leave the sellers' control after delivery. But services are controlled by the service provider from delivery to completion. Intangibles fall between sales of tangible goods and providing services and can be in the form of both sales (assigning the right to use) and services (licensing the right to use). It is also possible that a transaction of an intangible combines sales and services, for example, purchasing an application and enjoying the update and patches which are provided by the seller and can be downloaded.

The different features of goods, services, and intangibles have no effect on attributing the sales factor, especially in the digital economy. The destination principle applicable to goods, services, and intangibles is actually the same. In this Chapter, I still distinguish them to follow the practice in the literature. In section 4.4 and section 4.5, the discussions are still broken into three categories: goods, services, and intangibles.

4.2.1.3 The Sales by Destination Principle Should Apply Equally to B2B and B2C Transactions

In the current examples of deciding on the destination of sales (including EU VAT and US MTC Regulations), it is common to see legislators or rule-makers distinguish between B2B services and B2C services; or distinguish electronically delivered versus non-electronically delivered situations. It turned out that there are various proxies used for seeking destinations in current practice, and they do not necessarily represent the spirit of seeking consumption or customers but are chosen for convenience.

The distinction between B2B and B2C does not help deciding the market destination, nor contribute to selecting the proper proxy.[636] What really matters when deciding the neutral attribution rule of the sales factor is not to rigidly follow any specific field of tax law. Instead, the sales factor under the tax neutrality framework focuses on how taxpayers' customers make use of their services in a location. Although it is undeniable that to decide 'destination', we need some proxies, we should carefully choose the proxies which reflect the services being enjoyed by MNE taxpayers' customers and not choose the proxies which reflect taxpayers' contribution origin simply due to the concern about compliance because the labour and the assets factor already reflect the origin more properly. So, proxies that are in line with the neutrality requirement should be 'customer-based', not 'supplier- based'.

635. For example, although section 17 of MTC Regulation IV regulates the attribution rules for the service and intangibles in the same section, they are in different subsections. *See* section 4.4 of this.

636. Similar opinion to abolish the distinction between B2B and B2C service for searching market destination, John A Swain, Reforming the State Corporate Income Tax: A Market State Approach to the Sourcing of Service Receipts, 83 Tulane Law Review 285 (2008); Millar, *supra* n. 485.

The rationale of refocusing on customers is also reflected in the latest development in EU VAT reform and US reform on the sales factor. In the digital economy, many B2B businesses are actually targeting the same group of 'individual customers'. Therefore, when selecting proxies for destination, the physical locations of individual customers will play a more important role now than in the past.

4.2.2 The Paradigm Shift from the Origin Principle to the Destination Rationale for Service

4.2.2.1 The Sales by Destination Was Not the Only Policy Option in the US

The sales-by-destination logic for the sales factor might seem obvious, but it is not the case in history.[637] For example, in the draft discussions of UDITPA in the US in the mid-1950s, there were five options regarding the sales of goods, including:

(1) destination - sales shipped into or delivered to customers in the state;
(2) origin - sales of goods shipped from a location in the state;
(3) sales office - sales arising from negotiations at, from, or through an office or other place of business in the state;
(4) sales activity - sales resulting from employee activity in the state; and
(5) place of acceptance - sales responsive to orders accepted in the state.

At the end for the sales of goods, the sales-by-destination rationale was adopted. However, for services, UDITPA adopted a completely different approach.

4.2.2.2 The US's Outdated View on the Origin-Based Attribution Rule for Services (Cost-of-Performance Rule)

In the historical development of the FA system in the US, the attribution rules of the sales factor regarding services are different from the attribution of sales of goods. It might look quite illogical, the sales factor of providing services did not follow the sales-by-destination rule but instead the 'income-producing activity test', i.e., the COP. More specifically, the COP rule is regulated in section 17 UDITPA. Section 17 UDITPA provides a different idea of attributing sales of non-tangible properties, such as services and intangibles. Section 17 UDITPA provides 'the income-producing activity rule' to decide the attribution of the sales arising from intangibles or services. In other words,

637. *See* Hellerstein, Hellerstein & Swain, *supra* n. 349, 9.18[1], citing the historical record the Willis Committee Report, Special Sub-commission on State Taxation of Interstate Commerce of the House Comm. on the Judiciary, 'State Taxation of Interstate Commerce,' HR Rep. No. 1480, 88th Cong., 2d Sess. (1964); HR Reps. Nos. 565 and 952, 89th Cong., 1st Sess. (1965) [paginated 1-1255, A1-A752], at 181-183. In the CCCTB working documents, there were two options on the discussion table: sales-by-destination and sales by origin, *see* CCCTB Working Document No. 52.

the sales of the intangibles or services are attributed to the state where the income-generating activities take place.

As indicated above, the sales by destination did not apply to attributing services when UDITPA and MTC Regulations entered into force.[638] Such approach was a historical and political result. In the mid-twentieth century, the manufacturing-centred economy was the main economy in the US. Therefore, the receipts from services of UDITPA were attributed by the simple means of depending on the costs of the income-producing activities and attributing them to the jurisdiction where the majority of costs are spent.[639] The COP rule is an all-or-nothing rule. The one single jurisdiction that has the majority of the COP will be attributed to all the receipts earned from the service.[640] Moreover, there is no comparable 'throwback rule' in the sales factor for services because the attribution will be purely based on where the costs of performing the services are spent, and thus it is not necessary to design a 'throwback' rule.

The 'income producing activity rule/cost of performance' has been criticized for being contrary to the fundamental theory of the sales factor of FA.[641] The costs of income producing activities reflect the production side of the activities and overlap with labour costs. When there are plural states where income producing activities take place, it is quite possible that the one state in which the 'most' costs of production activities are spent may only exceed other states to a very small extent.

In fact, the drafters of the UDITPA were aware of the problem of the income producing activity rule because they had already excluded several service industries, such as financial institutions, from the scope of application of the UDITPA, and they also affirmed that the results of the income producing activity rule might be unfair and thus subject to equitable apportionment. The drafters of the UDITPA originally designed section 17 for attributing 'in-person services', not for 'non-in-person services', let alone computer and data processing services. The UDITPA drafters simply did not expect that the problems of the income producing activity rule would cause such large problems later.

When it comes to a cross-border service, it is more difficult to stick to the COP rule. Even in the pre-Internet era, there were various types of services with a mobility feature, such as transportation services: trucking, airlines, railroad transportation;

638. The history of UDITPA and MTC's attribution rules for services in the sales factor, *see* Pomp, *supra* n. 345, at 10-1.
639. For example, when taxpayers' income producing activities take place in three states, and the whole costs are divided as 30%, 35%, 25%. Only the state with 35% of the COP can be attributed to 100% of the receipts earned from providing services.
640. For example, if the taxpayer's income is business income, receipts from intangibles, such as patents and copyrights, will be attributed to the state where the patents and copyrights are managed because it is the state where the 'income producing activities' are performed. For another example, if the taxpayer's receipts arise from the performance of services, the receipts should be attributed to the state where the costs of these income-generating activities are spent. If the services are performed in more than one state, the receipts of the services will be attributed to the state where the activity costs are spent the most. There is only one single state which is attributed to the whole receipts/sales of performing services. It is an 'all-or-nothing' rule.
641. The COP rule has caused distortions, *see* Scott J Heyman & Marc Weinstein, Calculating the Sales Factor for Service Businesses, 4. The State and Local Tax Lawyer, 35 (1999).

media industry: television and broadcasting; publishing, advertising, etc. This flaw in the COP rule led to a prevailing phenomenon that in the US, states as well as the MTC adopted various special formulas for many service industries to replace the COP rule because the COP rule created unfair results.[642] A typical example is the MTC's special industry formula for financial institutions in 1994: its sales (receipts) factor is designed to reflect both 'money-centre state' and 'market state'.[643]

To sum up, the COP rule is theoretically faulty and non-proportionately attributes the receipts to one single state. This is also one of the reasons why the sales factor has been the most controversial factor in US state taxation.[644] The design of the COP rule is based on administrative reasons in the mid-twentieth century when the drafters could not envision that cross-border services could take place so frequently and so extensively throughout the world. Therefore, the reform of the COP rule was found to be necessary, and it is indeed the trend in practice.[645]

4.2.2.3 The US's Paradigm Shift Towards the Destination Rule for Services (Market Sourcing)

Many states in the US have adopted different rules to replace section 17 UDITPA. This new trend to adopt market-based sourcing for attributing the sales factor earned from performing services has created more diversities and thus needs some efforts aimed at creating uniformity.[646] In July 2014, Article IV section 17 MTC was amended. Article IV section 17 MTC adopted a totally different approach from the income producing activity/COP rule. The new method is the market-sourcing rule.[647] The contents of Article IV section 17 MTC and its implementation regulation[648] are lengthy and

642. Hellerstein, Hellerstein & Swain, *supra* n. 349, at 10.02. Regarding industry formulas, *see* Chapter 7 of this book.
643. *See* discussions in section 7.2.4 of this book.
644. Elizabeth C Burton, Importance of the Scales Factor, 1 Corporate Business Taxation Monthly 18 (1999).
645. Michael S Schadewald, Apportionment Rules Evolve as Business Environment Changes, 85 Taxes 39 (2007).
646. Examples from different states, *see* Catherine A Battin, Maria P Eberle & Lindsay M LaCava, Demystifying the Sales Factor: Market-Based Sourcing, State Tax Notes (2014); for developments, *see* comments by Blaise M Sonnier & Ricardo Colon, The Apportionment of Income from Licensing of Intangibles under MTC's Proposed Market-Based Sourcing Regulations, 35 Journal of State Taxation 23 (2016); Todd Lard & Stephanie Do, States Fine-Tune Market-Based Sourcing Rules Through Regulation 68 Tax Executive 29 (2016); Kelli P Murphy, Michigan Business Tax Apportionment and Sales Sourcing Provisions, 53 Wayne Law Review 1395 (2007).
647. Commentary and explanation of the reform, Richard Pomp's final hearing report, published also as Richard D Pomp, Reforming a State Corporate Income Tax, 32 Journal of State Taxation 13 (2013).
648. MTC model Regulation is the implementing regulation for MTC Article IV, so it contains more comprehensive rules to attribute sales of different types of the intangibles and services. The new section 17 will fully embrace the market-sourcing approach and abolish the costs of performance rule. The implementing regulation is approved in February 2017, so I discuss further on the new model regulation of implementing section 17 MTC Article IV. *See* Michael S Schadewald, Multistate Tax Commission's Market-Sourcing Regulations: Will They Promote Uniformity, 95 Taxes 23 (2017).

complex by selecting different proxies, but the underlying rationale coincides with the sales-by-destination rule.[649]

In my view, such complexity of the sales attribution rules for services is inevitably influenced by the prevailing trend[650] of the states adopting the single-sales-factor formula. The reformed MTC also allows different weightings for each factor.[651] When the sales factor is the only indicator of apportioning multistate income, the attribution rules would inevitably be very complex in order to fairly reflect the different states' interests involved in the supply chain. Fortunately, the starting point is correct: adopting the destination rule and seeking the 'market'.

From a survey of US state taxation of 2019, there is a trend that more and more states are adopting market-sourcing rules based on customers' activities (i.e., where the service is received),[652] not rules based on taxpayers' activities.[653] With thanks to Sicilian and Huddleston's article,[654] a summary of the market-sourcing rules until January 2019 is as follows (Table 1).

649. The MTC Regulation IV section 17 has two sets of important new rules useful for the CCCTB Directive. One is the new attribution rule for various types of services to ascertain the 'market' of the sales earned from the services (section 17(d) of MTC Reg. IV). The other is the rule for attributing the receipts from licensing and sales of intangibles (section 17(e) of MTC Reg. IV).
650. *See* section 3.4.2 of this book about USA's state taxation FA overview.
651. Section 9 of Multistate Tax Compact Article IV (as of February 2017).
652. The state Texas is a good example of the trend toward to adopting customer-based proxies to attribute the service. From the survey, Texas seems to still have the sourcing rules based on taxpayers' activities instead of customers, *see* Kenneth Laks, Sales Allocation Methods: Cost of Performance vs. Market-Based Sourcing, 89 CPA Journal 12 (2019).

But Texas has been reducing application of the income-producing rule in practice and extensively applies the market sourcing for attributing service to specific industries involving audience, such as advertisement or telephone companies. So, in reality, even though Texas seems to still adopt the traditional income-producing rationale, it also considers 'end-product act' that refers to the location of customers. In my view, it is also evidence that the (customer-centered) destination rationale has stronger and stronger influence. *See* Ray Langenberg & Matt Jones, Sourcing Service Receipts for Franchise Tax Apportionment in Texas, 49 Mary's Law Journal 583 (2017).
653. The survey in 2013 already shows this, *see* Michael S Shadewald, More States Adopt Market-Based Rule for Sourcing Sales of Services, 32 Journal of State Taxation 5 (2013).
654. Regarding this 2019 states taxation survey, *see* Sicilian & Huddleston, *supra* n. 387.

Table 1 A Survey of States' Rules for Sourcing Services in 2019

Market-Based Sourcing Customer Activity	*Market-Based Sourcing Taxpayer Activity*	*Cost of Performance*
Benefit Received	Service Delivered	- Alaska
- Arizona	- Alabama	- Arkansas
- California	- Colorado	- Delaware
- Georgia	- District of Columbia	- Florida
- Indiana	- Kentucky	- Idaho
- Iowa	- Louisiana	- Kansas
- Michigan	- Massachusetts	- Mississippi
- Missouri	- Montana	- North Carolina
- New Jersey	- New Hampshire	- North Dakota
- New York	- New Mexico	- Virginia
- Ohio	- Oregon	- West Virginia
- Rhode Island	- Pennsylvania	
- Utah	- Tennessee	
- Washington	- Vermont	
- Wisconsin	Service Performed	
Service Received	- New Jersey	
- Illinois	- South Carolina	
- Maine	- Texas	
- Minnesota		
Service Used		
- Connecticut		
- Hawaii		
Customer Located		
- Maryland		
- Nebraska		
- Oklahoma		

Source: Reproduced from Shirley K Sicilian and Joe B Huddleston (2020), *supra* n. 387, Table 2.2.

In section 4.2.3, I further elaborate on how the MTC's latest market-sourcing regulation (in fact as a recommendation for states) selects proxies to decide the market.

4.2.3 Proxies of Deemed Destination

Ascertaining the location(s) of individual customer(s) that receive goods or services has been difficult and complex for tax administrations. The difficulty in implementing the destination principle to services is not a brand-new issue. Even in the pre-Internet era, it was already a difficult issue, just as it is in the digital economy era. Therefore, legislators and scholars have admitted that it is administratively difficult, if not impossible, to fully implement the destination principle, which is why there are various 'proxies' which act as a substitute for 'destination' or 'where customers consume the goods/service'.[655]

This difficulty is intensified due to the rapid development of the Internet and consequent complications of all kinds of 'services' in a digital economy, especially when these involve the 'cloud'. It is disputable where the 'destination' of services actually is.[656] For example, cloud computing services, such as Drop-box/iCloud, or share economy platforms/intermediaries, such as Uber and Airbnb, have changed the business models of providing services. Many online services, such as Facebook, are provided in the form of 'free usage', while service providers earn income from advertising. These digitalized MNEs have customers/clients from all over the world, and the current FA and VAT rules both have difficulties in levying tax on digitalized MNEs properly.

Even for the purpose of administrative feasibility, selecting proxies for deemed destinations should still be cautious. Proxies should as closely as possible represent the ultimate customers' physical locations, and not merely function for administrative convenience. Neither market sourcing based on the destination principle nor the origin-based rule is inherently 'simpler' or 'less burdensome'.[657] Therefore, the administrative burden argument might not be the fundamental guideline but only the secondary guideline when designing the attribution rule.

In section 4.4, I demonstrate different proxies for attributing deemed destinations, and I explain why some proxies are not neutral for the sales factor.

4.3 THE DEFINITION OF THE SALES AND CONCERNS[658]

4.3.1 The Sales Factor Represents Taxpayers' Response to the Market by Receiving Remuneration

In the literature and practice in the US, since the terms sales factor and 'receipts' factor are interchangeable, I use the term sales as the main reference below.

As Chapter 3.4. demonstrates the sales factor is designed to reflect MNE taxpayers' market of their customers or clients, i.e., remuneration for taxpayers' providing goods or services. In other words, the sales factor reflects MNE taxpayers' response to demand, i.e., their customers and clients.

From the perspective of the benefit principle, the relevant public benefit is maintaining a customers' market. Moreover, the sales factor counterbalances the

655. Madeleine Merkx, *Establishments in European VAT* (Kluwer Law International 2013), at Chapter 2 and accompanying footnotes.
656. Michael Devereux & John Vella, Implications of Digitalization for International Corporation Tax Reform. University of Oxford Centre for Business Taxation, WP 17/07, Oxford UK (2017).
657. Swain, *supra* n. 636.
658. These paragraphs are used in Shu-Chien Chen, Tax Avoidance in the Sales Factor: Comparison Between the CCCTB and USA's Formulary Apportionment Taxation, Indian Journal of Tax Law (2017).

classical income-generating factors: capital and labour. The sales factor represents the demand side of the market and thus is justified.[659]

It seems that 'all' receipts earned from taxpayers' customers could and should be included in the sales factor. However, when monetary receipts are not the result of a response to the market, they should be excluded from the sales factor, even though these receipts are in the legal form of receipts in a sales-purchase contract or service provision contract.

Although the question is: what are 'sales' or 'receipts' that should be defined in the sales factor, it is difficult to provide a descriptive definition of 'sales'. As the flip side of the coin, what is not 'sales' in the context of FA? I continue this discussion in the following section.

4.3.2 Excluding 'non-sales' from the Sales Factor Is Market Neutral

The question of 'what should be excluded from the sales factor' has been addressed in two ways in the US. The first is to provide an 'exclusion list' of non-sales; the second is to adopt a 'throw-out' rule to exclude items from the numerator and denominator of the sales factor, mainly applicable to the intangible income such as interest, royalties, and dividends. The current CCCTB Directive Proposal adopts a hybrid approach combining these two, and it is quite understandable due to the legal transplantation process.[660]

Designing an exclusion list or a throw-out rule is not contrary to benefit-based MN. However, in some occasions, items are excluded from the sales factor, not because they do not respond to the market, but simply due to difficulties or uncertainty in attributing a correct destination. There are disputes, especially about intangibles. The design based on mere administrative convenience or a practical compromise is not consistent with the benefit principle because it gives up seeking the economic reality.

Although the legislation technique of adopting a list seems to provide certainty, it does not always follow a convincing underlying theory. Consequently, the MTC will need to continuously update and amend the list, in response to emerging new forms of transactions.

Furthermore, when a disputed monetary receipt is not on the exclusion list, a court will have to rule on the issue, but a court's decision is not always satisfactory, due to the imitation of the text of legislation; so, the court usually decides to exclude or partially exclude an item while answering the question of 'fairness' on a case-by-case

659. Weiner, *supra* n. 47.

660. *See* the historical record of CCCTB written by one of the American expert Joanna Weiner hired by the European Commission. Joann Martens Weiner, The Dream Is Alive: EU Tax Policy with a Common Consolidated Corporate Tax Base and Formulary Apportionment, in Krever & Vaillancourt (eds), *supra* n. 46.

From the European Commission's CCCTB working documents, it is clear that opinion from US experts play an important role. From the text of 2011 and 2016 CCCTB Directive Proposal, it is also evident that European Commission has adopted many comparable legal concepts in US state taxation.

basis instead of raising the fundamental question of who defines terms for the exclusion list.

Therefore, excluding and including items from the sales factor consistently is the only way to ensure the MN of the sales factor. The MTC's sales factor exclusion list for development shows the dynamic between legislators and courts on this issue, but benefit-based MN is not yet achieved.

4.3.2.1 The MTC's Exclusion List in 2001: Justifiable But Lacks a Consistent Rationale

In the beginning, in the US, MTC[661] decided the definition of receipts/sales by means of a list that excludes items 'that are not sales'. Such exclusion list has been developed and amended several times through time, with the result that the exclusion list has become longer and longer. It is worthwhile to revisit the historical development of this exclusion list for sales.

Under Article 15(a) MTC Regulation IV: 'gross receipts' means the amounts realized via various transactions, including 'sale or exchange of property', 'the performance of services', or 'the use of property or capital'. In other words, 'gross receipts' includes gross amounts of remuneration from all kinds of a taxpayer's business activities.

In 2001, Article 2(a)(5) MTC Regulation IV was amended, so there was a new definition of 'gross receipts'. In the amendment, there are 10 items expressly excluded from the sales factor, even if they are earned in the form of business income. The list of exclusions is not exhaustive but gives examples as guidance.[662]

These 10 items in the exclusion list are:

(1) repayment, maturity, or redemption of the principal of a loan, bond, or mutual fund or certificate of deposit or similar marketable instrument;
(2) the principal amount received under a repurchase agreement or other transaction properly characterized as a loan;
(3) proceeds from issuance of the taxpayer's own stock or from sale of treasury stock;
(4) damages and other amounts received as the result of litigation;
(5) property acquired by an agent on behalf of another;
(6) tax refunds and other tax benefit recoveries;
(7) pension reversions;
(8) contributions to capital (except for sales of securities by securities dealers);
(9) income from forgiveness of indebtedness; or

661. Section 15 of UDITPA (of the 1957 version) does not provide a definition of 'sales' or 'gross receipts', but the MTC's model regulation further provides more guidance about the sales factor.
662. The old version of the MTC Regulations before 2017 amendment is available and can be requested at MTC official website http://www.mtc.gov/.

(10) amounts realized from exchanges of inventory that are not recognized by the Internal Revenue Code (IRC).

The exclusion list seems to follow several rationales. Several items obviously do not exchange value in a commercial market. For example, repayment of the principal of a loan, damages, and other amounts received such as the result of litigation, tax refunds, etc. There are items in the list which obviously do not exchange value. (Nos 4, 5, 6, 7, 9, 10 above.) There are items related to taxpayers' own capital contribution: proceeds from issuance of the taxpayer's own stock or from sale of treasury stock (No. 3 above) and contributions to capital (except for sales of securities by securities dealers) (No. 8 above).[663]

Roughly speaking, the definition of 'sales/gross receipts' in the MTC Regulations seems to exclude items that do not exchange value or do not contribute to the market. Since the sales-factor formula is expected to represent the taxpayers' response to their clients' demand, excluding exchange-no-value items from the sales factor will ensure tax neutrality.

However, when we use the rationale of 'exchange-no-value' to exclude items from the sales factor, we still confront difficulties regarding receipts from financial instruments: a repurchase agreement (the so-called Repos, No. 2 in the list above) and receipts from investing in marketable instruments, such as bonds, mutual funds, certificates of deposit, etc. (No.1 above). It is arguable that these receipts are still exchanging value in another separate financial market. Unfortunately, even the MTC's latest amendment report[664] did not address these questions directly either.

In my opinion, the exclusion list of MTC Regulation IV of 2001 has a theoretical deficiency: it is not completely consistent with the underlying rationale of the sales factor: reflecting the taxpayer's response to the demand side of the market. McLure also criticized two items about financial instruments (No.1 and No. 2 on the exclusion list) as lacking consistency and theoretical foundation.[665] The 'exchange no value' rationale cannot distinguish the sales factor from other financial transactions, such as hedging transactions and redemption of marketable securities. From the perspective of a legal form, hedging transactions and redemption of marketable securities are perfectly in the form of a series of sales-purchase transactions, and thus it is difficult to argue that these transactions are 'exchanging no value'.

---

663. Issuing stock or selling treasury stock are the means of financing for the company but do not exchange value in a commercial market. The same rationale is applicable to the taxpayer's contributions to capital, except for sales of securities dealers.
664. Model General Allocation & Apportionment Regulations with Amendments Submitted for Adoption by the Commission February 24, 2017, which can be requested at the MTC official website http://www.mtc.gov/.
665. Mclure, *supra* n. 622, at 111.

4.3.2.2 *The MTC's Exclusion List in 2014 and Onwards: Borrowing the Unitary Business Concept*

In 2014, the MTC further launched a reform project about the definition of sales. In the end, the definition of sales was renamed 'gross receipts' and amended:

> Receipts means all gross receipts of the taxpayer that are not allocated under paragraphs of this article, and that are received from transactions and activity in the regular course of the taxpayer's trade or business; except that receipts of a taxpayer from hedging transactions and from the maturity, redemption, sale, exchange, loan or other disposition of cash or securities, shall be excluded.[666]

In other words, the cash management activities (via short-term marketable securities) and risk management activities (via hedging transactions) are not included in the sales factor.[667]

Regarding the rationale of excluding hedging transactions and redemption of securities from the gross receipts (sales) factor, the explanation in the 2017 MTC Apportionment Regulation[668] asserts that 'the new definition explicitly excludes receipts that give rise to income that would meet the functional, but not the transactional,

666. Section 1(g) of Multistate Tax Compact Article IV.
MTC Hearing Officer's Report on definition of receipts (as requested at November 20 meeting), 3 December 2014 and the complete working documents of MTC's market-sourcing regulations can be requested at the MTC official website http://www.mtc.gov/.

667. Such exclusion is triggered by the two California cases whose disputes are in regard to 'inflating the sales factor' by excluding these two types of receipts. I discuss these two representative cases in the next section.

668. Reg. IV.2.(a)(6) 'Receipts' means all gross receipts of the taxpayer that are not allocated under paragraphs of Article IV and that are received from transactions and activity in the regular course of the taxpayer's trade or business. The following are additional rules for determining 'receipts' in various situations:

> (A) In the case of a taxpayer engaged in manufacturing and selling or purchasing and reselling goods or products, 'receipts' includes all gross receipts from the sales of such goods or products (or other property of a kind which would properly be included in the inventory of the taxpayer if on hand at the close of the tax period) held by the taxpayer primarily for sale to customers in the ordinary course of its trade or business. Gross receipts for this purpose means gross sales less returns and allowances.
> (B) In the case of cost plus fixed fee contracts, such as the operation of a government-owned plant for a fee, 'receipts' includes the entire reimbursed cost plus the fee.
> (C) In the case of a taxpayer engaged in providing services, such as the operation of an advertising agency or the performance of equipment service contracts or research and development contracts, 'receipts' includes the gross receipts from the performance of such services, including fees, commissions, and similar items.
> (D) In the case of a taxpayer engaged in the sale of equipment used in the taxpayer's trade or business, where the taxpayer disposes of the equipment under a regular replacement program, 'receipts' includes the gross receipts from the sale of this equipment. For example, a truck express company that owns a fleet of trucks and sells its trucks under a regular replacement program the gross receipts from the sale of the trucks would be included in 'receipts.'
> (E) In the case of a taxpayer with insubstantial amounts of gross receipts arising from sales in the ordinary course of business, the insubstantial amounts may be excluded from the receipts factor unless their exclusion would materially affect the amount of income apportioned to this state.
> (F) Receipts of a taxpayer from hedging transactions, or from holding cash or securities, or from the maturity, redemption, sale, exchange, loan or other disposition of cash or

test for apportionable income. 'By using the transactional and functional tests[669] for deciding the unitary business, MTC argues that hedging transactions and marketable securities transactions can only fulfil the 'functional test' (as the integral part of or 'related' to the taxpayer's business) but fail the transactional test (not a typical transaction of taxpayer's primary business). According to the MTC, these types of transactions cannot be included in the sales factor, even though they constitute the unitary business.

With the same rationale, 2017 MTC Apportionment Regulation further provides specific examples[670] that should always be excluded. According to the MTC, these items fulfil both the functional test and the transactional test for the unitary business, but they still should be excluded from the sales factor.[671] The exclusion list is still only illustrative. These items largely repeat the exclusion list in the MTC Regulation IV of 2001:

(1) damages and other amounts received as the result of litigation;
(2) property acquired by an agent on behalf of another;
(3) tax refunds and other tax benefit recoveries;
(4) contributions to capital;
(5) income from forgiveness of indebtedness;

---

securities, shall be excluded. Receipts arising from a business activity are receipts from hedging, if the primary purpose of engaging in the business activity is to reduce the exposure to risk caused by other business activities. Whether events or transactions not involving cash or securities are hedging transactions shall be determined based on the primary purpose of the taxpayer engaging in the activity giving rise to the receipts, including the acquisition or holding of the underlying asset. Receipts from the holding of cash or securities, or maturity, redemption, sale, exchange, loan or other disposition of cash or securities are excluded from the definition of receipts whether or not those events or transactions are engaged in for the purpose of hedging. The taxpayer's treatment of the receipts as hedging receipts for accounting or federal tax purposes may serve as indicia of the taxpayer's primary purpose, but shall not be determinative.

(G) Receipts, even if apportionable income, are presumed not to include such items as, for example:
1) damages and other amounts received as the result of litigation;
2) property acquired by an agent on behalf of another;
3) tax refunds and other tax benefit recoveries;
4) contributions to capital;
5) income from forgiveness of indebtedness;
6) amounts realized from exchanges of inventory that are not recognized by the Internal Revenue Code; or
7) Amounts realized as a result of factoring accounts receivable recorded on an accrual basis.

Exclusion of an item from the definition of 'receipts' is not determinative of its character as apportionable or non-apportionable income. Certain gross receipts that are 'receipts' under the definition are excluded from the 'receipts factor' under section IV.17. Nothing in this definition shall be construed to modify, impair or supersede any provision of section IV.18.

669. The unitary business is introduced in section 3.2.3 of this book.
670. Model General Allocation & Apportionment Regulations with Amendments Submitted for Adoption by the Commission February 24, 2017, which can be requested at the MTC official website http://www.mtc.gov/.
671. *Ibid.*, 5. The explanation of the exclusion list: 'In addition, certain specific types of receipts are explicitly excluded even if they give rise to income that would meet the transactional test.'

(6) amounts realized from exchanges of inventory that are not recognized by the IRC; or
(7) amounts realized as a result of factoring accounts receivable recorded on an accrual basis.

In my view, although the transactional test and the functional test have long existed for deciding the scope of the tax base (unitary business income), they are not suitable for deciding the definition of the sales factor. It is because the unitary business concerns the relationship between different parts of the unitary group, whereas the sales factor concerns the enterprise's reaction to the market. The transactional test and the functional test still cannot explain why there are some items that still should be excluded from the sales factor, even though they fulfil both tests; not to say that the distinction between the transactional test and the functional test has been made muddier.[672]

Although the current MTC's reform still does not provide a good theory, it clearly shows that the MTC is aware of the phenomenon that some receipts from transactions do not always reflect the taxpayers' response to their customers' market, and so they should be excluded from the sales factor. Unfortunately, the MTC's approach of using the unitary business-related principles is not consistent with the tax-neutral sales factor.

In section 4.3.3, I explain how short-term marketable securities and hedging transactions caused disputes about the definition of sales before the Californian courts and in the end are excluded by legislation.[673]

4.3.3 'Inflating (= reducing) the sales factor' Cases in California: Difficult to Recover Market Neutrality

In California, it was disputed whether the gross receipts from redemption of short-term marketable securities[674] and hedging transactions[675] can be included in the sales factor. These two types of transactions are in the form of purchase-sales contracts, but they have a cash management function (marketable securities) and price fluctuation risk management function (hedging transactions), respectively.

What interests us most is that in these disputes, it is what taxpayers would like to include in their sales factor, to make the denominator large and consequently decrease the sales factor ratio in California. The tax authorities would like to exclude these items from the sales factor. Since the sales factor is a ratio, it is possible to inflate the ratio either by reducing the numerator or by increasing the denominator. The calculation is dynamic and thus complicated.

672. Hellerstein, Hellerstein & Swain, *supra* n. 349, at 9.05[2][a].
673. The development of MTC regulations and California's definition on 'gross receipts', *see* Chen, *supra* n. 658. The definition of 'sales'/'gross receipts' has been one of the most important issue in state taxation in US since early, *see* Paul H Frankel, Basic Principles and Significant Issues in State Taxation of Unitary Corporate Income, 37 Tax Executive 1 (1984).
674. *Microsoft Corp. v. Franchise Tax Board* No. S133343, 2006.
675. *General Mills v. Franchise Tax Board* No. A120492, 15 April 2009· [172 Cal.App.4th 1545].

In the two cases, the California tax authorities argued to exclude some items completely from the sales factor (from both the numerator and the denominator) to prevent 'inflation (read: decrease) of the sales factor' in California. In other words, the dispute about the definition of sales turned into a fairness/distortion issue. The California tax authorities not only argued to exclude the disputed items from the definition but also invoked the equitable apportionment provision[676] to argue that the standard formula is not fair to reflect multistate income attributed to California.

The legal consequences of the issues of definition and fairness might look similar, but the subtle distinction has an important meaning: as to the definition issue, we discuss the very fundamental feature of the 'sales' and it is objective; as to the fairness issue, we still accept an item as a type of sales but exclude it because of the result being unfair to a specific (state) jurisdiction, and the unfairness will be subject to a comparison test.

These two cases in California are strong evidence that the MTC's exclusion list and relying on 'the transactional test' still do not provide a consistent tool for the court to decide the definition of sales. There could be various transactions in the form of purchase-sales contracts. By revisiting and analysing features of the facts and arguments in these cases, it will be clear that the criterion of 'response to the market demand side' is the logical one.

4.3.3.1 Microsoft: Inclusion of the Net Amount of Marketable Securities

The Microsoft[677] case involved a dispute as to whether receipts from the redemption of marketable securities should be included in the sales factor. Here are the facts in the case: Microsoft mainly designs and sells operation systems for computers. Its headquarter is in the State of Washington, where no corporate tax is levied; and its production activities take place in California, so Microsoft has a nexus in California. In 1991, Microsoft had a gain of USD 10.7 million on its marketable securities, which yielded gross proceeds of USD 5.7 billion. These marketable securities are held and sold regularly for the treasury function. In other words, when Microsoft needs cash, it sells some securities to maintain its cash flow. These securities' liquidity is almost the same as cash trading, i.e., selling/redeeming and purchasing, so these marketable securities are similar to liquidating cash from a bank account and later saving it back. It is part of Microsoft group's cash management activities. The sale/redemption of these marketable securities only produce very marginal profits, but Microsoft conducts this type of transaction very frequently.

In the California tax authorities (Franchise Tax Board, FTB)'s view, the full amount of redemption of these short-term marketable securities are just bubbles and

676. It is the alternative apportionment provision, comparable to UDITPA section 18 and 2016 CCCTB Directive Proposal Article 58.

677. *Microsoft Corp. v. Franchise Tax Board*, 39 Cal. 4th 750, 139 P.3d 1169, 47 Cal. Rptr. 3d 216 (2006). Some general comments, *see* Michael Schadewald, Apportionment Issues-Redemptions of Short-Term Marketable Securities: The Microsoft Case, 25 Journal of State Taxation 9 (2006); a specific comparison to CCCTB, *see* Hellerstein, *supra* n. 549.

thus inflates the sales factor that could have been attributed to California. Including these short-term marketable securities makes the denominator of the sales factor of California very large. The amount of redemption of these short-term marketable securities are all attributed to the State of Washington where there is no CIT levied. The FTB then adjusted the sales factor of Microsoft's tax return to only include the consideration of the transaction, i.e., 'net amount' of redemption of short-term marketable securities, not the full amount.

The FTB argued that redemption of short-term marketable securities is different from selling securities to a third party. The FTB argued that only selling the securities to a third party is really a 'sale' but 'redemption' upon maturity of securities is not.[678] According to the FTB, the difference between sale of securities and redemption of securities lies on the other side of the transaction. The recipient of the sale of securities is a 'third party', whereas the recipient of redemption is the 'original issuer' of securities. The court rejected[679] this argument and ruled that there was no actual difference for the taxpayer in these two situations regarding 'selling'. These two situations have identical economic substances to the taxpayer and thus should be treated the same. The court concluded that the full redemption price, like the full sale price, must be treated as gross receipts.

The further question was whether the inclusion of the full redemption price in the sales factor would distort the fair representation of Microsoft's business activities. If the current result of calculation indeed distorts the apportionment of income, an alternative method of apportionment may be adopted. The court discussed and compared disputes about gross receipts related to the big treasury department of multinationals in other previous similar cases.[680] The court used a quantitative approach[681] to decide whether there was a distortion of the sales factor.

First, the court did not agree that there was a distortion simply due to including marketable securities. Rather, according to the court's analysis, the real problem was the scale of inclusion.[682] The profit margin of redemption of marketable securities was much lower than Microsoft's primary business activities, but inclusion of the entire amount of redemption was so huge in the denominator that the ratio of the sales factor of California became quite small. Compared to the hypothetical situation that only the sales from Microsoft's primary activities are included, there was a huge difference.

Also, according to the court,[683] inclusion of the full price of redemption of marketable securities attributed a great portion of Microsoft's business activities to the State of Washington (where Microsoft's headquarters are located). These marketable

678. *Microsoft Corp. v. Franchise Tax Board*, 39 Cal. 4th 750, 139 P.3d 1169, 47 Cal. Rptr. 3d 216 (2006), at 223.
679. *Ibid.*, 224.
680. *Ibid.*, 228-229. The court analyses cases including *Crisa Corp.*, *Merrill Lynch*, *Pacific Telephone & Telegraph*, *Sherwin-Williams Co. v. Johnson*, *American Telephone & Telegraph Co. v. State Tax Appeal Board*, etc.
681. *Microsoft Corp. v. Franchise Tax Board*, 39 Cal. 4th 750, 139 P.3d 1169, 47 Cal. Rptr. 3d 216 (2006), 229-230.
682. *Ibid.*, 229.
683. *Ibid.*, 230, the Court's footnote 19 calculated the profits margin of Microsoft's treasury department in Washington State.

securities from its treasury department are traded in the State of Washington. It is unfair. Based on these quantitative analyses, the alternative formula should be applied to adjust the unfair result of including the redemption of marketable securities into the sales factor.

Therefore, the court concluded that including the entire amount of its marketable securities would indeed distort the sales factor of the sharing formula adopted in California. The denominator would be huge and thus the ratio of apportioned tax base would be inflated. The court took a position partially in favour of the taxpayer, Microsoft: although the redemption amount is still conceptually included in the gross receipts, the precise extent to which Microsoft is entitled includes only the 'net' income of its securities transactions in its California sales factor.

In brief, the court took a compromise position: in principle, the entire amount of redemption of market securities was still defined as gross receipts, no doubts; however, in *Microsoft*, including the entire amount would distort the fair representation of Microsoft's business activities in California. The court adjusted the calculation of the total sales of Microsoft: Only the net amount of redemption should be included as 'sales' based on the equitable relief provision which is a case-by-case adjustment, so the tax authorities must invoke this against the taxpayer or bring the case to court each time there is an alleged distortion. In this regard, the California tax authorities did not win the whole case. If the California tax authorities wanted to adopt an alternative formula, they would have to bear the burden of proof to demonstrate distortion resulting from the standard formula in every single case regarding marketable securities.

Microsoft is especially significant in the development of case law on the sales factor[684] because it was the first time that a court concluded directly that marketable securities should be defined as 'gross receipts' according to the existing law at that time. Based on this precondition, the court decided further whether there was distortion. This ruling also influenced the amendment of the definition of sales in California's tax law[685] and later in the MTC's regulation. Legislation is amended expressly to exclude redemption of short-term marketable securities from the sales factor.

McLure describes California's legislative reaction to exclude short-term marketable securities as a 'throw-out approach' and endorses this legislative amendment over the Microsoft judgment: in McLure's view, full exclusion is more logical than including the net amount of redemption of short-term marketable securities. In McLure's analysis,[686] redemption of short-term marketable securities is no different from a general sales of 'inventory', from an economic perspective; the only difference between

684. Ossie Ravid & William Hays Weissman, Cash Management Activities and the Sales Factor: When Is Gross Really Gross and a Receipt Really a Receipt, 10. State & Local Tax Law 93 (2005).
685. The amendment bill is analysed by the expert at FTB, *see* FTB Analysis of Amended Bill (Bill Number: SBX3), 14 February 2009, 13-14, available at https://www.ftb.ca.gov/Archive/Law/legis/09_10bills/sbx3_15_021409.pdf.
In the record of the legislation note of February 14, 2009, the Microsoft and General Mills cases are not mentioned at all, though.
686. McLure, *supra* n. 622.

a financial instrument transaction and a general sales of goods or inventories is that it is impossible to define the origin as well as the destination of such financial cash flow, and therefore he endorses the 'throw-out approach'/ full exclusion, based on the theoretical soundness and simplicity.

In my view, I partially agree with McLure's observation. The dispute as to how short-term marketable securities should be treated in the sales factor results from the dispute about the fundamental rationale of the sales factor. I am of the same opinion as McLure that receipts from short-term marketable securities as such in *Microsoft* should not be defined as the sales of the taxpayers, from the very beginning. But I do not think that marketable securities are the same as 'selling inventories'. Selling inventories would be a typical response to market demand, and it is fine to include all receipts from selling inventories in the sales factor.

Differing from McLure's argument, I see MNE taxpayers 'trade' financial instruments, including short-term marketable securities, not as a response to the market where they market their goods or services. These financial transactions should not be included in taxpayers' sales factor because these financial transactions do not represent these taxpayers' reaction/response to the demand of their customers.[687]

In other words, MNE taxpayers are the 'customers' in the market of short-term securities. MNE taxpayers make use of the market of short-term securities to maintain their cash flow. Even though these financial transactions are an integral part of MNE taxpayers' business circle and in the form of sales transactions, these transactions are not responding to the demand of MNE taxpayers' clients, and thus the sales factor should not include them. This interpretation method is consistent with the neutrality principle that the sales factor should represent the demand side of the market.

4.3.3.2 General Mills: Inclusion of the Net Amount by Hedging Transactions

Another leading California case regarding the definition of gross receipts and sales is the *General Mills* case. General Mills is a commodities trader. In the agricultural commodities industry, the risk of price fluctuation is very high, and therefore commodity traders have developed a mechanism of mitigating the risk of price fluctuation: traders will sign the futures contract, i.e., delivery of a specific amount of goods at a specific price at a future date. The traders trade their commodities at 'the cash market' and use the 'futures market' to mitigate price fluctuation risk. The dispute is whether the hedging transactions in the futures market should be included in the sales of the taxpayers.

Here is the basic design of how 'hedge futures contracts' reduce risk from price fluctuations in the commodities market. First of all, the prices of commodities are

687. In Chapter 7, I discuss FA involving financial institutions as taxpayers. In that context, financial transactions are included in the sales factor for the special industry formula and calculated according to the net amount/interests because the principal of the monetary capital does not represent the response to the demand. That context is not the same in the context of the sales factor of the standard formula.

constantly changing because of bad weather or other natural causes. It is the inherent nature of agriculture. The risk of purchasing a commodity for a food manufacturer as a buyer, such as General Mills, is that the commodity's price rises before its delivery to the factory, which is the price a buyer should actually pay. Hedging means that the taxpayer sells its futures contracts in 'the futures market' and utilizes the profits from the futures market to compensate the adverse price fluctuation for its product materials in the commodity market, i.e., the 'cash market'. General Mills needs to 'buy' commodities in the cash market, and it 'sells' its futures contracts in the futures market. General Mills takes the buyer's position in the cash market and takes the seller's position in the futures market. This is what is known as 'opposite' positions in the hedging process.

The (simplified) process of hedging[688] is described as follows: General Mills signs a buyer's futures contract that stipulates the commodity's price at a specific price at a specific future time. The counterparty of this buyer's futures contract is the trading forum, as indicated above. Later, General Mills offsets its buying contract by signing another seller's futures contract at the moment that the price is lower. After offsetting, there will be a margin 'profits' recorded to its account at the trading forum; more importantly because of offsetting, there is no real delivery of agricultural products taking place. By utilizing the recorded profits, General Mills can compensate the commodity price rising later. In other words, its risk of a price rise has been mitigated and diminished.

The disputed points are: first, whether such hedging transactions are defined as gross receipts, and to what extent they should be included as gross receipts. Second, whether an alternative formula should be applied in this case. The taxpayer General Mills took the position that the full amount of these futures contracts should be included in the gross receipts. The FTB argued that none of the amounts received of futures contracts should be included. Alternatively, even if the court were to decide to include the futures contract in the gross receipts, an alternative formula should be applied in the current case. In either case, the FTB argued that the hedging transactions should be completely excluded from the sales factor, both in the numerator and in the denominator.

The court gave affirmative answers to the first question. The first question is whether the whole amount of each futures contract's value should be included in the gross receipt. The FTB argued that General Mills' 97% futures sales contracts were satisfied by merely offsetting, and never physically delivered, so these futures sales contracts did not warrant consideration and 'had no value'. The court rejected[689] these arguments and affirmed that futures sales contracts were in fact legally binding contracts to the full extent. The fact that these hedging contracts were offset with each other did not influence their legally binding nature.

688. Basic principles of hedging strategies using futures, *see* John C Hull, *Options, Futures, and Other Derivatives* (8th ed. Prentice Hall 2012), at 47.
689. *General Mills v. Franchise Tax Board*, 172 Cal.App.4th 1535, 92 Cal. Rptr. 3d 208, 218 (1st Dist. 2009).

Furthermore, the court affirmed that General Mills' 'future sales'/hedging transactions indeed reflect an integral part of its business. According to the court,[690] hedging its futures sales contracts is done on a daily basis and is so important to protect General Mills against the commodity price fluctuation. Hedging futures sales is done 'for the ultimate purpose of obtaining gains or profits' even though General Mills does not merely seek to make profits on its futures trade.

The court agreed that hedging is an 'integral part of the company's business activities', just as important as the physical delivery of its raw materials for its products manufacturing. According to the plain language of the definition of 'gross receipts', it is impossible to include only the net profits from hedging the futures contracts in the gross receipts. Therefore, the court concluded that the futures sales should be included in the gross receipts when calculating the formula's sales factor.

As for the second question of whether the alternative formula should be applied, the court of appeal further[691] required the lower court to examine facts and evidence. Based on the lower court's additional evidence and re-examination, the court ruled[692] ('*General Mills II*') that the full inclusion of General Mill's futures sales would distort the result of apportionment, and thus an alternative formula should be applied. The court of appeal conducted both the qualitative[693] and quantitative analyses.[694] Although General Mills' hedging activities are an integral part of its business activities, inclusion of all amounts of the futures contracts would make the standard formula not fairly represent General Mills' activities in California. Therefore, the court accepted the alternative method that only includes the net profits of the futures sales in gross receipts. The court recognized that full inclusion would result in distortion and unfair apportionment.[695]

In brief, in *General Mills*, the court addressed the issues of definition and distortion. The court concluded[696] that hedging activities should be included in the gross receipts when calculating the California standard formula's sales factor, but only to the extent of 'net profits', not to the entire value of futures contracts because the inclusion of the entire amount of futures contracts would lead to a distortive result of apportionment.

Although this result seems quite comparable and similar to *Microsoft*, the court still emphasized that the risk management activities, i.e., hedging transactions are different from the cash management activities, i.e., marketable securities.[697]

---

690. *General Mills v. Franchise Tax Board* No. A120492, April 15, 2009 [172 Cal.App.4th 1548].
691. *Ibid.*
692. *General Mills v. Franchise Tax Board* No. A131477. 208 Cal.App.4th 1290 (2012).
693. *Ibid.*, [208 Cal.App.4th 1304-1307].
694. *Ibid.*, [208 Cal.App.4th 1307-1313].
695. Different view, Diann L Smith & Miranda K Davis, No Hedging on Gross Receipts Inclusion in Sales Factor, Tax Analysts (2009).
    Smith and Davis simply argue that hedging is part of the business, and there is no justification to deviate from the text of 'gross'.
696. *General Mills v. Franchise Tax Board* No. A131477. 208 Cal.App.4th 1290 (2012) [208 Cal.App.4th 1316].
697. *Ibid.*, [208 Cal.App.4th 1301].

4.3.3.3 *'The Net Amount Calculation' Is Still Contrary to Benefit-Based Market Neutrality*

Both hedging transactions and trading short-term marketable securities are in the form of purchase-sale contracts, but they have different functions than the normal purchase-sales contracts. Technically, the court's approach is quite similar: only the net amounts received from the hedging transactions and marketable securities can be included in the sales factor.

The California court's compromise approach of including the net amount is not completely without sense. From the literal meaning of 'gross receipts' from sales, excluding gross receipts via marketable securities or hedging transactions is not legitimate; from the perspective of 'in the ordinary course of trade and business', these activities are crucial for maintaining the business smoothly, and it seems not legitimate to exclude them. But this is because the court is inherently restricted, so it may not go beyond what the tax law regulates.

In my view, the California court's decision of 'calculating the net amount' is still an unconvincing compromise. In *General Mills*, the court ruled that hedging transactions are defined as gross receipts mainly because of the restriction of the legislation at that time: hedging transactions are indeed legally binding and constitute an integral part of the business. Even from the 'transaction test' perspective, hedging transactions can pass the test because the futures contracts signed by General Mills are totally valid and enforceable contracts; the physical delivery of each futures contract does not take place because of the custom of offsetting.

From the benefit-based MN perspective for designing the sales factor, I especially agree with California's legislative tax reform decision to completely exclude hedging transactions. It is quite clear that in the commodities industry, the cash market and the futures market are two separate markets; hedging transactions take place in the futures market and function as a type of insurance. Therefore, the receipts from hedging transactions should not be included in the sales factor because hedging transactions do not represent the taxpayers' response to the demand of their clients. In the futures market, taxpayers are making use of this market to reduce their risk of their commodities market. Back to the imperative that the sales factor should represent the taxpayers' response to the market, hedging transactions do not fulfil this requirement and thus it is necessary to exclude them.

In short, including taxpayers' gross receipts via marketable securities or hedging transactions in the taxpayers' sales factor is contrary to the rationale that the sales factor should reflect the taxpayers' response to their customers. When conducting these two types of transactions: taxpayers like Microsoft or General Mills are not goods/service providers here. Therefore, although in the form of sales contracts, the amount of gross receipts from these forms of 'sales contracts' should not be included in the taxpayers' sales factor at all because taxpayers are 'clients' who make use of the securities and hedging transactions.

4.3.4 Excluding Intangible Income Purely Due to Uncertainty Is Not Market Neutral

4.3.4.1 Uncertain, So Throwing out Intangible Income

In addition to providing an exclusion list for the definition of sales, there is another way of excluding intangible income from the sales factor, in the form of a 'throw-out' rule. Quite a few states in the US have adopted the throw-out rule to exclude intangible income for which it is impossible to identify the locations.[698]

Conceptually speaking, the throw-out rule deals with the attribution, not the definition, but the effect of some throw-out rules is the same as the definition rule of the sales, when the throw-out rule excludes an item from both the numerator and the denominator. Since the 'complete' throw-out rule sometimes has the same function as the definition rule, many state taxation practitioners roughly call it the 'throw-out rule'.[699] The current practice of throw-out rules is so complicated and thus has been criticized for creating uncertainties, and taxpayers actually need experts to deal with various throw-out rules.[700]

4.3.4.2 The Background of the Throw-out Rule: The Difficulty of Ascertaining Intangibles' Location

As Weiner observes,[701] a typical example of invoking the throw-out rule is to exclude gross receipts earned from intangibles: such as royalties from patents and copyrights, dividends from stocks, or interest from bonds. These items are excluded from the sales factor completely when the throw-out rules apply. The main rationale of the throw-out rule is from the inherent indeterminacy of intangibles: it seems unfair no matter which state these receipts are attributed to because these receipts are earned from intangibles that cannot be identified to any physical jurisdiction.[702]

The throw-out rule for intangible income is developed from the inherent difficulty of deciding the geographical location and the contribution of intangibles. For a typical FA system in the US, any intangible income needs to constitute the unitary business to be apportionable. It is quite controversial to ascertain if an intangible function is part of the unitary business, or if 'factor representation requirement is fulfilled'.[703]

The Reg. IV.1(a)(5)(C) Multistate Tax Compact Regulation IV especially mentions that intangible income needs to have an 'operational function': 'under the

698. Weiner, *supra* n. 47.
699. For example, California tax authorities Franchise Tax Board's law amendment reason: 'Final Statement of Reasons. For Adoption of California Code of Regulations, Title 18, section 25137(C)(1)(D)', 2006.
700. Scott Austin, Hardeo Bissoondial & Ilya A Lipin, Throwing Out Uncertainty from the Throwout Rule, 76 State Tax Notes (2015).
701. Weiner, *supra* n. 47.
702. The development of throw-out rule, *see* Ilya A Lipin, Corporate Taxpayers' Sore Arm: Throw-Out Rule Litigation in State and Local Taxation, 66 Tax Lawyer 901 (2013).
703. Hellerstein, *supra* n. 100, at 5.03.

functional test, income from intangible property is apportionable income when the intangible property serves an operational function as opposed to solely an investment function'. In other words, intangible income must be 'operational' for the unitary business.

If being not apportionable, the intangible income is usually allocated to a single state:[704] historically, such intangible income is allocated to the taxpayer's commerce domicile (*mobilia sequuntur personam*) unless the acquisition of the intangible income constitutes a business status, then to that business status state. Nowadays, many states no longer follow the '*mobilia sequuntur personam*' rationale for intangible income, but allocate this non-apportionable intangible income to the 'state of use'.[705] In any case, the intangible income that is not apportionable will not be calculated in the sales factor.

4.3.4.3 *Unconditionally Throwing out Income from 'intangibles' Is Not Market Neutral*

Even when being apportionable, intangible income is still geographically indeterminate[706] and this is when some states decide to adopt the throw-out rule 'for intangibles whose geographic location is not readily ascertainable'.[707]

The rationale to exclude intangibles completely from the sales factor due to uncertainty also influenced the MTC's tax reform. Another example is the MTC's new section 17 of MTC Regulation IV on attributing sales earned from 'mixed intangibles'.[708] Mixed intangibles are intangibles that cannot be classified as a production intangible (a typical production intangible is patent or production know-how) or a marketing intangible (a typical marketing tangible is a trademark).

For attributing income from mixed intangibles in the sales factor, section 17 MTC Regulation IV throws out (i.e., excludes) all receipts from a sale of a mixed intangible that cannot be classified as a production intangible or a marketing intangible from the numerator and denominator of the sales factor.

From the benefit-based MN perspective, it is not tax neutral to exclude intangible income purely due to difficulty in ascertaining a geographical location. Moreover, although intangible income does not have a physical form to allocate the geographical location, neither it is an illusion nor does it appear out of nowhere; instead, intangibles

704. Hellerstein, Hellerstein & Swain, *supra* n. 349, at 9.08[1].
705. *Ibid.*
706. *Ibid.*, 9.18[4]:

> Because the location of intangible assets and the receipts they produce is geographically indeterminate, there is no generally accepted methodology for apportioning intangible income on a geographic basis. Under these circumstances, a rule assigning the factors associated with the intangible income according to the factors associated with the corporation's tangible operations is justified. The rule reflects the underlying theory on which the intangible income is being apportioned, namely, that it is related to the operation of the corporation's business.

707. Hellerstein, Hellerstein & Swain, *supra* n. 349, at 9.18[4][b]. There are examples of throwing out intangible income from the sales factor.
708. *See section* 4.4.4 of this book.

are created and utilized via a series of legal relationships; there are contribution costs to the intangible, and the intangible can also generate profits for the taxpayers in the market. Therefore, intangible income can also be the result of a response to the market and be attributed in the sales factor. In fact, instead of the throw-out approach, there are states adopting a more generic approach to attributing intangible income in the sales factor 'based on the management, control, or use of the intangible in the state'.[709] Throwing out intangible income from the sales factor based on difficulty in ascertaining a geographical location is not a tax-neutral option for the CCCTB to follow.

4.3.5 The Sales Factor Definition under the Current CCCTB Directive Proposal Has the Same Problem

4.3.5.1 The CCCTB's Approach to Excluding Intangible Income Is Not Market Neutral

According to Article 37 of the 2016 CCCTB Directive Proposal, sales is roughly defined as 'the proceeds of all sales of goods and supplies of services after discounts and returns, excluding VAT, other taxes and duties'.[710] Several items excluded from the sales factor, including intra-group sales, are always excluded; exempt revenues, interest, dividends, royalties, and proceeds from the disposal of fixed assets are in principle excluded, unless these items are earned 'in the ordinary course of trade or business'.

The reason for excluding exempt revenues, interest, dividends, and royalties is not clearly disclosed in the current CCCTB Directive Proposal's legislative record.[711] Despite the silence, it is reasonable to exclude exempt revenues from the sales factor for being not part of the consolidated tax base because there should be a symmetrical relationship between the weighting factor and the tax base.[712]

Regarding excluding 'intangible income' (i.e., interest, dividends, royalties,), it looks symmetrical for the assets factor to exclude intangibles.[713] But if interest,

---

709. Hellerstein, Hellerstein & Swain, *supra* n. 349, at 9.18[4][b].

710. Article 37 of 2016 CCCTB Directive Proposal

Article 37 Composition of the sales factor

1. The sales factor shall consist of the total sales allocated to a group member, including permanent establishments that are considered to exist pursuant to Article 22(3), as its numerator and the total sales of the group as its denominator.
2. Sales shall mean the proceeds of all sales of goods and supplies of services after discounts and returns, excluding value added tax, other taxes and duties. Exempt revenues, interest, dividends, royalties and proceeds from the disposal of fixed assets shall not be included in the sales factor, unless they are revenues earned in the ordinary course of trade or business. Intra-group sales of goods and supplies of services shall not be included in the sales factor.
3. Sales shall be valued in accordance with Article 20 of Directive 2016/xx/EU.

711. The relevant paragraph 15 and paragraph 50 in the CCCTB Working Document No. 60 are both silent.

712. Regarding this symmetry, *see* Chapter 8 of this book.

713. Paragraph 51 of the CCCTB Working Document No. 60.

dividends, and royalties are earned in response to clients' demand, there is no reason to exclude them from the sales factor.

Although Article 37 of the 2016 CCCTB Directive Proposal provides that intangible income 'earned "in the ordinary course of trade or business"' may be included in the sales factor, this extra clause does not make Article 37 tax neutral when read in combination with Article 38.

When an intangible income is earned in the ordinary course of trade and business, it can be included in the sales factor, and it is included in the sales factor of the 'beneficiary' of the intangible income according to Article 38(3).[714] Attributing intangible income to the beneficiary does not present the market side. So, when Article 37 and Article 38 jointly apply, it is clearly a non-neutral result because they deviate from the sales-by-destination principle. In other words, even putting these items in the CCCTB Directive Proposal's exclusion list back in the sales factor is still contrary to the tax neutrality principle.

In my view, the sales factor under the current CCCTB Directive Proposal is evidence of 'lost in translation'. When we compare Article 37(2) and Article 38(3) to the US's approach discussed above, we can see the influence and the attempt of legal transplantation. Article 37(2)'s clause 'in the regular course of trade and business' is quite similar to formulation of 'the transaction test' of MTC Regulation IV discussed above. Article 38(3) is also similar to the rule of 'assigning to the taxpayer's commerce domicile (*mobilia sequuntur personam*)' that was used by many states of the US in the past mentioned in section 4.3.4 above. But the European Commission's CCCTB Directive Proposal does not seem to be up to date with the latest developments in US tax law and has chosen an outdated option. Such option is not tax neutral.

4.3.5.2 The CCCTB's Sales Factor Is Unable to Exclude Non-sales

Moreover, presuming *Microsoft* and *General Mills* were under the current CCCTB Directive Proposal, the same disputes and distortions would still happen. As indicated above, Article 37 of 2016 CCCTB Directive Proposal provides that exempt revenues, interest, dividends, royalties, and proceeds from the disposal of fixed assets are in principle excluded from the sales factor, unless these items are earned 'in the ordinary course of trade or business'.

As to the interest on redemption of marketable securities or hedging transactions, they can both be interpreted as being earned 'in the ordinary course of trade or businesses'. The condition of 'in the ordinary course of trade or business' is extremely general and broad, so it is quite easy to qualify.

One might still argue to adopt the conclusion of *Microsoft* and *General Mills* (i.e., only including the net amount of the short-term marketable securities and hedging transactions) for interpreting the current CCCTB Directive Proposal, but it is not

714. Article 38 (3) of the 2016 CCCTB Directive Proposal: 'Exempt revenues, interest, dividends and royalties and the proceeds from the disposal of fixed assets that are included in the sales factor shall be attributed to **the beneficiary** of those revenues, interest, dividends, royalties and proceeds.'

feasible. Even if we accept that only the 'net' amount of these transactions should be included as 'sales', this argument is too optimistic to presume that there is not too much distortion. Short-term marketable securities and hedging transactions are both repetitive series of transactions which take place very often, and even if the net amount of the transactions is included, they can still inflate the sale factor when the transactions volume is large.

To sum up, according to Article 37 of the current CCCTB Directive Proposal, cash management and risk management activities still fall within the core part of business income earned 'in the regular course of trade and business'. Article 37 is not able to exclude them from the sales factor, and therefore the definition rule in Article 37 is not tax neutral because it is not able to exclude non-sales and its corresponding attribution rule is contrary to the destination principle.

4.4 THE ATTRIBUTION OF SALES: DESTINATION AND DEEMED DESTINATIONS

4.4.1 In the Name of Destination

4.4.1.1 Deviations from the Sales by Destination Rule Are Not Market Neutral

The concept of the destination principle has been widely used in different contexts.[715] There are different proxies used to decide the destination/customers' market. These proxies are not always consistent with the benefit-based MN framework. These proxies are chosen when the destination is not desirable[716] or when the destination is not convenient.[717]

In section 4.4.3, I demonstrate different examples that deviate from the destination principle based on customers' location, even if they might claim themselves in the name of destination principle. The discussion of this section is inspired by Swain's extensive survey on indirect tax models and income tax models. In both direct tax and indirect tax fields, there are rules for selecting proxies to reflect customers, i.e., the destination of a transaction.[718]

4.4.1.2 Deviating from the Destination Principle Creates Complexities

Among these attribution rules in VAT or FA, there is one feature in common: traditionally when it comes to attributing services, all these attribution rules inevitably

715. For example, Senyk has discussed the meaning of destination principle for VAT, in the OECD, WTO and EU contexts, *see* M Senyk, *The Origin and Destination Principles as Alternative Approaches Towards VAT Allocation: Analysis in the WTO, the OECD and the EU Legal Frameworks* (IBFD 2020).
716. The of 'no-where sales' which leads to various 'throw-back' rules, *see* section 4.4.2.1.
717. For administrative convenience, which is the main reason why many EU VAT attribution rules deviate from the destination principle, *see* section 4.4.3.3.2.
718. Swain, *supra* n. 636.

include the 'origin element' and do not consistently follow the destination rationale. This is the common feature in the FA (CIT) regime as well as the indirect tax regime, such as VAT. For example, the MTC's outdated 'income generating rule/cost of performance rule'[719] and the EU VAT's 'place of supply' rules for B2C service transactions are the typical examples of incorporating the origin element as deemed destinations.[720]

The deviation from the destination rationale is illogical from the perspective of consumption tax but is dominant out of administrative convenience concerns. It is not tax neutral either because the origin element of these rules does not quite represent an MNE taxpayer's 'response to their clients/customers'; the origin element focuses on service providers instead of customers.

Because of allowing deviations, there are again many 'exceptions' to the origin-based attribution rules, and these 'exceptions' are actually shifting back to the destination principle. For example, the MTC regulations provide various special formulas for service industries to circumvent the COP rule for attributing services;[721] the EU VAT Directive provides exceptions to 'place of supply'/'place of taxation' rule for B2C services and industry-specific industries.[722]

As a common problem in VAT as well as the MTC's market-sourcing rules, all these 'deviations' from the destination principle and 'the exceptions to the deviations' make the whole system complex and hard to follow.

4.4.1.3 Market Neutrality Implications of Existing Attribution Rules of Sales of Goods

In section 4.4.2, I discuss deviations from the destination principle where the attribution result is undesirable for the tax authorities. It is caused by the 'no-where sales of goods'.

The attribution rules of sales of tangible goods and the implications are outlined in Table 2.

Table 2 Attribution Rules of Sales of Tangible Goods

	The Throw-Back Rule	*The Throw-Around Rule*
Examples	- MTC. - CCCTB Article 38(1). - State taxation in the US (two variations on the Joyce rule and Finnigan rule).	Article 38(4) and (5) of the current CCCTB Directive Proposal.

719. *See section* 4.4.3 of this book.
720. Rita de la Feria refers this as a conceptual incoherence, *see* Rita de La Feria, *The EU VAT System and the Internal Market* (IBFD 2009), at 3.2.1.1.1, footnote 397.
721. The description of all these industry formulas is outside the scope of this chapter, *see* Hellerstein, Hellerstein & Swain, *supra* n. 349, at Chapter 10.
722. *See section* 4.5 of this book.

	The Throw-Back Rule	*The Throw-Around Rule*
Underlying Rationales	It addresses the fear of 'no-where sales'.	It addresses the nexus issue.
Neutrality Implications	Not market neutral because it does not reflect the market side.	Not market neutral when the nexus is still PE and being triggered too easily. When the taxable nexus follows the factor presence nexus test, the pro-rata throw-around rule is a logical way to ensure tax base erosion.

Source: The author.

4.4.1.4 Market Neutrality Implications of Existing Attribution Rules of Sales of Services

In section 4.4.3 regarding attributing services, I discuss different types of attribution rules for services and their tax neutrality implications, outlined in Table 3.

Table 3 Attribution Rules of Sales of Services

	The Origin-Based Approach	*The Destination-Based Approach*	*The Hybrid Approach*
Examples	- The MTC's traditional COP Rule. - EU VAT rules for B2C services (Suppliers' establishment is an origin-based element).	- The MTC's market sourcing (in theory). - OECD VAT guidelines (in theory). - EU VAT B2C service of some specific industries. - EU VAT reform package in 2015.	- EU VAT B2B services(Business Customers' establishment is not destination per se). - OECD VAT guidelines has some proxies based on administrate convenience (e.g., customers' residence). - Some supplementary proxies at the MTC's market sourcing for professional services and other services (e.g., the location of the ordering or the customer's billing address).

	The Origin-Based Approach	*The Destination-Based Approach*	*The Hybrid Approach*
Underlying Rationales	To balance the interest state of production; administrative convenience, historical reasons	To react to the rapid development of the technology and e-commerce.	As to VAT for services: for administrative convenience as feasible. While still in the name of the destination principle, there are proxies used for 'deemed' destination but in fact not focusing on customers' enjoyment or consumption. As to the MTC's market sourcing for professional services and other services, there are proxies for administration convenience.
Neutrality Implication	It is not neutral for the sales factor attribution.	It is neutral because the destination approach reflects the market side (taxpayers' response to their clients' market).	Selecting proxies as 'deemed destination' is still in the name of destination in reality deviating from the destination principle is not tax neutral, even though in the name of the destination principle.

Source: The author.

4.4.2 When the Destination Is Not Desirable: 'no-where' Sales of Goods

In Chapter 3, I concluded that the benefit-based market-neutral attribution rule for the sales factor should be 'customer-based'. Ideally speaking, the sales-by-destination rule is the only theoretically logical option for the sales factor. The sales factor of the current CCCTB Directive Proposal is designed under this rationale, and it is clearly expressed in its title.[723]

723. Article 38 of 2016 CCCTB Directive Proposal:

Article 38 Sales by destination

1. Sales of goods shall be included in the sales factor of the group member located in the Member State where the dispatch or transport of the goods to the person acquiring

However, from the very beginning of FA rules, there have been 'exceptions' to the sales-by-destination rule. The most typical is the 'throw-back rule' for sales of goods, developed in the US, and followed by the current CCCTB Directive Proposal with some modifications. The throw-back rule applies when out-of-state sales are classified as 'no-where sales'.[724]

'No-where sales'[725] refers not only to goods 'disappearing from the record' or not identifiable but also to some situations where it would seem unfair not to attribute some sales to the sales factor, though the state is not the destination.[726] The second type of situations is often based on political concerns or tax authorities' ad hoc concerns, and thus it create complexities to the system. In short, the throw-back rule (and current CCCTB Directive Proposal's throw-around rule, section 4.4.2.2) for out-of-state sales reflect the fear of losing revenue, even though it is in the name of ensuring 'full accountability' of the taxpayer. Only out-of-state sales could be classified as no-where sales.

4.4.2.1 *The Throw-back Rule Is Neutral Only for 'unidentifiable destination' Sales*

4.4.2.1.1 *Full Accountability of All Sales*

As indicated in section 3.4.2.2, the current CCCTB Directive Proposal demonstrates the destination principle in Article 38(1), the first sentence; and the last sentence is a

them ends. Where that place cannot be determined, the sales of goods shall be attributed to the group member located in the Member State of the last identifiable location of the goods.

2. Supplies of services shall be included in the sales factor of the group member located in the Member State where the services are physically carried out or actually supplied.
3. Exempt revenues, interest, dividends and royalties and the proceeds from the disposal of fixed assets that are included in the sales factor shall be attributed to the beneficiary of those revenues, interest, dividends, royalties and proceeds.
4. Where there is no group member in the Member State where the goods are delivered or the services are supplied, or where goods are delivered or services are supplied in a third country, the sales of goods and supplies of services shall be included in the sales factor of all group members in proportion to their labour and asset factors.
5. Where there is more than one group member in the Member State where the goods are delivered or the services are supplied, the sales shall be included in the sales factor of all group members located in that Member State in proportion to their labour and asset factors.

724. The purpose of the throw-back rule, *see* Walter Hellerstein, Construing the Uniform Division of Income for Tax Purposes Act: Reflections on the Illinois Supreme Court's Reading of the 'Throwback' Rule, 45 University of Chicago Law Review 3 (1978).
Hellerstein, Hellerstein & Swain, *supra* n. 349, 9.18[1][b].
The throw-back rule also has planning opportunities; *see* early discussions, Vernon B Savoie & Michael L Burr, The Throwback Rule: Concepts, Components and Planning Opportunities, 2 Journal of State Taxation 19 (1983).
725. Practitioners are criticizing the 'no-where income' as a myth and excuse for states expanding their extraterritorial taxing rights, *see* David J Shipley & Michael A Guariglia, NaCl-State and Local Taxes-Extraterritorial Taxation 101, 87 Tax Magazine 35 (2009).
726. For some discussions on the no-where activities, *see* John A Swain & Walter Hellerstein, State Jurisdiction to Tax Nowhere Activity, 33 Virginia Tax Review 209 (2013).

typical 'throwback' rule: 'Where that place cannot be determined, the sales of goods shall be attributed to the group member located in the Member State of the last identifiable location of the goods'.

CCCTB's throw-back rule is copied from the US's experience. In the US, the UDITPA and the MTC both follow the similar 'sales by destination rule' rationale.[727] Section 16(a)(6) MTC Regulation IV provides the throw-back rule: '(6) If the taxpayer is not taxable in the state of the purchaser, the sale is attributed to this state if the property is shipped from an office, store, warehouse, factory, or other place of storage in this state'.

The throw-back rules of section 16 (a)(7) where the goods are shipped by a third party directly to the purchaser also requires that the taxpayer is not taxable in the destination state:

> (7) If a taxpayer whose salesman operates from an office located in this state makes a sale to a purchaser in another state in which the taxpayer is not taxable and the property is shipped directly by a third party to the purchaser, the following rules apply:
> (A) If the taxpayer is taxable in the state from which the third party ships the property, then the sale is in that state.
> (B) If the taxpayer is not taxable in the state from which the property is shipped, then the sale is in this state.

In short, when the taxpayer is not taxable at the destination state of the goods, the sales should be reassigned to the state of goods' origin; if the taxpayer is not taxable at the state of goods' origin, the sales should be reassigned to the taxpayer's office state where it is taxable.

The 'not taxable' condition demonstrates that the rationale of the throw-back rule is to ensure 'full accountability' of taxable income.[728] The throw-back rule is a reassignment rule for the sales.[729] However, since not every state has implemented the throw-back rule,[730] this disparity makes application of the sales factor even more complicated.[731] In order to pursue full accountability, and to prevent no-where sales,

727. Section 16(a)(1) of MTC Apportionment Regulations IV provides that, sales of goods are attributed to the state when goods are 'delivered or shipped to a purchaser within this state'. Section 16(a)(2)-(5) further regulate how 'delivered or shipped to a purchaser within this state' is defined, including: 'the recipient is located in this state'; 'the shipment terminates in this state'; the ultimate recipient is in the state; the recipient is another state but the goods are en route to a purchaser in this state.
728. Hellerstein, *supra* n. 724; Michael S Schadewald, Primer on Sales Factor Throwback Rule, 29 Journal of State Taxation 9 (2010).
729. Hellerstein, *supra* n. 724.
730. *See* the survey from Editors of the Journal of State Taxation, Throwback Rules for Sales of Tangible Personal Property, 34 J. St. Tax'n 33 (2016); Tax Foundation published a survey in 2018, and it demonstrates the complicities and diversities of the throw-back rules in practice. *See* Katherine Loughead, Does Your State Have a Throwback or Throwout Rule?, 5 December 2018 at http://taxfoundation.org/throwback-rule-throwout-rule.
731. Margaret C Wilson, Apportionment Apoplexy: Throwback, Throwout, or Just Throw up Your Hands, 57 Tax Executive 357 (2005).

the sales-by-destination rationale is not fully followed, the attribution rule for the sales factor has become extremely complex and lost its conceptual coherency.[732]

4.4.2.1.2 The Precondition of 'not taxable at the destination': The Joyce-Finnigan Debate

Moreover, since different states have adopted different approaches to combined reporting, it is even more difficult to ascertain if a throw-back rule should be applicable or not.

To invoke the throw-out rule, its precondition of 'being subject to no tax' is not so easy to define. When a state taxation system also adopts combined reporting, i.e., the group taxation, the throw-back rule will face another question: what is the criterion that 'taxpayer is not taxable'.[733] This is the long-disputed 'Joyce-Finnigan' debate,[734] originally from the *Joyce*[735] and *Finnigan*[736] cases decided by the California tax authorities (SBE) in the 1960s and 1980s,[737] but this debate is also taking place in other states and goes beyond the throw-back rule and reaches the general sales attribution rule.[738] The debate is centred whether the criterion of 'not being taxable' should be based on the specific entity or on the whole group.

According to the 'Joyce rule', the throw-back rule can be triggered as long as the single entity that conducts the sales is not taxable in the destination jurisdiction. Even when another group member from the same unitary group is taxable in the destination jurisdiction, it is still allowed to invoke the throw-back rule. The Joyce rule is based on the strict territorial rationale. The out-of-state sales would be thrown back when the seller entity itself is not taxable at the destination, and the activities and the network established from the unitary group at the destination jurisdiction are not relevant.

In contrast, according to the 'Finnigan rule', the throw-back rule may not apply where at least one single group member in the unitary group is already taxable in the jurisdiction of the sales destination. In other words, according to the Finnigan rule,

---

732. *Ibid.*
733. Lisandra Ortiz, *Joyce v. Finnigan*: Adoption of the 'Best' Approach in Hopes of Some Uniformity, 67 Tax Lawyer 979 (2014). The content of 'Joyce' and 'Finnigan' rule, *see* footnote 742 below.
734. Some brief overview of *Joyce v. Finnigan* debate and the combed reporting, *see also* Noel & Lee, *supra* n. 377.
735. Case Appeal of Joyce, Inc. (No. 66 SBE 069).
736. Case Appeal of Finnigan Corporation (No. 88-SBE-022).
737. Appeal of Finnigan Corporation (No. 88-SBE-022). California court has been changing its approach between the Joyce rule and the Finnigan Rule on this issue. For example, in the Huffy case, it shifted back to the Joyce rule. Robert M Kozub, Readoption of Joyce in Huffy Affects the Sales Factor Determination of Unitary Businesses in California, 19 Journal of State Taxation 1 (2000); development, *see* William F. Fox & LeAnn Luna, *Combined Reporting with the Corporate Income Tax* (NCSL Task Force on State & Local Taxation of Communications and Interstate Commerce 2010).
738. For example, the New York case, Michael Schadewald, Apportionment Issues-Sales Factor of a Combined Unitary Group: The Disney Case, J. St. Tax'n 25 (2007), 9. In this case, the New York adopts the Finnigan rule, even in a non-throwback rule context but a standard attribution of sales context.

only when the whole unitary group that the seller belongs to is not taxable at the destination jurisdiction, can the throw-back rule applies.

In theory, it would be harder to trigger the throw-back rule under the Finnigan rule because the precondition of 'not being taxable' is harder to fulfil. In other words, as long as a sister company or a subsidiary or the parent company is taxable in the sales destination jurisdiction, the sales would not be thrown back even though the specific entity conducting the sales is not taxable.[739] The Finnigan rule is based on the unitary business rationale. Even though the selling entity is not taxable at the destination jurisdiction, it is quite possible that the selling entity is already making use of the business network and resources of another group member in that jurisdiction, such as the retail network.[740] In this regard, it is reasonable to include the sales of this entity for the purpose of calculating the apportionment result in order to reflect this entity's economic activity in relation to the group.

According to the MTC's report on the Joyce-Finnigan debate in 2018,[741] the US Supreme Court has not decided on this issue. There has been a trend towards the Finnigan rule, though there are still many varieties among states.[742] Therefore, although the MTC has not decided its position, it might tend to adopt a simplified Finnigan rule as an option for states.[743] When a throw-back rule is based on the Finnigan rule, although it might feel that a state's taxing right is going beyond the border, such throw-back rule would actually be less-often invoked because the no-tax requirement is more difficult to fulfil. Besides, the Finnigan rule would still be subject to the nexus requirement as well as the unitary business requirement for the apportionability. So, it would not really provide leeway for states to exercise 'exterritorial' taxing rights too much.

In short, the Joyce rule makes it easier to trigger the throw-back rule than the Finnigan rule because the precondition of 'not being taxable' is based only on one single group member. The Joyce rule would be inherently attractive for states' tax authorities. However, the Finnigan rule is much more consistent with thinking about combined reporting and group taxation.

In any case, from the perspective of tax neutrality, it is not tax neutral to deviate from the sales by destination, and thus a tax-neutral throw-back rule exists only when the destination is unknown and not identifiable. The no-tax precondition and the development of the Joyce rule or the Finnigan rule in the US are both inconsistent with tax neutrality, even though the Finnigan rule has largely reduced the possibility to invoke the throw-back rule.

---

739. 'Being not taxable status' can be out of any reason, such as Public Law 86-272 or simply not reaching the taxable nexus threshold of that destination state.
740. This argument is from the Disney case indicated, Schadewald, *supra* n. 738. A California-based company 'Buena Vista Home Video' belonged to the Disney unitary group was not taxable in New York due to Public Law 86-272, though it sold movie cassettes to New York. It made use of the Disney retail stores to sell movie cassettes. The Court has included its sales also in the sales factor of the New York tax return. *Disney Enters., Inc. v. Tax Appeals Tribunal of the State*, 888 N.E.2d 1029 *(N.Y.* 2008).
741. MTC Legal Staff, Finnigan Briefing Book Provided to Phil Skinner, Idaho (MTC 2018).
742. *Ibid.*, Annex E, the survey of states' position regarding the Joyce-Finnigan.
743. *Ibid.*, 7.

4.4.2.2 *The CCCTB's 'throw-around rule' Is Not Market Neutral Because It Combines the PE Threshold*

In addition to the throw-back rule of Article 38(1), Article 38(4) of the current CCCTB Directive Proposal further provides a 'throw-around' rule when there is no group member located in the Member State where the service is physically carried out. Article 38(4) reads:

> Where there is no group member in the Member State where the goods are delivered or the services are supplied, or where goods are delivered or services are supplied in a third country, the sales of goods and supplies of services shall be included in the sales factor of all group members in proportion to their labor and asset factors.

Article 38(4) of the current CCCTB Directive Proposal is not a typical 'throw-back' provision because it does not mention a specific group member to 'throw back'. The tax-neutral throw-back provision is like the last sentence of Article 38(1), which deals with the situation that the place of destination is not identifiable. In contrast, the clause in Article 38(4) deals with the situation that there is no group member that the receipts can be attributed to, despite the destination being clearly identified. Therefore, the place of destination is identifiable and certain, but there is no group member/PE there. Article 38(4) actually aims to solve a tax nexus issue.

Article 38(4) then provides that the 'no-where' sales should be attributed to all group members in proportion to their labour and asset factors. This is not a 'throw-back' provision but a 'throw-around' provision[744] because the sales and receipts will be attributed pro rata to all the group members according to the labour factor and the assets factor.

When the taxable nexus is still a 'PE', Article 38(4) of the current CCCTB Directive Proposal triggers the throw-around rule too easily and thus changes the sales factor's function. As the BEPS action plans demonstrate, the problem of avoiding a PE status is hard to address in the current digital economy, but the current CCCTB Directive Proposal's current sales factor attribution rule is as vulnerable as traditional international tax treaties. Based on Article 38(4), the sales-by-destination principle can be circumvented by avoiding a group member or simply avoiding the PE status in that jurisdiction. As long as there is no group member at the destination state, the destination principle no longer applies, but the throw-around rule applies instead. When Articles 38(4) applies, the reassigned sales no longer reflect the group members' economic activities in the destination state.

In my view, the throw-around rule under the current CCCTB Directive Proposal is not based on a tax-neutral position[745] but based on the fear of losing revenue in the

744. This term is from Hellerstein, *supra* n. 549, footnote 79; Durst also uses similar term, *see* M Durst, Analysis of a Formulary System, Part VII: The Sales Factor, 22 Bloomsberg BNA Tax Management Transfer Pricing Report 1414 (2014).

745. Different ideas on the throw-back rule, for example, Pereira, *supra* n. 81, at 399-400. Pereira argues that the CCCTB should be designed to ensure single taxation. So, the throw-back or the throw-out rule in state taxation is a good reference. With the same rationale, Pereira argues that

name of catching 'no-where sales'. Such fear is understandable but is not suitable for a tax reform because it is not theoretically sound or administratively simple. More importantly, the throw-around rule deviates from the economic reality, i.e., the destination of goods or services, and it seeks a seemingly fair arrangement to 'throw around' to other group members. Deviation from the sales-by-destination setting should be limited to the situation when the destination is not indefinable. The throw-back rule or throw-around rule can be neutral only when the destinations are not identifiable. The throw-back rule or throw-around rule is absolutely not a shift back to 'the sales by origin rationale' either, but it is just used by any state that wishes to include the out-of-state sales when they 'feel' or fear the result would be unfair.

When the attribution rules are neutral, the need to have attribution rules for special industries will naturally decrease. Complexities will also decrease as a consequence. Since the throw-back or throw-around rule is an exception to the main destination rule, they should only apply when necessary.

Last, as a sidenote, although Article 38(5) of the 2016 CCCTB Directive Proposal is a throw-around rule, it is redundant. Article 38(5) provides that when there is more than one group member located in the Member State where the service is physically carried out, the receipts are also attributed to all group members involved of that Member State, according to their labour and assets factor. It is redundant and illogical because when there is more than one group member in the destination state, there is no need to throw around because the sales can be attributed to the destination, and it is neutral. From the perspective of pursuing full accountability or preventing 'no-where sales', Article 38(5)'s throw-around rule still makes no sense. Therefore, it is also a non-neutral deviation from the sales-by-destination principle and cannot be justified in any case.

4.4.3 When the Destination Is Not Convenient: The Deemed Destinations by Proxies

In this section, I analyse attribution rules for services in detail. The following discussions involve three types of attribution rules for services: first, the current CCCTB Directive Proposal's attribution rule for services, which is still influenced by the COP Rule/Income-Generating Rule in the US.

Second, there are the destination-based attribution rules, by the MTC's latest tax reform to the traditional COP rule since 2014, the 'Market-Sourcing' rules. The MTC's market-sourcing regulations mainly involve various customer-related proxies to seek the 'market'. After that I summarize the latest developments and reforms on this issue in the US.

Third, there is a mixture of the destination and origin rules, a hybrid approach developed in the VAT regime. I discuss the OECD VAT guidelines and EU VAT Rules

CCCTB should adopt a more comprehensive switch-over clause to ensure effectively exercising taxing rights regarding the third countries to ensure single taxation. Pereira's benchmark is 'single taxation', neither tax neutrality nor the benefit principle, and thus her implication would not be consistent with my conclusion.

and revisit the VAT 'place of supply' rules in the context of the OECD and the EU. Even in the context of VAT that is supposed to reflect 'consumption' as its destination, there are still origin-based proxies that are selected for 'collection points', and these proxies deviate from the destination principle.

All these discussions aim to analyse what 'destination', 'deemed destination', and 'origin' are and whether they are consistent with the benefit-based MN framework.

4.4.3.1 *Attribution Rules of Sales of Services under the Current CCCTB Directive Proposal Repeats the US's Mistakes*

Article 38(2) of the current CCCTB Directive Proposal provides that 'Supplies of services shall be included in the sales factor of the group member located in the Member State where the services are physically carried out or actually supplied'.[746] The 2016 version added the phrase 'actually supplied' in the end of the sentence.

In the preamble of the current CCCTB Directive Proposal, the attribution rules for sales of services seems to also follow the 'sales by destination' rule; however, from the text of Article 38(2), it focuses on 'physical location of performance'. But in the case of cross-border services provided via telecommunication technology, we are still not really sure if Article 38(2) should be understood as where the services are performed or where the services are received. Both locations can be interpreted as 'physically carried out or actually supplied'. The text is not quite clear which location should be the answer. Article 38(2) does not fully implement the sales-by-destination principle.

Moreover, under Article 38(4) of the current CCCTB Directive Proposal, the throw-around rule also applies to the sales factor of services. The problems of the throw-around rule were discussed in the previous section. Just like cross-border sales of goods, cross-border sales of services can be conducted without a PE at the destination state. As long as the throw-around rule is still closely connected to the PE requirement as the taxable nexus requirement, it cannot be tax neutral.

4.4.3.2 *The New Destination Principle for Attributing Services in the US: 'market-sourcing'*

As discussed in section 4.2.2, there has been a paradigm shift in the US with regard to the attribution rule for services providing: from the origin-based COP Rule/Income-Generating Rule to the market-sourcing rule because the COP rule no longer represents the economic reality and has caused unreasonable results. The rest is history. The Article IV section 17 of the new Multistate Tax Compact and MTC Regulation IV are the latest developments.

746. In the 2011 version of the CCCTB Directive Proposal, the supplies of service shall be attributed to 'where the services are physically carried out'.

The Article IV section 17 of the new Multistate Tax Compact (as of 2015)[747] provides:

(a) Receipts, other than receipts described in Section 16, are in this state if the taxpayer's market for the sales is in this state. The taxpayer's market for sales is in this state:
  (1) in the case of sale, rental, lease or license of real property, if and to the extent the property is located in this state;
  (2) in the case of rental, lease or license of tangible personal property, if and to the extent the property is located in this state;
  (3) in the case of sale of a service, if and to the extent the service is delivered to a location in this state; and
  (4) in the case of intangible property,
    (i) that is rented, leased, or licensed, if and to the extent the property is used in this state, provided that intangible property utilized in marketing a good or service to a consumer is 'used in this state' if that good or service is purchased by a consumer who is in this state; and
    (ii) that is sold, if and to the extent the property is used in this state, provided that:
      (A) a contract right, government license, or similar intangible property that authorizes the holder to conduct a business activity in a specific geographic area is 'used in this state' if the geographic area includes all or part of this state;
      (B) receipts from intangible property sales that are contingent on the productivity, use, or disposition of the intangible property shall be treated as receipts from the rental, lease or licensing of such intangible property under subsection (a)(4)(i); and
      (C) all other receipts from a sale of intangible property shall be excluded from the numerator and denominator of the receipts factor.

(b) If the state or states of assignment under subsection (a) cannot be determined, the state or states of assignment shall be reasonably approximated.

(c) If the taxpayer is not taxable in a state to which a receipt is assigned under subsection (a) or (b), or if the state of assignment cannot be determined under subsection (a) or reasonably approximated under subsection (b), such receipt shall be excluded from the denominator of the receipts factor.

(d) [The tax administrator may prescribe regulations as necessary or appropriate to carry out the purposes of this section.]

As Hellerstein criticized, though section 17 new Multistate Tax Compact pays a lot of attention to 'market-sourcing' for attributing the sales, the definition of 'market' is still not clear. Even in the implementing regulation, the 'market' is not directly formulated. States now have implemented the new section 17 but not completely in the identical manner.[748]

The new section 17 covers all types of sales 'other than sales of movable tangible properties'. The attribution principle for services is to the location where the service is

747. The new section 17 is published and can be requested at the MTC official website http://www.mtc.gov/.
748. Blaise M Sonnier & Ricardo Colon, The Shift Toward Market-Based Sourcing for Multistate Apportionment of Income from Services, 34 Journal of State Taxation 21 (2015).

'delivered'. The ways of delivering for different types of services are regulated by the implementing regulation.[749] Without adopting a specific throw-back or throw-around rule, the new section 17(b) grants the tax authorities the ability to estimate the attribution of the sales factor within the state. The results of assigning the sales shall be 'reasonably approximated' when the tax authorities cannot determine the sales attribution. The more detailed approaches to 'reasonable approximation' will be regulated by the implementing regulation too.

In short, the most important amendments of Article IV section 17 Multistate Tax Compact involve the shift from 'costs of performance' to 'market-sourcing'.[750] The market-sourcing rationale is now more theoretically sound and consistent with economic activities.[751] However, the market-sourcing rules turn out to be quite complex and still raise a concern about uncertainty.

Section 17 MTC Regulation IV implemented Article IV section 17 Multistate Tax Compact in detail. It is a complex rule because it decides the destination of the sales of service (the market-sourcing) based on three cumulative sets of circumstances (the types of service, the status of the customer as a business customer or an individual customer, and the ways of delivering service via physical means or electronic means or on behalf of/through an intermediary). There are eight different situations, six different proxies, and one general free discretion clause for tax authorities to decide the proxy of destination. I have summarized section 17 MTC Regulation IV in Table 3 in the Annex attached to Chapter 4 and the overview decision flowchart in Figure 8 at the end of this section.

4.4.3.2.1 Three Different Types of Services Influence the Destination Proxy

Article IV section 17 Multistate Tax Compact is further implemented by section 17 MTC Regulation IV.[752] The attribution rules are designed according to three types of services: 'in-person services', 'professional services', and 'other services', neither in-person nor professional. Different types of services will be subject to different attribution rules, but they all refer to their 'destination', i.e., their customers' markets, but the distinctions lead to selecting different proxies. Not all these proxies provided are neutral from the sales-by-destination perspective, as I explain in the following paragraphs.

749. MTC Hearing officer's report (2016), which can be requested at the MTC official website http://www.mtc.gov/.
750. Richard Pomp, Report of the Hearing Officer Multistate Tax Compact Article IV [UDITPA] Proposed Amendments,available at https://ssrn.com/abstract=3853124.
751. The theory and practice do not always coincide from the beginning, but the state practice has evolved under the influence of the market-sourcing rationale. For example, *see* the development of creating a hybrid sourcing rules in Texas, Langenberg & Jones, *supra* n. 652.
752. MTC Regulation IV is published and can be requested at the MTC official website http://www.mtc.gov/.

4.4.3.2.2 *In-Person Services*

In-person services[753] refer to 'services that are physically provided in person by the taxpayer, where the customer or the customer's real or tangible property upon which the services are performed is in the same location as the service provider at the time the services are performed'. Typical in-person services include cleaning services, warranty and repair services, hair-cutting, child-care, etc.[754] This is similar to the 'on-spot service' concept in the VAT. The locations of the in-person service performance and receipt of service are usually the same. Therefore, the assignment (i.e., attribution) rules[755] of the sales from performing in-person services are 'where received';[756] when necessary, tax authorities decide appropriate 'reasonable approximation' methods to throw out some receipts.

4.4.3.2.3 *Professional Services*

Professional services[757] refer to 'services that require specialized knowledge and, in some cases, require a professional certification, license, or degree'. These professional services include legal, accounting, tax preparation, bank data processing service, etc.[758] As to professional services, the attribution rules of the sales are dependent on the types of customers: individual customers and business customers. To source receipts earned from these two types of customers, different rules apply. For individual customers, the sales are attributed to the primary residence or the billing address. The detailed rules for business customers are more complicated, depending on where the services could be attributed: the place of management, or place of order, or to billing address, depending on different situations. This is discussed in the following section.

4.4.3.2.4 *'Other Services': Linking Targeted Customers of Another Market*

In addition to in-person and professional services, MTC Regulation IV recognizes 'other services'. The feature of 'other services' is that a service is delivered to another targeted group of people other than the customers who order the service. Another group of people is the ordering customer's own or potential 'customers'. A typical example of such services is online advertising: the advertising companies' customers are enterprises which pay for the service, and the advertising services are performed towards an audience, viewers, and readers. In this case, an advertising service would involve customers of another related market.

753. Section 17(d)(2)(A) of MTC Regulation IV.
754. Examples are listed in section 17(d)(2)(A) of MTC Model Regulation IV.
755. Section 17(d)(2)(B)1 of MTC Regulation IV.
756. Such as 'attributed to the location of the real estate of the service'; 'attributing to the location of the customer's physical presence'; 'attributing to the location of the service received in case of shipping the customer's personal tangible property'.
757. Section 17(d)(4) of MTC Regulation IV.
758. For examples, *see* Proposed section 17(d)(4)(A) of MTC Regulation IV.

Another example of 'other services' is web-based services. With a similar structure, a web-based 'customer service' provider can provide their services to other enterprises that sell computer software or digital services, so customers can consult such web-based service provider while such extra services are included in the product or service price.[759] This type of service would involve third-party end users/viewers, and it is actually bundled with sales of goods or services provided by their customer, which is why these services are delivered 'to', 'on behalf of', and 'through' the customer.

If we understand the market of advertising services as only between the advertising companies and the companies that order advertising, we ignore the audience of the advertisement. In fact, information transmission is the key to the digital economy: via the Internet and data mining and analysing, controlling, and presenting information to the correct targeted audience and recipients has become the key to business success. The issue of audience actually existed even in the pre-Internet era,[760] but due to the rapid development in technology nowadays, the audience can influence the market deeply in the whole supply-demand chain. Therefore, it is quite wise that the MTC's market-sourcing rules address this type of service involving third-party recipients specifically, but its selected proxies are quite complicated.

4.4.3.2.5 *The Status as Business Customer Influences the Destination Proxy*

The MTC's new market-sourcing rules for professional services and other services distinguish B2B and B2C.[761] As to the individual customers, the location of their 'primary residence' or the location of the actual receipt of the service is the key proxy to source the market. As to business customers, the location of 'the contract being principally managed' is the key proxy to source the market.

Section 17(d) further provides alternative proxies for attributing professional services to business customers when the main proxy is not identifiable: professional services are attributed to the location of the contract being principally managed; when the location of the contract being principally managed cannot be identified, the sales

759. Section 17(d)(3) of MTC Regulation IV.

760. As to using the audience or subscribers as the weighting factor, in US state taxation practice, advertising is regulated by the special publishing industry formula recommendation adopted by MTC in US since 1993. It especially includes 'circulation factor', to reflect the subscribers' role in the formula.

The full text is available and can be requested at the MTC official website http://www.mtc.gov/.

See Chapter 7 of this book for the theory of adopting a special industry formula. For more details, *see* Hellerstein, Hellerstein & Swain, *supra* n. 349, at 10.4.

The special industry formula for publishing is not specifically addressed in this book because the CCCTB Directive Proposal does not address this industry separately. However, this is a typical example that 'destination' is relative and difficult to decide.

Multistate Taxation Commission has the special formula for Television and Radio Broadcasting since 1990. It adopts 'the audience factor' in the sales factor, to reflect the audience's importance for formula.

For more details *see*, Hellerstein, Hellerstein & Swain, *supra* n. 349, at 10.5.

761. As the same as the distinction of B2B and B2C services in the VAT.

may be attributed to the location where the order was placed. If the location of ordering is not identifiable, then the sale is attributed to the location of the customer's billing address.

However, when a taxpayer derives more than 5 % of its profits from one business customer, the taxpayer must identify the location of that business customer's contract being principally managed. This is because earning 5 % of its profits from one customer would mean a solid business relationship, so that the information received is supposed to be sufficient enough for the taxpayer to identify the location where its business customer principally manages the contract. Taxpayers cannot invoke other proxies. The same rationale applies to 'sales of performing professional services to individual customers'.[762]

For assigning the sales from professional services, there is an extra quantitative criterion: the safe harbour clause (also called the large volume of transactions clause).[763] When the safe-harbour clause is fulfilled, taxpayers can choose to use the convenient and simplified proxy of 'billing address' as its market destination. There are two cumulative conditions of the safe harbour clause for a taxpayer: (1) engages in substantially similar service transactions with more than 250 customers, whether individuals or businesses, and (2) does not derive more than 5 % of its receipts from sales of services from that customer (which is not a major customer in this case).

The rationale of the safe-harbour clause is to strike a balance between providing convenience while making sure that taxpayers do not abuse the business setting to manipulate the attribution result. The billing address is a convenient administrative proxy and can only be used in a situation that the taxpayer cannot easily manipulate. When taxpayers' volume of transactions is more than 5 %, it is reasonable to ascertain the real principal contract management location. For business customers, when the safe harbour clause does not apply, sales will be attributed to the location of the contract being principally managed by the business customers.

4.4.3.2.6 Means of Delivery Influences the Destination Proxy for Attributing 'other services'

The attribution rules for services involving third-party recipients (i.e., 'other services') are as follows. There are two types of means of delivery[764] according to section 17 MTC Regulation IV: '(1) physically delivered to the customer; (2) electronical means, being divided into three sub-types: electronically delivered 'to', 'on behalf of', or 'through' the customer'. This type of service arises at the core of the digital economy and is

762. For sales of performing professional services to individual customers, if the safe harbour clause does not apply, the sales shall be attributed to the location of the customer's primary 'residence'. If the customer's primary residence is not identifiable, then the sales shall be attributed to the individual customer's billing address. In other word, if the safe harbour clause does not fulfil the requirements, the individual customer's billing address will only be a residual rule not the main rule. However, when the taxpayer derives more than 5 % of profits from one individual customer, the taxpayer must identify that individual's primary residence.
763. Section 17(d)(4)(C)1.c of MTC Regulation IV.
764. Section 17(d)(3) of MTC Regulation IV.

heavily disputed because the means of delivery can create extra difficulties in ascertaining the market.

In the case of being delivered by physical means, the sales are assigned to the location of the delivery of the services.[765] Delivering services via a physical medium includes delivery of a brochure for advertising services, or delivery of a DVD for software upgrading services.[766] This type of software upgrading service is not delivered via downloading but through the delivery of a DVD. Since there is a physical medium, it is easier to trace, and therefore the location of the delivery of the physical medium is the key criterion.[767] If the taxpayer cannot determine the actual location of the service being delivered, then the sales are attributed according to the tax authorities' reasonable approximation.[768]

In the case of being electronically delivered to a customer directly, the attribution rules depend on the status of the customer: business or individual. It is the same as the attribution rule regarding professional services:

> If the customers are business customers, the attribution rules regarding the attribution of the professional services to business customers indicated above will apply too: that is, the main proxy is where the contracts are principle managed; but when the safe harbour clause[769] is fulfilled, the billing address can be the proxy.
>
> If the customers are individual customers, the sales from other services delivered electronically will be attributed to the location where the individual customers actually receive service.[770] If the tax authorities cannot make sure of the location of receiving service, the tax authorities can reasonably approximate based on the information they have. If they do not have sufficient information to approximate reasonably, the sales will be attributed to the location of the customers' billing address.

In the case of being delivered electronically 'through or on behalf of a customer', the sales are attributed to the location of the services being received by the end-users or third-party recipients. If the taxpayers do not have sufficient information to determine the location of the end-users or third-party recipients, the sales are attributed according to the tax authorities' reasonable approximation. The typical advertising's audience or viewers or web-customer service, and the sales are attributed to the end-customers. This type of market-sourcing rules are an important advancement because the MTC regulations have recognized that service-related markets can target the same group of individuals, and the means of electronic transmission make such target possible.

765. Section 17(d)(3)(B)1.a of MTC Regulation IV.
766. Section 17(d)(3) (B)1 of MTC Regulation IV.
767. Section 17(d)(3) (B)1.a of MTC Regulation IV.
768. Section 17(d)(3)1.b of MTC Regulation IV.
769. Section 17(d)(3)(B)2.b.iv of MTC Regulation IV.
770. Section 17(d)(3)(B)2.a of MTC Regulation IV.

4.4.3.2.7 *Dynamic Between Taxpayers' Obligation and Tax Authorities' Discretion*

4.4.3.2.7.1 Customers' Billing Address Allowed for Non-major Customers

It is worth noting that the customers' billing address can be the proxy under some specific circumstances, i.e., the safe harbour rule, or the large volume transaction rule, is fulfilled.[771] When the cumulative tests of the safe harbour clause are both met, the taxpayer may use the customers' billing address as the proxy for the market-sourcing. Such rule applies to all customers of the professional service providers or the business customers of other electronically direct delivered services. Such a safe harbour rule can effectively reduce administrative costs because it is easier to keep records of the billing address. Since the taxpayer's profits are not concentrated on a specific customer, the possibility of tax avoidance is also smaller. Therefore, customers' billing addresses will not be vulnerable and easily manipulated in this situation.

4.4.3.2.7.2 Taxpayers' Obligation to Ascertain Major Customers' Location(s)

While having the opportunity to use the simplified proxy of the billing address, taxpayers have an obligation to ascertain their own major customers' information under some circumstances. If the taxpayer in fact gains more than 5% of its profits from the specific customer, the taxpayer has the obligation to ascertain the business customer's location of the contract being managed or the location of the individual customer's primary residence. The taxpayer cannot claim its inability to ascertain locations in order to assign the receipts to the customer's billing address. The rationale of 'the more than 5% profits rule' is that the taxpayer should have the capacity and sufficient information on one important customer, i.e., 'a major customer'.[772]

4.4.3.2.7.3 Tax Authorities' Discretion to Reasonable Approximation and Caution to Related Party Transactions

The new section 17 also grants wide discretion for tax authorities to ascertain where the market is. This is known as the power of 'reasonable approximation'. Section 17 MTC Regulation IV provides primary[773] and secondary reasonable approximation[774] methods and allows tax authorities to use these methods when mentioned in the Regulation

771. There are two conditions of the safe harbour rule to decide the receipt from a customer: (1) the taxpayer engaging in substantially similar services with more than 250 customers, and (2) the taxpayer must not gain profits of more than 5% from one customer. In other words, that customer is not a major customer.
772. Schadewald, *supra* n. 648.
773. Section 17(d)(3)(B)2.b.ii of MTC Regulation IV: 'Rule of Reasonable Approximation. If the taxpayer cannot determine the state or states where the customer actually receives the service,

specifically. 'Reasonable approximation' is especially vital for 'other services' because services via electronic methods of delivery can reach many different customers in different places. The new section 17 grants wide discretionary powers to tax authorities to decide the reasonable assignment of the sales arising from the performance of services. There are other reasonable approximation methods for electronically delivered services involving the intended audience for tax authorities; MTC Regulation IV allow more indicators, such as subscription lists or the macro-data, such as population for advertising services.[775]

Moreover, the new MTC Regulation IV also recognizes that the market-sourcing rules might be manipulated in the case of 'related party transactions'. 'Related party'[776] is defined as a party that the taxpayer substantially controls, for example, it has more

---

but has sufficient information regarding the place of receipt from which it can reasonably approximate the state or states where the service is received, it shall reasonably approximate the state or states.'

774. Section 17(d)(3)(B)2.b.iii of MTC Regulation IV:

> Secondary Rule of Reasonable Approximation. In the case of the delivery of a service to a business customer by electronic transmission where a taxpayer does not have sufficient information from which it can determine or reasonably approximate the state or states in which the service is received, the taxpayer shall reasonably approximate the state or states as set forth in this regulation.
>
> In these cases, unless the taxpayer can apply the safe harbour set forth in Section 17(d).(3)(B)2.b.iv of MTC Reg. IV, the taxpayer shall reasonably approximate the state or states in which the service is received as follows: first, by assigning the receipts from the sale to the state where the contract of sale is principally managed by the customer; second, if the state where the customer principally manages the contract is not reasonably determinable, by assigning the receipts from the sale to the customer's place of order; and third, if the customer's place of order is not reasonably determinable, by assigning the receipts from the sale using the customer's billing address; provided, however, if the taxpayer derives more than 5% of its receipts from sales of services from any single customer, the taxpayer is required to identify the state in which the contract of sale is principally managed by that customer.

775. If the services involve advertising with subscription lists, the sales will be attributed and reasonably approximated according to the list; if the advertising services lack subscription lists, the attribution of sales will be reasonably approximated according to the population of the states involved. If the services involve the taxpayer's intermediary reselling of services, such as cable television programming service, advertising from network companies, etc., the population of the states involved will be taken into account.

See guidance about section 17 (d)(3)(B)3.c. of MTC Regulation IV Select Secondary Rules of Reasonable Approximation.

776. Section 17(a)(3)(H) of MTC Regulation IV 'Related party' means:

> (1) a stockholder who is an individual, or a member of the stockholder's family set forth in section 318 of the Code if the stockholder and the members of the stockholder's family own, directly, indirectly, beneficially or constructively, in the aggregate, at least 50 per cent of the value of the taxpayer's outstanding stock;
> (2) a stockholder, or a stockholder's partnership, limited liability company, estate, trust or corporation, if the stockholder and the stockholder's partnerships, limited liability companies, estates, trusts and corporations own directly, indirectly, beneficially or constructively, in the aggregate, at least 50 per cent of the value of the taxpayer's outstanding stock; or
> (3) a corporation, or a party related to the corporation in a manner that would require an attribution of stock from the corporation to the party or from the party to the corporation under the attribution rules of the Code if the taxpayer owns, directly, indirectly, beneficially or constructively, at least 50 per cent of the value of the corporation's outstanding stock. The attribution rules of the Code shall apply for

than a 50% shareholding, and thus it is easier to use related-party transactions as a tool to manipulate the sales assignment rule. For example, in the case of a related-party transaction of services electronically delivered to a business customer, taxpayers may not use the proxies of the secondary reasonable approximation methods (i.e., the formal proxies that might be manipulated: where the contract is principally managed, the place of order, the customer's billing address).[777] For another example, in the case of professional services provided to the related party, tax authorities may assign the receipts according to the related-party's payroll within the state.[778] In any case, tax authorities may use their wide discretion to decide where the market is in the case of a related-party transaction under the new MTC Regulation IV.

4.4.3.2.7.4 Proxies Reflecting Services Received in Customers' Physical Location(s) Are Neutral

To sum up, the new market-sourcing rule provided by MTC Regulation IV has provided many proxies to ascertain the destination. Many proxies are a true destination, such as 'where received' and ultimate users' location; this type of proxy is consistent with the

---

purposes of determining whether the ownership requirements of this definition have been met. [or insert state definition]

(B) 'State where a contract of sale is principally managed by the customer,' means the primary location at which an employee or other representative of a customer serves as the primary contact person for the taxpayer with respect to the day-to-day execution and performance of a contract entered into by the taxpayer with the customer.

777. For example, section 17(d)(3)(B)2.b.v. of MTC Regulation IV:

> Related Party Transactions. In the case of a sale of a service by electronic transmission to a business customer that is a related party, the taxpayer may not use the secondary rule of reasonable approximation in Reg. IV.17.(d).(3)(B)2.b.iii but may use the rule of reasonable approximation in Reg. IV.17.(d).(3)(B)2.b.ii, and the safe harbour in Reg. IV.17.(d).(3)(B)2.b.iv, provided that [the tax administrator] may aggregate sales to related parties in determining whether the sales exceed 5% of receipts from sales of all services under that safe harbour provision if necessary or appropriate to prevent distortion.

778. Section 17(d)(4)(C)4 of MTC Regulation IV:

> Related Party Transactions. In any instance in which the professional service is sold to a related party, rather than applying the rule for professional services delivered to business customers in Reg. IV.17.(d).(4)(C)1.b, the state or states to which the service is assigned is the place of receipt by the related party as reasonably approximated using the following hierarchy: (1) if the service primarily relates to specific operations or activities of a related party conducted in one or more locations, then to the state or states in which those operations or activities are conducted in proportion to the related party's payroll at the locations to which the service relates in the state or states; or (2) if the service does not relate primarily to operations or activities of a related party conducted in particular locations, but instead relates to the operations of the related party generally, then to the state or states in which the related party has employees, in proportion to the related party's payroll in those states. The taxpayer may use the safe harbor provided by Reg. IV.17.(d).(4)(C)1.c provided that [the tax administrator] may aggregate the receipts from sales to related parties in applying the 5% rule if necessary or appropriate to avoid distortion.

sales-by-destination rationale, and they are tax neutral. However, other proxies are proxies of deemed destinations. The rest of them are based on information related to individual and business customers, such as 'where the contract is principally managed', primary residence, place of order, billing address, etc. Therefore, it is clear that the MTC market-sourcing rules make a great effort to implement the destination principle.

The deemed destination proxies are not always tax neutral; only when these proxies reflect the customers' physical locations where services are received are these proxies tax neutral. MTC Regulation IV tries to strike a balance between anti-avoidance and tax administration convenience and therefore distinguishes the market-sourcing proxies from many perspectives. These various reasonable approximation methods can create possible inconsistencies and thus are not a good option for the CCCTB to adopt.

Section 17 MTC Regulation IV is illustrated in the decision flowchart in Figure 7. This flowchart demonstrates that in the end, section 17 MTC Regulation IV distinguishes eight different situations and six types of proxies are used to indicate the destination of services for the sales factor and provides tax authorities with quite wide discretion to decide the proxy of the destination (via 'reasonable approximation'), when necessary.

4.4.3.2.7.5 The Decision Flowchart of Section 17(d) MTC Regulation IV[779]

See Figure 7.

779. This figure is copied from Schadewald, *supra* n. 648. It is a brief version of the flowchart published by MTC in 2014.

Figure 7 The Decision Flowchart of Section 17(d) MTC Regulation IV

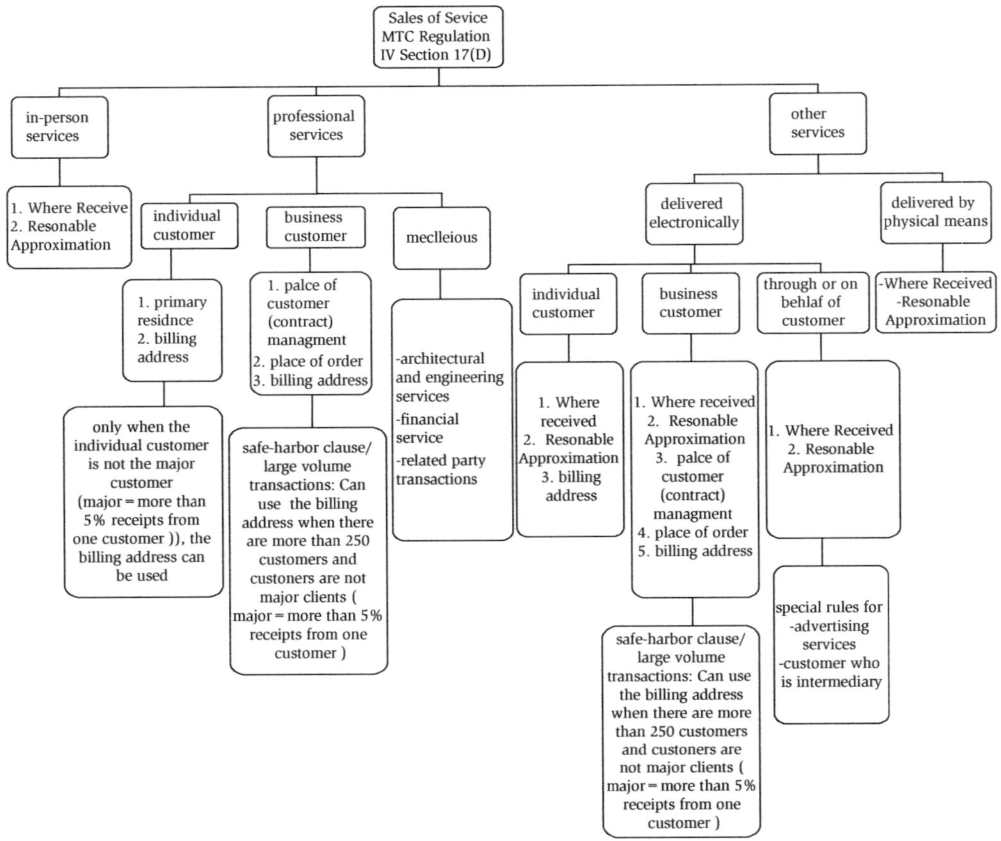

Source: Reproduced from Michael S Schadewald, 2017.

4.4.3.3 *Origin-Based Proxies as 'deemed destination' of Consumption in VAT as a Hybrid*

4.4.3.3.1 OECD VAT/GST Guidelines: The Destination Principle as a Slogan

VAT is a consumption tax, and therefore the destination seems the most logical and intuitive option. However, despite mentioning the 'destination principle' at a general conceptual level from the very beginning, there are actually different views on the actual design of the national VAT systems in practice.[780] The 'destination principle' and the 'origin principle'[781] have been widely discussed and debated in the field of VAT as equal options;[782] some scholars have seen this dichotomy as similar to the residence principle and the source principle in international tax law regarding direct taxation.[783] When we read the 'destination principle' in VAT closely, we can quickly realize that the destination principle in the general sense and the destination principle implemented in the VAT actual rules are 'false friends' that share the same name but do not exactly have identical contents.[784]

In the OECD VAT/GST guidelines, B2B and B2C transactions use different proxies to decide 'consumption/place of supplies': for B2B supplies of services, place of supplies is deemed to be the place of 'establishment of the business customer'; for B2C supplies of services, place of supplies is deemed to be the customer's location (in the case of on-the-spot services that customers and service providers are in the same location), with the proxy of the customer's residence.[785] Both options seem still roughly consistent with the destination principle.

From the level of ideology, the destination principle is still the fundamental rationale for a VAT system in the OECD VAT/GST guidelines; from the level of practice, the destination principle helps in selecting the proxy but does not provide much

780. As to destination principle concept in OECD's development of VAT guidelines from the Ottawa taxation framework in 1997 to the latest version of VAT/GST guidelines after the BEPS project, *See* Senyk, *supra* n. 715, at 5.2.
781. Although the mainstream of VAT scholars advocate the destination principle, there are also some reflections to adopt the origin element to improve the current VAT system. *See*, for example, Howell H Zee, A VAT Voucher System for Origin-Based Taxation, 20 EC Tax Review 75 (2011).
    Senyk observes that, OECD uses the origin principle and the destination principle not consistently, Senyk, *supra* n. 715, at 7.1.
782. Schenk, Thuronyi & Cui, *supra* n. 632, at 188.
783. Millar, *supra* n. 485. Millar argue, the 'origin element' in these VAT attributing rules for services above, echoes the phenomenon that the source concept of the international taxation. However, the traditional source concept (as well as the residence concept) in the international tax law regime is no longer adequate or appropriate for dividing a cross-border taxable income because the source concept can cover any involved jurisdiction and does not provide a clear indication in the context of digital economy. The origin concept in the VAT is facing the same problem as the 'source' concept.
784. Millar, *supra* n. 485; Senyk also extensively explored the different contents under the name of 'the destination principle' in different fields of tax law, *see* Senyk, *supra* n. 715.
785. Walter Hellerstein, An Introduction to the OECD's International VAT/GST Guidelines, Journal of Taxation 256 (2016).

guidance as to where the destination actually is.[786] Hellerstein vividly used the term of 'best guess' to describe the customer's residence as the deemed destination.[787] 'The individual customer's residence' as such is not a destination per se, compared to 'enjoyment' or 'consumption', but an acceptable proxy for levying VAT.

The destination principle is also implemented in B2B services but confronted new issues when the business customer has more than one location. For B2B services, the OECD VAT/GST guidelines further distinguish business customers as single location entities (SLE) customers and multiple location entities (MLE) customers.[788] Providing services to an SLE customer (which has only one establishment) involves only one jurisdiction; providing services to an MLE customer involves multiple jurisdictions.

As to services provided to an SLE business customer, the OECD VAT/GST guidelines suggest the place of taxation is the SLE business customer's establishment;[789] as to services provided to an MLE business customer, the OECD VAT/GST guidelines suggest that there can be three equally possible options: direct delivery, direct use, or a 'recharge' method to decide the place of taxation.[790] The 'recharge' method accepts that a service provided to an MLE can be attributed to different places and decides the place of taxation according to an 'internal arrangement' (read: self-assessment) between these multiple entities of the business.[791] From the perspective of tax neutrality, 'direct use' is the tax-neutral option or attributing sales of services; the 'internal arrangement/self-assessment' method might coincide with the direct use method, but the MNE customer's self-assessment cannot always reflect the plural locations of the services provided in reality.

The OECD VAT/GST guidelines suggest proxies for consumption, but these proxies do not always represent 'the market that Multinational Enterprises (MNEs) taxpayers have the response to'. The OECD guidelines are criticized for adding confusion to the concepts of destination and origin.[792] However, the OECD VAT/GST guidelines still indicate two valuable lessons that can be taken, especially for the CCCTB's sales factor: First, accepting that services or intangibles can be provided in

786. Michael Keen & Walter Hellerstein, Interjurisdictional Issues in the Design of a VAT, 63 Tax Law Review 359 (2009).
787. Hellerstein, *supra* n. 785.
788. Walter Hellerstein, A Hitchhiker's Guide to the OECD's International VAT/GST Guidelines, 18 Florida Tax Review 589 (2015).
789. It is combed with a 'reverse charge' mechanism (i.e., self-assessment) mechanism, that 'the SLE business customer' accounts for the tax due in the jurisdiction and bears the compliance burden. *See* Hellerstein *Ibid.*
790. *Ibid.*, 617.
791. Currently, EU VAT adopts Restricted Direct Use Method, not adopt the recharge method. Merkx argues that, the advantages of adopting the recharge method outweigh the advantages of the current Restricted Direct Use Method in EU VAT law. Merkx has examined the drawbacks of the current Restricted Direct Use Method as an all-or-nothing approach not reflecting multiple location of use and prevalent abusive practices and argued that, the recharge method should also be implemented by EU, and the compliance burden of the recharge method is not as heavy as critics thought. *See* Madeleine Merkx, Should EU VAT Apply the Recharge Method in the Place of Supply Rules for B2B Services?, 22 EC Tax Review 282 (2013).
792. Senyk, *supra* n. 715.

multiple jurisdictions, which is becoming more and more prevalent;[793] second, reaffirming the destination principle by using proxies related to 'customers' activities (even though customer's residence is not a theoretically perfect destination), whether for B2B or B2C.

The trend of gradually embracing individual customers' locations as proxies for consumption corresponds to EU VAT law's latest development for digital services, though the EU VAT system as a whole does not yet fully embrace the destination principle. I explain this in the following paragraphs.

4.4.3.3.2 EU VAT: The Trend Towards a Hybrid Incorporating the Destination of 'final customers'

4.4.3.3.2.1 A Hybrid Based on Both the Destination and the Origin

The EU VAT regime is another proof that the destination is not fully but only partially implemented. The current EU VAT regime is a hybrid system based on both the destination and the origin principle.[794] As to the EU VAT attribution rules, the key question is 'where to tax', i.e., 'place of taxation'. In the field of VAT, supplies of services and intangibles are subject to the same set of rules to decide 'place of supplies'. The EU VAT system has been developed from an origin-based system to a hybrid system.[795] After the European Commission's 2015 E-Commerce Package Proposal, there are more destination-based rules for the digital economy. In general, the EU VAT system has developed 'from a hybrid towards another hybrid system'.[796]

In the Annex attached to Chapter 4, I have summarized the proxies used in the EU VAT regime in Table 4 to Table 6, including rules for sales of goods, rules for B2C services, and rules for special industries. The following paragraphs describe these proxies in detail.

793. For an example, assume a MNE enterprises has purchased an online operation cloud environment service, and every employee of this group can be assigned an account and password, VPN, so each of them can work at different locations while logging into the MNE's purchased package.

794. The same remarks on the EU VAT system as a hybrid system, *see* Senyk, *supra* n. 715, at 7.3. and Lamensch, *supra* n. 633. The historical development of EU VAT demonstrates that, in the beginning, EU adopted a restricted origin principle, that the destination principle only applied for non-EU states. That was the history.

De la Feria also observed that, there was no clear-cut between the destination principle and origin principle in the EU VAT law. *See* De La Feria, *supra* n. 720, at 3.2.1, footnote 243.

Many EU VAT scholars were convinced that the origin principle is superior than the destination principle in the EU VAT, and asserted that it is impossible to implement the destination principle without the border control. *See* Ben Lockwood, David de Meza & Gareth Myles, On the European Union VAT Proposals: The Superiority of Origin over Destination Taxation, 16 Fiscal Studies 1 (1995).

795. The historical development of EU VAT, *see* Senyk, *supra* n. 715, at Chapter 6.

796. *Ibid.*, 7.3.

Under the EU VAT regime, the supply of goods rule follows the destination rationale in most cases.[797] The overview of EU VAT for sales of goods is illustrated in the Annex at the end of Chapter 4. These attribution rules for supply of goods all indicate various 'destinations' for the purpose of levying VAT.[798] In contrast to the supply of goods, the supply of services rules of the EU VAT Directive expressly deviate from the destination principle and adopt the origin principle at a technical level.[799] Such deviation from the destination principle is mainly due to reasons of administration because in many cases it is impossible or too burdensome to ascertain where a service is actually consumed, and thus feasible proxies are needed.[800]

Being similar to the OECD VAT/GST guidelines, the EU VAT Directive also distinguishes between B2B and B2C services. Under the EU VAT regime, B2C services are deemed to take place at the supplier's establishment as a proxy for the place of supply of services.[801] This is actually an origin-based design.[802] Although still recognizing VAT as a consumption tax, the supply of B2C services is in principle subject to the origin rule.[803] However, in order to adjust the consequences of this origin-based design, there are several special rules for industry-specific B2C services based on the destination principle to adjust to this main origin-based rule. *See* Table 7 in the Annex at the end of this chapter.[804]

Under the EU VAT regime, B2B services' place of taxation/place of supply is attributed to where the business customer's establishment is.[805] It looks like a destination-based design.[806] For deciding 'the business customer's establishment',

797. For an overview of EU VAT in the literature, *see* Walter Hellerstein & Timothy H Gillis, The VAT in the European Union, 127 Tax Notes 461(2010); Ben Terra & Julie Kajus, *Introduction to European VAT (Recast), Commentaries on European VAT Directives* (IBFD 2019).
798. *See* the table in the Annex at the end of this chapter. The place of supply for sales of goods under the EU VAT legal system, and the source is derived from Hellerstein with some modifications adapted from Hellerstein & Gillis, *ibid.*
799. Aleksandra Bal, EU VAT: New Rules on B2C Supplies of Digital Services from 2015, 54 European Taxation 300 (2014); Aleksandra Bal, The Sky's the Limit: Cloud-Based Services in an International Perspective (2014).
800. Thomas Ecker, *A VAT/GST Model Convention: Tax Treaties as Solution for Value Added Tax and Goods and Services Tax Double Taxation* (IBFD 2013), at 11.1.1.
801. Article 45 of the 6th EU VAT Directive.
802. Senyk, *supra* n. 715, at 6.5.2 As Senyk correctly states: 'the allocation of VAT in respect of business-to-consumer transactions within the European Union is generally based on the common market principle, which presupposes taxation of goods and services in the Member State of purchase (origin).There are a few derogations therefrom, where goods and services are taxed in the Member State of destination or in another Member State where the final consumption is deemed to occur'.
803. The EU VAT has followed the origin principle for intra-EU B2C services. The origin principle was the root of the VAT regime. For example, Ecker, *supra* n. 800, at 11.5.1; Schenk, Thuronyi & Cui, *supra* n. 632, at Chapter 15. It has been believed that the origin principle would be less burdensome, so the deviation from the origin principle/shift to the destination principle (for example, the telecommunication industry) would require heavier compliance obligation, and thus 'one-stop-shop' is needed. *See* Pernilla Rendahl, *Cross-Border Consumption Taxation of Digital Supplies* (IBFD 2009), at 6.2.2.
804. EU VAT B2C Services Special Industry Rules, adapted from Hellerstein & Gillis, *supra* n. 797.
805. Article 44 of EU VAT Directive.
806. Senyk, *supra* n. 715, at 6.5.1.

VAT rules incorporate the criterion of 'fixed establishment' (FE)[807] of the business customers as the proxy of consumption.[808] Business customers themselves also have a VAT registration for their establishment, and therefore VAT place of taxation for services would have some administrative advantages.

From the appearance, attributing to business customers' establishment also implements the 'destination principle' because business customers' establishment is a proxy derived from 'customers'. In reality, B2B services do not always involve a business customer with an establishment in a jurisdiction. For example, it has been argued where the place of taxation of the advertising services is for VAT. As to B2B advertising services, in *Athenas Druck*[809] the CJEU ruled that the advertising service provided by the Austrian advertiser representing his clients from Austria and Germany is to be attributed to where the advertising materials are disseminated. In this case, the jurisdiction where the advertising materials are disseminated is Italy, but neither the advertiser Athenas Druck nor its Austrian and German clients have an establishment in Italy. It is especially interesting that this case does not even involve the digital economy but just the advertising activity in the traditional media in Italy. Such dispute shows that to attribute services with a cross-border element is a very difficult issue in the VAT regime, even when there is no Internet involved. To require a 'fixed establishment' to decide the VAT's place of supply is not always reasonable.

For another example of EU VAT being a hybrid system: the EU VAT Directive provides several specific place-of-taxation rules for specific types of industry which apply to B2B and B2C services. These specific industry rules incorporate both the destination and the origin element, such as services connected with immovable property, passenger transport, and other services related to passenger transport, etc.[810] These special industry-specific 'place of taxation' rules have conveyed an important message that in the VAT regime, a reasonable place of taxation can be greatly influenced by features of the industry and following the rationale of destination or origin might not be intuitive per se. For example, the passenger transportation industry

807. Madeleine Merkx, Fixed Establishments in European Value Added Tax: Base Erosion and Profit Shifting's Side Effects?, 26 EC Tax Review 36 (2017). Merkx compares the different formulations between a PE under the OECD Model Convention and fixed establishment (FE) in the EU VAT rules. The most important difference is that EU VAT FE concept does not have the 'fixed place' element, though its term refers to 'fixed'. According to CJEU, it is possible that a moving object qualifies as a FE under the EU VAT rules. It is possible for establishments carrying out preparatory or auxiliary activities to qualify as an FE under the VAT according to Article 11 of EU VAT Directive implementing Regulations. EU VAT does not have the agency PE concept or provisions regarding building sites or construction or installation projects like Article 5 (3) OECD Model Convention.

808. We should be aware that in the context of the VAT, 'place of supply' is the counterpart to 'place of consumption'. The place of supply is not completely negating the destination principle, but it is indeed a deviation. In some jurisdictions, the term 'place of supply' in VAT laws, refers to 'place of consumption' as well. *See* Millar, *supra* n. 485.

809. Case C-1/08 *Athesia Druck Srl v. Ministero dell'Economia e delle Finanze and Agenzia delle Entrate.*

810. Here is the table of briefing, adapted from Hellerstein & Gillis, *supra* n. 797. *See* Annex at the end of the Chapter.

uses 'the place of departure'[811] as the place of taxation, though transportation services are actually used throughout the whole journey.

From the perspective of tax neutrality, the element of origin in the EU VAT attribution rules is not neutral for attributing the sales of services because they do not reflect the customers' market. De la Feria[812] has sharply and correctly criticized EU VAT place of supply as 'conceptual incoherencies' due to mixing the destination principle and the origin principle arbitrarily.[813] The EU VAT's place of taxation rules are just a historical and political compromise; they are designed for the purpose of administrative convenience and feasibility; the attribution rules make use of 'proxies' for customers' actual enjoyment of services.[814] However, we should never misunderstand that these origin-based proxies are inherently neutral and appropriate. In other words, there should always be the possibility to rebut the proxies which no longer reflect taxpayers' customers' consumption.

4.4.3.3.3 *The Digital Economy and EU VAT Reform: Towards the Destination Principle*

Due to the digital economy, it is quite easy to provide intangibles or digital services to individual customers in a jurisdiction where the provider is located; this has become a new default situation. In the past, it has been argued that implementing the destination principle/adopting the customer-related proxies (to levy VAT on B2C services) would cause too heavy a burden for compliance to service suppliers. Nowadays, we need to reconsider this proposition. But via digitalization, the distinction between the destination and the origin has become blurred. In many cases, it is even difficult conceptually, if the service provision, delivery, receipt, and enjoyment are all conducted in a digital environment.

In order to address digitally-provided B2C services, the EU VAT Directive, since 2015,[815] shifted from the origin principle to the destination principle.[816] Such shift has been criticized by tractional VAT scholars because ascertaining non-business customers can be too burdensome for VAT taxpayers. For example, Ecker[817] argues that place of effective management (POEM) and enjoyment should not be the main practical policy option for place of attribution of services, and such argument seems accepted in the traditional EU VAT scholarship.[818]

811. *See* Article 48 of the 6th VAT Directive.
812. De La Feria, *supra* n. 720.
813. Although Rita de La feria's criticism is based on EU VAT rules up to 2008, but until 2018 her points still stand, *see ibid.*
814. Gorka Echevarria Zubeldia, Introducing VAT in the Gulf States, 69 Tax Executive 63 (2017).
815. Bal, *supra* n. 799.
816. Aleksandra Bal, Taxation of Digital Supplies in the European Union and United States: What Can They Learn from Each Other?, 55 European taxation 245 (2015).
817. Ecker, *supra* n. 800, at 11.1.2.
818. For example, Bal, *supra* n. 816.

The EU's VAT reform regarding electronic commerce since 2017[819] further demonstrates that the EU VAT's origin-based design for B2C services cannot solve the new problems occurring in the digital economy, especially in three industries: B2C telecommunication, broadcasting and electronically supplied services (whether B2B or B2C), distance sale of goods (intra-Community as well as imported from third countries).[820] Therefore, such reform is further moving towards (or going back to) fully implementing the destination principle[821] based on individual customers. These industries of the digital economy are especially difficult to deal with because it is equally difficult to ascertain the origin and the destination of these digital services and goods. In the digital economy, both destination and origin could be controlled by the enterprise and become artificial and manipulated. Therefore, what we see from the reform efforts is that EU legislators re-emphasize the status of the 'customers' which receive the goods or services.

4.4.3.3.4 Reflections on VAT: Destination Is Wrongly Labelled as Burdensome and Manipulable

EU VAT experiences demonstrate that place of supply and place of taxation rules for goods and services do not necessarily follow a consistent rationale, even though they all mention the destination principle. Proxies are very often selected based on convenience and administration for VAT collection, not based on proxies closely related to customers.

Here arises a very intriguing contrast regarding the destination principle between the VAT literature and the FA literature. In the FA literature, it is widely accepted that the sales factor is less prone to manipulation by taxpayers because taxpayers cannot really control their customers.[822] Therefore the sales factor based on the destination principle is believed to be a more neutral approach. However, classical VAT scholars often argue that destination is easily manipulated. The current EU VAT system accommodates some tax avoidance and fraud scenarios such as VAT carousel fraud scenarios, partially due to the destination principle and the time gap of the VAT remittance system.[823] This contrast shows that the destination concept is fluid and hard to capture.

---

819. The VAT e-commerce package in the EU, https://ec.europa.eu/digital-single-market/en/new-eu-rules-e-commerce, *see* Marta Papis-Almansa, VAT and Electronic Commerce: The New Rules as a Means for Simplification, Combatting Fraud and Creating a More Level Playing Field?, *ERA Forum* (Springer 2019).
820. *Ibid.*
821. Lamensch, *supra* n. 633.
822. There are works advocating the sales factor for being more difficult to manipulate, for example, De Wilde, *supra* n. 76, at 6.4.5.2; Avi-Yonah & Benshalom, *supra* n. 46; Reuven S. Avi-Yonah & Kimberly Clausing, A Proposal to Adopt Formulary Apportionment for Corporate Income Taxation: The Hamilton Project, 2007.
823. As to VAT fraud, Cnossen has summarized several types, including the classical cross-border carousal fraud. S Cnossen, *Three VAT Studies* (Centraal Planbureau 2010).
These VAT fraud scenarios can take place partially because 'This fraud exploits two key features of the VAT system: the time gap between the collection of the tax and its remittance;

Another popular (but incorrect) argument against the destination principle in VAT is that the destination principle leads to a heavy compliance burden for business taxpayers and tax authorities. When there is no fixed establishment in the destination jurisdiction, business would not be subject to VAT. In other words, in the case of B2C cross-border services, implementing the destination principle seems too hard for the tax authorities of the origin jurisdiction as well as the tax authorities of the destination jurisdiction to monitor properly if business taxpayers file VAT in the destination jurisdiction.

This type of critical argument against the destination principle also appears regarding the distinction between the 'substantive jurisdiction' and the 'enforcement jurisdiction'[824] in the VAT regime. Substantive and enforcement jurisdictions of VAT ideally should be the same, but in reality, they are often not. Due to the administrative feasibility, it is not rare to choose the enforcement jurisdiction which does not coincide with the substantial jurisdiction. Many origin-based proxies in VAT are examples of a relatively 'easy' enforcement jurisdiction.

However, the difficulty of levying VAT in the digital economy does not merely involve difficulties from the enforcement jurisdiction,[825] so selecting origin-based proxies only temporarily (and not effectively) addresses the enforcement difficulties. The real difficulty arising from the digital economy results from the fact that the scope of substantive jurisdiction (consumption) has been widened. For example, in the digital economy, 'the destination of consumption' can be multiple when it comes to online cloud-computing services: the service is delivered and enjoyed online via computer servers and an Internet network. It is impossible under the traditional VAT regime to choose a proper proxy as consumption. Giving up the destination principle in the VAT regime is mainly based on administrative convenience and feasible enforceability, but such origin-based proxies do not make enforcement easier in the digital economy. Deviating from the destination principle is not as effective as expected.

Furthermore, the possibility of manipulation or concerns about administrative burden, though important, should not be the most decisive criterion to design a tax-neutral sales-factor attribution rule because they both can be arbitrary. When designing the sales factor attribution rule, the most decisive step is to follow the destination principle based on customers. There are other possible administration

and the destination principle, which requires all exports to be VAT-free, with the tax collected solely on imports.' *See* Rita de la Feria, Tax Fraud and the Rule of Law, Oxford Centre for Business Taxation Working Paper (2018).

Most VAT scholars are in favour of implementing the destination principle consistently to both B2B and B2C services.

824. There are quite a few works recognizing this distinction between the substantive jurisdiction and the enforcement jurisdiction. For example, Walter Hellerstein, Jurisdiction to Tax Income and Consumption in the New Economy: A Theoretical and Comparative Perspective, 38 Georgia Law Review 1 (2003); John A Swain, Misalignment of Substantive and Enforcement Tax Jurisdiction in a Mobile Economy: Causes and Strategies for Realignment, National Tax Journal 10 (2010); Millar, *supra* n. 485; Arthur J Cockfield, Jurisdiction to Tax: A Law and Technology Perspective, 38 Georgia Law Review 85 (2003); Devereux & De la Feria, *supra* n. 183.

825. *See* the debate record, Martijn L Schippers & Constantijn E Verhaeren, Taxation in a Digitizing World: Solutions for Corporate Income Tax and Value Added Tax, 27 EC Tax Review 61 (2018).

measures to equip the destination jurisdiction/substantive jurisdiction to levy tax effectively;[826] giving up the destination principle and selecting the origin-based proxies due to the difficulties mentioned is not consistent with the tax neutrality framework.

To sum up, the traditional VAT regime's approach to selecting proxies is not suitable for the sales factor of an FA because many proxies do not reflect the consumption/market but are selected due to administrative convenience and enforcement feasibility. These origin-based proxies used in the VAT regime are not suitable for the tax-neutral sales factor under the CCCTB Directive.

4.4.3.4 Final Remarks on Attributing Services: Individual Customers' Locations Prevail

When the destination is not convenient, proxies are needed. Selecting individual customer-based proxies is the logical and tax-neutral option, and such trend is occurring both in the new development of VAT regimes as well as in US state taxation.

Comparing VAT rules (from the EU or the OECD guidelines) and the MTC market-sourcing rules above, there are quite a few similarities.[827] The common feature of the new developments from both the OECD VAT guidelines and the MTC market-sourcing rules is attribution to the customers as closely as possible, provided that the proxies are not absolutely impossible to ascertain. This is why at the end of the day,

---

826. For example, *see* discussions regarding registration and collection mechanism, Walter Hellerstein, Stéphane Buydens & Dimitra Koulouri, Simplified Registration and Collection Mechanisms for Taxpayers That Are Not Located in the Jurisdiction of Taxation: A Review and Assessment, OECD Taxation Working Papers (2018).

    There is a trend to refer the 'technology-based' approach to deal with transactions and services in the digital economy. For VAT place of taxation rules of digital supplies, Lamensch closely analyses EU VAT Rules and OECD guidelines regarding online/digital supplies, and she critically concludes that, the current VAT rules from neither EU nor OECD can satisfy the need of the digital economy. Lamensch's suggestions are very interesting: she suggests two alternative 'technology-based' proposals to the current EU VAT Directive of digital supplies. The first one is 'the Know-Your-Customer (KYC) proposal' and the second one is 'Digital Certificate (DC) proposal', to decide the place of taxation. Lamensch's both proposals are based on the individual customers' information collected during the service provision, and such information is useful to decide the place of taxation. *See* Marie Lamensch, *European Value Added Tax in the Digital Era: A Critical Analysis and Proposals for Reform* (IBFD 2015).

    It is worth noticing that misalignment between the substantive and the enforcement jurisdiction has been recognized as a problem, but there is no consensus even between VAT researchers. Swain has proposed several suggestions, including harmonizing the rules for different states, simplifying compliance for foreign taxpayers, lowering nexus threshold, and 'reverse engineering' the substantive jurisdiction to be compatible with the enforcement jurisdiction. A typical example of such reverse engineering is the 'throw-back' rules. Although I agree with Swain that, there must be some actions to re-align (the misalignment of) the substantive and the enforcement jurisdiction, we should be cautious especially with 'reverse-engineering' approach because it is just a compromise and in fact digital supplies can be attributed to different destinations, and they are all justified. A throw-back rule as such should be used cautiously.
827. Both OECD VAT rules and MTC Market-sourcing rules distinguish B2B and B2C transactions. Both OECD VAT rules and MTC Market-sourcing rules have noticed that, intangibles can be used in multiple jurisdictions (no matter licensing/selling out marketing intangibles or production intangibles) and thus provide corresponding attribution rules.

individual customers' billing addresses would be selected as a proxy in the MTC market-sourcing rules in many occasions because it is a convenient proxy, but not because the billing address per se is a perfect indicator for the market.

Moreover, there is common development process in FA in the US among states and the MTC regarding the sales factor attribution rules for services: the rules evolve from the focus on 'income producing activity' going towards 'sourcing the market of customers'. The rationale of seeking the market of customers for the sales factor earned from providing services has become prevalent and popular.

To sum up, when the attribution rule for services is designed in a market-neutral manner with the appropriate rationale, it would no longer be necessary to provide additional special service industry formulas.

4.4.4 When the Destination Is Uncertain? The Case of Sales from the Intangibles

In addition to attributing gross receipts earned from services, attributing gross receipts earned from intangibles in the sales factor is another challenging issue. As discussed previously, gross receipts earned from intangibles can only be defined as sales when these receipts represent taxpayers' response to their customers' market.

4.4.4.1 CCCTB: Attributing to Intangible Beneficiaries' Sales Factor Is Still Not Neutral

Article 38(3) of the 2016 CCCTB Directive provides the attribution rule for receipts in the form of interest, dividends, royalties, and proceeds from the disposal of assets. In principle, these items are excluded from the sales factor according to Article 37(2), but when they are revenues earned 'in the ordinary course of trade or business', they can be included in the sales factor. Article 38(3) provides that 'where exempt revenues, interest, dividends and royalties and the proceeds from the disposal of assets are included in the sales factor, they shall be attributed to the beneficiary'.[828]

The beneficiary is the person which really enjoys the benefits in the form of interest, dividends, royalties, and proceeds. Therefore, it might sound reasonable that the receipts from these intangibles are attributed to the beneficiary rather than the nominal legal owner.

However, attributing receipts from intangibles to the beneficiaries is still contrary to the sales-by-destination principle, since when the intangibles licensee or assignee makes use of these intangibles in a different jurisdiction than where the beneficiary is

828. Furthermore, since Article 38(3) should be interpreted together with Article 37(2), it is obvious that only the intangible interest earned in the ordinary course of trade or business can be attributed to the beneficial owner. In other words, purely passive income attributed to a conduit company will not be qualified as a beneficiary under Article 38(3) because payment to a conduit company cannot be regarded as 'in the ordinary course of trade or business'. With regard to conduit companies and 'beneficial ownership', international tax law literature has widely discussed this issue. In the context of the CCCTB Directive, this issue is not the focal discussion point. Article 38(3) will not include conduit companies as beneficiaries.

established, the attribution result would immediately be illogical: the beneficiary has nothing to do with the market side that taxpayers respond to.[829] Article 38(2) is not tax neutral because it attributes the receipts from intangibles to the beneficiaries and does not seek 'the market'.

Attributing the sales from intangibles to the 'beneficiaries' is not consistent with the market-side theory of the sales factor. The current CCCTB Directive Proposal seems to escape the problem of deciding the precise market location, but it ignores that the beneficiaries can be established in a jurisdiction strategically and attract the sales factor from the intangibles.

4.4.4.2 *The MTC's New Market-Sourcing for Intangibles Is Partially Consistent with the Destination Principle*

As to the attribution of the receipts from licensing and sales of intangibles, new MTC Regulation IV has a separate provision. Section 17(e) the new MTC Regulation IV[830] is completely different from Article 38 of the current CCCTB Directive Proposal: Section 17(e) the new MTC Regulation IV seeks the location 'where the intangibles are actually used' and distinguishes different types of intangibles. Classifying different types of intangibles is not brand new, and we have observed that TP studies have created and used similar categories.[831] Different intangibles represent different ways of their utilization and functions.

Article IV section 17(a)(4) MTC Regulation IV distinguishes three types of intangibles and corresponding different attribution rules will apply consequently. There are three types of intangibles under discussion: production intangibles, marketing intangibles, and mixed intangibles. The first type is 'production intangibles' the receipts of which are attributed according to the state where these intangibles are 'used'. A typical example is a patent, which is licensed to a specific factory. The second type is 'marketing intangibles' the receipts of which are attributed according to the geographic area where this intangible is authorized, i.e., where the production intangible is used. A typical example of a 'marketing intangible' is a trademark, which is often authorized for a specific geographic market. The third type is an intangible that cannot be categorized as a marketing or a production intangible: it is a mixed-intangible.

It is worth noting that as to the mixed intangible, Article IV section 17(a)(4)(C) MTC Regulation IV excludes the receipts from this type of intangibles from the receipts factor's numerator and denominator completely. The rationale for complete exclusion seems that it is too difficult to properly attribute receipts from this type of intangibles

829. The illogical result will also take place when the asset factor attributes assets to 'economic owners', instead of to 'where assets are utilized', and I elaborate this issue in Chapter 6. This is an asymmetry and non-market-neutral result.
830. Discussions about the intangibles in the FA corporate tax system, Pomp, *supra* n. 647, at 16.
831. *See section* 6.5 and section 6.2.2 of Chapter 6 of this book. OECD's BEPS Action Plan 8-10 have discussed marketing intangibles, HTVI, etc.

and attributing to any jurisdiction would be unfair.[832] To exclude a mixed intangible completely from the sales factor purely due to administrative difficulties is not tax neutral, and this is already discussed in section 4.3 above.

Licensing intangibles resembles sales or providing services. As to the attribution rules of receipts earned from licensing or assigning/selling intangibles, it is tax-neutral and the sales-by-destination rule applies, and attribution is to end-users. The principle of attributing the sales factor of intangibles is to where the intangible is 'used' by the taxpayers' customers.

For production intangibles, it is easier to attribute because production intangibles would be used in another production process, combined with employees and tangible assets. Attributing marketing intangibles are more difficult. Marketing intangibles can be used on products further being distributed to other jurisdictions. Licensing or assigning marketing intangibles, such as copyrights, trademarks, logos, would usually make taxpayers' customers reach out to 'end' customers. It is consistent with the economic reality of marketing intangibles.

4.4.4.3 'Special Rules' for Software Transactions and Digital Goods or Services: The Destination Rationale Reaffirmed

As a side note: for software transactions and sales or licences of digital goods or services, in the past, it usually still involved a physical material such as CD-ROMs or USB sticks. Nowadays, downloading or cloud usage has become the new way of sales or licences of digital goods or services. Both ways are possible for delivering software services. Therefore, the MTC market-sourcing rules also provide special rules for software transactions and sales or licences of digital goods or services because software transactions and digital goods and services cannot be categorized as providing services in the traditional sense.

According to section 17(g)(1) MTC Regulation IV (for software transactions) and section 17(g)(2)(licences of digital goods or services), when software transactions in the form of 'sales of personal tangible property', such as CD-ROMs or USB sticks, should be treated according to sales of tangible properties. When software transactions via other means should be treated as sales of intangibles or licence of intangibles, and thus section 17(d), (e), and (f) may apply depending on the type of intangible of the software involved. Either way has followed the destination principle.

The destination principle is likely to be the guiding principle for tax authorities. According to the examples used in the MTC Regulation IV, drafters do not seem to know how to deal with more advanced technology, such as cloud services, which does not involve a 'delivery', and thus MTC Regulation IV leaves a wide discretion to the tax authorities to make a 'reasonable approximation'. As the discussions of MTC Regulation IV regarding services demonstrate, the rationale of sourcing the market by seeking customers' actual location/destination is the new trend in the digital economy. In the

832. Brian Hamer, Hearing Officer Report: Synopsis and Recommendations on Proposed Draft Amendments to the Commission's Model General Allocation and Apportionment Regulations, at 9, which can be requested at the MTC official website http://www.mtc.gov/.

future, it is quite possible that all the rules for the digital economy will be the main rule instead of the special rule. To seek the destination rule might still be difficult, but the consensus is to use proxies to reflect the taxpayers' real customers who make use of the services, not proxies that reflect taxpayers' income-generating activities. This consensus would also guide the tax authorities' discretion in making a 'reasonable approximation'.

4.5 MISSION IMPOSSIBLE TO ASCERTAIN INVISIBLE DESTINATION IN THE DIGITAL ECONOMY?

In this section, I discuss digitalized services and goods and clouds, explain why the existing rules in the current CCCTB Directive Proposal, the US tax regime or the EU VAT regime still cannot completely solve the difficulties we are facing now. In the end, I reaffirm that a sales-by-destination rationale will attribute digitalized services to the 'individual customers' location' in the digital economy, according to the tax neutrality framework developed in Chapter 3, and use two typical examples of the digital economy as an illustration.

4.5.1 Bundled Services and Cloud Services

Although the sales-by-destination rationale is the tax-neutral option, it is not always easy to ascertain the market and destination, as previous sections already indicated. Among all the difficulties mentioned above, the most difficult task to attribute sales is attributing sales in the context of the digital economy. Attributing sales in the digital economy is especially difficult due to two aspects: first, via a platform, many digitalized services are bundled[833] and provided altogether by different businesses, and thus it becomes conceptually difficult to ascertain the right destination; and second, it is doubtful if 'destination' still exists when it comes to cloud-computing technology. Sometimes the service or services being bundled and cloud service being in/via the cloud are both digitalized services, but they demonstrate different difficulties.

The emerging difficulties in the digital economy reaffirm that attributing services to individual customers' physical locations for the sales factor is not only theoretically logical and tax neutral but also administratively simple. Other proxies are not able to represent taxpayers' response to the market; individual customers are the market which enterprises respond to. Their locations are the real destination. This can be explained as follows.

In the current digital economy, many services are bundled via online websites, platforms. Individual customers enjoy 'free service'. For example, a digital service provider offers a 'free' digital platform or 'free' social media to individual customers. In return, platforms or websites charge the actual service providers fees for using the

833. This is what Devereux and Vella described 'two-sided market', *see* Michael Devereux & John Vella, Implications of Digitalization for International Corporation Tax Reform, *Digital Revolutions in Public Finance* (IMF 2017), at 107; a later version, *see* Devereux & Vella, *supra* n. 15.

platform or advertising. The business structure involves three sets of services: the platform service provided to individual customers; the online and targeted advertising[834] service or platform service to businesses; and the services businesses provide to individual customers. These giant platform companies, such as Uber/Airbnb and online social media like Instagram/Facebook/LinkedIn, are representative examples.

Since many digital services are bundled, the distinction between B2B services and B2C services is blurred, and 'P2P' (peer-to-peer) platforms have arisen.[835] Internet advertising nowadays can precisely target potential customers that have used 'free' search engines or social media. Multinationals such as Uber or Airbnb provide a platform in the software application where businesses and individual customers can conduct transactions with each other even with a Smartphone. At the end of the day, the market of advertising, search engine, online gaming, entertainment services, etc., are all bundled together. These services can be all digitalized and thus 'invisible'. It is obvious that the origin-based rule, such as COP rule, cannot provide a proper attribution.

The other difficulty in the digital economy is 'Cloud Computing Services'.[836] This is different from digital intermediary platforms. Digital platforms involve at least some 'physical' services, such as lodging or transportation, but cloud computing services involve a service for which customers only need to make use of the Internet and can enjoy the service 'everywhere'.[837] Cloud computing services are even more 'invisible'. Due to the development of technology, digital 'products' and 'services' have become even 'invisible', and transactions are completed totally 'in the cloud'. The service providers and service users who are located in different jurisdictions, via the Internet and the servers, can still make use of the cloud to carry out and enjoy the service. In the US, cloud computing is classified as SaaS (Software as a Service), PaaS (Platform as a

834. Even in the pre-Internet era, attributing sales of services involving 'audience', such as advertising, publishing, television, and broadcasting, is tricky. In fact, long before MTC's reform of the attribution rules for services, MTC has provided special industry formulas for publishing and television, and broadcasting industries, which include the 'circulation' factor and audience factor. *See* MTC Reg.IV.18.(j) Special Rules: Publishing (adopted 30 July 1993) and MTC Reg.IV.18(h) Special Rules: Television and Radio Broadcasting (adopted 31 August 1990; amended 25 April 1996).

See Hellerstein, Hellerstein & Swain, *supra* n. 349, Chapter 10; Allyson Pyrdek, Jon Sedon & Saabir Kapoor, Click This! Sales Factor Sourcing of Receipts from Internet Advertising - A Tangled Web Indeed, *The State and Local Tax Lawyer. Symposium Edition* (American Bar Association 2009).

835. Aqib Aslam & Alpa Shah, *Taxation and the Peer-to-Peer Economy* (IMF 2017).

836. Regarding the difficulty of taxing cloud service, W Hellerstein & J Sedon, State Taxation of Cloud Computing: A Framework for Analysis, 117 Journal of Taxation 11 (2012); Stephen J Lusch, State Taxation of Cloud Computing, 29 Santa Clara Computer & High Tech Law Journal 369 (2012); David J Shakow, The Taxation of Cloud Computing and Digital Content, in John A. Rothchild (eds), *Research Handbook on Electronic Commerce Law* (Edward Elgar 2016); Arthur J Cockfield, Walter Hellerstein & Marie Lamensch, Applying the United States Retail Sales Tax (RST) to Cross-Border Digital Commerce, in Arthur Cockfield, Walter Hellerstein & Marie Lamensch (eds), *Taxing Global Digital Commerce* (2nd ed. Kluwer Law International 2019), at 6.02.

837. Online platforms also involve issues regarding the labour factor, the discussions are at section 5.5 of this book.

Service), or IaaS (Infrastructure as a Service).[838] It involves various services provided via online environments.

The current cloud computing services do not even require users to download anything to their devices, and therefore the whole process of providing and receiving services takes place totally 'in the cloud'. Therefore, the service is even not 'electronically transferred' as a traditional software on the customer's side. Cloud computing has no conceptual physical location, and therefore it is quite difficult – almost impossible – to decide the place where 'the service is physically carried out'.

As to cloud computing services, the MTC's new market-sourcing rules do not provide a clear solution either. It is not clear if cloud services should be qualified as professional services or other services. There are so many different types of cloud computing, and qualifying them is already uncertain. As to PaaS and IaaS, they can be categorized as digital services, but SaaS can be categorized as a type of mixed contract of sales and services because the provider might upgrade or fix the bugs even after the transaction.

Briefly speaking, in the digital economy, it is indeed more difficult to attribute services. In the past, the difficulty lay in the conflicts between different jurisdictions in the physical sense: performance, delivery, receiving, or enjoyment still took place in a physical location, though they might refer to different jurisdictions. Nowadays, digital technology actually integrates different industries,[839] and for some digital services, the performance itself requires merely 'cloud computing' which exists conceptually in the servers. The traditional ways of attribution rules, in the international taxation or VAT regimes that already have difficulty with traditional cross-border services, are definitely incapable of dealing with them because the business models are revolutionarily changed. The current CCCTB Directive Proposal or the MTC's reform project on market sourcing does not provide useful solutions either.

---

838. Currently, there are three well-accepted models of cloud computing: Software as a Service (SaaS), the Platform as a Service (PaaS), and Infrastructure as a Service (IaaS). SaaS means that the customers can access the provider's applications located in the cloud. PaaS means that the customers launch their own applications on the cloud using programming languages and other tools supplied by the cloud service provider. IaaS means that the customers are provided access to processing, storage, networks and other computing resources to run software, applications, and operating systems. These types of cloud computing services are all functioning in the 'cloud' offered by the service provider.

The definition is provided by National Institute of Standards and Technology of the U.S. Department of Commerce, L Badger, NIST Draft Special Publication 800-146, DRAFT Cloud Computing Synopsis and Recommendations (Gaithersburg, MD: National Institute of Standards and Technology May 2011), quoting National Institute Of Standards & Tech., Special Pub. No. 800-145, available at http://csrc.nist.gov/publications/drafts/800-146/Draft-NIST-SP800-146.pdf. The definition and categories are also accepted and used by OECD BEPS Project. *See* OECD BEPS Action 1 Final Report, paragraph 143.

839. Cockfield also observed the integration of the whole market via digitalization in early 2000s, *see* Cockfield, *supra* n. 824.

4.5.2 The Market-Neutral Attribution Rules for Digitalized Services: Chasing the Individuals

The existing discussions on the reform of international taxation or FA focus on the 'Internet' and related difficulties. There are indeed difficulties, but a new thinking of attribution can streamline the attribution results even more. When we look at the economic activities, the development of technology just makes it easier to combine different services and goods markets.

Internet technology itself does not make customers disappear. Social media companies, such as Facebook, provide 'free services' to end-users but also earn income from advertising or via a webshop function. A Facebook customer can be a French company established in France, but its target audience is purely in the Netherlands. In this case, Facebook's advertising service is sold to a French 'customer', but the audience is in the Netherlands. With the IP address records, it is even easier for tax authorities to trace end-users. From the benefit principle perspective, the Netherlands is justified to have taxing powers to apportion these receipts because via the Internet infrastructure provided by the Dutch government, the Dutch customers' market is open to Facebook and its French advisor. Customers belong to a combined market, and they receive information and enjoy the 'free' services of Facebook, which are indirectly covered by advisors. Strictly speaking, social media services are never free of charge.

Nowadays, digital commerce is no longer a special type of business model because every transaction of an MNE is digitalized. Digitalization also brings in the phenomenon of bundling different types of services from different service sectors together. Ring-fencing the special industry as a digital service is not very wise because nowadays no single MNE possesses the digital means of conducting business. Fragmentation of 'digital service' seems unrealistic and creates unnecessary delineation problems. Digitalization also makes customers in the market more transparent and easier to trace. The traditional thinking about international taxation might find cross-border digital commerce difficult to capture, not to say to levy tax on. Nonetheless, I also see opportunities due to technology:[840] as long as tax authorities can control data of MNE taxpayers' relevant individual customers, it would be easier to align taxation with 'economic reality'.

Here I would like to provide two examples for illustrative purposes. The first example is a platform[841] demonstrating the difficulty of deciding the destination of cross-border services.

Presume Company 1 (in Country A) produce online games, which consist of a DVD-ROM to set up, and there is a monthly subscription for the game with new storylines in the game. Individual customers can play the online game with their play station anywhere in the world, provided that they have access to the Internet. Individual customers can order DVDs delivered by Company 3 (in Country C) and have

840. The same opinion, Cockfield, *ibid.*
841. The example is adapted from the VAT example from Keen & Hellerstein, *supra* n. 786, at 381. This revised example includes several digital economy features, including online remote retailers, social media's advertising.

a subscription with Company 1. Company 1 aims to develop their market in Country D and hires a social media giant Company 2 (in Country B) to conduct online advertising activities for potential customers in Country D. Assume all countries are EU Member States.

Figure 8 Cross-Border Services and Goods Providers

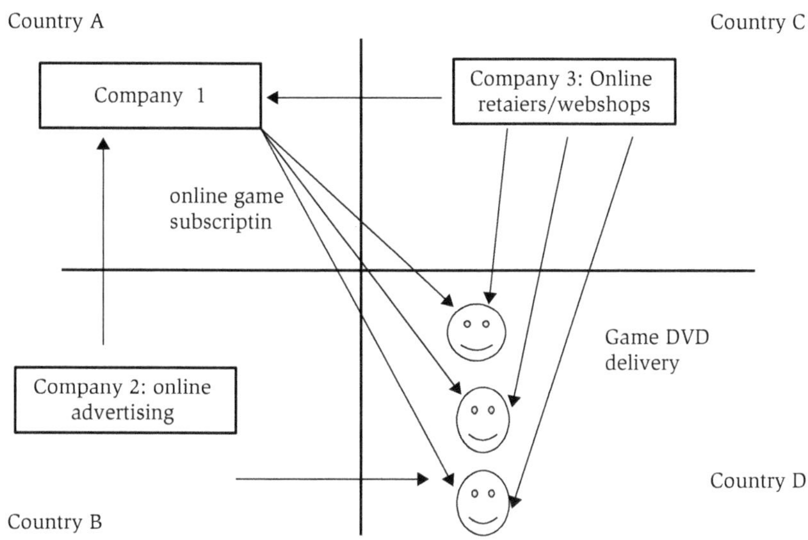

Source: The author.

In order to compare the different application results from the attributions, here is table which compares application of all the attribution rules discussed in this chapter. Quite a few disparities appear from this table. And though each attribution rule has its own rationale, it does necessarily refer to the ultimate customers.

What this chapter suggests is a simple and straightforward way to seek the ultimate customers' physical location because it is where Company 1, Company 2, and Company 3 have responded to the market. This approach is closer to the EU VAT reform package, but this book sees the end-users as the ultimate trigger of the market, and all companies' services respond to them.

Attribution	*Current CCCTB*[842]	*Multistate Tax Commission*[843]	*EU VAT (including 2015 Package)*	*This Book's Criterion*[844]
Company 1's sales factor	Sales of goods:	Sales of goods:	Sales of goods:[845]	Sales of goods:
	Country D	Country D	Country D	Country D
	Subscription service to individual customers: Not clear; no physical service involved.	Subscription service to individual customers: It is 'other services' electronically delivered directly to individual customers and attributed to where customers received the service: Country D	Subscription Game Service to individual customers:[846] Country D	Subscription service to individual customers: Country D
Company 2's sales factor	Advertising service:	Advertising service:	Advertising service:[847]	Advertising service:
	Possibly Country B (physically performed) or Country D (or actually received)	It is an 'other service', which is delivered electronically on behalf of the customer, so it would be where end-users receive the service: Country D	Country D	Country D

842. Article 38 of 2016 CCCTB Directive. The destination principle applies.
843. *See* Figure 7 at section 4.4.3.2 of this book.
844. The sales should be attributed to where individual customers are physically located because it is where the taxpayer responds to the customers' market.
845. EU VAT package 2015.
846. Online games are covered by the EU VAT package 2015, New Article 58 of VAT Directive. Annex II of the VAT Directive and of their examples in Annex I of the VAT Implementing Regulation.
847. Article 7 of VAT Implementing Regulation 'Electronically supplied services'.

Attribution	*Current CCCTB*	*Multistate Tax Commission*	*EU VAT (including 2015 Package)*	*This Book's Criterion*
Company 3's sales factor	Providing an online marketplace for Company 1: Not clear; no physical service involved. Delivery service for Company 1: Country D	Providing an online marketplace and delivery service for Company 1: It is a professional service, delivered to a business customer, by whom a contract is principally managed: Country A	Providing an online marketplace:[848] When the marketplace's service is for Company 1 (Article 44 of the VAT Directive, it is the same after 2015) Country A Delivery service for Company 1: Country D	Providing an online marketplace: Country D Delivery service for Company 1: Country D

The second example is a cloud computing service. Company 1 provides cloud computing services (an electronic working environment) for Company 2 (located in Country B), Company 2 has different employees physically located in different countries, and they log in to the electronic working environment and make use of the service.

Figure 9 Cross-Border Cloud Computing Service

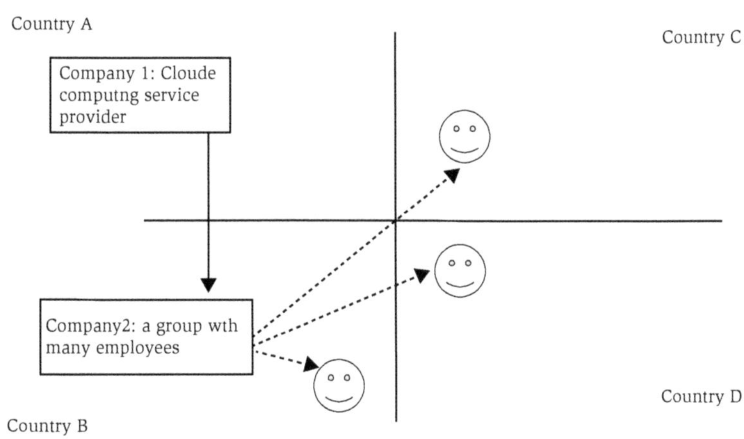

Source: The author.

848. It is electronically provided service to individual customers as well as the Company 1.

According to the different attribution rules discussed in this chapter, the sales of Company 1's cloud computing service might refer to different jurisdictions, as in the following table.

	Current CCCTB	*New MTC Section 17*	*EU VAT*	*This Book's Criterion*
Company 1's sales factor	Not clear; no physical service involved. Either Country A or Country B is possible.	Delivered electronically to a business customer, to the location where the business customers actually receive the service: Country B	It is an electronically provided service, attributed to the customer (Company 2)'s residence: Country B	Country B, C, or D because each employee makes use of this service in the jurisdiction where he or she is located. When the factor presence nexus is not met, the throw-around rule applies.

The two typical digital economy examples show that even when attribution rules claim the 'destination principle', the results could be different. In my view, in a digitalized era, the most practical approach is actually the most tax-neutral approach: to embrace fully the customers' market and use the ultimate users/viewers/individual consumers' physical location as the proxy of ascertaining the destination.

4.6 CONCLUSIONS AND SUGGESTIONS: MARKET NEUTRALITY REQUIRES A CUSTOMER-CENTRED SALES FACTOR

A tax-neutral sales factor represents the taxpayers' response to their customers because the sales factor in the formula is justified by the public benefit of a well-maintained and healthy market. Therefore, 'sales by destination' is the tax-neutral option.

Although the 'destination' is recognized as the market, the 'destination' concept is still difficult to capture, so it is decided by different proxies in different fields of tax law. This chapter has explored the development of the sales factor of a sharing formula in both the CCCTB and state taxation in the US as well as VAT regimes, including the difficulty arising from the digital economy. The research question of this chapter is simple: how should the sales factor in a formula be designed? The ultimate answer is also simple and straightforward: following the basic rationale of sales-by-destination/customers' market rule, and it refers to the ultimate individual customers' physical locations. This criterion is also suitable in the context of the digital economy.

This conclusion is based on a critical analysis of the US's FA developments as well as revisiting the VAT 'place of supply rules'. The sales factor represents the public benefit provided by the jurisdiction: the 'market where customers make use of goods or services provided from taxpayers'. This criterion should guide the design of the sales factor even in innovative and complex transactions.

When a definition or an attribution rule deviates from the fundamental sales-by-destination rationale of the sales factor, it does not match the function of sales factor nor represent the taxpayers' response to the demand side of the market. When the public benefit of maintaining the customers' market is ignored, such sales factor design is not market neutral. When implementing the sales-by-destination rationale comprehensively, the sales factor is consistent with MN.

As to the definition of sales, all receipts earned from providing services or goods should be included, including receipts in the form of royalties or renumeration earned from assigning or licensing taxpayers' intangibles to unrelated parities. Completely excluding 'income from intangibles from the sales factor' is not market neutral because it ignores taxpayers' response to the market via assigning or licensing intangibles. The current CCCTB Directive Proposal's sales factor is unfortunately still not completely market neutral.

The current CCCTB Directive's text accepts intangible income earned 'in the regular course of trade and business', but it is still not able to exclude receipts that are not the result of the response to the market, such as short-term marketable securities and hedging transactions. Taxpayers in the short-term marketable securities and hedging markets have a status as customers, not service or product providers. Therefore, the 'receipts' from short-term marketable securities and hedging transactions should not be included in the sales factor. The sales factor can only be market neutral when it represents the taxpayers' response to their customers, not when it represents taxpayers 'being' customers. By this rationale, even if there are more innovative forms of transactions in the future, there will be a market neutral and logical way to interpret the sales factor in the current CCCTB Directive Proposal.

Among the current attribution rules, the destination rationale is not strictly followed when the destination is not desirable (such as no-where sales), or the destination is not convenient (such as cross-border transactions). In the name of the destination principle, there are many proxies used as 'deemed' destination. De facto deviation from the destination principle is a prevalent phenomenon especially in VAT regimes as well as some of the US's market-sourcing rules in state taxation. But the fact that these deviations exist does not justify their legitimacy. 'Deemed' destinations are not market-neutral destinations per se.

As such, this chapter concludes that the market-neutral sales-by-destination attribution rule should attribute the sales of goods to the jurisdictions of end individual customers. Selection of proxies to decide 'destination' should be based on a customer-centred perspective. The billing addresses of customers or the residence of customers both can be a reasonable proxy, provided that these proxies coincide with the ultimate customers' physical locations. A throw-back rule or a throw-around rule is exceptional, and it should apply only when the destination of goods is factually unidentifiable. The current CCCTB Directive Proposal's throw-around rule is not market neutral because it only considers the fiscal interest of EU Member States and ignores the sales-by-destination rationale.

The sales-by-destination rule based on individual customers' physical location is also suitable for the digital economy. Via the Internet and new technology, an MNE not only provides borderless services but also makes different customers' markets bundled. Internet advertising services and social media services are bundled towards the same group of individual customers. At the end of the day, the sales factor should be based on the individual customers because these customers truly exist. Even 'invisible' services, such as cloud services, or share economy services based on digital technology, should follow the same rationale. It is tax neutral to clarify the related markets and admit that all MNE taxpayers from different sectors in fact target the same group of individual customers, who make use of various related services.

It should be noted that the Internet network and wireless network are a type of public goods that need to be established by local governments. Without this infrastructure, it would never be possible to access customers. Moreover, digital technology has made providing the service borderless, and digital technology also makes it easier to trace customers because all digital footprints are inevitably recorded. In other words, in addition to these challenges, the digital economy also creates new opportunities because customer-related information can be collected naturally in the process of various transactions and provision of services.

To sum up, the current CCCTB Directive Proposal's sales factor is not market neutral. The definition of 'sales' should be clarified again as gross receipts earned in response to the customers' market. The attribution rule of the sales of goods and services should both follow the sales-by-destination rule and seek the real 'customers' thus attributing the sales to where the goods are dispatched and where customers make use of the services.

For the sales factor of the EU's FA regime, this chapter recommends amending the provisions of the current CCCTB Directive Proposal accordingly as follows:

Article 37 Composition of the sales factor

1. The sales factor shall consist of the total sales allocated to a group member or a deemed group member where the factor presence nexus is established, as its numerator and the total sales of the group as its denominator.
2. Sales shall mean the proceeds of all sales of goods and supplies of services after discounts and returns, excluding value added tax, other taxes and duties. Exempt revenues shall not be included in the sales factor. Intra-group sales of goods and supplies of services shall not be included in the sales factor.
   intangible income, including but not limited to, interest, dividends, royalties and proceeds from the disposal of fixed assets shall be included in the sales factor, provided it is earned in response to the customers' market. The European Commission may provide an indicative list to exclude the earned receipts that do not respond to taxpayers' customers' market.
3. Sales shall be valued in accordance with Article 20 of Directive 2016/xx/EU *[undefined in source]*.

Article 38 Sales by destination

1. Sales of goods shall be included in the sales factor of the group member located in the Member State where the dispatch or transport of the goods to the person acquiring them ends. Where that place cannot be determined, the sales of

goods shall be attributed to the group member located in the Member State of the last identifiable location of the goods.

2. Supplies of services shall be included in the sales factor of the group member located in the Member State where the services are physically received by the ultimate individual customers of the market. The European Commission can provide a Regulation for selecting proxies to reflect the ultimate individual customers of the market when the physical place is not identifiable.
3. Interest, dividends and royalties and the proceeds from the disposal of fixed assets that are included in the sales factor shall be attributed to the group member earning those revenues, interest, dividends, royalties and proceeds in response to the customer's market.
4. Where it is not identifiable or no proper proxy selected where the goods are delivered or the services are supplied, or when the factor presence nexus is not met, the sales of goods and supplies of services shall be included in the sales factor of all group members in proportion to their labour and asset factors.
5. Where there is more than one group member in the Member State where the goods are delivered or the services are supplied, the sales shall be included in the sales factor of all group members located in that Member State in proportion to their labour and asset factors.

ANNEX TO CHAPTER 4

Overview of Section 17(d) of the Multistate Tax Commission Regulation IV on Market Sourcing

Table 4 Attribution Rules for Services under Section 17(d) of the New MTC Regulation IV

Service Type	*The Priority Rule (For Convenience)*	*The Standard Attribution Rule*	*The Residual Rule When Uncertain*
in-person service	No	The customer's physical presence; the real estate of the service involves a real estate; the shipping destination of the tangible property	Reasonable approximation; the throw-out rule applies if the location cannot be determined or the taxpayer is not taxable in the determined market state
Professional service			

Service Type	*The Priority Rule (For Convenience)*	*The Standard Attribution Rule*	*The Residual Rule When Uncertain*
to business customers	(The customer's billing address) the safe harbour rule is fulfilled when the taxpayer: (1) engages in substantially similar service transactions with more than 250 customers, whether individuals or businesses, and (2) does not derive more than 5% of its receipts from sales of services from one customer.	Where the contract is being principally managed by business customers; if not identified, the location of the ordering; if the location of ordering is not identifiable, the customer's billing address Exception: if the taxpayer derives more than 5% of its profits from one business customer, the taxpayer must identify the location of the contract being principally managed by the business customer	N/A
to individual customers	The safe harbour rule, i.e., the large volume transaction rule	The location of the customers' primary residence; if not identifiable, the individual customer's billing address Exception: if the taxpayer derives more than 5% of profits from one individual customer, the taxpayer must identify that individual customer's primary residence.	N/A
Other services (involving third-party recipients/intermediary)			
Delivered by physical means	No	The location of the services being delivered	

Service Type	*The Priority Rule (For Convenience)*	*The Standard Attribution Rule*	*The Residual Rule When Uncertain*
Delivered electronically to a business customer	The safe harbour rule	The location where the business customers actually receive service	'Reasonable approximations': to seek the location of the contract being principally managed by the customers; if not identified, the location of the ordering; if the location of ordering is not identifiable, then attributing to the location of the customer's billing address Exception: if the taxpayer derives more than 5% of its profits from one business customer, the taxpayer must identify the location of the contract being principally managed by the business customer
Delivered electronically to an individual customer	no	The location where the individual customers actually receive service	'Reasonable approximation' if they do not have sufficient information to approximate reasonably, the sales will be attributed to the location of the customers' billing address
Services delivered electronically through or on behalf of a customer	no	The location of the end-users	Reasonable approximation

Source: The author.

Overview of EU VAT Rules for Sales of Goods

Table 5 EU VAT Rules for Sales of Goods

Supply of Goods	*Rule*	*Rationale*	*Legal Source (Article Number)*
General rule	Where the goods are located at the time the supply takes place, if they are not dispatched or transported.	destination	31
Transported goods to taxable person - B2B	Where the goods are located when the dispatch or transport to the customer begins, if they are dispatched or transported by the supplier, the customer, or a third party.	destination	32
Transported goods to private consumer - B2C - Supplier above distance selling threshold	Where the goods are located when the dispatch to the customer ends for distance sales when the supplier's annual sales are above the threshold applied by the customer's Member State.	destination	33
Transported goods to private consumer - B2C - Supplier below distance selling threshold	Where the goods are located when the dispatch or transport to the customer begins for distance sales, if the supplier's sales are below the threshold applied by the customer's Member State (unless the supplier has opted to tax in the Member State of destination).	a deemed destination	34
Installation or assembly of goods - B2B and B2C	Where the goods are being installed or assembled, if done by the supplier.	destination	36

Supply of Goods	*Rule*	*Rationale*	*Legal Source (Article Number)*
Goods supplied onboard ships, planes, or trains - B2B and B2C	Where the point of departure is, if supplied during the section of a passenger transport operation effected within the EU.	a deemed destination	37
Electricity or natural gas to a taxable person - B2B	Where the taxable dealer is established when receiving electricity or gas supplied through the natural gas distribution system.	destination	38
Electricity or natural gas to private consumer - B2C	Where electricity or gas supplied through the natural gas system is effectively used or consumed by the private consumer.	destination	39
Intra-EU acquisition of goods by registered trader in a Member State from trader in another Member State - B2B	Where the goods are finally located after transport from another Member State. The place of acquisition is initially deemed to be the country having issued the VAT number under which the acquisition was made. If the goods are subsequently transferred to another Member State for use, VAT will be due based on where the goods are finally located after transfer and any tax due that the Member State having issued the VAT number, will be reduced accordingly.	destination	40 & 41

Supply of Goods	*Rule*	*Rationale*	*Legal Source (Article Number)*
All importation of goods into the EU – B2B and B2C	The Member State within whose territory the goods are located when they enter the Community. Any subsequent sales or transfers to a Member State would be subject to intra-EU rules.	destination	60

Source: The author.

Overview of EU VAT B2C Services Special Industry Rules (prior to 2015)

Table 6 EU VAT B2C Services Special Industry Rules prior to 2015

Item	*Rule*	*Rationale*	*Source*
Services provided by an intermediary – B2C	Where the underlying transaction, in which the intermediary intervenes, is taxable.	origin	46
Transport of goods other than intra-Community – B2C	Where the transport takes place, proportionate to the distance covered in any jurisdiction.	origin and destination pro rata	49
Transport of goods intra-Community – B2C	At the place of departure.	origin and destination coincide	50
Services ancillary to transport of goods (e.g., loading and unloading) – B2C	Where the services are physically carried out.	origin and destination coincide	54
Valuations of or work on movable tangible property – B2C	Where the services are physically delivered.	origin and destination coincide	54
Electronically supplied services provided by non-EU supplier to private consumers in the EU – B2C	Where the customer is established, resides, or has a permanent address.	a deemed destination	58

Item	*Rule*	*Rationale*	*Source*
Select services provided by EU suppliers to non-EU private consumers - B2C	Where the private customer is established, resides, or has a permanent address. Services covered include intangible transfers; advertising; consulting; banking; supply of staff; hiring of movable tangible property; access to electricity and natural gas; telecommunications; radio and television broadcasting; and electronically supplied services.	a deemed destination	59
Radio and TV broadcasting and telecommunications services provided by a non-EU supplier to private consumers in the EU - B2C	Where the customer effectively uses and enjoys the service.	destination	59b

Source: The author.

EU VAT Specific Industry Place of Supply Rules, whether B2B or B2C[849]

Table 7 EU VAT Specific Industry Place of Supply Rules, Whether B2B or B2C

B2B and B2C Services	*Rule*	*Rationale*	*Source (EU 6th VAT Directive)*
Services connected with immovable property	Where the immovable property is located.	destination	47

849. Hellerstein & Gillis, *supra* n. 797, at 1.

B2B and B2C Services	*Rule*	*Rationale*	*Source (EU 6th VAT Directive)*
Passenger transport	Where the transport takes place, proportionate to the distance covered in any jurisdiction.	pro-rata origin and destination	48
Services relating to cultural, artistic, sporting, scientific, educational, entertainment, and similar activities	Where the services are physically carried out. Effective 2 January 2011, these services will be taxed where the events take place.	destination	53
Restaurant and catering services not associated with passenger transport within the EU	Where the services are actually carried out.	origin and destination coincide	55
Restaurant and catering services supplied onboard ship, aircraft, or train during passenger transport in the EU	At the place of departure.	origin	57
Short-term hiring of means of transport	Where the means of transport is actually put at the disposal of the customer. Effective 1 January 2013, long-term hire of transport for B2C transactions will be taxed where the private customer is established.	destination	56

Source: The author, adapted from Hellerstein & Gillis, *supra* n. 797.

CHAPTER 5
Towards the Market-Neutral Labour Factor

Some are born great, some achieve greatness, and some have greatness thrust upon them.

Twelfth Night, or, What You Will, William Shakespeare[850]

5.1 INTRODUCTION

5.1.1 The Labour Factor Represents the Public Benefits Maintaining the Labour Market

In addition to the market side activities, it is quite common that a formula consists of a payroll factor representing input side activities. The payroll factor is a factor representing the input from human beings in the production process. As introduced in Chapter 3, in the US's FA experiences, the payroll factor has been widely adopted from the very beginning. The current CCCTB Directive Proposal follows the similar rationale but with a variation: the labour factor of the current CCCTB Directive Proposal is a factor consisting of two sub-factors: payroll and headcounts of employees. Payroll and headcounts are equally weighted in the labour factor.[851]

The research question of this chapter is: how should the market-neutral labour factor under the EU FA regime be designed? As Chapter 3 explicated, the public benefits that justify the labour factor are providing and maintaining a healthy labour market. Therefore, the market-neutral labour factor should cover all types of the human

850. William Shakespeare, Barbara A Mowat & Paul Werstine, *Twelfth Night, or, What You Will* (2019), Act 2 Scene 5.

851. The European Commission's BEFIT tax reform package has the same rationale to include both 'personnel and salaries'. European Commission, *supra* n. 117, at 12. https://ec.europa.eu/taxation_customs/sites/taxation/files/communication_on_business_taxation_for_the_21st_century.pdf.

resources used, and the attribution of human resources should be to the jurisdiction that provides the corresponding public benefits to support the labour market.

So, the sub-questions are: how should employees be defined? And how should employees be attributed? While answering these two questions, I explore how and why the current practices and proposals deviate from the market-neutral labour factor.

5.1.2 Justification for Carving-Out Genuine Independent Contractors

In order to provide the answers, I revisit the US's FA experiences in the payroll factor and the European Commission's relevant working documents. Furthermore, I explore the relevant discussions on the scope of 'employee' in the EU and US labour law and social security law. It is quite intriguing that the labour law literature indicates that the definition of employee is not only a labour law question but also a tax law question.[852] It is a field where labour law, social security law, and tax law are intertwined.

Therefore, Chapter 5 seeks a tailored solution to decide what constitutes employee for the EU FA regime's labour factor. While acknowledging diverse examples of 'employee' from different judications, I take a critical perspective when choosing suitable elements to apply and design the labour factor. I focus on the underlying rationale, development trends, and common elements, instead of the actual details of each test to decide the status of employees. This approach is especially inspired by the 'purposive approach' used in new labour law research.[853]

Comparing examples of the definition of employee demonstrates that the labour factor needs a broad and harmonized definition of employee. However, instead of giving a definition of employee at the EU level, it is feasible to adopt the test of 'independent contractors (i.e., true self-employees)' which excludes people who are not actually mobilized by MNE taxpayers. The approach of carving out only a limited scope of independent contractors is consistent with developments in labour law in the US too.

Genuine independent contractors are not human resources mobilized by the MNE taxpayer as if they were a production element, but they have an equal business relationship with the MNE taxpayer. In theory, such genuine independent contractors would act as if they can bargain with MNE taxpayers and also act as entrepreneurs.

852. This expression is borrowed from the comment on Uber/Lyft drivers' disputes in California, *see* Uber, Taxes, and the Question of Who's an Employee in the Gig Economy, 2020/08/25 at https://www.taxpolicycenter.org/taxvox/uber-taxes-and-question-whos-employee-gig-economy. 'Who counts an employee is a taxing question'.

853. For example, Guy Davidov, The Status of Uber Drivers: A Purposive Approach, Spanish Labour Law and Employment Relations Journal (2017). Marianne Jenum Hotvedt, The Contract-of-Employment Test Renewed: A Scandinavian Approach to Platform Work, 7 Spanish Labour Law and Employment Relations Journal 56 (2018). The recent labour law research on the sharing economy/gig economy/platform economy strategically uses the purposive approach, to seek a proper scope of employee and sufficient protection of level. Instead of analysing the meaning of a specific legal concept, the purposive approach is ready at any time to change the traditional understanding of the concept. Therefore, the concepts and practices in the existing law can be de-constructed and rebuild for the purpose of a law reform. In my view, it is similar to the functional approach in the comparative legal research discipline and focuses more on the direction of reform.

Since MNE taxpayers do not control and mobilized them, it is justified to exclude these genuine independent contractors from the labour factor. In practice, the number of genuine independent contractors that can be excluded from the labour factor is quite limited.

5.1.3 The Structure of This Chapter

The chapter is structured as follows. Section 5.2 revisits the rationale and theory of the labour factor and clarifies the intertwined relationship between labour law, social security law, and tax law. Section 5.3 focuses on the definition of employee, so I explore discussions under labour law and social security law.

Section 5.4 further discusses the attribution rule of employee. Theoretically speaking, a workforce is like a human being which is the means of production, and therefore where he or she physically performs the work. The location of physical performance is the tax-neutral location because it best represents the public benefit of maintaining the labour market. In practice, for administrative convenience, some attribution rules use 'renumeration paying employers' as the criterion. The employee attribution rule is usually designed as 'all-or-nothing'. However, when there is some cross-border element in the employment, the all-or-nothing attribution does not faithfully reflect how the human resources are utilized. Therefore, I recommend the pro-rata attribution method based on the time spent in the physical location.

Section 5.5 discusses the difficulties for the labour factor in the digital economy, especially involving online platforms. Unlike the market side of the digital economy, the labour side of the digital economy receives less attention in the field of tax law. However, new developments in technology not only influence the market/output side (destination) but also the input/labour side. As to the implications for formulas in the digital economy, section 5.5 is symmetric with section 4.5 in Chapter 4. Section 5.6 concludes and makes recommendations on amending the current CCCTB Directive Proposal for the EU's FA regime.

5.2 DECIPHERING THE THEORY UPHOLDING A MARKET-NEUTRAL LABOUR FACTOR

5.2.1 Maintaining a Healthy Labour Market Is the Public Benefit Justifying the Labour Factor

Historically, a three-factor sharing formula consisting of the sales factor, the labour factor, and the assets factor is not based on any specific economic theory in the US.[854] From a roughly theoretical point of view, the factors of the sharing formula aim to reflect the taxpayers' economic activities in each Member State. The asset factor and the labour factor both reflect the economic activities of the supply side, i.e., the

854. The presumption of 'no theory for the formula', *see* Musgrave, *supra* n. 150. William J Pierce, The Uniform Division of Income for State Tax Purposes, 35 Taxes 747 (1957).

production; the sales factor reflects the demand side, i.e., the market. This is reiterated by the working document of the current CCCTB Directive Proposal.[855]

As discussed in Chapter 3.4 for factor selection, market-neutral weighting factors of a formula are designed in line with the benefit theory. The labour factor represents the input from human resources of a jurisdiction where the production process takes place, and such input is only possible when relevant public benefits are provided in the jurisdiction. It is therefore consistent with the benefit principle to adopt the labour factor in a sharing formula. The public benefit that the labour factor represents is the 'labour market'[856] in the broad sense, as maintained in the jurisdiction.

It is true that there is no real freedom of contract in the 'labour market', especially from the perspective of job seekers and employees. However, from employers' perspective, qualified human resources provided in that jurisdiction present themselves like a 'market' for employers to choose from. Moreover, to maintain this 'labour market', there are also corresponding infrastructures, institutions, and systems, for example, an education system, a social security system, unemployment benefits, vocational training, healthy industrial relations, etc. These systems and institutions are all necessary to constitute a well-functioning labour market, and these are public benefits that private individuals or companies could not provide for themselves.

The labour factor is justified because MNE taxpayers make use of 'human resources from labour'. Together with the asset factor, the labour factor represents MNE taxpayers' supply/input side, i.e., the whole production process. As a pair from the input side, the assets factor represents the MNE taxpayers' utilization of material resources and the labour factor represents the MNE taxpayers' utilization of human resources. Therefore, the labour factor in fact reflects MNE taxpayers' capacity to mobilize human resources. The assets factor and the labour factor are two equally important pillars in the production process.

5.2.2 Consensus: Employees Are Human Resources Used at the Task-Performing Location

The 'employee' is the key human resource in the labour market, and labour law and social security law represent the public benefits to maintain and support a healthy labour market. Therefore, this chapter also revisit relevant information in these fields of law, for designing the neutral labour factor of the EU's FA regime.

It goes without saying that the definition of 'employee' is a difficult issue, and there is not yet (and possibly will never be) a clear consensus about a definition among EU Member States or internationally. Diversity does not prevent us from seeking a market-neutral definition of employee in the context of FA taxation. However, it is

855. CCCTB Working Document No. 47, paragraph 15.

856. Although the term of 'labour market' has been criticized for not reflecting the power imbalance between employers and employees so conveying a wrong implication that 'a de-regulated free market is ideal', I still decide to use the concept 'maintaining the labour market' to describe the public benefits that uphold and justify the labour factor in the sharing formula. Dukes, *supra* n. 551.

necessary to take a critical perspective to gain useful insights. Any definition of employee from a specific discipline needs to fulfil the purpose of the labour factor that represents a well-functioning labour market.

Attributing workers is not easy either. The mobility of employees nowadays has become a universal issue.[857] Workers can perform their work in different Member States or via the Internet or other digital means, thanks to developments in communication technology. The physical location where an employee is performing a task might be anywhere in the world other than the jurisdiction where the employer company is running the business. In a digitalized economy, not only a market jurisdiction can face difficulties capturing a nexus, but also a 'production' jurisdiction can face the same difficulties because via online platforms and the Internet, human beings can perform their work in an atypical, non-office-work way,[858] even cross-border.

Attributing cross-border employees is not a completely new issue. It arises in international tax law, EU law,[859] and social security law. These fields of law all have the common logic to seek 'where the employment takes place'. In this regard, international tax law, EU social security law, EU labour law, as well as the labour factor in the EU's FA have the same rationale, but existing practices cannot be copied directly for the labour factor because attribution rules do not necessarily use proxies reflecting actual utilization of the labour market.

Although using the same rationale, the existing attribution rules in practice often aim to seek the most suitable proxy to decide 'where the employment takes place' for their own regulatory purposes. Therefore, they are not necessarily suitable for FA. For example, in order to relieve double taxation, the international tax regime decides the 'single' jurisdiction as the source jurisdiction that has primarily the taxing right to the employment income, even though mobile employees might already involve multiple jurisdictions and spend almost an equal amount of time in each jurisdiction. The OECD Model Convention provides for employment income in the broad sense: from the employment income, director fees, and income from other special types of professionals, from Article 15 to Article 19 of the OECD Model Convention.

However, the OECD's model on allocating taxing powers on income derived by cross-border personnel is not useful for designing the labour factor in an FA system, even though both regimes (the labour factor and the employment income) seem to deal with the same issue. The OECD Model Convention aims to relieve double taxation but not to represent the labour market. As a result, the OECD Model Convention provisions will end up choosing one jurisdiction. For highly mobile workers who work in the transportation industry and involve several jurisdictions, Article 15 (3) of the OECD

857. Giorgio Beretta, Cross-Border Mobility of Individuals and the Lack of Fiscal Policy Coordination among Jurisdictions (Even) after the BEPS Project, 47 Intertax 91 (2019).

858. The outbreak of COVID-19 in 2020 has influenced how people work. Working from home and social distancing might become a new phenomenon for the purpose of controlling the pandemic crisis. Many jobs can be done from home. *See* Jonathan I Dingel & Brent Neiman, *How Many Jobs Can Be Done at Home?* (National Bureau of Economic Research 2020). Jean-Victor Alipour, Oliver Falck & Simone Schüller, Germany's Capacities to Work from Home, CESifo Working Paper No. 8227 (2020).

859. Bruno Peeters, Mobility of EU Citizens and Family Taxation: A Hard to Reconcile Combination, 23 EC Tax Review 118 (2014).

Model Convention is unable to provide a clear normative framework when physical locations are multiple.[860]

As another example, coordination of EU social security law has a similar rationale in its 'single state rule': to ensure employees can have legal certainty about the jurisdiction where they are entitled to social security benefits.[861] Coordination of EU social security law focuses on ensuring social security entitlements and the applicable law in a cross-border situation. It does not reflect the human resources mobilized by MNE enterprises.

As to the labour factor of the EU's FA regime, a benefit-based MN framework needs to closely reflect the labour market and how human resources are mobilized and utilized. In this regard, the existing attribution rules are not suitable because they focus on deciding an applicable law for ensuring that social security is not lacking and taxing rights are not doubled.

Therefore, a more flexible attribution rule, such as 'a formula in formula' based on the time spent in multiple jurisdictions, can be also acceptable as long as the attribution result reflects the corresponding labour markets. The discussions are elaborated in section 5.4.

5.2.3 The Murky Relationship Between Labour Law, Social Security Law, and Tax Law: 'fiscalization'

It is intriguing that, in practice, rules to decide the 'employee' status demonstrate that labour law, social security law, and tax law are already intertwined. The discussion about 'employee' is not only a labour law discussion but also a tax law discussion.[862] The relationship between these three fields of law is sometimes confusing.

To maintain a healthy labour market, different legal mechanisms are required. The essential element in the labour market is that every individual human being who performs a task is included in public benefits. Both labour law and social security law in modern society regulate issues related to working human beings. Labour law has the underlying rationale of protecting 'employees' as the weaker party in the inherently imbalanced employment relationship, to prevent exploitation and even 'self-exploitation'.[863] Therefore, the package of typical labour rights includes minimum wage, working hours, safe and healthy working conditions, and collective rights, such as collective bargaining, right to strike, and establishing trade unions, etc. Since labour law aims to protect the weaker party in the employment relationship, the labour law system has to establish the 'weakness' of employees, since 'weakness/subordination'

860. Hannelore Niesten, Revisiting the Fiscal and Social Security Status of Highly Mobile Workers in the Road and Railway Transportation: Quo Vadis?, 46 Intertax 836 (2018).
861. *See section* 5.4.4 below.
862. This expression is borrowed from the remarks from the blogpost on Uber drivers' employee status, https://www.taxpolicycenter.org/taxvox/uber-taxes-and-question-whos-employee-gig-economy. 'Who counts an employee is a taxing question'.
863. This term of 'self-exploitation' is from the description from Annette Thörnquist, False Self-Employment and Other Precarious Forms of Employment in the 'Grey Area' of the Labour Market, 31 International Journal of Comparative Labour Law and Industrial Relations (2015).

is a requirement of the status of employee. Then typical labour law rights not only ensure the level of rights related to working conditions and equal treatment but also provide rights to 'empower' employees to cooperate as a group, collectively.

Since the social security system is closely related to labour law,[864] many notions under labour law are also used in social security law. There are quite a few overlapping areas between social security law and labour law, especially when it comes to the scope of personal application.[865] But the focus of social security law is addressing various inevitable risks and consequent damages arising from life: being sick, injured, incapacitated, old, unemployed; and then providing relevant benefits to compensate and relieve damages. Such focus will also influence the definition of employee and the scope of personal application.

The ways of financing the social security system can also influence the scope of personal application. In a social security system, 'social insurance' is a typical measure, which especially covers healthcare insurance. This is also where tax law and social security law overlap in practice. There are two main models of social insurance: the Bismarckian and Beverdigean models.[866] The Bismarckian model of social insurance, originating from Germany, emphasizes that the social insurance system is financed from social security premiums paid according to employees' wages, and thus employees are also the insured persons. The Beverdigean model of social insurance, from the UK, in contrast, is financed by the state's budget from taxes, and the whole population is insured; but public social insurance in the Beverdigean model is at a minimum level; people purchase private insurance for additional benefits.[867] Whether adopting the Bismarckian or Beverdigean model or a hybrid like a Nordic model, social security premiums are quite often regulated in the form of levying tax.[868] Some taxes are levied for the specific part of the budget (a special fund), referred to as 'socially embarked tax'.[869]

This is where the concept of 'employee' of labour law, social security law, and tax law are interrelated, especially in the Bismarckian model where the concept of 'employee' directly influences the scope of the benefits enjoyed and required contributions. From an administrative viewpoint, national tax authorities are also

864. B Spiegel & others, The Relationship Between Social Security Coordination and Taxation Law, FreSsco, Brussels: European Commission (2014).
865. Many scholars do not strictly distinguish the personal application scope in the labour law and the social security law because, in practice, the concept of 'employee' in both fields is the same. For example, Karin Schulze Buschoff & Claudia Schmidt, Adapting Labour Law and Social Security to the Needs of the 'new Self-Employed' – Comparing the UK, Germany and the Netherlands, 19 Journal of European Social Policy 147 (2009).
866. Anja Rohwer, Bismarck Versus Beveridge: A Comparison of Social Insurance Systems in Europe, 4 CESifo DICE Report (2008). Jaan Paju, *The European Union and Social Security Law* (Bloomsbury 2017), at 2.1.
867. Paju, *ibid.*, 2.1.
868. Jean-Philippe Lhernould, *The Interrelation Between Social Security Coordination Law and Labour Law* (European Commission Directorate -General for Employment, Social Affairs and Inclusion 2017).
869. Spiegel & others, *supra* n. 864.

responsible for collecting social security taxes and contributions.[870] Questions may arise about the borderline between 'personal income tax' and 'social securities',[871] but for this discussion, the issue of distinguishing between the two is irrelevant because when designing the labour factor for apportioning a consolidated corporate tax base, there is no concern about double levy, as already discussed in section 3.4.3.2.

The intertwined feature of labour law, social security law, and tax law actually further influences the labour market composition and employers' decision-making. Labour law scholars observe the phenomenon of 'fiscalization', where employers enjoy more tax benefits or bear less of a burden of social security when hiring self-employees/independent contractors. 'Independent contractors' enjoy less social security protection, but they can get jobs and income more easily.[872] Therefore, not only false self-employees inevitably increase but also 'genuine'/voluntarily dependent self-employees increase. Social security law and tax law scholars usually formulate 'false self-employee' as a misapplication or tax avoidance/manipulation scenario,[873] and the problem of 'fiscalization' takes place not only in Europe[874] but also in the US.[875]

870. *Ibid.*, 11; Didier Verbeke, Analysis of the Main Systems of Social Security Contribution Collection in the European Union Based on the Experience of 12 Member States (European Commission DG EMPL 2012).
871. Marjon Weerepas, Tax or Social Security Contribution, a World of Difference?, 1 Nordic Tax Journal 18 (2018).
872. Zoe Adams & Simon Deakin, Institutional Solutions to Precariousness and Inequality in Labour Markets, 52 British Journal of Industrial Relations 779 (2014). The same phenomenon also takes place in USA, and there is an temptation to (mis)classify an employee as independent contractor for reducing costs, *see* John A Pearce & Jonathan P Silva, The Future of Independent Contractors and Their Status as Non-Employees: Moving on from a Common Law Standard, 14 Hastings Business Law Journal 1 (2018).
873. For example, Benshalom observes the problem of manipulating the distinction of employee and independent contractor, *see* Benshalom, The Quest to Tax Financial Income Virginia Tax Review, *supra* n. 54.
874. Werner Eichhorst & others, Social Protection Rights of Economically Dependent Self-Employed Workers WIFO Studies (2013), 58: 'Both employers and employee organisations recognise the main driving force towards genuine self-employment of workers within the construction industry as the desire for entrepreneurship and self-determination and expectation of a higher net income (by diminishing taxes and social contributions), even at the expense of less social protection'.

    The UK example of fiscalization, *see* Mark Freedland & Jeremias Prassl, Employees, Workers and the 'Sharing Economy' Changing Practices and Changing Concepts in The United Kingdom, 6 Spanish Labour Law and Employment Relations Journal 16 (2017), 28.

    According to Freedland and Prassl citing UK tax authorities' concern:

    > In the United Kingdom, self-employed workers are taxed (for national insurance purposes) at a lower rate than the employed; a rate which can be reduced further when services are offered through the worker's own limited liability company. The tax authorities (HMRC) have become worried about the 'unfair manipulation' of the applicable rules (IR35), which they suggest 'contribute to, and reinforce, the incentives for individuals to work through companies when they would otherwise be employees, and for businesses to engage individuals through companies, even if they are working in a similar way to their employees' – and thus a considerable loss of approximately £430m per annum to the Exchequer.

875. Sarah Leberstein, Independent Contractor Misclassification Imposes Huge Costs on Workers and Federal and State Treasuries, National Employment Project (2012).

The problem of fiscalization reveals the need to design the labour factor as market neutral and that it reflects the economic reality. The status quo of the labour law practice of distinguishing employees and non-employees is already often used as a tax avoidance/tax planning scenario. But when the human resources of the labour market can be covered by the labour factor, the EU's FA regime can mitigate the problem of fiscalization.

Since the labour/payroll factor of the formula represents the labour market, here I analyse 'what in the labour market is' that involves the definition of employee, and 'where the labour market is' that involves the attribution of employees, as represented by the neutral labour factor. This chapter revisits the options used in labour law and social security law and seeks insightful options for FA reform.

5.2.4 The Market-Neutral Employee Definition Is Broad Enough to Represent the Current Labour Market

Broadening the scope of employee for the payroll factor in the FA regime is tax neutral because such approach demonstrates a taxpayer's capacity to mobilize a workforce in various forms. In the existing FA literature, Benshalom[876] also endorses a broad definition of employee in the context of financial industries. Beyond the financial industry, Benshalom's argument still stands.[877] Benshalom argues, in principle, that the payroll factor is the most difficult to manipulate because payroll is paid to a specific individual, so it is more difficult for taxpayers to create a no-where payroll factor since payroll is linked to a worker's remuneration and cannot be easily circumvented. However, if the payroll factor/labour factor only includes the payroll received by traditional regular employees and excludes others, taxpayers may start again to manipulate this distinction.[878] What Benshalom describes coincides with labour law scholars' observation on 'fiscalization' of employment decisions. A purely formal distinction would cause unnecessary incentives for tax planning.

Therefore, although it is almost impossible to directly harmonize the definition of employee under EU law, or in any field of law, it is feasible for the EU's FA to have a broad scope of employee. Even though there is no harmonized definition, the scope is broad enough to cover all types of human resources being used by MNE taxpayers.

Instead of looking for a definition of 'employee', it is more feasible to adopt a legal presumption that an individual receiving payroll is presumed to be an employee,

876. Benshalom, The Quest to Tax Financial Income, *supra* n. 54.

877. In my view, the approach of adopting a broad definition for employees should not be limited to the financial industry. Although the current MTC Regulation IV's text seems conservative, its special formulas have demonstrated the need to broaden the scope of employees. For example, the MTC special industry formula for the television and radio broadcasting industry as laid down in Article 18(h)(iii)A provides that the payroll factor denominator shall include compensation paid to employees, including 'directors, actors, newscasters and other talent as employees.' Detailed discussion of the special formula of the television and radio broadcasting industry is not within the scope of this chapter, but it is a convincing evidence to show that the definition of employees can be broad and flexible.

878. Benshalom, The Quest to Tax Financial Income, *supra* n. 54.

unless the independent and commercial nature of the relationship is proven.[879] In this way, all typical employees and employee-like people are included in the labour factor, with the result that the labour factor is broad enough to reflect taxpayers' production side contributions by human resources and taxpayers' capacity to mobilize them. The scope of employees should not only cover typical employees who are working/performing in one Member State but also other types of employees, including posted employees and atypical employees, such as tele-employees (home workers), frontier workers, part-time employees, dependent contractors, etc.

Although my approach here looks similar to labour law's trend in extending the scope of protection, my argument to adopt a broad scope of employee for the labour factor of the EU's FA regime is not exactly the same as that of labour law/social security law to extend the scope of protection for the 'weaker party'. Instead, my core argument for the market-neutral labour factor is to represent the employer's capacity to mobilize human resources. Whether an individual is specifically classified as an employee or an employee-like person is not the main concern for the labour factor under the EU's FA regime.

5.3 WHAT IS IN THE LABOUR MARKET? THE DEFINITION AND VALUATION OF EMPLOYEES OF THE LABOUR FACTOR

5.3.1 Different Types of Workforce Involved

The scope of the labour factor is dependent on the definition of 'employee'. Even in labour law or social security law, there is no harmonized definition of employee internationally or under EU law.[880] These discussions are elaborated in section 5.3.2.

In this section, I discuss four types of 'employee-like' because they are all related to the idea of workforce in a labour market. These four types are: (1) employee under labour law, which focuses on 'control and subordination'; (2) employee under social security law in the EU and the US, which focuses on social security entitlement; (3) a hybrid type of 'worker' under EU law, which focuses on the impact of free movement of workers in the context of EU law; and (4) genuine self-employee/independent contractor, which are not classified as employee under a binary distinction.

These four types of workforce are briefly explained in Table 8.

879. This approach of 'rebuttable presumption' is often used in labour law to establish the employee status, *see* Nicola Countouris, *Defining and Regulating Work Relations for the Future of Work* (International Labour Organization 2019). International Labour Organization, Regulating the Employment Relationship in Europe: A Guide to Recommendation No. 198: European Labour Law Network (2013).

880. From CJEU's case law on free movement of workers, there is a definition of 'worker' according to Lawrie-Blum formula, but there is no harmonized definition for employees at the EU law level. CJEU in the social security law field also refers to national social security law to decide the employee *See* C-340/94 *De Jaeck v Staatssecretaris van Financiën*.

Table 8 Different Types of Workforce

	Employee under (National) Labour Law	*Employee under Social Security Law*	*'Worker' under EU Law*	*Genuine Self-Employee/ Independent Contractor/Entrepreneur*
Examples	• CCCTB (Member States' labour law). • Article 15 OECD Model Convention. • US Supreme Court's 'common law employee'. • Section 13 prior-2010 MTC Regulation IV 'common law employee'. • US IRS's 20 factor test. • ILO's 14 factors test.	• EU Regulation 833/2004. • CJEU's case law: definition of employee and self-employee: (CJEU Case C-340/94: referring to the national law where activities take place). • US: section 13 post-2010 MTC Regulation IV follows several federal social security regimes.	• Three elements from case law – the Lawrie-Blum formula: (i) economic activities (ii) subordination, and (iii) remuneration. • Workers under EU law can include self-employees who are not subordinated (Case C-107/94 P. *H. Asscher v. Staatssecretaris van Financiën*). • In the Posted Worker Directive (Directive 96/71/EC), the definition of worker is that which applies in the law of the Member State to whose territory the worker is posted.	Those who are not employees: • The Entrepreneur Opportunity Test (Fedex). • ABC Test for independent contractors. • The 're-targeting approach' of labour proposed by scholars.
Rationale	Focusing on the elements of 'control' and 'subordination' between the employee and employer, protecting the weaker party.	Focusing on the social security purpose and entitlements; looking at 'dependence' of employees instead of being controlled.	A general description of the features of a worker in the context of 'free movement of workers'.	To define independent contractors, to avoid difficulties of defining employee.

	Employee under (National) Labour Law	*Employee under Social Security Law*	*'Worker' under EU Law*	*Genuine Self-Employee/ Independent Contractor/Entrepreneur*
Neutrality implication for the labour factor	A typical employee that is subordinated to their employer should be included in the labour factor. But the element of subordination of the labour law employee makes the definition too narrow and cannot reflect the labour market, and thus it is not neutral and thus should not be the only criterion for the CCCTB labour law factor.	It is wide enough to cover typical and atypical employees in the labour market, and thus it is neutral.	A worker under EU law should be included, especially quasi-subordinated self-employees. It is market neutral when interpreting the Lawrie-Blum formula broadly.	A market-neutral labour factor should exclude true independent contractors, but should include misclassified, sham independent contractors.

Source: The author.

Generally speaking, the definition of employee in the social security regime would be wider than labour law because social security deals with compensating immediate risks which occur and which affect people, whereas labour law emphasizes empowering the weaker party of the employment relationship. Tax law often (though not always) is the follower of social security law and labour law, but the regulatory goals of these three fields of law do not always coincide.

5.3.2 The Typical Employee Is Not Always Sufficient to Cover the Labour Market

5.3.2.1 No Uniform Definition of 'employee' under EU Law; Mutual Recognition Cannot Solve All Disparities

The labour factor is provided for in Articles 32 and 33 of the 2016 Commission's CCCTB Directive Proposal.[881] Article 32 provides the qualification of the labour factor, including the number of employees and the amount of payroll and indicates the definition of an employee. Article 33 further provides the attribution rule of the labour factor.

Article 32 provides the scope of the labour factor:

Composition of the labour factor

> The labour factor shall consist, as to one half, of the total amount of the payroll of a group member as its numerator and the total amount of the payroll of the group as its denominator, and as to the other half, of the number of employees of a group member as its numerator and the number of employees of the group as its denominator. Where an individual employee is included in the labour factor of a group member, the payroll relating to that employee shall be allocated to the labour factor of the same group member.
>
> 1. The number of employees shall be measured at the end of the tax year.
> 2. The definition of an employee shall be determined by the national law of the Member State where the employment is exercised.

The current CCCTB Directive Proposal does not provide a definition of employee. Therefore Article 32(3) of the CCCTB Directive provides that '[t]he definition of an employee shall be determined by 'the national law' of the Member State where the employment is exercised'. Article 32(3) of the CCCTB Directive Proposal leaves it unharmonized, and Member States can formulate their own definition according to national legislation.

It is also unclear whether the definition of employee depends on national labour law or national tax law. It seems that the definition of employee might depend on the national labour law of the Member State where the workforce physically performs their activities. Moreover, although the term of 'the employment is exercised' is not explained in the CCCTB Working Document either, the term 'where the employment is exercised' can be interpreted as 'where employees are physically present and performing activities',[882] as in the international tax regime.

881. It is comparable to Article 90 and Article 91 of the 2011 CCCTB Directive Proposal.
882. In this regard, the OECD Model Convention has used the same term in the field of international tax law, so the CCCTB Directive Proposal, also as an instrument to allocate states' taxing powers, might take into account the OECD Model Convention to interpret the definition of 'where the employment is exercised'. *See* OECD, OECD Model Convention on Income and Capital, version 2017, Commentary on Article Concerning the Taxation of Income from Employment, paragraph 1.

Since there is no EU-level harmonized definition of employee,[883] CCCTB Working Document No. 60 mentions[884] that the current CCCTB Directive Proposal adopts the 'mutual recognition approach' to define employees, and thus once a workforce is defined as an employee in one national law, he or she is an employee in another Member State. At the EU secondary law level, it is quite often that Member States are left with the competence to decide the definition of employee.[885] Article 32 of the current CCCTB Directive Proposal follows this pattern.

It is intriguing that the current text in Article 32(3) does not expressly mention 'mutual recognition'. Consequently, it is still possible that a workforce is defined as an employee in one Member State but not recognized as employee in another Member State. But even when mutual recognition applies, disputes and inconsistencies might still occur when such workforce actually exercises his or her employment in multiple EU Member States which provide different qualifications of employee. Since EU Member States' social policy, labour law, and social security law are so diverse, such dispute is quite likely to happen, especially in the case of a cross-border secondment. Even mutual recognition cannot resolve all the problems.

5.3.2.2 Two Aspects of the Employee Definition in EU Member States: Control and Economic Dependence

Since there is no harmonized definition of employee at the EU level,[886] EU Member States provide their own definition of employee in their civil law, labour law, and social security law.[887] Even in one single state, the definition of 'employee' can differ in different fields of law.

Although the concept of employee is not completely the same across all EU Member States, there are some common features. According to the International

883. The definition of employee is not fully harmonized and very often left to the national law even in the field of EU labor law. This is a fundamental issue but also a sensitive issue in EU law. *See* the brief introduction on the definition of employee in EU labor law by Eurofound: http://www.eurofound.europa.eu/areas/industrialrelations/dictionary/definitions/employee.htm.
884. CCCTB Working Document No. 60, paragraph 22.
885. Frans Pennings & Claire Bosse, *The Protection of Working Relationships: A Comparative Study*, Vol. 39 (Kluwer Law International 2011). For example, the Acquired Rights Directive of 1977 (Council Directive 77/187, consolidated in Directive 2001/23); Directive 80/987 of 1980 on the protection of employees in the event of insolvency; Council Directive No. 2002/14, etc.
An introduction, *see* European Industrial Relations Dictionary (2017), https://www.eurofound.europa.eu/observatories/eurwork/industrial-relations-dictionary/employee.
886. E Verhulp, *The Notion of 'Employee' in EU-Law and National Laws* (The European Centre of Expertise (ECE) in the Field of Labour Law, Employment and Labour Market Policies 2017).
887. A comprehensive survey, *see* Bernd Waas & Guus Heerma van Voss (eds), *The Concept of Employee* (Hart 2017).

Labour Organization's (ILO's) 2006 recommendation,[888] there are common indicators[889] of the definition of employee from two perspectives: control and economic dependence.

According to the ILO, from the perspective of 'control', factors include: direct control/subordination/'behavioural dependence', integration in the organization,[890] mutuality of obligations, lack of freedom to choose place, time, and/or content of the work',[891] the worker's availability, the provision of tools, materials, and machinery by the party requesting the work, etc. The control/subordination aspect focuses more on the employer's right and power to exercise control.

From the perspective of 'economic dependence', it focuses on the worker's status of economic reliance in the form of payment of renumeration and benefits. Factors include 'periodic payment of remuneration to the worker that such remuneration constitutes the worker's sole or principal source of income; provision of payment in kind, such as food, lodging or transport; recognition of entitlements such as weekly rest and annual holidays; payment by the party requesting the work for travel undertaken by the worker in order to carry out the work; or absence of financial risk for the worker'.[892] The aspect of economic dependence focuses more on the worker's vulnerable status, even without specific and direct subordination or control from the employer. Deciding whether or not being dependent is sometimes challenging because two parties of the labour market are also to some extent inherently 'mutually

888. International Labor Organization (ILO), The Employment Relationship: An Annotated Guide to ILO Recommendation No. 198 (2006), 27-29.
889. Scholars call ILO's approach as 14 factor-test; some scholars identify 17 factors. Guy Davidov, Mark Freedland & Nicola Countouris, *The Subjects of Labor Law: 'Employees' and Other Workers, Comparative labor law* (Edward Elgar 2015).
890. The integration test is expressly mentioned in the employee definition of the UK and Portugal. *See* International Labour Organization, *supra* n. 879, at 41.

In my view, the integration test, can be used in the context of CCCTB, especially with the factor presence nexus: when we need to re-attribute an employee who physically perform tasks in a jurisdiction where the employer has no nexus. Since he or she is functionally integrated in an organization, there must be a reporting line in the organization, even in a relatively flat structure. An employee would need to deliver his or her work and has a function in the organization. Such modified integration test can be used for not only deciding the employee status but also the attribution rule for the CCCTB which regulates a cross-border group of companies.

We can see the integration element is used when deciding the idea control, in the German law when recognizing the quasi-subordinated employee, *see* Nicola Countouris, *The Changing Law of the Employment Relationship: Comparative Analyses in the European Context* (Routledge 2007).

The integration element is also discussed in the common law employee status of the outsourced engineers of Microsoft case in 1990, *see section* 5.3.4 below. In USA, 'integration' is recognized in both aspects of control and dependence. *See* Charles J Muhl, What Is an Employee – The Answer Depends on the Federal Law, 125 Monthly Labor Review 3 (2002).
891. International Labour Organization (2013), *supra* n. 879, at 36.
892. International Labour Organization, Employment Relationship Recommendation (2006), Article 11(b), *supra* n. 888.

dependent'.[893] Among these factors related to dependence, 'the ability to assume and spread risk' is representative.[894]

All these factors/indicators for an 'employment relationship' represent the power imbalance between employers and employees. Two aspects have some conceptual overlap too. Deciding whether a person has employee status needs a holistic but case-by-case analysis. Moreover, these common indicators are designed around 'the typical standard full-time employment relationship' as the norm and the prototype. Therefore, in addition to the inherent difficulty in assessing various factors/tests, there is a newly emerging difficulty in capturing the current labour market in the digital economy because the power imbalance between employers and employees can take on a new form. In section 5.5, I further elaborate on this issue, especially online platforms.

5.3.2.3 The Concept of Worker under EU Law: Control/Subordination Is Also Key

Although there is no harmonized definition of 'employee' under EU law,[895] there is a concept of 'worker' developed by the CJEU and applied in secondary law in the field of labour law, social security law, and the EU internal market on the free movement of persons. Although these two terms: 'worker' and 'employee' have the same function under EU law, their formulation is not entirely identical.[896] Theoretically speaking, since free movement of 'workers' is a freedom under TFEU, the scope of worker is supposed to be the widest, yet in practice this is not always the case.

The free movement of workers is the fundamental freedom provided by Article 45 TFEU, and the CJEU has adjudicated on the definition of worker on several occasions.[897] According to *Lawrie-Blum*, the leading CJEU judgment, the status of worker is decided by three elements: work (genuine economic activities), subordination, and remuneration. This is known as the 'Lawrie-Blum formula' – 'the essential feature of the employment relationship is that, for a certain period of time, one person performs services for and under the direction of another person in return for which he or she receives remuneration'.[898]

In different EU secondary laws, the term 'worker' is not uniformly formulated; the personal applicable scope of different social policy and labour protection Directives

893. Observations *see* Orly Lobel, The Gig Economy & the Future of Employment and Labor Law, 51 University of San Francisco Law Review 51 (2017), at 62. Lobel discussed USA law, but the 'dependence' element is also used in USA for deciding the employee status, *see* section 5.3.2.4.
894. Davidov, *supra* n. 853, at 11.
895. CJEU has been repeatedly stating that, '[T]here is no single definition of worker/employed or self employed person in Community law' Judgment of 16 July 2009, von Chamier-Glisczinski, C-208/07, ECLI: EU: C:2009:455, paragraph 68. *See* comments, Adam Sagan, The Classification as 'Worker' under EU Law, 10 European Labour Law Journal 353 (2019).
896. Lhernould, *supra* n. 868.
897. Case 66/85 *Deborah Lawrie-Blum v. Land Baden-Wurttemberg*; Case C-256/01 *Debra Allonby v. Accrington & Rossendale College and Others*.
898. Martin Risak & Thomas Dullinger, The Concept of 'Worker' in EU Law: Status Quo and Potential for Change, 140 ETUI Research Paper-Report (2018). Vincent Février, The Concept of 'Worker' in the Free Movement of Workers and the Social Policy Directives: Perspectives from the Case Law of the Court of Justice, European Labour Law Journal (2020).

varies.[899] As Sagan observes,[900] the CJEU in early cases almost leaves it all up to national law when a directive has only minimum harmonization; more recently, the CJEU uses both the formal approach, looking at the wording of directives and the material approach, emphasizing 'principles of equality and effectiveness'. In short, even among different secondary laws in the same field, there is no autonomous uniform concept of 'worker' because the CJEU does not have a uniform approach to interpreting the personal scope of 'worker' in secondary laws.

The 'Lawrie-Blum formula' is actually quite strictly formulated, and thus the concept of 'worker' under EU law is not as broad as expected.[901] Compared to the ILO's indicators for an employment relationship, the CJEU's interpretation of 'worker' emphases the element of 'control'.

For the CCCTB's labour factor, worker under the CJEU's case law and employee fulfilling the control test or economic dependence test under national labour law should both be included in the labour factor. However, if we use only the labour law definition based on the control/subordination test, it is too restrictive and cannot cover non-typical workforce. Therefore, by using the labour law definition of employee or the concept of worker under the Lawrie-Blum formula in EU law as the only criterion, it still cannot achieve a tax-neutral result.

5.3.2.4 *'Employee' in the US: Variety in Different Contexts and a Trend to Broaden the Scope*

The concept of employee is essential for the payroll factor. Section 13 (a)(1) MTC Regulation IV[902] provides that the payroll factor shall include 'the total amount paid by the taxpayer in the regular course of its trade or business for compensation during the tax period'.[903] Just like the labour factor under the current CCCTB Directive Proposal, neither the UDITPA nor MTC Regulation IV itself defines 'employees' directly.[904]

899. Martinez Sala, C-85/96, ECLI: EU: C:1998:217, paragraph 31.
900. Sagan, *supra* n. 895.
901. Taco Van Peijpe, EU Limits for the Personal Scope of Employment Law, 3 European Labour Law Journal 35 (2012) (arguing CJEU has too restricted definition for workers by incorporating the subordination element).
902. MTC Reg. IV.13.(a). Payroll Factor: In General.

(1) The payroll factor of the apportionment formula for each trade or business of the taxpayer shall include the total amount paid by the taxpayer in the regular course of its trade or business for compensation during the tax period.

903. The unitary business concept plays a role here: It should be noted that, UDITPA and MTC Regulation IV distinguish between business and non-business income. Only payroll contributed to business income (i.e., apportionable between States where the sharing formula is applicable) is included in the payroll factor. Payroll that is paid to generate non-business income would not be included in the payroll factor either. The explanatory example attached to the MTC Regulation section 13 further mentions that the salary paid to the employee who deals with non-business activities, for example, the taxpayer's investment portfolio via securities, should be excluded from the payroll factor of the sharing formula. Another explanatory example indicates that the wages paid to the construction workers who build a storage building that upon completion will be used for the taxpayer's regular trade and

The definition of employee is a complex legal question in the US, representing an intersection between tax law, social security law, and labour law, just like the concept of employee in the EU. The concept of employee in the US has been developed and used in different federal legislation. Different employees in different statutes enjoy different degrees of social protection.[905] But just like many EU Member States, the concept of employee in the US is also based on the binary distinction: employee versus independent contractor.

5.3.2.4.1 The Right to Control Test, the Economic Dependence Test in the US

To decide employee status in the US, there are two tests developed from the courts for different statutes: the (right to) control test, the economic realities test, and a hybrid test combining the control and the economic dependence test.[906] The control test focuses on employers' control over workers; the economic dependence test focuses on the economic dependence of the employee.[907] These two tests may overlap.[908] The

---

business should be included in the labour factor. Such a distinction is based on whether the payroll is related to production of business income.

Since the unitary business is the precondition of apportionment in USA, section 13(a)(2) excludes the payroll which is paid for the production of 'non-business income' because non-business income is not apportionable. Section 13(a)(2) is irrelevant for CCCTB.

See: MTC Reg. IV.13.(a).(2). The total amount 'paid' to employees is determined upon the basis of the taxpayer's accounting method. If the taxpayer has adopted the accrual method of accounting, all compensation properly accrued shall be deemed to have been paid.

904. Maureen Pechacek & Karen Nakamura, The Payroll Factor: Whose Factor Is It Anyway?, *The State and Local Tax Lawyer. Symposium Edition* (American Bar Association 2009).
905. Seth D Harris & Alan B Krueger, A Proposal for Modernizing Labor Laws for Twenty-First-Century Work: The 'Independent Worker' (The Hamilton Project 2015). Jane Dokko, Megan Mumford & DW Schanzenbach, Workers and the Online Gig Economy: A Hamilton Project Framing Paper, The Hamilton Project: Advancing Opportunity, Prosperity, and Growth (2015).
906. In the labour law literature of USA, scholars also use 'economic realities' test. But in this book, the term economic realities refer to a broader concept as the economic environment. So, I decide to use 'economic dependence' instead. As to the history of economic realities test, *see* Lewis L Maltby & David C Yamada, Beyond Economic Realities: The Case for Amending Federal Employment Discrimination Laws to Include Independent Contractors, 38 Boston College Law Review 239 (1996).

    Muhl, *supra* n. 890. Nancy E Dowd, The Test of Employee Status: Economic Realities and Title VII, 26 William & Mary Law Review 75 (1984).
907. Keith Cunningham-Parmeter, From Amazon to Uber: Defining Employment in the Modern Economy, 96 Boston University Law Review 1673 (2016), at 1696. The economic realities test is mainly used in Fair Labour Standards Act (FLSA), Age Discrimination in Employment Act, Americans with Disabilities Act, Title VII of the Civil Rights Act of 1964. According to Stelter, the following indicators should be taken into account for the economic realities test as a whole:

    > (1) the alleged employee's opportunity for profit or loss depending upon managerial skill; (2) the alleged employee's investment in equipment or materials required for the work; (3) whether the service rendered requires special skills; the degree of permanence in the working relationship; and (4) whether the service rendered by the individual is an integral part of the alleged employer's business.

    Judson D Stelter, The IRS' Classification Settlement Program: Is It an Adequate Tool to Relieve Taxpayer Burden for Small Businesses That Have Misclassified Workers as Independent Contractors, 56 Clev. St. L. Review 451 (2008).

economic realities test is formulated to expand various labour law and social security law protection to precarious workers, who are not obviously subject to direct control, but deserve and need these protection measures.[909] These two tests are similar to the two aspects of national labour law of European countries discussed earlier.

Although the economic realities test is presumed to apply to more employees than the control test because the right to control test is formulated quite restrictive, it is not necessarily the case.[910] When the concept of 'control' is interpreted widely, dependence is the natural result of being controlled. Therefore, scholars also argue that the control test is the most decisive criterion.[911] In both tests, control and dominance are the main indicators,[912] like two sides of one coin. When compared closely, both tests actually have several indicators in common, such as 'integration',[913] but observed from different perspectives. Many, though not all, courts use a hybrid of these two tests in practice,[914] or focus on the relative nature of the work between the pair of the employer and the employee.[915] In any event, the control and the dependence represent the power imbalance of the employment relationship from two counterpart perspectives.

5.3.2.4.2 The Common Law Employee and the Statutory Employee in US Tax Law

By focusing on the control test, the 'common law employee' developed by case law in the US is, in particular, widely used in the field of tax law. Since the core concept of the common law employee is 'control', thus a true independent contractor is not a common law employee because independent contractors are not in any way controlled by their principals for performing their tasks. According to the US Supreme Court,[916] the common law employee means: '[T]he employment relationship exists if the employer has rights to control the work process as determined by evaluating the totality of the circumstances and special factors'.[917]

908. Cunningham-Parmeter, *supra* n. 907, at 1696, footnote 153. The same observation, Marc Linder, The Joint Employment Doctrine: Clarifying Joint Legislative-Judicial Confusion, 10 Hamline Journal of Public Law and Policy 321 (1989).
909. Robert Sprague, Using the ABC Test to Classify Workers: End of the Platform-Based Business Model or Status Quo Ante?, 11 William & Mary Business Law Review 733 (2020), some historical development of the economic dependence test, at 742.
910. Cunningham-Parmeter, *supra* n. 907.
911. *Ibid.*
912. Richard R Carlson, Why the Law Still Can't Tell an Employee When It Sees One and How It Ought to Stop Trying, 22 Berkeley Journal of Employment and Labor Law 295 (2001).
913. *See* comparison of indicators of two tests, Muhl, *supra* n. 890.
914. Sprague, *supra* n. 909, at 744.
915. Julien M Mundele, Note-Not Everything That Glitters Is Gold, Misclassification of Employees: The Blurred Line Between Independent Contractors and Employees under the Major Classification Tests, 20 Suffolk Journal of Trial & Appellate Advocacy 253 (2015).
916. *Nationwide Mutual Insurance Co. v. Darden* 503 U.S. 318 (1992). Muhl, *supra* n. 890. Martin H Zern, Employee or Independent Contractor? Classification by The Internal Revenue Service, 12 North East Journal of Legal Studies 1 (2006).
917. Muhl, *ibid.*

In other words, the common law employee is established, depending on substantial requirements, not on the formal criterion of the contract. Under this common law employee test, when the taxpayer's workforce is not an employee, but an independent contractor, the taxpayer does not control the independent contractor's work process. The 'true' independent contractor's compensation is therefore not included in the payroll factor.

In the IRC, the most important federal level tax code in the US, mainly adopts the control test.[918] According to section 3121(d) IRC, an employee is defined in several types: (i) a common law employee, (ii) a 'statutory employee', which is the legal category from the Federal Insurance Contributions Act (FICA) and from the Federal Unemployment Tax Act (FUTA), and (iii) corporate officers and 'Section 218 employees that are state and local government employees for the purpose of the voluntary social security agreement'.[919] The common law employee and statutory employee are not strictly speaking two mutually exclusive categories,[920] but they are used in different contexts. In different types of social security regulations, the scope and the definition of employee can vary.[921]

Moreover, to implement the common law test, the federal IRS has also developed more detailed rules to decide the existence of the employment. In the early days, the IRS used the '20 factor test'[922] to decide the existence of employment. To simplify the complicated 20 factors, the IRS later developed guidance to take all facts into account to decide on the employee status. There are three types of control categories recognized by the IRS's practice: (i) behaviour control, (ii) financial control, and (iii) the parties' intention to establish the characterization of relationships. The IRS has accepted that indicators to establish an employee status can be multiple, and it is necessary to take all relevant circumstances into consideration. These three categories are not strictly exclusive. The 20-factor test and the IRS's guidance has also influenced labour law discussions. This is also evidence that developments in tax law influence the definition of employee in developments in labour law.

As to the statutory employee defined by the IRC, it was originally designed to give some non-common law employees a 'statutory' employee status for the purpose of a specific state; so, a 'statutory' employee in different states in theory has a different scope. In the IRC, statutory employees are both related to the social security system,

918. *Ibid.*

919. IRC section 218 employees refer to state and local government employees for the purpose of the voluntary social security agreement, so it is outside the scope of current discussion. Pechacek & Nakamura, *supra* n. 904, at 162.

920. The statutory employee is always decided after the common law employee condition is not fulfilled. *See* Zern, *supra* n. 916, at 13.

921. For example, the employee definition for federal unemployment tax purposes is different from the employee for social security and Medicare purpose, Pechacek & Nakamura, *supra* n. 904, at 165. The social security and Medicare is part of FICA, whereas for federal unemployment, tax is provided in FUTA.

922. Discussions, *see* Pechacek & Nakamura, *supra* n. 904. Susan A Berson, Distinguishing Between Independent Contractors and Employees: Part I, 4 Corporate Business Taxation Monthly 12 (2002).

i.e., the FICA[923] and FUTA. FUTA and FICA and the income tax act have the same definition of 'wages', but the definition of employee in FUTA and FICA are slightly different. A statutory employee has employee status, even though he or she does not fulfil the common law employee test.

Four types of workforce are per se statutory employees, regardless of whether they fulfil the common law test or not.[924] According to section 3121 IRC and IRS guidance 15A, the scope of statutory employee is extended beyond common law employee for the purpose of levying social security tax (i.e., the FICA tax).

According to the IRC, statutory employee refers to the four industrial groups: Group (A) to group (D) of workers and are defined as statutory employee for the purpose of FICA tax; for the purpose of the FUTA, only the following group (A) and group (D) can be defined as employee:

(A) as an agent-driver or commission-driver engaged in distributing meat products, vegetable products, fruit products, bakery products, beverages (other than milk), or laundry or dry-cleaning services, for her principal;
(B) as a full-time life insurance salesperson;
(C) as a home worker[925] performing work, according to specifications furnished by the person for whom the services are performed, on materials or goods furnished by such person which are required to be returned to such person or a person designated by her; or
(D) as a traveling or city salesman, other than as an agent-driver or commission-driver, engaged upon a full-time basis in the solicitation on behalf of, and the transmission to, his principal (except for side-line sales activities on behalf of some other person) of orders from wholesalers, retailers, contractors, or operators of hotels, restaurants, or other similar establishments for merchandise for resale or supplies for use in their business operations.

Moreover, according to the IRS's guidance 15A[926] about the statutory employee of section 3121 IRC, to qualify as statutory employee for FICA tax, that person should also fulfil the following three cumulative dependence conditions:

1. The service contract states or implies that substantially all the services are to be performed personally by them.
2. They don't have a substantial investment in the equipment and property used to perform the services (other than an investment in facilities for transportation, such as a car or truck).
3. The services are performed on a continuing basis for the same payer.

Therefore, although the IRC's common law employee is mainly based on the control test, when it comes to statutory employee, the IRS' guidance also combines

923. The supreme court case law, *Rowan Companies, Inc. v. United States*, 452 U.S. 247 (1981); Amanda Stein, FICA Taxation of Post-Employment Benefits: A Statutory Puzzle and Sociopolitical Conundrum, 91Washington University Law Review 203 (2013).
924. The explanation of statutory employee in IRC, *see* Robert W Wood & Christopher A Karachale, Home Workers and the Debate Over 'Who's a Statutory Employee' under the Internal Revenue Code, Business Law News (2010). Zern, *supra* n. 915.
925. Discussions about home worker, *see* Wood & Karachale, *Ibid.*
926. About Publication 15-A, Employer's Supplemental Tax Guide (Supplement to Circular E, Employer's Tax Guide, Publication 15).

dependence with control as the criterion to decide employee status when determining statutory employee status under the FICA tax.

When a person is classified as an employee under the FICA tax, his or her employer has to withhold FICA tax and pay the employer's share. It means higher hiring costs. Therefore, the fiscal and financial incentives to misclassify employee status exist for obvious reasons. The punishments and consequences from the IRS due to misclassification are also quite high.[927] Misclassification is a serious tax avoidance scenario in the US.

Since the common law employee and the statutory employee are designed in parallel, it is hard to say which concept is wider. There is also the trend that the courts or the IRS gradually recognize new types of 'control', and an employee under such control goes beyond the scope of traditional common law employees. But a specific statute for the purpose of social security entitlement regulates the statutory employee, and thus sometimes such statutory scope does not cover some new types of common law employees,[928] though as long as a worker is qualified as a common law employee, it would never invoke the statutory employee test.[929]

5.3.2.4.3 The Trend of Broadening the Scope of Employee Is Market Neutral

As indicated earlier, the definition of employee in the US varies in different acts of federal legislation. State taxation and the MTC Regulation refer to the IRC's definition of employee, and therefore the common law employee is still the most influential criterion for the payroll factor in state taxation.

The section 13 of the MTC Regulation on the scope of employee has been amended several times. Before 2010, since section 13 directly referred to the 'common law employee' of the IRC, it is possible that a 'statutory employee' (who does not fulfil the common law test) would not be an MTC Regulation employee.

After 2010, section 13 MTC Regulation IV was amended; the wording a 'common law employee' is deleted. But such amendment does not fully solve the disparity, it is still uncertain what employee would be included in the payroll factor. Such disparity seems inevitable because of the concept of common law employee and of statutory employee developed by different labour law and social security regimes. Furthermore, even in the social security regimes, such as FICA and FUTA, both have different scopes

927. *See* Jack N Kondrasuk, Lisa J Reed & James J Jurinski, The Dangers of Misclassifying 'Employees': Microsoft Litigation Emphasizes Distinctions Between Employees and Nontraditional Workers, 13 Employee Responsibilities and Rights Journal 165 (2001). Catherine Ruckelhaus & Celedih Gao, Independent Contractor Misclassification Imposes Huge Costs on Workers and Federal and State Treasuries, National Employment Law Project, Fact Sheet 1 (2017). Barry Leibowicz, Independent Contractor or Employee?, 81 CPA Journal 46 (2011). Amy L Short, Workers Misclassified as Independent Contractors Were Entitled to Retirement Benefits: *Vizcaino v. Microsoft Corp.*, 51 Tax Lawyer 405 (1998).
928. Pechacek & Nakamura, *supra* n. 904.
929. Susan A Berson, Distinguishing Between Independent Contractors and Employees: Part II, 4 Corporate Business Taxation Monthly 14 (2002). According to Berson, 'By definition, a worker cannot be a statutory employee if that worker is a common law employee.'

of employee for the purpose of the statute.[930] Therefore, reference to federal legislation, the IRC, does not eliminate disparity nor does it establish a clear scope of 'employee'.

But there is indeed a trend that many state tax authorities and courts have been broadening the scope of employee, to include not only direct employees but also 'indirect employees, such as employees from affiliated entities, transferred and leased employees, temporary help'. A 'leased' employee has been included in the payroll factor decided by several state court cases.[931] Although these US states do not always have identical judgments on these indirect employment relationships, the development of the 'common law employee' has evolved to broadly define the 'control' concept from behavioural, financial, and parties' intentions perspective.[932]

A wide scope of employee is more comprehensive than the scope of employee under the common law test because the wide scope of employee can cover various typical and atypical human resources that a taxpayer can make use of. Therefore, the trend of broadening the scope of employees is consistent with the MN framework, to represent the status quo of the labour market that has become more diverse.

5.3.3 Beyond a 'typical' Employee and the Binary Distinction Is Market Neutral, But to What Extent?

5.3.3.1 The Binary Distinction and the Grey Area of 'employee-like' People

Even though there is no clear consensus on the definition of employee, it is widely accepted that there is the binary distinction between worker/employee versus self-employee/independent contractors. The binary distinction is still prevalent in both Europe and the US, even though many labour law scholars have called for reforms (*see* discussions below).

For example, the CJEU does not directly provide a clear definition of 'employee' but does accept a binary distinction of employees versus 'self-employees' (i.e., entrepreneurs): the key criterion is whether the contractual relationship has the element of 'subordination'.[933] If the relationship has the element of subordination, then the relationship is defined as employment; if the answer is in the negative, then the relationship is self-employment, i.e., a service contract. In the US, the binary distinction between employee versus 'independent contractor' is also prevalent in case law and legislation.[934]

930. As Pachacek and Nakamura observed, the common law employee that the MTC Regulation section 13 (prior to 2010) referred to, does not completely coincide with IRC guidance's category 2 (employee under financial control) and category 3 (employee under a more 'indirect' control) of common law employee under.
931. Michael Schadewald, Appointment Issues-Payroll Factor-Leased Employees, 25 Journal of State Taxation 9 (2006).
932. Pechacek & Nakamura, *supra* n. 904, at 187-188.
933. Nicola Countouris, The Concept of 'Worker' in European Labour Law: Fragmentation, Autonomy and Scope, 47 Industrial Law Journal 192 (2018).
934. The binary of employee versus independent contractor is quite solid in USA, especially in the tax law field, *see* Berson, *supra* n. 922; Berson, *supra* n. 929. Wood & Karachale, *supra* n. 924. Pearce & Silva, *supra* n. 872. Sprague, *supra* n. 909.

The binary distinction of employee versus self-employee/entrepreneur has been recognized in the tradition of the labour law regime.[935] But from the very beginning, labour law scholars explored the grey area between these two and tried to create an 'umbrella category' to cover less-visible subordinated/continuous/formalized working relationships.[936] Therefore, in Europe, there is also a clear trend to broaden the scope of employee and ensure extensive protection in the field of labour law. In many EU Member States, a third category of 'employee-like persons' has arisen[937] which is between typical employees and self-employees. This category is also called 'dependent self-employee', 'false self-employee', 'sham self-employee', 'quasi-subordinated self-employee', 'independent worker', and/or 'dependent contractor' in the literature.[938] The workforce in this grey area is actually not homogeneous; sometimes working conditions are closer to traditional employees and sometimes working conditions look similar to entrepreneurs.

Employee-like persons, even when recognized by national law, usually enjoy minimal labour rights. According to Guy Davidov et al., those rights are: 'mostly limited to collective bargaining, health and safety, social security and tax treatment (at most). Most employment standards do not apply'.[939] In some countries, such as Spain,[940] the 'dependent self-employee' (Trabajador Autonomo Dependiente Economicamente, TRADE) has gradually enjoyed more and more labour rights, though still not sufficient and comparable to a typical employee.[941]

It should be emphasized that the CJEU has never accepted this separate third category in addition to the binary distinction between employee and self-employee,[942] though the CJEU's concept of worker, based on the binary distinction, is criticized as not being workable. But as a practical compromise, the CJEU also accepts that people who are 'less subordinated' in a company, i.e., who hold managerial positions, such as 'board member' 'in a company, can still be "worker" because that individual is "made" responsible for the fixed period in the integral part of the company of time and has to

935. Countouris, *supra* n. 890; Georges Cavalier & Robert Upex, The Concept of Employment Contract in European Union Private Law, 55 International & Comparative Law Quarterly 587 (2006); Countouris, *supra* n. 879.
936. Countouris, *supra* n. 879.
937. Bernd Waas & Guus Heerma van Voss (eds), *Restatement of Labour Law in Europe Vol I: The Concept of Employee* (Hart 2017).
938. Literature discussing this third category, Thörnquist, *supra* n. 863; Countouris, *supra* n. 890; Cavalier & Upex, *supra* n. 935; Buschoff & Schmidt, *supra* n. 865. Discussions focus more on USA, Harris & Krueger, *supra* n. 905; Miriam A Cherry & Antonio Aloisi, 'Dependent Contractors' in the Gig Economy: A Comparative Approach, 66 American University Law Review 635 (2017) (comparing the dependent contractor category of Canada, Italy and Spain).
939. Davidov, Freedland & Countouris, *supra* n. 889.
940. *Ibid.*
941. Adriin Todoli-Signes, Workers, the Self-Employed and TRADEs: Conceptualisation and Collective Rights in Spain, European Labour Law Journal (2019); Annamaria Donini & others, Towards Collective Protections for Crowdworkers: Italy, Spain and France in the EU Context, 23 Transfer: European Review of Labour and Research 207 (2017).
942. Countouris, *supra* n. 933. EF Grosheide & BP ter Haar, Employee-like Worker: Competitive Entrepreneur or Submissive Employee? Reflections on CJEU, C-413/13, FNV Kunsten Informatie, *Labour Law and Social Rights in Europe: The Jurisprudence of International Courts, Selected Judgements* (Gdańsk University Press 2017).

report to the company', as in *Danosa*.[943] In *FNV Kunsten Informatie en Media*,[944] the CJEU ruled that a substitute musician for an orchestra is an employee under EU law, although a substitute formally signs a service contract with the orchestra, under national law. A substitute follows the conductor's instructions, and as an integral part of the company, cannot decide the schedule of the integral part of the orchestra and does not share commercial risks with the orchestra. Therefore, a substitute musician is a false self-employee and should be re-characterized as an employee, according to the CJEU.

In other words, while still keeping the binary distinction, the CJEU has implicitly recognized that the employee/worker concept under EU law should cover the false or the disguised self-employee, whose contract is in its substance an employment contract but is formed as if a service contract for the purpose of avoiding the application of 'fiscal or labour regulations',[945] should be categorized as an employee, so that traditional labour law protection should still apply. The rationale of reclassifying such 'disguised self-employment' is to protect the weaker party.[946] Such approach should also apply to the labour factor of the CCCTB Directive.

5.3.3.2 The Other Way Around to Achieve Market Neutrality: Excluding Genuine Independent Contractors

The experiences of labour law development above in both Europe and the US show that to define an 'employee' or 'worker' involves multiple factors in various tests, totality of circumstances, etc. These case-by-case analyses are complicated and thus create uncertainties. The traditional binary distinction between employee and self-employee/independent contractor is often too rigid and vulnerable to manipulation. Therefore, in many national labour law systems, it is often common to adopt the rebuttable presumption approach to establish employee status by presumption.[947]

In Europe and the US, there is also a new practical approach to the difficulty of defining employee: to define positively the narrow definition self-employee,[948] or 're-targeting the labour law approach',[949] which presumes all workforce to be engaged in providing labour for another as employees 'while excluding only genuine own account businesses'. The self-employee is limited to those who conduct commercial activities for themselves.

943. In Case C-232/09 *Dita Danosa v. LKB Līzings SIA*, commentary, Siniša Petrović & Petar Ceronja, Corporate Effects of the Danosa Case: Is the Termination of Membership of the Board of Directors Allowed in the Case of a Pregnant Board Member?, 8 Croatian Yearbook of European Law & Policy 437 (2012).
944. Grosheide & Haar, *supra* n. 942.
945. Opinion AG Wahl Case C-413/13, 11 September 2014, FNV KIEM ECLI: EU:C:2014:2215, paragraph 52; European Commission, Green Paper 'Modernising Labour Law to Meet the Challenges of the 21st Century' (COM (2006) 708 Final), 10-12. *See also*, Catherine Barnard, *EU Employment Law* (OUP Oxford 2012), at 144-154.
946. Verhulp, *supra* n. 886.
947. International Labour Organization, *supra* n. 879.
948. Peijpe, *supra* n. 901, at 53.
949. Countouris, *supra* n. 879, at 15.

The effort to define self-employees and independent contractors in the US is more advanced than in Europe. In the US, in order to have a definition of 'independent contractor' that is clearer and more certain, and to prevent misclassification of employee, more than 15 states have adopted an 'independent contractor statute' since 2004[950] to clarify and provide a definition of independent contractor. This is what is called the 'ABC' test.[951]

The ABC test in the US is a simplified version of the common law employee indicated above, and it focuses on only three of the most important cumulative conditions to qualify as an independent contractor. This is categorized in three prongs:

- A prong: the workforce is free from control;
- B prong: the work involved is *outside* the usual course of business of the employer;
- C prong: the workforce has a profession which is an independently established trade or business.

As to the A prong, the indicators in the control test and the economic dependence test can also be useful. As long as a workforce is not free from any type of control, the A prong is not fulfilled. As to the B prong, it is essential to ascertain the scope of business of the employer. It is feasible to use the firm theory to interpret the commercial rationale.[952] As to the C prong, the workforce must have an independently established profession. To determine 'independence', in addition to looking at the profession involved, it is also useful to take the ability to assume and spread risk into account because risk-spreading is the key feature of entrepreneurship.[953]

The ABC test's three prongs are much more concise and easier to understand. It also prevents lengthy discussions on whether there is control or dependence. By applying such negative test, after excluding the true independent contractors, the scope of employee is also representative and wide enough to cover new types of workforce, including traditional employees and the employee-like people in the grey zone,

950. Introductions of various independent contractor statues, Mundele, *supra* n. 915.
951. Anna Deknatel & Lauren Hoff-Downing, ABC on the Books and in the Courts: An Analysis of Recent Independent Contractor and Misclassification Statutes, 18 University of Pennsylvania Journal of Law & Social Change 53 (2015); Sprague, *supra* n. 909. Pearce & Silva, *supra* n. 872 (The history of the ABC test and current overview among states in USA, at 27-29).
952. Inspired by Richard R Carlson, Employment by Design: Employees Independent Contractors and the Theory of the Firm, 71 Arkansas Law Review 127 (2018). Carlson argues that, hiring an employee or an independent contractor is consistent with the firm theory's analysis of 'make or buy', and either decision is not random. So analysing the commercial rationality behind, it helps courts to formulate the tests for the employee status. In the ABC test context, it is also important to ascertain what business the claimed employer is conducting. In fact, CJEU also adopts the similar approach to analyse Uber's activities as 'transportation' not merely 'information/intermediation' because the business model of Uber is 'intermediation plus control'. *See* Philipp Hacker, UberPop, UberBlack, and the Regulation of Digital Platforms after the Asociación Profesional Elite Taxi Judgment of the CJEU: Judgment of the Court (Grand Chamber) 20 December 2017, Asociación Profesional Elite Taxi (C-434/15), 14 European Review of Contract Law 80 (2018).
953. Analysing risk as an indicator as (in)dependence, *see* Davidov, *supra* n. 853.

especially for gig workers in the platform economy.[954] Such approach in combination with the popular method of 'rebuttable presumption' in Europe is a tax-neutral option for the labour factor for the EU's FA regime.

5.3.3.3 Excluding Genuine Independent Contractors Is Still Necessary

In both the EU and the US, ensuring social security protection is a reason to expand the concept of employee in the development of national law. Many national social security schemes also apply to 'employee-like persons', though they might not have formal employee status under their national labour law.[955] For example, in Germany and Italy,[956] the definition of employee under social security law is wider than under traditional labour law.[957] But a typical/standard employee still enjoys a broader scope of social security rights than non-employees or self-employees, even though non-employees or self-employees are also covered in the social security system.

As explained in section 5.2 above, especially in a Bismarckian style social insurance system, self-employees/independent contractors do not enjoy the same level of rights as an employee derived from labour law as well as social security law. This is because self-employees are not targeted as insured people and do not pay premiums, even though self-employees are covered and enjoy 'some' entitlements in the national social security system to a certain extent.

The expanded applicable personal scope also appears in EU social security law. For example, according to Regulation 883/2004,[958] the personal scope covers all the 'working population'.[959] In other words, true self-employees who do not have an employment contract with their 'principal' or 'client' are also covered under EU social security law.[960] Furthermore, in 2018, the European Commission proposed a Council Recommendation to provide equal access to social protection of employees and self-employees (roughly defined as 'working on their own behalf').[961] Some European

954. Keith Cunningham-Parmeter, Gig-Dependence: Finding the Real Independent Contractors of Platform Work, 39 Northern Illinois University Law Review 379 (2018) (explaining the history of excluding independent contractors; 409-411, analysing how ABC test is used - California Supreme Court's judgment on the delivery platform Dynamex in 2018).
955. Countouris, *supra* n. 890.
956. *Ibid.*, 67.
957. Michele Tiraboschi & Maurizio Del Conte, Employment Contract: Disputes on Definition in the Changing Italian Labour Law (2004).
958. It should be noted that Regulation 833/2004 'coordinates' EU social security systems, not 'harmonizes'. This is because the competence of social security is still mainly within the EU Member States, and thus Regulation 833/2004 and its precedents intentionally leave some national disparities in this field, only coordinating Member States, not harmonizing. *See* F Pennings, *European Social Security Law* (6th ed. Intersentia 2015), at Chapter 2.
959. Barnard, *supra* n. 945, at 457.
960. Countouris, *supra* n. 890, at 177-178. The personal scope of Regulation 883/2004 has been wide since it was adopted in the very beginning in 1971, as its previous version EC Regulation 1408/71 also has a wide personal scope, *see* commentary, AW Govers, Material and Personal Applicational Scope of EEC Regulation No. 1408/71, 6 Legal Issues of Eur. Integration 65 (1979), 76-78.
961. Proposal for a Council Recommendation on access to social protection for workers and the self-employed, COM/2018/0132 final _ 2018/059. In the field of social law in the EU, there is an

scholars advocate a broader definition of 'worker' under EU law for social protection, and further abandoning the distinction of employee and self-employee,[962] and decoupling enjoyment and employment.[963] Similarly, in the US, Orly Lobel argued for a reform to completely disconnect employee status and entitlement to welfare.[964] These reform proposals all point out the new developments in the labour market where more and more atypical and precarious workforces are active, and they also need social security protection against various risks.

The ultimate question then arises as to whether the labour factor of the EU's FA regime also follows developments in social security law, and in the end, no longer distinguishes between employees and independent contractors? Put differently, should the labour factor of the EU's FA regime include all types of human being workforce and abolish the distinction between employees and self-employed?

From the benefit-based MN framework, the answer is in the negative. In my view, the market-neutral labour factor covers human resources that MNE taxpayers make use of, and thus there is control to some extent. Even when being interpreted broadly, the labour factor of the EU's FA regime still cannot and should not include true independent contractors because the transactions and arrangements with true independent contractors are commercial activities with another enterprise. Such true independent contractors do not represent the labour factor the MNE taxpayer is making use of. For the labour factor of the EU's FA regime, maintaining the binary distinction and adopting the legal presumption in combination with the independent contractor test are market-neutral options.

5.3.4 Examples of a Non-typical Employee That Should Be Included in the Labour Factor

As indicated earlier, I propose that the labour factor of the EU's FA regime should use criterion like the ABC test to exclude human resources that are truly independent and not mobilized by the MNE taxpayer from the labour factor.

Here are several examples of 'non-typical employee' workforce in dispute. I explain how they should be included in the labour factor to be consistent with the tax-neutrality framework, by using the approach of 'excluding self-employees/independent contractors' indicated in the previous section.

---

idea emerging to enhance EU as not only an economic union but also a social union and thus equalize employees and self-employees' social rights, the view is also implemented by EU's another project: The European Pillar of Social Rights, to improve comprehensively the labour law standard. Garben, *supra* n. 561.

962. Countouris, *supra* n. 933. In most of the EU Member States' national legislation, more than 20 EU Member States do not promulgate a separate group of 'workers' in their national laws; only UK has expressly distinguished the concept of worker and employee and gives the worker a broader definition.

963. Sacha Garben & European Agency for Safety and Health at Work, Protecting Workers in the Online Platform Economy an Overview of Regulatory and Policy Developments in the EU (2017), 22-23.

964. Lobel, *supra* n. 893.

5.3.4.1 The Market-Neutral Labour Factor Should Include Managerial Workers

The first example is the managerial workforce (such as Chief Executive Officers (CEOs), Chief Fiancial Officers (CFOs), Chief Operating Officers (COOs), etc.) and members of the board. Managers or board members, though they have a managerial function in the company, they might not look as if they are subordinate when they perform their tasks. It is disputed whether or not such managerial workforce is an employee.

In the US, section 13 UDITPA on the payroll factor clearly excludes payroll attributable to management, i.e., salaries paid to CEOs or management level officers. It seems that the UDITPA payroll factor is aimed only at employees in the very narrow sense and excludes management personnel.

In some EU Member States, the managerial workforce might be classified as non-employee, as a service provider to the company. However, the degree of being controlled and being instructed when performing tasks is mainly based on individuals' capacity and experiences in relation to other co-workers. If we observe the companies' capacity to mobilize employees, for the purpose of the labour factor in the FA, it does not matter whether a human being is a manager or a lower-level employee, they are all human resources, being mobilized by MNE taxpayers' economic powers to contribute to the taxpayers' production activities.

Traditional labour law mainly regulates the relationship between employer and weaker parties, so managerial employees who are not that 'weak' might enjoy fewer labour law rights and (e.g., limitation on number of working hours or payment of overtime) bear heavier obligations (such as an additional obligation of confidentiality) under labour law.

But for the labour factor of FA of corporate taxation, managerial employees and other employees should be treated the same, and both should be included in the labour factor. The managerial workforce might be subject to less-factual control from the company due to its own capacities and functions, but managers are also the human resources being mobilized by the company. Therefore, they should be included in the labour factor. Moreover, when applying the ABC test to determine the status of independent contractor, the managerial workforce will not be classified as an independent contractor and therefore be included in the labour factor.

In this regard, in *Danosa* the CJEU discussed an example which supports this conclusion: although Danosa was a board member who exercises management competence but is neither instructed nor controlled in her daily work, she is still defined as an employee. The original design of section 13 UDITPA in the US, as mentioned above, is then already outdated and should not be included in the EU's FA regime.

5.3.4.2 *The Market-Neutral Labour Factor Should Include 'Outsourced' Human Resources That Are Integrated in the Business*

Another difficult issue is regarding outsourced workforce. The 'outsourced workforce' can be hired from a job agency that has signed a formal contract. It is also possible to arrange an intra-group secondment/outsourcing between group members. In any event, outsourced workforce involves a triangular arrangement in which the formalistic 'employer' is not the company for which the outsourced workforce actually performs tasks for. To some extent, these outsourced workers have 'two bosses' in reality. Thus, it is disputable which hiring entity the outsourced workforce should be attributed to. This question is puzzling even before the digital economy. Hellerstein[965] has a very vivid example: should the fees paid to truck drivers for the retailer multinational Walmart also be included in the payroll factor of Walmart?

Under the current CCCTB Directive Proposal, treatment of outsourced workforce is also disputed.[966] According to the CCCTB Working Document No. 52, the Commission distinguished between two types of outsourced employees: The 'genuine outsourced labour'[967] who are (sent from) truly independent service providers outside the group, versus the 'intra-group posted labour'[968] who are sent from one group member (I refer to this below as a sending group member) to another group member (I refer to this below as a receiving group member).

In the European Commission's view, the 'genuine' outsourced workforce is excluded from the labour factor because this outsourced labour is regarded as service providers rather than employees with 'core functions'. So, in the working document, the European Commission suggests[969] that the current CCCTB Directive Proposal should exclude the outsourced workforce from the labour factor, unless the outsourced workforce is actually provided by another group member. That is to say, the genuine outsourced workforce will not be included in the labour factor of any group member. In contrast, for an outsourced workforce from an intra-group arrangement, the Commission suggests including them as employees for the purpose of the current CCCTB Directive Proposal, as long as one is cautious about possible manipulation from intra-group outsourced arrangements.

When referring to 'genuine external outsourced workforce', the Commission specifically mentions 'cleaning, security, and in general any provision of services which goes beyond simply putting workers at the disposal of the company' from the labour factor, although it does not give clear reasons for mentioning those activities. One possible interpretation is that an external outsourced workforce does not involve the group's 'core' production activities, and the outsourced workforce receives instruction and supervision from the agency outside the group, not from any group member. Therefore, from the Commission's perspective, since the labour factor represents the

965. Hellerstein, *supra* n. 549.
966. CCCTB Working Document No. 52, paragraphs 22-30.
967. CCCTB Working Document No. 52, paragraph 23.
968. CCCTB Working Document No. 52, paragraph 26.
969. CCCTB Working Document No. 60, paragraph 24.

production side of the group member, the workforce, which is 'too far' from the core production of a group member, should consequently be excluded. I do not agree with the Commission's perspective because it views 'outsourced human resources' as an exception and inherently far from the core business (so it refers to examples of cleaning services or security). Such perspective on outsourcing is outdated, which I can explain as follows.

Excluding outsourced workforce unconditionally is, nevertheless, not market neutral because it is not consistent with the rationale of including human resources of the labour market. While expressly excluding the genuine outsourced workforce from the labour factor, the Commission suggests[970] that part-time and even temporary employment should also be included in the labour factor. Therefore, typical temporary employment contracts directly concluded with a group member can always be included, but the outsourced workforce is subject to several strict conditions to be included in the labour factor. It implies that even temporary employment by the group member reflects the group member's production side activities more accurately than the outsourced workforce. Such distinction is not consistent with the economic reality, and it creates opportunities for manipulation.

Furthermore, it is not always clear-cut if 'outsourced' activities are core activities,[971] but it is important to determine the 'regular course of business and trade' of the employer. Different industries may have different models of hiring outsourced labour. Companies can use outsourced labour for almost all activities, such as 'a virtual company',[972] or a Walmart department store,[973] which outsources its delivery activities to many truck drivers. It should be noted that in the era of the digital economy, even delivery activities might constitute core activities for many online retailers.[974] When the task performed is in the scope of the regular course of business and trade, such workforce will never pass the test of independent contractor, and therefore such workforce should be included in the labour factor as employee.

Hiring (and misclassifying) outsourced workforce is not limited to low-skilled workers either. For example, in the US during the late 1980s, Microsoft hired project-based engineers from external job agencies.[975] They signed a contract where intentionally and expressly they do not have employee status with Microsoft. These outsourced engineers have different badges from Microsoft's in-house employees, but their work is

970. CCCTB Working Document No. 60.
971. Walter Hellerstein, Formulary Apportionment in the EU and the US: A Comparative Perspective on the Sharing Mechanism of the Proposed CCCTB, in Dourado (ed.), *supra* n. 5.
972. Paul Kellogg, Independent Contractor or Employee: *Vizcaino v. Microsoft Corp.*, 35 Hous. Law Review 1775 (1998); Kondrasuk, Reed & Jurinski, *supra* n. 927.
    F Lee Perkins, Employment Law-*Vizcaino v. Microsoft Corp.*: Are Independent Contractors Eligible for Employee Benefits, 21 American Journal of Trial Advocacy 205 (1997); Short, *supra* n. 927; Hellerstein, *supra* n. 971.
973. *Ibid.*
974. In the current digital economy, the different/changed idea of a 'core activity' or a 'preparatory or auxiliary activity' influences not only the treatment of an outsourced workforce but also the definition of a 'permanent establishment' (PE). When some delivery activities of multinational online retailers constitute a (virtual) PE, the online retailers' tax base will be recaptured. The BEPS Report Action 7 also addressed this issue.
975. Kellogg, *supra* n. 972.

fully integrated in the normal course of Microsoft's software development activities. These engineers have to work on-site so they are given entrance cards, and some are offered to work on following projects on a continuing basis. The IRS audited Microsoft and decided that these project-based engineers are misclassified as independent contractors; they are common law employees, and Microsoft should levy FICA tax (i.e., social security levy).[976] After being aware of their common law employee status, a group of 'independent contractor/freelancer' engineers initiated a class action suit against Microsoft for misclassification and asked to join the benefits programmes designed for regular employees. Microsoft argued that these project-based temporary engineers were not common law employees from the very beginning, and thus they did not have the right to join Microsoft's employee benefit programmes. In the end, the court ruled in favour of these engineers and affirmed that, despite the express wording of 'being an independent contractor' in their contracts signed with Microsoft, the activities they performed qualified them as common law employees.

When we apply the independent contractor (ABC test) test indicated in section 5.3.3, it becomes quite clear that freelance engineers indirectly hired by Microsoft did not fulfil the conditions to be independent contractors. First, freelancer engineers were required to work on-site for specific projects for Microsoft, they were not free from control of the quality of their work and their way of working. Second, their work consisting of developing computer software was within the regular course of business and trade of Microsoft. Third, freelance engineers are not an independent occupation, and they are not able to assume and spread managerial risks for their own business. Therefore, such freelance engineers do not fulfil the conditions of independent contractor and should be defined as employees. Only when a freelance engineer (or any kind of freelancer) has fulfilled the test and demonstrates the extent of being an entrepreneur and having almost an equal position as the MNE taxpayer, should such freelancer be excluded from the labour factor.

To sum up, to decide if a specific workforce should be included in the labour factor under the EU's FA regime, it is not decisive if a workforce is formally hired via outsourcing or a regular employment contract, but if such workforce fulfils the conditions of being independent contractors. If not, that workforce should be included in the labour factor.

5.3.4.3 Reflections on Delivery Drivers Disputes in the US: Marginalized Autonomy Is Not True Independence

Another typical example of affiliated or leased workforce is in the logistics sector, such as workforce at drayage trucking and warehouse/distribution centres.[977] In the logistics sector, it is quite common that the parent company sets up local agencies to hire workers to perform tasks and sign arrangements to (mis)classify workers.

---

976. The case brief, *see* Susan L Coskey, *Vizcaino v. Microsoft Corporation*: A Labor and Employment Lawyer's Perspective (1997) 48 Labor Law Journal 91. Short, *supra* n. 927.

977. David Jaffee & David Bensman, Draying and Picking: Precarious Work and Labor Action in the Logistics Sector Working USA: The Journal of Labor and Society (2017).

For example, FedEx, a well-known package delivery service group in the US was confronted with a dispute as to whether their delivery drivers are employees. Unlike its main competitor UPS, FedEx hired their drivers under an independent contractor status, and this strategy was believed to have led to FedEx's fast growth and success.[978] There have been lots of class action suits against FedEx.[979] FedEx asserted that their drivers are entrepreneurs (i.e., independent contractors) and argued that FedEx does not exercise control. In the end, the courts ruled that FedEx has comprehensive control over drivers, from working time and routes, to appearance. In a series of class action suits, the employee status of FedEx drivers was established.[980]

Among the series of decisions, FedEx's most interesting counterargument was to invoke the 'entrepreneur opportunities test'; according to FedEx, their drivers have several rights including: 'the ability to sell, assign, or bequeath their contractual rights to third parties without FedEx's permission; the right to hire their own employees to assist in package delivery; and the right to contract for multiple routes'. From their appearance, FedEx drivers do have some freedom, autonomy, and discretion. FedEx asserted such arrangement makes drivers entrepreneurs because drivers have opportunities to decide how to perform their delivery tasks. Such assertion is not correct because it mixed the opportunities granted by the firm with true entrepreneur opportunities arising from the true market.[981] FedEx is the only 'buyer or client' of these drivers' 'service', and drivers' marginalized autonomy is also granted from FedEx as a firm. Therefore, if we apply the independent contractor test to FedEx drivers, FedEx drivers are not free from control (A prong, *see* above); and they cannot be classified as an independent occupation because they do not really enjoy the entrepreneur opportunities or have the capacity to bear, assume, and spread risks. FedEx's opportunity test argument is invalid.

Disputes concerning FedEx's drivers are quite similar to drivers hired by many online platforms such as gig workers.[982] Because of the flexibility arrangement, drivers' status might look different from the traditional employee which is under the direct control of an employer. Although FedEx uses a separate agency to hire drivers, these online platforms make use of the Internet to contact and influence drivers. As to the

978. David Bauer, The Misclassification of Independent Contractors: The Fifty-Four Billion Dollar Problem, 12 Rutgers Journal of Law & Public Policy 2 (2015).
979. Scott J Brewerton, Employment Law-FedEx Delivery Drivers Improperly Classified as Independent Contractors Rather Than Employees - *Alexander v. FedEx Ground Package System, Inc.*, 765 F. 3d 981 (9th Cir. 2014), 48 Suffolk University Law Review 537 (2015).Tina Quinn & Sangshin Pae, The Case of the Missing Employees: The Saga of Fedex, 2 Academy of Business Research 34 (2011). Whitney Rutherford, Fitting a Square Peg into a Round Hole: *Alexander v. FedEx Ground Package Systems* & the Sharing Economy, 11 Liberty UL Review 33 (2016). Julia Tomassetti, From Hierarchies to Markets: FedEx Drivers and the Work Contract as Institutional Marker, 19 Lewis & Clark Law Review 1083 (2015).
980. *See* Cunningham-Parmeter, *supra* n. 907, at 1714-1717.
981. Tomassetti, *supra* n. 980, at 1128.
982. Discussions linking FedEx misclassification disputes of drivers with gig workers like Uber/Lyft drivers, *see* Cunningham-Parmeter, *supra* n. 907. Peter Gibbins, Extending Employee Protections to Gig-Economy Workers Through the Entrepreneurial Opportunity Test of FedEx Home Delivery, 57 Washington University Journal of Law & Policy 183 (2018). Rutherford, *supra* n. 979.

latest developments regarding employee status in the gig economy/platform economy, I discuss these disputes in section 5.5.

When a workforce is formally hired by an affiliated entity/another group member to perform tasks, it still causes disputes. It is disputable if such workforce should be included in the payroll factor denominator, and if so, whose payroll factor numerator should include such workforce. As to the second question regarding attribution, I discuss this topic in section 5.4.

5.3.5 The Valuation Methods of Human Resources

From the discussions above, the scope of 'employee' of the labour factor under the EU FA regime should follow the rationale of excluding genuine independent contractors, i.e., fulfilling the cumulative prongs of the ABC test at section 5.3.3.2 above. We should first presume the workforce utilized to be included as employees, unless the ABC test is fulfilled.

When the employee status is established due to not fulfilling the ABC test, the scope of the labour factor is also established. The next question is the evaluation. The payroll is the most intuitive valuation method, which is also widely adopted in the US. The current CCCTB Directive Proposal provides an additional valuation method: 'headcount'. Both payroll and headcount of employees are consistent with the tax-neutrality framework because they both represent the employees in the labour market but from two different perspectives, as discussed below.

5.3.5.1 Payroll as the Primary Valuation Method of Human Resources

According to Article 32(1) of the current CCCTB Directive Proposal, the labour factor consists of the amount of payroll and the number of employees. These two sub-factors are equally half-weighted in the labour factor, so the labour factor of a group member is:

$$\left(\frac{1}{2}\frac{\textit{number of employees of the group member}}{\textit{number of employees of the group}} + \frac{1}{2}\frac{\textit{payroll of the group member}}{\textit{total payroll of the group}}\right)$$

According to the CCCTB Working Document, the underlying reason for the current CCCTB Directive Proposal to include not only the payroll factor[983] but also 'the number of employees' is to balance the interests of different EU Member States.[984] EU Member States have different average levels of wages due to their economic developments; therefore, only taking payroll in the labour factor into account may be unfair to some less-developed Member States with low-level wages. In other words, the same

983. The payroll is the only factor that the USA system adopts for the sharing formula, not the headcounts.
984. CCCTB Working Document No. 60, paragraph 26.

labour productivity in different EU Member States is valued differently: less economically developed Member States might provide the same quality of workforce, but due to their lower level of wages, the labour factor ratio would be consequently smaller if the labour factor only takes 'payroll' into account.

When payroll is used in the formula as a weighting factor, the following question is what item should be included in the payroll. With the same rationale of representing the labour market, the payroll should include all employees' sick benefits and vacation allowances should also be included in the payroll factor as part of remuneration, when an employee is sick or on vacation. This is rightly implemented in the current CCCTB Directive Proposal, which defines payroll as 'all costs of salaries, wages, bonuses and all other employee compensation, including related pension and social security costs'.

Some scholars doubt that since the labour factor in the FA system represents MNE taxpayers' production side activities, the labour factor/payroll factor should not include employees who are sick or on vacation because they do not work and thus do not contribute to production while on sick leave or vacation.[985] This is not completely correct. The labour factor as a whole represents the human resources in the labour market. Taking a metaphor of employees as a means of production which are comparable to a type of fixed assets for production, the payroll should include all relevant costs, including costs derived from labour law obligations, keeping this 'workforce asset' functioning well. The value of an employee's payroll is a package of all these relevant costs to maintain the workforce in good conditions to perform the work.

5.3.5.2 *History of 'Manufacturing Costs' or Payroll Debates in the US: Comprehensiveness Is the Key*

The payroll factor has a long history in the US. The sharing formula of the UDITPA has included a payroll factor since 1957. Under section 13 UDITPA,[986] payroll is a factor in the formula. Sections 13 and 14 of MTC Regulation IV provide further detailed rules. In fact, the difficulty of determining the definition of employee and the value of 'payroll' is already an old controversy that existed even prior to the adoption of UDITPA or the Multistate Tax Compact.

Although payroll is the main criterion to evaluate human resources, there are other possible evaluation methods.[987] In the past in the US, for evaluating human resources used for the FA, many states substituted 'payroll' for an even more general factor: 'manufacturing costs'.[988]

985. De Wilde, *supra* n. 76, at 6.4.4.2.
986. Section 13 UDITPA reads, 'Section 13. The payroll factor is a fraction, the numerator of which is the total amount paid in this state during the tax period by the taxpayer for compensation, and the denominator of-11-which is the total compensation paid everywhere during the tax period.'
987. Herbert C Manning, Problems in Application of State Tax Allocation Formulae to Oil and Gas Company Operations, 7 Proc. Ann. Inst. on Oil & Gas L. & Tax'n 447 (1956).
988. Louis G Langpop, Payroll, Manufacturing Costs and Other Factors, 7 Tax Executive (1954).

As Herbert observed in 1956, before UDITPA was adopted:

> As a substitute for the payroll factor, a number of states use the broader factor of 'manufacturing costs,' 'operating costs,' or 'direct costs'. Among the states which utilize manufacturing costs rather than payrolls are Alabama, Arizona, Arkansas, Kansas, South Carolina, North Carolina, Tennessee, and Wisconsin. Such states make little or no clarification whatsoever of the term except to state that manufacturing costs shall be computed under the best accounting practice customary in the industry.[989]

From a theoretical perspective, payroll is indeed more logical than 'manufacturing costs'.[990] Payroll has a more comprehensive scope and is not merely limited to 'manufacturing'; payroll also can cover the relevant production phases, such as designing, storing, and general administration.

From historical developments, we can already clearly see that there has been a trend to broaden the scope of 'employee' in the payroll factor for states because states would like to use a proxy that can capture multistate companies' input from human resources as comprehensively as possible. In the late twentieth century, more and more states followed UDITPA and adopted payroll instead of 'manufacturing costs', where payroll and manufacturing costs are both interpreted as extensively as possible to reflect the different phases of production. Such interpretation has existed as a norm to understand 'payroll' or 'manufacturing costs' in a sharing formula. Nowadays, I still see this old wisdom sheds light on understanding the concept of 'employee' in a sharing formula: the scope of employee and of payroll should be comprehensive and sufficiently broad. Moreover, in addition to 'net' wages, the payroll factor should also include all related pension and social security costs. In this regard, the current CCCTB Directive Proposal has followed the right path.

5.3.5.3 FTE Headcounts of Employees Is a Justified Evaluation Method

According to Article 32 of the current CCCTB Directive Proposal, the number of employees is a method of evaluating human resources, as a sub-factor, in addition to the payroll actually paid. Since the result of this sub-factor is a separate ratio and not mixed with the payroll factor, it is an acceptable method, as long as it is applied consistently.

According to CCCTB Working Document No. 60,[991] the number of employees should be calculated on a full time equivalent (FTE) basis. However, Article 32 of the current CCCTB Directive Proposal text does not follow the Working Document's 'full time equivalent' calculation method. Article 32 is unreasonable: a part-time and a fulltime employee are calculated as the same headcount and treated equally for the employee sub-factor. This is an inconsistency. If the labour factor aims to include the

989. Manning, *supra* n. 987.
990. John A Wilkie, A Theoretical Basis for the Allocation of Multi-State Income by the Unitary Businesses under State Corporate Net Income Taxes, 13 Tax Executive 157 (1960).
991. CCCTB Working Document No. 60, paragraph 28.

headcount as the sub-factor, the sub-factor has to take the FTE basis into account, so the headcount of the part-time and fulltime workforce is included by the same criterion.

It is unique that the current CCCTB Directive Proposal's labour factor consists of not only the payroll but also the number of employees. The European Commission decided to include the number of employees as a sub-factor because it would like to reflect the differences in salary levels of EU Member States.[992] Some scholars[993] criticized this design and argued that including headcounts in the labour factor is redundant, and the European Commission's consideration of different salary levels is not well-founded and seems to mix up the policy goals of a tax system with the goal of coordinating the different salary levels of EU Member States.

Criticism of the headcount of employees as a sub-factor is not completely meaningless because headcount as such is indeed too rough. Nevertheless, headcounts are indeed another way of evaluating human resources in the labour factor, when combined with the FTE scale. It would still be logical to evaluate an employee's 'value' to the company simply by headcount, in addition to remuneration. When calculating headcount, it is logical to combine it with the FTE ratio.

Therefore, the EU's BEFIT tax reform package should still adopt this approach to calculate headcount.

5.4 WHERE ARE HUMAN RESOURCES FUNCTIONING? THE ATTRIBUTION RULE OF THE LABOUR FACTOR

5.4.1 Different Rules of Attributing Employees But Most of Them Are the All-or-Nothing Rule

The following section demonstrates two criteria for attributing employees: by payment of payroll/salary and by physical performance. The current CCCTB Directive Proposal and the MTC's attribution rules are both hybrid rules. But these rules have one common feature: they both aim to seek a 'single' jurisdiction to include the workforce involved. This is the all-or-nothing approach mentioned below. The all-or-nothing approach has the ideal and advantage of 'being simple and certain' but, in fact, cannot reflect atypical employees nowadays.

Theoretically speaking, the labour factor attribution rule should be based on employees' physical location of performing their tasks; however, in practice, there are different threshold and hybrid approaches. Here I introduce the current CCCTB Directive Proposal, and the US, OECD, and EU social security law approaches, to demonstrate that seeking one single jurisdiction might be impractical as disparities still exist.

992. CCCTB Working Document No. 52, paragraph 28.
993. For example, De Wilde, *supra* n. 76, at 6.4.4.2.

Table 9 The Status Quo of Different Attribution Rules for Employees

	Where the Renumeration Paying Entity Is Located	*Where Workforce Is Physically Performing*	*A Hybrid Approach Based on Multiple Criteria*
Examples	CCCTB's main rule	- MTC 'Base of Operation' (all or nothing). - Dutch Supreme Court's pro-rata approach. - Oklahoma's payroll factor attribution.	- CCCTB's seconded employee rule: where employees actually perform work. - EU's social security law: The single state rule (two possibilities: 'country of employment' or 'country of residence rule', depending on cross-border, residence, and dominant part of the activity)
Underlying Rationale	It is clear to see who pays the renumeration.	To reflect the production activities conducted by employees.	For CCCTB: To prevent manipulating the paying entity by a seconded arrangement. For EU's social security law: To streamline and ensure the social security entitlements or employees.

	Where the Renumeration Paying Entity Is Located	*Where Workforce Is Physically Performing*	*A Hybrid Approach Based on Multiple Criteria*
Neutrality Implications	It is not neutral because it does not reflect the production activities done by employees, which is the core theory of the labour factor.	This is tax neutral, especially in combination with based on the time spent working in different states.	It is tax neutral when a hybrid approach is followed where employment is physically performed; however, the CCCTB's seconded employee rule still has a precondition threshold. As to the single state rule in the EU's social security law, the all-or-nothing approach and the country of residence rule cannot reflect the employment activities. It is not neutral for the labour factor.

Source: The author.

5.4.2 Attributing to the Remuneration-Paying Member

5.4.2.1 The CCCTB's Attribution Rule for Employees and Its Concerns about Anti-manipulation

Article 33 of the 2016 CCCTB Directive Proposal provides the attribution rule for the labour factor:

> **Allocation of employees and payroll**
>
> 1. Employees shall be included in the labour factor of the group member from which they receive remuneration.
> 2. By way of derogation from paragraph 1, where employees physically exercise their employment under the control and responsibility of a group member other than that from which they receive remuneration, those employees as well as the amount of payroll related to them shall be included in the labour factor of the former group member.
>
> This rule shall only apply where all of the following conditions are met:
>
> (a) the employment lasts for an uninterrupted period of at least three months;

(b) those employees represent at least 5 % of the overall number of employees of the group member from which they receive remuneration.
3. Employees shall include persons who, although not employed directly by a group member, perform tasks similar to those performed by employees.
4. Payroll shall include all costs of salaries, wages, bonuses and all other employee compensation, including related pension and social security costs borne by the employer as well as expenses of the employer corresponding to the cost of persons as referred to in paragraph 3.
5. Payroll costs shall be valued at the amount of expenses that are treated as deductible by the employer in a tax year.

As indicated, according to Article 33(1), an employee and his or her payroll is in principle attributed to who pays the renumeration. In other words, the attribution rule and the calculation rule are the 'all-or-nothing' method. If an employee performs his or her tasks for more than one group member, the attribution rule will decide that only one specific group member can include his or her labour and payroll in the labour factor. Moreover, if the employee works for one group member and receives renumeration, he or she will be attributed to only one group member, according to Article 33(2). Article 33(2) is still an all-or-nothing rule. Moreover, the attribution rule of the labour factor in Article 33 of the 2016 CCCTB Directive Proposal does not have the comparable 'throw-back' or 'throw around' rule in the sales factor (*see* Article 38(4) and Article 38(5) of the 2016 CCCTB Directive Proposal).

Article 33(2) is the rule for a seconded employee, and that employee is attributed to the group member that actually controls and is responsible for the work performed, when two cumulative conditions are met: (1) the employment lasts for at least three undisrupted months (the three-month working time requirement),[994] and (2) such employees represent at least 5% of the group member from which they receive remuneration (the 5% headcount requirement).

Based on these two conditions, here is the typical example of Article 33(2): a group has member company A and member company B in different Member States. Group member company A hires 100 employees, and five of A's employees need to work in another group member B for longer than three months, but they sign their formal employment contracts officially with company A. If these five people are defined according to company B's national law, they are included in company B and those five seconded employees will be included in the labour factor of the company that they really work for.

Moreover, Article 33(3) has a similarity test: indirectly hired employees are also included when they perform tasks similar to those performed by directly hired employees. Article 33(3) not only regulates the attribution but also influences the scope of employees included. Because the similarity test compares the content of functions performed of a seconded worker with other staying employees, this test would not merely involve where the workforce and the payroll should be attributed but also why such workforce with such work could be included in the labour factor. As Hellerstein

994. The three-months requirement reflects the discussion in Working Document No. 60 on 'de minis rule' to decide the 'location' of employees.

analyses,[995] how to define 'similarity' is a difficult question, and it is not clearly stated anywhere in the current CCCTB Directive Proposal. As to the meaning of similarity of tasks, the Commission is unfortunately silent throughout the working documents. What we can see is that under Articles 32 and 33, intra-group outsourced employees would be presumed as performing similar tasks per se and thus can be included in at least one group member's labour factor, and 'the similar tasks test' is not necessary.

It is possible that a cross-border seconded 'employee' cannot be included in any group member when that employee is seconded to a place where their employee status is not recognized, and they cannot be presumed to have employee status if they do not do comparable work as an employee in the receiving company. It is because Article 32 only uses 'where employment is exercised' as the criterion to decide employee status, Article 32 does not consider the situation where the sending company and receiving company might be subject to different national rules.

But when using the independent contractor test for the labour factor of the EU's FA regime to exclude true self-employees via the B prong, it is quite clear which group member's business activities accommodate the employee's task. To prevent the loophole of a 'no-where workforce', Articles 32 and 33 of the current CCCTB Directive Proposal should be interpreted in a way that accommodates a seconded workforce to the company which the employee actually works for.

In short, in order to fulfil the tax-neutrality principle, the seconded workforce should be attributed to where he or she actually physically performs the work as the primary rule; if the seconded workforce has to be thrown back to another group member due to uncertain location or not fulfilling the factor presence nexus, they should be thrown back to the company their work is integrated with, such as part of the team or being supervised and controlled. Moreover, the primary rule of attribution should also accept the possibility that an individual employee can work for more than one group member, and in this situation, it is possible to attribute their payroll and headcount pro rata according to the time spent.

5.4.2.2 The Formalistic Employer? A 'Common Paymaster' and a 'Common Pay Agent'

In the FA experience in the US, there have been typical tax planning scenarios[996] to manipulate the payroll factor: establishing a payroll paying company in the group to attribute payroll to a specific group member (a common paymaster) or hiring a professional agency outside the group to deal with payroll issues (a common pay agent or a professional employer organization, PEO). Although these scenarios originally are designed for MNE's administrative convenience and reducing various compliance costs related to social security or law, these scenarios turned out to be also used as tax avoidance techniques.

995. Hellerstein, *supra* n. 971, footnote 136.
996. Pechacek & Nakamura, *supra* n. 904, at 155-189.

From the experiences of the payroll factor in the US, many disputes arise regarding seconded workforce, regardless of intra-group arrangements or arrangements with a non-group company. The scenarios of setting up a 'common paymaster', 'common pay agent', or 'PEO' all indicate that attribution of the payroll factor might be vulnerable to some manipulation when such intermediaries are responsible for paying renumeration to individuals. Although the scenarios sometimes look similar, the term 'common paymaster' is designed for one employee with multiple employers, whereas the term 'common pay agent' is designed for one employer (a corporate group or a company) with multiple employees.

As to setting up a common paymaster, an employee can be hired by multiple companies, and these hiring companies together assign a 'common paymaster' to pay the employee. Such arrangement saves a lot of administrative costs.[997]

As to setting up a 'common pay agent', one corporate group may have multiple employees sign a contract with one group member while the work is in fact being performed for another group member. The employees receive remuneration from the group member (the common pay agent) with which they formally have a contract, and thus their payroll is attributed to the company that pays the remuneration and sends employees. The common pay agent deals with multiple employees for the corporate group. With the metaphor of seeing employees as assets, such scenario of setting up a common pay agent to attribute employees is similar to the scenario of setting up a holding company for intangibles.

In the US, the 'common pay agent' scenario is seen as a tax avoidance scenario and thus adjusted by the tax authorities in several states[998] based on the reason of substance over form, to attribute the payroll to where the employees actually perform their service.[999]

Hellerstein also indicates[1000] that the common pay agent scenario might happen under the current CCCTB Directive Proposal too, by way of assigning employees to a specific group member functioning as a 'human resources group member'. By making a specific group member, the company which signs contracts and pays the payroll, the MNE taxpayer can thus change the numerator of other group members' labour factors.[1001] While designing the labour factor under the CCCTB, the European Commission Working Group is aware of this scenario and mentioned it as 'shifting the labour factor to a specific group'. The Commission describes this possible manipulation as the 'seconded labour' problem in the working document.[1002] However, Article 33 of the 2016 CCCTB Directive Proposal does not solve this problem.

997. *Ibid.*, 177.
998. It has been used for long; *see* Keith B Giddens & Michael G Maxey, Common Payment Payroll Tax Planning 58 Taxes 189 (1980).
999. Hellerstein, Hellerstein & Swain, *supra* n. 349, at 9.17[1][a].
1000. Hellerstein, *supra* n. 971, at 17.4.2.1.
1001. *Ibid.*
1002. CCCTB Working Document No. 52, paragraph 24.

5.4.3 Attributing to the Physical Location of Performance and 'Base of Operation' Rule: The Multistate Tax Commission

Section 14[1003] of MTC Regulation IV provides the sourcing/attribution rule for the payroll paid by MNE taxpayers. MTC Regulation IV adopts the all-or-nothing approach. In other words, an employee and his or her wages can only be attributed to one jurisdiction.

The all-or-nothing attribution approach in the MTC Regulation has its historical and federal legislation origins. The 'wages' in section 13(c) MTC Regulation IV refers to 'Model Unemployment Compensation Act', which is already now integrated as the FUTA.[1004] FUTA follows the all-or-nothing attribution approach even when an individual employee renders services in more than one state. Accordingly, the MTC/UDITPA payroll test, following the rule of the Model Unemployment Compensation Act, also attributes an employee's compensation to a state on an all-or-nothing basis.[1005]

Section 14 MTC Regulation IV covers three situations. All of them are an all-or-nothing attribution rule. The first is when an employee's services are *performed within a state*, and the compensation paid is included in the payroll factor of that state. When an employee's services only involve one jurisdiction, it is simpler to attribute

1003. MTC Reg. IV.14. Payroll Factor: Compensation Paid in This State. Compensation is paid in this state if any one of the following tests, applied consecutively, are met:

(1) The employee's service is performed entirely within the state.
(2) The employee's service is performed both within and without the state, but the service performed without the state is incidental to the employee's service within the state. The word 'incidental' means any service which is temporary or transitory in nature, or which is rendered in connection with an isolated transaction.
(3) If the employee's services are performed both within and without this state, the employee's compensation will be attributed to this state:
    (A) if the employee's base of operations is in this state; or
    (B) if there is no base of operations in any state in which some part of the service is performed, but the place from which the service is directed or controlled is in this state;(B) or
    (C) if the base of operations or the place from which the service is directed or controlled is not in any state in which some part of the service is performed but the employee's residence is in this state.

The term 'place from which the service is directed or controlled' refers to the place from which the power to direct or control is exercised by the taxpayer.

The term 'base of operations' is the place of more or less permanent nature from which the employee starts his or her work and to which he or she customarily returns in order to receive instructions from the taxpayer or communications from his or her customers or other persons or to replenish stock or other materials, repair equipment, or perform any other functions necessary to the exercise of his or her trade or profession at some other point or points.

1004. Hellerstein, Hellerstein & Swain, *supra* n. 349, at 9.17 footnote 907. Joann M Weiner, 'Using the Experience in the US States to Evaluate Issues in Implementing Formula Apportionment at the International Level' (1999) 83 OTA paper.

1005. Hellerstein, Hellerstein & Swain, *supra* n. 349, at 9.17.

employees. The criterion of the work performed within the state refers to the 'physical' location.[1006]

The second situation is when employees' services are performed within and outside of a state, but the service outside the state is just 'incidental', then the payroll is still included in the payroll factor of that state.

The third situation is more complex; employees perform services both within and outside of the state, and the services outside the state are not just 'incidental'. Then the key criterion to accredit the compensation to the state is 'the employees' base of operation'. The base of operation is where the employees 'receive instructions from the taxpayer, communications from customers or other persons, replenish stock or other materials, repair equipment or perform other necessary functions'. If the base of operation is in the state, then the compensation is included in the payroll factor of that state. Moreover, section 14 provides a type of 'throw-back' clause for the payroll factor: if the base of operation is not within any state, but the service is directed or controlled in the state, then the compensation is still included in the payroll factor; if the base of operation is not in any state and the service is not directed or controlled in any state, when the employee's residence is within the state, the compensation is included in the payroll factor of the state of the employee's residence.

Even in case of a purely in-state (i.e., non cross-border) situation, it is not always clear which entity should include the wages in the payroll factor. For example, 'indirect' employment, such as temporary, leased and other indirect employees lead to disputes not only about the definition of employee but also the attribution rule, i.e., sourcing rules. From a formal perspective, employees are hired by PEOs which provide employee leasing services, and PEOs can provide leased employees to the client company, but these employees in fact perform tasks for the client company. In practice, US states do not all have completely the same approach to attribution. For example, Arkansas and Florida take a more formalistic approach, so payrolls of these leased employees are included in PEOs; whereas Delaware and Massachusetts, on the contrary, attribute payroll to the client company.[1007]

Sometimes taxpayers want to include affiliated or leased employees in the payroll factor because including the payroll factor would be favourable for the apportionment ratio, but they are rejected for not being formally the employer who pay the payroll. For example, the Supreme Court of Pennsylvania rejected UPS Worldwide's request to adopt the payroll factor and include its fully-controlled subsidiary (UPS Aviation Services)'s payroll.[1008] UPS Worldwide transferred amounts of money to the subsidiary UPS Aviation Services, and such 'payroll costs' were further paid to subsidiary UPS Aviation Services' employees. UPS Worldwide stipulated that it had no employees

1006. Hellerstein, *supra* n. 971, at 17.4.1.: 'The US payroll factors contain no provision analogous to the CCCTB rule that employees who physically exercise their employment under the control and responsibility of a group member other than the group member that compensates them are assigned to the group member that actually controls their employment.'

1007. Pechacek & Nakamura, *supra* n. 904.

1008. *UPS Worldwide Forwarding, Inc. v. Commonwealth*, 890 A.2d 368 (Pa. 2005), affg 843 A.2d 438, 442 (Pa. Commw. Ct. 2004); Comments, Schadewald, *supra* n. 931; Pechacek & Nakamura, *supra* n. 904.

itself but requested to include the subsidiary's employees' payroll as its payroll factor. The majority opinion of the court rejected this request and ruled quite formally that UPS Worldwide did not 'directly' pay the subsidiary's employees, and it admitted having no employees itself. The dissenting opinion of one judge is more convincing: 'the presence and absence of a payroll factor should depend on the actual business relationship between UPS Worldwide and the employees'.[1009]

Disputes arise when employees perform tasks in a jurisdiction other than where the headquarters (i.e., the salary paying company) are located. Compensation might be paid in the headquarters' jurisdiction, but tasks are performed in another jurisdiction. Due to the development of technology, such as the Internet, employees can easily perform their tasks in one jurisdiction while employers are located in another jurisdiction. US states have not established identical rules on this issue either.[1010]

Despite disparities regarding employees performing tasks in another jurisdiction other than the headquarters, we still can also observe a common feature of the key criteria used: tax authorities or courts examine the actual content of the employment and physical locations of performing tasks to decide which state(s) could include the payment to employees in the payroll factor. These indicators including office location, time spent, etc.

When the actual contents of the employment involve a localized link, the base of operation is established. As Pechacek and Nakamura's analysis shows, in *Photo-Marker Corporation of California,*[1011] the California tax authorities established the base of operation of the two New York hired and paid corporate officers because their work was actually implemented in California, and they just did short-term regular business trips to New York. In *O.H. Materials Co.*,[1012] the Ohio Court of Appeals ruled that an employee paid in Ohio and performing tasks in a New Jersey job site could also be included in Ohio's payroll factor numerator. In other words, services performed in Ohio and New Jersey should be both included to Ohio's payroll factor. In a Kentucky case,[1013] the court ruled that wages paid to a tugboat performing services along the Mississippi River, i.e., crossing several states, should not be included in Kentucky because the boat did not stop in Kentucky. Among these cases, it shows that physically staying in a jurisdiction and doing substantial activities clearly with a localized link is the decisive common feature to the 'base of operation', and it could be justified to attribute to the headquarters or the local site depending on the actual situation of the tasks performed.

To sum up, when it involves an indirect employment, such as loaned employees/seconded employees, or cross-border employee, there is always a tension between adopting the formal criterion and the substantial criterion for attributing the

1009. Dissent was written by Jude Cohn Jubelirer, joined by Judge Leadbetter & Judge Leavitt, *UPS Worldwide Forwarding, Inc. v. Commonwealth*, 890 A.2d 368 (Pa. 2005), affg 843 A.2d 438, 442 (Pa. Commw. Ct. 2004).
1010. Pechacek & Nakamura, *supra* n. 904; Hellerstein, Hellerstein & Swain, *supra* n. 349, at 9.17, Table 9-6.
1011. Photo-Marker Corp., 1986 Cal. Tax LEXIS 19, 1986.
1012. *O.H. Materials Co. v. Limbach*, No. 5-89-2, 1990 Ohio App. LEXIS 5277.
1013. *Marquette Transp. Co. v. Ky. Fin. & Admin. Cabinet*, No. K03-R-27, 2005 Ky. Tax LEXIS 132.

payroll. I agree with what Hellerstein argues,[1014] that fully switching to the substantial criterion and abandoning the formal criterion 'on the papers', seem unreasonable, even for the purpose of administrative convenience. From the perspective of representing the economic reality from MNE taxpayers' human input, I endorse the substantial criterion for attribution, i.e., where an employee physically performs the task and for whom the employee actually performs, in combination with the time spent, to decide the attribution. Therefore, the all-or-nothing sourcing approach should be reconsidered;[1015] a time and physical location combined pro-rata attribution rule is feasible (*See* section 5.4.5).

5.4.4 Attributing Cross-Border Employees: Seeking One Single Jurisdiction Is Not Tax Neutral

5.4.4.1 The International Tax Regime Ignores That the 'Employment Exercise Location' Can Be Plural

In the process of preparing and drafting the CCCTB Directive Proposal, the European Commission commented that the experiences of allocating taxing powers on cross-border employment income might be a useful reference,[1016] specifically 'Article 15 of the OECD Model Tax Convention', and expected that the experiences gained from allocating sovereign states taxing rights in the double taxation treaties could provide some insights. In reality, the international tax regime does not contribute much.

The latest version of Article 15 of the OECD Model Convention provides as follows:

Article 15 Income From Employment

1. Subject to the provisions of Articles 16, 18 and 19, salaries, wages and other similar remuneration derived by a resident of a Contracting State in respect of an employment shall be taxable only in that State unless the employment is exercised in the other Contracting State. If the employment is so exercised, such remuneration as is derived therefrom may be taxed in that other State.
2. Notwithstanding the provisions of paragraph 1, remuneration derived by a resident of a Contracting State in respect of an employment exercised in the other Contracting State shall be taxable only in the first-mentioned State if:

1014. Hellerstein, Hellerstein & Swain, *supra* n. 349, at 9.17 [1].
1015. Pechacek & Nakamura, *supra* n. 904, at 188.
1016. CCCTB Working Document No. 52, paragraphs 26-27.

> 26. The possible formula manipulations due to outsourced labour are even bigger in case of seconded employees, who are sent from one group company in a low tax MS to another group company in high tax MS. In this case, employees would be on the payroll of the low tax MS although they perform services for the benefit of the companies in the high tax MS and the intra-group payment would be eliminated due to the consolidation.
> 27. To prevent this, a method could be used to attribute the cost of the employees to the two companies involved. Among the possible methods, it was considered taking into account the rules that would be applicable to the personal income of the employee (Article 15 of the OECD Model Tax Convention).

a) the recipient is present in the other State for a period or periods not exceeding in the aggregate 183 days in any twelve-month period commencing or ending in the fiscal year concerned, and
b) the remuneration is paid by, or on behalf of, an employer who is not a resident of the other State, and
c) the remuneration is not borne by a permanent establishment which the employer has in the other State.

3. Notwithstanding the preceding provisions of this Article, remuneration derived by a resident of a Contracting State in respect of an employment, as a member of the regular complement of a ship or aircraft, that is exercised aboard a ship or aircraft operated in international traffic, other than aboard a ship or aircraft operated solely within the other Contracting State, shall be taxable only in the first-mentioned State.

The key criterion to allocate the taxing rights under Article 15 of the OECD Model Convention is again 'where employment is exercised'. This is actually tax neutral, and also the European Commission's position of where an employee is physically performing the task is indeed a criterion that is consistent with the economic rationale of representing the taxpayer's/employer's capacity to mobilize the human resources.

However, except for the main criterion from Article 15(1) of the OECD Model Convention, the international tax experiences from 'employment income' rights under Article 15(2) are not very useful for the attribution rule of the labour factor. Article 15(2) provides additional limitations to the main rule, and the 'sufficient economic allegiance' principle, applicable if an employee performs tasks but receives remuneration or is physically present in another jurisdiction.[1017] Moreover, Article 15 of the OECD Model Convention and the relevant practice have been criticized for lacking coordination and creating complexities and uncertainties for both highly mobile employees and tax authorities of different states, so it would be advisable to take a more critical perspective.[1018]

Therefore, Article 15(2) of the OECD Model Convention is not appropriate to the labour factor attribution because it actually still embraces the all-or-nothing approach (the 183 days rule) and ignores the fact that employment is often exercised in multiple jurisdictions. The approach of seeking one single jurisdiction only has the claimed administrative convenience and conceptually relieves double taxation. Such attribution rule deviates from the economic reality and is incompatible with the benefit-based MN framework. I explain this further in section 5.4.5.

Moreover, all the conditions in Article 15(2) of the OECD Model Convention are not directly related to the actual contents of the task performed, but how and where remuneration is paid (Article 15(2)(b)&(c)). Since these situations are not related to the task itself performed, they are not sufficient to reflect the employer's ability to mobilize the human resources in the production process, and therefore, Article 15(2) of the OECD Model Convention does not provide useful guidance for designing the attribution rule of the labour factor under the CCCTB.

1017. FPG Pötgens, *Income from International Private Employment: An Analysis of Article 15 of the OECD Model* (IBFD 2006), at 6.5.1-6.5.4.
1018. Niesten, *supra* n. 860.

Therefore, for designing the labour factor, Article 15 on employment income or Article 16 on director's fees of the OECD Model Convention do not provide useful insights for the scope of employee, nor do they really provide a meaningful allocation rule for the seconded employees either.

5.4.4.2 *The Single State Rule under the Social Security Law Regime Is Contrary to Benefit-Based Market Neutrality*

As to most attribution rules for payroll, it should be noted that social security law, in either US experiences or EU law, embraces the all-or-nothing approach to decide the applicable law or the sourcing rule for a cross-border employee. This is the exclusivity principle or 'the single state rule'.[1019] For employees working in one EU Member State, it is the law of the state of the employment; for employees working in more than one EU Member State, it is the law of the country of residence when the employee's residence is in the same jurisdiction as the office. When the employee's residence is in the same jurisdiction as the office, it is where the dominant activity takes place between the country of residence and the country of office.[1020]

The field of social security law aims to protect entitlements and administrative convenience. The field of social security law aims to ensure that an individual is entitled to social benefits, so that deciding an applicable national law and issuing benefits according to that specific applicable law needs to be clear and certain. 'The single state rule' would be more appropriate.

For reflecting on corporate taxpayers' ability to mobilize their employees in a sharing formula, the all-or-nothing approach/the single state rule would be illogical, especially since cross-border employment often takes place in Europe. In other words, 'the single state rule' is not compatible with the rationale of the labour factor's attribution rule because the single state rule would not be able to reflect taxpayers' capacity to mobilize and control employees in different states. Therefore, the all-or-nothing approach embedded in social security law should also be set aside when extracting useful lessons in the field of tax law for designing the labour factor attribution rule under the EU's FA regime.

5.4.5 The Tax-Neutral Attribution Method: Physical Location with Pro-Rata Time Spent

In most approaches to attribution used in the US, the international tax regime and EU social security law, they all aim to seek one single jurisdiction, and this is an

1019. F Pennings & GJ Vonk (eds), *Research Handbook on European Social Security Law* (Edward Elgar 2015), at 452. Spiegel (ed.), K Daxkobler, G Strban & AP van der Mei, Analytical Report 2014: The Relationship Between Social Security Coordination and Taxation Law, FreSsco, European Commission, April 2015. Spiegel & others, *supra* n. 864.
EU Regulation 833/2004 Article 11.

1020. To decide which national social security legislation is applicable, *see* Jan Cremers, Free Movement of Workers and Rights That Can Be Derived, 2012 FMW Online Journal on Free Movement of Workers Within the European Union 26 (2012), at 29.

all-or-nothing approach. It might sometimes feel administratively convenient and legally certain, but it does not always reflect the actual economic activities.

Where employment is exercised (i.e., a specific physical location) is actually a tax-neutral indicator, especially when 'seconded' employees are involved. Seconded employees, as the term suggests, perform tasks in a receiving company other than where they have a formal employment contract, and the sending company and receiving company are in different jurisdictions. When an employee works in fact in different jurisdictions, calculating pro rata depending on where the employment is actually exercised is not only a practical criterion but also a logical one because the time spent in working is a clear indicator of how a seconded employee works in different companies/different jurisdictions.[1021]

The Dutch Supreme Court adopted the pro-rata approach when interpreting the tax treaty provision comparable to Article 15 of the OECD Model Convention.[1022] The Dutch Supreme Court ruled that an employee working in different jurisdictions can divide the involved states' taxing rights on employment income according to the working time spent in the different jurisdictions. Nowadays, there are also scholars who argue that a 'pro rata'/fractional approach for social securities and personal income tax is more consistent with the goal of promoting mobility and moderating the conflicts between the working state and the residence state.[1023] I think the pro-rata approach is a neutral design for the labour factor attribution rule.

The pro-rata attribution rule based on the time spent within the state has also been adopted by some states in the US, such as Oklahoma. The payroll factor of the state of Oklahoma does not follow completely the MTC Model Regulation IV (which refers to the Model Unemployment Compensation Act). The numerator of the Oklahoma payroll factor is defined only when 'the compensation for services rendered in the state during the tax period'.[1024] Moreover, there is a specific provision for 'itinerant employees' (who travel to work) whose compensation is assigned to Oklahoma 'in the proportion that time spent in Oklahoma bears to total time spent in furtherance of the enterprise by such employees'.

To sum up, in order to represent the labour market, the attribution rule for cross-border employees should take into account the time, instead of the all-or-nothing attribution rule. Although deviating from the comfort zone of the all-or-nothing attribution rule would involve additional implementing administration work when adopting the EU FA, MNE employers already have the capacity to keep records of these mobile workers using modern communication technology.

1021. In case that an employee or only few employees work in a jurisdiction and there is no sufficient taxable nexus in that jurisdiction, such employee should be thrown back to where he or she is 'integrated' with the team and his or her function. The integration test, developed in some EU Member States' labour law, is usually used in the discussion of an employee status; sometimes the integration test is seen as a part of 'control test' when deciding if there is an employment relationship, *see* 5.4.1 and 5.4.2 'throw-back rule' above.

1022. De Wilde, *supra* n. 76, at 6.4.4.2.3 'Exploring suitable proxies for locating and evaluating firm inputs and firm outputs'.

1023. Niesten, *supra* n. 207.

1024. Hellerstein, Hellerstein & Swain, *supra* n. 349, at 9.17; Okla. Admin. Code § 710:50-17-71(3)(A) and (E)(Westlaw 2011).

When there is no sufficient nexus in the jurisdiction where employees physically perform tasks, the attributed employees should be thrown back to where their work is actually integrated, such as the same production line of another group member, or the parent company, if the direct reporting line is so designed. Such throwing-back of employees should be an exceptional situation, since the presence nexus factor (*see* Chapter 3) is easier to fulfil.

5.5 RETHINKING THE LABOUR FACTOR IN THE DIGITAL PLATFORM ECONOMY/GIG ECONOMY

5.5.1 Platforms to Mobilize on Demand Human Resources

Last, we zoom in on the 'sharing economy/gig economy',[1025] a subfield of the digital economy. The impact of the digital economy on the international tax regime market takes place not only in the customers' market but also in the labour market. Online platforms are a good example.

Depending on the content of services, platforms can be location-based and web-based.[1026] Location-based online platforms provide accommodation, transportation, and tasks services.[1027] Web-based platforms assign work to gig workers, and the finished work is transmitted back to the platform, so the platform can deliver to the ultimate task-giving client. The legal relationship between the individual worker and these online platforms is still a difficult issue in labour law[1028] and tax law.[1029]

However, the difficulty of regulating the sharing economy is not a completely new issue.[1030] The problems of online labour platforms already existed and are very similar to the triangular arrangements involving human resources agencies.[1031] A 'platform labour market' represents a new way of mobilizing human resources via

1025. Valerio De Stefano & Antonio Aloisi, European Legal Framework for 'Digital Labour Platforms', European Commission (2018).

1026. Janine Berg & others, *Digital Labour Platforms and the Future of Work: Towards Decent Work in the Online World* (International Labour Organization 2018), at 4 (Figure 1.1). Figure 1.1 from this ILO report is adapted from Florian A Schmidt, Friedrich-Ebert-Stiftung & Abteilung Wirtschafts- und Sozialpolitik, Digital Labour Markets in the Platform Economy: Mapping the Political Challenges of Crowd Work and Gig Work (2017).

1027. Hatzopoulos & Roma, *supra* n. 17. The online platforms are especially active on these three types of sectors.

1028. Brian Fabo, Jovana Karanovic & Katerina Dukova, In Search of an Adequate European Policy Response to the Platform Economy, 23 Transfer: European Review of Labour and Research 163 (2017).

1029. Pantazatou, *supra* n. 17, https://doi.org/10.1017/9781108255882 (accessed 3 June 2020). The European Commission's communication also mentioned taxation in the sharing economy as a priority and difficult regime, *see* COM(2016) 356 final, Communication from the Commission to the European Parliament, the Council, the European Economic and Social Committee and the Committee of the Regions, A European agenda for the collaborative economy {SWD(2016) 184 final} Brussels, 2.6.2016.

1030. Malcolm Sargeant, The Gig Economy and the Future of Work, 6 Ejournal of International and Comparative labour Studies 1 (2017).

1031. The same remark, Stuart Adam, Helen Miller & Thomas Pope, Tax, Legal Form and the Gig Economy 2017 Green Budget (2017).

technology. The platform economy reaffirms that the labour factor should be designed to be consistent with the capacity to mobilize human resources because the platforms make use of the workforce of a labour market much more intensively.

The advancement of technology makes classifying gig workers more difficult because the Internet and online platforms dilute the element of control in the traditional employment relationship. Gig workers seem to have more freedom, autonomy, and flexibility, and some of them even have their own facilities to perform tasks, like their own cars.[1032] Because of this 'autonomous element', some tests to establish employee status seem inapplicable from appearances, but such autonomy is illusory. Such illusory autonomy does not make gig workers entrepreneurs. Therefore, in the US, more and more Uber/Lyft drivers have won their class action lawsuits and successfully classified themselves as employees, for example, in California.[1033]

Not all courts[1034] rule in favour of gig workers in the US. In addition, the online platform enterprise, Handy, also managed to lobby in seven states[1035] to pass special rules for classifying gig workers as independent contractors until 2020 (the 'Marketplace Platform Statutes').[1036] In other words, these seven states intentionally labelled gig workers as independent contractors as long as this in explicit in a written clause of a contract. Even in states that adopted the ABC test (*see* section 5.3.3), such as Utah and Tennessee,[1037] they have statutes which can classify gig workers as independent contractors.

Interestingly, in the US not all platforms classify their workers as independent contractors, like Uber/Lyft, many online platforms, ranging from cleaning services, homecare, food shopping, and delivery to technology support, classify their workers as employees because most CEOs of these platforms believe treating employees well will bring in successful business.[1038] For another example, even classifying their gig workers as independent contractors, the platform TaskRabbit pays minimum wages

1032. Cunningham-Parmeter, *supra* n. 907, at 1717-1718.
1033. On series cases of Uber in USA, *see* Cunningham-Parmeter, *ibid.*; Andre Andoyan, Independent Contractor or Employee: I'm Uber Confused: Why California Should Create an Exception for Uber Drivers and the on-Demand Economy, 47 Golden Gate University Law Review 153 (2017). Nicholas L DeBruyne, Uber Drivers: A Disputed Employment Relationship in Light of the Sharing Economy 92 Chicago-Kent Law Review 289 (2017). Yasaman Maozami, UBER in the US and Canada: Is the Gig-Economy Exploiting or Exploring Labor and Employment Laws by Going Beyond the Dichotomous Workers' Classification, 24 U. Miami International & Comparative Law Review 609 (2016).
1034. For example, a Florida court ruled that Uber is a technology platform that connects drivers with paying customers seeking transportation services. *McGillis v. Dept. of Econ. Opportunity*, 210 So. 3d 220, 221 (Fla. 3d Dist. App. 2017), *see* Cunningham-Parmeter, *supra* n. 954, at 396-397.
1035. Michael C Duff, All the World's a Platform?: Some Remarks on 'Marketplace Platform' Employment Laws, https://ssrn.com/abstract=3520723; Sprague, *supra* n. 909, at 746.
1036. Rebecca Smith, 'Marketplace Platforms' and 'Employers' Under State Law—Why We Should Reject Corporate Solutions and Support Worker-Led Innovation (May 2018), https://www.nelp.org.
1037. Sprague, *supra* n. 909, at 746.
1038. *See* the survey in 2016, National Employment Law Project, Employers in the On-Demand Economy: Why Treating Workers as Employees Is Good for Business (16 March 2016), https://www.nelp.org.

and thus has not been confronted with any class actions suits.[1039] In short, developments in case law and legislation in the US demonstrate that the employee status of gig workers is still an ongoing debate. But there is a growing awareness that platforms can make use of these gig workers so extensively, that traditional labour law is facing challenges. There is indeed a trend to call for more social protection and more inclusivity for gig workers.[1040]

For the purpose of the labour factor under the CCCTB, it is market neutral to include all of the workforce mobilized by online platforms in these platform companies' labour factor for both the remuneration paid and headcounts. It is justified because these online platforms in the platform labour market have in fact a stronger status than these platform workers.[1041] To maintain a healthy and balanced labour market and industrial relations, more corresponding public benefits and policies are necessary.

5.5.2 Using the Independent Contractor Test to Classify Platform Workforce's Status

In both Europe[1042] and the US,[1043] the number of active platform workers performing on-demand tasks is increasing. These on-demand platform workers have a distinctive

1039. *See* Joseph W McHugh, Looking Through the (Mis) Classifieds: Why TaskRabbit Is Better Suited than Uber and Lyft to Succeed Against a Worker Misclassification Claim, 66 Clev. St. Law Review 649 (2017).

1040. Sacha Garben & European Agency for Safety and Health at Work, Protecting Workers in the Online Platform Economy: An Overview of Regulatory and Policy Developments in the EU (2017). Garben has conducted a survey of different Member States, European Commission, European Parliament, CJEU's reactions to gig workers, and concludes that, occupational safety and health risks to the gig workers are significant (in Garben's term, 'higher accident rates and stress incidence, and lower job security, with all its physical and psycho-social implications') but the protection is not sufficient, so it is called for a more extensive reform.

1041. Joyce Beebe, How Should We Tax the Sharing Economy? 10 Issue Brief (2018). 'Sharing economy workers experience higher income instability compared to traditional employees. Their work is mostly tied to a certain platform.' Problems and impacts from the digitalized labour market, *see* Christophe Degryse, Digitalisation of the Economy and Its Impact on Labour Markets, *ETUI Research Paper-Working Paper* (2016). The problems include blurring of work life and private life, inequality and wage stagnation, etc.

1042. For example, discussions on Uber drivers in UK, Ewan McGaughey, Uber, the Taylor Review, Mutuality and the Duty Not to Misrepresent Employment Status, 48 Industrial Law Journal 180 (2019) (indicating that malpresentation of employee status causes social cost; relying on tax authorities to define the employee status is too slow). Mark Freedland & Nicola Countouris, Some Reflections on the 'Personal Scope' of Collective Labour Law' 46 Industrial Law Journal 52 (2017) (arguing for a more inclusive and wide personal scope for labour law to include Uber drivers). Mark Freedland & Jeremias Prassl, Employees, Workers and the 'Sharing Economy' Changing Practices and Changing Concepts in The United Kingdom, 6 Spanish Labour Law and Employment Relations Journal 16 (2017) (analysing the Uber cases in UK and arguing for a third category of workers in addition to the binary system of 'employee versus self-employee', so these workers can benefit from some rights).

Discussions on gig workers in Spain, *see* Todoli-Signes, *supra* n. 941 (discussing the third category of workers, 'TRADE' (economically dependent self-employees) and argues that it is not a separate category but a subcategory of 'self-employee'); Donini & others, *supra* n. 941. Sacha Garben & European Agency for Safety and Health at Work, *supra* n. 1040 (This

feature compared to the traditional employee: they seem to enjoy wider autonomy, freedom, and flexibility regarding their work, they can decide if they take the work offer, and they may work in their available spare time, in addition to their main job or family commitments. At the same time, platform work is also criticized for being precarious, not bringing in stable income and is not even subject to minimum wage requirements in national law. But many gig workers express clearly that they want to be 'independent contractors' because they need such flexibility,[1044] which leads to self-exploitation. It is not a good sign for maintaining a healthy labour market.

For deciding the labour factor under the EU's FA regime regarding online labour platforms, it is tax neutral to follow the ABC test to exclude true independent contractors, as I discussed earlier.

In combination with legal presumption of employee status when being paid, this narrow and precise scope of independent contractor of the ABC test is compatible with the latest developments in EU law regarding the platform economy. Although the CJEU does not decide directly whether or not Uber drivers are employees, in December 2017, the CJEU ruled that[1045] Uber BV is not merely providing information as an intermediary but providing transportation services under EU law.

Under the rationale of independent contractor (ABC) test, Uber drivers are not free from the control of Uber because their rate and driving routes are closely monitored and decided; Uber drivers' activities are not outside the regular course of Uber's transportation service; Uber drivers do not have independent occupation in which they can assume and spread managerial risks. Since Uber drivers do not fulfil the three-prong independent contractor (ABC) test, they should be included in the payroll factor of Uber, when Uber is subject to the EU's FA regime.

---

report covers France, The United Kingdom, Denmark, Sweden, Finland, The Netherlands, Belgium, and Ireland).

1043. Regarding platform economy/gig economy/on-demand economy, discussions in USA are enormous. Similar to the European discussions, many works explore the possibility to have an extra intermediary category between employees and independent contractors. It should be noted that, in addition to drivers, there are many platforms dealing with different sectors.

See discussions on the platform economy in USA, especially on labour law perspective, Orly Lobel, The Gig Economy & the Future of Employment and Labor Law, 51 University of San Francisco Law Review 51 (2017). Orly Lobel, The Law of the Platform, 101 Minnesota Law Review 87 (2016).

1044. Many Uber drivers express that they do not want to be labelled as employees because they want more flexibility, and this is also used by Uber as arguing Uber drivers are not employees, *see* Veena Dubal, An Uber Ambivalence: Employee Status, Worker Perspectives, & Regulation in the Gig Economy, UC Hastings Research Paper No. 381 (2019).

1045. Case C-434/15 *Asociación Profesional Élite Taxi v. Uber Systems Spain SL*, comments and analysis, *see* Hacker, *supra* n. 952. Malgorzata Sieradzka, *Asociación Profesional Elite Taxi vs Uber Systems Spain SL*: Differences Between the Internet Platform and the Transport Service, 11 Journal of European Competition Law & Practice 263 (2020).

5.5.3 Examples of a Platform and a Task-Giving Company

I would like to wrap up this chapter with an example of an online labour platform to demonstrate that the existing options regarding defining and attributing employees discussed in Chapter 5 do not provide suitable solutions.

Assume Company 1 (in Country A) and Company 2 (in Country B) are unrelated companies, and thus the intra-group discussions are irrelevant. Company 2 is an online labour platform and matching workers and Company 1, so that workers from all over the world can perform tasks for Company 1. These workers are also called gig workers. In this case, from Countries B, C, D, there are platform workers registered in Company 2, doing tasks assigned by Company 1 via Company 2.

Figure 10 The Online Labour Platform

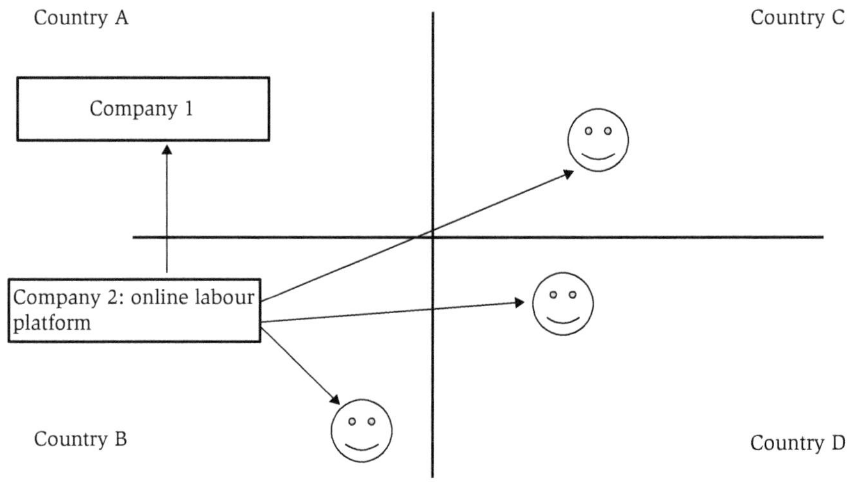

	The Current CCCTB	*US's Common Law Employee/Statutory Employee*	*EU Social Security Law 'Single State Rule'*	*This Book's Suggestion*
Company 1's labour factor	Depends on the national law of Countries B, C, D, if these platform workers are included. If the answer is in the affirmative, they might be included in Company 1's labour factor, so they will be attributed to Company A.	These platform workers are outsourced workers, and thus they might not always fulfil the common law employee or any statutory employee in some states (e.g., some states do not recognize Uber drivers as employees) If employee status is established (such as Microsoft project-based engineers), according to the MTC's base of operation rules, these platform workers might be attributed to Countries B, C, D and thrown back to Company A when conditions are met.	These platform workers might be qualified as employees under the social security law, attributed either to county of employment or country of residence.	If platform workers conduct the activities within the regular course of business of Company 1, not free from control, and not an independent occupation, these platform workers should be included in Company 1's labour factor. Workers should be attributed to Country B, C, D, respectively.

	The Current CCCTB	*US's Common Law Employee/Statutory Employee*	*EU Social Security Law 'Single State Rule'*	*This Book's Suggestion*
Company 2's labour factor	Depends on the national law of Countries B, C, D, if these platform workers are defined as employees of an online platform. If the answer is in the affirmative, they might be included in Company 2's labour factor, so they will be attributed to Company B.	These platform workers might fulfil the common law employee (IRS 20 factor test) of the online labour platform. California legislation[1046] approves employee status of Uber drivers.	These platform workers might be qualified as employees under social security law, either to county of employment or to country of residence.	If platform workers conduct activities within the regular course of business of Company 2, these platform workers should be included in Company 2's labour factor, based on their FTE basis. Workers should be attributed to Country B, C, or D, respectively.

Source: The author.

The figure above demonstrates how exiting attribution rules could apply to this case, but there are still quite a few uncertainties. In this Chapter, I have explored existing labour law and social security law, and they do share a consensus. However, by utilizing the 'independent contractor test', it is clear and easier to exclude a workforce that should not be included in the labour factor as employees.

About the scope of employees and where they are attributed, my suggested approach is: based on the broad scope of employees, gig workers should be defined as employees. Depending on the type of business being conducted, either the online labour platform or the task-giving company can include these gig workers. If gig workers work for multiple platforms or different task-giving companies, they are attributed pro rata according to their time spent.

Gig workers should be attributed to the location where they physically perform tasks, and the labour presence nexus test in the jurisdiction where gig workers physically perform tasks has to take them into account.

One might question that if 'both' the online platform and the task-giving company are entitled to include gig workers, wouldn't this result in double-counting or double taxation. This is a misunderstanding. By way of explanation, first, the labour factor is just the ratio which is part of the formula, it does not directly influence the size of the consolidated tax base. The online platform and the task-giving company have their own consolidated corporate tax base, and there is no 'overlap'. By applying the

1046. It is the AB5 gig-work bill, *see* Dubal, *supra* n. 1044.

independent contractor test, especially the second prong 'in the course of business', and as long as we determine the platform's business, it is easy to see which entity should include the gig worker. If the platform conducts the business of a specific service, like Uber being classified as providing transportation services, Uber drivers should be included in Uber's labour factor. If the platform only conducts human resources management and recruitment for the task-giving company, such as hiring project-based engineers for Microsoft or Amazon, these gig workers should be included in the task-giving company.

Second, in such triangular arrangement, gig workers are controlled by both the online platform and the task-giving company at the same time, so they are formally mobilized by both. The attribution depends on what gig workers do in relation to the business of the platform or the task-giving company.

Third, in many jurisdictions gig workers are classified as 'no-where workers' that cannot enjoy the same level of labour rights and social security entitlements as typical employees. Such underpayment has become a social problem and needs further 'tax-financed mechanisms'[1047] to re-enhance protection of these gig workers. Such enhancement is a government response to the digital economy through social policy measures, and these are necessary public benefits to maintain a good labour market. It is justified to include gig workers in both the online labour platform and the task-giving company because they are effectively mobilizing these flexible workforces, and often in a much more cost-efficient or even unfair way.[1048] Therefore, the suspicion and accusation of 'double counting one employee' is unfounded.

To sum up, for the digital economy, attribution of platform workers/gig workers should follow the same tax-neutral rationale: having a broad scope of employees and attributing to where they physically work, in combination with adopting the labour factor presence nexus.

5.6 CONCLUSIONS AND RECOMMENDATIONS: THE LABOUR FACTOR REPRESENTS TAXPAYERS' ABILITY TO MOBILIZE HUMAN RESOURCES

The ultimate rationale of the labour factor is to represent a company taxpayers' production side of activities, contributed by workforce. In other words, the labour factor should reflect the group's ability to mobilize human resources. The justification for adopting the labour factor is to represent the public goods and infrastructure provided in the labour market. In other words, the taxpayer's capacity to mobilize human resources is the indicator of the degree to which the taxpayer enjoys the public benefits from the jurisdiction involved.

This chapter has answered two core sub-questions: how the scope of employees should be decided and how employees should be attributed, according to the tax-neutrality principle based on the benefit principle. The definition of employee for the

1047. Janine Berg & others, *supra* n. 1026, at 110.
1048. *Ibid.*, 22 'Non-user-friendly adhesion contracts'.

labour factor of the EU FA regime is not necessarily the same as the definition of employee in any specific national labour law; instead, the scope of employee under the labour factor of the EU FA regime needs to be broad enough to cover typical employees, atypical employees, managers, directors, etc., if they are mobilized by the taxpayer. Only 'true independent contractor' can be excluded from the labour factor.

Instead of looking for the indicators of employee status, such as control and economic dependence, I recommend adopting the three-prong independent contractor test adapted from US states' statutes, and to change the assessment perspective: (A) the workforce is free from control; (B) the workforce's performance is outside the scope of the regular business and trade of the employer; and (C) the workforce holds an independent occupation. When the three prongs are not cumulatively fulfilled, the workforce is not an independent contractor and has to be included in the labour factor.

As to the attribution of employees for the purpose of deciding the labour factor, the EU FA regime should implement the rule of where the employment is exercised, that is, the location where the employee is physically working. In the case of employees working via a means of telecommunication, since employees do not perform their tasks in a physical location where other colleagues (including those who are responsible for supervising and controlling the work) are working, such employees should first be attributed to the physical location.

In my view, the location of employment is an EU law concept that should have an autonomous meaning.[1049] The attribution of employee under the EU FA regime should also have an autonomous meaning by adopting the 'physical and actual working location' approach, in combination with the pro-rata time dimension. The physical location of performing the task, as the main rule, in combination of the 'throw back to where the employee's work is integrated' as the rule only when the factor presence nexus threshold of where the workforce is performing the task is not met. By such design, the labour factor would be consistent with the economic reality of taxpayers' capacity to control and mobilize human resources.

In sum, for the labour factor for the EU's FA regime, this book recommends amending the provisions of the current CCCTB Directive Proposal accordingly as follows. These amended texts from the current CCCTB Directive Proposal are also 'digital economy proof'.

Article 32 Composition of the labour factor

1. The labour factor shall consist, as to one half, of the total amount of the payroll of a group member as its numerator and the total amount of the payroll of the group as its denominator, and as to the other half, of the number of employees of a group member as its numerator and the number of employees of the group as its denominator. Where an individual employee is included in the labour factor of a group member, the payroll relating to that employee shall be allocated to the labour factor of the same group member.
2. The number of employees shall be measured on a fulltime equivalent basis at the end of the tax year.

1049. Similar remarks, Pennings, *supra* n. 958, at 104.

3. The definition of an employee shall include all workforce that are not independent contractors mobilized by the Group. The independent contractors should fulfil three cumulative conditions: (A) being free from control of the taxpayer; (B) performing tasks outside the regular course of business and trade of the taxpayer; (C) holding an independent occupation.

Article 33 Allocation of employees and payroll

1. Employees shall be included in the labour factor of the group member where employees physically exercise their employment, when employees physically exercise their employment in multiple Member States.
2. By way of derogation from paragraph 1, where there is no taxable nexus at the Member State where employees physically exercise their employment, employees shall be attributed to where their employment is integrated, and if they are not integrated in any other jurisdictions, the labour factor shall be attributed in proportion to the average of the other two weighting factors.
3. Employees shall include persons who, although not employed directly by a group member, perform tasks similar to those performed by employees.
4. Payroll shall include all costs of salaries, wages, bonuses and all other employee compensation, including related pension and social security costs borne by the employer as well as expenses of the employer corresponding to the cost of persons as referred to in paragraph 3.
5. Payroll costs shall be valued at the amount of expenses that are treated as deductible by the employer in a tax year.

CHAPTER 6
Towards the Market-Neutral Asset Factor

When you find a diamond that belongs to nobody, it is yours. When you discover an island that belongs to nobody, it is yours. When you get an idea before anyone else, you take out a patent on it: it is yours. So, with me: I own the stars because nobody else before me ever thought of owning them.

'Yes, that is true,' said the little prince. 'And what do you do with them?'

'I manage them,' replied the businessman. 'I count them and recount them. It is difficult. But I am a man concerned with matters of consequence.'

The Little Prince[1050]

6.1 INTRODUCTION

6.1.1 The Public Benefits Justify the Asset Factor: An Environment for Production and Innovation

The asset factor of a sharing formula represents the production side of taxpayers' economic activities.[1051] As discussed in Chapter 3, including the asset factor in the formula is justified from the viewpoint of the benefit principle. When the production side of the economic activities includes labour and capital, the asset factor presents the element of 'capital' in the production process. Government provides the relevant public benefits, environment, and infrastructure, such as protection of property and encouragement of innovation, so that taxpayers can use material resources. The asset

1050. Antoine de Saint-Exupéry, *The Little Prince* (General Press 2018).
1051. Canada's FA does not include the property factor in the system. *See* Weiner, *supra* n. 47; Smart & Vaillancourt, *supra* n. 47.

factor also represents taxpayers' capability to mobilize non-human resources in the production process.

Another focus of this chapter is to explore how intangibles should be treated for the asset factor. There is a tradition, developed from the US and reflected in the current CCCTB Directive Proposal,[1052] that intangibles, in principle, are not included in the asset factor. One popular argument for excluding intangibles is anti-manipulation. The European Commission was aware of the possible tax avoidance scenario arising from the asset factor and thus excluded intangibles from the asset factor under the current CCCTB Directive Proposal. Nevertheless, there are still quite a few theoretical loopholes that make 'excluding intangibles' not tax neutral. BEFIT, the European Commission's new tax reform package of 2021, changes the traditional position of excluding intangibles and expressly mentions that BEFIT will include intangibles in the asset factor.[1053] So the next step is to design the proper method to treat intangibles in the asset factor.

The treatment of intangibles is still a difficult question in FA. Complete exclusion of intangibles from the asset factor is not market neutral, but which, and the extent to which, intangibles should be included are the ultimate questions. This chapter seeks answers that are consistent with the tax-neutrality principle.

Moreover, when attributing assets for the asset factor, the decisive criterion is where the assets are utilized, not legal ownership or economic ownership. Using the ownership concept to attribute assets is the cause of non-neutrality and does not align economic activities with the public benefits provided by the jurisdictions involved. The rationale of 'attributing assets by utilization' applies to both tangible and intangible assets. The current CCCTB Directive Proposal does not follow this rationale and already leads to unreasonable results. These mistakes should be prevented in the EU FA regime in the future.

To seek the 'market neutral' asset factor for the EU FA regime, I revisit the asset factor rules in the CCCTB Directive Proposal and further introduce the MTC's apportionment and allocation regulations in the US. For the treatment of tangible assets, I compare the CCCTB Directive Proposal with the MTC apportionment rules. For the treatment of intangibles, I revisit relevant TP standards adopted by the OECD. As to financial assets, I discuss them in Chapter 7 regarding the special industry formula for financial institutions.

6.1.2 The Structure of This Chapter

This chapter is structured as follows. Section 6.2 first revisits the rationale and theory upholding and negating the asset factor in the context of FA. Traditionally, only tangible assets are included in the asset factor, but this is already outdated, as discussed in Chapter 3. Section 6.2.2 also explains how intangibles should be included

1052. Preamble (10) of 2016 CCCTB Directive Proposal.
1053. European Commission, *supra* n. 117, at 12. https://ec.europa.eu/taxation_customs/sites/taxation/files/communication_on_business_taxation_for_the_21st_century.pdf.

in the asset factor and clarify some confusion regarding intangibles in different contexts.

Section 6.3 introduces the definition, scope, and valuation of the asset factor in the CCCTB Directive Proposal and the MTC Regulations, focusing on tangibles. Section 6.4 discusses attribution rules, including intangibles and real estate examples, to demonstrate why the assets attribution rule based on 'ownership' is not market neutral.

Section 6.5 explores the 'functional analysis' of intangibles in the TP Guidelines and Authorised OECD Approach (AOA). The functional analysis can provide insights into how an intangible is created and utilized. This is consistent with the tax neutrality of the asset factor: assets should be attributed to utilization. Section 6.6 concludes what the asset factor should look like and what amendments should be made to the current CCCTB Directive Proposal and suggestions to the EU FA in the future.

6.2 DECIPHERING THE THEORY UPHOLDING A TAX-NEUTRAL ASSET FACTOR

6.2.1 The Asset Factor Representing the Environment of Production Side Activities Taking Place

As discussed in Chapter 2, the design of a formula or selecting any specific factor should be consistent with the MN principle based on taxpayers' economic activities and corresponding to the public benefits enjoyed.

From the perspective of the 'production/input' side of economic activities, the asset factor representing the production process is justified; and the asset factor might look as if it overlaps with the labour factor since these two factors are both 'input'. But the input from assets and human resources are different types of inputs to production. It is meaningful to adopt both the labour factor and the asset factor in the formula.[1054] These weighting factors of the sharing formula 'proxies' are designed to conceptually measure MNE taxpayers' input and output activities and the public benefits they have enjoyed from the jurisdiction where their production activities and service performance take place.[1055] In other words, adopting the asset factor in the formula is consistent with the benefit principle in tax law.[1056]

1054. There might be an overlapping conceptual area between the asset factor and labour factor, which is taxing 'robots.' There have been discussions on levying tax on robots because robots are used to replace the jobs of human beings, i.e., replacing labourers. *See* Xavier Oberson, Taxing Robots? From the Emergence of an Electronic Ability to Pay to a Tax on Robots or the Use of Robots, 9 World Tax Journal 247 (2017). For this book, I will not further discuss taxation on robots or artificial intelligence (AI) because I still see such new technology as non-human resources not that can replace human resources. *See also* Giorgio Beretta, Literature Review: Xavier Oberson, Taxing Robots. Helping the Economy to Adapt to the Use of Artificial Intelligence, Edward Elgar, 2019, 48 Intertax 350 (2020).

1055. *See* section 3.4.2 of this book.

1056. Hellerstein, Hellerstein & Swain, *supra* n. 349, 8.06 [2]. Hellerstein further elaborates: they (the payroll factor and the property factor) reflect the geographic "source" of the taxpayer's income, which may reasonably be attributed to the locus of the taxpayer's property and

The history of adopting the asset factor in FA is long. In the US, the asset factor (in the US, the term is the 'property factor',[1057] so these terms are used interchangeably in this chapter) is used in various early formulas in states even prior to the UDITPA, such as the 'single asset factor' formula for apportioning property tax from the transcontinental railroad industry dating back to the nineteenth century[1058] and other state income tax formulas prior to the UDITPA and the MTC.[1059] Although there are more and more states in the US shifting to adoption of the single-sales-factor formula, the MTC Recommendation still keeps the asset factor in the standard formula.

Nowadays, the trend of adopting the single-sales-factor formula in states in the US is an example of abandoning the asset factor to attract investments. Moreover, as another example, Canada also excludes the asset factor and adopts a two-factor formula consisting of the sales factor and the payroll factor.[1060] According to Weiner, Canada has already decided that the asset factor is redundant because the sales factor and the payroll factor already represent the taxpayers' production and customers' market in balance.[1061]

Furthermore, there has been a popular argument for excluding the asset factor entirely from the formula: the asset factor represents the taxpayers' capital capacity, and such capital is under the taxpayers' control and thus easier to be manipulated.[1062] Such concern is related to the nature of 'assets'. It is undeniable that assets are an element of production controlled by the taxpayer per se, and taxpayers can freely use these assets. However, it is overly zealous to deny the essential role of 'assets' in the production process. The benefit-based MN principle means that the tax rules faithfully reflect taxpayers' economic activities, including the production side. Thus, completely negating the asset factor would be non-neutral because abolishing the asset factor

---

employees. On the other hand, they constitute rough indicia of the protection, benefits, and services that the state furnishes to the enterprise and of the costs that the enterprise imposes upon the state. These benefits and costs embrace such items as highways, streets, police, and fire protection, as well as services furnished to the employees of the business, through schools, recreational facilities, health care, and welfare benefits. There is also increasing awareness of the importance to business, and the heavy costs to governments, of providing a liveable physical environment through clean air, potable water, adequate sewage disposal, reduction of noise pollution, and an overall ambience in which to participate in or enjoy the leisure and cultural activities.

1057. Some early discussions on the property factor before UDITPA, *see* Edward Roesken, The Property Factor in State Income Tax Allocation, 24 Taxes 473 (1946). Adopting the property factor has a very long history among states in the US; many states even used the property factor as the single-factor allocation key. Sumerwell argued that there are two possible theories for the property factor: based on 'capital investment' or based on 'use of the property.' Sumerwell further argued that if the theory of the property factor is based on the 'use of a property,' the depreciation should be ignored. *See* RF Sumerwell, The Property Factor, 7 Tax Executive 30 (1954). In my view, the theory of the property factor should be a hybrid of both because these two aspects reflect taxpayers' capacity to mobilize the property.

1058. Weiner, *supra* n. 47, at 11.

1059. Weiner, *supra* n. 47.

1060. The Canadian formula is regulated by section 400 of the Income Tax Regulations, *see* Smart & Vaillancourt, *supra* n. 47, at 80.

1061. Weiner, *supra* n. 47, at 17.

1062. De Wilde, *supra* n. 76, at 6.4.5.2.

would be missing the factor representing the material resources provided in the jurisdiction.

Therefore, in order to design an asset factor that can reflect the production process, the scope of the asset factor should be broad enough to include assets that contribute to the production process. Items not having any production-related function should not be included.

In my view, the basic design of excluding all types of intangibles should be reconsidered and be amended, according to the nature of the intangibles. When intangibles are being utilized for taxpayers' production activities, it would be illogical to exclude them. The difficulty and opportunity for manipulation would exist, but there should be other solutions to address these problems, not by negating and excluding intangibles. This is elaborated in section 6.5.

6.2.2 Intangibles in Different Contexts

The classical argument for excluding intangibles is based on a concern about manipulation and difficulties in valuation. However, when revisiting the fundamental rationale of adopting the asset factor and how income is generated from assets, excluding items purely out of administrative convenience or anti-manipulation is not theoretically sufficient. It has been argued that only including tangible assets would be unfair for some industries, such as the financial industry,[1063] though it is undeniable that some intangibles' location is geographically indeterminable.[1064] Therefore, in the financial industry formula, financial assets are included in the asset factor and this is a widely accepted 'exception' for the asset factor of the standard formula.

In other words, 'only including tangibles in the asset factor' is never an unchangeable truth. Although financial assets are different from intangibles, the experiences from the financial industry have demonstrated the possibility to redesign the asset factor. Regarding financial assets, I discuss them separately in Chapter 7.

Intangibles are challenging to capture because there are too many perspectives to observe. When designing an asset factor that accommodates intangibles, one needs to be cautious about not making circular arguments. Different fields of law, including private law, accounting law, and tax law, have used the term 'intangibles' not identically.[1065] The OECD has also developed various concepts of intangibles:[1066] trade intangibles, marketing intangibles,[1067] hybrid intangibles,[1068] HTVI, etc. Some scholars

1063. The financial industry formula; *see* discussions in Chapter 7 of this book. MTC also has provided a special formula for the financial industry available at http://www.mtc.gov. General discussions on several industry formulas, *see* Weiner, *supra* n. 47.

1064. Hellerstein, Hellerstein & Swain, *supra* n. 349, at 9.16.

1065. Karin Winters & others, Concepts: IP Rights from a Legal, Accounting and Tax Point of View, in Isabel Verlinden & Anuschka Bakker (eds), *Mastering the IP Life Cycle from a Legal, Tax and Accounting Perspective* (IBFD 2018).

1066. *Ibid.*

1067. Marketing intangibles have been in the debate, including BEPS Action 8. This is because it is complex to decide the remuneration and value of marketing intangibles. Marc M Levey & others, The Quest for Marketing Intangibles, 34 Intertax 2 (2006); Chantal Roberge, Transfer Pricing in the Pharmaceutical Industry: The Remuneration of Marketing Intangibles, 20

distinguish between 'soft intangibles' and 'hard intangibles':[1069] soft intangibles cannot be owned and commercialized, such as locational savings, market power, assembled workforce, etc.; while hard intangibles, can be easily commercialized, such as patents, copyrights, and trademarks. Distinctions and categories of intangibles are endless, so I only focus on the contexts relevant to the asset factor of the current CCCTB Directive Proposal.

More precisely, for the EU's FA regime, the distinction between 'intellectual property (IP)' and 'intangible assets' is nevertheless still meaningful:[1070] intangible assets are all the elements of a business enterprise that exist separately from monetary and tangible assets. Intangibles are assets that do not have physical substance, grant rights and privileges to a business owner, and are inseparable from the enterprise. IP and intangible assets both lack physical form but are often discussed separately.[1071]

In this chapter, I argue that only IP should be in the asset factor because IP is the result of innovation, which coincides with the public benefits provided in the jurisdiction. IP rights (patent, copyright, trademark) enjoy more concrete legal protection than other types of intangibles, such as 'locational savings' or 'market power'.

In my view, intangibles and IP both involve a 'human element', so intangible assets/IP have a status falling between 'labour' and 'tangible assets'. This is also why the inclusion of intangibles in the asset factor might appear to be blurred with the labour factor: intangible assets involve human intellectual works.

6.2.3 Intangibles' Interaction with Formulary Apportionment in Three Contexts

Due to the diverse meaning of 'intangibles', there are three contexts[1072] involving interaction between intangibles and FA in the literature. These discussions sometimes overlap because they all involve FA. Still, for the purpose of this chapter, i.e., designing the market-neutral asset factor, we need to clarify first these different contexts.

The first context is to allocate income earned from 'intangibles'.[1073] This type of income includes royalties, dividends, interest, etc., because intangibles in this context include stock holdings, shareholdings, etc. Some scholars, such as Richter, advocate the regulated profit splitting (RPS) method to taxing royalty income from licensing IP.

International Transfer Pricing Journal (2013); Jasna Voje, Milestone Transfer Pricing Cases on IP, in Verlinden & Bakker (eds), *supra* n. 1065, at 15.3.

1068. Hybrid of a trade intangible and a marketing intangible.

1069. Mirna Screpante, Rethinking the Arm's Length Principle and Its Impact on the IP Licence Model after OECD/G20 BEPS Actions 8-10: Nothing Changed But the Change?, 11 World Tax Journal 557 (2019), at 3.2.2.

1070. For example, Russell L Parr, *Intellectual Property: Valuation, Infringement, and Joint Venture Strategies* (5th ed. Wiley 2018), at Chapters 2 and 3.

1071. *Ibid.*, 40.

1072. These three contexts are also evidence that, treatment intangibles will involve all weighting factors as well as the tax base level. *See section* 3.4 of this book.

1073. Wolfram F Richter, Taxing Intellectual Property in the Global Economy: A Plea for Regulated and Internationally Coordinated Profit Splitting CESifo Working Paper Series No. 6564 (2017); Hellerstein, *supra* n. 352.

Hellerstein analyses different possible formulas for allocation rules for different types of income from intangibles.[1074] In US state taxation cases, this issue is also discussed with the definition of 'unitary business' and 'factor representation'[1075] because sometimes it is arguable that specific income earned from an intangible might not be part of a unitary business, especially in the natural resources extractive industry.[1076] This is not what I discuss in the chapter. It should be clarified here because the terminology (intangible) is similar.

The second context is 'marketing intangible,' which is often transcribed as a ratio. In 2019, the OECD was considering using a ratio/FA to allocate taxing rights on income,[1077] and 'marketing intangible' as one type of formula apportionment method to allocate taxing rights on MNE's cross-border income.[1078] It resembles a single-sales-factor formula representing the market jurisdiction.

The third context discusses how to regulate intangibles in the asset factor to conform to the tax-neutrality normative framework. This chapter aims to answer the question in the third context, not the first and the second context.

Since this chapter concentrates on the function of intangibles in the production process to decide the scope, attribution, and valuation, the 'market status' of an intangible and estimation from 'market value/fair value' would not be appropriate. This is not because a market-based valuation method is inherently wrong; just because the 'market value' method is not suitable to reflect the input side. This rationale can also prevent one of the concerns of including intangibles in the asset factor: bringing back the risk and uncertainty due to the difficulty of allocating and valuating intangibles.

Furthermore, this rationale prevents the circular argument concerning when to include intangibles in the asset factor. FA is based on 'proxies,' i.e., weighting factors, to reflect taxpayers' economic activities and related public benefits provided by government. To attribute and valuate an intangible would inevitably make use of another proxy. In this regard, a proxy used to attribute and valuate intangibles must be concrete enough and not overlap with other weighting factors.

If we mix up the issues of apportioning 'income earned from intangibles' and making use of 'marketing intangibles' with the problem of designing the asset factor, we would end up using circular reasoning to justify the treatment of intangibles in the asset factor because we would need to use another proxy (such as market value or fair value) for the asset factor proxy.

In my view, difficulty or complexity in valuation is not the only reason for traditional FA to exclude intangibles from the asset factor. It is the concern about

1074. Hellerstein, *supra* n. 352.
1075. Hellerstein, *supra* n. 380; *see section* 3.2.3 of this book.
1076. Regarding the extractive industry's formula, *see* Chapter 7.4 of this book.
1077. OECD/G20 Base Erosion and Profit Shifting Project, Programme of Work to Develop a Consensus Solution to the Tax Challenges Arising from the Digitalization of the Economy Inclusive Framework on BEPS, May 2019. The new profits allocation rule options, such as 'Fractional apportionment method' and 'Distribution-based approaches,' are all FA-type solutions.
1078. Sigurd Næss-Schmidt & others, Future Taxation of Company Profits: What to Do with Intangibles?, Copenhagen Economics, February 2019 (Copenhagen Economics 2019).

circular reasoning that makes us uncomfortable. Therefore, when we focus on an intangible's function in the production process, we exclude intangibles that do not have a production function. We also maintain symmetry between the asset factor and factor presence nexus, which does create illogical circular reasoning.

In the following sections, I describe the asset factor rules in the current CCCTB Directive Proposal as well as US experiences and examine all the rules according to the rationale of 'being utilized in the production process'. When the result is consistent with this rationale, it is market neutral; when the result is not consistent, then such a rule would be contrary to the MN framework.

6.3 THE ASSET FACTOR IN THE CURRENT FORMULARY APPORTIONMENT SYSTEMS

6.3.1 The Asset Factor under the Current CCCTB Directive Proposal

The asset factor is one factor of the three-factor sharing formula of the current CCCTB Directive Proposal. Like the labour factor, the asset factor represents the 'production side' of the group members' activities.[1079] The asset factor of each group member is the fraction between the assets of the group member (the numerator) and the assets of the whole group (the denominator). Each group member must calculate its own asset factor according to the current CCCTB Directive Proposal.[1080] The detailed rules of the asset factor are laid down in Articles 34 to 36 of the 2016 CCCTB Directive.[1081] Article 34 of the current CCCTB Directive Proposal provides the composition of the asset factor; Article 35 provides the allocation rule for items in the asset factor; Article 36 provides the valuation method for items in the asset factor.

6.3.1.1 The Composition of the Asset Factor: Article 34

Article 34 of the 2016 CCCTB Directive Proposal provides that:[1082]

> **Composition of the asset factor**
>
> 1. The asset factor shall consist of the average value of all fixed tangible assets owned, rented or leased by a group member as its numerator and the average value of all fixed tangible assets owned, rented or leased by the group as its denominator.
> 2. In the five years that follow a taxpayer's entry into an existing or new group, its asset factor shall also include the total amount of costs incurred for research, development, marketing and advertising by the taxpayer over the six years that preceded its entry into the group.

1079. *See* the Commission's CCCTB Working Document No. 60, paragraph 48.
1080. The apportioned tax base is apportioned to each group member first, not directly to a Member State. Therefore, all the items in the weighting factors need to be allocated to one group member, and one item cannot be counted twice by two group members within the same group.
1081. It is comparable to Articles 92 through 94 of the 2011 CCCTB Directive Proposal.
1082. It is identical to Article 92 of the 2011 CCCTB Directive Proposal.

The asset factor is the fraction of the 'fixed tangible assets'[1083] 'owned, rented or leased' by a group member to the fixed tangible assets 'owned, rented or leased' by the whole group. Since the asset factor includes only 'fixed tangible assets', the stock or inventories are not included in the asset factor.[1084] In my view, to exclude inventories from the asset factor is justified under the tax-neutrality framework, not only due to concerns about 'manipulation/tax avoidance'[1085] but also due to the fact that inventories are no longer representing the production process as the input side. Inventories are more representative of the output/market side because they are ready to be sold and become the response to the market.

Article 34(1) of the 2016 CCCTB Directive Proposal also expressly excludes intangible assets from the asset factor. The underlying reason is anti-avoidance or anti-manipulation.[1086] According to the European Commission's preparation work on the CCCTB, intangibles have a mobile feature and ownership of intangibles seems to be easily transferable. Especially in combination with the tax-free intra-group asset transfer rule under the CCCTB,[1087] intangibles are easily manipulated and shifted to change the composition of the asset factor. The European Commission also reiterates exclusion of intangibles from the asset factor in Preamble (10)[1088] of the 2016 CCCTB Directive Proposal.

However, Article 34(2) provides one exception to the main rule of excluding intangibles: in the five years that follow a taxpayer's entry into an existing or new

---

1083. The fixed assets are defined by Article 4(19) of the 2016 CCCTB Directive Proposal. Article 4(14) of the 2011 CCCTB Directive Proposal provides that '"fixed assets" means all tangible assets acquired for value or created by the taxpayer and all intangible assets acquired for value where they are capable of being valued independently and are used in the business in the production, maintenance or securing of income for more than 12 months, except where the cost of their acquisition, construction or improvement are less than EUR 1,000. Fixed assets shall also include financial assets.'

1084. The underlying reason of excluding stocks and inventories of goods from the asset factor is the anti-avoidance concern from the experiences of the USA. This is the majority opinion of the experts in the CCCTB working group. *See* the CCCTB Working Document No. 60, paragraphs 30-31, 65 and CCCTB Working Document No. 64, paragraph 61.

Theoretically speaking, the stocks/inventories represent a very important part for some sectors, such as trading companies, and it seems still logical to include inventories. However, the European Commission decided not to include inventories in the asset factor. The reason is that inclusion of these stocks/inventories is prone to manipulation. According to the working document, stocks and inventories are quite mobile. If the stocks and inventories can be included in the asset factor, the taxpayer can establish a warehouse in a low-tax Member State and easily shift part of the tax base by increasing the warehouse's asset factor. This concern is incorporated by Article 34 because only 'fixed tangible assets' are included in the asset factor, and the inventories/stocks that have the mobile feature are excluded from the asset factor. The tax avoidance scenario of setting up a warehouse in a specific Member State to manipulate the asset factor is already addressed in Article 34.

1085. Hellerstein, *supra* n. 971.

1086. Preamble (10) of the 2016 CCCTB Directive. *See* the European Commission CCCTB Working Document No. 47, paragraphs 16, 17.

1087. *See* Article 59 of the 2016 CCCTB Directive Proposal.

1088. Preamble (10) of the 2016 CCCTB Directive Proposal. It is also comparable to Preamble (21) of the 2011 CCCTB Directive Proposal, which provides 'the asset factor should consist of all fixed tangible assets. Intangibles and financial assets should be excluded from the formula due to their mobile nature and the risks of circumventing the system.' There is a clear anti-avoidance concern over the sharing formula rules.

group, its asset factor shall also include 'the total amount of costs incurred for research, development, marketing and advertising by the taxpayer, over the six years that preceded its entry into the group'. In short, Article 34(2) accepts a special type of intangibles in the form of 'research, development, marketing and advertising' costs, to be included for a specific period of time.

The underlying reason for Article 34(2)'s last sentence is to balance the possible fiscal revenue decrease of the Member States where the expenses of the self-generated intangibles are incurred.[1089] After adopting the CCCTB Directive, the income earned from these self-generated intangibles is shared with the whole group by the formula, and all Member States involved also share taxing power on the income. The Member States where the self-generated intangibles are incurred often have provided tax relief or innovation promotion measures for taxpayers previously creating intangibles. Therefore, to counterbalance the possible negative impact from sharing the taxing rights due to adopting the CCCTB, the costs of research, development, marketing, and advertising shall be added back to the asset factor of the group member who originally incurred the costs.

The reason for 'protecting the Member States' fiscal interests' has been repeatedly raised in the working documents and also reflected in several provisions in the current CCCTB Directive Proposal. Regarding the 'costs of research, development, marketing, and advertising,' the provisions of Article 20[1090] are symmetrical to Article 34 at the tax base level. Article 20 deals with the consolidated tax base if self-generated intangibles leave the group; Article 34 deals with calculation of the intangibles in the asset factor. Both provisions use the 'costs of research, development, marketing, and advertising' as a proxy to decide the value of the (future) profit-making intangibles.

Articles 20 and 34 both demonstrate the underlying assumption that the Member States have provided public benefits to support the creation of self-generated intangibles. Therefore, although the European Commission does not directly recognize the necessity of including some intangibles in the asset factor, the underlying rationale of Articles 20 and 34 is already implicitly consistent with the tax-neutrality framework. As to intangibles, I further elaborate on this in section 6.4.

1089. *See* the European Commission's discussion room document, Workshop on the CCCTB (Common Consolidated Corporate Tax Base): Business Reorganization in the CCCTB, Room Document No. 2, paragraph 8, 20 October 2010.

1090. Article 20 of 2016 CCCTB Directive Proposal provides that:

Self-generated intangible assets

> Where a taxpayer which is the economic owner of one or more self-generated intangible assets leaves the group, an amount equal to the costs incurred in respect of those assets for research, development, marketing and advertising in the previous five years shall be added to the consolidated tax base of the remaining group members. The amount added shall not, however, exceed the value of the assets on the departure of the taxpayer from the group. Those costs shall be attributed to the leaving taxpayer and shall be treated in accordance with national corporate tax law that subsequently becomes applicable to the taxpayer or, if it joins another group, those costs shall be attributed in the tax year that the taxpayer joined that other group.

It is comparable to Article 68 of the 2011 CCCTB Directive Proposal.

6.3.1.2 Intra-Group Shift of Assets: Article 36(5)

The CCCTB Working Group has considered concerns about anti-avoidance[1091] while drafting the asset factor provision. Article 36(5) is a special anti-avoidance rule against manipulating the asset factor by an intra-group asset transfer.

Article 36(5) provides:

> An asset sold by a group member to a person outside the group following an intra-group transfer in the same or the previous tax year shall be included in the asset factor of the transferring group member for the period between the intra-group transfer and the sale to the person outside the group, except where the group members concerned demonstrate that the intra-group transfer was made for genuine commercial reasons.

Article 36(5) is an adjustment rule for attributing an asset if the asset is sold outside the group to manipulate group members' asset factor. It is an anti-avoidance rule. Such tax avoidance scenarios of manipulating the asset factor can be conducted via a prior intra-group asset transfer because the intra-group transaction is tax-free under the CCCTB Directive Proposal. For example, an asset is owned originally by group member A and was transferred to another group member B on 1 January of Year 1. After holding the asset for one year, B sells the asset outside the group on 1 January of Year 2. If there is no Article 36(5), the asset will be included in B's asset factor for the period between the intra-group asset transfer and the sale of the asset outside the group, i.e., the whole year of Year 1. In Year 1, B would be entitled to include the asset's value in its asset factor.

Without Article 36(5), A's asset factor will decrease, and B's asset factor will increase after the intra-group asset transfer. In combination with the sale of the asset outside the group and the realization of the hidden reserves afterward, although the profits arising from realized hidden reserves are still apportioned to all group members, B has an increased asset factor and thus can be apportioned a larger consolidated tax base. B may have a strong incentive to increase its asset factor when B is in a low-tax-rate Member State or B has a significant amount of pre-consolidation losses and wants to accelerate offsetting these losses.[1092]

The tax avoidance scenario of manipulating the asset factor via the asset transfer will be combated after applying Article 36(5). Article 36(5) will adjust the asset factor of the group members if the asset is sold outside the group very soon, i.e., in the same year or within one year after the intra-group asset transfer. However, if the asset is sold outside of the group after two years of the intra-group asset transfer, Article 36(5) will not apply, and the GAAR will not apply either. The one-year requirement of Article 36(5) is specific. As long as a taxpayer complies with this time restriction, its transaction of an asset following the intra-group asset transfer is legitimate.

1091. CCCTB Working Document No. 64, paragraphs 41-42.
1092. This strategy is elaborated at Chen, *supra* n. 82.

6.3.1.3 *Remarks: Complete Exclusion of Intangibles Is Not Justified*

As to the treatment of intangibles in the asset factor, the reason for their exclusion from the asset factor is also based on anti-avoidance. Intangibles seem to have a mobile nature and thus are prone to manipulation because it feels easy to set up the owner of the intangibles on paper easily. This feeling is not completely correct.

As to intangibles, such as self-generated intangibles like patent or trademark rights, they are not as mobile as we imagine, and they are very difficult to valuate within a comparable market. The main reason to exclude self-generated intangibles is out of the administrative difficulty they pose when it comes to valuating and allocating them to a specific group member. Moreover, they are (claimed to be) prone to manipulation because the taxpayer can claim these intangibles arbitrarily.

To sum up, excluding intangibles from the asset factor is not theoretically justified when intangibles contribute to the taxpayer's production process. Many intangibles are the consequence of self-produced efficiency (such as creating a new technology) or protected innovation result (such as a patent), so they are consistent with the fundamental rationale of the asset factor. From the perspective of the benefit-based MN principle, to generate intangibles would involve an environment that promotes knowledge-creation and sharing; such environment would accommodate knowledgeable workers, a culture of promoting innovation, and a good education system. Such innovation-promoting environment is a type of public benefit, and intangibles are a proxy to reflect such benefit. Such proxy does not overlap with the labour factor, which represents directly the human resources that taxpayers mobilize. Therefore, neglecting intangibles would neglect an important aspect in the production process which intangibles represent: efficient productivity.

6.3.2 The Multistate Tax Commission's Property Factor in the US

The MTC's Allocation and Apportionment Regulation IV (MTC Regulation IV) recommends a three-factor formula for apportioning multistate business income of a unitary business: the property factor, the payroll factor, and the sales factor. The property factor is comparable to the asset factor of the CCCTB Directive. Sections 10 through 12 MTC Regulation IV lay down the rules of the property factor. Section 10 provides the composition and the general rule of the property factor. Section 11 provides the general valuation rule, and section 12 provides the special valuation rule for properties that have substantial price fluctuations.

Section 10(a) MTC Regulation IV provides that the property factor includes all real and tangible personal property owned or rented by the taxpayer and used during the tax period in the regular course of the trade of business. Real and tangible personal property includes land, buildings, machinery, stock of goods, equipment, and other real and tangible properties but excludes coin or currency. It should be noted that 'intangibles' are not included in the property factor according to section 10.

There is a special item that is included in the property factor and mentioned in section 11(a): 'the capitalized intangible drilling and development costs'. Intangible drilling and development costs are expenses incurred especially in the oil and gas industry, but after being capitalized, they are regarded as a special intangible and shall be included in the property factor.[1093]

As to the composition of the asset factor, the treatment of inventories is different in the CCCTB and MTC Regulation IV. Under the CCCTB, inventories are excluded from the asset factor as discussed above. On the contrary, the asset factor of the MTC formula does not exclude inventories. As to the inventory of stock of goods and the property acquired by gift or inheritance, they both are still included in the property factor and valued according to federal tax law purposes.[1094] Inclusion of inventories would not be consistent with the tax-neutrality framework, and thus the current CCCTB Directive Proposal has corrected this mistake.

6.4 THE TANGIBLE ASSETS SHOULD BE ATTRIBUTED TO THE UTILIZATION LOCATION AND VALUED BASED ON COSTS

As to attributing tangible assets, there are several criteria under discussion. These criteria can be categorized under two categories: 'who' is making use of or owns the asset and 'where' the asset is being used.

In these two categories, the criteria of attributing an asset include three main indicators: ownership, effective usership, and utilization of the physical location. The CCCTB Directive Proposal has used a hybrid criterion, consisting of 'economic owner and effective user,' from the first category. On the contrary, the MTC/UDITPA uses the utilization location as the attribution criterion, which is based on the second category.

In my view, according to the benefit-based MN framework, the asset attribution rule should be 'attributing the asset to where it is used in the production process' because it corresponds to the public benefit of the environment with material resources in the jurisdiction. Ownership, whether legal ownership or economic ownership, cannot represent the public benefit that justifies the asset factor in the formula. Therefore, the attribution rule of the asset factor in the current CCCTB Directive Proposal is not market neutral, and such un-neutrality becomes quite apparent even when it comes to real estate, as elaborated in section 6.4.3.

1093. The criticism to MTC's design on the intangible drilling and development costs in the early literature, Steven S Bronson, Treatment of Expensed Intangible Drilling and Development Costs for Purposes of the Property Factor of the Multistate Tax Commission's Apportionment Formula, The Urban Lawyer 224 (1978). Bronson argues that it does not satisfy the need to deviate from the standard property factor to include these costs for taxing the oil and gas industry. Bronson also argued that the property factor should not include any intangible items, and the wells will later appear in the property factor. The same criticism, *see* Eugene F Corrigan, The IDC Property Factor Myth, 5 Journal of State Taxation 191 (1986).

1094. The relevant provisions in IRC, *see* 26 CFR 1.471-2 - Valuation of inventories.

6.4.1 The Current CCCTB Directive Proposal's Attribution Rule: The Hybrid of Economic Ownership and User

6.4.1.1 The Main Allocation Rule of the Asset Factor: To the 'economic owner'

Article 35 of the 2016 CCCTB Directive Proposal[1095] is the allocation rule for the asset factor. It heavily depends on the 'economic owner' as the main criterion of attribution, and the text reads:

> **Allocation of assets**
>
> 1. Without prejudice to Article 22(2) and (3), an asset shall be included in the asset factor of its economic owner. Where the economic owner cannot be identified, the asset shall be included in the asset factor of the legal owner.
>   However, an asset that is not effectively used by its economic owner shall be included in the factor of the group member that effectively uses that asset, provided that the asset represents more than 5% of the value for tax purposes of all fixed tangible assets of the group member that effectively uses it.
> 2. Except in the case of leases between group members, leased assets shall be included in the asset factor of the group member that is the lessor or the lessee of the asset. The same shall apply to rented assets.

Article 35(1) refers to 'economic owner,' and the definition of 'economic owner' is regulated in Article 4(28) of the 2016 CCTB Directive Proposal as 'the person who has substantially all the benefits and risks attached to a fixed asset, regardless of whether a person is a legal owner. A taxpayer who has the right to possess, use and dispose of a fixed asset and bears the risk of its loss or destruction shall in any event be considered the economic owner.'

The definition of economic owner is the counterpart of the concept of 'legal owner,' but the current CCCTB Directive Proposal does not define legal owner.[1096] As to allocating the asset, if the economic owner cannot be identified, the asset shall be included in the asset factor of the 'legal owner.'

Article 35(1) further provides: if the asset is not effectively used by the economic owner, the asset shall be included in the asset factor of the group member which effectively uses the asset. However, the rule of allocating assets to the effective user shall apply only if the assets represent '5% of the value for tax purposes of all fixed tangible assets of the group member that effectively uses the asset.' This 5% requirement precludes the situation where the asset user only randomly or ad hoc uses the asset owned by another economic owner. This is an adjustment rule.

The threshold of attributing to the effective user is more than 5% of the effective user's total fixed tangible assets. Without reaching this threshold, the asset user cannot

1095. It is comparable to Article 93 of the 2011 CCCTB Directive Proposal.
1096. The definition of the legal owner and economic owner of a leased asset may be further defined by the delegated acts by the European Commission, according to the Preamble (19) of the 2016 CCTB Directive Proposal, based on Article 290 of the TFEU.

include the asset in question in the asset factor. Therefore, the 5% threshold of Article 35(1) also has an implicit anti-avoidance function.

6.4.1.2 Leased Assets: Only One Group Member Who Actually Uses the Leased Asset Is Attributed

Article 35(2) provides that in the case of a non-intra-group lease, the group member which is either the lessor or lessee can include the leased assets in its asset factor. Article 35(2) treats intra-group asset leases and non-intra-group asset leases differently. In the case of an intra-group lease, the lessee member gets the asset; in the case of a non-intra-group lease, all leased assets can be included, regardless of whether the group member is a lessor or a lessee.

Furthermore, if a specific asset is leased between two group members, the lease contract is regarded as non-existent for CCCTB purposes, according to Article 9 of the 2016 CCCTB Directive Proposal. Although intra-group leases are regarded as eliminated, the leased asset still must be allocated to one group member. One asset cannot be counted twice in an intra-group arrangement. In this case, Article 35(1) still applies, i.e., the effective user of the asset and the 5% rule will prevail. In short, one single asset should not be counted twice in different group members' asset factors in an intra-group lease.[1097]

In the case of a lease, to decide the leased asset's economic owner under the current CCCTB Directive Proposal, it seems reasonable to consider the distinction provided by the internationally recognized International Financial Reporting Standards (IFRS)[1098] between financial/capital lease and operating lease before 2016,[1099] since the IFRS is regarded as an important starting point and the source for interpreting the current CCCTB Directive Proposal. The formulation of Article 4(28) of the 2016 CCTB Directive Proposal also significantly resembles the formulation in the IFRS regarding financial lease, as Article 4(28) of the 2016 CCTB Directive Proposal refers to 'benefits and risks' attached to the asset.

According to the old rules (International Accounting Standard (IAS) 17), IFRS treats 'a financial/capital lease' and 'operating lease' differently, and this difference will also influence the qualification of the economic owner. According to IAS 17, in the case of a financial/capital lease, the economic owner is the lessee because risks and rewards incidental to ownership of the leased asset are already transferred to the

1097. CCCTB Directive Proposal Article 36 (4); CCCTB Working Document No. 60, paragraphs 39-40.

1098. IFRS is the starting point for the CCCTB and is especially useful for the fundamental concepts and the types of assets. For the same opinion, *see* Iida Jaatinen, IAS/IFRS: A Starting Point for the CCCTB?, 40 Intertax 260 (2012); PHJ Essers & R Russo, *The Precious Relationship Between IAS/IFRS, National Tax Accounting Systems and the CCCTB* (Kluwer Law International 2009). PHJ Essers (ed.), The Influence of IAS/IFRS on the CCCTB, Tax Accounting, Disclosure and Corporate Law Accounting Concepts: A Clash of Cultures (Wolters Kluwer Law & Business 2009).

1099. Leases are regulated by IAS 17 Leases, available at http://ec.europa.eu/internal_market/accounting/docs/consolidated/ias17_en.pdf. It should be noted that IFRS 16 now is different from IAS 17.

lessee; whereas in the case of an operating lease, the economic owner is still the lessor because risks and rewards incidental to ownership are not transferred (and remain). Therefore, the lessor in an operating lease will maintain economic ownership. The distinction between a financial lease and a capital lease is more significant in the case of an intra-group lease. For the non-intra-group lease, the difference is less important because the group member can include the leased asset anyway, as long as it is a lessor or a lessee.

It should be noted that after the new IFRS 16 was adopted and replaced IAS 17 in 2016, there is no distinction between a 'financial/capital lease' and an 'operating lease'. IFRS 16 focuses on the 'right of use' instead of the 'benefit and risk' criterion of IAS 17.[1100] In the context of the asset factor, the implication of IFRS 16 is compatible with the benefit-based MN framework: when it comes to the asset, utilization plays the key role, not the 'economic owner'.

To sum up, under the current CCCTB Directive Proposal, attributing the asset to the effective user is consistent with the underlying theory of the asset factor in the sharing formula. The asset factor should represent the production side of the taxpayer, and thus the asset factor shall include assets that are effectively used and function to create products for the market. Most of the time, the economic owner, the legal owner, and the effective user refer to the same group member.

When there is a divergence between these three roles, allocating the asset to the effective user is the most rational solution. The current CCCTB Directive Proposal's attribution approach still has a problem, namely that sometimes the economic owner and the effective user can be two different group members. Moreover, the current CCCTB Directive Proposal strictly embraces an 'all-or-nothing' approach and that 'one asset cannot be counted twice' but neglects that the utilization location of an asset can play a role in the production process. These are problems that the EU's FA regime in the future should eliminate.

6.4.2 The Multistate Tax Commission's Property Factor: The Assets Attribution Rule Based on Utilization

Section 10(b) UDITPA lays down the most important fundamental principle for the property factor. Property shall be included in the property factor if it is used or is available for or capable of being used during the tax period in the regular course of the taxpayer's trade and business. Property or equipment 'under construction' shall be excluded in principle because they are not 'used' in the regular course of the taxpayer's trade and business unless such property under construction also constitutes 'inventoriable goods in process'. If such property under construction is still used in the regular course of the taxpayer's trade and business, it is includable in the property factor to the extent that it is being used.

1100. The introduction of IFRS 16, Marian Săcărin, IFRS 16 'Leases'–Consequences on the Financial Statements and Financial Indicators, 15 The Audit Financial Journal 114 (2017).

Section 10(c) UDITPA provides that there must be consistency in reporting the property factor. This applies when there are differences regarding the valuation of a property in a state taxation law. Such consistency requirement should ensure 'year-to-year consistency' and 'state-to-state consistency' in the tax return. The taxpayer shall disclose the modification if it includes, excludes, or changes the manner of valuation of the property; if the manner of valuation, inclusion, or exclusion of the property is not uniform under Article IV of the Multistate Tax Compact and the UDITPA, the taxpayer shall also disclose its variance of reporting to the state. Such consistency requirement is for the existing diversities between states that are not unified by the Multistate Tax Compact and the UDITPA. The taxpayer shall not take advantage of such diversities and is obliged to disclose to the state tax authorities.

Section 10(d) UDITPA provides the rules of calculating the numerator of the property factor. First, all the real and tangible personal property owned or rented by the taxpayer and used within the state in the regular course of trade or business of the taxpayer should be included in the property factor of that state. The property which is physically located within a state can be included in that state's property factor. These properties need to be calculated as the average value.

There is a clear difference in section 10(d) MTC Regulation IV: the location of the property is the key criterion for the inclusion of the numerator. Only properties within the state are includable. The reason for this is that MTC Regulation IV apportions the tax base 'to the state', unlike the CCCTB Directive Proposal, which apportions the tax base 'to the group member'. So, under the CCCTB, even if a property is not located within the same Member State as the economic owner, such property can still be included in the group member as the economic owner. Such a difference may raise some questions, especially regarding the calculation of real estate in the property/asset factor.

Moreover, in section 10(d) MTC Regulation IV, the 'property in transit' between the seller and buyer should be included in the property factor of the state of destination. Moreover, mobile and movable property, such as construction equipment, trucks, or leased electronic equipment that are located within and outside of the state, shall be calculated according to the period of their stay within the state. Therefore, an automobile assigned to traveling employees should be included in the property of the state 'of which the employee's compensation is assigned under the payroll factor' or the state 'in which the automobile is licensed'.

Section 10(d) reveals two difficulties and provides specific rules when calculating the numerator of the property factor. One difficulty is to trace a 'property in transit'. It provides that the property in transit shall be included in the numerator of the property factor of the state of destination. Another difficulty is that in the transportation industry, it is not easy to decide the location of automobiles. Section 10(d) provides two options for taxpayers, of which the employee's compensation is assigned under the 'payroll factor' or the state 'in which the automobile is licensed'.

It is not uncommon that the criterion of the property factor is dependent on another weighting factor in the formula. From the perspective of the supply side/input side theory, since both the payroll factor and the property factor represent the supply side of the taxpayer's economic activities in the market, borrowing the rules from the payroll factor to calculate the property factor in some difficult case seems logical because both payroll and the property are from the input side. The issue of attributing automobiles is also regulated by another MTC special industry formula for apportionment, which I discuss in Chapter 7.

6.4.3 Why Utilization Should Prevail over Ownership for Attributing Assets?

6.4.3.1 Utilization Represents the Resources in the Environment

The market-neutral attribution rule for the asset factor should be based on where the asset (including both tangible and intangible) is utilized and performs its function, not based on 'ownership', regardless of economic ownership or legal ownership or any type of variation because adopting the ownership concept as the attribution criterion would directly invite the possibility of disconnecting utilization and ownership. Such disconnection is directly contrary to the fundamental rationale of the asset factor: representing the production side of the activity.

Therefore, the 2016 CCCTB Directive Proposal's main attribution rule of 'attributing to the group member as the economic owner' as the main rule is not appropriate. As a consequence, it is possible that the real estate can be attributed to the 'foreign' economic owner which is located in another location other than the real estate's location. Such attribution result is not only counter-intuitive but also conflicts with the economic reality: it is a widely accepted consensus that the situs state has the closest economic link with the real estate.[1101]

Although the 2016 CCCTB Directive Proposal further provides supplementary attribution rules to legal owner or the effective user of the asset when the economic owner is not identified or the effective user holds more than 5% of the assets, these attribution rules cannot correct the non-neutral result.

In this regard, the MTC formula adopts the attribution to the states approach as its starting point. Furthermore, for tangible assets and real estate, the physical location is the key criterion of attribution. Disconnecting the physical location and the asset fact attribution is the fundamental difference between the current CCCTB Directive Proposal and the MTC.

6.4.3.2 Economic Ownership and Legal Ownership Are Redundant: The Real Estate Example

An obvious problem in the asset factor of the current CCCTB Directive Proposal is the disconnection between where the assets are utilized for production. The attribution rule is mainly based on the 'economic ownership' and the legal owner and the effective user as the supplementary rule. However, the attribution rule is based on 'ownership'

1101. The same remarks, *see* H Vermeulen & MFA Blaauw, The Tax Treatment of Directly Held Real Estate under the Proposed CCCTB Directive, 51 European Taxation (2011).

regardless of the type of ownership concept,[1102] which would create an unreasonable result even when attributing real estate.

As indicated above, the unreasonable result of attributing 'real estate' under the current CCCTB Directive Proposal has been criticized.[1103] Relying on the concept of 'economic ownership' still can make the attribution result of a real estate different from its physical and geographical location when the owner is a foreign company outside the real estate's situs jurisdiction. In the international tax law regime, the situs of real estate is still significant and is embodied in Article 6 of the OECD Model Convention.[1104] The situs is the most straightforward and reasonable attribution rule for real estate because the situs state has the closest economic link.

Vermeulen and Blaauw observe that the CCCTB Directive Proposal abandons *the situs principle* for attributing real estate, which might result in the Member States where real estate is located apportioning nothing from the asset factor because the CCCTB Directive Proposal embraces economic/legal ownership as the main rule. Vermeulen and Blaauw observed that such unreasonable result is partially due to the 2011 CCCTB Directive Proposal's nexus rule, so they suggest that a real estate property constitutes a deemed PE at its physical location state if it is owned by a real estate investment trust (REIT) company.[1105] Vermeulen and Blaauw's solution aims to reflect the situs state's fiscal interest and contribution. However, even there is a deemed PE from the real estate in the situs state, it is not always possible to claim that the deemed PE is the economic owner of the real estate; it is the REIT company that qualifies as the economic owner of the real estate.

In my view, to accept a deemed PE for real estate still does not escape the blind spot of attributing assets by 'ownership'. Moreover, the result of attributing real estate under Article 35 of the CCCTB Directive Proposal is just another convincing example that adopting a PE as nexus simply distorts the relationship between tax law and the economic reality.

1102. Martin Lagarden, Intangibles in a Transfer Pricing Context: Where Does the Road Lead, 21 International Transfer Pricing Journal (2014).

Lagarden has discussed four different types of 'ownership' concepts: legal ownership, contractual ownership, economic ownership, and beneficial ownership, that all can be used in the transfer pricing practice. He classifies 'legal ownership and contractual ownership' as 'judicial', whereas 'economic ownership and beneficial ownership' are not specifically related to a legal contract, so they are summarized as under the 'economic' perspective. In my view, these four concepts do not seem mutually exclusive but might be overlapping in the specific case. In the context of the asset factor of FA, neither of these ownership concepts is appropriate, though each of them might reflect part of economic reality from different viewpoints.

1103. Vermeulen & Blaauw, *supra* n. 1101.

1104. The current OECD Model Convention Article 6 has developed from different versions of drafts since 1923. *See* Jogarajan, *supra* n. 29, at 245. It is intriguing and surprising to see that, in early days around 1923, some experts and jurisdictions support attributing income from immovable property to taxpayer's residence because the prototype and the base case the immovable property provision is based on income from agricultural profits, *see* p. 23 and p. 80. Therefore, as the lesson of the history shows, it is not completely unthinkable to have a rule deviating from the situs principle. But in the CCCTB context as well as the international tax law regime, attributing immovable property to a jurisdiction other than the situs would be quite illogical.

1105. Vermeulen & Blaauw, *supra* n. 1101.

The economic owner and the actual user may sometimes coincide. The conceptual similarity arises because the asset factor represents the production activity side and the non-human resources mobilized by the taxpayer, so 'economic ownership' might look like an attractive criterion. But adopting the concept of (economic) ownership would add an unnecessary proxy to decide a specific asset's function. Creating a deemed PE for a real estate at the situs state or any rule lowering the PE threshold will not solve the problem of having an extra unnecessary proxy.

The current economic ownership-based attribution rule mentioned in the CCCTB Directive Proposal seems influenced by TP practice. It has the good intention of seeking the economic reality instead of legal formality. However, economic ownership focuses on taxpayers' risk-bearing or 'entitlements to profits earned' from the specific asset in the TP context but no longer represents the 'input' by making use of an asset in the production/service provision process.

In short, economic ownership is not suitable for attributing intangibles or tangible assets for the asset factor for the EU's FA regime because using 'ownership' as the attribution rule creates additional misalignment between the functions of the assets involved and the public benefits that the production process and the asset factor should represent. Therefore, the utilization location is the proper attribution criterion instead of legal ownership or economic ownership.

6.4.3.3 Out-Jurisdictional Assets?

Some assets inherently cannot be attributed to a physical location of any state jurisdiction; for example, satellites are orbiting in space. Satellites are high-value items in the telecommunications industry or television industry, but conceptually they are not performing their function in any state's jurisdiction, so they are classified as out-jurisdictional assets.[1106]

Disputes arise when a satellite is not within a state but is included in the asset factor's denominator. The asset factor ratio will become extremely small, which is a distortion for some tax authorities.[1107] To address this problem, the MTC adopts a special formula[1108] for the telecommunications industry to completely exclude satellites from the asset factor to address the distortion. However, from the perspective of

1106. Disputes on attributing satellites are actually not new and already took place in the 1980s in California, *see*, for example, *Communications Satellite Inc. v. Franchise Tax Board* (1984), 156 Cal. App.3d 726. Benjamin F Miller, Current Problems with UDITPA and Possible Solutions, 38 State Tax Notes (2005).

1107. Many telecommunication companies assert and argue that their sales factor numerator in their apportionment formula in California is zero, so California has no taxing right to apportion its taxable income. Such disputes result from the special feature of the telecommunication industry because it engages in many out-of-state facilities and services. Without a special formula, the apportionment result may be unfair and distortive because the standard formula cannot reflect the economic business activities in this industry. Therefore, MTC Regulation adopts a separate formula for the telecommunication industry in MTC Regulation IV Article IV 18(i). *See* Miller, *supra* n. 1106.

1108. MTC Reg. IV 18(i). Special Rules: Telecommunications and ancillary service providers (adopted July 31, 2008).

utilization of the asset, it would be more logical to divide the satellite among all jurisdictions on earth which the transmitted signals cover. The satellite is like a common asset shared and used by multiple jurisdictions but not the 'whole world'. In my view, it is not market neutral to exclude such high-value and important assets; the economic reality should prevail over the concerns about the administrative costs.

6.4.4 Valuation of Tangible Assets

6.4.4.1 Valuation of Assets: Market Value or Cost-Based Value?

The valuation of an asset is a difficult issue,[1109] and the difficulty in valuation is the Achilles heel of the asset factor because there is no single perfect valuation method. Understanding of the nature of the asset factor also influences the valuation method. In the early discussion, the Working Group demonstrated two different approaches to valuating the asset factor:[1110] one regards an asset as a 'flow' concept, the other regards an asset as a 'stock' concept. The flow asset concept takes into account the 'flow of capitals' when valuating the asset. Therefore, the valuation of a specific asset should be equal to the 'economic depreciation plus the financial cost of capital', i.e., the value that can be reflected by the market value. This stock asset concept, on the contrary, regards an asset as a stable status. Therefore, the value of an asset in the sharing formula is the same as the tax book value.[1111]

The 2016 CCCTB Directive Proposal[1112] and the MTC Formula both adopt the original cost method to valuate land and buildings and non-depreciable fixed tangible

The hearing officer's report Sheldon H Laskin, Report of the Hearing Officer Regarding Proposed Model Regulation for Apportionment of Income from the Sale of Telecommunications and Ancillary Services, April 2008.

1109. European Commission CCCTB Working Document No. 47, paragraphs 16-17.
1110. CCCTB Working Document No. 52, paragraph. 32.
1111. CCCTB Working Document No. 47, paragraph 16.
1112. Article 36 of the 2016 CCCTB Directive Proposal provides:

Valuation

1. Land and other non-depreciable fixed tangible assets shall be valued at their original cost.
2. An individually depreciable fixed tangible asset shall be valued at the average of its value for tax purposes at the beginning and at the end of a tax year.

   Where, as a result of one or more intra-group transactions, an individually depreciable fixed tangible asset is included in the asset factor of a group member for less than a tax year, the value to be taken into account shall be calculated with regard to the number of months that the asset was included in the asset factor of that group member.
3. The pool of fixed assets, as referred to in Article 37 of Directive 2016/xx/EU, shall be valued at the average of its value for tax purposes at the beginning and at the end of a tax year.
4. The renter or lessee of an asset of which it is not the economic owner shall value that rented or leased asset at eight times the net annual rental or lease payment due, less any amounts receivable from sub-rentals or sub-leases.

   A group member renting out or leasing an asset of which it is not its economic owner shall value that rented or leased asset at eight times the net annual rental or lease payment due.

assets. As to other depreciable tangibles, the current CCCTB Directive Proposal adopts the valuation method of the average value at the tax year's beginning and end.

Ideally, seeking a fair market value of a specific asset is not impossible. Still, it involves too many sophisticated considerations to ascertain the asset's 'fair value' while being utilized for the production process, including some estimate of future events. To avoid the burden and complexities like TP practice, the current CCCTB Directive Proposal adopts the origin cost approach. I endorse this approach because it reflects the historical aspect of the asset in use.

From the perspective of the production process, the asset factor should be valued from the original cost, not the market value. The assets' original costs (including purchase costs and maintenance costs) are the MNE taxpayer's investment to conduct production or service activities. Thus, these investments represent the taxpayer's ability to control and use these assets as the input.

The European Commission admits that the tax book value might not be the most precise approach, but it might be the most feasible approach to administration. Article 36[1113] of the 2016 CCCTB Directive Proposal incorporates both approaches. As to non-depreciable assets, they are valued as the original costs. As to individually depreciable fixed tangible assets and the pool of fixed assets, they are valued at the average value for tax purposes at the beginning and the end of the year. Although the tax book value is the main criterion, Article 36(2)'s average value method represents the 'flow' feature of a depreciable fixed asset. It considers fluctuations in value by calculating the average value of the whole year.

Although it is not clearly defined in the current CCCTB Directive Proposal, the 'original cost' is to be decided by the historical cost when these non-depreciable fixed tangible assets are acquired from the non-related seller outside the group. The intra-group asset transfer will be regarded as non-existent for tax purpose under Article 9 of the 2016 CCCTB Directive Proposal. Therefore, if an asset is acquired from another group member, the intra-group purchase price is not the 'original cost' and is already consolidated, and thus it represents the asset's adding-up value.

According to Article 36(1) of the CCCTB Directive Proposal, land and other non-depreciable fixed tangible assets are to be valued at their 'original cost'. The original cost is to be determined without depreciation. Otherwise, a fully depreciated asset cannot be included in the asset factor.[1114]

---

5. An asset sold by a group member to a person outside the group following an intra-group transfer in the same or the previous tax year shall be included in the asset factor of the transferring group member for the period between the intra-group transfer and the sale to the person outside the group, except where the group members concerned demonstrate that the intra-group transfer was made for genuine commercial reasons.

1113. It is comparable to Article 94 of the 2011 CCCTB Directive Proposal.
1114. CCCTB Working Document No. 64, paragraph 62.

6.4.4.2 *The Special Valuation Rule for Price Fluctuation: The Eight Times Rule*

As to rented assets, both the 2016 CCCTB Directive Proposal[1115] and the MTC/UDITPA formula[1116] adopt an adjusted valuation method: the rented assets are valued as 'eight times' of the value of the 'net annual rental or lease payment due'. US experiences directly influence the current CCCTB Directive Proposal; although neither the CCCTB working documents nor the MTC Regulation IV expressly indicates any specific empirical evidence how and why 'eight times of the value' is decided.

Moreover, when calculating the net annual rental or lease payment due, it is necessary to exclude 'any amounts receivable from sub-rental or sub-leases'. To exclude sub-rentals and sub-leases is to reflect precisely the value of the property used for production because the receivables of sub-rentals or sub-leases are not directly related to the production activities. Such exclusion of sub-rentals and sub-leases is consistent with the theory of the asset factor.

6.5 RETHINKING INTANGIBLES AS PART OF THE INPUT SIDE ACTIVITY

6.5.1 What Intangibles Can Be Included in the Asset Factor of the Formula?

For the asset factor of the standard formula, not including intangibles is not compatible with the benefit-based MN framework. So, the next step would be deciding what intangibles should be included.

1115. 2016 CCCTB Directive Proposal Article 36 (4).

1116. Section 11 of UDITPA provides the rules of valuation. As to the owned property, section 11(a) provides that it shall be valued at its original cost. The definition of 'the original cost' is the cost of the property 'for federal income tax purposes' (prior to any federal adjustments) at the time of acquisition by the taxpayer and adjusted by subsequent capital additions or improvements and partial disposition due to sale, exchange, abandonment, etc. If the original costs are uncertain, the fair market value of the date of acquisition is the deemed value of the property.

Section 11(b) UDITPA provides rules of valuation for rented property. The valuation of the rented properties is subject to a special rule: The value of the property rented by the taxpayer is valued at eight times its 'net annual rent rate'. The net annual rent rate is 'the annual rent rate' paid by the taxpayer less the aggregate annual sub-rental rates paid by the taxpayer's subtenants. The sub-rental rates are regarded as the income and thus deducted from the annual rent.

Calculating 'the annual rent rate' is based on the actual amount of annual rent collected and 'annualized', i.e., the amount divided over the tax period of 12 months. If the rental contract is longer than 12 months, it should only be calculated as 12 months; if the rental contract is less than 12 months, the annual rent rate should be calculated beyond the contract term. The 'annual rent rate' is a basis value and being averaged over the period of 12 months.

The annual rents of the asset exclude the following items: incidental day-to-day expenses, and royalties based on extraction of natural resources. These costs are excluded because they do not relate to the value of the rented property itself but relate to the taxpayer's activities. However, the improvement costs are included in the annual rent. The inclusion of improvement costs is logical because they help to maintain the value and the function of the rented property and thus should be reflected in the property factor.

Deciding what intangibles should be included in the asset factor is easy. Unlike tangible properties having a physical form, intangibles are created based on various legal relationships.[1117] These relationships create rights or non-right-status economic efficiencies or interests that MNE taxpayers could use to optimize further their input side (production/service provision) and develop their output side (customers' market). Intangibles, especially IP rights, involve innovation, effort, and design from individual human beings. The 'life circle'[1118] and 'value creation chain'[1119] of IP rights involve different stages of inputs and contributions from human beings.

It was almost impossible to define 'intangibles' in the international tax regime before the BEPS Action Plans.[1120] BEPS Action 8 still faces the challenge of defining and identifying intangibles as a type of asset or a bundled asset consisting of different relationships.[1121] Identification of an intangible itself is problematic when such intangible is not a specific legal right. Therefore, the definition of 'intangible' can vary in different contexts and is not generally defined in the context of TP. Currently, the OECD does not include 'financial asset' as an intangible in the discussion of BEPS.[1122] Intangibles under the OECD 2017 TP Guidelines are understood as all non-tangible assets but not including financial assets.

In other words, the context always matters for deciding the scope and definition of 'intangibles'. The justification for including intangibles in the asset factor is the public benefit of an environment promoting and encouraging innovation. Therefore, the intangibles in the asset factor should be IP rights because these IP rights represent the innovation and the environment promoting innovation. The asset factor should include both self-generated and purchased/licensed IP when they both contribute to the production process.

Under this rationale, the asset factor should not include 'goodwill'[1123] (although it is a well-known 'intangible') because goodwill is merely a calculated result of the 'difference between the aggregate value of an operating business and the sum of the values of all separately identifiable tangible and intangible assets,' according to Andreas Oestreicher; goodwill is neither self-generated nor purchased innovation efficiency or a resource that can contribute to the production process.[1124]

1117. In tax, law, accounting fields, intangibles refer to different concepts. *See* Winters & others, *supra* n. 1065.
1118. Anuschka Bakker & others, Increasing Importance of IP Rights, in Verlinden & Bakker (eds), *supra* n. 1065.
1119. *Ibid.*, Figure 1.1, reproduced from Figure 1.4 of WIPO, World Intellectual Property Report 2017: Intangible Capital in Global Value Chains, available at https://www.wipo.int/edocs/pubdocs/en/wipo_pub_944_2017.pdf.
1120. JS Wilkie, The Definition and Ownership of Intangibles: Inside the Box? Outside the Box? What Is the Box?, World Tax Journal (2012).
1121. JS Wilkie, Intangibles and Location Benefits (Customer Base), 68 Bulletin for International Taxation (2014).
1122. BEPS Action 8-10 Final Report, paragraph 6.6; JL Andrus & Richard Collier, *Transfer Pricing and the Arm's Length Principle after BEPS* (Oxford University Press 2017), at 6.53; Wilkie, *ibid.*
1123. Andreas Oestreicher, Transfer Pricing of Intangibles in Cases of Post-Merger Reorganization: Lessons from the Revised OECD Draft, 42 Intertax 509 (2014), at 512-513.
1124. Bakker & others, *supra* n. 1118, at 1.3.1.3.1.

Moreover, when no specific IP is being developed or improved, locational savings/location-specific advantages[1125] or group synergies should not be included in the asset factor either[1126] because locational savings do not represent taxpayers' innovation activities. In the TP literature, the reason to negate location savings as a type of intangible is that 'location savings are broad external environmental factors that cannot be controlled or owned by a taxpayer and cannot be the object of transactions'.[1127] 'Not being controlled/owned by the taxpayer' is different from the reason I recommend to exclude locational savings/location-specific advantages from the asset factor of the EU FA regime, though the results look similar.

Lastly, 'financial assets' are not included in the asset factor and should be separated from the IP rights discussions in this chapter. 'Financial assets' are mentioned in the 2016 CCTB Directive Proposal.[1128] Financial assets can also be classified as fixed assets for the purpose of calculating the tax base, but financial assets are not included in the asset factor of the formula. In other words, financial assets as such are not the same as IP rights. I agree with this approach because financial assets do not represent the innovation activities in the production process. Financial assets are not in line with the rationale of the asset factor of the standard formula. However, there should be special treatment of financial assets for the financial industry. Problems and treatment of financial assets under the CCCTB Directive Proposal are discussed in section 7.2.

1125. The same opinion, Wilkie, *supra* n. 1121.
1126. Bakker & others, *supra* n. 1118, at 1.3.1.3.2.
1127. *Ibid.*, at 1.3.1.3.1.
See also Jinyan Li & Stephen Ji, Location-Specific Advantages: A Rising Disruptive Factor in Transfer Pricing, 71 (5) Bulletin for International Taxation 259 (2017). Wilkie, *supra* n. 1121.
1128. 2016 CCTB Directive Proposal Article 4 (19):

> 'fixed assets' means tangible assets acquired for value or created by the taxpayer and intangible assets acquired for the value that is capable of being valued independently and that are used in the business for producing, maintaining, or securing income for more than 12 months, except where their acquisition or construction cost is less than EUR 1,000. Fixed assets shall also include financial assets, with the exception of financial assets held for trading in accordance with Article 21.

2016 CCTB Directive Proposal Article 4 (20):

> 'financial assets' means shares in, and loans to, associated enterprises as referred to in Article 56 of this Directive, participating interests as defined in Article 2(2) of Directive 2013/34/EU of the European Parliament and of the Council, loans to undertakings with which the taxpayer is linked by virtue of participating interests, investments held as fixed assets, other loans, and own shares to the extent that national law permits their being shown in the balance sheet;

6.5.2 Reflections on the 'functional analysis' for Intangibles

6.5.2.1 Seeking the Functions Which Represent Innovation

As indicated above, the market-neutral attribution rule for the asset factor is to attribute to where the asset is utilized. This rationale of attribution applies to both tangible and intangible assets. It is easier to decide tangible assets' utilization location because tangible assets have physical form. Ascertaining 'where intangibles are utilized', however, needs to rely on other proxies. A 'functional analysis' serves the need to search for where intangibles are used.

To decide on profits attribution of intangibles, the very first step of the analytical process of the OECD Transfer Pricing Guidelines[1129] and PE Guidelines[1130] is the 'functional and factual analysis'. Although the OECD Transfer Pricing Guidelines and PE Guidelines are designed based on the 'arm's length principle',[1131] the functions selected in the OECD Transfer Pricing Guidelines and PE Guidelines are still useful for designing the assets attribution rule for IP rights in the context of FA. It is because the post-BEPS OECD Guidelines already acknowledge the intertwined relationships between related parties in the same multinational group and accept a holistic approach to assessing assets, functions, and risks altogether,[1132] so the functional analysis developed by the OECD Transfer Pricing Guidelines and PE Guidelines still can be applied selectively to the asset factor of the EU's FA regime.

A typical functional analysis in the TP analysis starts with a comparison.[1133] It compares the controlled party's transactions with the uncontrolled party's transactions in the same industry and analyses the 'functions' involved. The basic underlying

---

1129. *OECD Transfer Pricing Guidelines for Multinational Enterprises and Tax Administrations*, different versions from 1995 until 2017, can be downloaded from https://www.oecd.org/ctp/transfer-pricing/resourcesfortransferpricing.htm.

1130. Regarding AOA, *see* https://www.oecd.org/tax/transfer-pricing/attributionofprofitstopermanentestablishments.htm.

About intangibles, OECD's PE guidelines especially involve discussions in the field of the banking industry. Kobetsky, *supra* n. 80, at Chapter 8, Intra-bank interest under the 2008 Report; Richard Collier & John Vella, Five Core Problems in the Attribution of Profits to Permanent Establishments, 11 World Tax Journal 159 (2019), at 2.2.4, regarding the financial sector.

As to the development of AOA and history, *see* Irene JJ Burgers, The New OECD Approach on Profit Allocation: A Step Forward Towards Neutral Treatment of Permanent Establishments and Subsidiaries, 10 Florida Tax Review 51 (2009). For early discussions on the banking industry and the PE issues, *see* IJJ Burgers, *Taxation and Supervision of Branches of International Banks: A Comparative Study of Banks and Other Enterprises* (IJJ Burgers 1991).

Oddleif Torvik, *Transfer Pricing and Intangibles: US and OECD Arm's Length Distribution of Operation Profits from IP Value Chains* (IBFD 2018), at Chapter 17 – The Allocation of Residual Profits to a Permanent Establishment and Chapter 25 – The Allocation of Residual Profits from Unique and Valuable IP to Permanent Establishments.

1131. Raffaele Petruzzi, The Arm's Length Principle: Between Legal Fiction and Economic Reality, in Lang & Storck, *supra* n. 20, at 16; OECD/G20 Base Erosion and Profit Shifting Project Aligning Transfer Pricing Outcomes with Value Creation, Actions 8-10: 2015 Final Reports, 1.162.

1132. Petruzzi, *ibid.*, 16; Andrus & Collier, *supra* n. 1122, at 4.07.

1133. Andrus & Collier, *supra* n. 1122, at 3.26-3.32.

assumption is the party where the more (significant) functions are performed, the more profits should be attributed to that party.

Functions include different business activities. For example, the 2010 OECD Transfer Pricing Guidelines[1134] have listed different functions for conducting a functional analysis, such as 'design, manufacturing, assembling, R&D, servicing, purchasing, distribution, marketing, advertising, transportation, financing and management'.

The OECD Permanent Establishment Guidelines (i.e., by AOA)[1135] also incorporate the step of functional analysis[1136] to decide the profits attributed to a PE, including profits from intangibles.[1137] Prior to 2010, the OECD had used 'key entrepreneurial

1134. Here, I cite the relevant paragraphs:D.1.2.2 Functional analysis

> 1.42 In transactions between two independent enterprises, compensation usually will reflect the functions that each enterprise performs (taking into account assets used and risks assumed). Therefore, in determining whether controlled and uncontrolled transactions or entities are comparable, a functional analysis is necessary. This functional analysis seeks to identify and compare the economically significant activities and responsibilities undertaken, assets used and risks assumed by the parties to the transactions. For this purpose, it may be helpful to understand the structure and organisation of the group and how they influence the context in which the taxpayer operates. It will also be relevant to determine the legal rights and obligations of the taxpayer in performing its functions.
>
> 1.43 The functions that taxpayers and tax administrations might need to identify and compare include, e.g., design, manufacturing, assembling, research and development, servicing, purchasing, distribution, marketing, advertising, transportation, financing and management. The principal functions performed by the party under examination should be identified. Adjustments should be made for any material differences from the functions undertaken by any independent enterprises with which that party is being compared. While one party may provide a large number of functions relative to that of the other party to the transaction, it is the economic significance of those functions in terms of their frequency, nature, and value to the respective parties to the transactions that is important.
>
> 1.44 The functional analysis should consider the type of assets used, such as plant and equipment, the use of valuable intangibles, financial assets, etc., and the nature of the assets used, such as the age, market value, location, property right protections available, etc.
>
> 1.45 Controlled and uncontrolled transactions and entities are not comparable if there are significant differences in the risks assumed for which appropriate adjustments cannot be made. Functional analysis is incomplete unless the material risks assumed by each party have been considered since the assumption or allocation of risks would influence the conditions of transactions between the associated enterprises. Usually, in the open market, the assumption of increased risk would also be compensated by an increase in the expected return, although the actual return may or may not increase depending on the degree to which the risks are realized.'

1135. Giammarco Cottani, Commissionaire Arrangements/Low Risk Distributors and Attribution of Profits to Permanent Establishments, in Lang & Storck, *supra* n. 20.

1136. Comparison between OECD and USA's approach and some historical background of attributing profits to PEs, *see* Torvik, *supra* n. 1130.

1137. *Ibid.*

Both transfer pricing Guidelines and PE Guidelines are implementing the ALP, though developing into divergent path. Deciding profit attribution to a PE, often involves business reconstructing that an asset is transferred from or to a PE from another group member. Before ascertaining the function and attribution of an asset, OECD's AOA approach would recognize the inter-group transaction between group members if there is one arrangement on the asset involved.

risk-taking (KERT) functions' as the criterion.[1138] In 2010, the OECD Permanent Establishment Guidelines renamed KERT functions and adopted the concept of significant people functions (SPF)[1139] to decide profits attributed to a PE. 'Risk control'[1140] is still the key indicator. In addition to personal functions, risks play a role in the functional analysis because risks are not only threats but also opportunities, and thus risk management is not merely about mitigating risk but also involves making use of strategic risk.[1141] The concept of SPF for the people who can take decisions emphasizes the concept of risk control in decision-making in the risk management process. SPF and risk are closely related but do not always coincide.

After the launch of the BEPS Project, the functional analysis has evolved to link 'function, asset, risk' more closely. As another example, according to the 2017 OECD Transfer Pricing Guidelines, the functional analysis is 'aimed at identifying the economically significant activities and responsibilities undertaken, assets used or contributed, and risks assumed by the parties to the transactions'. The functional analysis can be combined with the value chain analysis (VCA) to assess the relationship of assets, risks, and functions altogether;[1142] Such approach is quite popular because it coincides with the most important goal of the BEPS Project: to 'align transfer pricing outcomes with value creation'. When combining the value chain approach and formula weighting factors, a holistic approach can become a bridge between FA and the TP based on the ALP.[1143] I think this is also why the OECD Guidelines have linked 'risk', 'assets', and 'functions' with each other as 'a holistic approach'[1144] to decide attribution of the intangible-related profits and ownership. In other words, under the post-BEPS holistic approach, only performing a purely 'financial funding function'[1145] or being a simple legal owner of an intangible will not entitle a party to the total profits from the intangible, even though the funding entity might be an important investor.

1138. Wolfgang Schön, Attribution of Profits to PEs and the OECD 2006 Report, 46 Tax notes international 1059 (2007); Richard J Vann, Reflections on Business Profits and the Arm's-Length Principle, The Taxation of Business Profits under Tax Treaties (2003), at 378.

1139. Danny Oosterhoff, The True Importance of Significant People Functions, 15 International Transfer Pricing Journal 68 (2008).

1140. Sébastien Gonnet, Risks Redefined in Transfer Pricing Post-BEPS, in Lang & Storck, *supra* n. 20.

1141. Pim Fris, Sébastien Gonnet & Ralph Meghames, Understanding Risk in the Enterprise: The Key to Transfer Pricing for Today's Business Models, 21 International Transfer Pricing Journal (2014). Regarding different aspects of dealing with risks, *see* Mikael Hall & Stuart Wood, Base Erosion and Profit Shifting and Business Restructurings, 44 Intertax 769 (2016), at 771-772.

1142. A detailed analysis on how VCA applied to seek 'where value is created', *see* Ilhan, *supra* n. 44, at 3.2.

1143. Offermans & others, *supra* n. 325.

1144. Steef Huibregtse & others, Multinational Enterprises, Transfer Pricing and Value Chain Analysis in Latin America Following the OECD/G20 Base Erosion and Profit Shifting Initiative, 72 Bulletin for International Taxation 11 (2018).

1145. An entity only has funding function without bearing the risk or performing DEMPEs, is an 'investor' only, *see* Isabel Verlinden, Stefaan De Baets & Vasistha Parmessar, Grappling with DEMPEs in the Trenches: Trying to Give It the Meaning It Deserves, 47 Intertax 1042 (2019), at 1045.

Under the BEPS Project Actions 8-10, the functions in the analysis include 'important functions related to the development, enhancement, maintenance, protection, and exploitation' (DEMPE).[1146] DEMPE functions are also incorporated in the 2017 OECD Transfer Pricing Guidelines. The DEMPE functions analysis focuses on objective evidence of the DEMPE activities being conducted, so it is seen as more objective than the 2010 OECD Transfer Pricing Guidelines which focus on 'substance over form'.[1147] DEMPE functions analysis closely assesses 'who is doing what'.[1148]

So the question is: what functions should be selected as proxies for attributing IP in the asset factor for the EU's FA regime?

In my view, these indicators for functions in the pre-BEPS era as well as the post-BEPS era, including risk control, KERT functions 'SPF', 'DEMPE' or many other functions such as 'design, manufacturing, assembling, R&D, servicing, purchasing, distribution, marketing, advertising, transportation, financing and management', have one feature in common: These 'functions' are all linked to the human beings/people who implement these functions. 'Decision-making' is the essential element to economically significant functions. Functions, especially DEMPE functions, naturally involve human interactions.[1149]

Since IP included in the asset factor should represent the innovation-promoting environment, I am of the opinion that DEMPE functions are the market-neutral option to decide the 'location where IP is utilized' for the purpose of the asset factor of the EU's FA regime. 'Decision-making' is not the key criterion in this context because the decision-making person is not necessarily involved in the innovation activities. For example, a risk-assuming or decision-making function is often done by managerial leaders, such as regional directors, or CEOs, who do not directly perform innovation activities to create, enhance, and make use of a patented innovation.

Therefore, DEMPE functions are more suitable and tax neutral as the functions for attributing IP for the CCCTB asset factor; this approach matches the development of the latest OECD guidelines, though the underlying rationale is not precisely the same as TP practice because the CCCTB asset factor does not need to incorporate the risk and decision-making aspects used in the OECD's post-BEPS holistic functional analysis.

1146. Comments on DEMPEs, Verlinden, De Baets & Parmessar, *ibid.*
Mirna Solange Screpante, The Arm's Length Principle Evolves Towards a 'Value Creation Functional (Ie DEMPE) Formula Standard': A Barrier or a Gateway to Locational Business Planning?, 48 Intertax (2020); Mirna Screpante, Rethinking the Arm's Length Principle and Its Impact on the IP Licence Model after OECD/G20 BEPS Actions 8-10: Nothing Changed But the Change?' 11 World Tax Journal (2019). Relating DEMPE in the 2013 OECD Transfer Pricing Guidelines, *see* Lagarden, *supra* n. 1102.

1147. Screpante (2020), *ibid.*

1148. *Ibid.*

1149. *See* Verlinden, De Baets & Parmessar, *supra* n. 1145, at 1045.

6.5.2.2 *Intangibles Should Not Be Observed Only from the Perspective of Possible Abusive IP Migration*

There is a necessary adjustment from TP discussions of IP: IP rights are inherently mobile and are prone to manipulation, when we focus on how IP is created and utilized.

In the current academic analysis on intangibles/IP prior to BEPS as well as post-BEPS and, there is a feature in common: their narratives or scenarios on the IP always involve a similar story of 'IP structures':[1150] in a group, there is an entity 'controlling or owning or holding' an intangible, and there is another entity conducting the real R&D or decision-making or risk-taking activities. Between these two entities, there is a transfer of 'intangible'.[1151] Many discussions try to design 'anti-avoidance' measures[1152] for the 'scenario of migration of IP rights'[1153] based on the assumption that intangibles are 'mobile'. Such assumption describes intangibles, including self-generated know-how or technology, can be created and its ownership transferred to another entity to be further developed and transformed to be a mature legal right or a separate intangible. The dispute arises when this intangible-owning entity becomes a 'box' in a low-tax-rate jurisdiction, and such box is embedded in a tax reduction scheme. These 'IP structures' can also be implemented by setting up a cost-sharing agreement (CSA)[1154] between group members in order to shift income from intangibles to low-tax jurisdiction.

The observation of 'migrating/transferring' intangibles is not completely wrong, but it neglects to take account of the fact of exercising an intangible, such as a patent, is actually linked and limited to a specific jurisdiction, that is, the registration jurisdiction. A typical way of exercising a patent is to invoke the patent to stop other competitors from producing as well as from selling the product which is patented. This is the 'right to exclude'.[1155] The right to exclude a patent is a type of 'exploitation' in the

1150. For example, the following articles are based on this narrative: Andrea Musselli & Alberto Musselli, Rise of a New Standard: Profit Location in Countries of Important Intangible Functions Managers, 24 International Transfer Pricing Journal (2017); Screpante (2019), *supra* n. 1146, at 2.3: three types of IP structures. Pankiv, *supra* n. 331.

1151. For example, *see* Andreas Oestreicher, Transfer Pricing of Intangibles in Cases of Post-Merger Reorganization: Lessons from the Revised OECD Draft, 42 Intertax 509 (2014).

1152. R Vlasceanu, Intellectual Property Structuring in the Context of the OECD BEPS Action Plan, in Madalina Cotrut (ed.), *International Tax Structures in the BEPS Era: An Analysis of Anti-Abuse Measures* (IBFD 2015).

1153. L. Nouel et al., Planning for and Migration of IP Rights, in Verlinden & Bakker (eds), *supra* n. 1065; R Vlasceanu, *ibid*.

1154. Lisa De Simone & Richard C Sansing, Income Shifting Using a Cost-Sharing Arrangement, 41 Journal of the American Taxation Association 123 (2019); De Simone and Sansing observe how MNE uses CSA structures to shift income outside the USA and understate the market IP value: 'MNE is more likely to use a CSA to develop the IP when the MNE has valuable domestic operating intangibles, such as a global brand; the MNE is more likely to use a CSA if the nature of the IP development project allows the MNE to understate the fair market value of the IP.'

1155. Adam Mossoff, Exclusion and Exclusive Use in Patent Law, 22 Harvard Journal of Law & Technology 321 (2008).

DEMPE regime. In this regard, a registered patent is actually similar to a real estate because the patent also has a 'situs', i.e., the registration state.[1156]

It should be noted that here I am not arguing the 'registration state' as the only key criterion for attributing the intangible. What I advocate and endorse is to still attribute the intangible to 'where it performs the function'. In the case of a patent, it can be exercised within the jurisdiction where it is registered. As another example of an 'EU trademark' under EU law,[1157] a community trademark can be registered in any EU Member State, but the community trademark will be exercised and utilized in a specific jurisdiction within the EU. Where the IP is actually exercised and performing the function of being exploited is a factual situation that can be observed objectively from the relevant patent, copyright, or trademark law.

When we include the well-recognized IP (i.e., patent, trademark, copyright) in the asset factor and attribute them according to the DEMPE functions activities, the criterion is where these functions really take place. The attribution criterion is not how these IP rights are transferred, assigned, and licensed, nor how these IP rights are owned or held by a cash box or a holding company.

6.5.2.3 *The Asset Factor's Functional Analysis Should Focus on Innovation Activities, Not Ownership*

Moreover, while focusing on innovation, discussions of the ownership of intangibles are not relevant, including the concept of economic ownership. This rationale applies to both tangibles and intangibles.

Ownership of intangibles within the context of TP means 'entitlement to profits attributable to intangibles'.[1158] In addition to the legal ownership, there are other ownership concepts[1159] developed in the TP and international tax regime: contractual ownership, economic ownership, and beneficial ownership. These different concepts of 'ownership' are different justifications for entitlements of profits from intangibles for a non-legal owner. These concepts of ownership (other than the legal ownership) are used when discussing 'intangibles' because intangibles are made up of various legal relationships. Therefore, different concepts of ownership can provide a nuanced interpretation of these legal relationships and entitlements.

1156. Justine Pila & Paul Torremans, Introduction to European Patent Law, in Justine Pila & Paul Torremans, *European Intellectual Property Law* (Oxford University Press 2019).

1157. History of the EU trademark law, *see* T Cohen Jehoram, *Constantinus Johan Jozef Clemens van Nispen and JLRA Huydecoper, European Trademark Law: Community Trademark Law and Harmonized National Trademark Law* (Kluwer Law International; Sold and distributed in North, Central, and South America by Aspen Publishers 2010). An overview of the reforms, *see* European Union Intellectual Property Office, EU Trade Mark Reform Summary of Changes Applying from 1 October 2017 (European Union Intellectual Property Office 2017).

1158. JL Andrus & Richard Collier, *supra* n. 1122, at 6.63-6.65; Marta Pankiv, *Contemporary Application of the Arm's Length Principle in Transfer Pricing* (IBFD 2017), at 4.2.1.

1159. Lagarden, *supra* n. 1102.

An example of typical 'economic owner' mentioned in the TP literature[1160] is 'licensing an intangible': the owner can license its self-owned intangible to another; the licence is the economic owner. Since economic ownership seeks justified 'entitlements', the economic ownership focuses on 'control' of these functions, not what functions actually take place at what location.

In contrast, the intangibles of the asset factor in the EU FA regime would represent the public benefit of the innovation environment, and therefore the DEMPE activities are the proxy as to how much the taxpayer has made use of these public benefits. Who owns the intangible is not the criterion. So, it would be unreasonable to use the economic ownership concept in the asset factor because such adoption cannot faithfully reflect the fundamental rationale of the asset factor. Adopting the economic ownership concept in the EU FA regime causes problems for attributing not only tangible assets/real estate (*see* section 6.4.3) but also intangibles because the concept of economic ownership focuses on entitlement and ignores the real meaning of IP: representing innovation.

6.5.3 The Cost-Based Valuation Method Corresponding to DEMPE Activities

How to valuate assets, especially intangibles, is difficult. There are ample discussions about the valuation of intangibles in the context of TP practice.[1161] There are various valuation methods[1162] for IP and intangible assets, including a cost approach, a market approach, and an income approach.[1163] Each valuation method is a different perspective to describe the status of the intangible involved, and because each of them has its strength and weakness.[1164] For example, the market approach might face the difficulty that there is not yet an external market for an intangible.[1165] The cost approach has the weakness that valuates intangibles by the costs of 'replacing the intangible involved', so the cost approach has limited application to IP but might be useful for other intangibles.[1166] The income approach is now the most recommended method for valuating intangibles.[1167] In the US, the preferred methods of valuating intangibles are mostly based on statistics, by using approximation and proxies.[1168] Since every valuation method could have its own strengths and weakness, for the purpose of

1160. For example, Screpante, *supra* n. 1146; Marta Pankiv, *Contemporary Application of the Arm's Length Principle in Transfer Pricing* (IBFD 2017). Verlinden & Bakker (eds), *supra* n. 1065, at 6.2.
1161. Regarding valuation of intangibles, Philippe Rasquin & others, The Importance of Valuation, in Verlinden & Bakker (eds), *supra* n. 1065; Lagarden, *supra* n. 1102.
1162. Parr, *supra* n. 1070.
1163. In addition to these three typical methods, there are other valuation approaches, *see* Lagarden, *supra* n. 1102, Figure 7.
1164. Yariv Brauner, Value in the Eye of the Beholder: The Valuation of Intangibles for Transfer Pricing Purposes, 28 Virginia Tax Review 79 (2008), at 106.
1165. *Ibid.*
1166. *Ibid.*
1167. Ravi Kant Gupta, *Recent Trends in Transfer Pricing: Intangibles, GAAR and BEPS* (Sunil Gupta ed., Bloomsbury 2017), at 5.16.3.
1168. Brauner, *supra* n. 1164, at 158.

deciding intangibles in the asset factor, we do not need to follow one specific approach but should select strategically.

Among these different valuation methods, there are two perspectives: from the (historical) cost side (i.e., the cost approach) and from the (future) market side (i.e., the market approach). As to the income approach, it is observed from a combined perspective of present and future, focusing on the discounted cash flow (DCF)[1169] 'by calculating the present value of future economic benefits expected from ownership and exploitation of the property'.

Since the asset factor aims to reflect the production process, it is logical to choose the cost-based method, not to choose the 'market-based' approach, even for valuating intangibles. However, the cost approach does not refer to the 'estimated cost that can replace the involved intangible';[1170] instead, costs related to research, develop, and maintain an intangible seem more consistent with the fundamental rationale of the asset factor. In this regard, the cost can reflect the intangibles' value in the asset factor, so the valuation should be based on the cost of the DEMPE functions.

The approach of using DEMPE functions for valuation is quite familiar already for the European Commission. Article 34 of the 2016 CCCTB Directive Proposal, for example, has already incorporated the spirit of including IP and valuating IP on the cost-based approach. According to Article 34(2), costs of 'research, development, marketing and advertisement' should be included in the asset factor as a type of special intangible. It is justified to include R&D as part of the production process. But it is illogical to use the costs of marketing and advertising as an intangible in the asset factor unlimitedly provided such costs are unrelated to the production process. Marketing and advertisement costs should be included in the asset factor when they are related to 'enhancing' trademarks or identifiable brands. By incorporating the costs of DEMPE functions, the valuation of intangibles of the asset factor is tax neutral for the EU's FA regime.

6.6 CONCLUSIONS: TOWARDS A MARKET-NEUTRAL ASSET FACTOR REPRESENTING PRODUCTION AND INNOVATION

The asset factor is consistent with the tax-neutrality principle when the design represents the public benefits providing the environment and non-human resources for production and innovation within the jurisdiction.

First, all assets that contribute to the production process should be included. Therefore, inventories should be excluded from the asset factor from the very beginning because inventories are the end result of production, and they no longer contribute to the process. Owned and rented assets should both be included in the asset factor, provided that an asset is utilized for the production process. Self-generated and purchased/licensed intangibles are both included in the asset factor as long as they are being used as the input side activity. In other words, not only tangible assets but also

1169. Gupta, *supra* n. 1167, at 16.3.
1170. Brauner, *supra* n. 1164.

well-recognized IP rights, i.e., patents, trademarks, and copyrights, should also be included in the asset factor.

Second, based on the same rationale, the attribution rule should be based on the location where the asset is utilized, not attributing to the economic owner. In the case of an intra-group agreement on renting or lending a tangible asset, the attribution should follow the same rule, i.e., where the tangible asset is actually utilized. Third, as to the valuation, in principle, the historical cost method/the original cost method is appropriate for tangible properties. The current CCCTB Directive Proposal and the US adopt the same special rule for calculating the value of the rented assets (i.e., the eight times rule). Still, the specific calculation does not seem to have a solid rationale.

The current CCCTB Directive Proposal is not entirely consistent with the benefit-based MN framework, partly due to legal transplantation from the US, such as excluding intangibles which is in part due to the influence from international taxation practice, such as using the concept of economic ownership. These old practices do not represent the public benefits provided by jurisdictions where material resources are utilized and innovation is encouraged.

The deviation from MN can be corrected by returning to the fundamental rationale of the asset factor: the asset factor is not easily manipulated because the rules as designed are based on the economic reality of the production process.

The inclusion of IP rights in the asset factor is different from the long-existing practice of FA developed in the US and the current CCCTB Directive Proposal. However, the worldwide trend is to recognize IP rights as the most valuable assets for MNE taxpayers. The design of a supranational corporate tax system like the CCCTB should not just escape into traditional practice. When including intangibles in the asset factor, it would be logical to include IP rights in the asset factor and attribute intangibles to where they are functionally utilized.

As to valuating intangibles, it is necessary to use proxies, provided these proxies are not contrary to the inherent rationale of the asset factor. Therefore, DEMPE costs are reasonable proxies for patents and copyrights; marketing and advertisement costs are relevant proxies for valuating the intangibles in the asset factor when these costs are related to a specific brand or trademark.

In sum, for the asset factor of the EU FA regime, I recommend amending the provisions of the current CCCTB Directive Proposal accordingly as follows:

Article 34 Composition of the asset factor

1. The asset factor shall consist of the average value of all fixed tangible assets owned, rented, or leased by a group member and the intellectual property rights (patent, copyright, trademark) that contribute to the taxpayer's production process as its numerator and the average value of all fixed tangible assets owned, rented, or leased by the group as its denominator.
2. In the five years that follow a taxpayer joining an existing or new group, its asset factor shall also include intellectual property rights for which the total amount of costs incurred for development, enhancement, maintenance, protection, and/or enforcement (DEMPE) functions by the taxpayer over the six years that preceded its joining the group.

Article 35 Allocation of assets

1. Without prejudice to Article 22(2) and (3), an asset shall be included in the asset factor to the location where it is used. Tangible assets are allocated to where they are physically used; intangible assets are allocated to where the development, enhancement, maintenance, protection, or exploitation takes place, depending on the function of the intangible asset.
2. Except in the case of leases between group members, leased assets shall be included in the asset factor of the group member that is the lessor or the lessee of the asset. The same shall apply to rented assets.

Article 36 Valuation

1. Land and other non-depreciable fixed tangible assets shall be valued at their original cost.
2. An individually depreciable fixed tangible asset shall be valued at the average of its value for tax purposes at the beginning and at the end of a tax year.

   Where, as a result of one or more intra-group transactions, an individually depreciable fixed tangible asset is included in the asset factor of a group member for less than a tax year, the value to be taken into account shall be calculated having regard to the number of months that the asset was included in the asset factor of that group member.
3. The pool of fixed assets, as referred to in Article 37 of Directive 2016/xx/EU, shall be valued at the average of its value for tax purposes at the beginning and the end of a tax year.
4. The renter or lessee of an asset of which it is not the economic owner shall value that rented or leased asset at eight times the net annual rental or lease payment due, less any amounts receivable from sub-rentals or sub-leases.

   A group member renting out or leasing an asset of which it is not its economic owner shall value that rented or leased asset at eight times the net annual rental or lease payment due.
5. An asset sold by a group member to a person outside the group following an intra- group transfer in the same or the previous tax year shall be included in the asset factor of the transferring group member for the period between the intra-group transfer and the sale to the person outside the group, except where the group members concerned demonstrate that the intra-group transfer was made for genuine commercial reasons.
6. Intangible assets that are included in the asset factor shall be valued based on the costs of development, enhancement, maintenance, protection, and/or exploitation that take place, depending on the function of the intangible asset.

CHAPTER 7

Towards Market-Neutral Industry-Specific Formulas: Rediscovering the Roots of Formulary Apportionment

A page of history is worth a volume of logic.

Justice Oliver Wendell Holmes[1171]

7.1 INTRODUCTION: INDUSTRY FORMULAS REPRESENT SPECIAL PUBLIC BENEFITS

7.1.1 Deciphering the Theory Upholding Industry-Specific Formulas: The Root, Not the Exceptions

In addition to a standard formula based on the prototype of the manufacturing industry, in most FA jurisdictions, there are also industry-specific formulas. There are a large number of examples, especially in US state taxation practices.[1172] This chapter discusses three types of industry-specific formulas: the financial industry, the transportation industry, and the extractive (oil and gas) industry.

In the early literature regarding FA, the view was that the standard formula, which was based on the manufacturing industry model, is the 'principle', and the transportation industry, financial industry, and extractive industry are 'exceptional'. Such view is incorrect.

Thinking from FA's original purpose, i.e., to solve the difficulty of taxing cross-border and integrated economic activities of MNE taxpayers, these industries are typical industries that nevertheless need FA as much as the cross-border car manufacturing industry. The unitary business concept that supports the FA system evolved

1171. *New York Trust Co. v. Eisner*, 256 U.S. 345 (1921).
1172. Hellerstein, Hellerstein & Swain, *supra* n. 349, at 8.06[1].

from the 'unit rule' developed in the railroad industry in the nineteenth century in the US.[1173] It is a misunderstanding to assert that the need for special industry formulas is the failure of an FA system as such or consider them as exceptional.

Therefore, although this book still uses the term 'special industry formula', these special industries are not exceptions to the fundamental rationale of FA. Rather, they have solid ground on which to adopt a formula.

To adopt these special industry formulas is justified by the benefit principle. Each industry formula represents a specific relationship with the jurisdiction(s) involved and the relevant public benefits. Each special relationship creates the need to adjust the content of the 'standard' formula discussed in Chapters 3 to 6. For the financial industry, monetary capital is the key for jurisdictions to supervise and regulate intensively; for the transportation industry, the transportation activity, as its inherent mobility, will involve a departure, voyage, and arrival jurisdiction. For the oil and gas industry, its input side activity involves natural resources which might look like a free gift or blessing but also require the origin jurisdiction to manage these natural resources and take care of other consequent impacts, to prevent 'resources curse'.

From the experiences from the US, there are many more industry formulas than formulas discussed in this chapter, such as for pipelines, telecommunications, publishing, broadcasting,[1174] etc. These formulas have been created mainly due to the historical reason that in US state taxation, many service industry formulas are designed due to the illogical 'cost of performance' rule (i.e., the origin-based income-generating rule) used for attributing the gross receipts earned from performing services in the sales factor.[1175] In section 4.2 above, I explained the paradigm shift from the COP rule to destination-based market shifting in the US. Therefore, these examples are not discussed in this chapter because these 'special' industries could be fairly apportioned under the standard formula with the sales-by-destination rule.

As a side note, there are indeed various new industries emerging in the digital economy, such as online platforms, cloud services, online gaming, 3D printing, advertising and social media, etc. In my view, with the reformed standard formula discussed in Chapters 3 to 6, there is no need to design industry formulas for these new industries due to digitalization. Chapter 7 instead focuses on the industries that a reformed standard formula cannot solve due to their special relationship with public interests.

1173. Hellerstein (1992), *supra* n. 352.
1174. Hellerstein, Hellerstein & Swain, *supra* n. 349, at Chapter 10 as well as MTC's website. https://www.mtc.gov.
1175. Heyman & Weinstein, *supra* n. 641.

7.1.2 The Common Features of Financial, Transportation, and Extractive Industries

7.1.2.1 Positive Externality to Facilitate Other Cross-Border Activities

These industry-specific formulas of the financial, transportation, and extractive industries share two features in common: mobility and remoteness of the economic activities. In addition to being mobile in their business models, the financial industry, transportation industry, and extractive (oil and gas) industry all have another common feature: these industries are essential to facilitating cross-border activities of other industries. Financial institutions involve the core of the free movement of capital; the transportation industry, including the aviation industry, is the driving force of free movement; and the extractive industry directly involves the energy market of the EU.

These industries are all within the shared competence[1176] of the EU and EU Member States under EU law, in the internal market, transportation, and energy, respectively. They also belong to policy areas or emerging actions that pursue further EU integration, such as the Capital Market Union (CMU),[1177] Single European Sky (SES),[1178] and the Energy Union.[1179]

What does this feature mean to the EU's FA regime as a corporate tax reform? In my view, these industries represent the driving force for conducting cross-border activities. From the perspective of establishing a border-free and more integrated internal market, these industries are especially worth encouraging for a well-functioning internal market. If we assumed that tax is only a DWL, we could come to the conclusion that these special industries should be subject neither to corporate tax at all, nor to the EU's FA regime scope of application.

However, as discussed in Chapter 2, when we see corporate tax also as a measurement unit of public benefits, we accept that these special industries, with positive externality to other industries, would need additional public benefits from the government to maintain and manage conditions in these industries. Such additional public benefits would justify an emphasis on the selection and content of the weighting factor because such industry would inevitably make use of more public benefits, and the design of the formula would need to reflect this aspect.

1176. Article 4 of the TFEU. Some theoretical explanation of the shared competence of EU, Alan Dashwood, The Relationship Between the Member States and the European Union/European Community, 41 Common Market Law Review 355 (2004). Robert Schütze, *From Dual to Cooperative Federalism* (Oxford University Press 2009).
1177. As to the tax issues and Capital Markets Union, *see* Loredana Carpentieri & Stefano Micossi, Removing Cross-Border Tax Barriers, in Danny Busch, Emilios Avgouleas & Guido Ferrarini (eds), *Capital Markets Union in Europe* (1st ed. Oxford University Press 2018), at 189.
1178. 'Single European Sky' *see* https://ec.europa.eu/transport/modes/air/ses_en.
1179. 'Energy Union' *see* https://ec.europa.eu/energy/en/topics/energy-strategy-and-energy-union.

7.1.2.2 *Seeking Special Public Benefits That Justify Special Industry Formulas: Reflections on US Experiences*

In the US, similar arguments of 'instrumentalities' have been appearing in the Commerce Clause discussions on whether state taxation should be imposed on these industries. For example, financial institutions, like banks, had been tax exempt from state taxation until 1976[1180] because they were regarded as a governmental instrumentality for interstate commerce. In the US, an intergovernmental instrumentality should be exempt from state tax,[1181] and banks were regarded as playing a similar role of an intergovernmental instrumentality. However, banks' immunity to state taxation in case law was designed in the early nineteenth century when the US was really in need of banks. As Justice Marshall so strongly stated: 'the power to tax is the power to destroy', to negate taxation levied on banks. Such statement seems outdated in the twenty-first century where complicated financial industries need comprehensive regulation and infrastructures, financed by taxation from the government.

As to other types of instrumentalities of interstate commerce, such as transportation, we can also see a similar paradigm shift, from being cautious about the state tax itself, to focusing on if state taxation represents service, as in the four-prong test of the Commerce Clause developed in case law, including *Complete Auto Transit (1977)*[1182] (*see* section 3.2.3.4).

Although states' power to levy property tax on properties used by railroads and other overland transportation in interstate commerce has never been questioned,[1183] levying tax on the oil and gas industry[1184] and transportation[1185] could also trigger concerns about infringing the Commerce Clause[1186] because these industries are 'instrumentalities of interstate commerce' or 'instrumentalities of foreign commerce'. In the past, the US Supreme Court's early case law established the 'doctrine of

1180. Hellerstein, Hellerstein & Swain, *supra* n. 349, at 6.30.
Jerome R Hellerstein, Current Issues in Multistate Taxation of Banks, 30 Tax Law Review 155 (1974). Also *see* M Pashman, Taxation of Government Instrumentalities, 1 NJL Rev. University of Newark 98 (1935). State immunity of banks can be traced back to the case law in the early nineteenth century, *McCulloch v. Maryland*, 17 U.S. 316 (1819).
1181. Walter Hellerstein, The United States, in Gianluigi Bizioli & Claudio Sacchetto (eds), *Tax Aspects of Fiscal Federalism: A Comparative Analysis* (IBFD 2011).
1182. *Complete Auto Transit, Inc. v. Brady*, 430 U.S. 274 (1977). *See* Chapter 3 of this book.
1183. Hellerstein, Hellerstein & Swain, *supra* n. 349, at 4.13.
1184. Early literature, *see* Paul J Hartman, The Commerce Clause and the States Power to Tax the Oil and Gas Industry, 7 Proc. Ann. Inst. on Oil & Gas L. & Tax'n 387 (1956). Hellerstein, *supra* n. 405. In some cases, income earned from the oil and gas from the lease of state land is immune from state taxation because the lease constituted a government instrumentality of the state. *See* Joseph W Burns, Taxation of Federal and State Instrumentalities, 10 Tax Magazine 208 (1932).
1185. George D Brabson, Multistate Taxation of the Transportation Industry, 18 Ohio St. LJ 22 (1957).
1186. The jurisprudence of US Supreme Court on state taxation and the Commerce clause, *see* Walter Hellerstein, State Income Taxation of Multijurisdictional Corporations: Reflections on Mobil, Exxon, and HR 5076, 79 Michigan Law Review 113 (1980). Hellerstein, *supra* n. 380. Walter Hellerstein, State Income Taxation of Multijurisdictional Corporations and the Supreme Court, National Tax Journal 401 (1982).

nontaxability of inseparably intermingled instrumentalities of commerce',[1187] but its applicable scope of this doctrine was strictly limited.

It is also worth noting that the original UDITPA also expressly excluded these special industries of the 'activity of public utilities' from apportionment.[1188] A public utility is defined as 'any business entity which owns and operates for public use any plant, equipment, property, franchise, or license for the transportation of goods or persons or the production, storage, transmission, sale, delivery or furnishing of electricity, water, steam, oil, oil products or gas', according to the UDITPA. It is because of the political concern that states might wish to enact separate legislation to regulate these industries. But these industries which exhibit a feature of a public utility can involve cross-border unitary business,[1189] and even though the UDITPA does not apply to these industries, many US states still established their own special industry formulas. Such phenomenon backs up my argument that these special industry formulas are actually the root that promotes the development of FA, long before the enactment of the UDITPA or the Multistate Tax Compact.

In my view, the US Supreme Court's current approach in *Complete Auto Transit* to the first prong: 'sufficient nexus' and the fourth prong: 'the tax was not fairly related to services provided by the State' should be analysed.[1190] Although currently US states assume when the nexus is found to exist, and the fourth prong is satisfied, no extra examination is needed.[1191] The fourth prong can still provide justification of an indication of sufficient nexus (the first prong) as well as fair apportionment (the second prong) based on the benefit principle.

Therefore, the main point to designing special industry formulas is to seek the key proxy when designing the weighting factor, to reflect the logical public benefit, and not to discriminate. As long as the right proxy is established, the design will not be arbitrary or discriminatory. Instead, the different design is justified for the different business model and different public benefits involved.

As to the three industries in this chapter, I use 'monetary capital' as the key proxy for financial institutions; 'departure and arrival' as the key proxy for the transportation industry;[1192] and the 'natural resource origin' as the key proxy for the oil and gas industry. These key proxies represent the link to the jurisdictions providing public benefits related to sustaining the economic activities of these industries.

1187. Jerome R Hellerstein, Recent Developments in Commerce Clause Limitations on State Taxation, 10 Tax Executive 117 (1957), at 230.
1188. John A Wilkie, Income Apportionment of Unitary Public Utility Corporations, 15 Tax Law Review 467 (1959).
1189. *Ibid.*
1190. Hellerstein, Hellerstein & Swain, *supra* n. 349, at 4.13[3][a].
1191. Philip M Zinn, The Requirements of 'Substantial Nexus' and 'Fairly Related' Under the Commerce Clause, *The State and Local Tax Lawyer. Symposium Edition* (American Bar Association 2007).
1192. Hellerstein, Hellerstein & Swain, *supra* n. 349, at 4.13, Home Port doctrine.

7.1.2.3 *Treating a Mixed Group in the Formula as a Whole, Not Carving out or Ring-Fencing*

Last but not least, it is questionable what the relationship between the standard formula and the special industry formula is, when it comes to a mixed group which involves a special industry and a non-special industry. It is not rare to establish a mixed group consisting of special industries and non-special industries, especially for MNE taxpayers that are able to integrate their business from diversified perspectives. The 'special industries' are quite often economically integrated with non-special industries. For example, automobile retailers like Harley-Davidson have developed their supporting financial services for their customers by setting up some special purpose entities (SPEs).[1193] As another example, MNEs of the air transportation industry also involve various supporting services, which are often conducted by different group members.[1194] The oil and gas industry is again a typical example of integrating the upstream, midstream, and the downstream industry, and this is also a reason that many leading cases of state taxation adjudicated by the US Supreme Court involve the oil and gas industry[1195] and the transportation industry.[1196] It is not coincidental that the European Commission selected these industries as 'special industries' under the current CCCTB Directive Proposal because they indeed merit extra attention.

FA researchers have been noticing the difficulty of applying the special industry formula to a mixed group.[1197] This question is similar to the difficult question of whether a unitary business relationship exists. On the one hand, we hope the industry formula can clearly demonstrate the special feature of that industry, so it seems illogical to apply the industry formula to a mixed group as a whole. But on the other hand, if we still apply the industry formula to a mixed group as a whole, there would be concerns that such industry formula does not sufficiently reflect economic activities from the special industry and makes the group fragmented. There is an inherent dilemma in adopting any special industry formula.

There are three approaches used to design special industry formulas in the US and the CCCTB. The first approach is 'carving out' or 'ring fencing' the special industry group member, either by creating a separate formula[1198] or by completely excluding the industry from the FA.[1199] The second approach is to create a new sub-factor[1200] or a

1193. *See* section 7.2.4.5.
1194. *See* section 7.3.
1195. For example, *Exxon Corp. v. Wisconsin Department of Revenue*, 447 U.S. 207 (1980); *Mobil Oil Corp. v. Commissioner of Taxes*, 445 U.S. 425 (1980).
1196. *Container Corp. v. Franchise Tax Bd.*, 463 U.S. 159 (1983).
Japan Line, Ltd. v. County of Los Angeles, 441 U.S. 434 (1979). *General Motors Corp. v. Tracy*, Tax Commissioner of Ohio, 519 U.S. 278 (1997).
1197. For example, Weiner, *supra* n. 47. Vieri Ceriani, CCCTB and the Financial Sector, 17 EC Tax Review 159 (2008).
1198. Such as CCCTB's financial industry formula, insurance industry formula, and MTC's financial institutions formula in USA, *see* below at section 7.4.2.
1199. Such as CCCTB's transportation industry formula, at section 7.4.3.
1200. Such as and USA states' shipping industry formula, adopting the port-day or by the voyage-day ratio, *See* section 7.3.2; Alaska's 'extraction factor' for the oil and gas industry, *see* section 7.4.

separate ratio[1201] to adjust the standard formula. The third approach is to adjust the items in the factor, either by changing the attribution rule,[1202] valuation rule,[1203] or by adding new items.[1204] These three approaches can also be used as a hybrid. The diversity of these approaches is also the reason why special industry formulas look complex and arbitrary.

In my view, keeping the three-factor formula structure, but in combination with some special rules embedded in each factor respectively, is a feasible solution. The relationship between the standard formula and the special industry formula is not the principle with exceptions; instead, special industry formulas embody the standard formula. Therefore, in a mixed group, the special industry formula should apply to the whole group and is still consistent with the standard formula.

A mixed group has chosen to integrate different fragments into a group, and each single part has its own role for the whole group. A special industry formula's special element in the standard three-factor formula structure not only reflects the part of the special industry but also the relationship between the special industry and the non-special industry in a group. Finding that key proxy for each industry formula could achieve this goal.

7.1.3 The Structure of This Chapter

This chapter is divided as follows. Section 7.2 discusses the financial industry under the current CCCTB Directive Proposal and US state taxation experiences. Section 7.3 discusses the transportation industry, in international tax law, the current CCCTB Directive Proposal, and the US. Section 7.4 discusses the extractive (oil and gas) industry. As to the key proxy in each industry that represents the special public benefit, section 7.2[1205] focuses on monetary capital because it is the driver of the entire financial industry. Section 7.3 discusses transportation activities' mobile process and the need to take departure and arrival into account. Section 7.4 discusses the importance of the origin of a natural resource.

In each subsection, I follow the same structure: the theory, the examples of the specific industry formulas (discussing the applicable scope and the factors involved), and treatment when involving a mixed group. In each subsection, examples from US states are discussed.

1201. Such as MTC's air transportation industry formula 'departure ratio' and railroad industry formula 'in-state miles travel ratio', *See* section 7.3.2.
1202. Such as CCCTB's oil and gas industry formula's sales factor.
1203. Such as California's 20% valuation rule for the financial assets on a financial industry/non-financial industry group; and CCCTB's 10% rule for the sales factor and the asset factor of the financial industry.
1204. Such as Alaska's jurisprudence on the asset factor for the oil and gas industry, to include the intangible drilling costs, Outer Continental Shelf (OCS), non-production oil wells, etc. *See section* 7.4.4.
1205. This section has used paragraphs from the essay published in Shu-Chien Chen, Tracing Capital: Toward a Neutral Specialized Formula for Financial Institutions under Common Consolidated Corporate Tax Base (CCCTB), 12 Bocconi Legal Papers 71 (2018).

7.2 FINANCIAL INDUSTRY: TRACING CAPITAL

7.2.1 Apportioning Income Earned Monetary Capital in the Financial Industry

7.2.1.1 The Necessity for a Special Formula Due to Fungibility and Mobility of Money: A Review of Current Discussions

In the FA literature, it is widely accepted that the standard three-factor formula cannot properly reflect the financial industry. The fundamental rationale for such special formula is that the input (production/supply) side has a significantly different feature from the manufacturing industry on which the standard formula is based: the financial industry involves a lot of 'financial assets' and provides the service of leveraging these financial assets for its clients.

The classical service in the financial industry is banks' lending and borrowing practices: nowadays, many banks not only provide the classical borrowing service but also sell innovative financial assets to corporate clients for their profit-seeking investments, risk or cashflow management, etc. The financial industry can include various types of institutions: banks, mutual funds, and trusts, and these institutions can have legal personality or not. The common feature of all financial institutions and their various financial products remains the same: the monetary capital plays the most important role. In other words, money itself is the key production element in the financial industry. The value of such production element is inevitably influenced by the actual transactions in financial markets. Therefore, both the sales and the assets factor should be adjusted for the financial industry formula.

As Benshalom's observes,[1206] the unique feature of economic activities in the financial industry is its 'fungibility' and 'mobility'. Fungibility means that financial flows can be structured in numerous ways to achieve the same economic effect, and financial institutions will very likely choose the most tax-efficient way. Moreover, current financial transactions are so complicated and can be even structured as derivatives the value of which is created from a composite value of other types of intangibles. For many financial transactions, a conceptual exchange of ownership does not even need to take place. Such complications of the financial market provide opportunities to manipulate the proceeds from these financial assets/transactions either as capital gains or as ordinary income.[1207] Therefore, it can be difficult to valuate financial income because of the sophisticated structure of the transactions. It is also clear that mobility is the inherent feature of financial assets: storing and transferring them to investment vehicles, such as funds or trusts, is almost free of charge.

Based on these two unique features of monetary capital, Benshalom expresses doubts about the function of the sales factor in the formula and argues that the specialized formula for the financial industry should abandon it and adopt the

1206. Benshalom, The Quest to Tax Financial Income, *supra* n. 54.
1207. *Ibid.*, 172.

two-factor formula based on payroll and tangible assets.[1208] His main argument is that it is impossible to seek a comparable market price for financial transactions, and therefore, the TP practice does not help much. In addition to the (tangible) assets factor, Benshalom's proposal heavily relies on the payroll factor as the important benchmark to apportion financial income and income from intangibles. He argues that the sales factor is too easy to be manipulated because financial institutions can conduct their transactions with their counterparties in a low-tax-rate jurisdiction, where these counterparties might also establish a subsidiary or a holding company. Therefore, it is easy to conduct financial transactions in a low-tax-rate jurisdiction to manipulate the ratio of the sales factor.

I do not fully agree with Benshalom's argument because Benshalom's presumption of manipulating the sales factor is based on the cooperation between financial institutions and their non-related counterparties. However, it is sometimes too complex and risky to conduct tax planning and tax avoidance scenarios outside of the group with non-related business counterparties.

McLure also analyses the 'fungibility' of monetary capital in the context of 'financial transactions'.[1209] McLure argues that there is no distinction between origin and destination, and therefore it would be difficult to decide the destination of a financial transaction for the sales factor.[1210]

Sadiq proposes a different formula from Benshalom's labour and tangible asset formula. While accepting Benshalom's observations on the financial industry, Sadiq proposes a two-factor formula based on the payroll and the sales factor.[1211] She recognizes the difficulty in attributing financial assets to the assets factor but argues that a sales-by-destination factor in the formula would be less vulnerable to manipulation because even banks cannot completely control their counterparties. Célestin[1212] discussed FA experiences from the US IRS's guidelines, arguing that the 'risk factor' should also play a role when trying to design a formula for the financial industry.

Last but not least, among this research and studies, Weiner's research has especially great influence on the European Commission. Based on Weiner's studies,[1213] the European Commission also follows a similar rationale to design the special formula for financial institutions under the current CCCTB Directive Proposal. The Commission is clearly aware that, because of the special characteristics of financial industries, the standard formula might not adequately reflect the economic activities.[1214] There is

1208. *Ibid.*, 207.
1209. McLure, *supra* n. 622.
1210. Section 4.3.3 of this book.
1211. Sadiq (2014), *supra* n. 318.
1212. Célestin, *supra* n. 54, available at http://hdl.handle.net/2123/846.
Similar opinion, *see* Leung, *supra* n. 319.
1213. Weiner, *supra* n. 47.
1214. CCCTB Working Document No. 60, paragraph 69:

> 69. In view of the specific characteristics of some economic sectors, a single apportionment formula covering all economic sectors may not adequately reflect the importance of the various factors generating profits in each sector. Thus, another issue, on which expert input is sought, is for which sectors (if any) a specific formula should be foreseen and how any specific formulae and factors could be defined for such sectors (keeping

undoubtedly a consensus that financial institutions need their own special formula other than the standard formula,[1215] but it is difficult to answer what such special industry formula would look like. According to Weiner's studies,[1216] financial institutions' sales factors may also contain receipts from intangible assets, which is always the centre of disputes due to their mobility and how difficult they are to calculate and locate. Thus, a special sales factor is also needed.

The blurred boundary between the sales factor and the property factor for the financial industry seems inevitable because monetary capital as a type of production/input element cannot be fully isolated from the consumer/market/output side. When it comes to FA, the standard formula based on the manufacturing industry must adapt in order to accommodate monetary capital. Money, as an atypical type of production element, is fluid in nature and closely linked to the sales side and the production side.

7.2.1.2 Reaffirmation of the Labour Factor's Function for Financial Institutions

As to the labour factor, human resources are essential and play an important role. The core of financial engineering and designing of various financial products heavily rely on financial engineers and researchers working in the industry.

As Benshalom's and Celestin's analyses above reaffirm, human resources actually play a very significant role in the financial industry. Financial engineering, estimating risks, and building models for financial products still heavily rely on financial engineers' brains and design. Nowadays, even though artificial intelligence technology has been developing fast, the application of AI to financial models is still not mature.

From the perspective of the existing rules of the MTC's recommendations and California's rules, the payroll factor is still a cornerstone. It is especially worth noting that California has indeed followed the trend of adopting a single-sales-factor formula as its standard formula since 2011, keeping, however, the three-factor formula for financial institutions and thus, the payroll factor still plays an important role. Therefore, for the financial industry formula, the labour factor is still a justified factor and should be kept also for the EU's FA regime.

There is indeed some difficulty arising, however, when we try to attribute the payroll factor to employees because financial engineers can work from any place

---

in mind that there was general agreement that sector-specific formulae should be as limited as possible). In the current view of the Commission Services the following sectors seem to need special formulae: financial services, transportation services such as airlines and railways, and television and broadcasting services.

1215. *See also* the CCCTB Working Document No. 52, Common Consolidated Corporate Tax Base Working Group (CCCTB WG), An overview of the main issues that emerged during the discussion on the mechanism for sharing the CCCTB, 13 March 2007, paragraph 47: '47. Few experts commented on this point, mainly considering that there should be as little differences as possible, the financial sector being one potential candidate to a 'special' formula.'

1216. Weiner, *supra* n. 47.

around the world when creating and designing financial products. However, such difficulty should not be a reason to exclude the labour factor in the formula for the financial industry formula. In fact, these financial engineers should be attributed to where they physically work because these 'working from home' financial engineers are sustained by the public benefits jurisdiction where they are actually located, including the local healthcare system. This rationale is consistent with the labour factor of the standard formula discussed in Chapter 5.

7.2.1.3 Lessons from the US: Conflict Between Money-Centre States and Market States

In the US, MTC's FA recommendation to the financial industry was not fully developed until 1994. Financial institutions were not in the scope of application of the UDITPA (1957)/Multistate Tax Compact (1967) because national banks had been immune from state taxation until 1976 according to federal legislation.[1217] This is due to a historical reason. Federal legislation restricts states' taxing powers upon 'national banks'. This is the 'doctrine of immunity from state taxation'. States could still impose state taxation on state banks which only conduct in-state activities and did not infringe the doctrine of immunity mentioned above.

Since 1976, the federal restrictions on states' taxing powers on national banks have been removed.[1218] After decades, the interstate lending business has grown, even though the doctrine of immunity from state taxation has been kept to the side. The growth of the interstate lending business has created the necessity to coordinate the division of multistate taxable income between states: banks and their clients can be located in different states, and thus how the taxing powers between states should be divided is under dispute.[1219] Just like other industries involving cross-border economic activities, the input (production/service provision) and the output (clients and customers) could belong to different states which can have a conflict of interest regarding taxing such economic activities. In the context of the financial industry, such conflict is obvious when it involves an interstate loan arrangement: clients are located in the 'market states', whereas the financial institutions are located in money-centre states.

In order to address the issue of taxing income earned from financial institutions, in the early 1990s, the MTC initiated a project to adopt a specialized formula model statute for financial institutions for use by states.[1220] In 1994, the specialized formula

1217. Hellerstein, Hellerstein & Swain, *supra* n. 349, at 6.30.

1218. *Ibid.*

Regarding the history of state taxation immunity for banks, *see* Sandra B McCray, State Taxation of Interstate Banking, 21 Georgia Law Review 283 (1986); Hellerstein, *supra* n. 1180.

1219. The market state can be very aggressive in extending its taxing power to the out-of-state financial institutions if the great amount of consumers are located within the state; for the early discussions before 1994 MTC Financial Institutions Formula was adopted, *see* John S Jagiela & Martin A Culhane III, A Taxing Situation for Out-of-State Financial Institutions: Minnesota Sets the Stage by Adopting MTC Proposed Regulations, 8 Journal of State Taxation 35.

1220. There are more than 50 articles in the MTC working group's dossier when they discuss this tension between the market state and the money centre state. For example, FE Ferguson, State

for financial institutions was adopted. Many states have followed this model statute and implemented it into their state legislation.

Since there have been a few problems and difficulties which have arisen since 2007 while implementing the 1994 financial institutions formula, the MTC again initiated the reform project to amend the 1994 financial institutions formula.[1221] In December 2014, a new specialized formula (valid since 1 January 2016) for financial institutions was adopted,[1222] and this reform is based on experiences of implementing the 1994 financial institutions formula.[1223]

The new 2016 MTC financial institutions formula amends the 1994 MTC financial institutions formula in several aspects, but the definition of financial institutions is not changed. The 2016 MTC financial institutions formula makes several amendments to the 1994 MTC financial institutions formula, but still retains much of it intact, such as the definition of financial institutions

In this section, both the 1994 MTC financial institutions formula and the 2016 MTC financial institutions formula are discussed aiming to seek the underlying normative framework and not limiting the discussion to a specific recommendation.

Both the 1994 MTC financial institutions formula and the 2016 MTC financial institutions formula demonstrate the importance of monetary capital and the tension of money-centre states and market states. The 1994 MTC financial institutions formula adopted a three-factor formula but provided a special sales factor (which is changed to the receipts factor; in this chapter, the terms receipts factor and sales factor are used interchangeably) and a property factor. Compared to the standard formula at that time, the 1994 MTC financial institutions formula's receipts factor already deviated from the COP rule (*see* Chapter 4). It is evidence of the unreasonableness of the COP rule, but the ambition of 'taking into account both money-centre states and market states' can lead to unnecessary complexities, as I elaborate on section 7.2.3.

Since the central debate focuses on the tension between 'money-centre states' and 'market states', it is crucial to strike a balance of taxing powers among money-centre states and consumer/market states in interstate banking activities. In the original MTC's financial institutions formula, the receipts factor tends to reflect the market states' interests, and the property factor tends to reflect the money-centre states' interest.[1224]

Taxation of Financial Institutions, in *Bank Administrative Institute-Multistate Taxation of Banking*, 1990 (Exhibit K17). The discussions before 1994 are collected in MTC's archive and can be requested at https://www.mtc.gov/.

1221. Michael A Garst, An Overview of the Sales Apportionment Factor and Its Application to Sales of Financial Instruments, 26 Journal of State Taxation 15 (2007).

1222. Resolution Adopting Recommended Amendments to the Formula for the Apportionment and Allocation of Net Income of Financial Institutions, MTC, 22 December 2014, which can be requested at https://www.mtc.gov/.

1223. For the resolution and the amended formula, these documents can be requested at https://www.mtc.gov/.

For the explanation of 2016 MTC financial institutions formula, *see* Sheldon H Laskin, 'Final Report of the Hearing Officer Regarding Proposed Amendments to the Formula for the Apportionment and Allocation of Net Income of Financial Institutions', which can be requested at https://www.mtc.gov/.

1224. Hellerstein, Hellerstein & Swain, *supra* n. 349, at 10.8.

However, the original intention is not fully implemented and this is not the end of the story. The effort of trying to strike a balance has also influenced the composition of both the sales and the property factor. In the 2016 MTC financial institutions formula, there are items in the sales factor that represent the money-centre state's interest, not the market state's interest. The same phenomenon also appears in the property factor: some items are included to represent the consumer/market state's interest, not the money-centre state's interest.[1225] The blurred boundary between the function of the sales factor and the property factor is also a feature of monetary capital. The borrower is the one who needs the financial service and capital injection, but the borrower is also the key contributor to the bank's capital by paying interest. Although the bank is established in the money-centre state, the bank's income will depend mostly on its clients, either by them purchasing financial products or by their deposits. Given this, it cannot be denied that the market state plays a role in the industry.

However, the money-centre state is as important as the market state where sales take place. The money-centre state provides a safe financial environment for financial institutions to make use of the deposits made by their clients. Financial institutions also have to fulfil all the compliance obligations in money-centre states. Therefore, from the 'input' side, the money-centre state also plays an important role.

7.2.2 Towards the Market-Neutral Subjective Scope of Financial Institutions

7.2.2.1 What Are 'financial institutions' for the Current CCCTB Directive Proposal?

Although it looks like a consensus, the European Commission's CCCTB Working Documents have never directly provided the underlying rationale for the special formula for financial institutions. It is not clear what kind of industry should be defined as a financial industry, as well as in other preparatory work.[1226]

1225. *See* the following table of the receipt factor and the attribution rule in section 3 of the 1994 MTC financial institutions formula.

1226. As part of the preparatory work, the Commission's CCCTB proposal also considers PwC's research report in 2008. The research report mentions several regulatory needs for financial industries and classified the financial industries as the banking sector and the insurance sector.

PwC, Study on the Possible Adjustments for Financial Institutions of the General Rules of the Common Consolidated Corporate Tax Base (CCCTB) as the Annex of the CCCTB Working Document No. 60.

PwC research report takes a broad definition of financial institutions, including insurance industry.

The classification in the PwC's research report is also reflected in the CCCTB Directive Proposal in 2011: Article 98 deals with financial institutions in the strict sense, i.e., the banking sector, and Article 41 deals with insurance undertakings. Unfortunately, the PwC report is only based on the CCCTB Working Document No. 57, which discusses only the technical details about the consolidated tax base, not the sharing mechanism and thus it does not mention the formula for special industries at all. This is because the sharing mechanism

Article 40 of the 2016 CCCTB Directive Proposal[1227] provides a special formula for 'financial institutions'. The definition of financial institutions in Article 40 is referred to in Article 4(29) (a), (d), (e), (f), (g), (h), and (i) of the 2016 CCTB Directive. According to Article 4(29):[1228]

> (29) 'Financial undertaking' means any of the following entities:

---

falls outside the scope of Working Document No. 57. Therefore, the PwC report is not a good reference to seek the underlying rationale of a special formula.

Regarding the subjective scope, it is silent in the Commission Services, Room Document #2, Working Party on Tax Questions - Direct Taxation 28 September 2012, not published, requested from the Council Register for Access for the documents.

1227. Article 40 of the 2016 CCCTB Directive Proposal:

> Calculation of the asset and sales factors for financial institutions
>
> The asset factor of a financial institution, as referred to in point (29)(a), (d), (e), (f), (g), (h) and (i) of Article 4 of Directive 2016/xx/EU, shall be 10% of the value of financial assets, with the exception of own shares and of participations that give rise to tax exempt income. Financial assets shall include assets held for trading as referred to in Article 21 of Directive 2016/xx/EU. Financial assets shall be included in the asset factor of the group member that had those assets recorded in its books when it became a member of the group.
>
> The sales factor of a financial institution, as referred to in point (29)(a), (d), (e), (f), (g), (h) and (i) of Article 4 of Directive 2016/xx/EU, shall be 10% of its revenues in the form of interest, fees, commissions and revenues from securities, excluding value added tax, other taxes and duties. Intra-group sales shall not be included. For the purposes of Article 38(2), financial services shall be considered to be carried out, in the case of a secured loan, in the Member State in which the security is situated or, if that Member State cannot be identified, the Member State in which the security is registered. Other financial services shall be considered to be carried out in the Member State of the borrower or of the person who pays fees, commissions or other revenue. Where the borrower or the person who pays fees, commissions or other revenue cannot be identified or if the Member State in which the security is situated or registered cannot be identified, the sales shall be attributed to all group members in proportion to their labor and asset factors.

It is comparable to Article 98 of the 2011 CCCTB Directive Proposal.

1228. Article 4(29)(a), (d), (e), (f), (g), (h) and (i) are within the scope of Article 40 of the 2016 CCCTB Directive Proposal; as to insurance companies and reinsurance companies, they are within the scope of Article 41 of 20116 CCCTB Directive Proposal. Comparing to Article 98(1) of the 2011 CCCTB Directive Proposal, Article 40 of the 2016 CCCTB Directive adopts a different legislative technique by numerating types of financial institutions clearly. According to Article 98(1) of the 2011 CCCTB Directive Proposal, the financial institutions include two types of entities: (1) credit institutions which are within the scope of Directive 2006/48/EC, and

(2) entities, except for insurance undertakings, that hold financial assets amounting to 80% or more of all their fixed assets. The second type of financial institution is a quite broad scope.

However, Article 40 of the 2016 CCCTB Directive Proposal, in combination with Article 4(29) of the 2016 CCTB Directive Proposal, has obviously missed the definition of one important category: 'credit institution'. Article 4(29)(a) of the 2016 CCTB Directive Proposal lists several Directives to indicate 'a credit institution or an investment firm', but none of the Directives listed in Article 4(29)(a) refers to banks, the most common financial institution. New Article 4(29)(a) of the 2016 CCTB Directive Proposal missed the definition of a credit institution whereas Article 98 of the 2011 CCCTB Directive Proposal refers to a credit institution by Directive 2006/48/EC. Directive 2006/48/EC is already replaced by Directive 2013/36/EU. It is obvious that the 2016 CCTB Directive Proposal and 2016 CCCTB Directive Proposal made a legislative mistake by forgetting to refer to the Directive regulating a credit institution like banks.

(a) a credit institution or an investment firm as defined in point (1) of Article 4(1) of Directive 2004/39/EC of the European Parliament and of the Council, an AIFM as defined in point (b) of Article 4(1) of Directive 2011/61/EU of the European Parliament and of the Council, or a management company as defined in point (b) of Article 2(1) of Directive 2009/65/EC of the European Parliament and of the Council;
(b) an insurance undertaking as defined in point (1) of Article 13 of Directive 2009/138/EC of the European Parliament and of the Council;
(c) a reinsurance undertaking as defined in point (4) of Article 13 of Directive 2009/138/EC;
(d) an institution for occupational retirement provision as defined in point (a) of Article 6 of Directive 2003/41/EC of the European Parliament and of the Council, unless a Member State has chosen not to apply that Directive in whole or in part to that institution in accordance with Article 5 of that Directive, or the delegate of an institution for occupational retirement provision as referred to in Article 19(1) of Directive 2003/41/EC;
(e) a pension institution operating pension schemes which qualify as social security schemes covered by Regulation (EC) No 883/2004 of the European Parliament and of the Council and by Regulation (EC) No 987/2009 of the European Parliament and of the Council, as well as any legal entity set up for the purpose of investment in such pension schemes;
(f) an AIF as defined in point (a) of Article 4(1) of Directive 2011/61/EU, which is managed by an AIFM as defined in point (b) of Article 4(1) of Directive 2011/61/EU, or an AIF supervised under national law;
(g) a UCITS as defined in Article 1(2) of Directive 2009/65/EC;
(h) a CCP as defined in point (1) of Article 2 of Regulation (EU) No 648/2012 of the European Parliament and of the Council;
(i) a central securities depository as defined in point (1) of Article 2(1) of Regulation (EU) No 909/2014 of the European Parliament and of the Council.

As to the definition of financial institutions, there is a change in Article 4 and Article 40 of the 2016 CCCTB Directive Proposal and makes the definition more limited than the previous version of the CCCTB Directive: in addition to credit institutions, Article 98 of the 2011 CCCTB Directive Proposal includes a general type of 'financial institution': '(b) entities, except for insurance undertakings (...), which hold financial assets amounting to 80% or more of all their fixed assets, as valued in accordance with the rules of this Directive'.[1229]

Article 98 of the 2011 CCCTB Directive Proposal further has an open category of a financial institution: entities holding financial assets more than 80% of all their fixed assets. This category is too general.

1229. Article 98 of the 2011 CCCTB Directive Proposal:

Financial institutions

The following entities shall be regarded as financial institutions:

(a) credit institutions authorised to operate in the Union in accordance with Directive 2006/48/EC of the European Parliament and of the Council;
(b) entities, except for insurance undertakings as defined in Article 99, which hold financial assets amounting to 80% or more of all their fixed assets, as valued in accordance with the rules of this Directive.

Article 40 of the 2016 CCCTB Directive Proposal is an appropriate amendment because the new scope of financial institutions no longer includes a group member with the treasury function as a financial institution. A headquarter or a holding company in a low-tax-rate jurisdiction is not qualified as a financial institution under the 2016 CCCTB Directive Proposal. A treasury function group member could own many financial assets or receivables, but such treasury function group member does not have the status of providing financial services for outside customers. Rather, such treasury function group member is merely an in-house treasury department, and they conduct 'financial transactions' for their own need to receive capital on behalf of the whole group as a 'customer', not a financial institution which is often subject to heavy banking and financial regulation.

The desire to include many types of financial institutions can be traced from the CCCTB Directive Working Document No. 27. In addition to banks and insurance companies, the CCCTB Working Document No. 27 mentions that financial institutions under the CCCTB shall also include: collective investment vehicles, pension funds, and venture capital.[1230] These institutions in some Member States' national law do not have legal personality and are established in different legal forms.[1231]

To sum up, since Article 40 of the 2016 CCCTB Directive will only apply to institutions that are listed in Article 4(29) of the 2016 CCTB Directive, a non-corporate financial institution will not necessarily fall within the scope of Article 40 of the 2016 CCCTB Directive Proposal, although under the current Article 5 of the 2016 CCCTB Directive Proposal, a non-corporate financial institution might still constitute a PE.[1232]

The asset factor of a financial institution shall include 10% of the value of financial assets, except for participating interests and own shares. Financial assets shall be included in the asset factor of the group member in the books of which they were recorded when it became a member of the group.

The sales factor of a financial institution shall include 10% of its revenues in the form of interest, fees, commissions and revenues from securities, excluding value added tax, other taxes and duties. For the purposes of Article 96(2), financial services shall be deemed to be carried out, in the case of a secured loan, in the Member State in which the security is situated or, if this Member State cannot be identified, the Member State in which the security is registered. Other financial services shall be deemed to be carried out in the Member State of the borrower or of the person who pays fees, commissions or other revenue. If the borrower or the person who pays fees, commissions or other revenue cannot be identified or if the Member State in which the security is situated or registered cannot be identified, the sales shall be attributed to all group members in proportion to their labour and asset factors.

1230. CCCTB Working Document No. 27, paragraphs 18-23.

1231. *Ibid.*, paragraphs 17 and 23.

1232. For example, a securitization Special Purpose Entity (SPE)/Special Purpose Vehicle (SPV) might constitute a PE of a group member under the CCCTB Directive or defined as a type of financial institution in the national tax law, but it is not automatically a financial institution under Article 40 of the 2016 CCCTB Directive Proposal. Furthermore, Article 5 of the 2016 CCCTB Directive Proposal does not preclude any entity which is not listed in Annex 1 and Annex 2 from qualifying a PE. Such non-corporate financial entities can qualify as a PE of another group member.

Regarding securitization SPE and SPV qualified as a PE, *see* Christiana HJI Panayi, Agency Permanent Establishments in Securitization Transactions, 33 Intertax 286 (2005).

In this regard, the scope of Article 40 of the 2016 CCCTB Directive Proposal is more limited than Article 98 of the 2011 CCCTB Directive Proposal: the 2016 CCCTB Directive Proposal no longer includes any entity whose 80% fixed assets are financial assets. By limiting the definition of a financial institution, it also reduces the possibility to form a 'mixed group' because a subsidiary which holds financial assets for the group would not be defined as a financial institution under the current CCCTB Directive Proposal.

7.2.2.2 The MTC's Scope of Financial Institutions:[1233] 'banks and entities in competition with banks'

When the MTC designed the 1994 financial institutions formula, it had already taken the tension between money-centre states and consumer/market states into account. The 1994 financial institutions formula is a three-factor formula, including the sales factor, the payroll factor, and the property factor. As Hellerstein observes,[1234] the sales factor tends to reflect the market states' interests, while the property factor tends to reflect the money-centre states' interests. There are also 'balanced' rules that consider the interests of both market states and money-centre states.

The 1994 MTC financial institutions formula does not directly define a financial institution. Instead, Appendix A of the 1994 MTC financial institutions formula provides a list of examples of financial institutions and expressly mentions that this list should be a starting point for discussions for states, but it indeed fails to provide a harmonized definition. States may exclude any person from application of the apportionment rules for financial institutions. The underlying principle of Appendix A[1235] is to cover banks as well as entities in competition with banks. Appendix A was retained in the 2016 MTC financial institutions formula.

In short, the prototype 'financial institution' in the 1994 MTC financial institutions formula is a bank which conducts lending, leasing, or other dealings in monetary capital. The entities which conduct the same activities and compete with banks are also regarded as financial institutions. Although Appendix A still does not provide a

1233. *See* the overview of 1994 MTC financial institutions formula, Scott R Schumacher, Adoption of MTC Regulations Relating to Apportioning Income of Financial Institutions, 18 Journal of State Taxation 45 (1999).

1234. Hellerstein, Hellerstein & Swain, *supra* n. 349, 10.8.

1235. Appendix A (1) to (8) lists various types of corporations as financial institutions: a bank holding company, a national bank, a savings association or federal savings bank, any bank or thrift institution, fiscal agents, any agency or branch of a foreign depository, a state credit union, a production credit association. Appendix A(1) to (8) are defined in separate federal laws. In addition to specific listed institutions, Appendix A section (9) to section (11) further provide other types of financial institutions. Appendix A subsection (9) provides that except for an insurance company, any corporation 'whose voting stock is more than fifty percent (50%) owned, directly or indirectly, by any person or business entity described in subsections (1) through (8)' is also a financial institution. In other words, these institutions mentioned in subsections (9) to (11) are relevant counter parties or de facto financial institutions, which in fact mainly conduct from the same financial activities the specific financial institutions.
The whole list can be requested at https://www.mtc.gov/.

comprehensive definition, its rationale is to include banks and other entities which compete with them as financial institutions.[1236]

It is also noteworthy that Appendix A of the 1994 MTC financial institutions formula expressly excludes insurance companies, real estate brokers, and securities dealers from the definition of financial institutions. The exclusion is explained by the hearing officer's report.[1237] The hearing officer indicates the concern that including all these three types of industries as financial institutions might distort the result of the apportionment. The MTC hearing officer recommends that states can still include such industries as financial institutions if they can ensure such inclusion will result in a fair apportionment of the net income derived from such activities.

7.2.2.3 Is the 'insurance industry' Also the Financial Industry?

According to Article 4 of the 2016 CCTB Directive Proposal, insurance companies and re-insurance companies are classified as 'financial institutions', and this is why Articles 41 and 40 are quite similar in content. In my view, the current Article 41 should be amended because the insurance industry is not completely the same as credit institutions like banks. This can be explained as follows.

The assets factor of the insurance industry formula in Article 41 is identical to the asset factor of the financial industry formula in Article 40 of the 2016 CCCTB Directive Proposal. The preparatory works of the Commission show that[1238] the insurance industry is categorized as a special type of financial institution. The CCCTB Directive Proposal is similar to the OECD's approach to classify insurance companies as part of the financial industry in the broad sense.[1239]

1236. Although the 1994 MTC financial institutions formula has suggested the list of financial institutions, in practice, only a few states followed this suggestion. Most jurisdictions adopt a more restricted scope and only includes traditional banks or savings and loans companies. *See* the analysis, Jeffrey M Serether, Maria P Eberle & Michael L Colavito Jr, Can You Take This to the Bank? State Taxation of Financial Institutions, 59 State Tax Notes 717 (2011).

1237. *See* the Hearing Officer's Report on MTC's financial institutions' formula in 1994, AH Friedman, Final Report of Hearing Officer Regarding Proposed Multistate Tax Commission Formula for the Uniform Apportionment of Net Income from Financial Institutions, which can be requested at the MTC official website http://www.mtc.gov/.

1238. *See* CCCTB Working Document No. 27, 2006, paragraph 16.

1239. *See*, for example, OECD, Taxing Insurance Companies, OECD Tax Policy Studies, No. 3, OECD Publishing, Paris, 2001.

DOI: http://dx.doi.org/10.1787/9789264188396-en. According to this report, the authors think that the insurance companies and banks do compete with each other and thus should be treated similarly, at p. 19:

The reality is however that financial products in different subsectors do compete. And this competition has become more explicit as institutions have found ways to tailor their products to provide the types of benefits more traditionally found in the products of other institutions. For example, life insurers have traditionally provided annuities. With a life annuity or deferred annuity there is a strong insurance component as the amount of payment is a function of the life expectancy of the annuitant. However defined period annuities, which may be transferable on death to the beneficiaries, function economically like a certificate of deposit in a bank, even if the legal form is different.

Accordingly, in many jurisdictions the old regulatory distinction among the different pillars is breaking down. The change recognizes economic reality and is intended to promote competition and more efficient financial arrangements.

As to the assets factor, banks (or other credit institutions) and insurance companies have one feature in common: they all use monetary capital as their 'production element'. Unlike the manufacturing industry or other service industries where monetary capital plays the role of purchasing materials/tangible assets or paying salaries, in the financial industry, monetary capital, such as insurance premiums or interest on loans, is invested in making more profits. The feature that 'money makes money' has resulted in financial institutions owning a lot of receivables from investments. The assets factor in the standard formula cannot properly represent the financial assets because only tangible assets and IP rights are included (*see* Chapter 6). From the perspective of the need to have a special assets factor, insurance companies and credit institutions, like banks, have the same need and it is justified.

Different from the current CCCTB Directive Proposal, insurance companies in the US are not regarded as a type of financial institution, so the formula for insurance companies (when there is one) does not resemble formulas for financial institutions. First, Appendix A of the 1994 MTC financial institutions formula expressly excludes insurance companies.[1240] Second, most states in the US do not levy CIT on insurance industries but instead levy a 'premiums tax'.[1241] Premiums are the payments to the insurers and the key obligation of an insurance contract. Only a few states[1242] in the US still levy CIT on insurance companies, and their formulas are not identical. In other words, there is no consensus on the necessity to adopt a separate special formula for the insurance industry in the US. But we can observe that the 'received premium' of insurance companies is a vital factor in these state insurance industry formulas. Among the eight states that still levy CIT on insurance companies, five states[1243] adopted the 'single premium factor' formula to apportion the taxable income of insurance companies.

In my view, treating the sales factor of insurance companies the same as the sales factor of banks is a misunderstanding. The CCCTB should treat insurance companies and credit institutions/banks differently for the sales factor because they have different business models. Although there are indeed some similar features between banks and insurance companies, such as having a lot of receivables and producing financial products that might compete with each other, the banks' lending services are still different from the insurance industry. Insurance companies do not enhance their clients' credibility or financial capacity, and they do not have to pay interest regularly to their clients and only pay claims when an insured damage occurs. The insurance industry does not need a special sales factor in the formula because received premiums are the key element and the standard sales factor already includes insurance premiums.

1240. 1994 MTC financial institutions formula is also referred to as 'pre-2015' version.
1241. CCH Editors, 2015 U.S. Master Multistate Corporate Tax Guide, CCH Group, 2014, at 281.
1242. As of 2014, these states are Florida, Illinois, Louisiana, Mississippi, Nebraska, New Hampshire, Oregon, Wisconsin, *see* CCH Editors, 2015 U.S. Master Multistate Corporate Tax Guide, CCH Group, 2014.
1243. The states adopting the single premiums factor formula are Florida, Illinois, Mississippi, Nebraska, Wisconsin, *see* CCH Editors, *ibid.*

7.2.3 Towards a Market-Neutral Sales Factor for a Special Formula for Financial Institutions

7.2.3.1 No Justification for the 10% Rule for the Sales Factor of the CCCTB's Current Financial Industry Formula

Article 40(2) of the 2016 CCCTB Directive Proposal[1244] provides a special sales factor for 'financial institutions':

> **Calculation of the asset and sales factors for financial institutions**
>
> (b) (....)
>
> 2. The sales factor of a financial institution, as referred to in points (29)(a), (d), (e), (f), (g), (h) and (i) of Article 4 of Directive 2016/xx/EU, shall be 10% of its revenues in the form of interest, fees, commissions and revenues from securities, excluding value added tax, other taxes and duties. Intra-group sales shall not be included. For the purposes of Article 38(2), financial services shall be considered to be carried out, in the case of a secured loan, in the Member State in which the security is situated or, if that Member State cannot be identified, the Member State in which the security is registered. Other financial services shall be considered to be carried out in the Member State of the borrower or of the person who pays fees, commissions or other revenue. Where the borrower or the person who pays fees, commissions or other revenue cannot be identified or if the Member State in which the security is situated or registered cannot be identified, the sales shall be attributed to all group members in proportion to their labor and asset factors.

Unlike the sales factor of the standard formula in Article 37 of the 2016 CCCTB Directive Proposal, which in principle excludes receipts that are earned through the sale or licence of intangible or financial assets, the sales factor in the formula for financial institutions includes various receipts earned from intangibles and financial assets. According to Article 40(2), interest, fees, commissions, and revenues from securities are included in the sales factor of a financial institution after excluding VAT and other taxes and duties. The value of these sales from intangible or financial assets is calculated, however, only to the extent of 10% of their whole value. The 10% rule has no clear rationale from the CCCTB Directive Proposal itself, or from the Commission's working documents. In my opinion, this 10% rule might be the counterpart of the asset factor in Article 40(1).

From the legislative record of drafting the CCCTB Directive Proposal, we can also observe that there are two key US experts contributing to the financial institutions formula: Joanna Weiner and Benjamin Miller.[1245] They both mention the 20% valuation rule in California law regarding financial institutions. Based on these contributions, the European Commission amended the 20% valuation rule to the 10% valuation

1244. It is comparable to Article 98 of 2011 CCCTB Directive Proposal.
1245. Benjamin F Miller (2007), Comments on Document CCCTB/WP060 Common Consolidated Corporate Tax Base Working Group Possible Elements of a Sharing Mechanism, at https://taxation-customs.ec.europa.eu/system/files/2016-09/millercomments_wp060.pdf.

rule and applied it to the design of the assets factor and the sales factor of the CCCTB's financial institutions formula.

The attribution rule in Article 40(2) distinguishes between three types of sales. As for financial services, they are assigned to the location where they are carried out. This rationale is the same as the standard formula's 'sales destination principle' in Article 38(2) of the CCCTB Directive.

As for interest from a secured loan, the financial service is regarded as carried out wherever the security is registered. If the security is a real property, the location of registration is its physical location, but if the security is a non-real property, the location of registration can be the site of the headquarters of the debtor. Security is essential for enforcement of the loan, and thus attributing the loans based on where security can be executed is consistent with the sales-by-destination rationale too because the location of the security is the proxy of where the customers' market is.

As for other financial services, they are regarded as carried out in the state of the borrower or the person who pays fees, commissions, or other revenues. If no member state above is identified, the sales factor will be attributed to all group members in proportion to the labour and asset factors. This is also consistent with sales-by-destination rationale.

To sum up, the sales factor of the formula should reflect a financial institution taxpayer's reaction to its clients in the service market, and in this regard sales-by-destination principle should still apply. Article 40(2) of the current CCCTB Directive Proposal has followed the sales-by-destination rule, and therefore the attribution rule of the sales factor of the financial institutions formula is tax neutral. However, the valuation method of the service provided by financial institutions does not follow any specific economic rationale. Further discussion is found in section 7.2.3.4.

7.2.3.2 The Special Sales Factor of the 1994 MTC Financial Institutions Formula: Reconciling the Conflicts Between Money-Centre States and Market States

Section 3 of the 1994 MTC financial institutions formula provides the sales factor and items that are included in the sales factor and the attribution rules. In order to have an overview, I illustrate them in Table 10.

The first column lists the legal basis, and the second column lists the includable items. The third column indicates the attribution rule of these items to the numerator. Since the MTC formula is unilateral, the items attributed to the numerator must be 'within the state' or calculated on a pro-rata basis and regarded as they are within the state. The fourth column indicates the implications of the rule involved: whether it considers the interest of money-centre states or market states.

Table 10 The Receipts Factor and the Attribution Rule in Section 3 of the 1994 MTC Financial Institutions Formula

Legal Basis	*Items*	*Attribution Rule*	*Implications for the Tension Between the Market State and the Money-Centre State*
Section 3(b)	Receipts from the lease of real property	The real property's location	Market states
Section 3(c)	Receipts from the lease of tangible personal property	The property's location	Market states
Section 3(c)	Receipts from the lease of transport of tangible personal property	To the extent that the property is used	Market states
Section 3(d)	Interest from loans secured by real property	The real property's location	Market states
Section 3(e)	Interest from loans not secured by real property	The borrower's location	Market states
Section 3(f)(2)	Net gains from the sale of loans not secured by real property	The borrower's location (at the pro-rata basis of the fraction in (e))	Market states
Section 3(g)	Receipts from credit card receivables	The billing address of the cardholder	Market states
Section 3(h)	Net gains from the sale of credit card receivables	The billing address of the cardholder at the pro rata basis of the fraction in (g)	Market states
Section 3(i)	Credit card issuer's reimbursement fees	The billing address of the cardholder at the pro-rata basis of the fraction in (g)	Market states
Section 3(j)	Receipts from merchant discount	The commercial domicile of the merchant	Market states
Section 3(k)(1)(A)	Loan servicing fees from secured real property	The real property's location at a pro-rata basis of the fraction in (d)	Market states

Legal Basis	*Items*	*Attribution Rule*	*Implications for the Tension Between the Market State and the Money-Centre State*
Section 3(k)(1)(B)	Loan servicing fees not secured by real property	The borrower's location (at the pro-rata basis of the fraction in (e)	Market states
Section 3(l)	Receipts from (other) services	Service providing location based on the cost of performance rule[1246]	Money-centre states
Section 3(m)	Receipts from investment assets and activities and trading assets and activities	The regular place of business of the taxpayer	Money-centre states

Source: The author.

Although in theory, the sales/receipts factor is expected to reflect the market states' interests, from Table 10, we can observe that the attribution rules of the sales factor in the 1994 MTC financial institutions formula are not purely designed for the interests of the market states. For example, receipts from services other than lending services and receipts from investment, as well as assets and activities and trading assets and activities, are attributed according to the 'cost of performance rule' (Section 3(l)) and the 'regular place of business of the taxpayer (Section 3(m))', respectively. These two attribution rules reflect the interests of money-centre states. Therefore, the sales factor in section 3 of the 1994 MTC financial institutions formula has tried to strike some balance between money-centre states and market states. We should understand that adopting the COP rule is a historical result and compromise with the old paradigm for attributing services.

7.2.3.3 The Special Receipts Factor of the 2016 MTC Financial Institutions Formula: Towards the Market States' Interests

The 2016 MTC financial institutions formula renamed the sales factor as the 'receipts factor', and 'ATM fees' were added as an item to the new section 3(k). ATM fees are attributed to the state where the ATM machines are located. Therefore, it reflects the market states' interests.

Furthermore, several attribution rules of the receipts factor were also amended. The receipts factor of the 2016 MTC financial institutions formula includes rules which can reflect market states more closely than the 1994 MTC financial institutions formula.

1246. Regarding the problems of COP rule that is based on the origin rationale and leads to an all-or-nothing result, *see* Chapter 4.

The amendments to the receipts factor in the 2016 MTC financial institutions formula are in line with the market-sourcing principle/the destination principle, that the sales factor/the receipts factor should reflect the economic output side and taxpayers' reaction to customers/clients.

Such amendment is consistent with the amendment of the new MTC standard formula's sales factor regarding the attribution of receipts from services, i.e., section 17 of the MTC Regulation IV in 2015 (discussed in Chapter 4). In the old MTC standard formula as well as section 3(l) of the 1994 MTC financial institutions formula, the attribution rule for receipts earned from providing services or intangibles was still the 'cost of performance' rule, i.e., attributing the cross-border service to one single state where the greatest costs are generated for the provision of the services or intangibles.

The traditional COP rule does not reflect the market side of activities, and thus the new section 17 of the MTC Regulation IV, i.e., the sets of sophisticated market-sourcing rules, was also amended in 2015. The new section 3(m) (old section 3(l)) of the 2016 MTC financial institutions formula regarding 'receipts from services' also amends the COP rule and adopts the market-sourcing rules instead. The 2016 financial institutions formula still keeps the COP rule for incidental receipts for administrative convenience and political reasons in the context of the US, expecting that most states will still keep COP rule for incidental receipts.[1247] In this regard, the COP rule is not useful for the sales factor of the financial industry formula in the EU's FA regime.

7.2.3.4 Remarks for the Tax-Neutral Sales Factor: Abolishing the 10% Valuation Rule and Embracing the Destination Principle

After analysing the sales factor for the financial industry in the MTC formula and California laws closely, it is clear that adopting the 10% rule for the sales factor for the financial industry formula in Article 40 of the 2016 CCCTB Directive Proposal has created some misunderstanding. The 20% rule of California law is designed specifically for the assets factor of a mixed group. Applying the 10% rule to the sales factor has no logical reason and should not be used.

Furthermore, the valuation of loans in the sales factor for the financial industry factor should be calculated according to *the rationale of net gains*, without including the capital principal because the capital principal should be reflected in the assets and not in the sales factor. The sales factor should represent taxpayers' 'response to their clients'. In this regard, the actual remuneration for providing a financial product or a typical loan, only the interest or the service fees, is logical to be included in the sales factor; the principals that the customers have to return are not the taxpayers' response to their customers but banks' production elements.

1247. Laskin, *supra* n. 1223, at 8.

7.2.4 Towards a Market-Neutral Asset Factor for Financial Institutions

7.2.4.1 Financial Assets Should Be Attributed to Where They Are Being Utilized

Since monetary capital performs the function of production means for financial institutions, financial assets should be properly taken into account in the assets factor because it represents the input side of financial institutions. Financial assets have different functions for non-financial institutions as discussed in section 6.5.1.

According to the definition in Article 4(20) of the 2016 CCTB Directive Proposal, financial assets include:

> shares in, and loans to, associated enterprises as referred to in Article 56 of this Directive, participating interests as defined in Article 2(2) of Directive 2013/34/EU of the European Parliament and of the Council, loans to undertakings with which the taxpayer is linked by virtue of participating interests, investments held as fixed assets, other loans, and own shares to the extent that national law permits their being shown in the balance sheet.

Article 40(1) of 2016 CCCTB Directive Proposal is not consistent with the normative framework because financial assets are included in the assets factor of the financial institution in which these assets are recorded: so, the financial assets are always attributed to the group member in which they are first recorded. In other words, Article 40(1) of the 2016 CCCTB Directive Proposal will result in all loan receivables being attributed to the financial institutions' nominator of their assets factor, i.e., the lender, because the loans are recorded. If the financial institution enters into a loan agreement with borrowers in other Member States, regardless of whether or not the financial institution has a subsidiary in the borrower's Member State, the intangibles are always in the lender financial institution because the financial assets are recorded by the lender.

Moreover, the financial assets are included in the assets factor of the financial institution 'that had those assets recorded in its books when it became a member of the group'. There is no explanation from the European Commission of this specific time of when these assets are recorded 'when it (the owner of financial assets) becomes a group member'. It seems that Article 40(1)'s timing restriction for recording the financial assets can have an anti-shifting effect against an abusive intra-group asset transfer. But transactions of financial assets can take place quite often in financial institutions after they join a CCCTB group. Article 40(1)'s specific timing restriction for recording the financial assets in the asset factor does not always reflect the economic reality.

Another question arising from Article 40(1) is if a recorded financial asset of one group member is later transferred to a third party outside the group or to another group member, should the financial asset still be taken out from the assets factor? The answer should be affirmative because the original financial institution does not own the financial assets any longer. Nevertheless, Article 40(1)'s text refers to the opposite. From the text of Article 40(1), the financial assets, which are already recorded in the assets factor, will still be recorded there. Such an interpretation is quite unreasonable, and it is an overly zealous consequence of the anti-shifting concern.[1248]

In short, attributing financial assets according to the initial recording under the current CCCTB Directive Proposal is contrary to the economic reality and deviates from the rationale of attributing assets to where the assets are 'utilized'. Therefore, such attribution rule is not consistent with benefit-based MN.

7.2.4.2 The MTC's Asset Factor for Financial Institutions: Also an Effort to Reconcile Money-Centre States and Market States

As indicated above, the MTC in the US adopted a special formula for financial institutions. The underlying rationale of the MTC's special industry formula is to reconcile the tension between money-centre states and market states, especially in the case of cross-border banking services. We can see this rationale embodied in the property factor of the MTC's financial institutions formula.

7.2.4.2.1 The Special Property Factor of the 1994 MTC Financial Institutions Formula: The 'SINAA' Test for Loan Receivables

Section 4 of the 1994 MTC financial institutions formula provides the special property factor, as summarized in Table 11. Financial institutions hold many more intangibles than the manufacturing corporations, and this is the industry feature of financial institutions. Therefore, the property factor of the standard formula cannot fairly reflect their properties. In addition to the tangibles and real properties, section 4 of the 1994 MTC financial institutions formula includes two additional special intangibles: loan receivables and credit card receivables.[1249] Other types of intangibles, such as patents, copyrights, etc., are still excluded from the property factor. To sum up, the property factor of the 1994 MTC financial institutions formula includes four types of properties:

1248. Furthermore, according to the text itself, such an anti-avoidance rule is inherently vulnerable: it cannot combat the tax avoidance scenario if the group transfers receivables to a company first, then makes it a group member later. In such a case, the transferred receivables can be included in the asset factor of the transferee because they are already recorded in the transferee's balance sheet 'when the transferee becomes a group member'; however, they are not leaving the transferee's asset factor, according to Article 40. It is indeed such a transaction of the receivables outside the group that will inevitably trigger taxation from realizing the hidden reserves, but the benefits sometimes can outweigh the costs. The same financial assets can be counted legally twice and thus distort the sharing formula of all other group members. Such a scenario can directly change the asset factor and even the sales factor of the old group member, but the Article 40(1)'s time restriction does not deal with this scenario.

1249. Section 4(c) to (e) provides the valuation rules for these properties. As to properties owned by the taxpayers, real property and tangible personal property are valued according to the original costs. The value of the owned properties that is included in the property factor is decided annually at the average value of the first day and the last day of the taxable year. The loans and credit cards receivables are valued at their 'outstanding principal balance', without regard to any reserve for bad debts. This is different from the valuation method of other tangible and real properties.

real properties, tangible personal properties (including transportation properties and aircraft), loan receivables, and credit card receivables.

As to the attribution rules, depending on the properties, different rules apply. In theory, the property factor should reflect the money-centre states' interests. These attribution rules of the property factor have different implications for the tension between market states and money-centre states.[1250] The attribution rules for loans and credit card receivables are the key ones. Section 4(g) provides that loans are attributed to the state of the 'regular place of business of the taxpayer with which it has a preponderance of substantive contacts' and provides five indicators to decide the 'preponderance of substantive contacts'. The five indicators should be taken together to decide the location of the loan. The five indicators represent the different chronological stages of a loan agreement, including 'solicitation', 'investigation', 'negotiation', 'approval', and 'administration'. This is called the 'SINAA' test. The SINAA test, in fact, represents both money-centre states' and market states' interests.

The SINAA test is another example demonstrating that the 1994 MTC financial institutions formula tries to strike a balance between the conflicting interests of money-centre states and market states. As a consequence, the property factor does not merely represent the production side; it is also expected to represent the market side. But this is not consistent with the theory. Therefore, the EU's formulary apportionment should not follow this option for attributing financial assets in the assets factor.

Table 11 The Property Factor and the Attribution Rule in Section 4 of the 1994 MTC Financial Institutions Formula

Legal Basis	*Items Included in the Property Factor*	*Attribution Rule for the Numerator*	*Implications Between the Market State and Money-Centre State*
Section 4(f)(1)	real property and tangible personal property owned by or rented to the taxpayer	the physical location	irrelevant
Section 4(f)(2)	transportation property	to the extent of in-state use	irrelevant
Section 4(f)(2)	aircrafts	to the extent of in-state use is calculated as the ratio of 'in-state landings to the total landings'	irrelevant

1250. Except for financial institutions' tangible assets, such as real estates, transportation properties, which are attributed to the physical location of where they are used.

Legal Basis	*Items Included in the Property Factor*	*Attribution Rule for the Numerator*	*Implications Between the Market State and Money-Centre State*
Section 4(g) and (h)	loans and credit card receivables	a regular place of business of the taxpayer with which it has a preponderance of substantive contacts, based on the following indicators as an overall analysis (the SINAA test)	both money-centre states and market states
		solicitation	market states
		investigation	market states
		negotiation	money-centre states
		approval	money-centre states
		administration	money-centre states

Source: The author.

7.2.4.2.2 *The Special Property Factor of the 2016 MTC Financial Institutions Formula: Excluding the Loans and Credit Card Receivables*

As to the property factor, the 2016 MTC financial institutions formula has a revolutionary amendment: the loans and credit card receivables are excluded from the property factor, and thus the complicated SINAA test will no longer apply. The MTC Working Group reached the practical conclusion[1251] that it is too difficult to properly regulate the loan and credit card receivables in the property factor, so they should no longer be included in the property factor.

Industry representatives expressed to the MTC Working Group that retaining the loans and credit card receivables in the property factor for financial institutions was still preferable.[1252] Despite the concerns from industry representatives, the 2016 MTC financial institutions formula excludes loan and credit card receivables from the property factor and abolishes the SINAA test. This revolutionary change to the property factor is the response to the criticism of the SINAA test. The SINAA test's deciding the 'location of loans' was criticized for its difficulty and high uncertainty.[1253] Since the

1251. Laskin, *supra* n. 1223, at 6.
1252. *Ibid.*
1253. The criticism of the SINAA test, *see* the MTC working document archive, Financial Institution Industry Thoughts/Reactions, Attached to the Status Report re Financial Institutions Work Group in 2013, available and can be requested at the MTC official website http://www.mtc.gov/.

loan and credit card receivables are inherently intangible, it is not surprising that attributing them to a location is difficult. The MTC Working Group seemed to embrace administrative practicality again. Since it is too difficult, or even impossible, to attribute the loan and credit card receivables, the MTC Working Group decided to exclude them completely.

It should be noted that such exclusion is out of concern for administrative difficulty of attributing these loan receivables and credit card receivables, not out of any economic rationale. The direct consequence is that the property factor of the formula for financial institutions would be the same as the property factor of the MTC standard formula: only tangible properties are included in the property factor.

To sum up, the amendment to exclude loan receivables and credit card receivables is mainly due to administrative convenience and the wish to eliminate the difficulty of applying the SINAA test to search for the location of the loan receivable. Such amendment seems overly zealous and still neglects the importance of such receivables in the financial industry,[1254] and it is not insightful for designing the CCCTB's financial industry formula.

7.2.4.3 The CCCTB's 10% Valuation Rule for the Assets Factor Needs a New Interpretation

The current CCCTB's standard sharing formula's asset factor does not include any intangible assets because the taxpayer might be able to shift intangibles arbitrarily.[1255] However, excluding all intangible assets from the assets factor is not consistent with the economic reality that many intangibles, such as IP rights, are the key driver for value creation. Therefore, in Chapter 6, I explained that IP rights, such as patents, trademarks, copyrights, should be included in the assets factor (*see* Chapter 6.4).

It should be noted that the assets factor in the standard formula proposed in Chapter 6 is still not suitable (enough) for financial institutions because 'financial assets' are not IP rights, which means that the assets factor in the standard formula cannot address them. For financial institutions, such as banks, loan receivables might be one of the most important items in the assets factor.

In this regard, Article 40 of the current CCCTB Directive Proposal has taken the specialty of financial institutions into account and allows financial assets to be included in the assets factor. More precisely, Article 40(1) provides that only 10% of the value of the financial assets should be included in the assets factor for financial institutions.

1254. This position is also raised by participating industry members of MTC in the discussion: 'Participating industry members are of the view that the property factor should be retained and that the need for including loans in the property factor for financial institutions is supported by case law.' *Crocker Equipment Leasing, Inc. v. Department of Revenue*, 838 P.2d 552 (OR 1992).

1255. Preamble (21) of the 2016 CCCTB Directive Proposal.

The estimated percentage of the 10% approach seems to have originated from Weiner's research report[1256] and Miller's contribution for the European Commission,[1257] which were inspired by California law.[1258] As Miller explained, California law has provided a special asset factor of the apportionment formula for financial institutions, which is similar to the 10% rule of the current 2016 CCCTB Directive Proposal. This special California rule is only applicable when a group consists of both financial institutions and 'non-financial institutions', but the predominant income of the whole group is still earned from non-financial activities.[1259] That is, California has a special rule for calculating the financial assets' value for a conglomerate group consisting of both financial and non-financial institutions. For example, retailers or manufacturers that established financial subsidiaries to facilitate their sales are conglomerate groups.

California's special formula calculates the financial institutions' asset factor by including 20% of the face value. Miller explains that the '20% figure was derived from the relationship between the value of the property of financial and of other industries'.[1260] Miller's contribution for the European Commission roughly suggests that 10% might be a reasonable level at which to include the value of financial assets in a special formula for a conglomerate group. It seems that the Commission has adopted Miller's suggestion in Article 40(1). Throughout all other CCCTB working documents, there is no recorded justification or explanation for the 10% rule.[1261]

Article 40(1) seems to over-implement the California expert Miller's suggestion.[1262] The 20% face value rule that Weiner and Miller mentioned is section 25137-10 of the California Revenue & Tax Code Regulation, which only applies to a conglomerate group whose predominant activities are non-financial.[1263] In contrast, Article 40(1) of the current CCCTB Directive Proposal applies to all groups containing a financial institution. In California, for a group whose predominant incomes are earned from financial institutions, another special formula[1264] should be applied. Furthermore, similar to section 25137-10 of the California Revenue & Tax Code Regulation, which mentions 'face value' of the financial assets, Article 40(1) seems to decide the value of the financial assets according to their book value. However, Article 40(1) ignores the

1256. Weiner, *supra* n. 47, at 25.
1257. Miller, *supra* n. 1245.
1258. California Revenue & Tax Code Regulation section 25137-10.
1259. Benjamin F Miller, States' Approaches to Combination of Dissimilar Businesses, State Tax Notes (1995).
1260. Miller, *supra* n. 1245.
1261. CCCTB Working Documents No. 47, No. 52 and No. 60.
1262. In 2015 in the tax summer institute at University of California, Davis, School of Law in California, I talked to Mr Benjamin Miller in person specifically on this issue. Mr Miller recalled the meeting for the CCCTB and opinion he submitted to the European Commission working group, and he confirmed with me that the later development of the CCCTB Directive Proposal's financial industry formula's 10% rule for the sales factor has indeed deviated from California rules and does not make sense to him either.
1263. For the application of California Revenue & Tax Code Regulation section 25137-10, *see* James D Goeller, California Taxation of Entities in Banking Groups: The Crucial Calculation of Financial Versus General, 19 Journal of Taxation and Regulation of Financial Institutions 21 (2005).
1264. California Revenue & Tax Code Regulation section 25137-4.2 implements the MTC's 1994 Recommendation for the formula for the financial institutions.

fact that a loan receivable's value continuously varies over time, and therefore, adopting such a static criterion of valuation is also quite questionable.

The key feature of financial assets is that the very existence of any financial asset is based on monetary capital, i.e., the principal. When a financial asset is offered in the market, there will be interest based on agreements between the financial institutions and clients. However, when we need to evaluate a 'financial asset', it is quite disputable which evaluation method should be used. A typical example of a financial asset is a loan receivable. From the general view, it can argue that either the interest is the value or the principal is the value or even the total amount of the interest, as well as the principal, should be the value of the loan receivable. Therefore, we need to focus only on the purpose of the asset factor in FA. Since the asset factor should reflect the taxpayer's input side, either by production or by service performance, it should reflect the taxpayer's ability to control and make use of the assets, regardless of their tangible or intangible/financial nature.

Therefore, the valuation of a loan receivable for the purpose of the asset factor of a sharing formula should reflect the financial institution's ability to leverage and create such a loan receivable from the very beginning. This is the asset factor's fundamental rationale: to reflect the taxpayer's economic input side and ability to mobilize material resources. In the financial industry, the ability to mobilize the material resources to provide financial services should be decided by the monetary capital. In this regard, we can interpret the 10% evaluation rule as representing the amount of monetary capital that a bank can actually manage and control.

As to the attribution of loan receivables, the SINAA test in the 1994 MTC financial institutions formula in the US is also not suitable for attributing the loan receivables in the asset factor of the financial industry formula of the EU's FA regime. The SINAA test included considerations for both money-centre states and market-centre states. Although the SINAA test had the ambition to reach a compromise between money-centre states and market-centre states, such test deviated from the purpose of the asset factor and created a lot of confusion.

In my view, the EU's FA regime should not follow the 2016 MTC financial institutions formula that excludes loan receivables and credit card receivables completely from the property factor of the bank, in order to escape the SINAA test. It would be overly zealous to negate the importance of loan receivables in the asset factor of a bank. In my view, based on the rationale of the asset factor, receivables should be attributed to the member which manages these receivables, i.e., where these receivables are recorded and actually managed.

7.2.5 Towards a Formula Applicable to Financial Institutions of Mixed Groups

7.2.5.1 Limiting the Definition of Financial Institutions and Realigning the Functions of the Sales Factor

Last but not least, a mixed/conglomerate group needs a separate discussion. A mixed/conglomerate group consists of both financial and non-financial institutions, but the main income is earned by non-financial institutions. The Harley-Davidson group is a typical example of a mixed group: it has its own financial institutions to assist purchasers' mortgage arrangements.

A mixed group adds another layer of complexity to a financial industry formula. On the one hand, some scholars, such as Ceriani, argue that a special financial industry formula should be applicable only to a purely financial group; on the other hand, the 2016 CCCTB Directive Proposal seems to allow the special financial industry formula to be applicable to a mixed group, and other scholars, such as Weiner, have been indicating that there should be a special rule for such conglomerate group. In my opinion, these disputes miss the real issue and the fundamental rationale of a receipts/sales factor.

It is indeed true that, in a conglomerate group, how a financial asset should be valuated in the assets factor is an important issue because a financial asset in a conglomerate group mainly serves the capital needs of the whole group. In a purely financial group, financial assets play the role of the production means for taxpayers (banks or similarly-functioning institutions competing with banks) by enhancing credibility and service to their clients.

As indicated in section 7.2.2, I argue that the definition of a financial institution should not be defined as broadly as in Article 98 of the 2011 CCCTB Directive Proposal that includes any entities whose 80% fixed assets are financial assets. Instead, the definition of financial institutions should be limited. The current 2016 CCCTB Directive Proposal has adopted an appropriate approach.

Limiting the scope of financial institutions can clarify the function of the sales factor as well. A group member which deals with treasury functions for the group can also hold a lot of financial assets exclusively and trade short-term marketable securities frequently to maintain the cashflow for the group, although such group member would not qualify as a financial institution.

A treasury function group member is not a financial institution automatically, so that the whole group would not even be qualified as a mixed/conglomerate group: for example, the multinational group Microsoft has such a group member in the state of Washington, but this does not make Microsoft a mixed group in California. Since a treasury function group member is not a financial institution for the purpose of the CCCTB, the sales factor of such group member would not apply the financial industry formula and should not include receipts earned from trading these short-term marketable securities in the sales factor because the treasury function group member is not the financial service provider like a bank but the client which deals with its own cashflow issues.[1265]

In contrast, as to the securitization of SPEs in the Harley-Davidson group (the case discussed below), they are actually the agent of the bank to facilitate and manage purchasers' mortgages. Therefore, these SPEs can be regarded as in competition with other banks. I explain this further in the following section.

7.2.5.2 *California Experiences Refocusing on the Market State and Lowering the Nexus Threshold*

As indicated above in sections 7.2.3 and 7.2.4, for the valuation of the sales factor and the asset factor of financial institutions, legal transplantation of the current CCCTB Directive Proposal has unfortunately over-simplified California's rules and thus missed the real insights to be gained from the California experiences. The important lessons given by California's legislation are about 'mixed group', as discussed directly below.

In addition to the standard formula (which is the single sales factor), California has additional sets of formula rules[1266] to regulate different situations of the financial industry. First, California law specifically carves out financial institutions and subjects them to a three-factor formula,[1267] even though California has provided the single-sales-factor formula as the standard formula since 2011.[1268] Second, a purely financial group and a mixed group are treated differently. California also adopts a very restricted definition of financial institution: 'Corporations that predominantly deal in money or moneyed capital in substantial competition with the business of national bank'. Therefore, a financial institution should involve supply and manage the monetary capital for clients, and the prototype is a bank.

Moreover, like many other states, California has changed its receipts (i.e., sales) factor's attribution rule into the market-sourcing rationale, to customers/clients, both for the standard formula as well as for the financial institutions formula. Emphasis on the market side influences not only the attribution rule but also the taxable nexus rule. Generally speaking, a business is only subject to a state tax when its activities have reached the taxable nexus threshold; each state can set its own nexus rule in its legislation, and nexus can also be developed by the courts. California has long followed the 'factor presence test' that nexus is established if the taxpayer (i) is commercially domiciled in California; (ii) has over USD 500,000 in California-sourced sales; (iii) has over USD 50,000 in California-sourced payroll or property; or (iv) has over 25% of its

1265. This dispute has been discussed in the California state taxation case Microsoft: *Microsoft Corp. v. Franchise Tax Board* No. S133343, 17 August 2006. *See* Chapter 4 of this book. As for similar cases regarding calculating the sales from securities before the Microsoft case, *see* Ravid & Weissman, *supra* n. 684.

1266. John Harper, Marianne Evans & Rick Najjar, Harley-Davidson, Factor Presence Nexus, and Market Sourcing: How California's Expansive and Evolving Definitions of 'Financial Corporations' and 'Doing Business' Create Unforeseen Hazards for Taxpayers, 29 Journal of Taxation & Regulation of Financial Institutions (2016).

1267. Cal. Rev. 8c Tax. Code section 25137.

1268. Cal. Rev. 8c Tax. Code sections 23101, 25128, 25128.5, 25128.7, 25136, 25136.1.

property, payroll, or sales in California.[1269] However, what a 'California-sourced' business is can still be arguable in a specific case.

The *Harley-Davidson* case[1270] in California demonstrates the difficulty and complex issues of taxable nexus and apportionment when it involves a mixed multinational group whose main business activity is trading motorcycles to customers and its outside-California financial service subsidiary. It seems that both the California courts and tax authorities are becoming more inclined to embrace the customer state over the money-centre state and to affirm the customers' market side.

Harley-Davidson is a globally well-known motorcycle manufacturing company. In order to integrate and streamline the supply chain to its customers, the whole group, including several subsidiaries, conducts two lines of business which are unitary: a motorcycle business and a financial services business.[1271] Harley-Davidson only sells motorcycles to California remotely and does not establish distribution centres in California. Its financial services business line is to facilitate motorcycle purchasers' financial arrangements, including financing and insurance. The company has set up several subsidiaries and SPEs that conduct securitization to provide financial services when facilitating purchasers' mortgages, but they have no physical presence in California, and these two financial subsidiaries only contact California customers remotely. More specifically, these financial subsidiaries facilitate purchasers in obtaining a loan from Harley-Davidson affiliated banks and conduct securitization of motorcycle purchasers' loan receivables. These SPEs have no offices, agents, employees, or property in California. In fact, they have no employees at all. These SPEs do not advertise or solicit business in California either, and nearly all their functions are completed entirely in Illinois and Nevada.

Although Harley-Davidson argued that all these financial services do not constitute a California nexus, the court did not agree on such argument and affirmed California's position: California customers of Harley-Davidson already had sufficed to meet the taxable nexus requirement of the securitization by SPEs. The court's key reasoning was that the securitization by SPEs interacted with California customers on behalf of Harley-Davidson and assisted customers in having a finance arrangement with the Harley-Davidson affiliated bank. The court's approach was obviously emphasizing the interest of the market state (in this case California), and it was also coherent with the trend of focusing on the sales factor and the destination rule.

7.2.5.3 The Proposed Financial Industry Formula for a Mixed Group with Financial Assets Recorded Separately

Another question regarding Article 40 of the 2016 CCCTB Directive Proposal is how the special industry formula and the standard formula should apply to 'a conglomerate

1269. Cal. Rev. 8c Tax. Code section 23101(b). These amounts are indexed to inflation.
1270. *Harley-Davidson, Inc. v. Cal. Franchise Tax Bd.*, 187 Cal. Rptr.3d 672 (Cal. Ct. App. 28 May 2015).
1271. *Ibid.*, 5.

group',[1272] i.e., a mixed group. A conglomerate group consists of financial institution members and non-financial institution members. According to the statutory language, Article 40 applies not only to the 'purely financial institution group' but also to a mixed/conglomerate group. In other words, the denominator of a conglomerate group's asset factor and sales factor will apply to financial institution group members as well as non-financial institution group members.

Consequently, the apportionment ratio for a non-financial group member in a conglomerate group will be influenced by Article 40 because its asset factor denominator, i.e., the group common denominator, will be the same as that of the financial institution. The whole group's common denominator of the asset factor and the sales factor will include the financial assets and the sales earned from them. Therefore, although Article 40 has the title of 'financial institutions', it will influence a non-financial institution's denominator if it forms a CCCTB group with a financial institution. This might give rise to some concerns.

In the literature prior to the 2011 CCCTB Directive Proposal being released, Ceriani argued for complete separation of financial institutions and non-financial institutions and criticized an industry formula applicable to both a purely financial group and a conglomerate group as such[1273] Ceriani argued that such a special formula should apply exclusively to a subgroup consisting of only financial institutions because the value of financial assets can be huge,[1274] which can distort the apportionment result of the non-financial institution group members.

In other words, Ceriani argued for a complete carve-out approach: in a conglomerate group, the financial institutions should form a separate subgroup and the special formula only applies to the subgroup; the other non-financial group members are subject to the standard formula. Ceriani claimed that application of a special formula to a conglomerate group would distort the apportionment result because such special formula would influence the non-financial institution group member's denominator by including too much of the value of the financial assets.

In my view, Ceriani's completely carving out financial institutions from a mixed group is not compatible with the normative framework because this approach does not reflect the close relationship between these members. Instead, I think the financial institutions formula proposed in this chapter is suitable to a mixed group for the following reasons.

First, the financial assets are recorded separately and valued as only 10% under the proposed formula. Financial assets are not mixed with tangible assets or IP rights, and the 10% rule already represents the relationship between group members of the financial industry and non-financial industry. Therefore, the concern about exaggerating the value of financial assets above is solved.

Second, the definition of financial institutions is limited to those listed in Article 4 (29) of the CCCTB Directive Proposal, which include banks and similar entities

1272. The terminology 'conglomerate group' is used in the CCCTB Working Document No. 56 and No. 60. The 2011 CCCTB Directive Proposal does not use it officially.
1273. Ceriani, *supra* n. 1197.
1274. *Ibid.*, 168.

competing with banks. By limiting the definition of financial institution, the so-called mixed group would be reduced.

Third, the design of the CCCTB Directive Proposal's financial institutions formula is based on the standard formula, and then adjusting the valuation of the sales factor and the asset factor to represent the special feature of the financial industry that 'money' as the main production means. Since the 'special' relationship between the financial industry formula and the standard formula does not aim to derogate from or exclude the other, the financial industry formula and the standard formula are compatible with each other. The amended financial industry formula will apply to the mixed group, while financial assets will be recorded separately in the group's total assets as the denominator and only be attributed to the financial institution member.

7.2.6 Conclusions of This Section: Correcting Mistakes in the Process of Legal Transplantation and Back to Market Neutrality

To answer the ultimate question of section 7.2 – what a formula for the financial institutions under the EU's FA regime should be, the conclusion is based on the experiences and insights learned from the US. It should be noted that the experiences from the US are not the only truth, so one should be cautious in transplanting specific rules.

The standard formula I propose for the EU's FA regime is a three-factor formula. And this three-factor formula is also suitable for financial institutions because the three-factor formula represents the public benefits and value-creation chain from the input side to the output side. The sales factor, the assets factor, and the labour factor are all justified in the financial industry formula. The relationship between the financial industry formula and the standard formula is not one of derogation but of nuanced implantation.

Special rules for valuation of the sales factor is necessary. As to valuation of the sales factor, receipts from providing financial services should all be included in the scope of the sales factor: service fees and commissions should be calculated at the full amount and net gains (such as interests, dividends, etc.) earned from loans should be included. It is because only receipts that really represent the taxpayer's response to its client market should be included in the sales/receipts factor. In this regard, the rationale of net gain should apply in the receipts factor since this is the real response to customers. The principal of the financial products that will be returned to the financial institutions should be included in the input side of the financial institutions.

The sales factor should attribute these receipts to the jurisdiction where financial institutions' customers are receiving the service. When it involves a remote service via telecommunications technology or the Internet, these receipts should still be attributed to customers. The financial industry formula's sales factor should also implement the destination principle based on customers. Empirically, to implement the sales-by-destination rule for the sales factor of financial institutions is a common and logical trend included both in the MTC's recommendations and developments in California.

As to the asset factor, the financial industry involves various financial assets and thus the asset factor needs some special rules. First of all, financial assets should be included in the asset factor as the current Article 40 does and the valuation should be 10% of the book value/original cost. These financial assets should be attributed to the group member which actually controls and manages them, not to the 'first registered group member'. When a financial asset is transferred and registered in another group member, it should be attributed to the second group member's asset factor. Such design is consistent with both the function of the asset factor and the features of the financial industry. The 10% rule should be interpreted as the estimation of monetary capital that a financial institution could control and manage as reserves.

Implementing an FA system to the financial industry involves quite a few technical complexities and conceptual difficulties. This is because monetary capital has the feature of being mobile and fungible, and the entire financial industry nowadays relies on such complex technicalities to reap a profit. Due to the fluid feature of monetary capital, income from a financial transaction's origin or destination might not easily be distinguished, as McLure[1275] observes. Such mixture of the origin and destination also leads to myths and misunderstandings both in the US and in the current CCCTB Directive Proposal. Current US practices and the current CCCTB Directive Proposal both still have some conceptual mistakes: the CCCTB Directive Proposal adopts a 10% valuation rule for the sales factor, which is not based on any solid theory; the 2016 MTC financial institutions formula excludes loan receivables and ATM fees from the property factor and does not completely abandon the cost-of-performance rule for 'incidental receipts' in the sales factor.

As discussed above in sections 7.2.3 and 7.2.4, the sales factor and the asset factor in the MTC's (1994 and 2016) financial institutions formula still aim to strike a balance between money-centre states and market states. It would be more logical and simpler to let the sales factor follow the sales-by-destination rule and let the asset factor represent the interest of money-centre states. The EU's FA should also follow this path.

7.3 TRANSPORTATION INDUSTRY FORMULA(S): MOBILITY AS THE KEY PROBLEM[1276]

The economic activities of transportation industry, including air transportation, shipping and land transport, are mobile and often cross-border. Tax authorities are also facing challenges of taxing MNEs of the international transportation industry because of the increasing frequency of cross-border transportation activities and the multiple jurisdictions involved.[1277]

1275. Mclure, *supra* n. 622.
1276. The following graphs are published at Shu-Chien Chen, Toward a Neutral Corporate Tax for the Transportation Industry – Rethinking the Transportation Industry Formula of the Common Consolidated Corporate Tax Base Directive Proposal under EU Law, 30 ID-DRITT Journal (2020).
1277. A Hemmelrath & L Marquardsen, Direct Taxation of Air Transport Activities, in G Maisto, *supra* n. 45.

This section answers the question: what are market-neutral rules for a transportation industry formula under the EU's FA regime?

As indicated in Chapter 2, the benefit-based MN framework means that the formula design represents the taxpayer's economic activities and corresponding public benefits. The transportation industry needs a special rule within the three-factor formula framework because transportation activities are inherently mobile.

In order to analyse taxing rights of the transportation industries, in addition to the CCCTB working documents, I first explore the relevant discussions in international tax law. The international tax regime is an all-or-nothing approach, whereas in US state taxation, there are different transportation industry formulas.

7.3.1 Taxing Right on Cross-Border Transportation Industries: The All-or-Nothing Approach Is Not Tax Neutral

As to allocating taxing rights on income from cross-border transportation industries between different jurisdictions, there are two approaches: either the all-or-nothing approach - selecting one specific criterion to allocate the taxing right to one single jurisdiction; or the FA approach - allocating taxing rights, so that only one jurisdiction will be entitled to a partial taxing right of the income.

7.3.1.1 The CCCTB Carves out Several Transportation Industries

As for shipping, inland waterways, and air transport industries, Article 43 of the 2016 CCCTB Directive Proposal provides a special formula. Article 43 provides:

> **Shipping, inland waterways transport and air transport**
>
> The revenues, expenses and other deductible items of a group member whose principal business is the operation of ships or aircraft in international traffic or the operation of boats engaged in inland waterways transport shall be excluded from the consolidated tax base and not be apportioned in accordance with the rules laid down in Article 28. Instead, those revenues, expenses and other deductible items shall be attributed to that group member on a transaction-by-transaction basis and be subject to adjustments for pricing in accordance with Article 56 of Directive 2016/xx/EU.
>
> Participations in and by the group member shall be taken into account for the purpose of determining whether there is a group as referred to in Articles 5 and 6.[1278]

Article 43 applies to three industries: sea transportation, inland waterways transportation, and air transportation. Although the term 'shipping' or 'operation of

1278. It is comparable to Article 101 of 2011 CCCTB Directive:

> The revenues, expenses and other deductible items of a group member whose principal business is the operation of ships or aircraft in international traffic or the operation of boats engaged in inland waterways transport shall not be apportioned according to the formula referred to in Article 86 but shall be attributed to that group member. Such a group member shall be excluded from the calculation of the apportionment formula.

ships' seems broad, Article 43 refers to the water transportation industry only. This interpretation can be more clearly found in the Dutch and French versions of Article 101 of the 2011 CCCTB Directive Proposal.[1279] Only sea transportation, inland waterway transportation, and air transportation industries are within the scope of Article 43.

It should be noted that Article 43, i.e., the formula for shipping companies, does not apply to shipping companies under the special tonnage tax regime, according to Article 2(4) of the 2016 CCCTB Directive Proposal. Furthermore, Article 43 is based on Article 8 of the OECD Model Convention, which does not include tonnage tax.[1280] The 2012 Commission's CCCTB Room Document affirms this perspective.[1281]

Article 43 completely excludes the application of a standard formula from the taxable income earned by a group member whose principal business is sea, inland waterways transportation, or air transportation. In other words, if a CCCTB group consists of members conducting these water transportation activities as well as others, the group may only calculate the sharing formula based on group members not conducting sea, inland waterways, or air transportation activities. As for tax base from group members conducting these transportation activities, the tax base will be neither consolidated nor subject to the apportionment formula.

But the underlying reason for or explanation of Article 43 was missing. CCCTB Working Document No. 60 does not even mention 'inland waterways transportation' or 'shipping' as a type of special industry, but it mentions only the airline and the 'railway' industry. However, in the end, the railway industry is left out in the current text. There is no explanation why the railway industry is left out in Article 43 in the CCCTB Working Document. There is no explanation why other types of transportation industry, such as the trucking industry, do not need a separate industry formula in the CCCTB Working Document.

1279. The Dutch version of Article 101 of the CCCTB Directive:

Artikel 101 Zeescheepvaart, binnenscheepvaart en luchtvaart

> De opbrengsten, kosten en andere aftrekbare posten van een groepsmaatschappij waarvan het hoofdbedrijf bestaat in de exploitatie van schepen of luchtvaartuigen in internationaal verkeer of in de exploitatie van binnenschepen worden niet verdeeld volgens de formule van artikel 86 maar toegerekend aan die groepsmaatschappij. Een dergelijke groepsmaatschappij wordt uitgesloten van de berekening van de toerekening.

The French version of Article 101 of the CCCTB Directive:

> Article 101 Transport maritime, transport fluvial et transport aérien
>
> Les produits, charges et autres éléments déductibles d'un membre du groupe dont l'activité principale consiste en l'exploitation de navires ou d'aéronefs aux fins du trafic international ou en l'exploitation de navires dans le cadre du transport fluvial ne sont pas répartis conformément à la formule visée à l'article 86 mais sont attribués à ce membre du groupe. Le membre du groupe concerné est exclu du calcul de la répartition.

1280. Guglielmo Maisto, Article 8: International Transport and Other Operations, IBFD (ed.), *Global Tax Treaty Commentaries* (IBFD 2015).

1281. Commission Services, Room Document No. 2, Working Party on Tax Questions - Direct Taxation, 28 September 2012, Proposal for a CCCTB Chapter XVI - Apportionment of the consolidated tax base, not published, requested from the Council Register for Access for the document.

In the 2012 Commission's CCCTB Room Document, the Commission explains the rationale of the special formula for shipping, inland waterways transport, and air transport:[1282]

> A group member whose principal business is the operation of ships or aircraft in international traffic or the operation of boats engaged in inland waterways transport shall be excluded from the calculation of the apportionment formula. The revenues, expenses and other deductible items shall be attributed to the group member instead. The provision is drafted in the lines of Article 8 of the OECD Model Double Tax Convention according to which the profits of these activities are taxable only in the Contracting State in which the place of effective management of the enterprise is situated. The shipping or air transport companies shall continue to be group members but do not consolidate their revenues with the other group members. Article 101 (of the 2011 CCCTB Directive Proposal, comparable to Article 43 of 2016 CCCTB Directive Proposal) shall be read in conjunction with Articles 59, 78 and 79 (of the 2011 CCCTB Directive Proposal), as the revenues of these companies shall be determined on an arm's length basis.

There is still some confusion about the European Commission's 2012 Room Document. First, the method of calculating the consolidated tax base of a consolidated group containing the transportation industry group member is not clear. As Simonis sharply asks,[1283] should the loss-offsetting rules for the group still apply to these transportation group members? According to the Commission's 2012 Room Document, since the rules for consolidation should not apply, the revenues earned by these companies or losses generated by them will not be consolidated with other group members either. The transportation industry will not be able to enjoy the main advantage of the CCCTB system.

Second, it is not clear how to address intra-group transactions. These special group members are still part of the group, although their taxable incomes are not consolidated for the purpose of calculating other non-air or non-water shipping industry group members' apportioned tax base. In this regard, the European Commission's 2012 explanation clarifies that within the non-transportation subgroup, intra-group transactions are regarded as eliminated. As to transactions between non-transportation companies and transportation companies, these transactions should be calculated and adjusted according to the ALP. The ALP applies to transactions between transportation group members with the non-transportation group members, according to the text of Article 43. But it is not clear how to deal with the intra-group transactions between two members of the transportation industry. The European Commission's 2012 explanation seems to treat the non-transportation group members in a consolidated subgroup, but treat the transportation group members as 'separate entities' for the purpose of consolidation and apportionment. If so, even transactions between two transportation group members should be subject to the ALP.

1282. Commission Services, Room Document No. 2, Working Party on Tax Questions – Direct Taxation, 28 September 2012, not published, requested from the Council Register for Access for the documents.

1283. P Simonis, Commentary to the Common Consolidated Corporate Tax Base, Highlights and Insights on European Taxation, June 2011, (2011), 68.

The relation between Article 43 and other Articles of the CCCTB Directive is illustrated as follows. An airline or water transportation group needs to follow different articles of the CCCTB Directive Proposal. According to Article 43, there will be a subgroup of all non-transportation subsidiaries which are subject to the sharing formula when the tax base of the transportation member does not form part of the consolidated tax base nor is it subject to the sharing formula. The transactions between the transportation group members and the non-transportation group members are not 'intra-group transactions' and need to be consistent with the ALP. In other words, the carving-out approach will create a subgroup with a group. Such approach might result in more complexities instead of the expected simplification by carving-out.

7.3.1.2 *Taxing Transportation Industries in the International Tax Regime: 'POEM' or a National Unilateral Formula*

In the international tax regime, allocating international transportation income has been decided in Article 8 of the OECD Model Convention as well as in Article 8 of the UN Model Convention.[1284] These two model conventions adopt the same criterion of the 'place of effective management' for the taxation of profits from maritime and air activities for a bilateral tax treaty. The POEM criterion grants the exclusive taxing right to the state where effective management takes place.[1285] This is also the basis for Article 43 of CCCTB Directive Proposal.[1286]

The POEM criterion itself has some problems. In addition to the difficult question of where effective management takes place,[1287] it should be noted that the POEM criterion is an all-or-nothing approach similar to a typical tax treaty provision: only one state is granted/assigned the taxing power, and there is no possibility of 'sharing or apportioning' by the POEM criterion. The historical reason for POEM is administrative convenience because it does not check the existence of a PE and thus prevents technical difficulties.[1288] POEM inevitably leads to possible non-taxation in the POEM

1284. I Richelle, Place of Effective Management Versus Residence, in Maisto, *supra* n. 45.
Reflections on POEM and its outdated feature in the digital economy, *see* Rafał Lipniewicz, Place of Effective Management in the Digital Economy, 48 Intertax (2020).
1285. The overview of different ways of allocating taxing rights on international shipping industry, *see* Tatiana Falcão, Taxing Carbon Emissions from International Shipping, 47 Intertax 832 (2019).
1286. Commission Services, Room Document No. 2, Working Party on Tax Questions – Direct Taxation, 28 September 2012, not published, requested from the Council Register for Access for the documents.
1287. Lipniewicz, *supra* n. 1284.
1288. GW Kofler, Article 8 OECD Model: Time for a Change?, in Maisto, *supra* n. 45.
Kofler cites Double Taxation and Tax Evasion – Report and Resolutions Submitted by The Technical Experts to the Financial Committee of the League of Nations (Document F.212, 7 February 1925), at 31. 'When an industrial concern carries on its activities throughout the whole world, the importance of the actual headquarters, or the "brain" of the enterprise, becomes paramount; and, above all, very serious technical difficulties may be encountered in determining an apportionment of the profits. The representatives of the Maritime Sub-Committee of the League of Nations have asked how it is possible to determine the profits earned in each of the twenty or twenty-five ports at which a vessel belonging to a

state such as in the case of the tonnage tax system.[1289] Furthermore, Article 8 of the OECD Model Convention is quite limited and only covers air transportation and water transportation, not land transportation. There is no specific explanation of this omission in Article 8, but some national treaties have been extended to include transport by road vehicle or railway.[1290]

Moreover, BEPS problems also happen to the transportation industry. Due to the inherent mobility feature of transportation activities[1291] and specific maritime law practice such as 'flag of convenience', tax planning issues are already detected for the transportation.[1292] Non-taxation of the shipping industry at the international level is as problematic as the shifting of intangibles.[1293] This is because, under the current international tax regime, it is quite easy to divide the transportation activities and 'the place of management' of a corporate transportation group. To adopt a formal criterion, such as POEM, not only failed to address BEPS problems but also has become an invitation for an MNE taxpayer to conduct aggressive tax planning, and it is also contrary to alignment of value creation.

Most importantly, the POEM criterion can neither match the mobility feature of transportation activities nor represent the public benefits provided in the multiple jurisdictions where transportation activities take place. Therefore, such all-or-nothing criterion is not tax neutral, as is the binary residence-source system in the international tax regime.

Instead of adopting the 'all or nothing' attribution rule of POEM, or the residence rule in the international tax law regime, some jurisdictions such as Hong Kong[1294] have developed their own FA provision in their national tax law applicable for shipping industries. These examples are the maritime formula and the Calcutta formula. Although the name of 'maritime formula' refers to 'maritime', such formula is also

---

trans-Atlantic company may have loaded or discharged cargo, when ten or fifteen different countries have to be taken into consideration.'

It is archived also at http://adc.library.usyd.edu.au/view?docId=split/law/xml-main-texts/brulegi-source-bibl-2.xml;database=;collection=;brand=default.

1289. *Ibid.*, 7.2.3.

1290. *Ibid.*, 7.3.3, these countries include Turkey, Bulgaria, Croatia, Russia, and South Africa, Serbia, *see* the in-chapter companying footnote 84.

1291. Hemmelrath & Marquardsen, *supra* n. 1277.

1292. Sang Man Kim & Jingho Kim, Flags of Convenience in the Context of the OECD BEPS Package, 49 Journal of Maritime Law & Commerce (2018). The tax planning data from Japanese multinationals of the shipping industry by using the flag of convenience (FOC), *see* Ryo Izawa, Who, Me? Tax Planning and Japanese Multinational Enterprises, 1887–2019.

1293. Richard J Vann, Current Trends in Balancing Residence and Source Taxation, in Y. Brauner & P. Pistone (eds), *BRICS and the Emergence of International Tax Coordination* (IBFD 2015).

1294. Cap. 112 Inland Revenue Ordinance – section 23B Ascertainment of the assessable profits of a ship-owner carrying on business in Hong Kong, 23B(3):

> Subject to subsections (4), (4AA) and (5) and section 26AB, where a person is deemed to be carrying on a business as an owner of ships in Hong Kong under subsection (1) or (2), as the case may be, the assessable profits of that person from that business for a year of assessment shall be the sum bearing the same ratio to the aggregate of the relevant sums earned by or accrued to that person during the basis period for that year of assessment as that person's total shipping profits for the basis period bear to the aggregate of the total shipping income earned by or accrued to that person during that basis period for that year of assessment. (Amended 27 of 2018 s. 32)

applicable to the aircraft transportation industry.[1295] Based on these actual examples, we can observe that a formula-based rule for the transportation industry actually has a long history in US state taxation and also exists in a piece of tax legislation even in a non-FA jurisdiction as a useful technique to levy tax on inherently mobile income earned from this industry.

7.3.2 Formulary Apportionment Experiences of Transportation Industries in the US

In US state taxation, transportation industry formulas have a longer history than the 'three-factor Massachusetts formula'. In the early twentieth century, there was already a formula specific for the railroad industry.[1296] Such formula was in the form of the 'unit rule' which is actually the origin of the FA, or unitary taxation in US state taxation.[1297]

MTC regulations currently provide three regulations for transportation industries, including airlines,[1298] railroad,[1299] and trucking.[1300] Transportation industries have the following feature in common: they all involve mobile activities, including properties and employees. Therefore, various pro-rata calculation methods are applied to calculate their 'in-state activities', i.e., the numerator of all the weighting factors.

7.3.2.1 The Shipping Industry: Diverse Formulas with the Spatial Dimension or the Time Dimension

There are states in the US which have adopted the special formula for the shipping industry which is different from the MTC's recommended formulas.[1301] These state formulas for the shipping industries are not uniform, and include one-factor,[1302]

1295. International Air Transport Association (IATA), Guidelines for Taxation of International Air Transport Profits, Appendix 7 and Appendix 8.
The maritime formula is based on the ratio of the revenue of the specific jurisdiction (the numerator) and the global revenue (the denominator).
1296. The early history of 'the Unit Rule' as one origin for current FA, *see* Elcanon Isaacs, The Unit Rule, 35 The Yale LJ 838 (1926).
1297. Wilkie, *supra* n. 1188.
1298. Multistate Tax Commission Recommendation Reg. IV.18.(e) Special Rules: Airlines (adopted 14 July 1983), which can be requested at https://www.mtc.gov/.
1299. *See* Multistate Tax Commission Recommendation Reg. IV.18.(f) Special Rules: Railroads (adopted 16 July 1981), which can be requested at https://www.mtc.gov/.
1300. *See* Multistate Tax Commission Recommendation Reg IV.18.(g) Special Rules: Trucking Companies.
(Adopted 11 July 1986; amended 27 July 1989), which can be requested at https://www.mtc.gov/.
1301. The survey, *see* CCH editors, 2015 U.S. Master Multistate Corporate Tax Guide, Chart 113 (Wolters Kluwer 2014), at 167-169. There are 16 states adopting a special formula for the shipping industry. These states are Alaska, California, District of Columbia, Florida, Hawaii, Illinois, Indiana, Iowa, Kentucky, Louisiana, Maryland, Michigan, New Hampshire, Oregon, Pennsylvania, and South Carolina.
1302. For example, Florida adopts a single revenue-mileage factor formula, Florida Stat. Ann. § 220.151(2)(c).

two-factor,[1303] and three-factor formulas.[1304] Among these formulas, the weighting factors range from the voyage-days factor,[1305] voyage-hours factor, 'revenue-tons factor',[1306] to 'mileage factor',[1307] etc. All these factors aim to describe the mobile shipping transportation activities, which might be difficult for the standard formula to capture.

These weighting factors represent the different aspects of shipping activities, including time, space, and quantity of shipping: the voyage-days factor employs the element of time; the mileage factor employs the element of space; and revenue-tons factor employs the measurement of cargos, the element of shipment. All these factors are designed to describe in-state shipping transportation activities.

Adopting the element of time in the weighting factor is a smart approach because there might be some difficulty in recording the mileage on the high seas and within the state's territorial waters, and the time element factor, such as 'port days' or 'voyage days', describes the shipping activities from another objective view. In any event, these special formulas are designed to catch 'shipping transportation activities' within the state.

7.3.2.2 The Airline Industry Formula: The MTC's Flight Departures Ratio

Typical cross-border transportation involves 'departure', 'voyage', and 'arrival'. This is the nature of transportation. Regarding air transportation, the voyage part of the activity is also called 'overflight'. Due to the mobility of airline transportation which involves several jurisdictions, it could be argued which jurisdiction is justified to levy or be apportioned the taxable income of the airline industry.[1308]

In practice, states in the US adopt different types of rules for apportioning the multistate taxable income of the airline industry.[1309] Some states follow the MTC Regulation, and some adopt other various formulas, such as the single growth receipts factor, a single-factor flight mileage formula, or a traditional three-factor formula with variations in order to fit the mobile nature of the airline business. Section 18(e) of MTC Regulation IV uses the indicator 'the aircraft's departure' in all three factors instead of using mileage as a proxy in state taxation practice, in order to reduce the problem of 'no-where income' in the airline industry.[1310]

Section 18(e) of MTC Regulation IV provides a three-factor formula consisting of property, payroll, and sales for the airline industry, but items that form the numerators

1303. The state of Louisiana adopts a two-factor formula consisting of the property and income, LA Rev Stat § 47:287.95C.
1304. For example, Hawaii adopts a three-factor formula consisting of 'revenue tons,' 'voyage hours,' and 'originating revenue', Haw. Code R. § 18-235-38-06.01.
1305. California, Cal. Rev. & Tax. Code § 25101; Cal. Code Regs. tit. 18, § 25101(b).
1306. For example, South Carolina, SC Code Ann. § 12-6-2310(6).
1307. Florida, Florida Stat. Ann. § 220.151(2)(c).
1308. Oregon has argued for its taxing rights based on overflight, *see* Elizabeth A. Gordon, The Sky's the Limit: The Apportionment of Overflights and Property Taxation after Alaska Airlines v. Department of Revenue, Willamette Law Review 26 711 (1990).
1309. The overview explanation, *see* Hellerstein, Hellerstein & Swain, *supra* n. 349, at 10.03[6][c].
1310. Hellerstein, Hellerstein & Swain, *supra* n. 349, at 10.03[6][c], the companying footnote 129.

of the three factors are all adjusted by the special ratio based on 'in-state aircraft departures'. The precise ratio is calculated as:

$$\frac{\textbf{departures of aircraft of a specific type departing from the locations in this state}}{\textbf{aircraft of the same or a specific type departing from everywhere}}$$

It is based on the value of the departure flights (the 'flight departures ratio'). It should be noted that the flight departure ratio from different types of aircraft should be calculated differently. For example, 747 and 727 aircrafts' departure ratio are calculated separately.[1311]

The airline industry formula also has a special rule for the payroll factor. The payroll of non-flight personnel and flight personnel are calculated differently. With regard to non-flight personnel, compensation paid to such employees is to be fully included in the numerator. Regarding flight personnel (the air crew aboard an aircraft assisting in the operations of the aircraft or the welfare of passengers while in the air), compensation paid to such employees is to be included but must be multiplied by 'flight departures ratio'.

As to the sales factor, it is in fact a 'transportation revenue factor': all the transportation revenue derived from transactions and activities in the regular course of trade or business of the taxpayer, and miscellaneous sales of merchandise, etc., are all included in the denominator. However, passive income items such as interest, rental income, dividends, and the proceeds or net gains or losses from the sale of aircraft will not be included. As for the numerator of the sales factor, there is a special rule that distinguishes two types of items: (1) the in-state flight revenue is calculated as the total flight revenue multiplied by the above-mentioned 'flight departures ratio', and (2) the non-flight revenue attributed to the state is attributed to the geographic state.

As to the property factor, the denominator of the property factor is the average value of all of the taxpayer's real and tangible personal property owned or rented and used during the income year. The airline formula provides a special rule for the numerator of the property factor. In principle, the property factor includes the taxpayer's real and tangible personal property owned or rented and used in this state during the income year. However, the property factor of the MTC's airline industry formula treats 'aircraft ready for flight' differently. The 'aircraft ready for flight' is still included in the numerator of the property factor at the 'flight departures ratio'.

1311. In the MTC's airline industry formula, the departure ratio is formulated as 'departures of aircraft from locations in this state weighted as to the cost and value of aircraft by type compared to total departures similarly weighted', which is not quite clear. In combination with the explanatory example attached in the MTC's airline industry formula, it clearly means that different types of aircrafts' departure ratio should apply to the aircrafts' valuation in the property factor differently.

7.3.2.3 *Other MTC Transportation Industry Formulas: Focus on 'in-state' Spatial Element*

7.3.2.3.1 *The Railroad Industry*

In addition to the airline industry, MTC Regulation IV further provides special formulas for the railroad industry and the trucking industry. The rationale for these two transportation industry formulas is to provide a fair apportionment result for the mobile transportation activities, especially when these transportation activities are conducted across states.

For the railroad industry, its weighting factors are calculated by the special ratios. This is also because the railroad industry has mobile features, and some states have even adopted the single-factor revenue miles formula.[1312] Section 18(f) of MTC Regulation IV provides a three-factor formula adjusted by special ratios.

According to section 18(f) of MTC Regulation IV, the railroad industry formula,[1313] the property factor has some special items. As to 'mobile or movable property', such as passenger cars, freight cars, locomotives, and freight containers, the value included in the numerator should be multiplied by the ratio of $\frac{\text{in-state locomotive miles}}{\text{everywhere locomotive miles}}$ and $\frac{\text{in-state car miles}}{\text{everywhere car miles}}$, respectively.

The payroll factor numerator has special rules for payroll of enginemen and trainmen performing services on interstate trains. The value of their compensation in the numerator should be calculated as the ratio of $\frac{\text{their services performed in this state}}{\text{their services performed everywhere}}$ because their services on the interstate trains are performed both within the state and outside the state. The ratio is to decide the extent to which the services are performed within the state.

The sales factor of the railroad industry formula distinguishes 'sales from hauling freight, mail, express' and 'sales from passengers'. The taxpayer's receipts from hauling freight, mail, express, and passengers purely in-state, i.e., originating and terminating within the same state, are fully included in the numerator of the sales factor. However, receipts from hauling freight, mail, and express while passing through/into/out of the state should be included in the numerator at the ratio of $\frac{\text{in – state miles travelled of such movement}}{\text{total miles travelled of such movement from origin to destination}}$. Moreover, the taxpayer's receipts from transportation of passengers passing through/out/into the state are included in the numerator of the sales factor at the ratio of $\frac{\text{in – state passenger miles}}{\text{total passenger miles}}$.

1312. For the overview explanation, *see* Hellerstein, Hellerstein & Swain, *supra* n. 349, at 10.03 [2][a].
1313. *Ibid.*

7.3.2.3.2 The Trucking Industry

For the trucking industry, section 18(g) of MTC Regulation IV also provides a special formula.[1314] The trucking industry formula has three weighting factors: property, payroll, and sales. Similar to the railroad industry formula, the trucking industry formula distinguishes between mobile property and non-mobile property. Mobile property means all motor vehicles, including trailers, engaged directly in the movement of tangible personal property. The value of the taxpayer's mobile property included in the numerator of the property factor is to be calculated at the ratio of

$$\frac{\text{in} - \text{state mobile property miles}}{\text{the total mobile property miles}}.$$

The payroll factor of the trucking industry formula also distinguishes between personnel performing services both within and outside of the state (the cross-border personnel) and personnel performing services exclusively within the state (in-state personnel). As to the compensation paid to in-state personnel, the value is fully included in the numerator of the payroll factor. However, the value of compensation paid to the cross-border personnel must be calculated at the ratio of

$$\frac{\text{in} - \text{state service performed based on mobile property miles}}{\text{everywhere service performed based on mobile property miles}}.$$

As to the sales factor, the trucking industry formula is very similar to the railroad industry formula. The taxpayer's receipts of hauling freight, mail, and express originating and terminating within the state, i.e., the intrastate sales, are fully included in the numerator of the sales factor; whereas the mobile property miles travelled by such movements must be calculated at the ratio of

$$\frac{\text{in} - \text{state mobile property miles travelled by such movements}}{\text{the total mobile property miles travelled by such movements everywhere}}.$$

These special ratios of the trucking industry and the railroad industry have one feature in common: the special ratios are applicable to the mobile items, and these ratios are decided by the type of mileage in each transportation industry.

7.3.2.4 Surface Travel, Flow-Through, and Pass-Through Distance Correspond to No Public Benefits

In state taxation cases regarding transportation industries, there are discussions about taxing rights of 'surface travel' and 'pass-through' jurisdictions. The core question is whether such pass-through transportation activities constitute a nexus and justify apportionment of the tax base.

1314. For the overview explanation, *see* Hellerstein, Hellerstein & Swain, *supra* n. 349, at 10.03 [3].

For the airline industry, there is a consensus that overflights[1315] should neither constitute a nexus nor justify apportionment because the mere fact of flying through does not avail itself of the public services or market of the jurisdiction, and this does not justify exercise of a taxing right.

As to the shipping industry, there are still diverse approaches[1316] regarding a voyage on the high seas or a voyage outside the waters of the jurisdiction. Some states in the US have adopted the voyage-days formula, so there will be 'no-where income' from a voyage on the high seas or non-taxable waters; other states have adopted the 'port day' formula, so a voyage on non-taxable waters would not be considered anyway.

As to land transportation and pipeline transportation, the answer is a bit more controversial. For example, prior to 2009, Illinois adopted[1317] 'pass-through miles' for motor carriers (land transportation), and the court also supported this formula. This is because motor carriers do have physical contact with the jurisdiction while 'passing through', even if they do not stop for picking up or delivering.

As Justice Black remarked on a 'physical basis' in *Northwest Airlines, Inc. v. Minnesota*:[1318]

> A state has a different relation to rolling stock of railroads than it has to airplanes. Rolling stock is useless without surface rights and continuous structures on every inch of land over which it operates. Surface rights the railroad has acquired from the state or under its law. There is a physical basis within the state for the taxation of rolling stock which is lacking in the case of airplanes.

It seems true that land transportation activities do create some more connections to the pass-through jurisdiction than air transportation does, and in some cases nexus and apportionment by the pass-through jurisdiction is justified.

However, from the perspective of providing public benefits, when there is no stopping point to deliver or collect goods or passengers, taxpayers of land transportation cannot fulfil the factor presence nexus threshold because they have no customers' market (the sales factor) or service provision (the labour factor) in the pass-through jurisdiction. The only possible factor presence threshold would be the asset factor, but it would be hard to argue that vehicles could be attributed to the pass-through jurisdiction if they do not stop at all. As to the land accommodating the railroad tracks, highways, and pipelines, it is true that taxpayers make use of them by passing through, but I would argue that without the related sales factor and the labour factor, the land accommodating the railroad tracks, highways, and pipelines do not represent the taxpayers' capacity to mobilize these facilities.

Therefore, in my view, transportation industry formulas should focus on the departure and arrival jurisdictions and not on the pass-through jurisdictions.

1315. *Ibid.*, 10.03[6][b][i] Treatment of overflight or flyover time or mileage.
1316. *Ibid.*, 10.03[5][a] Specialized Statutory and Regulatory Provisions.
1317. *Ibid.*, 10.03[3][b][v] Pass-through miles.
1318. *Northwest Airlines, Inc. v. Minnesota* (1944) Comments on the case, Zinn, *supra* n. 1191, at 66.

7.3.2.5 *Summary of the Transportation Industry Formulas in the US*

In the context of state taxation in the US, the transportation industry needs special rules for apportionment. This is not only because the standard formula is based on a manufacturing industry's model, but also because the transportation industry by its nature involves a lot of cross-border provision of services. The state formula aims to decide the taxability within the state, and thus there must be some indicators to estimate the reasonably attributable extent of these activities.

In the MTC transportation industry formulas, various proxies in the form of a ratio are used for different industries to estimate their in-state activities. The airline formula takes the flight's departure as a proxy; the railroad formula and the trucking industry take the mileage as the main proxy. Since the state formula is unilaterally applied to the taxpayers, these ratios are necessary to limit the states' powers to apportion the tax base.

7.3.3 Conclusions of This Section: Departure and Arrival Are Both Essential for a Tax-Neutral Transportation Industry Formula

Due to the inherent feature of mobility of transportation activities, the income earned will inevitably involve the departure, voyage, and arrival jurisdictions. From the perspective of the benefit principle, the departure jurisdiction and the arrival jurisdiction provide the main customer markets for MNE taxpayers. Therefore, both the departure and the arrival jurisdiction should be understood as source as well as 'destination' in the context of the sales factor.

From the examples of the transportation industry formulas developed by MTC and states in the US mentioned above, it is common to apply an extra ratio to the weighting factor(s). Some are based on the spatial criterion (such as the MTC's railroad and trucking industry formula and mileage factor) and some are based on time criterion (such as the port-days formula or voyage-days formula).

For the current CCCTB Directive Proposal, its 'carving-out' approach for the shipping industry, influenced by the OECD's POEM criterion, is mainly for the purpose of administrative convenience. Administrative convenience is only one side of the story about taxing the transportation industry.

FA actually can also be an alternative to taxing cross-border income earned transportation activities and has been used in practice, either on a small scale as in Hong Kong or at a state level in the US. In my view, due to the transportation industry's mobile feature, it is also reasonable to adopt the sales factor which equally weights the dimension of both arrival and departure.

In my view, for the shipping and the airline industry under the EU's FA regime, the rationale of the standard formula continues to apply. To represent the mobility feature of the transportation activities, the renumeration from transportation should be pro rata divided between the departure and the arrival jurisdiction according to the ratio of time being spent because these two jurisdictions are qualified as 'destination' of the sales. Passengers and goods are physically present in both jurisdictions. As to the asset factor and the labour factor, the payroll and the ships/aircraft should be attributed to where employees and ships/aircraft are performing tasks and utilized, also according to the ratio of time being spent within the departure and the arrival jurisdiction. The time dimension of each voyage is clear and recorded. Each jurisdiction where departures and arrivals take place could be attributed to the ratio of the payroll/employee headcounts and the value of ships/aircraft.

As a closing remark, in my view the EU FA regime does not have to include the trucking or railroad industries as 'special industries' like the US. However, for the mobile feature, these transportation industries should also be included in this provision.

7.4 EXTRACTIVE (OIL AND GAS) INDUSTRY: INTEGRATION OF UPSTREAM, MIDSTREAM, AND DOWNSTREAM[1319]

7.4.1 The Theory of the Extractive Industry's Formula

7.4.1.1 The Importance of Natural Resources

Currently there are only a few theoretical discussions[1320] on designing FA for the oil and gas industry, though it is a wide consensus that the extractive industry has its own unique feature. It is widely accepted that the typical three-factor Massachusetts formula does not reflect the uniqueness of the extractive industry, but there is no consensus on how to solve this problem.

As discussed in section 7.1, the underlying rationale of adopting a special industry formula is that the economic reality and the business model of that specific industry involve different public benefits. It is indeed the case of the oil and gas industry.

The oil and gas industry has the feature that its profits heavily rely on the natural resource itself. Profitability at the extractive stage of production, i.e., the upstream, is

1319. This section has used paragraphs from my published article Shu-Chien Chen, Lost in Translation?: Rethinking the Oil and Gas Industry Formula under the Common Consolidated Corporate Tax Base Directive Proposal, 7 Societas et iurisprudentia 108 (2019).

The following section does not include other type of mining industries because the EU's CCCTB working group has made this decision too. *See* CCCTB Working Document No. 60 and No. 68.

To distinguish the oil and gas industry between other natural extractive industries in the tax law seems unnecessary. Besides, from the perspective of free competition, such distinction is also illogical. In my view, since other types of extractive industries can demonstrate the quantity of natural extraction, the following discussions on the oil and gas industry also apply to them.

1320. For example, Erika Dayle Siu & others, Unitary Taxation in the Extractive Industry Sector, ICTD Working Paper 35 (2015).

There are some case studies on FA and the mining industry, *see* Einsny Phionesgo, Using Global Formulary Apportionment for International Profit Allocation: The Case of Indonesia's Mining Industry (Master Thesis, Queensland University of Technology 2015).

Some general theory and policy discussions about taxation on the oil and gas industry, *see* Philip Daniel, Michael Keen & Charles P McPherson (eds), *The Taxation of Petroleum and Minerals: Principles, Problems and Practice* (Routledge/IMF 2010).

greater than the later stages, i.e., the midstream and downstream.[1321] Therefore, the standard formula cannot reflect the contribution from the oil reserves, which the extractive industry makes profits from because they are typically not 'assets' of the company for any length of time.[1322] It seems that the jurisdiction where a mine is located should have some kind of priority, but the classical three-factor formula does not reflect its importance enough. Here we can summarize this rationale as the 'importance of resource origin' principle for the oil and gas industry.

The rationale of the 'importance of resource origin' has been long recognized and applied in the field of levying tax in the mining industry; the amount of production has been a key criterion to design royalties or tax levy.[1323] The mining industry and the oil and gas industry share the feature in common that the natural resource origin is the ultimate driver for the economic activities of the supply chain.

The complexity of cross-border taxation in the oil and gas industry also results from the vertically integrated feature of an oil and gas group: a group can consist of members conducting quite different economic activities. The tension between the mining jurisdiction, the transit jurisdiction, and the sales jurisdiction then becomes clear too. One oil and gas group can involve these three types of jurisdictions at the same time. In the current TP practice, it is also difficult to allocate profits from oil and gas MNE groups[1324] just like the difficulty embedded in the MNE groups in other industries.

The same difficulty of cross-border taxation also happens when adopting the FA approach: if the standard three-factor formula applies to the oil and gas group, it is very likely that the transit jurisdiction will be apportioned an even larger share than the mining jurisdiction because in the transit jurisdiction, the costs to establish a transition pipeline network for the oil and gas can be enormous and consequently increase the asset factor attributed to the transit jurisdiction. Such apportionment result seems contrary to the principle of the 'importance of resource origin' and causes some unfairness.

7.4.1.2 Public Benefit Provided by the Resource Origin Jurisdiction?

A formula applicable to multiple jurisdictions is tax neutral when it can reflect the economic reality of the MNE taxpayers in each jurisdiction, and it can correspond to the public benefits provided by these domestic governments, as elaborated in Chapter 3.

Here the question is: does the resource origin jurisdiction provide a specific public benefit to justify the weighted calculation when designing the formula? It is

1321. James L Johnston & Alan Reynolds, A Natural Resource Theory of Unitary Taxation, 6 The Energy Journal (1985).
1322. Avi-Yonah, *supra* n. 327.
1323. Lauri Finér & Matti Ylönen, Tax-Driven Wealth Chains: A Multiple Case Study of Tax Avoidance in the Finnish Mining Sector, 48 Critical Perspectives on Accounting 53 (2017).
1324. Jack Calder, Transfer Pricing-Special Extractive Issues, in Philip Daniel (ed.), *International Taxation and the Extractive Industries* (Routledge, an imprint of the Taylor & Francis Group 2017), at 79-110.

undeniable that natural resources, like the sunshine of a tropical island,[1325] is a natural coincidence of God's gift for the resource origin jurisdiction. A resource origin jurisdiction does not provide extra public benefits to have natural oil and gas reserves. However, we should observe the public benefit involved from the perspective of the consequences and regulatory needs to deal with the oil and natural gas resources. In this regard, the resource origin jurisdiction is entitled to taxing rights because it has a heavier responsibility to maintain the infrastructure.

A resource origin jurisdiction not only grants access for MNEs to explore a mine and further produce oil and gas products, but it also bears an extra burden to maintain the domestic economy. As many economists have observed, a resource-rich state can suffer from the 'natural resource curse'[1326] where exploration, production, and exportation of the non-renewable resource can contribute to the state's economic growth for the short term, but in the long term, the economy does not necessarily prosper, and local people suffer from inequalities. In any event, the resource origin state must provide additional public services to manage the local environment due to developments in the oil and gas industry.

Because of the responsibility to create and manage corresponding infrastructure and maintaining the side-effects from exploring natural resources, it is justified that the importance of the resource origin jurisdiction should also be taken into account for the CCCTB's oil and gas formula. In the following section, I analyse closely the status quo of the 2016 CCCTB Directive Proposal.

7.4.2 The Too-limited Scope of Application of the Oil and Gas Industry Formula under the Current CCCTB Directive Proposal

Despite acknowledging the necessity of adopting special industry formulas,[1327] the European Commission is still very cautious with creating industry formulas because too many special formulas might hinder the important goals of pursing simplicity and reducing compliance costs.

Due to being cautious about providing a separate industry formula, the Commission designed the oil and gas industry formula (Article 42) which closely approximates the form of the standard formula. Article 42 of the 2016 CCCTB Directive Proposal chooses the same three factors: the labour, the assets, and the sales as the standard.

It is worth noting that Article 42 is not to be understood or interpreted as a single-sales-factor formula, but it merely provides a special rule for the sales factor. Therefore, the labour factor and the assets factor in the three-factor formula should still apply because Article 42 follows the general rule, unless otherwise provided, from the viewpoint of systematic interpretation. The only difference in Article 42 is the

1325. Regarding uncontrolled natural phenomenon, tax law scholars usually are reluctant to use it as a criterion as taxability. Similar discussions take place in the context of 'locational savings/location-specific advantages' in the transfer pricing discussions, *see* Li & Ji (2017), *supra* n. 1127, at 262 which cites Hugh Ault, Some Reflections on the OECD and the Sources of International Tax Principles, 70 Tax Notes International 1195 (2013).
1326. World Trade Organization (ed.), *Trade in Natural Resources* (WTO 2010).
1327. CCCTB Working Document No. 60, paragraph 69.

attribution rule for the sales factor: Article 42 of the CCCTB Directive Proposal adopts the sales by origin rule, instead of the sales-by-destination rule. Being still quite similar to the standard three-factor formula, the oil and gas industry formula reflects the European Commission's effort to seek a proper formula for this industry and to pursue simplicity at the same time.

Article 42 of the 2016 CCCTB Directive Proposal sets out:

Article 42 Oil and gas

> By way of derogation from Article 38(1), (2) and (3), sales of a group member conducting its principal business in the field of the exploration or production of oil or gas shall be attributed to the group member in the Member State where the oil or gas is to be extracted or produced.
>
> By way of derogation from Article 38(4) and (5), where there is no group member in the Member State of exploration or production of oil and gas or the exploration or production takes place in a third country where the group member that carries on the exploration or production of oil and gas does not maintain a PE, the sales shall be attributed to that group member.

Although Article 42 is short, there are quite a few implications worth analysing. Article 42(2) is designed as an exception/derogation to Article 38(4) and Article 38(5). Instead of a throw-around provision in the standard formula, for oil and gas exploration and production group members, the sales which cannot be attributed to the place of origin should be attributed to the specific group members carrying on the exploration or production of oil and gas. In other words, Article 42(2) is the comparable provision to the 'throw-around' provision in the standard formula (Article 38 (4) and Article 38 (5)) in case of no-where sales or uncertain-where sales. But Article 42(2) adopts the 'fully throw-back rule' to one EU Member State approach, not the 'throw-around' rule.

The applicable scope of the 'oil and gas industry' in Article 42 seems quite restrictive. This is contrary to the economic reality of the oil and gas industry. In reality, the oil and gas industry covers a wide range of industries, including the upstream, midstream, and downstream industries and other relevant service industries.[1328] Upstream industries include production and exploration, and midstream and downstream industries include transportation, storage, wholesale, refining, purifying, and even some financial services. A typical oil or gas corporate group is fully integrated from the upstream industry to the downstream industry.

From the terminology in Article 42, Article 42 only applies to group members whose principal activities are exploration and production. The 'exploration and production' belongs to the oil and gas upstream industry. In other words, midstream industry is not in the scope of Article 42. Group members in the oil and gas midstream industries will be subject to the standard formula of Article 28. In other words, the scope of Article 42 of the CCCTB Directive Proposal is quite limited and does not include the pipeline industry (This is quite different than Alaska, *see* further).

1328. Kim Talus, *EU Energy Law and Policy: A Critical Account* (Oxford University Press 2013), at 114.

The Commission's idea on the necessity of a special formula for the oil and gas industry can be traced back to Weiner's consultation paper for the European Commission.[1329] Weiner mentioned that the underlying reason for a special formula was that the standard formula cannot reflect the unique feature of the pipeline industry. Not only the US but also Canada have such special industry formula. Since the pipeline is so important to the pipeline operator, 'the miles of pipelines in the province' replaces the sales factor in the special sharing formula for the pipeline generator companies because the pipelines are valuable assets. However, in the current CCCTB Directive Proposal, Article 42 does not include the pipeline industry because the pipeline industry is not in the scope of 'exploration and production'. The limited scope of application of Article 42 seems only to solve a very small part of the problem in the oil and gas industry.

The current design of Article 42 seems not to be consistent with the Commission's original intention to provide a proper special formula for the oil and gas industry. An oil and gas multinational is usually highly vertically integrated and can consist of subsidiaries and branches from upstream, midstream, and downstream industries. Different subsidiaries conduct different activities. Unfortunately, Article 42 is limited to upstream activities.

7.4.3 Towards the Market-Neutral Sales Factor: Amending the Sales-by-Origin Factor

7.4.3.1 The Sales-by-Origin Rule and the Throw-Back Rule Are Illogical and Not Tax Neutral

Unlike the sales-by-destination principle of the sales factor in the standard formula, the oil and gas industry formula provides that the sales of the oil and gas members should be attributed in the group member's sales factor to where the oil or gas is to be 'extracted or produced'. In other words, the sales factor for the oil and gas industry should be decided by the origin principle rather than the destination principle according to the European Commission.[1330]

The underlying reason for the oil and gas industry's special formula is explained in the CCCTB Working Document No. 68: 'extracting oil is not a trading activity and

1329. Weiner, *supra* n. 47.

1330. This is actually a common misunderstanding, IMF policy paper Corporate Taxation in The Global Economy (2019) also claims that 'sale by origin' rule is adopted by USA state for the oil and gas industry. This is not completely correct. International Monetary Fund, *supra* n. 25.

See discussions in section 7.4.3 of this book. Alaska has used an 'extractive factor' in the formula, not to deviate from the sales-by-destination factor. In the US state taxation cases, it is true that, the court adopted 'sales by origin' as an alternative approach to adjust the unfairness for a taxpayer of metal mining industry, not the oil and gas industry, for example, *Kennecott Copper Corp. v. State Tax Comm'n*, 27 Utah 2d 119, 493 P2d 632 (1972), appeal dismissed, 409 US 973, 93 S. Ct. 323 (1972).

Hellerstein, Hellerstein & Swain, *supra* n. 349, at 9.20[7][c] Deviation From Sales Destination Test under Equitable Apportionment Provision. *See* further section 8.3.4.3 of this book.

should be treated on an origin basis'.[1331] The Commission further expressed that such a special oil and gas industry formula will not apply to other mineral resource industries because the Commission presumes that only the oil and gas industry, after the CCCTB is adopted, will substantially influence EU Member States.[1332] Therefore, other mineral resource industries will still adopt the destination rule for deciding the sales factor in the standard formula.

A typical example that can fall within the conditions of Article 42(1) is a corporate group member which extracts, produces and sells the oil and gas products from exploration and production (E&P) activities to irrelevant third parties directly. In this regard, the origin of the sales corresponds to the place of E&P. The sales-by-origin rule seems only able to represent the interest of extraction and production origin state. In the European Commission's simple presumption, the origin of sales of oil and gas products is the same jurisdiction where E&P activities take place.

Under the same rationale, Article 42(2) provides the exception to 'the throw-around rule' of the standard sales factor. There are three situations in Article 42(2): (i) when there is no group member in the Member State where E&P activities take place, (ii) when the group member carries out E&P activities at a third country; and (iii) when the group member carries out E&P activities in a Member State where no PE is established. In these three situations, the special 'throw-back' rule applies: the sales should be attributed to the group member within an EU Member State.

The first and the third situation of 'no group member in the Member State of E&P of oil and gas' or there is no PE, might not happen very often because the PE threshold under the current CCCTB Directive Proposal is quite low: 'a mine, an oil or gas well, a quarry or any other place of extraction of natural resources'[1333] can be regarded as a PE. A qualifying subsidiary and a PE are both qualified as a 'group member'.

Compared to other definitions of PE in tax treaties, the PE threshold of the CCCTB Directive Proposal for the oil and gas industry is quite low because it does not require a separate time-threshold.[1334] In other words, the definition of PE of the CCCTB Directive Proposal is quite easy to fulfil. In this regard, it is less likely that exploration and production activities do not constitute a PE in the source state. Thus Article 42(2) might not be applicable very often in the case of 'no group member in the Member State of E&P of oil and gas'.

In the case of the second situation of 'exploration or production takes place in a third country', it might take place more often. For example, Norway is a third country under EU law. In this case, Article 42(2) throws the sales back to the 'group member' of the EU Member State. Article 42(1) is concerned much more about the fiscal interest

1331. CCCTB Working Document No. 68, paragraphs 47-48.
1332. *Ibid.*, paragraph 49.
1333. Article 5(2)(f) of the 2016 CCTB Directive Proposal, COM(2016) 685 Final. 2016/0337 (CNS). Proposal for A. Council Directive on a Common Corporate Tax Base.
1334. This is not always the case in a bilateral tax treaty. For example, Article 23 of the Denmark-Germany Income, Capital, Inheritance and Gift Tax Treaty (1995) provides several time-thresholds for drilling activities and pipelines to constitute a PE. *See* Maja Stubbe Gelineck, Permanent Establishments and the Offshore Oil and Gas Industry – Part 1, 70 Bulletin for International Taxation 1 (2016).

of the EU Member States, rather than for the purpose of a consistent rationale for the oil and gas industry. It also deviates from the policy goal of emphasizing the importance of the origin.

7.4.3.2 The Throw-Back Rule Ignores the Highly Integrated Features of the Oil and Gas Industry

Article 42 of the 2016 CCCTB Directive Proposal has the good intention to reflect the oil and gas industry's economic reality and take the oil production state into account. However, the design of the oil and gas industry formula has several theoretical flaws due to it deviating from the fundamental rationale of the sales factor. The flaws will lead to an unfair result, and sometimes the attribution can be neither the origin nor the destination, elaborated as follows.

The sales-by-origin rule in Article 42(1) can be easily circumvented because sales of extracted products can be conducted in an intra-group manner. As one example of Article 42(1): a German oil parent company has a Danish subsidiary, and the Danish subsidiary conducts oil exploration and production in the North Sea. In this group, there is a Dutch subsidiary to conduct marketing and sales activities in the Netherlands. The oil is transmitted via the pipeline network to the Netherlands. The oil product produced by the Danish subsidiary is directly sold to Dutch customers. According to Article 42, the sales of the Danish subsidiary to the Netherlands should be attributed to the Danish subsidiary, i.e., Denmark. However, if the Danish subsidiary conducts an intra-group sale of the oil, first to the Dutch subsidiary, such intra-group sales are eliminated and regarded as non-existent. Furthermore, the sales from the Dutch subsidiary to Dutch customers are still subject to the scope of the sales-by-destination rule because the Dutch marketing company will have to follow the standard formula. Article 42(1) can be easily circumvented by making use of an intra-group transaction. Such scenario is similar to the old 'setting up an intermediary' scenario of the standard formula to manipulate or reduce the sales factor. In the oil and gas industry, the upstream and the downstream industry is typically vertically integrated, and such intra-group transactions are just normal business practice.

The throw-back rule of Article 42(2) also has problems. Suppose in the same group, the German parent cooperates with a local Norwegian producer and trades the oil and gas products directly to the Netherlands on a project basis. The European Economic Area (EEA) agreement does not cover direct taxation competence, and thus the CCCTB would not apply to Norway.[1335] Therefore, in this example, the sales of the oil from Norway will be attributed to the German parent company, according to Article 42(2), because it qualifies 'exploration or production of oil and gas takes place in a third country'. The sales would be thrown back to that group member; in this case, the sales of oil and products produced in Norway would be attributed to the German parent. In

1335. Pereira, *supra* n. 81, at 2.1.5.2.
Johan Bernhard Hort, Kyrre Isaksen & Rino S Lystad, Norway, in Michael Lang (ed.), *Procedural Rules in Tax Law in the Context of European Union and Domestic Law* (Kluwer Law International 2010).

other words, Article 42(2)'s throw-back rule deviates from the underlying imperative in the oil and gas industry: the production origin state's interest should be fairly emphasized.

In this case, the sales of oil and gas products from Norway by a German parent, in fact, is attributed to neither the origin (Norway) nor the destination (the Netherlands), but merely a jurisdiction where the group headquarters are established. Such result has also missed the rationale of the sales factor. In other words, Norway, a third-country jurisdiction where the quantity of oil and gas products is large, can be easily manipulated for the purpose of the CCCTB under Article 42(2). Designing the oil and gas formula in this way is not only unfair for the resource origin state, i.e., Norway, but also harmful for the CCCTB system itself for creating an opportunity for manipulation.

7.4.3.3 Clarification of Misunderstandings about the Sales Factor's Function

The rationale of adopting 'sales by origin' for the oil and gas industry, according to the European Commission's working document, is that: 'extracting the oil is not a trading activity and should be treated on an origin basis'. The origin basis seems to correspond to the idea of E&P of oil and gas.

The Commission's starting point of its reasoning seems right but ends up in the wrong direction. The European Commission has made a conceptual mistake regarding the idea of sales. Since extracting the oil is not a trading activity per se, choosing the sales factor in the formula is incorrect and illogical from the very beginning, regardless of the attribution rule being 'sales-by-destination' or 'sales-by-origin'.

The sales factor is expected to represent the demand side of the taxpayer's economic activities, and therefore a non-trading activity cannot be reflected by the sales factor because sales, per se, are defined as activities related to the market and thus cannot be completely separated from trading. As the working document record shows, the European Commission believes that adopting an origin-based sales factor in the sharing formula can serve the need of representing a non-trading activity and 'output' of the taxpayer in the oil and gas industry. Such belief is merely a misunderstanding. The European Commission chooses a wrong tool to reflect 'output' of the oil and gas industry.

The sales by origin principle cannot serve the need of the importance of the resource origin theory because exploration and production of oil is inherently different from sales, regardless of destination or origin. The European Commission wrongly made use of the sales factor hoping to achieve the aim of taking the production jurisdiction into account.

Therefore, the sales factor of the oil and gas group should still follow the sales-by-destination rule, and it will be calculated by the actual amount of receipts earned. The sales-by-destination rule can reflect the jurisdiction where the downstream industry takes place. It is a fair attribution rule and should not be altered simply because of the need to accommodate the importance of the resource origin theory.

In my view, 'exploration and production' are conceptually closer to the production side. Therefore, the asset factor is a better alternative to achieve the aim of emphasizing the importance of the origin. I elaborate on this further in section 7.4.4.

7.4.4 Towards a Market-Neutral Assets Factor for the Oil and Gas Industry

7.4.4.1 The Assets Factor of the Standard Formula Does Not Emphasize the Origin Enough

The 2016 CCCTB Directive Proposal does not provide a special asset factor for the oil and gas industry. Therefore, the standard formula's assets factor applies as default. As Chapter 6 demonstrates, the assets factor represents the material resources and public benefits provided in the jurisdiction of the input/production side. I have elaborated in this chapter that the assets factor should include fixed tangible assets and IP rights because they all contribute to the production process.

The assets included in the assets factor are production elements. In this sense, the oil and gas extracted from the reserves are not the production means but the preliminary result of the exploration and production. Therefore, in the standard formula, the extraction result cannot be represented in the assets factor.

As indicated in section 7.4.1, the resource origin is the key value-creation driver, so granting a more weighted taxing right to the resource origin jurisdiction is justified. However, the assets factor of the standard formula cannot achieve this goal because the assets factor is supposed to include tangibles and IP rights that 'contribute' to production, not the result of the production. Since the assets factor of the standard formula cannot achieve the goal of allocating weighted taxing rights to the resource origin jurisdiction to represent the public benefits provided there, it is not tax neutral.

In the following section, I explain how the Alaska experience can give some insights into solving this problem.

7.4.4.2 Oil and Gas Formulas in US State Taxation and the Alaska Experience

Most states in the US do not have a special formula for the pipeline or upstream industry, and they still use their standard three-factor or single-sales-factor formula for the oil and gas industry. This is because most of US states do not have a special need to regulate the oil and gas industry.

There are still quite a few examples of oil and gas industry formulas in different states. The midstream industry, such as the pipeline industry and the upstream industry, such as oil exploration and production, are often regulated differently by states, though these two types of industries both need to deviate from the standard formula. For example, there are a few US states, including Pennsylvania, Tennessee, and Oklahoma, that have already adopted a special formula other than the standard three-factor formula for the pipeline industry.[1336]

A further question arises as to what formula should be applicable when a group consists of different types of industries at the same time, as a 'divided business' or 'conglomerate group'. As to an oil and gas industry group, it is quite possible that group members belong to the upstream, the midstream, and the downstream industry. Therefore, it is arguable how the scope of application of a special industry formula should be designed. Among these states, Alaska has provided a quite comprehensive statutory oil and gas industry formula for the upstream industry as well as the midstream industry. For the EU's FA regime, Alaska might provide some insight.

Alaska adopted a set of special formulas applicable to the pipeline industry and the oil and gas industry[1337] which is quite unique and thus merits discussion. Alaska's apportionment rules for the oil and gas industry are provided in section 43.20.144 of the Alaska Statutes since 1981.[1338] Section 43.20.144 provides a very comprehensive formula for oil and gas industry companies, including pipeline companies and extracting companies. In other words, not only the upstream but also the midstream oil and gas industries are subject to the special industry formula. This is quite different from Article 42 of the current CCCTB Directive Proposal because Alaska's oil and gas industry formula has a broader scope of application.

As to the downstream industries, such as marketing companies, they are still subject to Alaska's standard formula,[1339] which is a three-factor formula consisting of the sales factor, the payroll factor, and the property factor. As to the upstream and midstream industries, section 43.20.144[1340] of the Alaska Statutes provides three formulas for oil and gas production companies, the transporting companies, and 'conglomerate' companies, respectively. Conglomerate companies both produce and transport oil and gas.

For oil and gas production companies not engaged in transportation, i.e., a purely upstream oil and gas extracting company, the formula has two factors: the property factor and the extraction factor.[1341] In Alaska, the purely pipeline transportation industry, i.e., the purely midstream company, is subject to the formula that consists of two factors: the property factor and the sales factor.[1342] As to the taxpayer engaging in both production and transportation of oil and gas, the formula has three factors: the property, the sales, and the extraction factor.[1343] In Alaska's oil and gas industry formula, the payroll factor is completely left out.

1336. Hellerstein, Hellerstein & Swain, *supra* n. 349, at 10.03[4].
1337. Siu & others, *supra* n. 1320.
1338. Alaska Department of Revenue – Tax Division, Corporate Income Tax Historical Overview, http://tax.alaska.gov/programs/programs/reports/Historical.aspx?60380 (accessed on 3 October 2022).
1339. *See* Alaska Statutes section 43.20.143 referring to 43.19.010, which incorporates the Multistate Tax Compact.
1340. Alaska Statutes section 43.20.144(c)(2).
1341. Alaska Statutes section 43.20.144(c)(1).
1342. Alaska Statutes section 43.20.144(c)(2), Alaska Statutes section 43.20.144(d).
1343. Alaska Statutes section 43.20.144(c)(3).

The 'extraction factor' is a factor based on the extraction activities. It is an independent factor and calculates the 'quantity of production' by the number of barrels of oil production and the number of the Mcf (1,000 cubic feet, a quantity unit of measure in the oil and gas industry for natural gas) of the gas production. 'Barrel' and 'Mcf' are both measurements of production. Therefore, the extraction factor is closely related to the results of extraction activities.[1344] The 'extraction factor' reflects the extraction activities in the oil and gas industry, and thus it has a closer link than the 'sales by origin' principle adopted by Article 42 of the CCCTB Directive Proposal. Alaska's extraction factor is especially reflective of the origin state's interest. Therefore, the extraction factor is more appropriate than the sales-by-origin principle to represent the origin state's interests.

Before laying down the statutory oil and gas formula, there have been other state taxation disputes on the oil and gas industry in Alaska, dating back to the 1980s. The disputes are centred on the property factor. As Hellerstein has discussed,[1345] it was argued whether or not intangible drilling costs,[1346] the outer continental shelf (OCS),[1347] and non-production oil wells[1348] should be included in the asset factor. Alaska's legislation and the Alaska Supreme Court have given affirmative answers in legislation and the Court's rulings. In other words, intangible drilling costs, OCS, and non-production oil well are all included in the assets factor. Although the arguments in each case are formulated differently, the common rationale developed in these rulings is that the oil and gas resource origin is the key element of the industry. Therefore, production efforts related to the resource origin are all included in the assets factor to represent the origin jurisdiction's taxing powers.

In addition to the importance of the resource origin rationale, the Alaska Supreme Court also reaffirmed the integrated feature of the oil and gas industry with the definition of unitary business. When the unitary business between an in-state company

---

1344. Alaska Statutes section 43.20.144(f). Alaska Statutes section 43.20.144(f) provides:

> The extraction factor of a taxpayer subject to this section is a fraction,
> (1) the numerator of which is the sum of the following for the tax period:
> (A) the number of barrels of the taxpayer's oil (net of royalty to an unrelated party) produced from or allocated to leases or properties of the taxpayer in this state; and
> (B) one-sixth of the number of Mcf of the taxpayer's gas (net of royalty to an unrelated party) produced from or allocated to leases or properties of the taxpayer in this state, excluding reinjected gas; and
> (2) the denominator of which is the sum of the following for the tax period:
> (A) the number of barrels of oil of the taxpayer's consolidated business (net of royalty to an unrelated party) produced from or allocated to leases or properties of the taxpayer's consolidated business everywhere; and
> (B) one-sixth of the number of Mcf of gas of the taxpayer's consolidated business (net of royalty to an unrelated party) produced from or allocated to leases or properties of the taxpayer's consolidated business everywhere, excluding reinjected gas.

1345. W Hellerstein, Recent Judicial Developments in State Income Taxation of the Oil and Gas Industry, 34 Oil Gas Tax Quarterly (1986).
1346. The current Alaska Statutes section 43.20.144(1)(1)(B).
1347. Des. No. 83-30, Alaska Department of Revenue, 7 September 1983.
1348. *State Department of Revenue v. Amoco Production Co.*, 676 P/2d 595 (Alaska 1984).

and the out-of-state affiliates is established, a state can have the taxing powers to apportion the whole unitary group's taxable income to the extent attributable. In 2013, in *Tesoro*, an Alaskan court ruled on unitary business and the formula.[1349] The ruling clearly reiterated that the integration between the upstream industry, the midstream industry, and the downstream industry is so strong as to constitute a unitary business, and thus the state of Alaska has the taxing power to apportion part of the taxable income from Tesoro group. Tesoro is a well-known oil and gas group, and its headquarters are established in Texas. Tesoro has been conducting retail and marketing services in Alaska since 1969, and Tesoro's exploration and production activities take place largely in Texas and Bolivia. In 1995, Tesoro acquired a pipeline company KPL, which serves its refinery business in Alaska. Tesoro argued that Kensai Pipeline did not constitute a unitary business with other business segments of the Tesoro group. However, the court ruled that there were indeed functional integration, centralized management, and economies of scale between the pipeline company Kensai Pipeline and other affiliates of Tesoro. Such unitary business justifies Alaska's nexus apportionment.

Comparing the CCCTB's oil and gas formula to Alaska's special formula for the oil and gas industry, Alaska's formula's asset factor is more dedicated. Alaska's formula takes the feature of production and extraction activity into account, and thus includes the 'extraction factor' in the special industry formula for the taxpayer conducting production and extraction activities. The extraction factor is based on the quantity of extraction and production, and it thus reflects the extraction activities in the oil and gas industry. The extraction factor obviously has a direct and close link, unlike the sales-by-origin principle adopted by Article 42 of the CCCTB Directive Proposal.

Though I am indeed inspired by Alaska's comprehensive rules, it should be clarified that here I do not argue that Alaska's oil and gas industry formula is the only correct or perfect approach to apportioning the consolidated tax base. Alaska's formula is a unilateral formula that reflects the interests of its own jurisdiction, so it is not wise to just copy it to the EU's FA regime. Since the EU's FA regime is a supranational formula, it must strike a balance between the interests of different EU Member States in advance.

In this regard, Alaska's oil and gas industry formula is indeed a convincing perspective to remind us of the economic reality of the oil and gas industry. The 'extraction factor' in Alaska's oil and gas formula does convey a key message that the production of crude oil should play a role in FA because extraction also represents an important aspect in the production process. Alaska's oil and gas formula replaces the payroll factor by the extraction factor, but in my view the EU's FA regime does not need to abandon the labour factor for the oil and gas industry because the oil and gas industry still makes use of the labour factor. When keeping the three-factor structure as the standard formula, it is comprehensively consistent with the public benefits.

1349. *Tesoro Corporation and Subsidiaries, Appellants, v. State of Alaska*, Department of Revenue, Appellee, No. S-14326, 25 October 2013.

7.4.5 Conclusions of This Section: Towards a Formula Applicable to the Highly Vertically Integrated Oil and Gas Group

One feature of the oil and gas industry is its vertical integration of the upstream, midstream, and downstream industries. Therefore, a mixed group is the normal and default situation. Therefore, the approach of 'carving-out' or 'creating' an industry formula for the pure 'exploration and production' group is not feasible nor does it represent the economic reality.

In my view, to reflect the economic reality of an integrated oil and gas group, the traditional three-factor formula still should apply. The oil and gas industry formula should still consist of the labour factor, the sales (by destination) factor, and the assets factor, whereas the asset factor should be adjusted. The sales factor reflects the economic activity from the downstream industry; and the assets factor reflects the economic activity from the midstream and upstream industry. Therefore, there should be some other types of special items to be included in the assets factor. The crude oil, which represents the extraction result and can be refined as product, should also be included in the assets factor.

There are two possible options to adjust the assets factor for the oil and gas industry. As the first option, like Alaska's legislation, is to add an extra sub-factor 'extraction' factor based on the exploration and production quantity of oil and gas in the assets factor, and weighted 50% of the assets factor, so that the assets factor of the oil and industry formula would be 1/3 (1/2 of the standard formula's assets factor + 1/2 of the extraction factor). The second option is to transcribe the exploration and production quantity of oil and gas according to a specific commodity price benchmark, such as Brent Crude, and then directly include the priced extraction result in the assets factor. Both options are familiar to the European Commission's CCCTB Working Group. The first option is similar to the approach adding the sub-factor of 'employee headcounts' in the labour factor (*see* Chapter 5); the second option is similar to the approach of adding research, development, marketing, and advertisement costs as a special intangible in the assets factor (*see* Chapter 6).

In my view, the first option of adopting the extraction factor as the sub-factor is consistent with the benefit-based MN framework. Valuation of crude oil and gas in the second option cannot easily refer to a historical cost method, and any oil benchmark is inevitably decided by the market. Since the oil and gas extraction result represents the production side, being included in the asset factor, it is logical to choose the first option. Alaska's experiences have shown that the extraction quantity is an objective criterion. Therefore, inclusion of the extraction factor in the assets factor for the oil and gas industry formula has achieved the importance of natural resource origin as well as represents the production side activity. It is tax neutral.

7.5 CONCLUSIONS: INDUSTRY FORMULAS ARE FORMULARY APPORTIONMENT'S ROOT

7.5.1 The CCCTB Is Suitable for Industries Other Than the Manufacturing Industry

The special industries in the current CCCTB Directive Proposal have a feature in common: they all have positive externality for other industries to conduct cross-border activities. In the context of the US, they can be categorized as 'instrumentalities of commerce', so there is always a concern that levying taxation would hinder them. Such argument can sometimes lead to opposing the FA regime as a whole: the fact that the current CCCTB Directive Proposal carves out the shipping industry and the air transportation industry from the scope of application shows similar concerns.

However, if we revisit the two aspects of taxation: benefit or DWL, addressed in Chapter 2, the concern of taxation hindering/distorting cross-border economic activities is actually only one side of the story. In my view, a well-designed FA taxation system at the EU level could promote the integration of the internal market and the exercise of fundamental freedoms. Such tax system is not distortion. We would exert effort to eliminate corporate tax 'obstacles', not to eliminate any 'corporate tax'.

The current CCCTB Directive Proposal is right to select special industries to design special rules, but the existing industry formulas are not completely consistent with the tax-neutrality principle. As discussed above, the financial institutions formula and the oil and gas industry formula of the current CCCTB Directive Proposal are both examples of transplantation with some misunderstanding. The 10% rule for valuating the financial assets and sales in the financial institutions formula of the current CCCTB Directive Proposal is merely a partial copy of California legislation. The 'sales by origin' rule of the CCCTB's oil and gas industry is also a misunderstanding of the sales factor. The carving-out rule for the shipping and the air transportation industry also lacks any solid theoretical ground, and it just copied the formulation of Article 8 of the OECD Model Convention. These incorrect efforts at legal transplantation should be reconsidered.

The most effective strategy to improve the current CCCTB Directive Proposal is to realign the current design with the benefit-based MN framework elaborated in Chapter 2 so that it reflects the corresponding public benefits provided by Member States. These industries need additional dedicated public infrastructures to maintain and manage a well-functioning market environment. These industries' key proxies are not the 'exception' to nor do they derogate from the standard formula but instead implement the benefit principle more nuancedly.

7.5.2 Clarifying a Mixed Group: High Integration Is the New Paradigm

Therefore, based on the observations above, all these industry formulas are not an 'exceptional rule' to the standard formula based on the manufacturing industry model. Instead, these industry formulas are different reflecting the features of 'remoteness' and 'mobility' of MNEs' activities and the development of the current economy. In fact, several transportation industry formulas date back far earlier than UDITPA/MTC's three-factor formula in the mid-twentieth century.

When a special industry formula is decided, the following question would be: 'how should the standard formula and the special industry formula interact with each other' when a group consists of group members of the special industry and the non-special industry at the same time? Even in the US state taxation experiences, there is no clear answer. Scholars such as Weiner and Célestin do indicate this issue but do not give a truly convincing instruction either.

Experiences from the oil and gas and financial industry formula in the US show that most states would carve out the company of the special industry. For example, California's financial industry formula is only applicable to financial institutions, and there are disputes whether a company qualifies as a financial institution. The current CCCTB Directive Proposal's shipping industry formula has adopted the same approach, and even completely excluded the shipping industry from the scope of the current CCCTB Directive Proposal.

In my opinion, the carving-out approach is not appropriate for the EU's FA regime, and it will simply create a subgroup in one consolidated group, and it would deviate from the fundamental purpose of group taxation: to comprehensively reflect the close economic relationship between group members. Furthermore, when we analyse the standard three-factor formula, it is also based on a mixed group in which different group members perform different functions: manufacturing, transporting, and selling. When we design a 'special industry formula', we still maintain the input-output structure and only adjust the content of the weighting factor to represent the relationship with a specific jurisdiction (such as resource origin, monetary capital, etc.) and naturally reflect such relationship between group members.

In other words, when designing a special industry formula for the CCCTB Directive, carving out or creating a subgroup would not make sense since we aim to pursue tax neutrality that can reflect the public benefits provided by the jurisdictions involved and integrated business by MNE taxpayers. The current CCCTB Directive Proposal does not follow this rationale and inevitably creates complex subgroups when it involves the financial industry, air and water shipping industry, and the oil and gas industry. In my view, such design clearly got 'lost in translation' when the European Commission tried to conduct legal transplantation from the US to the EU.

7.5.3 Recommendation for the Suggested Wording of the Industry Formulas for the EU's Formulary Apportionment Regime

In sum, for the EU's FA regime, I recommend amending the provisions of the special industry formulas of the CCCTB Directive Proposal, as follows:

Article 40 Calculation of the asset and sales factors for financial institutions

The asset factor of a financial institution, as referred to in point (29)(a), (d), (e), (f), (g), (h) and (i) of Article 4 of Directive 2016/xx/EU, shall be 10% of the value of financial assets, with the exception of own shares and of participations that give rise to tax exempt income. Financial assets shall include assets held for trading as referred to in Article 21 of Directive 2016/xx/EU. Financial assets shall be included in the asset factor of the group member that had those assets recorded in its books when it became a member of the group.

The sales factor of a financial institution, as referred to in point (29)(a), (d), (e), (f), (g), (h) and (i) of Article 4 of Directive 2016/xx/EU, shall be all the net amount of interest, fees, commissions and revenues from securities, excluding value added tax, other taxes and duties. Intra-group sales shall not be included. For the purposes of Article 38(2), financial services shall be considered to be carried out, in the case of a secured loan, in the Member State in which the security is situated or, if that Member State cannot be identified, the Member State in which the security is registered. Other financial services shall be considered to be carried out in the Member State of the borrower or of the person who pays fees, commissions, or other revenue. Where the borrower or the person who pays fees, commissions or other revenue cannot be identified or if the Member State in which the security is situated or registered cannot be identified, the sales shall be attributed to all group members in proportion to their labour and asset factors.

Article 41 Calculation of the asset and sales factors for insurance undertakings

The asset factor of insurance undertakings, as referred to in point (29)(b) and (c) of Article 4 of Directive 2016/xx/EU, shall be 10 % of the value of the financial assets referred to in Article 40(1).

Article 42 Oil and gas

The asset factor of a group member conducting its principal business in the field of the exploration or production of oil or gas shall include the extraction factor on the basis of the quantity of oil and gas production.

Article 43 Shipping, inland waterways transport and air transport

A group member whose principal business is the operation of ships or aircraft in international traffic or the operation of boats engaged in inland waterways transport shall be subject to the consolidated tax base and the standard formulary apportionment. The sales of transportation services shall be allocated to departure and arrival jurisdictions according to the ratio of time spent.

CHAPTER 8

The Procedural Weapon Towards a Market-Neutral Apportionment Result: The Safeguard Clause

'Would you tell me, please, which way I ought to go from here?'

'That depends a good deal on where you want to get to,' said the Cat.

Alice's Adventures in Wonderland[1350]

8.1 INTRODUCTION

In an FA tax system, it is typical to have an 'alternative apportionment' or 'equitable apportionment' as in the US states taxation context, or a 'safeguard clause' as in the current CCCTB Directive Proposal context, in order to adjust an 'unusual' or 'unfair' apportionment result. In the experiences of FA in Europe, such as in Switzerland[1351] and Germany,[1352] such adjustment mechanism also exists.

From the normative framework established in Chapter 2, MN for the EU's FA regime means that the formula design and apportioned results would reflect the relevant Member States' public benefits enjoyed by MNE taxpayers. The safeguard clause as such is a procedure that takes the unfair apportionment back to the 'benefit-based market neutral' status. When economic activities in a specific Member State are substantial whereas the apportionment tax base is obviously small, it would be unfair to provide the public benefits with such a low tax return.

Although the safeguard clause is a procedural provision, it could influence or, more specifically, correct the apportionment results substantially. This chapter focuses

1350. Lewis Carroll, *Alice's Adventures in Wonderland* (Random House 1865).
1351. Mayer, *supra* n. 48, at 3.4.6.3 (adjustment by Court).
1352. *Ibid.*, 3.5.5.3.

on the function of such mechanism and explores experiences with and reform attempts of the equitable apportionment provision in the US.

The central question of this chapter is: how should the safeguard clause of the EU FA regime be designed in order to ensure or, bring back, the tax neutrality of the formula? The sub-questions are: what should 'unfair apportionment' mean? Who may invoke the safeguard clause and how should the burden of proof be allocated? What role should the European Commission play in this procedure for the purpose of 'bringing back tax neutrality'?

The structure of this chapter is as follows: section 8.2 introduces the current CCCTB Directive Proposal's safeguard clause, including its rationale and function, and legislative records from the European Commission working documents. Section 8.3 introduces the development and reform project of the MTC's equitable apportionment (i.e., section 18 UDITPA). Section 8.4 discusses and compares problems arising from two systems and makes recommendations.

8.2 THE SAFEGUARD CLAUSE UNDER THE CURRENT CCCTB DIRECTIVE PROPOSAL

8.2.1 The Safeguard Clause: Content and Concerns

Article 29 of the current CCCTB Directive Proposal,[1353] the 'safeguard clause', sets out:

> **Article 29 Safeguard clause**
>
> As an exception to the rule set out in Article 28, if the principal taxpayer or a competent authority considers that the outcome of the apportionment of the consolidated tax base to a group member does not fairly represent the extent of the business activity of that group member, the principal taxpayer or competent authority may request the use of an alternative method for calculating the tax share of each group member. An alternative method can be used only if, following consultations among the competent authorities and, where applicable, discussions held in accordance with Articles 77 and 78, all these authorities agree to that alternative method. The Member State of the principal tax authority shall inform the Commission about the alternative method used.

Article 29 of the 2016 CCCTB Directive Proposal applies when the outcome of apportionment does not 'reflect the business activities of the group members'. It means that application of the sharing formula in the CCCTB Directive results in unreasonable and unfair outcomes. Member States can argue unfairness if they find the tax base is not sufficiently apportioned to them to reflect taxpayers' activities within their jurisdiction.

Taxpayers can also argue unfairness with the tax authorities if they think the apportionment results are not reasonable. After consultations among all the national

1353. It should be noted that the content of Article 29 of the 2016 CCCTB Directive Proposal is exactly identical to Article 87 of the 2011 CCCTB Directive. Therefore, the relevant working documents and literature regarding Article 87 of the 2011 CCCTB Directive will also be discussed.

competent authorities concerned and discussions with the Committee organized by the Commission, an alternative method may be agreed by all parties involved, and it will apply to the specific case. Therefore, such an alternative method as Article 29 is only applicable in a case under dispute on an ad hoc basis in a form of a tax ruling but does not function as legislation that is applicable to all other similar cases in the future. It only applies to exceptional cases and does not mean reintroducing SA.[1354]

The underlying reasoning of Article 29 is indicated in the CCCTB Working Document No. 65. In this Working Document, manipulation of weighting factors is discussed together with the GAAR and SAARs such as the CFC rule. It seems that the Commission regards unfair apportionment results due to manipulating the CCCTB sharing formula as a type of tax avoidance. Therefore, the safeguard clause that can adjust the unfair apportionment is classified as a type of anti-avoidance rule in the Commission's original design.

The procedure of Article 29 of the current CCCTB Directive Proposal is designed in a form of a mutual agreement procedure (MAP) in international tax law[1355] or in Article 6 of the European Arbitration Convention, but it allows more than two Member States concerned to join the proceedings and is not limited to TP disputes. When the Member States concerned achieve agreement on the alternative method, the alternative method will replace the FA rules of the current CCCTB Directive Proposal. In this case, the taxpayers will be subject to the method that is not regulated in the current CCCTB Directive Proposal. If the taxpayer does not agree with such an alternative method, according to the text of Article 29, it does not seem to have the right to further request another method because Article 29 does not have direct effect under EU law. However, as to the legal concept of 'fairly represent' in Article 29, the national courts of the Member States have the competence to refer a preliminary question[1356] to the CJEU.

Last but not least, according to the statutory text of the administrative provisions of the current CCCTB Directive Proposal, taxpayers do not seem to have the competence to appeal against the decision of adopting an alternative apportionment because such decision is not within the scope of Article 66 of the 2016 CCCTB Directive Proposal, which regulates the acts that can be appealed. This has been criticized as a loophole in Article 124 of the 2011 CCCTB Directive Proposal.[1357] It is an obvious loophole and needs to be amended.[1358]

1354. Regarding the safe-guard clause, *see* Cerioni, *supra* n. 269, at 166.
1355. *See* Article 25 of OECD Model Convention.
1356. Article 267 of TFEU.
1357. Arjo van Eijsden, The One-Stop-Shop Approach: A Discussion of the Administrative and Procedural Aspects of the CCCTB Draft Directive, 20 EC Tax Review 217 (2011).
1358. According to Article 66 of CCCTB Directive Proposal, taxpayers can appeal acts including:
    (a) a decision rejecting a notice to create a group;
    (b) a notice requesting the disclosure of documents or information;
    (c) an amended tax assessment;
    (d) an assessment of the failure to file a consolidated tax return;
    (e) an invalidation of the original notice to create a group by the principal tax authority as referred to in Article 49(2).

    Unless we interpret the alternative apportionment as 'an amended tax assessment', the alternative apportionment is not a decision that can be appealed.

8.2.2 Interpreting the Safeguard Clause as a 'balanced allocation of taxing powers'

Article 29 of the current CCCTB Directive Proposal aims to ensure a fair apportionment of the consolidated tax base and therefore provides the alternative apportionment method in the case of unfairness or distortion. Pursuing a fair result from the allocation of taxing powers is not a brand-new imperative in EU law. In the case law of the CJEU, 'balanced allocation of taxing powers' has been used as an accepted justification for the restriction to EU fundamental freedoms caused by a national measure.

The justification of 'ensuring balanced allocation of taxing powers' has been invoked and discussed in *Marks & Spencer*,[1359] *Oy AA*,[1360] *SGI*,[1361] and *Emerging Markets Series of DFA Investment Trust Company*.[1362] This justification is a separate and independent justification from the justification for 'combating tax avoidance'. Compared to the justification for 'combating tax avoidance', 'ensuring balanced allocation of taxing powers' seems more relaxed and easier to qualify.[1363] 'Balanced' allocation of the tax revenue has been an additional accepted justification for national measures to restrict fundamental freedoms and disadvantage cross-border activities.

Even though ensuring the balanced allocation of taxing powers is a separate and independent justification, it does not allow Member States to invoke it simply when there is a reduction in revenue comparing the hypothetical domestic situation. In other words, restrictions to EU fundamental freedoms still cannot be justified simply due to the Member States' reduction in tax revenue.[1364] Therefore, the national TP rules such as in *SGI*, loss-offsetting rules such as in *Marks & Spencer*, and tax exemption rules such as in emerging markets may limit cross-border activities from enjoying complete tax benefits or legal effects, but they are still subject to quite restrictive scrutiny. The mere fact of reduction of tax revenue does not seem to qualify as a valid justification.

1359. Case C-446/03 *Marks & Spencer plc v. David Halsey*.
1360. Case C-231/05 Oy AA.
1361. Case C-311/08 SGI.
1362. Case C-190/12 Emerging Markets Series.
1363. Violeta Ruiz Almendral, Tax Avoidance, the 'Balanced Allocation of Taxing Powers' and the Arm's Length Standard: An Odd Threesome in Need of Clarification, in I Richelle, W Schön & E Traversa (eds), *Allocating Taxing Powers Within the European Union* (Springer 2013).
1364. The CJEU has repeatedly mentioned it as the established, for example, the judgment Case C-324/00, *Lankhorst-Hohorst GmbH v. Finanzamt Steinfurt* '36 It is settled law that reduction in tax revenue does not constitute an overriding reason in the public interest which may justify a measure which is in principle contrary to a fundamental freedom (*see* Case C-264/96 *ICI* [1998] ECR I-4695, paragraph 28; *Verkooijen*, cited above, paragraph 59; *Metallgesellschaft and Others*, cited above, paragraph 59, and Case C-307/97 *Saint-Gobain ZN* [1999] ECR I-6161, paragraph 51).'

Another example, the Case C-196/04 *Cadbury Schweppes plc and Cadbury Schweppes Overseas Ltd v. Commissioners of Inland Revenue*, 'The need to prevent the reduction of tax revenue is not one of the grounds listed in Article 46(1) EC or a matter of overriding general interest which would justify a restriction on a freedom introduced by the Treaty (*see*, to that effect, Case C-136/00 *Danner* [2002] ECR I-8147, paragraph 56, and *Skandia and Ramstedt*, paragraph 53)'.

Early literature on justifications, *see* Mattias Dahlberg, *Direct Taxation in Relation to the Freedom of Establishment and the Free Movement of Capital*, Vol. 9 (Kluwer Law International 2005).

As to the interpretation of Article 29 of the 2016 CCCTB Directive, case law regarding balanced allocation of taxing powers needs to be considered. It also means that the application of Article 29 should not be invoked by Member States too broadly or too easily, simply due to the decrease in tax revenue. The meaning of 'not fairly representing the extent of the business activity' needs to be interpreted as the taxpayer's tax return and apportionment results already causing an unbalanced allocation of Member States' taxing powers. Mere reduction or decrease of a Member State's tax revenue should not be qualified as 'not fairly representing' the extent of the business activity and thus not sufficient to trigger Article 29.

8.2.3 The Factual Difficulty of Invoking the Safeguard Cause

There is an obvious disadvantage in Article 29 because, in practice, it is very difficult to invoke it. When a national authority or a principal taxpayer invokes Article 29 to seek an alternative apportionment method, such method needs to be agreed by all tax authorities involved. The original intention of requiring such consensus is to prevent inconsistency between Member States, but such requirement also makes it extremely difficult to invoke Article 29.

Furthermore, in the process of deciding on an alternative method, the Commission plays a relatively passive role. The Commission is not responsible for initiating or coordinating the alternative apportionment but is only consulted during the discussions and informed when all the competent authorities agree on the alternative method.[1365] Even if Article 29 is successfully invoked, Article 29 has then easily become a tool with which Member States fight for their taxing rights. It is not an opportunity, however, to pursue a common EU interest or correct the unfairness while implementing the current CCCTB Directive Proposal. Due to the procedures and the assignment of powers in Article 29, it is an article that is difficult to invoke and easily becomes a field of political conflict rather than a chance to correct injustice from a legal perspective.

8.2.4 The Relationship Between GAAR and the Safeguard Clause Is Not Clear

The critical question in adopting Article 58 of the 2016 CCTB Directive (CCCTB GAAR) and Article 29 of the 2016 CCCTB Directive (the safeguard clause) is how their scope of application is distinguished. There are several differences between GAAR and the safeguard clause. First of all, GAAR can be interpreted in the context of the development of CJEU case law regarding the GAAR, and therefore we need to take the subjective and objective elements of a disputed tax avoidance scenario into account.

1365. The Commission's role is quite passive in the current Article 87, which may fail to achieve its supervisory function. Herrera and Montera have concluded that the Commission should be the active body to interpret the sharing mechanism, *see* PM Herrera & A Montero, Supervisory Function of European Institutions?, in Lang & others, *supra* n. 5.

However, Article 29 is a new concept that has not existed before in EU tax law because the FA system has not been adopted at the EU level and rarely at the Member State level. The only example might be Germany. Germany indeed has an FA system to apportion trade tax at subnational regions. However, the German formulary system is not a CIT, and thus the German experience might not be so useful for the discussions here. Interestingly, in this German FA system, there is also a provision that adopts 'allocation rather than apportionment, in case of extraordinary unfair circumstances'.[1366] Therefore, an alternative method to replace the standard formula under some unfair circumstances already exists in the German formulary system. This is a rare example that cannot really provide insights for the EU's FA regime.

Examined purely from the text of Article 29, it seems that the subjective element is not the condition. As long as the objective outcome of the apportionment is unfair, the tax authority or the taxpayer may invoke it. Second, the legal consequences of these two articles are different. GAAR provides only one option: to ignore the artificial arrangements. Article 29 allows alternative apportionment methods, and thus it does not preclude the possibility of ignoring some of the taxpayers' arrangements. Therefore, Article 29's legal consequences are broader than GAAR. Third, the scope of application of these two could be separate if the texts are interpreted restrictively. According to Lang's interpretation, GAAR is not applicable to the manipulation of the sharing formula because GAAR only deals with 'the tax base' issues, not the apportionment issues.

The conditions of these two articles are not identical, but their underlying purpose and function are still similar when tax authorities invoke them. Both of them aim to adjust the result of the application of the existing rules because the outcome is abusive or unfair. The anti-abuse purpose of these two provisions is reflected in Working Document No. 65, in which the Commission in fact regards the rules to resolve the factor manipulation problem as a type of anti-avoidance rule.[1367] It seems that the Commission recognizes that SAAR and the safeguard clause both are measures and examples that embody GAAR. Therefore, conceptually speaking, it is still possible that GAAR and the safeguard clause might overlap in a specific case. Thus, the requirements discussed for a GAAR in the safeguard clause should also apply because they in fact have the same function in the CCCTB Directive Proposal.

Other evidence that also indicates the convergence and overlap of GAAR and the safeguard clause is the convergence of 'preventing tax avoidance'[1368] and 'balanced

1366. *See* Mayer, *supra* n. 48, at 3.5.5.3.
1367. *See* the Commission's CCCTB Working Document No. 65, paragraph 10.
1368. This justification is often discussed as a synonym of 'preventing abuse of law'. There have been numerous academic works on it. Since GAAR or Principle Purpose Test (PPT) are not within the scope of this book, here I only list a few main works that related to case law development of CJEU.

Luca Cerioni, Abuse of Rights in EU Company Law and EU Tax Law: A Re-Reading of the ECJ Case Law and the Quest for a Unitary Notion, 21 European Business Law Review 783 (2010); Koen Lenaerts, The Concept of 'Abuse of Law' in the Case Law of the European Court of Justice on Direct Taxation, 22 Maastricht Journal of European and Comparative Law 329 (2015); De La Feria, *supra* n. 86; Adam Zalasinski, Some Basic Aspects of the Concept of Abuse in the Tax Case Law of the European Court of Justice, 36 Intertax 156 (2008); Adam

allocation of taxing powers' when the CJEU analyses them. As Schaper[1369] comments, the justification of 'preventing tax avoidance' in fact constitutes a composition of another justification of 'balanced allocation of taxing powers'. These two justifications have semantic similarities, and in many cases, the CJEU combines the two justifications in its reasoning. For example, in the cases discussed above, *Cadbury Schweppes* (paragraph 55), *Thin Cap Group Taxation* (paragraph 74), and *Glaxo Wellcome* (paragraph 84) all refer to wholly artificial arrangements that attempt 'to escape the tax normally due on the profits generated by activities carried out on the national territory', i.e., the territoriality of taxing rights, which is equal to 'balanced allocation of taxing powers'. There are also other cases[1370] using the same approach to describe the wholly artificial arrangements. Therefore, I am of the same opinion that GAAR and the safeguard clause might have similar functions when national tax authorities invoke it.

Then the crucial issue persists: how should Article 29 incorporate case law on anti-avoidance and statutory GAAR? As to the alternative apportionment method achieved by Article 29 of the CCCTB Directive, it does in fact function as an ad hoc anti-avoidance rule made by two or more Member States. Member States should ensure that their alternative method is only applicable to wholly artificial arrangements the sole purpose of which is to manipulate the sharing formula and does not reflect economic reality.

To sum up, GAAR of the 2016 CCTB Directive and Article 29 of the 2016 CCCTB Directive function on different levels of the CCCTB Directive. In specific cases, they can overlap. Article 29 has a broader scope than GAAR, but when Member States agree to adopt the alternative method via Article 29, Member States should focus on the economic reality of each weighting factor or the consequences. In practice, for tax authorities, it might be easier to invoke the safeguard clause than GAAR, provided that the alternative apportionment is agreed by all tax authorities involved.

Zalasinski, Proportionality of Anti-Avoidance and Anti-Abuse Measures in the ECJ's Direct Tax Case Law, 35 Intertax 310 (2007); Adam Zalasinski, Case-Law-Based Anti-Avoidance Measures in Conflict with Proportionality Test: Comment on the ECJ Decision in Kofoed, 47 European taxation 571 (2007); Paolo Piantavigna, Tax Abuse in European Union Law: A Theory, 20 EC Tax Review 134 (2011); Frans Vanistendael, Halifax and Cadbury Schweppes: One Single European Theory of Abuse in Tax Law?, 15 EC Tax Review 192 (2006); Dennis Weber, Abuse of Law in European Tax Law: An Overview and Some Recent Trends in the Direct and Indirect Tax Case Law of the ECJ-Part 1, 53 European Taxation 251 (2013); Dennis Weber, Abuse of Law in European Tax Law: An Overview and Some Recent Trends in the Direct and Indirect Tax Case Law of the ECJ-Part 2, 53 European Taxation 313 (2013).

1369. Marcel GH Schaper, The Need to Prevent Abusive Practices and Fraud as a Composite Justification, 23 EC Tax Review 220 (2014).

1370. Case C-282/12 Itelcar, paragraph 34; Case C-105/07 NV Lammers paragraph 28; Case C-347/04 Rewe Zentralfinanz, paragraph 42, etc.

8.3 EXPERIENCES FROM THE US: THE MULTISTATE TAX COMMISSION'S RECOMMENDATIONS AND IMPLEMENTATION BY STATES

From the European Commission's working documents,[1371] we can observe that the US FA experiences on state taxation are expected to enlighten the design of the CCCTB Directive's sharing mechanism. This key reference is section 18 UDITPA. It would be useful to observe how the US deals with the issue of 'unfair apportionment'.

8.3.1 'Unfair' Apportionment: Constitutional Challenges and State Implementation Practices

8.3.1.1 Unconstitutional Unfair Apportionment in the US: What Can the EU's Formulary Apportionment Regime Learn?

According to Lee and Noel,[1372] there are mainly two types of circumstances in which an alternative apportionment might be invoked: (1) per se use of alternative apportionment, and (2) applied use of alternative apportionment. The first type of challenge refers to constitutional arguments: whether an FA state taxation as a whole is infringing constitutional clauses, such as the Dormant/Interstate Commerce Clause or the Due Process Clause.[1373] When infringing these constitutional clauses, they are inherently invalid because they are unconstitutional.[1374]

The second type of unfairness refers to the unfair apportionment result which takes place in an individual case. A state's tax legislation is not unconstitutional per se, but the apportionment result is unfair. Section 18 UDITPA is applicable to the second type of challenge. In any case, invoking Article IV section 4 UDITPA/MTC Regulations is based on a case-by-case analysis.[1375]

As to the per se use of alternative apportionment, there are three key norms developed in the US: the internal consistency test, the external consistency test, and the factor representation requirement.[1376] The 'internal consistency' test and 'external consistency' test were first developed by the US Supreme Court in the early 1980s to address the argument as to whether the Dormant Commerce Clause is infringed due to the apportionment result.

1371. For example, CCCTB Working Documents No. 47 and No. 60.
1372. Lee & Noel (2009), *supra* n. 512.
1373. *See* section 3.2.2 of this book.
1374. Charlette Noel & Kristi L Stathopoulos, Is There a Constitutional Standard for UDITPA section 18 Alternative Apportionment, 8 Corporate Business Taxation Monthly 31 (2006).
1375. Discussions from taxpayers' perspective while invoking UDITPA section 18, Fields CB, Newmark MA & Gibilaro EJ, 'Unfair Apportionment: Consider the Alternatives' 69 Tax Executive 21 (2017).
1376. General introduction of the constitutional restraints, *see* Hellerstein, Kofler & Mason, *supra* n. 271.

Briefly speaking, as we already elaborated in section 3.2.2 regarding US state taxation, the internal consistency test[1377] examines whether a state taxation infringes the Dormant Commerce Clause and makes interstate commerce more burdensome than intrastate commerce. The internal consistency test would first make the hypothesis that every state adopts this legislation all in the same way. The second step would analyse if more than 100% of the income is subject to tax, and when the answer is in the affirmative, such legislation is unconstitutional. So, the internal consistency test examines the 'risk' of double taxation, not the actual result of double taxation.[1378] The internal consistency test is similar to the non-discrimination test in combination with the non-double taxation mandate.

Another test is the external consistency test. External consistency exists when the factors reasonably reflect how the income was generated. It is similar to the principle of territoriality.[1379] States should be able to demonstrate the legitimacy of levying state taxation based on these factors. The external consistency test examines if a state levies extraterritorial taxation. If the answer is in the affirmative, such state tax infringes external consistency.

Lastly, although not having a constitutional status, 'factor representation'[1380] also plays a role when deciding if apportionment is fair.[1381] This concept mainly deals with the income earned from intangibles. It has been argued in an intangible income case whether factors can represent how intangible incomes are generated. In the discussions on whether marketable securities constitute 'gross receipts', taxpayers also argue the issue of 'factor representation'.[1382]

In section 3.2.3, the internal consistency test, the external consistency test, and factor representation test developed from the Commerce Clause of the US Constitution are all consistent with the benefit principle. Therefore, for the CCCTB system, unfair apportionment means the design of the formula or the apportionment result leads to asymmetry between the apportioned tax base and public benefits. This criterion can cover two types of unfair apportionment in the context of the US.

8.3.1.2 *Unfair Apportionment of Section 18 UDITPA: A Weapon for Both Sides*

To adjust unfair apportionment, the key provision is section 18 UDITPA. Section 18, the 'distortion relief' or the 'equitable apportionment' provision,[1383] deals with the

1377. *See* discussions, Hellerstein, *supra* n. 411.
1378. Hellerstein, Kofler & Mason (2008), *supra* n. 271.
1379. Joondeph, *supra* n. 410.
1380. Hollis L Hyans & R Gregory Roberts, When Is Symmetry Between the Tax Base and Sourcing Rules Required?, *The State and Local Tax Lawyer. Symposium Edition* (American Bar Association 2009).
1381. *U.S. Supreme Court case: Mobil Oil Corp. v. Commissioner of Taxes*, 445 U.S. 425 (1980); Hellerstein, *supra* n. 352; Arrache, *supra* n. 380.
1382. *See* Chapter 4 of this book.
1383. *See* Hellerstein, Hellerstein & Swain, *supra* n. 349, at 9.20.

situation that the results of applying the apportionment or allocation rules cannot 'fairly represent the extent of the taxpayer's business in the state'.

Section 18 UDITPA provides that:

> If the allocation and apportionment provisions of this Article do not fairly represent the extent of the taxpayer's business activity in this State, the taxpayer may petition for or the tax administrator may require, in respect to all or any part of the taxpayer's business activity, if reasonable:
>
> (a) separate accounting;
> (b) the exclusion of any one or more of the factors;
> (c) the inclusion of one or more additional factors which will fairly represent the taxpayer's business activity in this State; or
> (d) the employment of any other method to effectuate an equitable allocation and apportionment of the taxpayer's income.

According to the UDITPA drafter Professor William Pierce,[1384] the purpose of section 18 is merely to adjust those individual cases where the tax base is not fairly apportioned or allocated. He emphasized that section 18 does not solve the issue of tax base but the issue of apportionment. Furthermore, according to the drafter, the original purpose of section 18 is not to lay down other general FA regulations for different industries but only to address individual unfair cases rather than systematic unfairness.[1385] However, more and more states are using section 18 to promulgate special rules for taxpayers of non-manufacturing and non-mercantile industries. In addition to providing industry-wide formulas, section 18 is also used by the MTC to regulate transactions or specific exclusions for the formula.[1386]

In the original sense, section 18 could only be invoked in an 'unusual situation'. Before 2010, 'MTC Model Regulation interpreting UDITPA' (the MTC Article IV Regulation) Article IV section 18(a)[1387] explicitly mentioned that 'Article IV.18. may be invoked only in specific cases where unusual fact situations (which ordinarily will be unique and non-recurring) produce incongruous results under the apportionment and allocation provisions contained in Article IV'. Nevertheless, after 2010, the MTC Regulation was amended and the condition of 'an unusual situation' was deleted. The amendment also means that an unfair result of apportionment cannot be justified by the argument that the whole industry has similar results. In other words, the distortion and unfairness under section 18 are necessarily unique or non-recurring, but they might be a phenomenon that prevails in the whole industry.

Section 18 UDITPA further indicates four types of distortion relief, i.e., the adjustment measures from the standard formula. However, these four measures are illustrative rather than definitive. Section 18(d) almost covers any possible type of

1384. Pierce, *supra* n. 854. *See also* the analysis from Hellerstein, Hellerstein & Swain, *supra* n. 349, at 9.20, 9-373.
1385. Pierce, *supra* n. 854.
1386. *See* Hellerstein, Hellerstein & Swain, *supra* n. 349, at 9.20[2], 9-377, The special industry formula regulations recommended and issued by MTC can be requested at http://www.mtc.gov.
1387. The old text of Article IV section 18 and the amendment history can be requested at http://www.mtc.gov.

alternative approach. As the development of case law in state taxation, these four types of measures cover various measures. Tax authorities have used creative approaches to relieve distortions.

In addition to being invoked by tax authorities, section 18 can also be invoked directly by taxpayers if they find unfair apportionment results or distortions.[1388] In other words, section 18 is a double-sided equitable apportionment provision which can be invoked not only by tax authorities but also by taxpayers. The practice of section 18, or the alternative apportionment, has been criticized for being unevenly used by the authorities to deviate from the text of the legislation.[1389] However, more and more requests are invoked by taxpayers too.[1390]

As to the anti-tax avoidance solutions being discussed here, the cases regarding taxpayers invoking section 18 are less relevant. I focus on the application of section 18 by tax authorities and the courts when it is used to solve the tax avoidance scenarios.

8.3.2 The MTC's Recommendation Proposal for Section 18 UDITPA (2012)

In 2012, the MTC published its reform proposal of UDITPA. After more than 50 years, many rules from the UDITPA are regarded as obsolete and in need of reform.[1391] One of the important issues in the reform proposal is about the distortion relief, or equitable apportionment provision, i.e., the UDITPA/Multistate Tax Compact Article IV section 18. The proposed Article IV section 18 (hereafter 2012 proposed Article IV 18) sets out:

Article IV.18.

(a) If the allocation and apportionment provisions of this Article do not fairly represent the extent of the taxpayer's business activity in this State, the taxpayer may petition for or the tax administrator may require, in respect to all or any part of the taxpayer's business activity, if reasonable:
   (1) separate accounting;
   (2) the exclusion of any one or more of the factors;
   (3) the inclusion of one or more additional factors which will fairly represent the taxpayer's business activity in this State; or
   (4) the employment of any other method to effectuate an equitable allocation and apportionment of the taxpayer's income.

(b) (1) If the allocation and apportionment provisions of this Article do not fairly represent the extent of business activity in this State of taxpayers engaged in a particular industry or in a particular transaction or activity, the tax administrator may, in addition to the authority provided in section (a),

1388. This is a key difference from the safeguard clause (Article 29 of 2016 CCCTB Directive Proposal) because Article 29 does not seem to have direct effect. Taxpayers can still try to persuade national courts to refer a preliminary question.
1389. Christopher T Lutz, Robert P Merten & Nicholas J Kump, Trends and Developments in Alternative Apportionment of State Income, 84 State Tax Notes (2017), 559.
1390. Fields, Newmark & Gibilaro (2017), *supra* n. 1375.
1391. In 2006, MTC asked Uniform Law Commission to amend UDITPA but was rejected in 2009. MTC then began their own amendment process.

establish appropriate rules or regulations for determining alternative allocation and apportionment methods for such taxpayers.

(2) A regulation adopted pursuant to this section shall be applied uniformly, except that with respect to any taxpayer to whom such regulation applies, the taxpayer may petition for, or the tax administrator may require, adjustment pursuant to section 18(a).

Compared to the original section 18, the 2012 proposed MTC Article IV 18 adds two provisions in paragraph (b). First, MTC Article IV 18(b)(1) clearly delegates the power to the tax administrator to establish alternative appropriate rules if they find out unfair results of tax apportionment or allocation. Such alternative rules include 'industry-wide' and 'issue-wide' special apportionment rules. MTC Article IV 18(b)(1) reaffirms that Article IV 18 can be the legal basis for tax authorities to provide special FA rules for specific industries. In this regard, such special relief rules are usually in the form of regulations applicable to all the taxpayers of the whole industry. MTC Article IV 18(b)(2) further emphasizes that such adjustment can be applied on an ad hoc basis to solve the unfairness case by case. In this regard, the relief can even be a form of a tax ruling, applicable specifically to the taxpayer.

8.3.3 Development of Section 18: The MTC Hearing Officer's Proposal (2013) and the Recommendation Adopted (2015)

In 2013, the MTC hearing Officer Professor Richard Pomp completed research and published his recommendations for the MTC's Article IV 18 reform proposal.[1392] According to Pomp's recommendations ('Pomp's 2013 Proposal'), there were several necessary amendments for the MTC's Article IV section 18 reform proposal.

Pomp's 2013 Proposal sets out:

18.

(a) If the allocation or apportionment provisions of this Act do not fairly represent the extent of the taxpayer's business activity in this state, the taxpayer may petition for, or the [tax administrator] may require, in respect to all or any part of the taxpayer's business activity, any reasonable method to effectuate an equitable allocation and apportionment of the taxpayer's income.

(b)(1) If the allocation or apportionment provisions of this Article do not fairly represent the extent of business activity in this State of taxpayers that are engaged in, or representative of, a particular industry, or that engage in a particular transaction or activity of general applicability, then a [tax administrator] that requires a reasonable method to effectuate an equitable allocation and apportionment of income that it applies uniformly to such industry, or to such transactions or activities, shall publish that method in appropriate rules or regulations.

(b)(2) Rules or regulations adopted pursuant to this Section shall be applied uniformly, except that with respect to any taxpayer to whom such regulation

1392. Richard Pomp, Report of the Hearing Officer Multistate Tax Compact Article IV [UDITPA] Proposed Amendments (2013), 35.

applies, the taxpayer may petition for, or the [tax administrator] may require, adjustment pursuant to Section 18(a).

(c) The party petitioning for, or the [tax administrator] requiring, the use of any method to effectuate an equitable allocation and apportionment of the taxpayer's income pursuant to (a), must prove by [Drafter's note: insert standard of proof here]: (1) that the allocation or apportionment provisions of this Article do not fairly represent the extent of the taxpayer's activity in this State; and (2) that the alternative to such provisions is reasonable. The same burden of proof shall apply whether the taxpayer is petitioning for, or the [tax administrator] is requiring, the use of any reasonable method to effectuate an equitable allocation and apportionment of the taxpayer's income.

(d) If the [tax administrator] requires any method to effectuate an equitable allocation and apportionment of the taxpayer's income, he or she cannot impose any civil or criminal penalties solely because the taxpayer reasonably relied on the allocation and apportionment provisions of this Article in filing a return.

(e) A taxpayer that has been permitted by the [tax administrator] to use a reasonable method to effectuate an equitable allocation and apportionment of the taxpayer's income shall not have that permission revoked with respect to transactions and activities that have already occurred unless there has been a material change in, or a material misrepresentation of, the facts provided by the taxpayer upon which the [tax administrator] reasonably relied.

In Pomp's 2013 Proposal on amending Article IV 18, the list of illustrative alternative methods was deleted, and Article IV 18(a) provides a residual rule which has a broader range for tax authorities to adopt alternative methods. According to Pomp's explanation,[1393] in the original section 18(a) UDITPA, three methods are merely examples. In the past, such examples were useful because there was no judicial interpretation when the UDITPA was adopted. Nowadays, since there is a long history of judicial interpretation, those three examples are less important for interpreting and implementing the rule. By deleting the list, Article IV 18 became more flexible for tax authorities and courts to use.

Furthermore, Pomp's 2013 Proposal emphasized that although section 18 could be used to promulgate industry formula regulations by state tax authorities, they need to be used sparingly. Also, in order to pursue uniformity, it is the MTC that should be mainly responsible for initiating or drafting industry formula regulations.[1394] The MTC adopted quite a broad range of model industry apportionment regulations for states, and as a leader of the Multistate Tax Compact member states, its role is more appropriate when adopting industry-wide regulations.

When tax authorities adopt the alternative method, regardless of the form of a tax ruling or a regulation, it should be consistent with the legislation intention.[1395] In other words, the alternative method is adopted to achieve the original legislative intent that is not achieved in a specific case or industry. Tax authorities may not deviate from the legislation. Furthermore, an alternative method can be adopted on an ad hoc basis or

1393. *Ibid.*, 35.
1394. *Ibid.*
1395. *Ibid.*, 31.

published as a generalized regulation for other taxpayers with the same conditions in the future. It is unrealistic to always require tax authorities to adopt the generalized regulation in order to invoke the alternative method. However, Pomp also emphasized that for widespread and general problems, tax authorities should adopt a regulation with wider applicability. Although a regulation enhances transparency, at the same time it can apply to similar taxpayers uniformly. Therefore, although the ad hoc alternative method can function as an adjustment in each tax ruling, a public regulation is better for pursuing transparency and uniformity.

Pomp also indicates that[1396] taxpayers should not be penalized for following the standard formula if the alternative apportionment method is adopted by the tax authorities later.[1397] His report emphasized this point because in practice, many states implement section 18 UDITPA or their own alternative apportionment rules with imposing penalties, sometimes even automatic penalties.[1398] In response to the amended UDITPA, tax legislation should also be amended because imposing penalties as the consequence of the alternative apportionment is not consistent with the purpose of section 18 UDITPA.

According to Pomp's 2012 Proposal, states' tax legislation can still lay down their own provisions for penalties, but it is not allowed to invoke section 18 UDITPA to adjust the apportionment result and at the same time impose penalties on taxpayers. Section 18 UDITPA is designed quite differently from GAAR as provided in IRC §7701. As Pomp's 2013 Proposal indicates, in non-abusive situations, section 18 UDITPA may still be invoked to adjust distortion, and taxpayers should not be penalized when they already follow the current apportionment rules. Therefore, according to Pomp, the alternative apportionment cannot be the basis for imposing penalties.

The most important recommendation in Pomp's 2013 Proposal is to allocate the burden of proof clearly to the party which invokes the alternative apportionment provision. It was not completely clear in the UDITPA and thus creates disputes and disparities. As Rose and Dow's analysis[1399] shows, in practice, there are many tax authorities,[1400] such as New Jersey, Virginia, Alaska, and Maryland, that clearly put the burden of proof on taxpayers regardless of who invokes the alternative apportionment. In other words, even when state tax authorities invoke the alternative apportionment method, it is the taxpayer that bears the burden of proof to prove that the original apportionment method is 'fair'. The phenomenon of shifting the burden of proof to taxpayers is sometimes even affirmed by state courts,[1401] even though it is not reasonable.

1396. *Ibid.*
1397. *Ibid.*, 29.
1398. *See also*, Peter L. Faber, Defending an Equitable Apportionment Case, State Tax Notes (2014).
1399. Arthur R. Rosen & Alexander Dowd, Alternative Apportionment: Who Bears the Burden of Proof and What Standard of Proof Applies, Tax Management Weekly State Tax Report (2014).
1400. *Ibid.*
1401. For example, the Equifax case is a famous one. *Equifax, Inc. v. Miss. Dep't of Revenue*, 125 So. 3d 36 (Miss. 2013). The Court upheld the tax authorities that the taxpayer should bear the burden of proof when the tax authorities invoke the alternative apportionment rule. In response to this ruling, the Mississippi Legislature passed House Bill 799 on 1 April 2014 and

Therefore, according to Pomp's 2013 Proposal, if tax authorities invoke the alternative apportionment method in relation to specific taxpayers, those taxpayers should bear the burden of proof to establish the unfair outcome of its application. The burden of proof rule for the alternative apportionment recommended by Pomp's 2013 Proposal is quite different from the economic substance doctrine indicated earlier: taxpayers are required to prove their economic reasons or business purpose for the disputed transactions.

In July 2015, a new section 18 was adopted.[1402] The MTC, in principle, followed the Pomp's recommendations and adopted a new section 18 as follows:

(a) If the allocation and apportionment provisions of this Article do not fairly represent the extent of the taxpayer's business activity in this State, the taxpayer may petition for or the tax administrator may require, in respect to all or any part of the taxpayer's business activity, if reasonable:
  (1) separate accounting;
  (2) the exclusion of any one or more of the factors;
  (3) the inclusion of one or more additional factors which will fairly represent the taxpayer's business activity in this State; or
  (4) the employment of any other method to effectuate an equitable allocation and apportionment of the taxpayer's income.

(b) (1) If the allocation and apportionment provisions of this Article do not fairly represent the extent of business activity in this State of taxpayers engaged in a particular industry or in a particular transaction or activity, the tax administrator may, in addition to the authority provided in section (a), establish appropriate rules or regulations for determining alternative allocation and apportionment methods for such taxpayers.
  (2) A regulation adopted pursuant to this section shall be applied uniformly, except that with respect to any taxpayer to whom such regulation applies, the taxpayer may petition for, or the tax administrator may require, adjustment pursuant to Section 18(a).

(c) The party petitioning for, or the [tax administrator] requiring, the use of any method to effectuate an equitable allocation and apportionment of the taxpayer's income pursuant to subsection (a) must prove by [Drafter's note: insert standard of proof]*[undefined in source]*: (1) that the allocation and apportionment provisions of this Article do not fairly represent the extent of the taxpayer's activity in this State; and (2) that the alternative to such provisions is reasonable.

The same burden of proof shall apply whether the taxpayer is petitioning for, or the [tax administrator] is requiring, the use of any reasonable method to

---

clearly indicated that the burden of proof should be allocated to the party invoking the alternative apportionment rule. The underlying reason of amendment is to overrule the case Equifax.

The new law is effective from 1 January 2015. The new rule provides, 'In any instance in which a taxpayer requests or the commissioner requires the use of any of the alternative apportionment methods..., the party requesting or requiring the method shall bear the burden of proving by preponderance of the evidence in any administrative or judicial proceeding that the methods set forth in this section or the commissioner's regulations do not fairly represent the extent of the taxpayer's business activity in this state and that the proposed method more fairly represents that activity than any other reasonable method available.' *See* Miss. Code Ann. § 27-7-24.

1402. Resolution Adopting Recommended Amendments to section 18 of model Multistate Tax Compact Article IV [UDITPA], which can be requested at http://www.mtc.gov.

effectuate an equitable allocation and apportionment of the taxpayer's income. Notwithstanding the previous sentence, if the tax administrator can show that in any two of the prior five tax years, the taxpayer had used an allocation or apportionment method at variance with its allocation or apportionment method or methods used for such other tax years, then the tax administrator shall not bear the burden of proof in imposing a different method pursuant to (a).

(d) If the [tax administrator] requires any method to effectuate an equitable allocation and apportionment of the taxpayer's income, the [tax administrator] cannot impose any civil or criminal penalty with reference to the tax due that is attributable to the taxpayer's reasonable reliance solely on the allocation and apportionment provisions of this Article.

(e) A taxpayer that has received written permission from the [tax administrator] to use a reasonable method to effectuate an equitable allocation and apportionment of the taxpayer's income shall not have that permission revoked with respect to transactions and activities that have already occurred unless there has been a material change in, or a material misrepresentation of, the facts provided by the taxpayer upon which the [tax administrator] reasonably relied.

The only substantial difference between the Pomp's recommendations and the article adopted lies in the burden of proof, i.e., section 18(c)(2). The newly adopted section 18, in principle, allocates the burden of proof to the party who invokes section 18 for an alternative apportionment method. However, a tax authority does not bear the burden of proof 'if the tax administrator can show that in any two of the prior five tax years, the taxpayer had used an allocation or apportionment method at variance with its allocation or apportionment method or methods used for such other tax years, then the tax administrator shall not bear the burden of proof in imposing a different method pursuant to (a)'. In other words, the tax authority still enjoys a more lenient rule in a case where the taxpayer has used a different apportionment method than the previous standard apportionment method. Such allocation of the burden of proof also grants the tax authorities more discretion to freely decide the alternative method, since it is not their obligation to prove the unfairness of the standard method.

8.3.4 Different Equitable Apportionment Methods Used in US State Taxation Cases

Section 18 UDITPA has been disputed and interpreted in state taxation case law. It has been widely used to deal with various issues regarding FA. As section 18(b)-(d) indicates, the possible alternative methods have a very wide scope and apply flexibly.

Hellerstein et al. have selected representative and leading state taxation case law regarding alternative apportionment scenarios when section 18 UDITPA is invoked.[1403] In this section, I re-classify selected section 18 UDITPA cases from Hellerstein's analysis into main five types regarding the formula ranging from the selection of the factors, and the definition and scope rules of the factors, to the attribution rule of the factors or creating a special industry formula or adjusting the tax base.

1403. Hellerstein, Hellerstein & Swain, *supra* n. 349, at 9.20.

From these cases, we observe the function of section 18 to adjust the apportionment outcomes by the courts. From the following scenarios, we can clearly see that tax authorities freely make use of section 18 UDITPA to develop various 'alternatives'.

It should be noted that the following cases only demonstrate that section 18 UDITPA can be widely and flexibly invoked and used. This does not mean that I agree with the adjustments made by courts or tax authorities nor does it imply that these alternative apportionments are 'more neutral'. Instead, in this section, these different equitable apportionment methods can be regarded as the evidence that a safeguard clause like section 18 UDITPA is not a panacea either. The EU's FA regime should not copy the flexibility of section 18 UDITPA because in many situations section 18 UDITPA is invoked to correct inherent non-neutrality, such as the COP rule. The EU can already address this problem by correctly designing an alternative method from the outset.

8.3.4.1 Changing the Choice of Weighting Factors

States courts can use the alternative apportionment method to choose or eliminate weighting factors. To exclude one or more weighting factors is one possible alternative method in section 18(b).

An example of eliminating factors from the standard formula as the alternative method is to combat aggressive tax planning done by intangible holding companies (IHCs). Being incorporated in a state that does not levy CIT, such as Delaware, IHCs usually have no property factor or payroll factor in other states. An IHC's sales or receipts factor is often null because its receipts are derived from intangibles and thus are attributed to the state where the costs are highest (the 'Cost of Performance' principle in section 17 UDITPA, *see* Chapter 4). Therefore, all the factors of the sharing formula are null, and therefore, the IHC will not be subject to any apportionment.

Setting an intangible holding company is a classic tax-planning scenario in US state taxation. In a New Mexico case, *Kmart Properties, Incorporated,*[1404] the Kmart Corporation established a wholly-owned subsidiary, Kmart Properties, Incorporated, in Michigan in 1991, and transferred its trademarks, trade names, and service marks to the subsidiary Kmart Properties, Incorporated. Kmart Corporation paid royalties to Kmart Properties, Incorporated to use the trademarks, trade names, and service marks and deducted the royalties from its New Mexico tax return. The creation of the subsidiary dramatically reduced Kmart's tax liability within New Mexico. Such scenario is also a typical BEPS strategy widely discussed.[1405]

Consequently, the New Mexico tax authorities issued an assessment by adopting an alternative formula that ignored the property factor and the payroll factor completely and only used the sales factor. The sales factor is the attributed receipts, including sales, that generated the royalties income. Therefore, after establishing the table nexus of Kmart Properties, Incorporated, the court held that apportionment of

1404. *Kmart Properties, Inc. v. Taxation and Revenue Department of the State of New Mexico*, 139 N.M. 177, 131 P.3d 27 (Ct App 2001).
1405. For example, Pankiv describes as 'Typical IP structures'. *See* Pankiv, *supra* n. 331.

Kmart Properties, Incorporated's royalties income to New Mexico was calculated only by the sales factor and naturally increased the apportionment to New Mexico.[1406]

8.3.4.2 Changing the Definition of Weighting Factors

In some cases, courts invoke equitable apportionment to redefine the meaning of a specific weighting factor. A famous example is the *Microsoft* case in California discussed in Chapter 4. The case involved calculation of the sales factor and the included amount of the sales of marketable securities. The software developing company Microsoft purchased and redeemed the marketable securities in the state of Washington regularly to maintain its cash flow, and therefore the gross amount of such transactions included the return of principals of the securities. The court ruled that only the net amount of the redemption should be included in the sales factor denominator and should therefore substantially change the definition of 'gross receipts' because inclusion of the gross amount of securities redemption would be distortive in calculating the sales factor and inflating the sales factor for California.

Another example is *Union Pacific Railroad* in Idaho,[1407] where the court also excluded sales account receivables from the sales factor and ruled that it overlapped with previous sales. Union Pacific Railroad sold its account receivables based on its freight sales. Such receivables should not be included in the sales factor, otherwise it would count the receipts twice from the taxpayer's freight income and thus would not fairly represent the taxpayer's business activities.

As to the payroll factor, the best example is in an old case, *Lancaster Colony Corp. v. Limbach*[1408] in Ohio. In the former tax code, Ohio still adopted the three-factor formula. Taxpayers used independent contractors to make all of its sales. The court ruled that on the basis of the equitable apportionment provision, the payroll factor should include the wages paid to independent contractors used by the taxpayer. In this case, the court also changed the definition of 'payroll'.

As to the property factor, in *Twentieth Century-Fox Film Corp. v. Department of Revenue*[1409] in Oregon, the court ruled that based on the equitable apportionment provision, the value of the intangibles, i.e., the value of the taxpayer's film negatives, is also included in the property factor, which only includes tangible property according to state legislation.

1406. Even prior to the BEPS project in the domestic context in USA, establishing an intangible holding company has been a 'classical' tax planning scenario to avoid state taxation. With similar case facts, sometimes the tax authorities invoke the economic substance doctrine (a type of GAAR in USA), *see Sherwin-William Co. v. Commissioner* (Sherwin-Williams (MA)) and *Sherwin-Williams Co. v. Tax Appeals Tribunal* (Sherwin-William (NY)), Gore. Here we can clearly see that the equitable apportionment provision and the economic substance doctrine are sometimes dealing with the same problem and conceptually overlapping in the US. This is the same puzzle taking place in the CCCTB Directive Proposal.

1407. *Union Pac. Corp. v. Idaho State Tax Comm'n*, 136 Idaho 34, 28 P3d 375 (2001).

1408. *Lancaster Colony Corp. v. Limbach*, 37 Ohio St. 3d 198, 524 NE2d 1389 (1988).

1409. *Twentieth Century-Fox Film Corp. v. Department of Revenue*, 299 Or. 220, 700 P2d 1035 (1985).

8.3.4.3 *Changing the Attribution Rule of Weighting Factors*

According to the UDITPA and MTC regulations, the numerator of each weighting factor, i.e., the in-state numerator, is decided by the attribution rule and directly influences the amount that a state can be apportioned. Changing the attribution rule can be a type of alternative apportionment method.

For example, in *Kennecott Copper Corp. v. State Tax Commission*,[1410] a Utah court approved a deviation from 'the sales by destination rule' for the sales factor numerator in Utah. The taxpayer Kennecott Copper and its subsidiaries conduct a worldwide mining, refining, and metal-fabricating business. They own mines and refineries and other property in Utah and three neighbouring states. Utah adopted a three-factor formula. In the years 1967 and 1968, Kennecott Copper's Utah property factors were 42% and 36%, respectively, and their payroll factors were 43% and 33%, respectively, but their sales factor was less than 1% because almost all of Kennecott Copper's products were shipped to out-of-state consumers. The Utah tax authorities determined that Kennecott Copper Corp's tax return did not fairly reflect the extent of its activities in Utah. The Utah tax authorities then attributed all of the taxpayer's sales to Utah, i.e., using the 'sales by origin rule', and substantially increased Utah's apportioned tax due to approximately USD 2.5 million. The court upheld this adjustment.[1411]

Another example of changing the attribution rule is *GTE Automatic Elec., Inc. v. Allphin*[1412] in Illinois. Illinois has a 'throw-back' provision for the sales factor if the taxpayer is not taxable in the state of origin or the state of destination of shipment. Illinois' throw-back rule only applies to the shipments originating from Illinois. Based on section 18 UDITPA, the Illinois tax authorities expanded the applicable scope of the 'throw-back' provision. The Illinois tax authorities determined that GTE Automatic's 'drop shipments' should also be subject to the throw-back rule (and thus attributed to Illinois' sales factor numerator), even though drop shipments do not originate from the retailer. Illinois instructs the manufacturer or the wholesaler to ship a product directly to the customer. The court also upheld the decision to use the alternative method to expand the application scope of the throw-back rule.

Even the traditional attribution rule for sales arising from providing services, i.e., section 17 UDITPA, may be adjusted based on section 18 UDITPA. In *Bellsouth Advertising*,[1413] the Tennessee tax authorities adopted the 'market state approach' to attribute the taxpayer's, a yellow page company, receipts of its advertising revenue to the state where the telephone directories are distributed rather than the state where the costs of producing the directories were incurred. In other words, the tax authorities adopted the market-sourcing approach to attribute sales to replace the traditional

1410. *Kennecott Copper Corp. v. State Tax Comm'n*, 27 Utah 2d 119, 493 P2d 632 (1972), appeal dismissed, 409 US 973, 93 S. Ct. 323 (1972).
1411. The dissenting opinion of the judge indicates that such decision is equal to repeal and amend the legislation. It is therefore highly questionable. *See* Hellerstein, Hellerstein & Swain, *supra* n. 349, at 9.20[7][c].
1412. *GTE Automatic Elec., Inc. v. Allphin*, 68 Ill. 2d 326, 369 NE2d 841 (1977).
1413. *Bellsouth Adver'g & Publ'g Corp. v. Chumley*, 308 SW3d 350 (Tenn. App. 2009).

approach, the 'Cost of Performance' method provided by section 17 UDITPA.[1414] The court affirmed the distortion arising from applying section 17 UDITPA to a cross-state advertising company and sustained the tax authorities' alternative method.

8.3.4.4 Adopting Special Industry Formulas and Special Rules in the Industry Formulas

Although it may be contrary to the UDITPA drafters' intentions, many states have used the alternative apportionment provision to further adopt industry-wide special formulas.[1415] Such implementation is also reflected in the amendment proposal of the Multistate Tax Compact Article IV.[1416] State legislators or state tax authorities have the competence to adopt special industry formulas in order to get fair apportionment and prevent distortion of the standard formula. In fact, the MTC also recommended rules for several special industry formulas, based on Article IV section 18 Multistate Tax Compact.[1417]

Here a question arises: can the alternative apportionment provision be applicable to a special industry formula? Can a special industry formula also have a further special rule? The Montana Supreme Court[1418] answered these questions in the affirmative and held that the equitable apportionment provision is also applicable to the special transportation industry formula when the apportionment result of the special industry formula is unfair. The alternative apportionment provision can also prevent distortion arising from application of a special industry formula.

8.3.4.5 Changing the Tax Base Calculation Rule to the Combined Reporting Method

As indicated above, the UDITPA originally regulated the apportionment method, not calculation of the tax base. To require combined reporting nevertheless already

1414. As introduced in Chapter 4 of this book, according to section 17 of UDITPA, the receipts earned from providing services are attributed to the state where the income producing activities occur or based on 'costs of performance' rule for attributing the receipts from cross-state services. In other words, the state where the amount of costs of the income producing activities is the greatest will be attributed to all the receipts to the state's sales factor numerator. For example, if the taxpayer's service is provided in state A and state B, and the costs attributing to state A takes 51% and the costs attributing to state B is 49%, the entire receipts will be attributed to state A's sales factor numerator. The COP rule embedded in UDITPA section 17 has been criticized for being easily distorted and now is under reform. *See* Hellerstein, Hellerstein & Swain, *supra* n. 349, at 9.18[3][b][iii].

1415. Hellerstein selects some industry formulae from individual state taxation rules, Hellerstein, Hellerstein & Swain, *supra* n. 349, at 10.
A latest comprehensive survey, *see* CCH Tax Law Editors, *U.S. Master Multistate Corporate Tax Guide (2020)* (CCH 2019).

1416. Shirley Sicilian, Multistate Tax Compact Article IV Recommended Amendments, 2012.

1417. The special industry formula regulations recommended and issued by MTC are discussed in Chapter 7 of this book.

1418. *Montana Dep't of Revenue v. United Parcel Serv., Inc.*, 252 Mont. 476, 830 P2d 1259 (1992).
Hellerstein, Hellerstein & Swain, *supra* n. 349, at 9.20[7][o].

influences the calculation of the tax base. In other words, from the cases indicated above, section 18 UDITPA is not only used to adjust the apportionment method but also used to decide the apportionable tax base.[1419] Such an approach is the evidence that the distinction between 'deciding the tax base' and 'the method of apportionment' can sometimes be blurred in cases where section 18 UDITPA is invoked by state tax authorities.

8.3.5 Final Remarks: What Can the EU's FA Regime Learn?

From the (types) of cases discussed here, we can observe that US state tax authorities have adopted various methods to adjust distortion in apportionment. Section 18 UDITPA is broad enough to cover all these methods.[1420] As to the states which do not adopt UDITPA, they still use similar provisions to deal with distortion in apportionment, though such provision is under the discussion of 'the economic doctrine'. In some cases, an equitable/alternative apportionment clause even overlaps with the GAAR and the alternative apportionment provision.[1421] The possible use of an alternative apportionment clause is really broad.

1419. Hellerstein, Hellerstein & Swain, *supra* n. 349, at 9.20[7][g] Combined Reporting as an Equitable Apportionment referring to 8.12[2] and 8.12[3].

1420. Gamage and Shanske ask a very interesting question: Since the single-sales-factor formula seems to become a popular trend among states in USA now, what can UDITPA section 18 do? Can UDITPA section 18 be applicable widely as in the past or not? *see* David Gamage & Darien Shanske, A New Theory of Equitable Apportionment, 85 State Tax Notes 267 (2017).

1421. One example is Maryland which is not a UDITPA state, *see* the case *Gore Enter. Holdings, Inc. v. Comptroller*, 87 A.3d 1263 (Md. 2014), aff'g *Comptroller v. Gore Enter. Holdings, Inc.*, 209 Md. App. 524 (Md. Ct. Spec. App. 2013), aff'g *W.L. Gore & Assocs., Inc. v. Comptroller*, Nos. 07-IN-OO-0084, 07-IN-OO-0085, 07-IN-OO-00862010, 2010 WL 5927989 (Md. Tax Ct. 9 November 2010). Discussions, William Joel Kolarik & Steven N Wlodychak, The Economic Substance Doctrine in Federal and State Taxation, 67(4) Tax Lawyer (2014).

As to Delaware IHCs, Maryland courts have developed and broadened the application scope of the doctrine. A series of Maryland cases also involve application of the economic substance doctrine to Delaware IHCs, and the Maryland Courts use the economic substance doctrine to establish the state's taxable nexus upon Delaware's IHCs in Maryland and the justification for tax authorities to adopt an alternative apportionment method.

Gore is a company incorporated in Delaware. It incorporates two Delaware intangible holding subsidiaries to manage its intangibles. One subsidiary, GEH, is responsible for managing Gore's entire patent portfolio, and the other, FVI, is responsible for managing Gore's excessive capitals. Gore pays royalties to GEH for using patents and pays interests to FVI. In Maryland, Gore operates several factories to manufacture Gore's fabric, medical devices, electronics, and industrial products, and the factories also use Gore's patents. Gore is subject to Maryland tax for its business via factories in Maryland. In other words, Gore has taxable nexus in Maryland, which is not disputed by the Gore or Maryland tax authorities. The Maryland tax authorities audit and reassess that Gore's Delaware IHCs are the unitary business of the whole Gore Group and thus should also be apportioned according to the Maryland law. Based on the nexus, the Maryland tax authorities also adopt the alternative apportionment method. Besides, Maryland tax authorities even impose penalties upon Gore.

The Court of Appeals of Maryland reviewed the case. It ruled that the two Delaware intangible holding subsidiaries do not have economic substance of their own separate existence but merely part of the parent Gore's business activities. Since the parent Gore has nexus in Maryland, the two Delaware IHCs also have nexus in Maryland. Furthermore, the Court also affirms the tax authorities' decision that using an alternative formula because the standard two-factor formula, which only consists of the property factor and the payroll factor,

Although the current CCCTB Directive Proposal's safeguard clause does not give examples as section 18 UDITPA does, the applicable scope of the safeguard clause can be very broad from US experiences due to the general formulation of the safeguard clause. If the safeguard clause is allowed to be applied easily, it can become a backdoor that creates many more special formulas which deviated from the standard formula. Therefore, invoking the safeguard clause should be done cautiously when there is indeed an asymmetry between the apportionment results and the public benefits within the jurisdiction. Since the concept of '[does] not fairly represent taxpayers' activities' is a new legal concept introduced by the current CCCTB Directive Proposal in EU law, it would be necessary for national courts to refer preliminary questions to the CJEU to obtain consistent interpretation.

8.4 CONCERNS ARISING FROM THE SAFEGUARD CLAUSE: WHO IS SAFEGUARDING WHAT?

8.4.1 What Should 'unfair apportionment' Mean under the EU's FA Regime?

The existence of unfair apportionment is the precondition to invoking the safeguard clause. The core question is what 'unfair apportionment' really means. From the experiences from the US, the equitable apportionment clause can be invoked by both tax authorities and taxpayers, so the basic trigger for tax authorities is the fact or suspicion that the apportioned share is 'less than expected'.

However, the single fact that the apportioned share is 'less than expected' does not sufficiently justify deviation from the statutory text of tax law or should not constitute 'unfair apportionment' from the perspective of the tax-neutrality principle based on the benefit principle. The underlying justification is actually the asymmetry between nexus and apportionment result of the jurisdiction involved. In other words, when there is a disproportionate relationship between the taxable nexus and the apportionment result, such disproportion justifies invoking the alternative apportionment provision and means 'unfairness' in the field of FA.

As indicated in Chapter 3, this book advocates the 'factor presence nexus' for the EU FA regime instead of the PE threshold of the current CCCTB Directive Proposal, even after taking the result of BEPS Action Plan 7 into account. The PE threshold might have the benefit of being familiar to current international tax law practitioners, but it is only when there is an asymmetry or disproportion between MNE taxpayer taxable nexus and apportionment result, is it possible to invoke the safeguard clause. It would also be logical, since symmetry between nexus and the apportionment rule and factor representation are both essential to designing a 'fair formula'.

---

cannot fairly reflect the Delaware IHCs' economic activities in Maryland because they do not have any tangible properties or pay compensation to employees in Maryland. In the end, the tax authorities calculate the two Delaware subsidiaries' apportioned income by multiplying the royalties and interests paid respectively by the parent company Gore, times the Maryland formula.

In fact, when we regard all weighting factors should represent some relationship and corresponding public benefits between the MNE taxpayer with the jurisdiction. When unfairness takes place, it is because the nexus, factor, and apportionment result do not match.

8.4.2 Burden of Proof on Who Invokes the Safeguard Clause

One of the most controversial issues in the procedure in the safeguard clause under the current CCCTB Directive Proposal is how the burden of proof should be allocated.[1422] It is also widely discussed in the reform project of Article IV section 18 Multistate Tax Compact, as discussed above. In the US state taxation experiences, the burden of proof is not always on the party who invokes the equitable apportionment (i.e., alternative apportionment) clause. In several states, nevertheless, it is always the taxpayer that must bear the burden of proof even when tax authorities invoke the equitable apportionment clause to argue the unfair apportionment result. It is quite unreasonable to put the burden of proof always on the taxpayer's side because the adjustment deviates from the normal application and interpretation of the FA rules. It would also be unreasonable to require a taxpayer that does not ask for the deviation to prove the fairness of the apportionment result because it already complies with the apportionment rules when filing its corporate tax return. This is also why the reformed Article IV section 18 Multistate Tax Compact has clearly indicated that the burden of proof in a case where section 18 is invoked should be borne by the party which argues for an alternative adjustment.

Why would the rule of the burden of proof in the alternative apportionment clause in state taxation practice be designed in an 'unreasonable' way in US state practice so that the taxpayer always bears the burden of proof? Taxpayers are in a better position to control business data that can prove the correct calculation of the corporate tax base. Besides, it seems that in a multistate tax alternative apportionment dispute, the taxpayer involved is usually an MNE taxpayer, and an MNE taxpayer already has the capacity to hire professionals to conduct their tax planning scenarios. Under the presumption that MNE taxpayers can take care of themselves and optimize their tax burden by planning, tax authorities would tend to require MNE taxpayers to prove the original apportionment result is 'fair', even when it is tax authorities that invoke the alternative apportionment provision. Such presumption is not reasonable and directly contrary to legal certainty.

1422. In addition to Richard Pomp's hearing officer report in 2013, *supra* n. 1392, this issue is controversial as the consensus in the state and local tax (SALT) community in USA. It is also reiterated, for example, at the 1 November 2013 panel discussion on the MTC's rewrite of the Uniform Division of Income for Tax Purposes Act (UDITPA). Moderated by Christopher Bergin, Tax Analysts President and Publisher, and featuring Shirley K Sicilian, Prentiss Willson, Richard Pomp, Arthur R Rosen, recording archived at https://youtu.be/lZt4M5 MiM3w, 37:17 onwards.

8.4.3 Concerns of Illegitimate Compromises Between Tax Authorities or Between a Tax Authority and Specific Taxpayers

Another concern that can arise in the safeguard clause in the context of EU law is state aid control and selectivity. When the tax authorities of the Member States involved invoke and agree upon an alternative apportionment method, it would be in the form of a tax ruling, deviating from a general corporate tax rule, issued together by the other Member State(s) involved. It would potentially constitute state aid because an alternative apportionment is decided for a specific individual MNE taxpayer.

Although issuing a tax ruling or an industry-based alternative apportionment under the current CCCTB Directive Proposal is not unlawful state aid per se,[1423] a tax ruling from the safeguard clause reveals the new dynamic between the EU, Member States, and MNE taxpayers. When tax authorities from different Member States try to reach a consensus on adopting an alternative apportionment, there is an opportunity that Member States can reach a consensus by 'give-and-take' in different individual alternative apportionment cases. In other words, Member State A might give in one case, to reach a compromise with Member State B in another case. When two (or more) Member States achieve a consensus on issuing a favourable tax ruling to a specific MNE taxpayer for an alternative apportionment, the selective benefit is issued from two or more Member States.

Traditionally, to evaluate whether an arrangement constitutes state aid, we would focus on the relationship between the arrangement and one Member State; similarly, to evaluate harmful tax competition, we would look at the tax competition between each Member State. However, in the context of the EU FA regime, the safeguard clause provides an opportunity for two (or more) Member States to 'group up' and achieve a compromise with each other. It is possible that this group of Member States might grant unlawful and selective state aid to a specific MNE taxpayer, and such aid comes from the state resources from two (or more) Member States together. Instead of competing with one another, it is also possible for 'a group of Member States' to conduct tax competition with another Member State or another 'group' of Member States.

8.4.4 The Position of the European Commission: A Mediator

When implementing the safeguard clause in the EU FA regime, the European Commission could have some functions similar to the MTC, but some modifications would be necessary.

1423. The state aid and tax rulings, *see* Raymond Luja, State Aid Benchmarking and Tax Rulings: Can We Keep It Simple?, in Wolfgang Schön, Isabelle Richelle & Edoardo Traversa (eds), *State Aid Law and Business Taxation* (Springer 2016).
Whether arrangements to a specific industry constitute a state aid is in the discussion regarding selectivity, *see* Wolfgang Schön, Tax Legislation and the Notion of Fiscal Aid: A Review of 5 Years of European Jurisprudence, in Schön, Richelle & Traversa (eds), *State Aid Law and Business Taxation*; Michael Lang, State Aid and Taxation: Selectivity and Comparability Analysis, in Schön, Richelle & Traversa (eds), *State Aid Law and Business Taxation*. Briefly speaking, it is not so easy to qualify as a state aid, even for an industry-based tax ruling.

As indicated in Chapter 7, the MTC has issued various recommendations for industry formulas. For the European Commission, it may not issue such recommendations, and it should not do so. Adopting the FA regime has as a fundamental purpose the elimination of unnecessary discrepancies and the streamlining of tax administration for MNE taxpayers. Issuing non-legally binding recommendations might just create more legal uncertainties.

The current Article 29 of the 2016 CCCTB Directive Proposal is difficult to invoke, and it can only be applied to an individual unfair apportionment case. To strike a balance between the simplicity principle and the consistency principle, the Commission should play a more active role[1424] when Article 29 applies. If the unfair apportionment is an industry-wide phenomenon, Article 29 the 2016 CCCTB Directive Proposal should grant the Commission powers to provide a special formula for that specific industry. The special industry formula created to address systematic unfair apportionment is widely adopted in the US. To avoid inconsistencies resulting from different national tax authorities, it is the Commission that should take the responsibility for initiating such special formulas for the Member States involved.

In my view, the European Commission, which independently represents the EU's interest, is the appropriate actor to prevent the safeguard clause from becoming a new source of legal uncertainty that unlimitedly allows '*ad hoc*' solutions which are a compromise between Member States' tax authorities. When a dispute regarding unfair apportionment takes place, either invoked by tax authorities or invoked by taxpayers via the preliminary procedure, the European Commission should be actively involved, while being a mediator, to help interpret the CCCTB formula. If unfairness takes place due to rapid developments in a specific industry that EU legislators and policy makers could not foresee, the European Commission should propose an amendment to CCCTB Directive (via the review process provided by Article 79 of the 2016 CCCTB Directive Proposal), so the adjustment is not merely ad hoc but applicable to all Member States.

8.5 CONCLUSIONS

'How fair is fair enough?'[1425] is the ultimate question of this chapter. While it examines the result of the application of the formula, it actually examines the symmetric relationship between the nexus, the factor interpretation, and the apportionment result.

Theoretically speaking, when the EU's FA standard formula's definition and attribution rule are redesigned according to the tax-neutrality principle, as discussed in Chapters 3 to 6, the occasions for invoking the safeguard clause should be reduced accordingly. From the experiences of state taxation in the US, the alternative apportionment provision has been widely used to address the definition issue (such as

1424. For the same opinion, *see* PM Herrera & A Montero, Supervisory Function of European Institutions?, in Lang & others, *supra* n. 5.

1425. This statement is borrowed from David J Shipley, The Limits of Fair Apportionment: How Fair Is Fair Enough?, *The State and Local Tax Lawyer: Symposium Edition* (American Bar Association 2007).

marketable securities), the attribution issue (such as the weakness of the COP rule), either by litigating an individual case or by promulgating a special industry formula. But when the formula is designed as including both the input side and output side, and interpreting the weighting factors according to their fundamental rationale, many disputes involving the alternative apportionment would not take place from the very beginning.

Therefore, the safeguard clause under the EU's FA regime should be used with caution, and both tax authorities and taxpayers should be competent to invoke the safeguard clause because unfair apportionment is an objective fact if the specific apportionment result has caused asymmetry. The way of invoking the safeguard clause is to eliminate the asymmetry, by (re-)interpreting the factors consistently with their fundamental rationale in the sharing formula. The intention of the safeguard clause is not to create new rules, or open a backdoor to the SA approach. The safeguard clause should not become a hidden table for negotiations for tax authorities from different Member States to do trade-offs.

In sum, for the safeguard clause, this book recommends amending the provisions of the CCCTB Directive Proposal as follows:

Article 29 Safeguard clause

As an exception to the rule set out in Article 28, if the principal taxpayer or a competent authority considers that the outcome of the apportionment of the consolidated tax base to a group member does not fairly represent the extent of the business activity of that group member, the principal taxpayer or competent authority may request the use of an alternative method for calculating the tax share of each group member. The party which invokes the safeguard clause bears the burden of proof. An alternative method can be used only if, following consultations among the competent authorities and, where applicable, discussions held in accordance with Articles 77 and 78, all these authorities agree to that alternative method. The Member State of the principal tax authority shall inform the Commission about the alternative method used. The alternative method used should be applicable to all comparable cases. The dispute over the applicability and the apportionment result of the safeguard clause is open to adjudication by the courts.

CHAPTER 9
Conclusions

Blame is simply the discharging of discomfort and pain. It has an inverse relationship with accountability.

Brené Brown[1426]

9.1 RETHINKING NEUTRALITY AS THE NORMATIVE CONTENT OF THE CORPORATE TAX REFORM: THE BENEFIT PRINCIPLE-BASED RATIONALE

The goal of this book is to provide an alternative approach to allocating taxing rights to MNEs' cross-border income, and this goal is also embedded in the current trend of international tax reform. Policy makers are trying hard to make MNEs fully accountable and pay a fair share of tax, and this effort should start from an awareness of systemic problems and leading to systemic solutions, instead of naming and blaming any specific jurisdictions, taxpayers, or industries.

This book has explored FA for the EU as an alternative solution to the current failures of the international tax law regime by analysing the current CCCTB Directive Proposal and US state taxation experiences for further improving the EU internal market. To find the answers, this book revisits different tax law principles and theories developed by economists and redesigns the normative framework that is suitable for a regionally integrated market like the EU.

The cornerstone of the normative framework for evaluating the EU's FA regime, as discussed in Chapter 2, is benefit-based MN. Since tax is seen not only as resulting in DWL but also as conceptual units of public benefits, levying tax would not be a

1426. This statement is quoted from the transcript of Brené Brown's speech 'The Power of Vulnerability' in 2013. This distinction between blaming and accountability has been appearing in her other books, including Brené Brown, Rising Strong (Random House 2017), at 196-198.; Brené Brown, Dare to Lead (Random House 2018), at 191.
The speech video is available at https://www.youtube.com/watch?v = RZWf2_2L2v8.

distortion per se as long as it is justified by the benefit principle. Tax neutrality should not be decided based on a 'no-tax world' but the public benefits baseline. In this regard, MN is compatible with the benefit principle in tax law.

9.2 FORMULARY APPORTIONMENT AS THE ALTERNATIVE TO THE TRADITIONAL TAXONOMY OF SOURCE VERSUS RESIDENCE PRINCIPLE

At the beginning part of Chapter 3, this book clarified the arguments regarding distortions caused by FA, explored the development of FA from the international tax law regime as well as from US state taxation experiences. There is a clear trend that FA has been utilized in the international tax regime or in TP methods. In the context of conducting tax reforms for the digital economy, the OECD has been considering 'fractional apportionment' and 'marketing intangibles' as two possible solutions, and both are in the form of FA. The OECD's Pillar One Project also incorporates an FA method. In other words, FA has become an accepted alternative in the international regime.

The state taxation experiences from the US are especially valuable because they involve a lot of discussions about cases involving constitutionality. These cases, especially the Dormant Commerce Clause in the US, provide insights into how the internal market should be functioning and what a constitutional and reasonable relationship between the federal government and states should be to cooperate and make the market and commerce flourish, while keeping states' diversity and autonomy. Most importantly, the internal consistency test and the external consistency test developed from the Dormant Commerce Clause in the US cases involving questions about constitutionality are all consistent with the benefit principle.

An undeniable advantage of FA is its flexibility, though opponents would claim it is arbitrary. The basic assumption of FA is to admit a broad sense of 'source' for MNEs' cross-border income. Some FA scholars argue that it is impossible to ascertain the real source, while other FA scholars argue that every jurisdiction involved is source. Although these two narratives look incompatible, they both support a 'formula' that can embrace multidimensional activities. Therefore, FA would be more feasible than the traditional distinction of the source principle versus the residence principle which allocate taxing powers by the all-or-nothing approach.

A market-neutral formula should consist of weighting factors from both the input side and the output side. The output side is represented by the sales factor and the input side is represented by the assets factor and the labour factor. In my view, it is not neutral to adopt a single-sales-factor formula, even though there is the trend in the US towards a single/heavily-weighted sales-factor formula. The trend in the US is based on the belief that adopting a single-sales-factor formula has the embedded economic incentive for MNEs to invest in more labour and assets. Such arguments for a built-in incentive was based on empirical research in the early 2000s and is being challenged by new research and new data after 2016.

In addition, there is no solid empirical evidence showing us the real tax incidence of corporate tax, or in the context of FA. Therefore, it would be short-sighted to see the labour factor or the assets factor in the formula as a potential burden. Instead, adopting a formula consisting of these three factors is sufficiently comprehensive to reflect MNEs' economic activities and corresponding public benefits.

In this regard, the OECD's Pillar One Project published in 2021 seems to only consider the interest of the client-market jurisdiction but neglects the labour-market jurisdiction. The EU's FA system should take a balanced approach.

9.3 ADOPTING A FORMULA REPRESENTING BOTH THE INPUT SIDE AND THE OUTPUT SIDE OF ECONOMIC ACTIVITIES

9.3.1 The Output Side as a Criterion of Value Creation, Representing the Response to the Customers' Market

The sales factor is the most controversial factor in FA, but it still can be designed as tax neutral. The sales factor should represent taxpayers' response to their customers' market. Although the destination for sales seems obvious, the current CCCTB Directive Proposal as well as state taxation experiences in the US are not entirely consistent with these two fundamental rationales. There are many examples of deviating from the destination principle, including the attribution rule for services for the sales factor. The deviations from the 'destination principle' are mainly due to administrative convenience and historical reasons in the US, and the current CCCTB Directive Proposal has transplanted the system as well as the deviations from the US. Such transplantation results in not only 'lost in translation' but also 'outdated in translation'. These would make tax reform efforts much less effective. The EU's FA regime should correct the mistakes from the US and the current CCCTB Directive Proposal.

By following the rationale of 'response to the customers' market', the definition/scope rule and the attribution rule of the sales factor are streamlined. In US FA experiences, a lot of discussions are about whether specific amounts of receipts are earned from 'unitary business' and 'in the course of ordinary business', and not to evaluate if it is the result of the MNE taxpayers' response to their market. Therefore, it would be disputed whether cash management by trading short-term marketable securities (the *Microsoft* case in California) or risk management by conducting hedging transactions (the *General Mills* case in California) takes place 'in the course of ordinary business'. On the contrary, when we follow the rationale of response to the customers' market consistently, it is quite clear that receipts from cash management and risk management, though very similar in the appearance of a continuous purchase-sales contract (redemption and hedging), they should not be defined as sales because these activities do not involve taxpayers' response to the market.

To decide the attribution rule for the sales factor, the key question is 'what is the destination?' In the US, the origin-based COP rule for attributing receipts earned from providing services has been proven outdated. The market-sourcing rule for providing services is the new widely accepted trend in US state taxation, but there is no clear criterion of 'destination'. I have explored EU VAT laws and OECD VAT guidelines on 'supply rules' in Chapter 4 because VAT is claimed to be designed based on the 'destination principle'. What it shows us is that EU VAT supply rules and OECD VAT guidelines do not implement the destination rationale thoroughly. Instead, there are many deviations from the destination principle to the origin-based rationale, in the name of 'proxies', mainly due to practical concerns and administrative convenience. The EU's FA regime should extract insights from these designs selectively.

Moreover, 'the response to the customers market rationale' can also address the concern of 'no-where sales', which already leads to overly complicated throw-back/throw-around rules inserted in a typical design of the sales factor. If there is the taxpayers' response to their customers, that is the market and destination where the sales should be attributed. A well-designed destination rule should not easily allow the throw-back or throw-around rule to change the fundamental rationale merely because of the worry of losing tax revenue or claimed 'no-where sales'.

9.3.2 The Input Side Can Still Be Designed as Manipulation-Proof and Market Neutral

In Chapter 5 and Chapter 6, I discussed how the labour factor and assets factor should be designed to comply with benefit-based MN. To follow the fundamental rationale, the assets factor and the labour factor are claimed to be subject to manipulation of factor shifting because their scope, attribution, and evaluation are decided according to the functions performed. However, when these two factors are designed according to their functions performed instead of administration convenience, the worry of being manipulated would be largely reduced because taxation would follow a consistent theory, not a convenient political compromise.

As to the design of the labour factor, in Chapter 5, I explored the scope of employees used in the payroll factor in the US and the concept of employee in labour law and social security law. Since the labour factor represents MNE taxpayers' ability to mobilize human resources and make use of the labour market, the 'subordination element' developed in the concept of employee in labour law is a useful tool to develop the scope of employees for the labour factor. Although the subordination element itself does not give a clear and easy definition of employee and results in various indicators of 'employee status', the subordination element shows that MNE taxpayers can have comprehensive powers to the human resources used. Therefore Chapter 5 argues for the approach of 'defining and excluding truly independent contractors' from the labour factor. In this way, the problem of being unable to directly define employee is solved.

As to the attribution of employees, the 'one single jurisdiction rule' in social security law is not consistent with the functional view of the labour factor, and thus the labour factor of the EU's FA should not follow it. The 'one single jurisdiction rule' in social security law is to ensure the entitlement to and enjoyment of social security benefits for each individual, and therefore, this single state principle does not serve the need of attribution of employees to the labour factor. The pro-rata approach, based on the time spent on performing in different states, to attribute the mobile workforce, is more logical.

As to the assets factor, Chapter 6 explored the current CCCTB Directive Proposal and the US's FA experiences with tangible and intangible assets, from the perspective of 'capacity to mobilize non-human resources in the production process'.

Using ownership for attribution rules for the assets factor is not tax neutral, regardless of legal or economic ownership. It is because the concept of 'ownership' does not directly relate to the function of the asset in the production process, and it creates an extra layer which hinders the alignment between the asset and where it serves its function. A clearly unreasonable example is that even real estate under the current CCCTB Directive Proposal could be attributed to a jurisdiction other than the situs state. Therefore, the attribution rule should be based on where the asset is utilized instead of ownership.

It is not market neutral to completely exclude intangibles from the assets factor even for anti-manipulation purposes. In Chapter 6, however, I argue for conditional inclusion of IP in the assets factor. I have observed that there are three contexts for the interaction between intangibles and FA regarding: income earned from intangibles, the OECD's discussions of the digital economy and marketing intangibles, and the treatment of intangibles in the assets factor. In the third context, a specific intangible should be included in the assets factor as long as it performs its innovation function in the production process. Therefore, intellectual properties (IP), i.e., copyright, patent, trademarks, should be included in the assets factor. From the perspective of the ability to utilize non-human resources, both tangible and intangible assets are important for MNEs. Although intangibles are in the form of a legal relationship or legal right, not in physical form, they can still contribute to the taxpayers' production and service provision process.

As to the attribution of IP rights in the assets factor, the attribution rule based on where the IP right is utilized is market neutral and will naturally coincide with human resources costs of creating and maintaining the intangible. As to the valuation of IP in the assets factor, the cost-based approach instead of any market-based approach is logical because the assets factor of a sharing formula should represent taxpayers' input side, not focusing the output side. The costs and functions of DEMPE are the suitable reference for attributing and evaluating IP in the assets factor.

9.4 INDUSTRY FORMULAS REFLECT THE ROOT OF FORMULARY APPORTIONMENT

In Chapter 7, I analysed three types of industries, i.e., financial institutions, transportation, and oil and gas industry which the current CCCTB Directive Proposal treats differently and provides special industry formulas or excluded them from the scope of application. However, we should not understand these special industry formulas as the exception to or failure of the standard formula; instead, these industries represent the roots and original intent of FA: dividing multijurisdictional income.

9.4.1 Monetary Capital Is the Key and Fungible for Financial Institutions

There is a wide consensus that the financial industry needs a special formula other than the standard formula. The consequent question is, 'how special should it be?'. As I explored the development of the financial industry formula in the US, monetary capital is the key proxy for financial institutions. Furthermore, the financial industry is a highly regulated industry, states that need to supervise and manage monetary capital are justified in levying tax because those states need to prevent the 'financial curse'.

Due to monetary capital's fungible feature, the sales factor and the assets factor of the financial industry formula should be amended accordingly: only the 'interest', i.e., the 'net amount' earned from financial transactions and sales of financial assets and corresponding service fees should be included in the sales factor because these amounts represent financial institutions' response to their clients. As to the assets factor, the financial assets should be included in the assets factor and evaluated as 10 % of the book value that can represent the monetary capital that the financial institution has the capacity to manage and control.

By adopting the three-factor formula structure for financial institutions, with the special modifications to the assets factor and the sales factor, income earned from a mixed group of financial institutions and non-financial institutions can also be apportioned properly because the special rules for these two weighting factors already consider the effect of monetary capital on the entire group.

9.4.2 Transportation Activities: Departure and Arrival Are Both Necessary

In Chapter 7.3, I explored various industry formulas for different transportation industries including land, maritime, and aviation in the US and other jurisdictions. It demonstrated that dividing taxing rights on multijurisdictional income of the transportation industry belongs to the original roots of FA. It demonstrated that the approach of excluding the shipping and air transportation industry from the current CCCTB Directive Proposal is illogical and creates more inconsistencies in a transportation group.

Moreover, even in the jurisdictions that do not use the FA approach for their international tax regime, such as Hong Kong and Australia, they adopt some pro rata or a ratio to decide income earned from international shipping activities in their domestic tax law. Therefore, an FA system as such better represents the mobile business activities of the shipping industry because adopting a pro-rata approach or a ratio is much more flexible and economically sound than the 'place of effective management' criterion adopted by Article 8 of the OECD Model Convention for income earned from the shipping industry. POEM is still based on the all-or-nothing rationale, so it has the same problems as the residence principle. POEM is not suitable for the EU's FA regime, and it cannot address the old BEPS problems either.

As to the transportation industry, the key proxies are departure and arrival because they are the goal of transportation: a successfully completed journey. Therefore, to decide the destination of the sales factor, both departure and arrival represent the taxpayers' response to their clients' market. Therefore, a journey's departure and arrival jurisdiction can be attributed 50% of the sales earned by the transportation service. As to the voyage jurisdiction(s) where transportation vehicles pass through or fly across, they are not the key proxy in the transportation industry formula because passing through or flying across jurisdictions provides quite marginal public infrastructures and thus does not justify apportionment.

9.4.3 Natural Resources Are the Key Value Driver for the Oil and Gas Industries

As to the oil and gas industry, natural resources should play the key role in the formula, and this is justified by the benefit principle because natural resources are the key value driver of the industry. Moreover, the states of a specific natural resource have a higher responsibility to prevent the 'resources curse', which is a negative effect for jurisdictions of the natural non-renewable resources.

However, the 'sales by origin rule' for the oil and gas industry under the current CCCTB Directive Proposal is not tax neutral even though it tries to emphasize the importance of the origin for the oil and gas industry formula because the 'sales by origin rule' has mixed up the functions of the sales factor and the assets factor. The 'sales by origin rule' for the oil and gas industry is another example of 'lost in translation'.

In this regard, the state of Alaska has provided a very good reference, to base the extraction factor on the quantity of production. In my view, the underlying rationale of the extraction factor illustrates a special item in the assets factor. In the context of the EU's FA regime, the quantity of production and exploration should be included in the asset factors as a sub-factor. Including the result of oil and gas exploration and production in the assets factor is justified because such result also represents taxpayers' capacity to control and make use of the natural resources.

9.5 NEW OPPORTUNITIES AND UNSOLVED PROBLEMS IN THE DIGITAL ECONOMY

9.5.1 Digitalization Is the New Industrial Revolution

The digital economy has become the background of international tax law reform, but the BEPS phenomenon is not brand new or happening merely because of the digital economy. Instead, from the very beginning of the development of the international tax law regime in the 1920s, the experts of the League of Nations were aware of base erosion problems;[1427] the current policy options, such as applying FA at the international level 'as the last resort' is not new and was also discussed by Mitchell B. Carroll in 1934.[1428] Nothing seems new. We can also say that the international tax regime (as well as its reform) is evolutionary but not truly revolutionary.

What we cannot deny, however, is that digitalization has completely changed the business models and made the BEPS problems more prominent. Digitalization has been the new industrial revolution in our era since the 1990s. Therefore, digitalization could inevitably cast doubts on an FA design and question if the weighting factors of a formula can address the issues in the digital economy. In my view, the answer is affirmative. To address the taxing rights issues of the digital economy by FA, it is not necessary to adopt a separate 'digital factor', but we indeed need to observe the economic activities, including the input side as well as the output side from a 'digitalized' viewpoint. The twenty-first century is an era where not only accessing customers and clients is 'digitalized', but so also is the way of utilizing human resources, such as employees working via telecommunication technology, and the more sophisticated non-human resources, such as artificial intelligence, algorithms (as intangible assets), or robots. It would be a bit naive if we think we can separate the 'digital economy' from the non-digital economy.

When we take a new 'digitalized' perspective on FA, it is a revolutionary view, but such revolutionary view has been evolving from the development of the international tax regime. By doing so, the EU's FA regime could be a pioneer to comprehensively address the BEPS issues that are worse under the digital economy.

9.5.2 Using the EU Formulary Apportionment Regime as a Pioneer in the Digital Economy

One of the prevailing statements against a supranational level FA is that such reform would require too much effort to build a whole new system, and tax administration and exchange of information between sovereign states would be difficult. Such concerns regarding difficulties in administration might have been true prior to the BEPS project. However, in the context of the digital economy, digitalized business activities are the actual reality, and it is now easier to trace all relevant information for customers and cross-border activities from the digital record. Therefore, to build up a support system for a supranational FA system for the EU is not as hard as in the past thanks to the development of technology. The digital economy does create difficulties in taxing multinationals fairly; the digital economy also ushers in opportunities for international tax reform because transaction data regarding customers is all digitally accumulated (and this data is of high economic value as 'big data'). Therefore, the necessary information, including foreign customers' information, for taxing the digital economy

1427. Jogarajan, *supra* n. 29, at 254. Comments by Reuven Avi-Yonah & Gianluca Mazzoni, Literature Review: Sunita Jogarajan, Double Taxation and the League of Nations, Cambridge University Press, 2018, (2018) 46(12) *Intertax*, 1027-1029.

1428. Mitchell B Carroll, Allocation of Business Income: The Draft Convention of the League of Nations, 34 Columbia Law Review 473 (1934).

is not that difficult to collect. The alleged administrative difficulty in FA could be reduced in the digital economy also by technology.

Especially from the analysis in Chapters 3 to 6, I observed that the market-neutral way of attributing the market destination, the asset functioning, the workforce performing tasks, is referring to the common destination: 'individuals'. When MNE taxpayers are conducting business, by making another MNE taxpayers' service (either by advertising services like Facebook or by an online matching platform like Uber/Airbnb, online labour platforms such as Fiverr), it is individual customers who are the ultimate trigger of the customers' market; it is individual workforces, regardless of whether or not the employees are legal, who are the human resources that can be used by MNEs. Also by today's technology, it is much easier to track individuals' activities than ever before. MNE taxpayers will be more active than ever, and it is common practice that multiple MNE taxpayers conduct cross-border activities. In my view, FA and the digital economy create opportunities together: the neutral design of an FA system elegantly solves the attribution issues arising from the digital economy in a convincing and intuitive way.

The challenges that the EU's FA regime could further face is the interaction with non-EU states. Since most other non-EU states do not adopt an FA system, the EU would need to confront the interaction between its own FA regime and the international tax regime. Even if other non-EU states follow one of the FA policy options of the digital economy proposed by the OECD's inclusive framework of BEPS in 2019, there will be an interaction between two (or more) FA systems. It is inevitable that the EU's FA regime will have to interact with systems still following TP practices and the ALP. Partially implementing the EU's FA in an MNE group is still consistent with the benefit-based MN framework. Ideally, when the three-factor formula is adopted globally, the benefit-based MN can be achieved. Before that ideal status is achieved, we are only in the process of moving 'towards' MN.

In my view, the EU as a global actor would need to explore the impact and consequences that the EU's FA regime could bring to the rest of the world. The EU's reformed FA regime, even when it is well designed, would not be the 'end of history'[1429] as to international tax reform. Instead, it would serve as an alternative to the current international tax reform and revive and re-implement the benefit principle. In other words, it would be a new starting point for further exploration.

1429. This expression is borrowed from Francis Fukuyama, The End of History and the Last Man (Simon & Schuster 2006).

Bibliography

Adam S, Miller H & Pope T, 'Tax, Legal Form and the Gig Economy' (2017) IFS Green Budget 2017

Adams Z & Deakin S, 'Institutional Solutions to Precariousness and Inequality in Labour Markets' (2014) 52 British Journal of Industrial Relations 779

Agúndez-García A, 'The Delineation and Apportionment of an EU Consolidated Tax Base for Multi-Jurisdictional Corporate Income Taxation: A Review of Issues and Options' (Directorate General Taxation and Customs Union, European Commission 2006)

Aikins M, 'Common Control and the Delineation of the Taxable Entity' (2011) 121 Yale Law Journal 624

Alipour J-V, Falck O & Schüller S, 'Germany's Capacities to Work from Home' (2020) CESifo Working Paper No. 8227

Almendral VR, 'Tax Avoidance, the "Balanced Allocation of Taxing Powers" and the Arm's Length Standard: An Odd Threesome in Need of Clarification', in *Allocating Taxing Powers Within the European Union* (I Richelle, W Schön & E Traversa (eds), Springer 2013)

Almudí Cid J, Ferreras Gutiérrez JA & Hernández González-Barreda PA (eds), *Combating Tax Avoidance in the EU: Harmonization and Cooperation in Direct Taxation* (Kluwer Law International 2019)

Altshuler R & Grubert H, 'Formula Apportionment: Is It Better than the Current System and Are There Better Alternatives?' (2010) 63 National Tax Journal, December 1145

Alvarez-Martinez M & others, 'How Large Is the Corporate Tax Base Erosion and Profit Shifting? A General Equilibrium Approach' (2022) 34 Economic Systems Research 2

Amand C, 'VAT Neutrality: A Principle of EU Law or a Principle of the VAT System?' (2013) 2 World Journal of VAT/GST Law 163-181

Amit R & Zott C, 'Value Creation in E-Business' (2001) 22 Strategic Management Journal 493

Andersson K, 'An Optional Common Consolidated Corporate Tax Base in the European Union', in *National Tax Policy in Europe* (K Andersson, E Eberhartinger & L Oxelheim (eds), Springer 2007)
Andoyan A, 'Independent Contractor or Employee: I'm Uber Confused: Why California Should Create an Exception for Uber Drivers and the on-Demand Economy' (2017) 47 Golden Gate University Law Review 153
Andrews AG, 'Lessons from Wynne: Why New York City's Internally Consistent Income Tax Nonetheless Violates the Dormant Commerce Clause' (2018) 50 Connecticut Law Review 1077
Andrus JL & Collier R, *Transfer Pricing and the Arm's Length Principle after BEPS* (Oxford University Press 2017)
Arnold B, *An Introduction to Tax Treaties* (United Nations 2013)
Arnold BJ, *International Tax Primer* (Kluwer Law International 2019)
Arnold BJ & Zolt EM (ed.), *The Taxation of Business Profits under Tax Treaties* (Canadian Tax Foundation 2003)
Arrache MR, 'Factor Representation in the Apportionment of Income from Intangibles' (1995) 36 Santa Clara Law Review 485
Arulampalam W, Devereux M & Maffini G, 'The Direct Incidence of Corporate Income Tax on Wages' (2012) 56 European Economic Review 1038
Aslam A & Shah A, *Taxation and the Peer-to-Peer Economy* (IMF 2017)
Auerbach A & others, 'Destination-Based Cash Flow Taxation WP 17/01' (2017) University of Oxford Centre of Business Taxation Working Papers
Auerbach AJ, 'Who Bears the Corporate Tax? A Review of What We Know' (2006) 20 Tax Policy and the Economy 1
Auerbach AJ & Smetters KA (eds), *The Economics of Tax Policy* (Oxford University Press 2017)
Ault H, 'Some Reflections on the OECD and the Sources of International Tax Principles' (2013) 70 Tax Notes International 1195
Austin S, Bissoondial H & Lipin IA, 'Throwing Out Uncertainty from the Throwout Rule' (2015) 76 State Tax Notes
Avi-Yonah RS, 'The Rise and Fall of Arm's Length: A Study in the Evolution of US International Taxation' (1995) 15 Virginia Tax Review 89
Avi-Yonah RS, 'International Taxation of Electronic Commerce' (1996) 52 Tax Law Review 507
Avi-Yonah RS, 'Globalization, Tax Competition, and the Fiscal Crisis of the Welfare State' (2000) Harvard Law Review 1573
Avi-Yonah RS, 'International Tax as International Law' (2003) 57 Tax Law Review 483
Avi-Yonah RS, 'All of a Piece Throughout: The Four Ages of US International Taxation' (2005) 25 Virginia Tax Review 313
Avi-Yonah RS, 'Federalism and the Commerce Clause: A Comparative Perspective', *The State and Local Tax Lawyer. Symposium Edition* (American Bar Association 2007)
Avi-Yonah RS, 'Tax Competition, Tax Arbitrage, and the International Tax Regime' (2007) University of Michigan Law & Economics, Olin Working Paper

Avi-Yonah RS, 'Between Formulary Apportionment and the OECD Guidelines: A Proposal for Reconciliation' (2010) 2(1) World Tax Journal

Avi-Yonah RS, 'Virtual PE: International Taxation and the Fairness Act' (2013) University of Michigan Public Law Research Paper

Avi-Yonah RS, 'Who Invented the Single Tax Principle: An Essay on the History of US Treaty Policy' (2014) 59 New York Law School Law Review 305

Avi-Yonah RS, 'Full Circle? The Single Tax Principle, BEPS, and the New US Model' (2015) The Single Tax Principle, BEPS, and the New US Model (13 October 2015) University of Michigan Public Law Research Paper 1

Avi-Yonah RS, 'Three Steps Forward, One Step Back? Reflections on "Google Taxes" and the Destination-Based Corporate Tax' (2016) Nordic Tax Journal 69

Avi-Yonah RS, 'Designing a 21st Century Taxing Threshold: Some International Implications of South Dakota vs. Wayfair' (2018) University of Michigan Public Law Research Paper

Avi-Yonah RS, *Advanced Introduction to International Tax Law* (Edward Elgar 2019)

Avi-Yonah RS & Benshalom I, 'Formulary Apportionment: Myths and Prospects' (2011) 3(3) World Tax Journal

Avi-Yonah RS & Clausing KA, *Reforming Corporate Taxation in a Global Economy: A Proposal to Adopt Formulary Apportionment* (Brookings Institution Washington, DC 2007)

Avi-Yonah RS, Clausing KA & Durst MC, 'Allocating Business Profits for Tax Purposes: A Proposal to Adopt a Formulary Profit Split' (2009) Florida Tax Review

Avi-Yonah RS & Halabi O, 'A Model Treaty for the Age of BEPS' (2014) University of Michigan Public Law Research Paper 14

Avi-Yonah RS & Lang M, *Comparative Fiscal Federalism* (Kluwer Law International 2016)

Avi-Yonah RS, Sartori N & Marian O, *Global Perspectives on Income Taxation Law* (Oxford University Press 2011)

Avi-Yonah RS & Xu H, 'Evaluating BEPS: A Reconsideration of the Benefits Principle and Proposal for UN Oversight' (2016) 6 Harvard Business Law Review 185

Badger L, 'NIST Draft Special Publication 800-146, DRAFT Cloud Computing Synopsis and Recommendations' (2011) Gaithersburg, MD: National Institute of Standards and Technology

Bagran Ilhan C, 'The Use of Value Chain Analysis in a Profit Split' (2018) 25(4) International Transfer Pricing Journal

Baker R, *Taxation and Operations Abroad: By Russell Baker Ua Symposium Conducted by the Tax Institute December 3-4, 1959* (Tax Inst 1960)

Baker RW, *Capitalism's Achilles Heel: Dirty Money and How to Renew the Free-Market System* (John Wiley & Sons 2005)

Bakker A & others, 'Chapter 1: Increasing Importance of IP Rights', in I Verlinden & A Bakker (eds), *Mastering the IP Life Cycle from a Legal, Tax and Accounting Perspective* (IBFD 2018)

Bal A, 'EU VAT: New Rules on B2C Supplies of Digital Services from 2015' (2014) 54 European Taxation 300

Bal A, *The Sky's the Limit: Cloud-Based Services in an International Perspective* (2014)

Bal A, 'Taxation of Digital Supplies in the European Union and United States: What Can They Learn from Each Other?' (2015) 55 European Taxation 245
Bal A, '(Mis)Guided by the Value Creation Principle: Can New Concepts Solve Old Problems?' (2018) 72(11) IBFD Bulletin for International Taxation
Bank SA, *Anglo-American Corporate Taxation: Tracing the Common Roots of Divergent Approaches* (Cambridge University Press 2011)
Bank SA, 'The Globalization of Corporate Tax Reform' (2012) 40 Pepperdine Law Review 1307
Barker J, Asare K & Brickman S, 'Transfer Pricing as a Vehicle in Corporate Tax Avoidance' (2017) 33 Journal of Applied Business Research 9
Barker P, 'Big Ticket Auditing: A Review of the Structures of the European Court of Auditors' (2006) 13 Irish Accounting Review
Barnard C, *EU Employment Law* (Oxford University Press 2012)
Barnard C, *The Substantive Law of the EU: The Four Freedoms* (4th ed., Oxford University Press 2013)
Battin CA, Eberle MP & LaCava LM, 'Demystifying the Sales Factor: Market-Based Sourcing' (2014) State Tax Notes
Bauer D, 'The Misclassification of Independent Contractors: The Fifty-Four Billion Dollar Problem' (2015) 12 Rutgers Journal of Law & Public Policy 2
Bauer M, 'Digital Companies and Their Fair Share of Taxes: Myths and Misconceptions' (2018) ECIPE Occasional Paper
Baxter CM, Asghar H & Border JR, 'Conclusions from a Business Point of View', in *Taxation of Shipping and Air Transport in Domestic Law, EU Law and Tax Treaties* (G Maisto (ed.), IBFD 2016)
Becerra JA, *Interpretation and Application of Tax Treaties* (IBFD 2007).
Becerra JA, *Interpretation and Application of Tax Treaties in North America* (2nd rev. ed., IBFD 2013)
Becker A, 'Japanese Tax Reforms Square Up to BEPS Action 1 to Tackle Tax Challenges of the Growing Digital Economy' (2018) 72 IBFD Bulletin for International Taxation
Becker J & Englisch J, 'A European Perspective on the US Plans for a Destination Based Cash Flow Tax' (2017) University of Oxford Centre of Business Taxation Working Papers
Becker J & Englisch J, 'Taxing Where Value Is Created: What's "User Involvement" Got to Do with It?' (2019) 47 Intertax 161
Beebe J, 'How Should We Tax the Sharing Economy?' (2018) 10 Issue Brief
Bellingwout J, 'Blueprint for a New Common Corporate Tax Base' (2015) 55 European Taxation 3
Bennett MC & Dunahoo CA, 'Attribution of Profits to a Permanent Establishment: Issues and Recommendations' (2005) 33 Intertax 51
Benshalom I, 'Taxing the Financial Income of Multinational Enterprises by Employing a Hybrid Formulary and Arm's Length Allocation Method' (2008) 28 Virginia Tax Review 619
Beretta G, 'Cross-Border Mobility of Individuals and the Lack of Fiscal Policy Coordination Among Jurisdictions (Even) After the BEPS Project' (2019) 47 Intertax 91

Berg J & others, *Digital Labour Platforms and the Future of Work: Towards Decent Work in the Online World* (International Labour Organization 2018)
Bernthal J & others, 'Single Sales-Factor Corporate Income Tax Apportionment: Evaluating the Impact in Wisconsin', The Wisconsin Department of Revenue (2012)
Berson SA, 'Distinguishing Between Independent Contractors and Employees: Part I' (2002) 4 Corporate Business Taxation Monthly 12
Berson SA, 'Distinguishing Between Independent Contractors and Employees: Part II' (2002) 4 Corporate Business Taxation Monthly 14
Bettendorf L & others, 'Corporate Tax Harmonization in the EU' (2010) 25 Economic Policy
Bhandari M, *Philosophical Foundations of Tax Law* (Oxford University Press 2017)
Biegalski A, 'The Arm's Length Principle: Fiscalism or Economic Realism? A Few Reflections' (2010) 38 Intertax 177
Biek JA, 'Alternative Formulary Apportionment Under the Multistate Tax Compact' (2013) 16 Journal of Passthrough Entities 41
Bishop-Henchman J, 'The History of Internet Sales Taxes from 1789 to the Present Day: South Dakota v. Wayfair' (2018) Cato Supreme Court Review
Bizioli G, 'Fairness of the Taxation of the Digital Economy', in *Tax and the Digital Economy: Challenges and Proposals for Reform* (WC Haslehner & others (eds), Kluwer Law International 2019)
Bizioli G & Sacchetto C (eds), *Tax Aspects of Fiscal Federalism: A Comparative Analysis* (IBFD 2011)
Blay PA, 'Reviving Transfer Pricing Enforcement Through Formulary Apportionment' (2017) 7 Tax Development Journal
Boadway R & Tremblay J-F, 'Reassessment of the Tiebout Model' (2012) 96 Journal of Public Economics 1063
Bohle D, 'Race to the Bottom? Transnational Companies and Reinforced Competition in the Enlarged European Union', in *Contradictions and Limits of Neoliberal European Governance* (B Van Apeldoorn, J Drahokoupil & L Horn (eds), Springer 2009)
Borg JC, 'Tax Treatment of Losses under the Proposed Common Consolidated Corporate Tax Base Directive' (2013) 41 Intertax 581
Bowen M, 'Slicing the Pie: A Call for Congress to Enact Single-Factor Payroll Apportionment of Interstate Business Revenue' (2017) 4 Belmont Law Review 187
Brabson GD, 'Multistate Taxation of the Transportation Industry' (1957) 18 Ohio State Law Journal 22
Bräumann P, 'Digital Permanent Establishments on Its Way to Becoming a Reality? The EU Commission's Proposal on Taxing "Significant Digital Presence"', in *Tax and the Digital Economy: Challenges and Proposals for Reform* (WC Haslehner & others (eds), Kluwer Law International 2019)
Brauner Y, 'Value in the Eye of the Beholder: The Valuation of Intangibles for Transfer Pricing Purposes' (2008) 28 Virginia Tax Review 79

Brauner Y, 'Formulary Taxation and Transfer Pricing: The Good, the Bad and the Misguided', in *Movement of Persons and Tax Mobility in the EU: Changing Winds* (AP Dourado (ed.), IBFD 2013)

Brauner Y, 'Formula Based Transfer Pricing' (2014) 42 Intertax 615

Brauner Y, 'What the BEPS?' (2014) 16 Florida Tax Review

Brauner Y, 'Changes? BEPS, Transfer Pricing for Intangibles, and CCAS', *University of Florida Levin College of Law Research Paper No. 16-14* (2016)

Brauner Y, 'Transfer Pricing Aspects of Intangibles: The Cost Contribution Arrangement Model', in *Transfer Pricing in a Post-BEPS World* (M Lang & A Storck (eds), Kluwer Law International 2016)

Brauner Y, 'International Tax Policy: Between Competition and Cooperation' (2019) 22 Florida Tax Review 571

Brauner Y, 'Between Arm's Length and Formulary Apportionment', in *The Allocation of Multinational Business Income: Reassessing the Formulary Apportionment Option* (RE Krever & F Vaillancourt (eds), Kluwer Law International 2020)

Brauner Y & Pistone P (eds), *BRICS and the Emergence of International Tax Coordination* (IBFD 2015)

Brauner Y & Pistone P (eds), 'Adapting Current International Taxation to New Business Models: Two Proposals for the European Union' (2017) 71 IBFD Bulletin for International Taxation 681

Brauner Y & Pistone P (eds), 'Some Comments on the Attribution of Profits to the Digital Permanent Establishment' (2018) 72 IBFD Bulletin for International Taxation

Brenninkmeijer A & others, 'Auditing Standards and the Accountability of the European Court of Auditors (ECA)' (2018) 14 Utrecht Law Review 1

Brewerton SJ, 'Employment Law-FedEx Delivery Drivers Improperly Classified as Independent Contractors Rather than Employees-Alexander v. FedEx Ground Package System, Inc., 765 F. 3d 981 (9th Cir. 2014)' (2015) 48 Suffolk University Law Review 537

Brill A & others, 'Amicus Brief in Wayfair v. South Dakota' (2018) South Dakota (5 March 2018)

Broekhuijsen DM, *A Multilateral Tax Treaty: Designing an Instrument to Modernise International Tax Law* (Kluwer Law International 2018)

Brokelind C, 'Coordination of Negotiation of Member States' Double Tax Treaties with Third States in a Post-BEPS and Post-ATAD Era: The Case of Hybrid Mismatches', in *The External Tax Strategy of the EU in a Post-BEPS Environment* (AJM Jiménez & Group for Research on European International Taxation (eds), IBFD 2019)

Brokelind C & Group for Research on European International Taxation (eds), *Principles of Law: Function, Status and Impact in EU Tax Law* (IBFD 2014)

Bronson SS, 'Treatment of Expensed Intangible Drilling and Development Costs for Purposes of the Property Factor of the Multistate Tax Commission's Apportionment Formula' (1978) The Urban Lawyer 224

Brooks K, 'Learning to Live with an Imperfect Tax: A Defence of the Corporate Tax' (2003) 36 University of British Columbia Law Review 621

Brown B, *Rising Strong* (Random House 2017)

Brown B, *Dare to Lead* (Random House 2018)
Brown JS, 'Formulary Taxation and NAFTA' (1993) 49 Tax Law Review 759
Bunn D, 'A Summary of Criticisms of the EU Digital Tax' (2018) Tax Foundation
Burgers IJ, 'The New OECD Approach on Profit Allocation: A Step Forward Towards Neutral Treatment of Permanent Establishments and Subsidiaries' (2009) 10 Florida Tax Review 51
Burgers IJJ, *Taxation and Supervision of Branches of International Banks: A Comparative Study of Banks and Other Enterprises* (IJJ Burgers 1991)
Buriak S & Lazarov I, 'Between State Aid and the Fundamental Freedoms: The Arm's Length Principle and EU Law' (2019) 56 Common Market Law Review.
Burton EC, 'Importance of the Scales Factor' (1999) 1 Corporate Business Taxation Monthly 18
Busch D, Avgouleas E & Ferrarini G (eds), *Capital Markets Union in Europe* (1st ed., Oxford University Press 2018)
Buschoff KS & Schmidt C, 'Adapting Labour Law and Social Security to the Needs of the "New Self-Employed": Comparing the UK, Germany and the Netherlands' (2009) 19 Journal of European Social Policy 147
Calder J, 'Transfer Pricing: Special Extractive Issues', in *International Taxation and the Extractive Industries* (P Daniel (ed.), Routledge 2017)
Carlos dos Santos A, 'What Is Substantial Economic Activity for Tax Purposes in the Context of the European Union and the OECD Initiatives Against Harmful Tax Competition' (2015) 24 EC Tax Review 166
Carlson RR, 'Why the Law Still Can't Tell an Employee When It Sees One and How It Ought to Stop Trying' (2001) 22 Berkeley Journal of Employment and Labor Law 295
Carlson RR, 'Employment by Design: Employees Independent Contractors and the Theory of the Firm' (2018) 71 Arkansas Law Review 127
Caroll L, *Alice's Adventures in Wonderland* (Random House 1865)
Carpentieri L & Micossi S, 'Removing Cross-Border Tax Barriers', in *Capital Markets Union in Europe* (D Busch, E Avgouleas & G Ferrarini G (eds), 1st ed., Oxford University Press 2018)
Carroll MB, 'Allocation of Business Income: The Draft Convention of the League of Nations' (1934) 34 Columbia Law Review 473
Cavalier G & Upex R, 'The Concept of Employment Contract in European Union Private Law' (2006) 55 International & Comparative Law Quarterly 587
CCH Tax Law Editors, *U.S. Master Multistate Corporate Tax Guide (2020)* (CCH Incorporated 2019)
Célestin LMFC, *Formulary Approach to the Taxation of Transnational Corporations: A Realistic Alternative?* (University of Sydney PhD thesis 2000)
Ceriani V, 'CCCTB and the Financial Sector' (2008) 17 EC Tax Review 159
Cerioni L, 'Abuse of Rights in EU Company Law and EU Tax Law: A Re-Reading of the ECJ Case Law and the Quest for a Unitary Notion' (2010) 21 European Business Law Review 783
Cerioni L, *The European Union and Direct Taxation: A Solution for a Difficult Relationship* (Routledge 2015)

Cerioni L, 'The Quest for a New Corporate Taxation Model and for an Effective Fight Against International Tax Avoidance within the EU' (2016) 44 Intertax 463

Chen S-C, 'Tax Avoidance in the Sales Factor: Comparison Between the CCCTB and USA's Formulary Apportionment Taxation' (2017) Indian Journal of Tax Law

Chen S-C, 'Neutrality as Tax Justice: The Case of Common Consolidated Corporate Tax Base under the EU Law' (2018) 5 European Studies – The Review of European Law, Economics and Politics 33

Chen S-C, 'Tracing Capital: Toward a Neutral Specialized Formula for Financial Institutions under Common Consolidated Corporate Tax Base (CCCTB)' (2018) 12 Bocconi Legal Papers 71

Chen S-C, 'Lost in Translation?: Rethinking the Oil and Gas Industry Formula under the Common Consolidated Corporate Tax Base Directive Proposal' (2019) 7 Societas et iurisprudentia 108

Chen S-C, 'The Strategy of Shifting-To-Losses: The Case of Common Consolidated Corporate Tax Base (CCCTB) in the European Union' (2019) 2 UCPH Fiscal Relations Law Journal (FIRE Journal)

Chen S-C, 'Toward a Neutral Corporate Tax for the Transportation Industry – Rethinking the Transportation Industry Formula of the Common Consolidated Corporate Tax Base Directive Proposal under EU Law' (2020) 30 ID-DRITT Journal

Cherry MA & Aloisi A, '"Dependent Contractors" in the Gig Economy: A Comparative Approach' (2017) 66 American University Law Review 635

Chesalina O, 'Access to Social Security for Digital Platform Workers in Germany and in Russia: A Comparative Study' (2018) 7 Spanish Labour Law and Employment Relations Journal 17

Choi W & Rienstra JG, *United States: Corporate Taxation, Country Tax Guides* (IBFD 2020)

Christians A, 'Hard Law, Soft Law, and International Taxation' (2007) 25 Wisconsin International Law Journal 325

Christians A, 'Taxing According to Value Creation' (2018) 90 Tax Notes International

Christians A & Ezenagu A, 'Kill-Switches in the New US Model Tax Treaty' (2016) 41 Brooklyn Journal of International Law

Christians A & Van Apeldoorn L, 'Taxing Income Where Value Is Created' (2018) 22 Florida Tax Review 1

Clausing KA, 'In Search of Corporate Tax Incidence' (2011) 65 Tax Law Review 433

Clausing KA, 'Who Pays the Corporate Tax in a Global Economy?' (2013) 66 National Tax Journal 151

Clausing KA, 'Lessons for International Tax Reform from the US State Experience under Formulary Apportionment' (2014) Available at SSRN 2359724

Clausing KA & Avi-Yonah RS, 'Reforming Corporate Taxation in a Global Economy: A Proposal to Adopt Formulary Apportionment. The Hamilton Project' (Discussion Paper 2007-2008 Brookings Institution, Washington, DC 2008) https://www.brookings.edu/research/reforming-corporate-taxation-in-a-global-economy-a-proposal-to-adopt-formulary-apportionment

Cleveland MM, 'A Classical Model of Distribution, Productivity and Growth: Adam Smith Was Right' (2003) Distribution, Productivity & Growth

Cline WR, 'Will Corporate Tax Cuts Cause a Large Increase in Wages?' (2017) Policy Briefs PB17-30, Peterson Institute for International Economics

Cnossen S (ed.), *Taxing Capital Income in the European Union: Issues and Options for Reform* (Oxford University Press 2000)

Cnossen S, *Three VAT Studies* (Centraal Planbureau 2010)

Cockfield AJ, 'Jurisdiction to Tax: A Law and Technology Perspective' (2003) 38 Georgia Law Review 85

Cockfield AJ, 'Reforming the Permanent Establishment Principle Through a Quantitative Economic Presence Test' (2003) 38 Canadian Business Law Journal 400

Cockfield AJ, 'Shaping International Tax Law and Policy in Challenging Times' (2018) 54 Stanford Journal of International Law 223

Cockfield AJ, Hellerstein W & Lamensch M, 'Applying the United States Retail Sales Tax (RST) to Cross-Border Digital Commerce', in *Taxing Global Digital Commerce* (AJ Cockfield, W Hellerstein & M Lamensch (eds), Kluwer Law International 2019)

Cockfield AJ, Hellerstein W & Lamensch M, *Taxing Global Digital Commerce* (2nd ed., Kluwer Law International 2019)

Cohen Jehoram T, Nispen CJJC van & Huydecoper JLRA, *European Trademark Law: Community Trademark Law and Harmonized National Trademark Law* (Kluwer Law International 2010)

Collier R & Vella J, 'Five Core Problems in the Attribution of Profits to Permanent Establishments' (2019) 11 World Tax Journal 159

Commission of the European Communities (eds), *Report of the Committee of Independent Experts on Company Taxation (Ruding Report)* (Office for Official Publications of the European Communities 1992)

Cooper GS, 'The Benefit Theory of Taxation' (1994) 11 Australian Tax Forum 397

Corrigan EF, 'The IDC Property Factor Myth' (1986) 5 Journal of State Taxation 191

Corujo BS, 'The "Gig" Economy and Its Impact on Social Security: The Spanish Example' (2017) 19 European Journal of Social Security 293

Coskey SL, '*Vizcaino v. Microsoft Corporation*: A Labor and Employment Lawyer's Perspective' (1997) 48 Labor Law Journal 91

Cotrut M (ed.), *International Tax Structures in the BEPS Era: An Analysis of Anti-Abuse Measures* (IBFD 2015)

Cottani G, 'Commissionaire Arrangements/Low Risk Distributors and Attribution of Profits to Permanent Establishments', in *Transfer Pricing in a Post-BEPS World* (M Lang & A Storck (eds), Kluwer Law International 2016)

Cottani G, 'Formulary Apportionment: A Revamp in the Post-Base Erosion and Profit Shifting Era?' (2016) 44 Intertax 755

Countouris N, *The Changing Law of the Employment Relationship: Comparative Analyses in the European Context* (Routledge 2007)

Countouris N, 'The Concept of "Worker" in European Labour Law: Fragmentation, Autonomy and Scope' (2018) 47 Industrial Law Journal 192

Countouris N, *Defining and Regulating Work Relations for the Future of Work* (International Labour Organization 2019)

Couzin R, 'Policy Forum: The End of Transfer Pricing' (2013) 61 Canadian Tax Journal 159
Cram by RL, 'No Shade for Cloud Computing Income under P.L. 86-272' (2018) State Tax Notes
Crawford LV, 'Alternatives to Worldwide Unitary Apportionment: An Analysis' (1984) 36 University of Florida Law Review 1051
Cremers J, 'Coordination of National Social Security in the EU: Rules Applicable in Multiple Cross Border Situations' (2010), AIAS Working Paper
Cremers J, 'Free Movement of Workers and Rights That Can Be Derived' (2012) FMW Online Journal on Free Movement of Workers Within the European Union 26
Cui W, 'Destination-Based Cash-Flow Taxation: A Critical Appraisal' (2017) 67 University of Toronto Law Journal 301
Cui W, 'Minimalism about Residence and Source' (2017) 38 Michigan Journal of International Law 245
Cui W, 'The Digital Services Tax: A Conceptual Defense' (2019) 73 Tax Law Review 69
Cunningham-Parmeter K, 'From Amazon to Uber: Defining Employment in the Modern Economy' (2016) 96 Boston University Law Review 1673
Cunningham-Parmeter K, 'Gig-Dependence: Finding the Real Independent Contractors of Platform Work' (2018) 39 Northern Illinois University Law Review 379
Cussons P & Casley A, 'United Kingdom-Reactions to the Common Consolidated Corporate Tax Base Proposals of the European Commission' (2011) 18 International Transfer Pricing Journal 358
Da Silva B, *The Impact of Tax Treaties and EU Law on Group Taxation Regimes* (Kluwer Law International 2016)
da Silva B, 'Cross-Border Loss Relief under the Proposed CCTB Directive' in *The EU Common Consolidated Corporate Tax Base: Critical Analysis* (D Weber & J van de Streek (eds), Kluwer Law International 2018)
Dagan T, *International Tax Policy: Between Competition and Cooperation* (Cambridge University Press 2018)
Dahlberg M, *Direct Taxation in Relation to the Freedom of Establishment and the Free Movement of Capital*, Vol. 9 (Kluwer Law International 2005)
Daniel P (ed.), *International Taxation and the Extractive Industries* (Routledge, an imprint of the Taylor & Francis Group 2017)
Darby J & Lemaster K, 'Double Irish More than Doubles the Tax Saving: Hybrid Structure Reduces Irish, US and Worldwide Taxation. Practical US' (2007) 11 International Tax Strategies 2
Dashwood A, 'The Relationship Between the Member States and the European Union/European Community' (2004) 41 Common Market Law Review 355
Davidov G, 'The Status of Uber Drivers: A Purposive Approach' (2017) 6(1/2) Spanish Labour Law and Employment Relations Journal 6-15
Davidov G, Freedland M & Countouris N, 'The Subjects of Labor Law: "Employees" and Other Workers', *Comparative Labor Law* ((M Finkin & G Mundlak (eds), Edward Elgar 2015)
Davidson NM, Infranca J & Finck M, *The Cambridge Handbook of Law of the Sharing Economy* (Cambridge University Press 2018)

Davies RB & Vadlamannati KC, 'A Race to the Bottom in Labor Standards? An Empirical Investigation' (2013) 103 Journal of Development Economics 1
Davis A & Hageman AM, 'An Exploration of the Antecedents and Consequences of State Income Tax Nexus: Does Economic Nexus Really Benefit States?', *AAA Annual Meeting-Tax Concurrent Sessions* (July 18, 2012) Available at SSRN: https://ssrn.com/abstract=2112503
Dayle Siu E & others, 'Unitary Taxation in the Extractive Industry Sector' (2015) ICTD Working Paper 35
de Graaf A & Visser K-J, 'BEPS: Will the Current Commitments and Peer Review Model Prove Effective?' (2018) 27 EC Tax Review 36
De La Feria R, 'Prohibition of Abuse of (Community) Law: The Creation of a New General Principle of EC Law through Tax' (2008) 45 Common Market Law Review 395
de la Feria R, 'Tax Fraud and the Rule of Law' (2018) Centre for Business Taxation Working Paper
de la Feria R, 'EU General Anti-(Tax) Avoidance Mechanisms: From GAAP to GAAR', *The Dynamics of Taxation* (G Loutzenhiser & R de la Feria (eds) Hart 2020)
de La Feria R & Vogenauer S, *Prohibition of Abuse of Law: A New General Principle of EU Law?* (Bloomsbury 2011)
De Lillo F, 'In Search of Single Taxation', in *Single Taxation?* (J Wheeler (ed.), IBFD 2018)
De Mooij RA, 'A Minimum Corporate Tax Rate in the EU Combines the Best of Two Worlds' (2004) 39 Intereconomics 180
de Mooij RA, Klemm MAD & Perry MVJ, *Corporate Income Taxes under Pressure: Why Reform Is Needed and How It Could Be Designed* (IMF 2021)
De Simone L & Sansing RC, 'Income Shifting Using a Cost-Sharing Arrangement' (2019) 41 Journal of the American Taxation Association 123
De Stefano V & Aloisi A, 'European Legal Framework for "Digital Labour Platforms"' (2018) European Commission, Luxembourg
De Stefano VM & Countouris N, 'New Trade Union Strategies for New Forms of Employment' (2019) New Trade Union Strategies for New Forms of Employment 1
de Wilde M, 'Tax Competition Within the European Union – Is the CCCTB Directive a Solution?' (2014) 7 Erasmus Law Review 24
de Wilde M, 'Sharing the Pie: Taxing Multinationals in a Global Market' (2015) 43 Intertax 438
de Wilde M, 'Lowering the Permanent Establishment Threshold via the Anti-BEPS Convention: Much Ado About Nothing?' (2017) 45 Intertax 556
de Wilde M, *Sharing the Pie: Taxing Multinationals in a Global Market* (IBFD 2017)
de Wilde M, 'The CCCTB Relaunch: A Critical Assessment and Some Suggestions for Modification' (2017) SSRN Electronic Journal https://www.ssrn.com/abstract=3040739 (accessed 17 June 2020)
de Wilde M, 'Tax Competition Within the European Union Revisited: Is the Relaunched CCCTB a Solution?', in *The EU Common Consolidated Corporate Tax Base: Critical Analysis* (DM Weber & J van de Streek (eds), Kluwer Law International 2018)

de Wilde M, 'Om de Toekomst van de Belastingheffing van Ondernemingswinsten in Europa (Oratie)' (2019) 13 TPE Digitaal 60

de Wilde M, 'On the Future of Business Income Taxation in Europe' (2019) https://www.ssrn.com/abstract=3424681 (accessed 27 May 2020)

de Wilde M & Wisman C, 'New Trends in the Definition of Permanent Establishment: The Netherlands' (2018) Available at SSRN 3307326

de Wilde M & Wisman C, 'OECD Consultations on the Digital Economy: "Tax Base Reallocation" and "I'll Tax If You Don't"?' (2019) Available at SSRN 3349078

Deakin S, 'The Changing Concept of the "Employer" in Labour Law' (2001) 30 Industrial Law Journal 72

DeBruyne NL, 'Uber Drivers: A Disputed Employment Relationship in Light of the Sharing Economy' (2017) 92 Chicago-Kent Law Review 289

Deknatel A & Hoff-Downing L, 'ABC on the Books and in the Courts: An Analysis of Recent Independent Contractor and Misclassification Statutes' (2015) 18 University of Pennsylvania Journal of Law & Social Change 53

Desai MA & Hines Jr JR, 'Evaluating International Tax Reform' (2003) National Tax Journal 487

Devereux M, 'The Ruding Committee Report: An Economic Assessment' (1992) 13 Fiscal Studies 96

Devereux M, 'Taxation of Outbound Direct Investment: Economic Principles and Tax Policy Considerations' (2008) 24 Oxford Review of Economic Policy 698

Devereux M, 'Residual Profit Allocation by Income' (2019) Oxford University Centre for Business Taxation Working Paper WP19/01

Devereux M & De la Feria R, 'Designing and Implementing a Destination-Based Corporate Tax' (2014) University of Oxford Centre of Business Taxation Working Papers

Devereux M & Vella J, 'Implications of Digitalization for International Corporation Tax Reform', in *Digital Revolutions in Public Finance* (S Gupta & others (eds), IMF 2017)

Devereux M & Vella J, 'Debate: Implications of Digitalization for International Corporate Tax Reform' (2018) 46 Intertax 550

Dickens C, *A Tale of Two Cities* (Dover Publications 1999)

Dietsch P, *Catching Capital: The Ethics of Tax Competition* (Oxford University Press 2015)

Dimitropoulou C, 'The Digital Services Tax and Fundamental Freedoms: Appraisal Under the Doctrine of Measures Having Equivalent Effect to Quantitative Restrictions' (2019) 47 Intertax 201

Dingel JI & Neiman B, 'How Many Jobs Can Be Done at Home?' (National Bureau of Economic Research 2020)

Dixit AK & Pindyck RS, *Investment under Uncertainty* (Princeton University Press 1994)

Dodge JM, 'Theories of Tax Justice: Ruminations on the Benefit, Partnership, and Ability-to-Pay Principles' (2004) 58 Tax Law Review 399

Dokko J, Mumford M & Schanzenbach DW, 'Workers and the Online Gig Economy: A Hamilton Project Framing Paper' (2015) The Hamilton Project: Advancing Opportunity, Prosperity, and Growth

Donini A & others, 'Towards Collective Protections for Crowdworkers: Italy, Spain and France in the EU Context' (2017) 23 Transfer: European Review of Labour and Research 207

dos Santos AC & Lopes CM, 'Tax Sovereignty, Tax Competition and the Base Erosion and Profit Shifting Concept of Permanent Establishment' (2016) 25 EC Tax Review 296

Douma S, *Optimization of Tax Sovereignty and Free Movement*, Vol. 21 (IBFD 2011)

Douma SCW, *Legal Research in International and EU Tax Law: Rede in Verkorte Vorm* (Kluwer 2014)

Dourado AP (ed.), *Movement of Persons and Tax Mobility in the EU: Changing Winds* (IBFD 2013)

Dourado AP, 'Debate: Digital Taxation Opens the Pandora Box: The OECD Interim Report and the European Commission Proposals' (2018) 46 Intertax 565

Dourado AP & De la Feria R, 'Thin Capitalization Rules in the Context of the CCCTB' (2008) 804 Working Papers from Oxford University Centre for Business Taxation

Douvier P-J & Daudé M, 'France-Common Consolidated Corporate Tax Base' (2011) 18 International Transfer Pricing Journal

Dowd NE, 'The Test of Employee Status: Economic Realities and Title VII' (1984) 26 William & Mary Law Review 75

Dubal V, 'An Uber Ambivalence: Employee Status, Worker Perspectives, & Regulation in the Gig Economy' (2019) UC Hastings Research Paper No. 381

Duff MC, 'All the World's a Platform?: Some Remarks on "Marketplace Platform" Employment Laws' https://ssrn.com/abstract=3520723

Dukes R, 'From the Labour Constitution to an Economic Sociology of Labour Law' (2018) 9 Jurisprudence 418

Durst M, 'Analysis of a Formulary System for Dividing Income, Part II: Examining Current Formulary and Arm's Length Approaches' (2013) 22 Bloomsberg BNA Tax Management Transfer Pricing Report 270

Durst M, 'Analysis of a Formulary System, Part IV: Choosing a Tax Base' (2013) 22 Bloomberg BNA Tax Management Transfer Pricing Report 771

Durst M, 'Analysis of a Formulary System, Part VII: The Sales Factor' (2014) 22 Bloomsberg BNA Tax Management Transfer Pricing Report 1414

Durst MC, 'Tax Management Transfer Pricing Report' (2013) The Bureau of National Affairs

Durst MC, 'The Tax Policy Outlook for Developing Countries: Reflections on International Formulary Apportionment' (2015) ICTD Working Paper 32

Dziurdź K, 'Attribution of Functions and Profits to a Dependent Agent PE: Different Arm's Length Principles under Articles 7 (2) and 9?' (2014) 2 World Tax Journal 135

Eberhartinger E & Petutschnig M, 'CCCTB: The Employment Factor Game' (2017) 43 European Journal of Law and Economics 333

Echevarria Zubeldia G, 'Introducing VAT in the Gulf States' (2017) 69 Tax Executive 63

Ecker T, *A VAT/GST Model Convention: Tax Treaties as Solution for Value Added Tax and Goods and Services Tax Double Taxation* (IBFD 2013)
Eichhorst W & others, Social Protection Rights of Economically Dependent Self-Employed Workers (European Parliament 2013)
Eijsden A van, 'The One-Stop-Shop Approach: A Discussion of the Administrative and Procedural Aspects of the CCCTB Draft Directive' (2011) 20 EC Tax Review 217
Eisenstein MI & Bessey NA, 'Public Law 86-272: Sunlight for a Cloud Service,' (2018) State Tax Notes
Elliffe C, 'The Meaning of the Principal Purpose Test: One Ring to Bind Them All?' (2019) 11 World Tax Journal
Elliot CB, 'Taxation of the Sharing Economy: Recurring Issues' (2018) 72 IBFD Bulletin for International Taxation
Engel DC, 'Would Formula Apportionment for International Transactions Be a More Efficient Approach' (1998) 24 International Tax Journal 23
Erasmus-Koen M, 'International-Common Consolidated Corporate Tax Base: A "Fair Share" of the Tax Base?' (2011) 18 International Transfer Pricing Journal 237
Escribano E, 'Is the OECD/G20 BEPS Initiative Heading in the Right Direction? Some Forgotten (and Uncomfortable) Questions' (2017) 71 IBFD Bulletin for International Taxation
Escribano E, 'A Preliminary Assessment of the EU Proposal on Significant Digital Presence: A Brave Attempt Requires and Deserves Further Analysis', in *Combating Tax Avoidance in the EU: Harmonization and Cooperation in Direct Taxation* (JM Almudí Cid, JA Ferreras Gutiérrez & PA Hernández González-Barreda (eds), Kluwer Law International 2019)
Escribano E, *Jurisdiction to Tax Corporate Income Pursuant to the Presumptive Benefit Principle: A Critical Analysis of Structural Paradigms Underlying Corporate Income Taxation and Proposals for Reform* (Kluwer Law International 2019)
Essers PHJ (ed.), *The Influence of IAS/IFRS on the CCCTB, Tax Accounting, Disclosure and Corporate Law Accounting Concepts: A Clash of Cultures* (Wolters Kluwer Law & Business 2009)
Essers PHJ & Russo R, 'The Precious Relationship Between IAS/IFRS, National Tax Accounting Systems and the CCCTB', *The Influence of IAS/IFRS on the CCCTB, Tax Accounting, Disclosure and Corporate Law Accounting Concepts* (PHJ Essers, T Raaijmakers, R Russo, P van der Schee, L van der Tas & P van der Zanden (eds) Kluwer Law International 2009)
European Commission, 'Green Paper "Modernising Labour Law to Meet the Challenges of the 21st Century" (COM (2006) 708 Final)' (European Commission 2006)
European Commission, 'Communication from the Commission to the European Parliament, the Council: Business Taxation for the 21st Century' (2021) Communication COM (2021) 251 final
European Commission, 'Impact Assessment Accompanying Document to the Proposal for a COUNCIL DIRECTIVE on a Common Consolidated Corporate Tax Base (CCCTB) {COM(2011) 121 Final} {SEC(2011) 316 Final}' (European Commission 2011)

European Commission, 'Proposal for a COUNCIL DIRECTIVE on a Common Consolidated Corporate Tax Base (CCCTB) {SEC(2011) 315} {SEC(2011) 316}' (2011)

European Commission, 'Impact Assessment Accompanying the Document Proposals for a Council Directive on a Common Corporate Tax Base and a Common Consolidated Corporate Tax Base (CCCTB) {COM(2016) 683 Final} {SWD(2016) 342 Final}' (European Commission 2016)

European Commission, 'Proposal for a COUNCIL DIRECTIVE on a Common Consolidated Corporate Tax Base (CCCTB) {SWD(2016) 341 Final} {SWD(2016) 342 Final}' (European Commission 2016)

European Commission, 'Proposal for a Council Directive on the Common System of a Digital Services Tax on Revenues Resulting from the Provision of Certain Digital Services, EUR COMM'N COM(2018) 148 Final (21 March 2018)' (European Commission 2018)

European Union Intellectual Property Office, 'EU Trade Mark Reform Summary of Changes Applying from 1 October 2017' (European Union Intellectual Property Office 2017)

Ezenagu A, 'Faltering Blocks in the Arguments Against Unitary Taxation and the Formulary Apportionment Approach to Income Allocation' (2017) 17 Asper Review of International Business & Trade Law 131

Ezenagu A, 'Unitary Taxation of Multinational Enterprises for a Just Allocation of Income: Nigeria as a Case Study of Africa's Largest Economies' (PhD Thesis, McGill University 2019)

Fabo B, Karanovic J & Dukova K, 'In Search of an Adequate European Policy Response to the Platform Economy' (2017) 23 Transfer: European Review of Labour and Research 163

Falcão T, 'Taxing Carbon Emissions from International Shipping' (2019) 47 Intertax 832

Faulhaber LV, 'Sovereignty, Integration and Tax Avoidance in the European Union: Striking the Proper Balance' (2009) 48 Columbia Journal of Transnational Law 177

Faulk D, 'Do State Economic Development Incentives Create Jobs? An Analysis of State Employment Tax Credits' (2002) 55 National Tax Journal 263

Feinschreiber R, 'Allocation and Apportionment of Interest' (1976) 3 International Tax Journal 538

Feinschreiber R, 'Final Regulations for Allocating and Apportioning Deductions' (1976) 3 International Tax Journal 278

Feinschreiber R, 'Allocation and Apportionment of Miscellaneous Deductions' (1977) 4 International Tax Journal 653

Feinschreiber R, 'Allocation and Apportionment of Research Expenses' (1977) 4 International Tax Journal 902

Feinschreiber R, 'Analysis of the Allocation and Apportionment Cases: 1934 to Present' (1977) 4 International Tax Journal 769

Feinschreiber R, 'Analysis of the Allocation and Apportionment Cases: The Early Years' (1977) 4 International Tax Journal 745

Feinschreiber R, 'Analysis of the Allocation and Apportionment Examples – Part I' (1977) 4 International Tax Journal 1027
Feinschreiber R, 'Treaty Provisions for Allocating and Apportioning Deductions' (1977) 4 International Tax Journal 995
Feinschreiber R, 'Analysis of the Allocation and Apportionment Examples – Part II' (1978) 5 International Tax Journal 45
Feldstein M, 'Tax Avoidance and the Deadweight Loss of the Income Tax' (1999) 81 Review of Economics and Statistics 674
Fernández MJG-T, 'Corporate Tax Harmonization: Key Issues for Ensuring an Efficient Implementation of the CCCTB' (2012) 40 Intertax 598
Février V, 'The Concept of "Worker" in the Free Movement of Workers and the Social Policy Directives: Perspectives from the Case Law of the Court of Justice' (2020) 12(2) European Labour Law Journal
Fields CB & McLoughlin MW, 'An Analysis of the Historical Development of the Dormant Commerce Clause in State Tax Cases', *The State and Local Tax Lawyer. Symposium Edition* (American Bar Association 2007)
Fields CB, Newmark MA & Gibilaro E, 'Fair Is Fair-How to Assert for and Defend Against Alternative Apportionment' (2018) 70 Tax Executive 61
Fields CB, Newmark MA & Gibilaro EJ, 'Unfair Apportionment: Consider the Alternatives' (2017) 69 Tax Executive 21
Finch AR, 'Slow Connections for E-Tailer Nexus: Bringing Sales and Use Taxes up to Speed in an E-Commerce Economy' (2012) 42 Stetson Law Review 293
Finér L & Ylönen M, 'Tax-Driven Wealth Chains: A Multiple Case Study of Tax Avoidance in the Finnish Mining Sector' (2017) 48 Critical Perspectives on Accounting 53
Fleming Jr JC, Peroni RJ & Shay SE, 'Fairness in International Taxation: The Ability-to-Pay Case for Taxing Worldwide Income' (2001) 5 Florida Tax Review 299
Fleming Jr JC, Peroni RJ & Shay SE, 'Formulary Apportionment in the US International Income Tax System: Putting Lipstick on a Pig?' (2015) 36(1) Michigan Journal of International Law
Fox WF & Yang Z, 'Destination Taxation: Road to Economic Success?' (2016) 69 National Tax Journal 285
Francis D, 'The Decline of the Dormant Commerce Clause' (2016) 94 Denver Law Review 255
Frankel PH, 'Basic Principles and Significant Issues in State Taxation of Unitary Corporate Income' (1984) 37 Tax Executive 1
Freedland M, 'From the Contract of Employment to the Personal Work Nexus' (2006) 35 Industrial Law Journal 1
Freedland M & Countouris N, 'Some Reflections on the "Personal Scope" of Collective Labour Law' (2017) 46 Industrial Law Journal 52
Freedland M & Prassl J, 'Employees, Workers and the "Sharing Economy" Changing Practices and Changing Concepts in the United Kingdom' (2017) 6 Spanish Labour Law and Employment Relations Journal 16
Freedman J, 'Tax and Brexit' (2017) 33 Oxford Review of Economic Policy S79

Freedman J & Macdonald G, The Tax Base for CCCTB: The Role of Principles (2008), Working Paper No. 0807, Oxford University Centre for Business Taxation

Friedman AH, 'Final Report of Hearing Officer Regarding Proposed Multistate Tax Commission Formula for the Uniform Apportionment of Net Income from Financial Institutions' (Multistate Tax Commission, 1994)

Fris P, Gonnet S & Meghames R, 'Understanding Risk in the Enterprise: The Key to Transfer Pricing for Today's Business Models' (2014) 21 International Transfer Pricing Journal

Fuest C, 'Who Bears the Burden of Corporate Income Taxation' (2015) ETPF Policy Paper

Fuest C & Fuest W, 'A Minimum Corporate Tax Rate Would Be Harmful for Both High and Low Tax Countries' (2004) 39 Intereconomics 183

Fuest C, Peichl A & Siegloch S, 'Do Higher Corporate Taxes Reduce Wages? Micro Evidence from Germany' (2018) 108 American Economic Review 393

Fuest C & Riedel N, 'Tax Evasion, Tax Avoidance and Tax Expenditures in Developing Countries: A Review of the Literature' (2009) 44 Report prepared for the UK Department for International Development (DFID)

Fukuyama F, *The End of History and the Last Man* (Simon & Schuster 2006)

Gaisbauer HP, Schweiger G & Sedmak C, *Philosophical Explorations of Justice and Taxation: National and Global Issues* (Springer 2015)

Galka K, 'Borderless Market Legislation Practice in EU and USA: Competence of Central Authorities in the Federal Model' (2013) 4 Marble Research Papers

Galle B, 'Designing Interstate Institutions: The Example of the Streamlined Sales and Use Tax Agreement (SSUTA)' (2006) 40 UC Davis Law Review 1381

Galle B, 'Kill Quill, Keep the Dormant Commerce Clause: History's Lessons on Congressional Control of State Taxation' (2017) 70 Stanford Law Review Online 158

Gamage D & Shanske D, 'A New Theory of Equitable Apportionment' (2017) 85 State Tax Notes 267

Gammie M, *The Ruding Committee Report: An Initial Response* (Institute for Fiscal Studies London 1992)

Gao F & Ting A, 'Is Arm's Length Profit Split Methodology Morphing into a Formulary Apportionment Hybrid: The Chinese Example', in *The Allocation of Multinational Business Income: Reassessing the Formulary Apportionment Option* (RE Krever & F Vaillancourt (eds), Kluwer Law International 2020)

Garbarino C, 'An Evolutionary Approach to Comparative Taxation: Theory, Methods and Agenda for Research' (2008) Bocconi Legal Studies Research Paper

Garbarino C, 'Permanent Establishments and BEPS Action 7: Perspectives in Evolution' (2019) 47 Intertax 365

Garben S, 'The European Pillar of Social Rights: Effectively Addressing Displacement?' (2018) 14 European Constitutional Law Review 210

Garben S &, *Protecting Workers in the Online Platform Economy: An Overview of Regulatory and Policy Developments in the EU* (European Agency for Safety and Health at Work 2017)

Garcia Anton R, 'The Limits of Tax Sovereignty Imposed by the Interpretation of Supranational Law', in *European Tax Integration: Law, Policy and Politics* (P Pistone (ed.), IBFD 2018)

García EG, 'The Single Tax Principle: Fiction or Reality in a Non-Comprehensive International Tax Regime?' (2019) 11 World Tax Journal 497

Garst MA, 'An Overview of the Sales Apportionment Factor and Its Application to Sales of Financial Instruments' (2007) 26 Journal of State Taxation 15

Gelineck MS, 'Permanent Establishments and the Offshore Oil and Gas Industry – Part 1' (2016) 70 IBFD Bulletin for International Taxation 1

Genschel P, Kemmerling A & Seils E, 'Accelerating Downhill: How the EU Shapes Corporate Tax Competition in the Single Market' (2011) 49 Journal of Common Market Studies 585

Genschel P & Schwarz P, 'Tax Competition: A Literature Review' (2011) 9 Socio-Economic Review 339

Gereffi G & Fernandez-Stark K, 'Global Value Chain Analysis: A Primer' (2011] Center on Globalization, Governance & Competitiveness (CGGC), Duke University, North Carolina, USA

Gianni MB, 'Transfer Pricing and Formulary Apportionment' (1996) 74 Taxes 169

Gibbins P, 'Extending Employee Protections to Gig-Economy Workers Through the Entrepreneurial Opportunity Test of FedEx Home Delivery' (2018) 57 Washington University Journal of Law & Policy 183

Giddens KB & Maxey MG, 'Common Payment Payroll Tax Planning' (1980) 58 Taxes 189

Goeller JD, 'California Taxation of Entities in Banking Groups: The Crucial Calculation of Financial Versus General' (2005) 19 Journal of Taxation and Regulation of Financial Institutions 21

Gonnet S, 'Risks Redefined in Transfer Pricing Post-BEPS', in *TP in a Post-BEPS World* (M Lang & A Storck (eds), Kluwer Law International 2016)

González SM & Diaz-Palacios JAS, 'The Common Consolidated Corporate Tax Base: Treatment of Losses', in *Common Consolidated Corporate Tax Base* (MLang & others (eds), Linde Verlag 2008)

Goolsbee A, 'Taxes, Organizational Form and the Deadweight Loss of the Corporate Income Tax' (1998) 69 Journal of Public Economics 143

Goolsbee A & Maydew EL, 'Coveting Thy Neighbor's Manufacturing: The Dilemma of State Income Apportionment' (2000) 75 Journal of Public Economics 125

Goolsbee A & Maydew EL, 'The Economic Impact of Single Factor Sales Apportionment for the State of New York' (2000) The Public Policy Institute of New York State, New York

Gordon EA, 'The Sky's the Limit: The Apportionment of Overflights and Property Taxation after Alaska Airlines v. Department of Revenue' (1990) 26 Willamette Law Review 711

Gorter J & Parikh A, 'How Sensitive Is FDI to Differences in Corporate Income Taxation Within the EU?' (2003) 151 De Economist 193

Govers AW, 'Material and Personal Applicational Scope of EEC Regulation No. 1408/71' (1979) 6 Legal Issues of European Integration 65

Graetz MJ, 'The David R. Tillinghast Lecture Taxing International Income: Inadequate Principles, Outdated Concepts, and Unsatisfactory Policies' (2000) 54 Tax Law Review 261

Graetz MJ & Doud R, 'Technological Innovation, International Competition, and the Challenges of International Income Taxation' (2013) Columbia Law Review 347

Gravelle J, 'Corporate Tax Incidence: Review of General Equilibrium Estimates and Analysis' (2013) 66 National Tax Journal 185

Gravelle J, 'Corporate Tax Incidence with Excess Profits', *Proceedings. Annual Conference on Taxation and Minutes of the Annual Meeting of the National Tax Association* Vol. 108 (National Tax Association 2015)

Gravelle JG & Smetters KA, 'Does the Open Economy Assumption Really Mean That Labor Bears the Burden of a Capital Income Tax?' (2006) 6 BE Journal of Economic Analysis & Policy

Greil S, 'The Dealing at Arm's Length Fallacy: A Way Forward to a Formula-Based Transactional Profit Split?' (2017) 45 Intertax 624

Greil S, 'The Arm's Length Principle in the 21st Century – Alive and Kicking?' (2019) SSRN Electronic Journal https://www.ssrn.com/abstract=3379092 (accessed 14 November 2019)

Grinberg I, Formulating the International Tax Debate: Where Does Formulary Apportionment Fit? in *The Allocation of Multinational Business Income: Reassessing the Formulary Apportionment Option* (RE Krever & F Vaillancourt (eds), Kluwer Law International 2020)

Grosheide EF & ter Haar BP, 'Employee-like Worker: Competitive Entrepreneur or Submissive Employee? Reflections on CJEU, C-413/13, FNV Kunsten Informatie', *Labour Law and Social Rights in Europe: The Jurisprudence of International courts, Selected Judgements* (M Łaga, S Bellomo, N Gundt &JM Miranda Boto (eds), Gdańsk University Press 2017)

Gruber J, *Public Finance and Public Policy* (6th ed., Macmillan International Higher Education 2019)

Gupta R, 'Analysis of Intellectual Property Tax Planning Strategies of Multinationals and the Impact of the BEPS Project' (2018) 33 Australian Tax Forum 185

Gupta RK, *Recent Trends in Transfer Pricing: Intangibles, GAAR and BEPS* (Sunil Gupta ed., Bloomsbury 2017)

Gupta S & others (eds), *Digital Revolutions in Public Finance* (IMF 2017)

Hacker P, 'UberPop, UberBlack, and the Regulation of Digital Platforms after the Asociación Profesional Elite Taxi Judgment of the CJEU: Judgment of the Court (Grand Chamber) 20 December 2017, Asociación Profesional Elite Taxi (C-434/15)' (2018) 14 European Review of Contract Law 80

Haibach G, 'The Interpretation of Article 30 of the EC Treaty and the "Dormant" Commerce Clause by the European Court of Justice and the US Supreme Court' (1999) 48 International & Comparative Law Quarterly 155

Hall M & Wood S, 'Base Erosion and Profit Shifting and Business Restructurings' (2016) 44 Intertax 769

Hamer B, 'Hearing Officer Report: Synopsis and Recommendations on Proposed Draft Amendments to the Commission's Model General Allocation and Apportionment Regulations' (1 May 2016)

Hanley RP (ed.), *Adam Smith: His Life, Thought, and Legacy* (Princeton University Press 2016)

Harberger A & Just R, 'A Conversation with Arnold Harberger' (2012) 4 Annual Review of Resource Economics 1

Harberger AC, *The Corporation Income Tax: An Empirical Appraisal. Tax Revision Compendium 1 (House Committee on Ways and Means, 86th Congress, First Session), 231-240* (US Government Printing Office 1959)

Harberger AC, 'The Incidence of the Corporation Income Tax' (1962) 70 Journal of Political Economy 215

Harberger AC, 'Three Basic Postulates for Applied Welfare Economics: An Interpretive Essay' (1971) 9 Journal of Economic Literature 785

Harberger AC, *Taxation and Welfare* (Little Brown 1974)

Harberger AC, 'Tax Neutrality in Investment Incentives' (1980) Economics of Taxation 299

Harper J, Evans M & Najjar R, 'Harley-Davidson, Factor Presence Nexus, and Market Sourcing: How California's Expansive and Evolving Definitions of "Financial Corporations" and "Doing Business" Create Unforeseen Hazards for Taxpayers' (2016) 29 Journal of Taxation & Regulation of Financial Institutions

Harris SD & Krueger AB, 'A Proposal for Modernizing Labor Laws for Twenty-First-Century Work: The "Independent Worker"' (Hamilton Project 2015)

Harriss CL, 'Economic Aspects of Interstate Apportionment of Business Income' (1959) 37 Taxes 327

Hartman PJ, 'The Commerce Clause and the States Power to Tax the Oil and Gas Industry' (1956) 7 *Proceedings of the Annual Institute on Oil and Gas Law and Taxation* 387

Hasen D, 'Tax Neutrality and Tax Amenities' (2012) 12 Florida Tax Review 57

Haskic N, 'The Arm's Length Principle and the CCCTB (Common Consolidated Corporate Tax Base): Solutions to Transfer Pricing Issues for Individual Countries and the European Union?' (2009) 19 Revenue Law Journal 71

Haslehner W, '"Consistency" and Fundamental Freedoms: The Case of Direct Taxation' (2013) 50 Common Market Law Review 737

Haslehner WC & others (eds), *Tax and the Digital Economy: Challenges and Proposals for Reform* (Kluwer Law International 2019)

Hatzopoulos V & Roma S, 'Caring for Sharing? The Collaborative Economy under EU Law' (2017) 54 Common Market Law Review 81

Hellerstein JR, 'Recent Developments in Commerce Clause Limitations on State Taxation' (1957) 10 Tax Executive 117

Hellerstein JR, 'Current Issues in Multistate Taxation of Banks' (1974) 30 Tax Law Review 155

Hellerstein JR, 'Foreword: State Taxation under the Commerce Clause: An Historical Perspective' (1976) 29 Vanderbilt Law Review 335

Hellerstein JR, Hellerstein W & Swain JA, *State Taxation* (3rd ed., Thomson Reuters/Tax & Accounting 2015)
Hellerstein W, 'Construing the Uniform Division of Income for Tax Purposes Act: Reflections on the Illinois Supreme Court's Reading of the "Throwback" Rule' (1978) 45 University of Chicago Law Review 3
Hellerstein W, 'State Income Taxation of Multijurisdictional Corporations: Reflections on Mobil, Exxon, and HR 5076' (1980) 79 Michigan Law Review 113
Hellerstein W, 'State Taxation in the Federal System: Perspectives on Louisiana's First Use Tax on Natural Gas' (1980) 55 Tulane Law Review 601
Hellerstein W, 'State Income Taxation of Multijurisdictional Corporations and the Supreme Court' (1982) National Tax Journal 401
Hellerstein W, 'State Income Taxation of Multijurisdictional Corporations, Part II: Reflections on ASARCO and Woolworth' (1982) 81 Michigan Law Review 157
Hellerstein W, 'Recent Judicial Developments in State Income Taxation of the Oil and Gas Industry' (1986) 34(3) Oil and Gas Tax Quarterly
Hellerstein W, 'Is "Internal Consistency" Foolish?: Reflections on an Emerging Commerce Clause Restraint on State Taxation' (1988) 87 Michigan Law Review 138
Hellerstein W, 'State Taxation of Corporate Income from Intangibles: Allied-Signal and Beyond' (1992) 48 Tax Law Review 739
Hellerstein W, 'Jurisdiction to Tax Income and Consumption in the New Economy: A Theoretical and Comparative Perspective' (2003) 38 Georgia Law Review 1
Hellerstein W, 'Is Internal Consistency Dead: Reflections on an Evolving Commerce Clause Restraint on State Taxation' (2007) 61 Tax Law Review 1
Hellerstein W, 'A Primer on State Tax Nexus: Law, Power, and Policy, Testimony of Walter Hellerstein Francis Shackelford Professor of Taxation University of Georgia Law School Before the Subcommittee on Commercial and Administrative Law of the Committee on the Judiciary United States House of Representatives Hearing on State Taxation: The Role of Congress in Defining Nexus' (The Council on State Taxation, 2010) https://cost.org/globalassets/cost/state-tax-resources-pdf-pages/other-state-tax-studies-articles-reports/hellerstein-testimony-on-nexus.pdf
Hellerstein W, 'The United States', in *Tax Aspects of Fiscal Federalism: A Comparative Analysis* (G Bizioli & C Sacchetto (eds), IBFD 2011)
Hellerstein W, 'Tax Planning under the CCCTB's Formulary Apportionment Provisions: The Good, the Bad and the Ugly', in *CCCTB: Selected Issues* (D Weber (eds), Kluwer Law International 2012)
Hellerstein W, 'Formulary Apportionment in the EU and the US: A Comparative Perspective on the Sharing Mechanism of the Proposed CCCTB', in *Movement of Persons and Tax Mobility in the EU: Changing Winds* (AP Dourado (ed.), IBFD 2013)
Hellerstein W, 'A Hitchhiker's Guide to the OECD's International VAT/GST Guidelines' (2015) 18 Florida Tax Review 589
Hellerstein W, 'An Introduction to the OECD's International VAT/GST Guidelines' (2016) 125(6) Journal of Taxation 256

Hellerstein W, 'The Application of Formulary Apportionment to Related Entities: Lessons from the US Experience', in *The Allocation of Multinational Business Income: Reassessing the Formulary Apportionment Option* (RE Krever & F Vaillancourt (eds), Kluwer Law International 2020)

Hellerstein W, *State and Local Taxation: Cases and Materials* (10th ed., West Academic Publishing 2014)

Hellerstein W, Buydens S & Koulouri D, 'Simplified Registration and Collection Mechanisms for Taxpayers That Are Not Located in the Jurisdiction of Taxation: A Review and Assessment' (OECD 2018) OECD Taxation Working Papers

Hellerstein W & Gillis TH, 'The VAT in the European Union' (2010) 127 Tax Notes 461

Hellerstein W, Kofler GW & Mason R, 'Constitutional Restraints on Corporate Tax Integration' (2008) 62 Tax Law Review 1

Hellerstein W & Sedon J, 'State Taxation of Cloud Computing: A Framework for Analysis' (2012) 117 Journal of Taxation 11

Helminen M, 'The Principle of Elimination of Double Taxation under EU Law-Does It Exist?', in *Principles of Law: Function, Status and Impact in EU Tax Law* (C Brokelind & Group for Research on European International Taxation (eds), IBFD 2014)

Hemerijck A & Eichhorst W, 'Whatever Happened to the Bismarckian Welfare State? From Labor Shedding to Employment-Friendly Reforms', in *A Long Goodbye to Bismarck: The Politics of Welfare Reform in Continental Europe* (Bruno Palier (ed.), Amsterdam University Press 2009)

Hemmelrath A & Marquardsen L, 'Direct Taxation of Air Transport Activities', in *Taxation of Shipping and Air Transport in Domestic Law, EU Law and Tax Treaties* (G Maisto (ed.), IBFD 2017)

Hennings KH, 'Capital as a Factor of Production', in *Capital Theory* (J Eatwell, M Milgate & P Newman (eds), The New Palgrave. Palgrave Macmillan 1990)

Henszey BN & Koot RS, 'Is a Three Factor Apportionment Formula Fair' (1982) 35 Tax Executive 141

Herrera PM & Montero A, 'Supervisory Function of European Institutions?', in *Common Consolidated Corporate Tax Base* (M Lang (ed.), Linde 2008)

Herzfeld M, 'The Case against BEPS: Lessons for Tax Coordination' (2017) 21 Florida Tax Review 1

Herzig N, Teschke M & Joisten C, 'Between Extremes: Merging the Advantages of Separate Accounting and Unitary Taxation' (2010) 38 Intertax 334

Hey J, 'EU Common Consolidated Corporate Tax Base: Guided Variety versus Strict Uniformity – Lessons from the US States' Tax Chaos' (Jean Monnet Chair 2008)

Hey J, '"Taxation Where Value Is Created" and the OECD/G20 Base Erosion and Profit Shifting Initiative' (2018) 72 IBFD Bulletin for International Taxation

Heyman SJ & Weinstein M, 'Calculating the Sales Factor for Service Businesses' (1999) The State and Local Tax Lawyer 35

Hines JR, 'Three Sides of Harberger Triangles' (1999) 13 Journal of Economic Perspectives 167

Hines JR, 'What Is Benefit Taxation?' (2000) 75 Journal of Public Economics 483

HM Simonis P, 'CCCTB: Some Observations on Consolidation from a Dutch Perspective' (2009) 37 Intertax 19

Holderness HR, 'Taking Tax Due Process Seriously: The Give and Take of State Taxation' (2016) 20 Florida Tax Review 371

Holley A & Evans M, 'The Pros and Cons of Combined Reporting: A Compendium of Arguments for and Against Combined Reporting', *The State and Local Tax Lawyer. Symposium Edition* (American Bar Association 2008)

Hongler P, *Justice in International Tax Law: A Normative Review of the International Tax Regime* (IBFD 2019)

Hongler P & Pistone P, 'Blueprints for a New PE Nexus to Tax Business Income in the Era of the Digital Economy' (2015), WU International Taxation Research Paper Series no. 2015-152586196

Hort JB, Isaksen K & Lystad RS, 'Norway', in *Procedural Rules in Tax Law in the Context of European Union and Domestic Law* (M Lang (ed.), Kluwer Law International 2010)

Huddleston J & Sicilian S, 'History and Considerations for Combined Reporting: Will States Adopt a Model Combined Reporting Statute?', *The State and Local Tax Lawyer. Symposium Edition* (American Bar Association 2008)

Huddleston J & Sicilian S, 'Should UDITPA Be Revisited?', *The State and Local Tax Lawyer. Symposium Edition* (American Bar Association 2009)

Huibregtse S & others, 'Multinational Enterprises, Transfer Pricing and Value Chain Analysis in Latin America Following the OECD/G20 Base Erosion and Profit Shifting Initiative'(2018) 72(11) IBFD Bulletin for International Taxation

Hull JC, *Options, Futures, and Other Derivatives* (8th ed., Prentice Hall 2012)

Huntington SP, 'The Clash of Civilizations' (1993) 72(3) Foreign Affairs 22-49

Huntington SP, *The Clash of Civilizations and the Remaking of World Order* (Simon & Schuster 2011)

Hyans, HL & Roberts RG, 'When Is Symmetry Between the Tax Base and Sourcing Rules Required?', *The State and Local Tax Lawyer. Symposium Edition* (American Bar Association 2009)

International Air Transport Association (IATA), 'Guidelines for Taxation of International Air Transport Profits' (International Air Transport Association (IATA), 2015) https://www.iata.org/contentassets/a72d8d3cfaf84529bcdef6b2dc59f224/taxation_intl_air_transport20profits_final.pdf

International Labour Organization, *Regulating the Employment Relationship in Europe: A Guide to Recommendation No. 198 : European Labour Law Network (ELLN)* (International Labour Organization 2013)

International Monetary Fund, *Corporate Taxation in the Global Economy* (IMF 2019)

Isaacs E, 'The Unit Rule' (1926) 35 Yale Law Journal 838

Izawa R, 'Who, Me? Tax Planning and Japanese Multinational Enterprises, 1887–2019'(2019), Working Paper Series (Faculty of Economics, Shiga University) no. 291

Jaag C & Rohner TF, 'Why Corporate Taxation Should Mean Source Taxation: A Response to the OECD's Actions Against Base Erosion and Profit Shifting' (2017) 9 World Tax Journal 352

Jaatinen I, 'IAS/IFRS: A Starting Point for the CCCTB?' (2012) 40 Intertax 260
Jaffee D & Bensman D, 'Draying and Picking: Precarious Work and Labor Action in the Logistics Sector' (2017) WorkingUSA: Journal of Labor and Society
Jagiela JS & Culhane III MA, 'A Taxing Situation for Out-of-State Financial Institutions: Minnesota Sets the Stage by Adopting MTC Proposed Regulations' (1989) 8 Journal of State Taxation 35
Janssens C, *Principle of Mutual Recognition in EU Law* (Oxford Scholarship Online 2013)
Jenum Hotvedt M, 'The Contract-of-Employment Test Renewed: A Scandinavian Approach to Platform Work' (2018) 7 Spanish Labour Law and Employment Relations Journal 56
Jiménez AJM & Group for Research on European International Taxation (eds), *The External Tax Strategy of the EU in a Post-BEPS Environment* (IBFD 2019)
Jogarajan S, 'The Conclusion and Termination of the "First" Double Taxation Treaty' (2012) 3 British Tax Review
Johnston JL & Reynolds A, 'A Natural Resource Theory of Unitary Taxation' (1985) 6 The Energy Journal
Joondeph BW, 'The Meaning of Fair Apportionment and the Prohibition on Extraterritorial State Taxation' (2002) 71 Fordham Law Review 149
Joondeph BW, 'Exploring the Myth of Parity in State Taxation: State Court Decisions Interpreting Public Law 86-272' (2003) 13 Washington University Journal of Law & Policy 205
Kahn DA, 'The Two Faces of Tax Neutrality: Do They Interact or Are They Mutually Exclusive?' (1990) 18 Northern Kentucky Law Review 1
Kane MA, 'Strategy and Cooperation in National Responses to International Tax Arbitrage' (2004) 53 Emory Law Journal 89
Kaufman NH, 'Fairness and the Taxation of International Income' (1997) 29 Law & Policy International Business 145
Kaye TA & Mahoney MK, 'Various Approaches to Sourcing Multijurisdictional Values: Sourcing Options Available to Tax Policy Makers', *The State and Local Tax Lawyer. Symposium Edition* (American Bar Association 2009)
Keen M & Hellerstein W, 'Interjurisdictional Issues in the Design of a VAT' (2009) 63 Tax Law Review 359
Keen MJ & others, *Spillovers in International Corporate Taxation* (IMF 2014)
Kellogg P, 'Independent Contractor or Employee: *Vizcaino v. Microsoft Corp.*' (1998) 35 Houston Law Review 1775
Kemmeren E, 'Source of Income in Globalizing Economies: Overview of the Issues and a Plea for an Origin-Based Approach' (2006) 60 IBFD Bulletin for International Taxation 438
Kemmeren EC, 'Should the Taxation of the Digital Economy Really Be Different?' (2018) 27 EC Tax Review 72
Kemmeren EC & Smit DS, 'Taxation of EU-Non-Resident Companies under the CCCTB System: Analysis and Suggestions for Improvement', in *Corporate Income Taxation in Europe* (M Lang, P Pistone, J Schuch, C Staringer & A Storck (eds) Edward Elgar 2013)

Kennedy T, 'The Court of Auditors', in *Oxford Principles of European Union Law: The European Union Legal Order: Volume I* (R Schütze &T Tridimas (eds), Oxford University Press 2018)

Kern A, 'Illusions of Justice in International Taxation' (2020) 48 Philosophy & Public Affairs 151

Kiekebeld BJ, *Harmful Tax Competition in the European Union: Code of Conduct, Countermeasures and EU Law* (Kluwer 2004)

Kim SM & Kim J, 'Flags of Convenience in the Context of the OECD BEPS Package' (2018) 49 Journal of Maritime Law & Commerce

Kjærsgaard LF & Schmidt PK, 'Allocation of the Right to Tax Income from Digital Intermediary Platforms – Challenges and Possibilities for Taxation in the Jurisdiction of the User' (2018) 1 Nordic Journal of Commercial Law 27

Klassen KJ & Shackelford DA, 'State and Provincial Corporate Tax Planning: Income Shifting and Sales Apportionment Factor Management' (1998) 25 Journal of Accounting and Economics 385

Klaver JA & Timmermans AJ, 'EU Taxation: Policy Competition or Policy Coordination' (1999) 8 EC Tax Review 185

Klein WA, 'The Incidence of the Corporation Income Tax: A Lawyer's View of a Problem in Economics' (1965) Wisconsin Law Review 576

Kleinbard ED, 'Throw Territorial Taxation from the Train' (2007) 46 Tax Notes International 63

Kleinbard ED, 'Stateless Income' (2011) 11 Florida Tax Review 699

Kleinbard ED, 'The Lessons of Stateless Income' (2011) 65 Tax Law Review 99

Kleinbard ED, 'Stateless Income and Its Remedies' (2014) USC CLASS Research Papers Series No. CLASS14-12

Kleist D, 'The Multilateral Convention to Implement Tax Treaty Related Measures to Prevent BEPS: Some Thoughts on Complexity and Uncertainty' (2018) Nordic Tax Journal 31

Knobbe-Keuk B, 'Ruding Committee Report – An Impressive Vision of European Company Taxation for the Year 2000' (1992) 1 EC Tax Review 22

Knoll MS, 'Reconsidering International Tax Neutrality' (2010) 64 Tax Law Review 99

Knoll MS & Mason R, 'The Economic Foundation of the Dormant Commerce Clause' (2017) Virginia Law Review 309

Kobetsky M, *International Taxation of Permanent Establishments: Principles and Policy* (Cambridge University Press 2011)

Kofler G, Mayr G & Schlager C, 'European Union-Taxation of the Digital Economy: "Quick Fixes" or Long-Term Solution?' (2017) 57 European Taxation 523

Kofler G, Mayr G & Schlager C, 'International-Taxation of the Digital Economy: A Pragmatic Approach to Short-Term Measures' (2018) 58 European Taxation 123

Kofler G & Sinnig J, 'Equalization Taxes and the EU's "Digital Services Tax"' (2019) 47 Intertax 176

Kofler GW, 'Article 8 OECD Model: Time for a Change?', in *Taxation of Shipping and Air Transport in Domestic Law, EU Law and Tax Treaties* (G Maisto (ed.), IBFD 2017)

Kokott J & Sobotta C, 'The Charter of Fundamental Rights of the European Union after Lisbon' (2010) Working Paper, EUI AEL, 2010/06, Distinguished Lectures of the Academy

Kolozs B, 'Neutrality in VAT', in *Value Added Tax and Direct Taxation: Similarities and Differences* (M Lang (ed.), IBFD 2009)

Kondrasuk JN, Reed LJ & Jurinski JJ, 'The Dangers of Misclassifying "Employees": Microsoft Litigation Emphasizes Distinctions Between Employees and Nontraditional Workers' (2001) 13 Employee Responsibilities and Rights Journal 165

Koukoulioti V, 'User Contribution to Value Creation: The Benefit Principle in the Spotlight', in *Taxing the Digital Economy: The EU Proposals and Other Insights* (P Pistone & D Weber (eds), IBFD 2019)

Kozub RM, 'Readoption of Joyce in Huffy Affects the Sales Factor Determination of Unitary Businesses in California' (2000) 19 Journal of State Taxation 1

Krever RE & Mellor P, 'History and Theory of Formulary Apportionment', in *The Allocation of Multinational Business Income: Reassessing the Formulary Apportionment Option* (Krever RE & Vaillancourt F (eds), Kluwer Law International 2020)

Krever RE & Vaillancourt F, *The Allocation of Multinational Business Income: Reassessing the Formulary Apportionment Option* (Kluwer Law International 2020)

Kroppen H-K, Dawid R & Schmidtke R, 'Profit Split, the Future of Transfer Pricing? Arm's Length Principle and Formulary Apportionment Revisited from a Theoretical and a Practical Perspective', in *Fundamentals of International Transfer Pricing in Law and Economics* (W Schön & KA Konrad (eds), Springer 2012)

Kroszner R & Putterman LG (eds), *The Economic Nature of the Firm: A Reader* (3rd ed., Cambridge University Press 2009)

Kuzniacki B, 'The Principal Purpose Test (PPT) in BEPS Action 6 and the MLI: Exploring Challenges Arising from Its Legal Implementation and Practical Application' (2018) 10 World Tax Journal 233

La Feria R de, *The EU VAT System and the Internal Market* (IBFD 2009)

Laffan B, 'Auditing and Accountability in the European Union' (2003) 10 Journal of European Public Policy 762

Laffer AB, 'The Laffer Curve: Past, Present, and Future' (2004) 1765 Backgrounder 1

Lagarden M, 'Intangibles in a Transfer Pricing Context: Where Does the Road Lead' (2014) 21 International Transfer Pricing Journal

Laks K, 'Sales Allocation Methods: Cost of Performance vs. Market-Based Sourcing' (2019) 89 CPA Journal 12

Lamb CS & others, 'Report of Committee on the Apportionment Between States of Taxes on Mercantile and Manufacturing Business', *Proceedings of the Annual Conference on Taxation under the Auspices of the National Tax Association* (National Tax Association 1922)

Lamensch M, *European Value Added Tax in the Digital Era: A Critical Analysis and Proposals for Reform* (IBFD Publications 2015)

Lamensch M, 'European Commission's New Package of Proposals on E-Commerce: A Critical Assessment' (2017) 28 International VAT Monitor

Lang M (ed.), *Procedural Rules in Tax Law in the Context of European Union and Domestic Law* (Kluwer Law International 2010)

Lang M, 'State Aid and Taxation: Selectivity and Comparability Analysis', in *State Aid Law and Business Taxation* (W Schön, I Richelle, & E Traversa (eds), Springer 2016)

Lang M, *Transfer Pricing and Intangibles: Current Developments, Relevant Issues and Possible Solutions* (Linde Verlag Ges.m.bH 2019)

Lang M, 'Double Taxation and EC Law', in *Comparative Fiscal Federalism: Comparing the European Court of Justice and the US Supreme Court's Tax Jurisprudence* (RS Avi-Yonah, JR Hines, JR & M Lang (eds), Kluwer Law International 2007).

Lang M, *Common Consolidated Corporate Tax Base* (Linde 2008)

Lang M (ed.), *Value Added Tax and Direct Taxation: Similarities and Differences* (IBFD 2009)

Lang M (ed.), *Corporate Income Taxation in Europe: The Common Consolidated Corporate Tax Base (CCCTB) and Third Countries* (Edward Elgar 2013)

Lang M, *GAARs: A Key Element of Tax Systems in the Post-BEPS World* (IBFD 2016)

Lang M, *Introduction to European Tax Law on Direct Taxation* (Linde Verlag GmbH 2018)

Lang M & Storck A, *Transfer Pricing in a Post-BEPS World* (Kluwer Law International 2016)

Langenberg R & Jones M, 'Sourcing Service Receipts for Franchise Tax Apportionment in Texas' (2017) 49 Mary's Law Journal 583

Langpop LG, 'Payroll, Manufacturing Costs And Other Factors' (1954) 7 Tax Executive

Langstraat CJ & Lemmon ES, 'Economic Nexus: Legislative Presumption or Legitimate Proposition' (1999) 14 Akron Tax Journal 1

Lard T & Do S, 'States Fine-Tune Market-Based Sourcing Rules Through Regulation' (2016) 68 Tax Executive 29

Lard TA, 'Domicile Versus Source Based Taxation: Must One Define the Other?', *The State and Local Tax Lawyer. Symposium Edition* (American Bar Association 2009)

Laskin SH, 'Report of the Hearing Officer Regarding Proposed Model Regulation for Apportionment of Income from the Sale of Telecommunications and Ancillary Services, April 2008' (Multistate Tax Commission, 2008)

Laskin SH, 'Final Report of the Hearing Officer Regarding Proposed Amendments to the Formula for the Apportionment and Allocation of Net Income of Financial Institutions' (Multistate Tax Commission, 2014)

Leberstein S, 'Independent Contractor Misclassification Imposes Huge Costs on Workers and Federal and State Treasuries' (2012) National Employment Project

Lee CJ & Noel C, 'Per Se Versus "As Applied" Challenges and the Use of Alternative Apportionment Provisions', *The State and Local Tax Lawyer. Symposium Edition* (American Bar Association 2009)

Leibowicz B, 'Independent Contractor or Employee?' (2011) 81 CPA Journal 46

Lenaerts K, 'Exploring the Limits of the EU Charter of Fundamental Rights' (2012) 8 European Constitutional Law Review 375

Lenaerts K, 'The Concept of "Abuse of Law" in the Case Law of the European Court of Justice on Direct Taxation' (2015) 22 Maastricht Journal of European and Comparative Law 329

Lennard M, 'The UN Model Tax Convention as Compared with the OECD Model Tax Convention – Current Points of Difference and Recent Developments' (2009) 29 Asia-Pacific Tax Bulletin 4

Lennard M, 'Act of Creation: The OECD/G20 Test of "Value Creation" as a Basis for Taxing Rights and Its Relevance to Developing Countries' (2018) 25 Transnational Corporations 55

Lenz CO, 'The Jurisprudence of the European Court of Justice in Tax Matters' (1997) 6 EC Tax Review 80

Leung KK, 'Taxing Global Trading: An Appropriate Testing Ground for Formula Apportionment' (1992) 1 Minnesota Journal of Global Trade 201

Levey MM & others, 'The Quest for Marketing Intangibles' (2006) 34 Intertax 2

Levin-Epstein M, 'What to Watch for in 2015' (2015) 67 Tax Executive 27

Levy R, 'Managing Value-for-Money Audit in the European Union: The Challenge of Diversity' (1996) 34 JCMS: Journal of Common Market Studies 509

Lhernould J-P, 'The Interrelation between Social Security Coordination Law and Labour Law' (European Commission Directorate-General for Employment, Social Affairs and Inclusion 2017)

Li J, 'Global Profit Split: An Evolutionary Approach to International Income Allocation' (2002) 50 Canadian Tax Journal 823

Li J, Bao NJ & Li HC, 'Value Creation: A Constant Principle in a Changing World of International Taxation' (2019) 67 Canadian Tax Journal 1107

Li J & Ji S, 'Location-Specific Advantages: A Rising Disruptive Factor in Transfer Pricing' (2017) 71 (5) IBFD Bulletin for International Taxation 259

Libson A, 'Is the Deadweight Actually Dead-Real Option Value and Taxation of Oil and Gas' (2015) 45 Seton Hall Law Review 833

Ličková M, 'European Exceptionalism in International Law' (2008) 19 European Journal of International Law 463

Limbach K, *Uniformity of Customs Administration in the European Union* (Bloomsbury 2015)

Linder M, 'The Joint Employment Doctrine: Clarifying Joint Legislative-Judicial Confusion' (1989) 10 Hamline Journal of Public Law and Policy 321

LIPIN IA, 'Corporate Taxpayers' Sore Arm: Throw-Out Rule Litigation in State and Local Taxation' (2013) 66 Tax Lawyer 901

Lipniewicz R, 'Place of Effective Management in the Digital Economy' (2020) 48 Intertax

Lirette R & Viard AD, 'Putting the Commerce Back in the Dormant Commerce Clause: State Taxes, State Subsidies, and Commerce Neutrality' (2016) 24 Journal of Law and Policy 467

Ljungqvist A & Smolyansky M, 'To Cut or Not to Cut? On the Impact of Corporate Taxes on Employment and Income' (National Bureau of Economic Research 2014)

Llopis EL, 'Formulary Apportionment in the European Union' (2017) 45 Intertax 631

Lobel O, 'The Law of the Platform' (2016) 101 Minnesota Law Review 87

Lobel O, 'The Gig Economy & the Future of Employment and Labor Law' (2017) 51 University of San Francisco Law Review 51

Lockwood B, de Meza D & Myles G, 'On the European Union VAT Proposals: The Superiority of Origin over Destination Taxation' (1995) 16 Fiscal Studies 1

Long C & Miller M, 'Taxation and the Sustainable Development Goals: Do Good Things Come to Those Who Tax More?' (2017) Overseas Development Institute (ODI) Briefing Note 1

Loomis SC, 'The Double Irish Sandwich: Reforming Overseas Tax Havens' (2011) 43 Mary's Law Journal 825

Loutzenhiser G & De La Feria R (eds), *The Dynamics of Taxation: Essays in Honour of Judith Freedman* (Hart 2020)

Lowe SK, Chandler CW & Staples J, 'Supreme Court Ruling in South Dakota v. Wayfair Inc. Updates Physical Nexus Standards and Sales Tax Collection Policies' 2019 http://www.subr.edu/assets/subr/COBJournal/8.28.19-Sales-Tax-Draft.pdf

Luja R, 'State Aid Benchmarking and Tax Rulings: Can We Keep It Simple?', in *State Aid Law and Business Taxation* (W Schön, I Richelle & E Traversa (eds), Springer 2016)

Lusch SJ, 'State Taxation of Cloud Computing' (2012) 29 Santa Clara Computer & High Tech Law Journal 369

Lutz CT, Merten RP & Kump NJ, 'Trends and Developments in Alternative Apportionment of State Income' (2017) 84 State Tax Notes

Lutz M & Yesnowitz J, 'Wayfair: Practical Implications for the Business World' (2018) Tax Executive, https://taxexecutive.org/wayfair-practical-implications-for-the-business-world/

MacDonald J, *Travels in Various Parts of Europe, Asia and Africa* (1790), printed for the author, and sold by J. Forbes.

Mahoney MK, 'Recommending an Apportionment Formula for the European Union's Common Consolidated Corporate Tax Base' (2009) 34 Seton Hall Legislative Journal 313

Maisto G, 'The "Shipping and Air Transport" Provision (Art. 8) in the Italy-USA Double Taxation Agreement' (1995) 23 Intertax 146

Maisto G, 'The History of Article 8 of the OECD Model Treaty on Taxation of Shipping and Air Transport' (2003) 31 Intertax 232

Maisto G, 'Taxation of Groups and CCCTB', in *Movement of Persons and Tax Mobility in the EU: Changing Winds* (AP Dourado (ed.), IBFD 2013)

Maisto, G, 'Article 8: International Transport and Other Operations', *Global Tax Treaty Commentaries* (Pistone, Nogueira & Wheeler (eds), IBFD 2015)

Maisto G (ed.), *Taxation of Shipping and Air Transport in Domestic Law, EU Law and Tax Treaties* (IBFD 2017)

Malherbe J, 'The Impact of the Rulings of the European Court of Justice in the Area of Direct Taxation (2008)' (2008) http://www.europarl.europa.eu/RegData/etudes/etudes/join/2008/404888/IPOL-ECON_ET(2008)404888_EN.pdf

Malherbe J, 'The Impact of the Rulings of the European Court of Justice in the Area of Direct Taxation (2010)' (2010) http://www.europarl.europa.eu/document/activities/cont/201203/20120313ATT40640/20120313ATT40640EN.pdf

Maltby LL & Yamada DC, 'Beyond Economic Realities: The Case for Amending Federal Employment Discrimination Laws to Include Independent Contractors' (1996) 38 Boston College Law Review 239

Manaa M & others, 'Crypto-Assets: Implications for Financial Stability, Monetary Policy, and Payments and Market Infrastructures' (2019) ECB Occasional Paper

Manning HC, 'Problems in Application of State Tax Allocation Formulae to Oil and Gas Company Operations' (1956) 7 Proc. Ann. Inst. on Oil & Gas L. & Tax'n 447

Manski C, 'Removing Deadweight Loss from Economic Discourse on Income Taxation and Public Spending' (2013) VoxEU

Manski CF, 'Choosing Size of Government under Ambiguity: Infrastructure Spending and Income Taxation' (2014) 124 Economic Journal 359

Maozami Y, 'UBER in the US and Canada: Is the Gig-Economy Exploiting or Exploring Labor and Employment Laws by Going Beyond the Dichotomous Workers' Classification' (2016) 24 University of Miami International & Comparative Law Review 609

Markham M, *The Transfer Pricing of Intangibles* (Kluwer Law International 2005)

Marres O, 'The Principle of Territoriality and Cross-Border Loss Compensation' (2011) 39 Intertax 112

Martinez AL, 'Are IFRS Standards a Good Starting Point for a Corporate Tax Base? Tax Principles for a CCCTB' (2019), Faculdade de Direito da Universidade de Coimbra

Mas LMF, 'Commentary on Chapter 2: CCCTB Relaunch: Why a Destination-Based Model Would Not Work', in *European Tax Integration: Law, Policy and Politics* (P Pistone (ed.), IBFD 2018)

Mason R, 'Made in America for European Tax: The Internal Consistency Test' (2008) 49 Boston College Law Review 1277

Mason R, 'Tax Rulings as State Aid – Part 4: Whose Arm's-Length Standard?' (2017) 155 Tax Notes

Mason R, 'Case Law Note: Implications of Wayfair' (2018) 46 Intertax 810

Mason R, 'The Transformation of International Tax' (2020) 114(3) American Journal of International Law 353-402

Mason R & Parada L, 'Digital Battlefront in the Tax Wars' (2018) Virginia Law and Economics Research Paper

Mason R & Parada L, 'The Legality of Digital Taxes in Europe' (2020) 40 Virginia Tax Review 175

Matheson T & others, 'Chapter 14 Formulary Apportionment in Theory and Practice', in *Corporate Income Taxes under Pressure : Why Reform Is Needed and How It Could Be Designed* (RA de Mooij, AD Klemm & VJ Perry (eds) IMF 2021)

Mawani R, 'Archival Legal History' (2018) The Oxford Handbook of Legal History 291

Mayer S, *Formulary Apportionment for the Internal Market*, Vol. 17 (IBFD 2009)

Mazerov M, *The 'Single Sales Factor Formula for State Corporate Taxes* (Center on Budget and Policy Priorities 2005)

Mazerov M, 'State Corporate Tax Shelters and the Need for "Combined Reporting"' (2007) 46 State Tax Notes 621

McCray SB, 'State Taxation of Interstate Banking' (1986) 21 Georgia Law Review 283

McDaniel PR, 'Formulary Taxation in the North American Free Trade Zone' (1993) 49 Tax Law Review 691
McGaughey E, 'Uber, the Taylor Review, Mutuality and the Duty Not to Misrepresent Employment Status' (2019) 48 Industrial Law Journal 180
McHugh JW, 'Looking Through the (Mis) Classifieds: Why TaskRabbit Is Better Suited than Uber and Lyft to Succeed Against a Worker Misclassification Claim' (2017) 66 Cleveland State Law Review 649
McIntyre MJ, 'Design of a National Formulary Apportionment Tax System' (1991) 84 *Proceedings of the Annual Conference on Taxation Held under the Auspices of the National Tax Association-Tax Institute of America* 118–124.
McIntyre MJ, 'The Design of Tax Rules for the North American Free Trade Alliance' (1993) 49 Tax Law Review 769
McLure CE, *State Corporate Income Tax: Lambs in Wolves' Clothing?* (Office of Tax Analysis, US Treasury Department 1977)
McLure CE, 'The Elusive Incidence of the Corporate Income Tax: The State Case' (1981) 9 Public Finance Quarterly 395
McLure CE, 'Defining a Unitary Business: An Economist's View' (National Bureau of Economic Research 1983)
McLure CE, 'International Aspects of Tax Policy for the 21st Century' (1989) 8 American Journal of Tax Policy 167
McLure CE, 'Coordinating Business Taxation in the Single European Market: The Ruding Committee Report' (1992) 1 EC Tax Review 13
McLure CE, 'Achieving Neutrality Between Electronic and Non-Electronic Commerce' (1999) 17(3) State Tax Notes
McLure CE, 'Implementing State Corporate Income Taxes in the Digital Age' (2000) 53 National Tax Journal 1287
McLure CE, 'A Comprehensive and Sensible UDITPA' (2005) 37 State Tax Notes 929
McLure CE, 'Legislative, Judicial, Soft Law, and Cooperative Approaches to Harmonizing Corporate Income Taxes in the US and the EU' (2007) 14 Columbia Journal of European Law 377
McLure CE, 'The Long Shadow of History: Sovereignty, Tax Assignment, Legislation and Judicial Decisions on Corporate Income Taxes in the US and the EU', in *Comparative Fiscal Federalism: Comparing the Court of Justice and the US Supreme Court's Tax Jurisprudence* (RS Avi-Yonah, JR Hines & M Lang (eds), Kluwer Law International 2007)
McLure CE, 'Harmonizing Corporate Income Taxes in the US and the EU: Legislative, Judicial, Soft Law and Cooperative Approaches', *CESifo Forum* (Institute-Leibniz Institute for Economic Research at the University of Munich 2008)
McLure CE, 'Understanding Uniformity and Diversity in State Corporate Income Taxes' (2008) National Tax Journal 141
McLure CE, 'How Should the UDITPA Sales Factor Treat Receipts from Transactions Involving Financial Instruments?', *The State and Local Tax Lawyer. Symposium Edition* (American Bar Association 2009)
McLure CE, 'The Difficulty of Getting Serious About State Corporate Tax Reform' (2010) 67 Washington & Lee Law Review 327

McLure CE & Martinez-Vazquez J, 'The Assignment of Revenues and Expenditures in Intergovernmental Fiscal Relations' (2000) Core Course on Intergovernmental Relations and Local Financial Management, World Bank Institute, Washington, DC: World Bank

McLure CE & Weiner JM, 'Deciding Whether the European Union Should Adopt Formula Apportionment of Company Income', Taxing Capital Income in the European Union–Issues and Options for Reform (S Cnossen (ed.), Oxford University Press 2000)

Meharia P, 'E-Commerce and Taxation: Past, Present and Future' (2012) 11 IUP Journal of Accounting Research & Audit Practices

Mendoza EG & Tesar LL, 'Why Hasn't Tax Competition Triggered a Race to the Bottom? Some Quantitative Lessons from the EU' (2005) 52 Journal of Monetary Economics 163

Merkx M, *Establishments in European VAT* (Kluwer Law International 2013)

Merkx M, 'Should EU VAT Apply the Recharge Method in the Place of Supply Rules for B2B Services?' (2013) 22 EC Tax Review 282

Merkx M, 'Fixed Establishments in European Value Added Tax: Base Erosion and Profit Shifting Side Effects?' (2017) 26 EC Tax Review 36

Merriman D, 'A Replication of "Coveting Thy Neighbor's Manufacturing: The Dilemma of State Income Apportionment"' (Journal of Public Economics 2000)' (2015) 43 Public Finance Review 185

Meussen G, 'The EU-Fight against Harmful Tax Competition; Future Developments' (2002) 11 EC Tax Review 157

Milanez A, 'Legal Tax Liability, Legal Remittance Responsibility and Tax Incidence: Three Dimensions of Business Taxation' (2017) OECD Taxation Working Papers 32

Millar R, 'Echoes of Source and Residence in VAT Jurisdictional Rules', in *Value Added Tax and Direct Taxation: Similarities and Differences* (M Lang (ed.), IBFD 2009)

Miller BF, 'States' Approaches to Combination of Dissimilar Businesses' (1995) State Tax Notes

Miller BF, 'Current Problems with UDITPA and Possible Solutions' (2005) 38 State Tax Notes

Miller BF, 'Comments on Document CCCTB/WP060 Common Consolidated Corporate Tax Base Working Group Possible Elements of a Sharing Mechanism' (European Commission 2007)

Miller DS, 'Tax Planning under the Destination Based Cash Flow Tax: A Guide for Policymakers and Practitioners' (2017) 8 Columbia Journal of Tax Law 295

Miller SR, 'First Principles for Regulating the Sharing Economy' (2016) 53 Harvard Journal on Legislation 147

Mintz J & Weiner JM, 'Exploring Formula Allocation for the European Union' (2003) 10 International Tax and Public Finance 695

Mirrlees JA, 'An Exploration in the Theory of Optimum Income Taxation' (1971) 38 Review of Economic Studies 175

Mitroyanni I, *Integration Approaches to Group Taxation in the European Internal Market.* (Wolters Kluwer Law & Business 2008)

Mitroyanni I & Putzolu C, 'CCCTB and Business Reorganizations: The Common Consolidated Corporate Tax Base and Business Reorganizations' (2009) 37 Intertax 436

Moens GA & Trone J, 'The Principle of Subsidarity in EU Judicial and Legislative Practice: Panacea or Placebo' (2014) 41 Journal of Legislation 65

Monsenego J, *Taxation of Foreign Business Income within the European Internal Market: An Analysis of the Conflict Between the Objective of Achievement of the European Internal Market and the Principles of Territoriality and Worldwide Taxation*, Vol. 22 (IBFD 2012)

Moreno AB, 'GAARs and Treaties: From the Guiding Principle to the Principal Purpose Test. What Have We Gained from BEPS Action 6?' (2017) 45 Intertax 432

Morse SC, 'Revisiting Global Formulary Apportionment' (2009) 29 Virginia Tax Review 593

Morse SC, 'Value Creation: A Standard in Search of a Process' (2018) 72(4/5) IBFD Bulletin for International Taxation 196

Mosley L & Uno S, 'Racing to the Bottom or Climbing to the Top? Economic Globalization and Collective Labor Rights' (2007) 40 Comparative Political Studies 923

Mosquera Valderrama IJ, 'BEPS Principal Purpose Test and Customary International Law' (2020) 33(3) Leiden Journal of International Law

Mossoff A, 'Exclusion and Exclusive Use in Patent Law' (2008) 22 Harvard Journal of Law & Technology 321

Moyal SS, 'Back to Basics: Rethinking Normative Principles in International Tax' (2019) 73 Tax Lawyer

MTC Legal Staff, 'Finnigan Briefing Book Provided to Phil Skinner, Idaho' (Multistate Tax Commission, 2018)

Mueller P, 'Formula Apportionment – Approaches to Reduce Tax Planning Incentives' (2010) Available at SSRN 1730178

Muhl CJ, 'What Is an Employee? The Answer Depends on the Federal Law' (2002) 125 Monthly Labor Review 3

Mullins P, 'Moving to Territoriality? Implications for the United States and the Rest of the World' (2006) IMF Working Papers 1

Multistate Tax Commission, 'Response of the Multistate Tax Commission Public Consultation Document on the Report on the Tax Challenges Arising from Digitalisation Report on Pillar One Blueprint – Items III and IV' (Multistate Tax Commission 2020)

Mundele JM, 'Note-Not Everything That Glitters Is Gold, Misclassification of Employees: The Blurred Line Between Independent Contractors and Employees under the Major Classification Tests' (2015) 20 Suffolk Journal of Trial & Appellate Advocacy 253

Murphy KP, 'Michigan Business Tax Apportionment and Sales Sourcing Provisions' (2007) 53 Wayne Law Review 1395

Murphy L & Nagel T, *The Myth of Ownership: Taxes and Justice* (Oxford University Press 2002)

Musgrave PB, 'Economic Criteria, Principles and Policies of the Taxation of Foreign Investment Income', in *Taxation of Foreign Investment Income: An Economic Analysis* (PB Musgrave (ed.), Johns Hopkins Press 1963)

Musgrave PB, *Taxation of Foreign Investment Income: An Economic Analysis* (Johns Hopkins Press 1963)

Musgrave PB, 'Principles for Dividing the State Corporate Tax Base', in *The State Corporation Income Tax: Issues in Worldwide Unitary Combination*, Vol. 1984 (Charles E. McLure (ed.), Stanford University Press 1984)

Musgrave PB, 'Interjurisdictional Equity in Company Taxation: Principles and Applications to the European Union', in *Taxing Capital Income in the European Union: Issues and Options for Reform* (S Cnossen (ed.), Oxford 2000) 46

Musgrave PB, *Tax Policy in the Global Economy* (Edward Elgar 2002)

Musgrave PB, 'Comments on Two Musgravian Concepts' (2008) 32 Journal of Economics and Finance 340

Musgrave RA, 'Criteria for Foreign Tax Credit', in *Taxation of Operations Abroad, The Tax Institute* (Baker (ed.), Princeton 1959)

Musgrave RA, *The Theory of Public Finance: A Study in Public Economy* (McGraw Hill 1959)

Musselli A & Musselli A, 'Rise of a New Standard: Profit Location in Countries of Important Intangible Functions Managers' (2017) 24 International Transfer Pricing Journal

Nachbar ML & Browdy BL, 'The Single Sales Factor Apportionment Method Origins and Development' (2008) 27 Journal of State Taxation 31

Næss-Schmidt HS & others, 'Simplifying and Modernising VAT in the Digital Single Market for E-Commerce' (European Parliament 2012)

Næss-Schmidt HS & others, 'Future Taxation of Company Profits: What to Do with Intangibles?, Copenhagen Economics, February 2019' (Copenhagen Economics 2019) https://www.copenhageneconomics.com/dyn/resources/Publication/publicationPDF/4/474/1550496379/future-taxation-of-company-profits_15022019_finalreport.pdf

Nallareddy S, Rouen E & Suárez Serrato JC, 'Do Corporate Tax Cuts Increase Income Inequality?' (National Bureau of Economic Research 2018)

Neighbour J & Owens J, 'Transfer Pricing in the New Millennium: Will the Arm's Length Principle Survive' (2001) 10 George Mason Law Review 951

Nerudová D & Solilová V, 'The Impact of the Introduction of a CCCTB in the EU' (2019) 54 Intereconomics 160

Nerudová D, Solilová V & Dobranschi M, *Sustainability-Oriented Future EU Funding: The Case of a C(C)CTB* (Umeaa Universitet 2016)

Niazi SU & Krever R, 'Romance and Divorce Between International Law and EU Law: Implications for European Competence on Direct Taxes' (2017) 53 Stanford Journal of International Law 129

Niazi SUK, 'Re-Launch of the Proposal for a Common Consolidated Corporate Tax Base (CCCTB) in the EU: A Shift in Paradigm' (2017) 44 Legal Issues of Economic Integration 293

Nicodème G, 'Corporate Tax Competition and Coordination in the European Union: What Do We Know? Where Do We Stand' (2007) International Taxation Handbook 171

Nicodème G, 'Taxation Papers: Corporate Income Tax and Economic Distortions' (2009) European Union

Nicodème G, 'Corporate Income Tax and Economic Distortions' (Directorate General Taxation and Customs Union, European Commission 2009) Taxation Paper 15 https://econpapers.repec.org/paper/taxtaxpap/0015.htm (accessed 22 May 2020)

Nieminen M, 'Debate on the CCCTB: Destination-with-Credit Formula: A Simple Add-On That Would Make the CCCTB More Resilient in the Face of Tax Competition and Tax Planning' (2019) 47 Intertax 490

Nieminen M, 'Destination-with-Credit Formula: A Simple Add-On That Would Make the CCCTB More Resilient in the Face of Tax Competition and Tax Planning' (2019) 47 Intertax 490

Niesten H, 'Growing Impetus for Harmonization of Personal and Family Allowances: Current State of Affairs of the Schumacker-Doctrine after Imfeld and Garcet' (2015) 24 EC Tax Review 185

Niesten H, 'Personal and Family Tax Benefits in the EU Internal Market: From Schumacker to Fractional Tax Treatment' (2018) 55 Common Market Law Review 819

Niesten H, 'Revisiting the Fiscal and Social Security Status of Highly Mobile Workers in the Road and Railway Transportation: Quo Vadis?' (2018) 46 Intertax 836

Noel C & Lee CJ, 'Would States Adopt a Uniform Model Combined Reporting Statute in a New Wave of Combined Reporting?', *The State and Local Tax Lawyer. Symposium Edition* (American Bar Association 2008)

Noel C & Stathopoulos KL, 'Is There a Constitutional Standard for UDITPA section 18 Alternative Apportionment?' (2006) 8 Corporate Business Taxation Monthly 31

OECD, 'The Arm's Length Principle' in OECD, *OECD Transfer Pricing Guidelines for Multinational Enterprises and Tax Administrations 2017* (OECD 2017)

OECD, 'Addressing the Tax Challenges of the Digitalisation of the Economy – Policy Note' (OECD 2019)

Oestreicher A, 'Transfer Pricing of Intangibles in Cases of Post-Merger Reorganization: Lessons from the Revised OECD Draft' (2014) 42 Intertax 509

Offermans R & others, 'European Union – Bridging the CCCTB and the Arm's Length Principle – A Value Chain Analysis Approach' (2017) 57 European Taxation 466

Office for Official Publications of the European Communities (ed.), *Company Taxation in the Internal Market* (European Commission 2002)

Ogawa H, Sato Y & Tamai T, 'A Note on Unemployment and Capital Tax Competition' (2006) 60 Journal of Urban Economics 350

Okten R, 'A Comparative Study of Cost Contribution Arrangements: Is Active Involvement Required To Share in the Benefits of Jointly Developed Intangible Property?' (2013) 20 International Transfer Pricing Journal 1

Olbert M & Spengel C, 'International Taxation in the Digital Economy: Challenge Accepted' (2017) 9 World Tax Journal 3

Olbert M & Spengel C, 'Taxation in the Digital Economy: Recent Policy Developments and the Question of Value Creation' (2019) ZEW-Centre for European Economic Research Discussion Paper

Oosterhoff D, 'The True Importance of Significant People Functions' (2008) 15 International Transfer Pricing Journal 68

Oosterhoff D & Wingerter B, 'Netherlands - The Dutch View on the Common Consolidated Corporate Tax Base' (2011) 18 International Transfer Pricing Journal 352

Ortiz L, 'Joyce v. Finnigan: Adoption of the "Best" Approach in Hopes of Some Uniformity' (2014) 67 Tax Lawyer 979

Örücü E, *The Enigma of Comparative Law: Variations on a Theme for the Twenty-First Century* (Springer 2013)

O'Shea T, 'European Tax Controversies: Fiscal Neutrality and EU Law', in *CFE Tax Advisors Europe: 60th Anniversary – Liber Amicorum* (S Van Thiel, P Valente & SR Calvo (eds), IBFD 2019)

Otusanya OJ, 'The Role of Multinational Companies in Tax Evasion and Tax Avoidance: The Case of Nigeria' (2011) 22 Critical Perspectives on Accounting 316

Overesch M & Rincke J, 'What Drives Corporate Tax Rates down? A Reassessment of Globalization, Tax Competition, and Dynamic Adjustment to Shocks' (2011) 113 Scandinavian Journal of Economics 579

Paju J, *The European Union and Social Security Law* (Bloomsbury 2017)

Panayi C, 'Agency Permanent Establishments in Securitization Transactions' (2005) 33 Intertax 286

Panayi C, 'European Union. The Common Consolidated Corporate Tax Base-Issues for Member States Opting out and Third Countries' (2008) 48 European Taxation 114

Panayi C, 'Reverse Subsidiarity and EU Tax Law: Can Member States Be Left to Their Own Devices?' (2010) 3 British Tax Review 261

Panayi C, 'The Common Consolidated Corporate Tax Base and the UK Tax System' (2011) Institute for Fiscal Studies

Panayi C, 'The Anti-Abuse Rules of the CCCTB' (2012) 66 IBFD Bulletin for International Taxation 256

Panayi C, 'CFC Rules Within the CCCTB', in *Corporate Income Taxation in Europe: The Common Consolidated Corporate Tax Base (CCCTB) and Third Countries* (M Lang (ed.), Edward Elgar 2013)

Panayi C, *European Union Corporate Tax Law* (Cambridge University Press 2013)

Panayi C, *Advanced Issues in International and European Tax Law* (Hart 2015)

Panayi C, 'The Globalisation of Tax Good Governance' (2018) Singapore Management University School of Accountancy Research Paper 74

Pankiv M, 'Post-BEPS Application of the Arm's Length Principle to Intangibles Structures' (2016) 23 International Transfer Pricing Journal 463

Pankiv M, *Contemporary Application of the Arm's Length Principle in Transfer Pricing* (IBFD 2017)

Pantazatou K, 'Taxation of the Sharing Economy in the European Union', in *The Cambridge Handbook of Law of the Sharing Economy* (NM Davidson, M Finck & JJ Infranca (eds), Cambridge University Press 2018)

Papis-Almansa M, 'VAT and Electronic Commerce: The New Rules as a Means for Simplification, Combatting Fraud and Creating a More Level Playing Field?' (2019), 20 *ERA Forum*

Parada L, 'Full Taxation: The Single Tax Emperor's New Clothes' (2021) 24 Florida Tax Review 729

Parr RL, *Intellectual Property: Valuation, Infringement, and Joint Venture Strategies* (5th ed., Wiley 2018)

Pashman M, 'Taxation of Government Instrumentalities' (1935) 1 New Jersey Law Review 98

Pearce JA & Silva JP, 'The Future of Independent Contractors and Their Status as Non-Employees: Moving on from a Common Law Standard' (2018) 14 Hastings Business Law Journal 1

Pechacek M & Nakamura K, 'The Payroll Factor: Whose Factor Is It Anyway?', *The State and Local Tax Lawyer(Symposium Edition)* (American Bar Association 2009)

Peeters B, 'International: Article 15 of the OECD Model Convention on "Income from Employment" and Its Undefined Terms' (2004) 44 European Taxation 72

Peeters B, 'Mobility of EU Citizens and Family Taxation: A Hard to Reconcile Combination' (2014) 23 EC Tax Review 118

Pennings F, *European Social Security Law* (6th ed., Intersentia 2015)

Pennings F, 'Barriers to Free Movement Due to Mismatches of Cross Border Tax and Social Security Instruments' (2018) 25 Studia z zakresu prawa pracy i polityki spo\lecznej 307

Pennings F & Bosse C, *The Protection of Working Relationships: A Comparative Study*, Vol. 39 (Kluwer Law International 2011)

Pennings F & Vonk GJ (eds), *Research Handbook on European Social Security Law* (Edward Elgar 2015)

Pereira TA, *International Aspects of the CCCTB in Europe* (Maastricht University 2014)

Perkins FL, 'Employment Law – *Vizcaino v. Microsoft Corp.*: Are Independent Contractors Eligible for Employee Benefits' (1997) 21 American Journal of Trial Advocacy 205

Peters C, *On the Legitimacy of International Tax Law* (IBFD Amsterdam 2014)

Peters JH & Miller BF, 'Apportionability in State Income Taxation: The Uniform Division of Income for Tax Purposes Act and Allied-Signal' (2006) 60 Tax Lawyer 57

Pethig R & Wagener A, 'Profit Tax Competition and Formula Apportionment' (2007) 14 International Tax and Public Finance 631

Petrović S & Ceronja P, 'Corporate Effects of the Danosa Case: Is the Termination of Membership of the Board of Directors Allowed in the Case of a Pregnant Board Member?' (2012) 8 Croatian Yearbook of European Law & Policy 437

Petruzzi R, 'The Arm's Length Principle: Between Legal Fiction and Economic Reality', in *Transfer Pricing in a Post-BEPS World* (M Lang & A Storck (eds), Kluwer Law International 2016)

Petruzzi R & Buriak S, 'Addressing the Tax Challenges of the Digitalization of the Economy – A Possible Answer in the Proper Application of the Transfer Pricing Rules' (2018) 72 IBFD Bulletin for International Taxation
Phionesgo E, 'Using Global Formulary Apportionment for International Profit Allocation: The Case of Indonesia's Mining Industry' (Master's Thesis, Queensland University of Technology 2015)
Piantavigna P, 'Tax Abuse in European Union Law: A Theory' (2011) 20 EC Tax Review 134
Piantavigna P, 'Tax Competition and Tax Coordination in Aggressive Tax Planning: A False Dichotomy' (2017) 9 World Tax Journal 477
Picciotto S, *Towards Unitary Taxation of Transnational Corporations* (Tax Justice Network 2012)
Picciotto S, 'Taxing Multinational Enterprises as Unitary Firms' (2016) ICTD Working Paper 53
Pierce WJ, 'The Uniform Division of Income for State Tax Purposes' (1957) 35 Taxes 747
Piketty T, *Capital in the Twenty-First Century* (Arthur Goldhammer tr.) (Harvard University Press 2017)
Pila J & Torremans P, *European Intellectual Property Law* (2nd ed., Oxford University Press 2019)
Pila J & Torremans P, 'Introduction to European Patent Law', in *European Intellectual Property Law* (J Pila & P Torremans (eds), Oxford University Press 2019)
Pinto C, 'EU and OECD to Fight Harmful Tax Competition: Has the Right Path Been Undertaken' (1998) 26 Intertax 386
Pinto D, *E-Commerce and Source-Based Income Taxation*, Vol. 6 (IBFD 2003)
Pinto D, 'The Need to Reconceptualize the Permanent Establishment Threshold' (2006) 60 Bulletin for International Taxation 266
Pîrvu D, *Corporate Income Tax Harmonization in the European Union* (Palgrave Macmillan 2012)
Pistone P, 'The Impact of European Law on the Relations with Third Countries in the Field of Direct Taxation' (2006) 34 Intertax 234
Pistone P (ed.), *European Tax Integration: Law, Policy and Politics* (IBFD 2018)
Pistone P, *Fundamentals of Taxation: An Introduction to Tax Policy, Tax Law and Tax Administration* (IBFD 2019)
Pistone P, Nogueira J, & Wheeler J (eds), Global Tax Treaty Commentaries (IBFD 2015)
Pistone P & Weber D (eds), *Taxing the Digital Economy: The EU Proposals and Other Insights* (IBFD 2019)
Pomp RD, 'Issues in the Design of Formulary Apportionment in the Context of NAFTA' (1993) 49 Tax Law Review 795
Pomp RD, 'Reforming a State Corporate Income Tax' (2013) 32 Journal of State Taxation 13
Pomp RD, 'Report of the Hearing Officer Multistate Tax Compact Article IV [UDITPA] Proposed Amendments' (Multistate Tax Commission, 13 October 2013)
Pomp RD, 'Revisiting Miller Brothers, Bellas Hess, and Quill' (2015) 65 American University Law Review 1115

Pomp RD, *State & Local Taxation* (RD Pomp 2015)
Pomp RD, 'Wayfair and the Myth of Substantial Nexus' (2018) 36 Journal of State Taxation 21
Pomp RD, 'Foreign Remote Vendors and the Possibility of Non-Compliance: Is the Only Thing We Have to Fear Is the Fear Itself?' (2019) 37 Journal of Taxation 39
Pomp RD, 'Wayfair: Its Implications and Missed Opportunities' (2019) 58 Washington University Journal of Law & Policy 1
Portuese A, 'The Principle of Subsidiarity as a Principle of Economic Efficiency' (2010) 17 Columbia Journal of European Law 231
Pötgens FPG, *Income from International Private Employment: An Analysis of Article 15 of the OECD Model* (IBFD 2006)
PwC, 'Study on the Possible Adjustments for Financial Institutions of the General Rules of the Common Consolidated Corporate Tax Base (CCCTB)' (European Commission, 2006), https://taxation-customs.ec.europa.eu/system/files/2016-09/ccctb_for_financial_institutions_en.pdf.
Pyrdek A, Sedon J & Kapoor S, 'Click This! Sales Factor Sourcing of Receipts from Internet Advertising A Tangled Web Indeed', *The State and Local Tax Lawyer. Symposium Edition* (American Bar Association 2009)
Quinn T & Pae S, 'The Case of the Missing Employees: The Saga of Fedex' (2011) 2 Academy of Business Research 34
Radaelli CM, 'The Puzzle of Regulatory Competition' (2004) 24 Journal of Public Policy 1
Rasquin P & others, 'The Importance of Valuation', in *Mastering the IP Life Cycle from a Legal, Tax and Accounting Perspective* (I Verlinden & A Bakker (eds), IBFD 2018)
Ravid O & Weissman WH, 'Cash Management Activities and the Sales Factor: When Is Gross Really Gross and a Receipt Really a Receipt' (2005) 10 State & Local Tax Law 93
Reese JM, 'Does the Streamlined Agreement Signal the End of Quill in the Area of E-Commerce?' (2003) 29 State Tax Notes
Rentrop T, 'The Services Directive: What Is Actually New?' (2007) 2 EIPAScope 1
Repetti JR, 'The Appropriate Roles for Equity and Efficiency in a Progressive Income Tax' (2020) 23 Florida Tax Review 522
Reurink A & Garcia-Bernardo J, 'Competing for Capitals: The Great Fragmentation of the Firm and Varieties of FDI Attraction Profiles in the European Union' (2020) 28 Review of International Political Economy 5
Richelle I, 'Place of Effective Management Versus Residence', in *Taxation of Shipping and Air Transport in Domestic Law, EU Law and Tax Treaties* (G Maisto (ed.), IBFD 2017)
Richelle I, Schön W & Traversa E (eds), *Allocating Taxing Powers Within the European Union* (Springer 2013)
Richter WF, 'Taxing Intellectual Property in the Global Economy: A Plea for Regulated and Internationally Coordinated Profit Splitting' (2017) Working Paper Series No. 6564

Riedel N, 'Quantifying International Tax Avoidance: A Review of the Academic Literature' (2018) 69 Review of Economics 169
Rienstra JG, 'United States-Corporate Taxation' (2015) IBFD database - Country surveys
Risak M & Dullinger T, 'The Concept of "Worker" in EU Law: Status Quo and Potential for Change' (2018) 140 ETUI Research Paper-Report
Roberge C, 'Transfer Pricing in the Pharmaceutical Industry: The Remuneration of Marketing Intangibles' (2013) 20 International Transfer Pricing Journal
Robillard R, 'BEPS: Is the OECD Now at the Gates of Global Formulary Apportionment?' (2015) 43 Intertax 447
Röder E, 'Proposal for an Enhanced CCTB as Alternative to a CCCTB with Formulary Apportionment' (2012) 4 World Tax Journal 125
Roesken E, 'The Sales Factor in State Franchise Tax Allocation' (1945) 23 Taxes 157
Roesken E, 'The Property Factor in State Income Tax Allocation' (1946) 24 Taxes 473
Rogers-Glabush J & International Bureau of Fiscal Documentation (eds), *IBFD International Tax Glossary* (7th rev. ed., IBFD 2015)
Rohwer A, 'Bismarck Versus Beveridge: A Comparison of Social Insurance Systems in Europe' (2008) 4 CESifo DICE Report
Roin J, 'Taxation Without Coordination' (2002) 31 Journal of Legal Studies S61
Roin J, 'Can the Income Tax Be Saved?: The Promise and Pitfalls of Adopting Worldwide Formulary Apportionment' (2007) 61 Tax Law Review 169
Rønfeldt T, 'Anti-Abuse Clause or Harmonization?' (2011) 39 Intertax 12
Rosenzweig AH, 'Harnessing the Costs of International Tax Arbitrage' (2006) 26 Virginia Tax Review 555
Rothbard MN, 'The Myth of Neutral Taxation' (1981) 1 Cato Journal 519
Ruckelhaus C & Gao C, 'Independent Contractor Misclassification Imposes Huge Costs on Workers and Federal and State Treasuries' (2017) National Employment Law Project, Fact Sheet 1
Rudisill CM, 'Container Corporation of America v. Franchise Tax Board: California's Three-Factor Apportionment Formula for Taxing US Corporations' Foreign Subsidiaries Held Constitutional' (1983) 9 North Carolina Journal of International Law and Commercial Regulation 337
Runkel M, 'In Favor of Formulary Apportionment A Comment on Kroppen/Dawid/Schmidtke: "Profit Split, the Future of Transfer Pricing? Arm's Length Principle and Formulary Apportionment Revisited from a Theoretical and a Practical Perspective"', in *Fundamentals of International Transfer Pricing in Law and Economics* (W Schön & KA Konrad (eds), Springer 2012)
Runkel M & Schjelderup G, 'The Choice of Apportionment Factors under Formula Apportionment' (2011) 52 International Economic Review 913
Rutherford W, 'Fitting a Square Peg into a Round Hole: Alexander v. FedEx Ground Package Systems & the Sharing Economy' (2016) 11 Liberty University Law Review 33
Sadiq K, 'Unitary Taxation of the Financial Sector' (2014) ICTD Working Paper 25
Sadiq K, 'The Case for Unitary Taxation with Formulary Apportionment in the Finance Sector and the Effect on Developing Nations' (2015) 44 Australian Tax Review 75

Sadiq K, 'A Framework for Assessing Business Sector Formulary Apportionment', in *The Allocation of Multinational Business Income: Reassessing the Formulary Apportionment Option* (RE Krever & F Vaillancourt (eds), Kluwer Law International 2020)

Sagan A, 'The Classification as "Worker" under EU Law' (2019) 10 European Labour Law Journal 353

Said E, *Orientalism: Western Concepts of the Orient* (Pantheon 1978)

Saint-Exupéry A de, *The Little Prince* (General Press 2018)

Sallee JM, 'The Surprising Incidence of Tax Credits for the Toyota Prius' (2011) 3 American Economic Journal: Economic Policy 189

Samuelson PA, 'Tax Deductibility of Economic Depreciation to Insure Invariant Valuations' (1964) 72 Journal of Political Economy 604

Sandmo A, 'Adam Smith and Modern Economics' in *Adam Smith: His Life, Thought, and Legacy* (RP Hanley (ed.), Princeton University Press 2016)

Sargeant M, 'The Gig Economy and the Future of Work' (2017) 6 Ejournal of International and Comparative Labour Studies 1

Savoie VB & Burr ML, 'The Throwback Rule: Concepts, Components and Planning Opportunities' (1983) 2 Journal of State Taxation 19

Saydé A, *Abuse of EU Law and Regulation of the Internal Market* (Bloomsbury 2014)

Schadewald M, 'Appointment Issues-Payroll Factor-Leased Employees' (2006) 25 Journal of State Taxation 9

Schadewald M, 'Apportionment Issues-Redemptions of Short-Term Marketable Securities: The Microsoft Case' (2006) 25 Journal of State Taxation 9

Schadewald MS, 'Apportionment Rules Evolve as Business Environment Changes' (2007) 85 Taxes 39

Schadewald MS, 'Primer on Sales Factor Throwback Rule' (2010) 29 Journal of State Taxation 9

Schadewald MS, 'Multistate Tax Commission's Market-Sourcing Regulations: Will They Promote Uniformity' (2017) 95 Taxes 23

Schaper MG, *The Structure and Organization of EU Law in the Field of Direct Taxes* (IBFD 2013)

Schaper MG, 'The Need to Prevent Abusive Practices and Fraud as a Composite Justification' (2014) 23 EC Tax Review 220

Schenk A, Thuronyi V & Cui W, *Value Added Tax: A Comparative Approach* (2nd ed., Cambridge University Press 2015)

Schippers ML & Verhaeren CE, 'Taxation in a Digitizing World: Solutions for Corporate Income Tax and Value Added Tax' (2018) 27 EC Tax Review 61

Schmidt FA, Friedrich-Ebert-Stiftung & Abteilung Wirtschafts- und Sozialpolitik, *Digital Labour Markets in the Platform Economy: Mapping the Political Challenges of Crowd Work and Gig Work* (Friedrich Ebert Stiftung 2017)

Schön W, 'Tax Competition in Europe – the Legal Perspective' (2000) 9 EC Tax Review 90

Schön W, 'Tax Competition in Europe – General Report', Tax Competition in Europe (IBFD 2003)

Schön W, 'Attribution of Profits to PEs and the OECD 2006 Report' (2007) 46 Tax Notes International 1059

Schön W, 'Group Taxation and The CCCTB' (2007) 48 Tax Notes International 1063

Schön W, 'International Tax Coordination for a Second-Best World (Part I)' (2009) 1 World Tax Journal 67

Schön W, 'International Tax Coordination for a Second-Best World (Part II)' (2010) 2 World Tax Journal 65

Schön W, 'International Tax Coordination for a Second-Best World (Part III)' (2010) 2 World Tax Journal 227

Schön W, 'Neutrality and Territoriality - Competing or Converging Concepts in European Tax Law' (2015) 69 Bulletin for International Taxation (IBFD-Bulletin) 271

Schön W, 'Tax Legislation and the Notion of Fiscal Aid: A Review of 5 Years of European Jurisprudence', in *State Aid Law and Business Taxation* (W Schön, I Richelle & E Traversa (eds), Springer 2016)

Schön W, 'Ten Questions about Why and How to Tax the Digitalized Economy' (2018) 72 Bulletin for International Taxation (IBFD-Bulletin) 278

Schön W, 'Value Creation, the Benefit Principle and Efficiency-Related Allocation of Taxing Rights', *EATLP International Tax Series* (2021) https://www.ssrn.com/abstract=3849322

Schön W & European Association of Tax Law Professors (eds), *Tax Competition in Europe* (IBFD Publications 2003)

Schott MC, 'Inconsistency with the Internal Consistency Test' (2016) 77 Lancaster Law Review 947

Schoueri LE, 'Arm's Length: Beyond the Guidelines of the OECD' (2015) 69 Bulletin for International Taxation 690

Schoueri LE & Galdino G, 'Single Taxation as a Policy Goal: Controversial Meaning, Lack of Justification and Unfeasibility', in *Single Taxation?* (J Wheeler (ed.), IBFD 2018)

Schoukens P & Barrio A, 'The Changing Concept of Work: When Does Typical Work Become Atypical?' (2017) 8 European Labour Law Journal 306

Schratzenstaller M & others, 'EU Taxes as Genuine Own Resource to Finance the EU Budget - Pros, Cons and Sustainability-Oriented Criteria to Evaluate Potential Tax Candidates' (2016) WIFO Studies

Schreiber U, 'The Taxation of Hidden Reserves under the Common Consolidated Corporate Tax Base' (2009) 49 European Taxation 84

Schreiber U, 'Sales-Based Apportionment of Profits' (2018) 72 Bulletin for International Taxation 1

Schreiber U & Fell LM, 'International Profit Allocation, Intangibles and Sales-Based Transactional Profit Split' (2017) 9 World Tax Journal 1

Schubert W, 'A Note on Eliminating the Corporate Income Tax' (2017) 17 Journal of Accounting and Finance

Schumacher SR, 'Adoption of MTC Regulations Relating to Apportioning Income of Financial Institutions' (1999) 18 Journal of State Taxation 45

Schütze R, *From Dual to Cooperative Federalism* (Oxford University Press 2009)

Screpante M, 'Rethinking the Arm's Length Principle and Its Impact on the IP Licence Model after OECD/G20 BEPS Actions 8-10: Nothing Changed But the Change?' (2019) 11 World Tax Journal 557

Screpante MS, 'The Arm's Length Principle Evolves Towards a "Value Creation Functional (Ie DEMPE) Formula Standard": A Barrier or a Gateway to Locational Business Planning?' (2020) 48 Intertax 861

Seiler M, *GAARs and Judicial Anti-Avoidance in Germany, the UK and the EU: Schriftenreihe IStR Band 98* (Linde Verlag GmbH 2016)

Šemeta A, 'EU Commissioner for Taxation and Customs Union, Audit and Anti-Fraud "Competitive Tax Policy and Tax Competition in the EU" 2nd Taxation Forum of Diario Economico/OTOC' (SPEECH/11/712 2011)

Senyk M, *The Origin and Destination Principles as Alternative Approaches Towards VAT Allocation: Analysis in the WTO, the OECD and the EU Legal Frameworks* (IBFD 2020)

Serether JM, Eberle MP & Colavito Jr ML, 'Can You Take This to the Bank? State Taxation of Financial Institutions' (2011) 59 State Tax Notes 717

Shadewald MS, 'More States Adopt Market-Based Rule for Sourcing Sales of Services' (2013) 32 Journal of State Taxation 5

Shaheen F, 'International Tax Neutrality: Reconsiderations' (2007) 27 Virginia Tax Review 203

Shaheen F, 'International Tax Neutrality: Revisited' (2010) 64 Tax Law Review 131

Shakespeare W, Mowat BA & Werstine P, *Twelfth Night, or, What You Will* (Simon & Schuster 2019)

Shakow DJ, 'The Taxation of Cloud Computing and Digital Content', in *Research Handbook on Electronic Commerce Law* (JA Rothchild (ed.), Edward Elgar 2016)

Shannon III HA, 'Comparison of the OECD and US Model Treaties for the Avoidance of Double Taxation' (1986) 12 International Tax Journal 265

Shanske D, 'A New Theory of the State Corporate Income Tax: The State Corporate Income Tax as Retail Sales Tax Complement' (2012) 66 Tax Law Review 305

Shaviro D, 'The Two Faces of the Single Tax Principle' (2015) SSRN Electronic Journal http://www.ssrn.com/abstract=2664680 (accessed 14 November 2019)

Shaviro DN, *Fixing U.S. International Taxation* (Oxford University Press 2014)

Shelton N, *Interpretation and Application of Tax Treaties* (LexisNexis UK 2004)

Shevlin T & others, 'Who Bears the Costs of the Corporate Income Tax? Evidence from State Tax Changes and Accounting Data', 2018, http://hdl.handle.net/10125/59340

Shipley DJ, 'The Limits of Fair Apportionment: How Fair Is Fair Enough?', *The State and Local Tax Lawyer. Symposium Edition* (American Bar Association 2007)

Shipley DJ & Guariglia MA, 'NaCl-State and Local Taxes-Extraterritorial Taxation 101' (2009) 87 Tax Magazine 35

Shoenfeld S, 'Much Ado about Nexus: The States Struggle to Impose Sales Tax Obligations on Out-of-State Sellers Engaged in E-Commerce' (2013) 24 Fordham Intellectual Property, Media and Entertainment Law Journal 260

Short AL, 'Workers Misclassified as Independent Contractors Were Entitled to Retirement Benefits: *Vizcaino v. Microsoft Corp.*' (1998) 51 Tax Lawyer 405

Shoven JB, 'The Incidence and Efficiency Effects of Taxes on Income from Capital' (1976) 84 Journal of Political Economy 1261

Sicilian S & Huddleston J, 'The US States' Experience with Formulary Apportionment', in RE Krever & F Vaillancourt (eds), *The Allocation of Multinational Business Income: Reassessing the Formulary Apportionment Option* (Kluwer Law International 2020)

Sieradzka M, '*Asociación Profesional Elite Taxi vs Uber Systems Spain SL*: Differences Between the Internet Platform and the Transport Service' (2020) 11 Journal of European Competition Law & Practice 263

Sikka P & Willmott H, 'The Dark Side of Transfer Pricing: Its Role in Tax Avoidance and Wealth Retentiveness' (2010) 21 Critical Perspectives on Accounting 342

Simonis P, 'Commentary to the Common Consolidated Corporate Tax Base' (2011) 4(6) Highlights and Insights on European Taxation

Singh KD, 'Tax Implications of Brexit – The Road Ahead' (2017) 5 Kathmandu School of Law Review 39

Skavlem JP & Schmitz AR, 'State & Local Tax Due Diligence: A Practical Approach' (2015) 34 Journal of State Taxation 17

Smart M & Vaillancourt F, 'Formulary Apportionment in Canada and Taxation of Corporate Income in 2019: Current Practice, Origins and Evaluation', in *The Allocation of Multinational Business Income: Reassessing the Formulary Apportionment Option* (RE Krever & F Vaillancourt (eds), Kluwer Law International 2020)

Smit DS, *Freedom of Investment Between EU and Non-EU Member States and Its Impact on Corporate Income Tax Systems Within the European Union* (Tilburg University 2011)

Smit DS, *EU Freedoms, Non-EU Countries and Company Taxation* (Kluwer Law International 2012)

Smit DS, *International Income Allocation under EU Tax Law: Tinker, Tailor, Soldier, Sailor* (Kluwer Law International 2016)

Smit DS, 'The Arm's Length Standard: A Blind Spot in the CC(C)TB Proposal', in *The EU Common Consolidated Corporate Tax Base Critical Analysis* (D Weber & J van de Streek (eds), Kluwer Law International 2018)

Smith A, *An Inquiry into the Nature and Causes of the Wealth of Nations*, Vol. 1 (Librito Mondi 1791)

Smith DL & Davis MK, 'No Hedging on Gross Receipts Inclusion in Sales Factor' (2009) Tax Analysts 415

Smith J, 'UDITPA Turns 50' (2006) 25 Journal of State Taxation 13

Smith MB, *The Taxing Road to Sustainable Growth: Resource Productivity and Corporate Taxation* (IBFD 2013)

Snape J, *The Political Economy of Corporation Tax: Theory, Values and Law Reform* (Hart 2011)

Sokatch J, 'Transfer-Pricing with Software Allows for Effective Circumvention of Subpart F Income: Google's "Sandwich" Costs Taxpayers Millions' (2011) The International Lawyer 725

Sonnier BM & Colon R, 'The Shift Toward Market-Based Sourcing for Multistate Apportionment of Income from Services' (2015) 34 Journal of State Taxation 21

Sonnier BM & Colon R, 'The Apportionment of Income from Licensing of Intangibles under MTC's Proposed Market-Based Sourcing Regulations' (2016) 35 Journal of State Taxation 23

Sørensen PB, 'Company Tax Reform in the European Union' (2004) 11 International Tax and Public Finance 91

Sørensen PB, 'Measuring the Deadweight Loss from Taxation in a Small Open Economy: A General Method with an Application to Sweden' (2014) 117 Journal of Public Economics 115

Spencer D, 'Transfer Pricing: Formulary Apportionment Is Not a Panacea, Part 1' (2014) Journal of International Taxation

Spengel C &others, 'A Common Corporate Tax Base for Europe: An Impact Assessment of the Draft Council Directive on a CC (C) TB' (2012) 4 World Tax Journal

Spengel C &others, *The Impact of the CCTB on the Effective Tax Burden of Corporations: Results from the Tax Analyzer Model-Final Report*, Vol. 75 (Publications Office of the European Union 2019)

Spengel C & Zöllkau Y (eds), *Common Corporate Tax Base (CC(C)TB) and Determination of Taxable Income: An International Comparison* (Springer 2012)

Spiegel B & others, 'The Relationship Between Social Security Coordination and Taxation Law' (2014) FreSsco, Brussels: European Commission

Sprague R, 'Using the ABC Test to Classify Workers: End of the Platform-Based Business Model or Status Quo Ante?' (2019) 11 William & Mary Business Law Review 733

Stein A, 'FICA Taxation of Post-Employment Benefits: A Statutory Puzzle and Socio-political Conundrum' (2013) 91 Washington University Law Review 203

Stelter JD, '"The IRS" Classification Settlement Program: Is It an Adequate Tool to Relieve Taxpayer Burden for Small Businesses That Have Misclassified Workers as Independent Contractors' (2008) 56 Cleveland State Law Review 451

Stewart M, 'The Tax State, Benefit and Legitimacy' (2015) TTPI – Working Paper 1/2015

Stöwhase S, 'Tax-Rate Differentials and Sector-Specific Foreign Direct Investment: Empirical Evidence from the EU' (2005) 61 FinanzArchiv: Public Finance Analysis 535

Streek J van de, 'The CCCTB Concept of Consolidation and the Rules on Entering a Group' (2012) 40 Intertax 24

Streek J van de, 'Some Introductory Remarks on the Re-Launched CCTB/CCCTB Proposals from a Policy Perspective', in *The EU Common Consolidated Corporate Tax Base: Critical Analysis* (DM Weber & J van de Streek (eds), Kluwer Law International 2018)

Sumerwell RF, 'The Property Factor' (1954) 7 Tax Executive 30

Sutton G, Yesnowitz JC & Jones C, 'Breaking State and Local Developments: 2010 Nexus Developments' (2010) 29 Journal of State Taxation 37

Swain JA, 'State Sales and Use Tax Jurisdiction: An Economic Nexus Standard for the Twenty-First Century' (2003) 38 Georgia Law Review 343

Swain JA, 'Reforming the State Corporate Income Tax: A Market State Approach to the Sourcing of Service Receipts' (2008) 83 Tulane Law Review 285

Swain JA, 'Misalignment of Substantive and Enforcement Tax Jurisdiction in a Mobile Economy: Causes and Strategies for Realignment' (2010) 63 National Tax Journal 4

Swain JA & Hellerstein W, 'The Political Economy of the Streamlined Sales and Use Tax Agreement' (2005) 58 National Tax Journal 605

Swain JA & Hellerstein W, 'State Jurisdiction to Tax Nowhere Activity' (2013) 33 Virginia Tax Review 209

Swenson C, 'On the Effectiveness of Single Sales Factors for State Taxation' (2011) University of Southern California Working Paper

Szudoczky R, 'Is the CCCTB Proposal in Line with the Principle of Subsidiarity? Negative Opinions Submitted by National Parliaments in the "Yellow Card Procedure"', in *CCCTB: Selected Issues* (D Weber (ed.), Kluwer Law International 2012)

Szudoczky R, 'Convergence of the Analysis of National Tax Measures under the EU State Aid Rules and the Fundamental Freedoms' (2016) 15 European State Aid Law Quarterly 357

Talus K, *EU Energy Law and Policy: A Critical Account* (Oxford University Press 2013)

Tatarowicz PM, 'A History of the State and Local Taxes Committee and Its Most Recent Quarter Century of Work' (2014) 68 Tax Lawyer 595

Tax Analysts & Herzfeld M (eds), *U.S. State Tax Considerations for International Tax Reform* (Tax Analysts 2014)

TAXATION ABASO, 'Comments on the Multistate Tax Commission's Proposed Draft Amendments to Its Model General Allocation and Apportionment Regulations' (2016) Tax Lawyer 769

Terra B & Kajus J, *Introduction to European VAT (Recast), Commentaries on European VAT Directives* (Online Books IBFD 2019)

Terra BJM & Kajus J, *A Guide to the European VAT Directives* (IBFD 2015)

Terra BJM & Kajus J, *A Guide to the European VAT Directives: Volumes 1&2* (IBFD 2019)

Thiel S van, Valente P & Raventós Calvo S (eds), *CFE Tax Advisors Europe: 60th Anniversary – Liber Amicorum* (IBFD 2019)

Thimmesch AB, 'The Illusory Promise of Economic Nexus' (2012) 13 Florida Tax Review 157

Thörnquist A, 'False Self-Employment and Other Precarious Forms of Employment in the "Grey Area" of the Labour Market' (2015) 31 International Journal of Comparative Labour Law and Industrial Relations

Tiebout CM, 'A Pure Theory of Local Expenditures' (1956) 64 Journal of Political Economy 416

Ting A, 'Multilateral Formulary Apportionment Model-A Reality Check', (2010) 25(1) *Australian Tax Forum*

Ting A, *The Taxation of Corporate Groups under Consolidation: An International Comparison* (Cambridge University Press 2013)

Ting A, 'ITax-Apple's International Tax Structure and the Double Non-Taxation Issue' (2014) British Tax Review 40

Ting A, 'Intangibles and the Transfer Pricing Reconstruction Rules: A Case Study of Amazon' (2020) British Tax Review 302

Tiraboschi M & Del Conte M, 'Employment Contract: Disputes on Definition in the Changing Italian Labour Law' (JILPT Report 2004)

Titus A, 'The Promise of Non-Arm's Length Practices: Is the Destination-Based Cash Flow Tax or Unitary Taxation the Panacea of Which Developing Countries Are in Search?', in *Taxation, International Cooperation and the 2030 Sustainable Development Agenda* (IJM Valderrama, D Lesage & W Lips (eds) Springer 2021)

Todolí-Signes A, 'The End of the Subordinate Worker?: Collaborative Economy, on-Demand Economy, Gig Economy, and the Crowdworkers' Need for Protection' (2017) 33(2) International Journal of Comparative Labour Law & Industrial Relations

Todolí-Signes A, 'The "Gig Economy": Employee, Self-Employed or the Need for a Special Employment Regulation?' (2017) 23 Transfer: European Review of Labour and Research 193

Todolí-Signes A, 'Workers, the Self-Employed and TRADEs: Conceptualisation and Collective Rights in Spain' (2019) 10(3) European Labour Law Journal

Tomassetti J, 'From Hierarchies to Markets: FedEx Drivers and the Work Contract as Institutional Marker' (2015) 19 Lewis & Clark Law Review 1083

Tørsløv TR, Wier LS & Zucman G, 'The Missing Profits of Nations' (2018) National Bureau of Economic Research Working Papers No. 24701

Torvik O, *Transfer Pricing and Intangibles: US and OECD Arm's Length Distribution of Operation Profits from IP Value Chains* (IBFD 2018)

Traversa E, 'Interest Deductibility and the BEPS Action Plan: Nihil Novi Sub Sole?' (2013) 2013(5) British Tax Review 607

Traversa E, 'Commentary on Chapter 13: The Magic Triangle of Sovereignty, Cooperation and Transparency in International Taxation' in *European Tax Integration: Law, Policy and Politics* (P Pistone (ed.), IBFD 2018)

Traversa E & Flamini A, 'Fighting Harmful Tax Competition Through EU State Aid Law' (2015) 14 European State Aid Law Quarterly 323

Trotter R, 'United Parcel Service-Federal Express-National Labor Relations Act-Railway Labor Act-Union Employee-Independent Contractor-FedEx-Current Developments of the Legal Status of FedEx Workers- and the Trend of Employers Classifying Employees as Independent Contractors' (2013) 13 American Journal of Management 67

Tryfonidou A, 'Further Steps on the Road to Convergence among the Market Freedoms' (2010) 35 European Law Review 36

Ture N, 'Taxing Foreign Source Income' (1975) 37 US Taxation of American Business Abroad

Unnikrishnan A & Nagappan M, 'Virtual Permanent Establishments: Indian Law and Practice' (2018) 46 Intertax 520

Valente P, 'Digital Revolution-Tax Revolution' (2018) 72 Bulletin for International Taxation

Van Apeldoorn B, Drahokoupil J & Horn L, *Contradictions and Limits of Neoliberal European Governance from Lisbon to Lisbon* (Palgrave Macmillan 2009)

Van Apeldoorn L, 'BEPS, Tax Sovereignty and Global Justice' (2018) 21 Critical Review of International Social and Political Philosophy 478

Van Apeldoorn L, 'A Sceptic's Guide to Justice in International Tax Policy' (2019) 32 Canadian Journal of Law & Jurisprudence 499

Van Apeldoorn L, 'Exploitation, International Taxation, and Global Justice' (2019) 77 Review of Social Economy 163

Van den Hurk H, 'The Common Consolidated Corporate Tax Base: A Desirable Alternative to a Flat EU Corporate Income Tax?' (2011) 4 Bulletin for International Fiscal Documentation 260

van der Ploeg F, 'Do Social Policies Harm Employment and Growth? Second-Best Effects of Taxes and Benefits on Employment', in *Tax Policy and Labor Market Performance* (J Agell & PB Sørensen (eds) MIT Press 2006)

Van Es M, *Stereotypes and Self-Representations of Women with a Muslim Background: The Stigma of Being Oppressed* (Palgrave Macmillan 2016)

Van Peijpe T, 'EU Limits for the Personal Scope of Employment Law' (2012) 3 European Labour Law Journal 35

Vandenbroucke F, 'Why We Need a European Social Union' (2013) 52 Reflets et perspectives de la vie économique 97

Vandenbroucke F, Barnard C & Baere G de (eds), *A European Social Union after the Crisis* (Cambridge University Press 2017)

Vandenbroucke F, 'The Idea of a European Social Union: A Normative Introduction' *A European Social Union after the Crisis* (Cambridge University Press 2017)

Vanistendael F, 'Comments on the Ruding Committee Report' (1992) 1 EC Tax Review 3

Vanistendael F, 'The Ruding Committee Report: A Personal View' (1992) 13 Fiscal Studies 85

Vanistendael F, 'The Role of the European Court of Justice as the Supreme Judge in Tax Cases' (1996) 5 EC Tax Review 114

Vanistendael F, 'Halifax and Cadbury Schweppes: One Single European Theory of Abuse in Tax Law?' (2006) 15 EC Tax Review 192

Vanistendael F, 'Single Taxation in a Single Market?', in *Single Taxation?* (J Wheeler (ed.), IBFD 2018)

Vann RJ, 'Reflections on Business Profits and the Arm's-Length Principle', in *The Taxation of Business Profits under Tax Treaties* (B Arnold, J Sasseville & EM Zolt (eds), Canadian Tax Foundation 2003)

Vann RJ, 'Policy Forum: The Policy Underpinnings of the BEPS Project-Preserving the International Corporate Income Tax?' (2014) 62 Canadian Tax Journal 433

Vann RJ, 'Current Trends in Balancing Residence and Source Taxation', in *BRICS and the Emergence of International Tax Coordination* (Y Brauner & P Pistone (eds), IBFD 2015)

Varyani N, 'Taxing Electronic Commerce: The Efforts of Sales and Use Tax to Evolve with Technology' (2014) 39 Oklahoma City University Law Review 151

Varyani N, 'A Contract among States: Capturing Income of the World's Multijurisdictional Taxpayers' (2016) 1 University of Bologna Law Review 219
Vega A, 'International Governance Through Soft Law: The Case of the OECD Transfer Pricing Guidelines' (2012) Max Planck Institute for Tax Law and Public Finance Working Paper No. 2012-05
Vella J, 'Value Creation and the Allocation of Profits under a Formulary Apportionment System', in *The Allocation of Multinational Business Income: Reassessing the Formulary Apportionment Option* (RE Krever & F Vaillancourt (eds), Kluwer Law International 2020)
Verbeke D, 'Analysis of the Main Systems of Social Security Contribution Collection in the European Union Based on the Experience of 12 Member States' (European Commission DG EMPL 2012)
Verhulp E, 'The Notion of "Employee" in EU-Law and National Laws' (The European Centre of Expertise (ECE) in the field of labour law, employment and labour market policies 2017)
Verlinden I, Bakker A & International Bureau of Fiscal Documentation (eds), *Mastering the IP Life Cycle from a Legal, Tax and Accounting Perspective* (IBFD 2018)
Verlinden I, De Baets S & Parmessar V, 'Grappling with DEMPEs in the Trenches: Trying to Give It the Meaning It Deserves' (2019) 47 Intertax 1042
Vermeulen H & Blaauw MFA, 'The Tax Treatment of Directly Held Real Estate under the Proposed CCCTB Directive' (2011) 51 European Taxation
Vlasceanu R, 'Intellectual Property Structuring in the Context of the OECD BEPS Action Plan', in M Cotrut (ed.), *International Tax Structures in the BEPS Era: An Analysis of Anti-Abuse Measures* (IBFD 2015)
Vlasceanu R, 'Does Location Matter? Early-Stage Planning and Migration Strategies', in *Mastering the IP Life Cycle from a Legal, Tax and Accounting Perspective* (I Verlinden & A Bakker (eds), IBFD 2018)
Vliegenthart A & Overbeek H, 'Corporate Tax Reform in Neoliberal Europe: Central and Eastern Europe as a Template for Deepening the Neoliberal European Integration Project?', in *Contradictions and Limits of Neoliberal European Governance From Lisbon to Lisbon* (B Van Apeldoorn, J Drahokoupil & L Horn (eds), Springer 2009)
Vogel K, 'Worldwide vs. Source Taxation of Income: A Review and Re-Evaluation of Arguments (Part I)' (1988) 16 Intertax 216
Vogel K, 'Worldwide vs. Source Taxation of Income: A Review and Re-Evaluation of Arguments (Part II)' (1988) 16 Intertax 310
Vogel K, 'Worldwide vs. Source Taxation of Income: A Review and Re-Evaluation of Arguments (Part III)' (1988) 16 Intertax 393
Vogel K, 'Which Method Should the European Community Adopt for the Avoidance of Double Taxation?' (2002) 56 Bulletin for International Fiscal Documentation 4
Vogel K & Brands J, *Taxation of Cross-Border Income, Harmonization, and Tax Neutrality under European Community Law: An Institutional Approach*, Vol. 2 (Kluwer Law International 1994)
Voje J, 'Milestone Transfer Pricing Cases on IP', in *Mastering the IP Life Cycle from a Legal, Tax and Accounting Perspective* (I Verlinden & A Bakker (eds), IBFD 2018)

Waas B & Voss GH van (eds), *Restatement of Labour Law in Europe Vol I: The Concept of Employee* (Hart 2017)
Wagener A, 'Evolutionary Tax Competition with Formulary Apportionment' (2017) WU International Taxation Research Paper Series
Ward BT & Sipior JC, 'To Tax or Not to Tax E-Commerce: A United States Perspective' (2004) 5 Journal of Electronic Commerce Research 172
Wattel PJ, 'Red Herrings in Direct Tax Cases before the ECJ' (2004) 31 Legal Issues of Economic Integration 81
Wattel PJ, 'Stateless Income, State Aid and the (Which?) Arm's Length Principle' (2016) 44 Intertax
Weatherill S, *The Internal Market as a Legal Concept* (Oxford University Press 2016)
Weber D, 'Proposal for a Council Directive on a Common Consolidated Corporate Tax Base (CCCTB)–Comments' (2011) 4 Highlights and Insights on European Taxation 5
Weber D, 'Abuse of Law in European Tax Law: An Overview and Some Recent Trends in the Direct and Indirect Tax Case Law of the ECJ-Part 1' (2013) 53 European Taxation 251
Weber D, 'Abuse of Law in European Tax Law: An Overview and Some Recent Trends in the Direct and Indirect Tax Case Law of the ECJ-Part 2' (2013) 53 European Taxation 313
Weber D & Amsterdam Centre for Tax Law (eds), *CCCTB: Selected Issues* (Kluwer Law International 2012)
Weber DM & Streek J van de (eds), *The EU Common Consolidated Corporate Tax Base: Critical Analysis* (Kluwer Law International 2018)
Weerepas M, 'Tax or Social Security Contribution, a World of Difference?' (2018) 1 Nordic Tax Journal 18
Weiner J, 'Formulary Apportionment and the Future of Company Taxation in the European Union: Company Taxation and the Internal Market', *CESifo Forum* (München: ifo Institut für Wirtschaftsforschung an der Universität München 2002)
Weiner J, 'The CCCTB, Brexit, and Unitary Taxation', *Proceedings. Annual Conference on Taxation and Minutes of the Annual Meeting of the National Tax Association* Vol. 109 (National Tax Association 2016)
Weiner JM, 'Using the Experience in the US States to Evaluate Issues in Implementing Formula Apportionment at the International Level' (1999) 83 OTA Paper
Weiner JM, *Company Tax Reform in the European Union: Guidance from the United States and Canada on Implementing Formulary Apportionment in the EU* (Springer 2005)
Weiner JM, 'Formulary Apportionment and Group Taxation in the European Union: Insights from the United States and Canada' (Directorate General Taxation and Customs Union, European Commission 2005)
Weiner JM, 'Practical Aspects of Implementing Formulary Apportionment in the European Union' (2006) 8 Florida Tax Review 629
Weiner JM, 'Formula One – The Race to Find a Common Formula to Apportion the EU Tax Base' (2008) 17 EC Tax Review 100

Weiner JM, 'An Economist's View of Income Allocation under the Arm's Length Standard and Under Formulary Apportionment', *The State and Local Tax Lawyer. Symposium Edition* (American Bar Association 2009)

Weiner JM, 'CCCTB and Formulary Apportionment: The European Commission Finds the Right Formula', in *CCCTB: Selected Issues* (D Weber (eds), Kluwer Law International 2012)

Weiner JM, 'The Dream Is Alive: EU Tax Policy with a Common Consolidated Corporate Tax Base and Formulary Apportionment', in *The Allocation of Multinational Business Income: Reassessing the Formulary Apportionment Option* (1st ed., Kluwer Law International 2020)

Weinzierl M, 'Revisiting the Classical View of Benefit-Based Taxation' (2018) 128 Economic Journal F37

Weisbach DA, 'The Use of Neutralities in International Tax Policy' (2015) 68 National Tax Journal 635

Wells B & Lowell C, 'Tax Base Erosion and Homeless Income: Collection at Source Is the Linchpin' (2011) 65 Tax Law Review 535

Wells B & Lowell CH, 'Income Tax Treaty in the 21st Century: Residence vs. Source' (2013) 5 Columbia Journal of Tax Law 1

Wheeler J (ed.), *Single Taxation?* (IBFD 2018)

White RM, 'The Constitutionality of the Multistate Tax Compact' (1976) 29 Vanderbilt Law Review 453

Wijnen W & de Goede J, 'The UN Model in Practice 1997-2013' (2014) 68(3) IBFD Bulletin for International Taxation

Wilkie JA, 'Income Apportionment of Unitary Public Utility Corporations' (1959) 15 Tax Law Review 467

Wilkie JA, 'A Theoretical Basis for the Allocation of Multi-State Income by the Unitary Businesses under State Corporate Net Income Taxes' (1960) 13 Tax Executive 157

Wilkie JS, 'Reflecting on the "Arm's Length Principle": What Is the "Principle"? Where Next?', in *Fundamentals of International Transfer Pricing in Law and Economics* (W Schön & KA Konrad (eds), Springer 2012)

Wilkie JS, 'The Definition and Ownership of Intangibles: Inside the Box? Outside the Box? What Is the Box?' (2012) 4(3) World Tax Journal

Wilkie JS, 'Intangibles and Location Benefits (Customer Base)' (2014) 68(6/7) IBFD Bulletin for International Taxation

Wilkie JS, 'Transfer Pricing Aspects of Intangibles: The License Model', in *Transfer Pricing in a Post-BEPS World* (M Lang & A Storck (eds), Kluwer Law International 2016)

Wilson MC, 'Apportionment Apoplexy: Throwback, Throwout, or Just Throw up Your Hands' (2005) 57 Tax Executive 357

Winters K & others, 'Concepts: IP Rights from a Legal, Accounting and Tax Point of View', in *Mastering the IP Life Cycle from a Legal, Tax and Accounting Perspective* (I Verlinden & A Bakker (eds), IBFD 2018)

WIPO, 'World Intellectual Property Report 2017: Intangible Capital in Global Value Chains' (World Intellectual Property Organization 2017)

Wood RW, 'Can Franchisees Be Recast as Employees?' (2011) 130 Tax Notes

Wood RW & Karachale CA, 'Home Workers and the Debate Over "Who's a Statutory Employee" under the Internal Revenue Code' (2010) 2010(4) Business Law News, the California Lawyers Association

World Trade Organization (ed.), *Trade in Natural Resources* (WTO 2010)

Wright DR & others, 'The BEPS Action 8 Final Report: Comments from Economists' (2016) 23 International Transfer Pricing Journal 1

Zalasinski A, 'Case-Law-Based Anti-Avoidance Measures in Conflict with Proportionality Test: Comment on the ECJ Decision in Kofoed' (2007) 47 European Taxation 571

Zalasinski A, 'Proportionality of Anti-Avoidance and Anti-Abuse Measures in the ECJ's Direct Tax Case Law' (2007) 35 Intertax 310

Zalasinski A, 'Some Basic Aspects of the Concept of Abuse in the Tax Case Law of the European Court of Justice' (2008) 36 Intertax 156

Zalasinski A, 'Limits of the EC Concept of Direct Tax Restriction on Free Movement Rights, the Principles of Equality and Ability to Pay, and Interstate Fiscal Equity' (2009) 37 Intertax 282

Zalasinski A, '35 Years of ECJ Direct Tax Case Law: An Historical Overview on the Occasion of the 60th Anniversary of European Taxation' (2021) 61 European Taxation

Zee HH, 'A VAT Voucher System for Origin-Based Taxation' (2011) 20 EC Tax Review 75

Zelinsky EA, 'Rethinking Tax Nexus and Apportionment: Voice, Exit, and the Dormant Commerce Clause' (2008) 28 Virginia Tax Review 1

Zern MH, 'Employee or Independent Contractor? Classification by the Internal Revenue Service' (2006) 12 North East Journal of Legal Studies 1

Zhan JJ, 'An Outlook on Intangible Assets and Transfer Pricing in China' (2018) 25 Revenue Law Journal 6752

Zimmer F, 'In Defence of General Anti-Avoidance Rules' (2019) 73 Bulletin for International Taxation 4

Zinn PM, 'The Requirements of "Substantial Nexus" and "Fairly Related" Under the Commerce Clause', *The State and Local Tax Lawyer. Symposium Edition* (American Bar Association 2007)

Table of Cases

European Union

US Federal Case Law

US State Case Law

Alaska

California

Florida

Idaho

Illinois

Kentucky

Maryland

Mississipi

Montana

New Mexico

Court of Appeals of New Mexico: *Kmart Properties, Inc. v. Taxation and Revenue Department of the State of New Mexico,* 139 N.M. 177, 131 P.3d 27 (Ct App 2001), 401

New York

Appellate Division of the Supreme Court of New York, Third Department: *Sherwin-Williams Co. v. State,* 12 A.D.3d 112, 784 N.Y.S.2d 178 (N.Y. App. Div. 2004), 161

Court of Appeals of the State of New York: *Disney Enters. v. Tax Appeals,* 10 N.Y.3d 392, 2008 N.Y. Slip Op. 2677, 859 N.Y.S.2d 87, 888 N.E.2d 1029 (N.Y. 2008), 178

Ohio

Supreme Court of Ohio: *Lancaster Colony Corp. v. Limbach,* 37 Ohio St. 3d 198, 524 N.E.2d 1389 (Ohio 1988), 402

Ohio Court of Appeals: *O.H. Materials, Co. v. Limbach,* No. 5-89-2 (Ohio Ct. App. 26 November 1990), 267

Oregon

Oregon Supreme Court: *Twentieth Century-Fox Film Corp. v. Department of Revenue,* 299 Or. 220, 700 P2d 1035 (1985), 402

Oregon Supreme Court: *Crocker Equipment Leasing, Inc. v. Department of Revenue,* 838 P.2d 552 (1992), 347

Tennessee

Court of Appeals of Tennessee: *Bellsouth Advertising & Publishing. Company v. Chumley,* 308 S.W.3d 350 (Tenn. Ct. App. 2009), 403

Utah

Utah Supreme Court of Utah: *Kennecott Copper Corp. v. State Tax Comm'n,* 27 Utah 2d 119, 493 P2d 632 (1972), appeal dismissed, 409 US 973, 93 S. Ct. 323 (1972), 372, 403

Table of Legislation and Proposals

European Union

Regulation

Regulation (EC) No. 883/2004 of the European Parliament and of the Council of 29 April 2004 on the coordination of social security systems, OJ L 166, 30.4.2004, 249

Directives

Directive 96/71/EC of the European Parliament and of the Council of 16 December 1996 concerning the posting of workers in the framework of the provision of services, OJ L 18, 21.1.1997, 233

Council Directive 80/987/EEC of 20 October 1980 on the approximation of the laws of the Member States relating to the protection of employees in the event of the insolvency of their employer, OJ L 283, 28.10.1980.

Council Directive 2001/23/EC of 12 March 2001 on the approximation of the laws of the Member States relating to the safeguarding of employees' rights in the event of transfers of undertakings, businesses or parts of undertakings or businesses, OJ L 82, 22.3.2001

Council Directive 2009/133/EC of 19 October 2009 on the common system of taxation applicable to mergers, divisions, partial divisions, transfers of assets and exchanges of shares concerning companies of different Member States and to the transfer of the registered office of an SE or SCE between Member States (Codified version), OJ L 310, 25.11.2009.

Council Directive 2011/96/EU of 30 November 2011 on the common system of taxation applicable in the case of parent companies and subsidiaries of different Member States (recast), OJ L 345, 29.12.2011.

Proposals

Proposal for a Council Directive on a Common Consolidated Corporate Tax Base (CCCTB), COM/2011/0121 final - 2011/0058 (CNS)

US

Canada

Index

O

P

Q

R

S

EUCOTAX Series on European Taxation

(1) Peter HJ Essers, Guido JME de Bont & Eric CCM Kemmeren (eds), *The Compatibility of Anti-Abuse Provisions in Tax Treaties with EC Law*, 1998 (ISBN 90-411-9678-1).
(2) Gerard TK Meussen (ed.), *The Principle of Equality in European Taxation*, 1999 (ISBN 90-411-9693-5).
(3) Michael Lang (ed.), *Tax Treaty Interpretation*, 2001 (ISBN 90-411-9857-1).
(4) Pasquale Pistone, *The Impact of Community Law on Tax Treaties: Issues and Solutions*, 2002 (ISBN 90-411-9860-1).
(5) René Offermanns, *The Entrepreneurship Concept in a European Comparative Tax Law Perspective*, 2002 (ISBN 90-411-9887-3).
(6) Michael Lang & Mario Züger, *Settlement of Disputes in Tax Treaty Law*, 2002 (ISBN 90-411-9904-7).
(7) Carlo Pinto, *Tax Competition and EU Law*, 2003 (ISBN 90-411-9913-6).
(8) Michael Lang, Hans-Jörgen Aigner, Ulrich Scheuerle & Markus Stefaner, *CFC Legislation, Tax Treaties and EC Law*, 2004 (ISBN 90-411-2284-2).
(9) Mattias Dahlberg, *Direct Taxation in Relation to the Freedom of Establishment and the Free Movement of Capital*, 2005 (ISBN 90-411-2363-6).
(10) Michael Lang, Judith Herdin & Ines Hofbauer, *WTO and Direct Taxation*, 2005 (ISBN 90-411-2371-7).
(11) Dennis Weber, *Tax Avoidance and the EC Tray Freedoms: A Study of the Limitations under European Law for the Prevention of Tax Avoidance*, 2005 (ISBN 90-411-2402-0).
(12) Félix Alberto Vega Borrego, *Limitations on Benefits Clauses on Double Taxation Conventions*, 2005 (ISBN 90-411-2370-9).
(13) Michael Lang, Josef Schuch & Claus Staringer, *ECJ-Recent Developments in Direct Taxation*, 2006 (ISBN 90-411-2509-4).
(14) Reuven S. Avi-Yonah, James R. Hines Jr. & Michael Lang, *Comparative Fiscal Federalism. Comparing the European Court of Justice and the US Supreme Court's Tax Jurisprudence*, 2007 (ISBN 978-90-411-2552-1).
(15) Christiana HJI Panayi, *Double Taxation, Tax Treaties, Treaty-Shopping and the European Community*, 2007 (ISBN 978-90-411-2658-0).
(16) Dennis Weber, *The Influence of European Law on Direct Taxation: Recent and Future Developments*, 2007 (ISBN 978-90-411-2667-2).
(17) Michael Lang & Pasquale Pistone, *The EU and Third Countries: Direct Taxation*, 2007 (ISBN 978-90-411-2665-8).
(18) Oskar Henkow, *Financial Activities in European VAT: A Theoretical and Legal Research of the European VAT System and Preferred Treatment of Financial Activities*, 2007 (ISBN 978-90-411-2703-7).
(19) Michael Lang (ed.), *Tax Compliance Costs for Companies in an Enlarged European Community*, 2008 (ISBN 978-90-411-2666-5).

(20) Michael Lang (ed.), *Source versus Residence. Problems Arising from the Allocation of Taxing Rights in Tax Treaty Law and Possible Alternatives*, 2008 (ISBN 978-90-411-2763-1).
(21) Ioanna Mitroyanni, *Integration Approaches to Group Taxation in the European Internal Market*, 2008 (ISBN 978-90-411-2779-2).
(22) Rolf Eicke, *Tax Planning with Holding Companies. Repatriation of US Profits from Europe: Concepts, Strategies, Structures*, 2008 (ISBN978-90-411-2794-5).
(23) Peter Essers et al. (ed.), *The Influence of IAS/IFRS on the CCCTB, Tax Accounting, Disclosure and Corporate Law Accounting Concepts: 'A Clash of Cultures'*, 2008 (ISBN 978-90-411-2819-5).
(24) Tonny Schenk-Geers, *International Exchange of Information and the Protection of Taxpayers*, 2009 (ISBN 978-90-411-3142-3).
(25) Raymond Adema, *UCITS and Taxation: Towards Harmonization of the Taxation of UCITS*, 2009 (ISBN 978-90-411-2839-3).
(26) Michael Lang, Jianwen Liu & Gongliang Tang (eds), *Europe–China Tax Treaties*, 2010 (ISBN 978-90-411-3216-1).
(27) Michael Lang, Pasquale Pistone, Josef Schuch & Claus Staringer (eds), *Procedural Rules in Tax Law in the Context of European Union and Domestic Law*, 2010 (ISBN 978-90-411-3376-2).
(28) Sjaak J.J.M. Jansen, *Fiscal Sovereignty of the Member States in an Internal Market: Past and Future*, 2011 (ISBN 978-90-411-3403-5).
(29) Dennis Weber & Bruno da Silva, *From Marks & Spencer to X Holding: The Future of Cross-Border Group Taxation*, 2011 (ISBN 978-90-411-3399-1).
(30) Claus Bohn Jespersen, *Intermediation of Insurance and Financial Services in European VAT*, 2011 (ISBN 978-90-411-3732-6).
(31) Sabine Heidenbauer, *Charity Crossing Borders: The Fundamental Freedoms' Influence on Charity and Donor Taxation in Europe*, 2011 (ISBN 978-90-411-3813-2).
(32) Michael Lang, et al., *The Future of Indirect Taxation: Recent Trends in VAT and GST Systems around the World*, 2012 (ISBN 978-90-411-3797-5).
(33) Harm van den Broek, *Cross-Border Mergers within the EU: Proposals to Remove the Remaining Tax Obstacles*, 2012 (ISBN 978-90-411-3824-8).
(34) Michael Lang, et al. (eds), *Tax Treaty Case Law around the Globe – 2011*, 2012 (ISBN 978-90-411-3876-7).
(35) Dennis Weber (ed.), *CCCTB: Selected Issues*, 2012 (ISBN 978-90-411-3872-9).
(36) Daniël Smit, *EU Freedoms, Non-EU Countries and Company Taxation*, 2012 (ISBN 978-90-411-4041-8).
(37) Rita de la Feria, *VAT Exemptions: Consequences and Design Alternatives*, 2013 (ISBN 978-90-411-3276-5).
(38) Karin Simader, *Withholding Taxes and the Fundamental Freedoms*, 2013 (ISBN 978-90-411-4842-1).
(39) Madeleine Merkx, *Establishments in European VAT*, 2013 (ISBN 978-90-411-4554-3).
(40) Carla De Pietro, *Tax Treaty Override*, 2014 (ISBN 978-90-411-5406-4).

(41) G.K. Fibbe & A.J.A. Stevens (eds), *Hybrid Entities and the EU Direct Tax Directives*, 2015 (ISBN 978-90-411-5942-7).
(42) Gerard Staats, *Personal Pensions in the EU*, 2015 (ISBN 978-90-411-5953-3).
(43) Michael Lang & Ine Lejeune (eds), *VAT/GST in a Global Digital Economy*, 2015 (ISBN 978-90-411-5952-6).
(44) Massimo Basilavecchia, Lorenzo del Federico & Pietro Mastellone (eds), *Tax Implications of Environmental Disasters and Pollution*, 2015 (ISBN 978-90-411-5611-2).
(45) Cristina Trenta, *Rethinking EU VAT for P2P Distribution*, 2015 (ISBN 978-90-411-6137-6).
(46) Marie Lamensch, Edoardo Traversa & Servaas van Thiel (eds), *Value Added Tax and the Digital Economy: The 2015 EU Rules and Broader Issues*, 2016 (ISBN 978-90-411-6612-8).
(47) Raffaele Petruzzi, *Transfer Pricing Aspects of Intra-Group Financing*, 2016 (ISBN 978-90-411-6732-3).
(48) Mario Grandinetti (ed.), *Corporate Tax Base in the Light of the IAS/IFRS and EU Directive 2013/34: A Comparative Approach*, 2016 (ISBN 978-90-411-6745-3).
(49) Bruno da Silva, *The Impact of Tax Treaties and EU Law on Group Taxation Regimes*, 2016 (ISBN 978-90-411-6905-1).
(50) Michael Lang, Alfred Storck & Raffaele Petruzzi (eds), *Transfer Pricing in a Post-BEPS World*, 2016 (ISBN 978-90-411-6710-1).
(51) Marta Papis-Almansa, *Insurance in European VAT: Current and Preferred Treatment in the Light of the New Zealand and Australian GST Systems*, 2017 (ISBN 978-90-411-8360-6).
(52) Wolfgang Speckhahn, *Real Estate Investment Trusts In Europe: Europeanising Tax Regimes*, 2017 (ISBN 978-90-411-8360-6).
(53) Frank J.G. Nellen, *Information Asymmetries in EU VAT*, 2017 (ISBN 978-90-411-8837-3).
(54) Erik Ros, *EU Citizenship and Direct Taxation*, 2017 (ISBN 978-90-411-8584-6).
(55) Werner Haslehner, Georg Kofler & Alexander Rust (eds), *EU Tax Law and Policy in the 21st Century*, 2017 (ISBN 978-90-411-8815-1).
(56) Claudia Sanò, *National Legal Presumptions and European Tax Law*, 2018 (ISBN 978-90-411-6613-5).
(57) Christoph Marchgraber, *Double (Non-)Taxation and EU Law*, 2018 (ISBN 978-90-411-9410-7).
(58) Dennis Weber & Jan van de Streek (eds), *The EU Common Consolidated Corporate Tax Base: Critical Analysis*, 2018 (ISBN 978-90-411-9233-2).
(59) Werner Haslehner (ed.), *Investment Fund Taxation: Domestic Law, EU Law, and Double Taxation Treaties*, 2018 (ISBN 978-90-411-9669-9).
(60) Jérôme Monsenego, *Selectivity in State Aid Law and the Methods for the Allocation of the Corporate Tax Base*, 2018 (ISBN 978-90-411-9413-8).
(61) José Manuel Almudí Cid, Jorge A. Ferreras Gutiérrez & Pablo A. Hernández González-Barreda (eds), *Combating Tax Avoidance in the EU: Harmonization and Cooperation in Direct Taxation*, 2019 (ISBN 978-94-035-0154-3).

(62) Werner Haslehner, Georg Kofler & Alexander Rust (eds), *Time and Tax: Issues in International, EU, and Constitutional Law*, 2019 (ISBN 978-94-035-0354-7).

(63) Nathalie Wittock, *Sales Promotion Techniques and VAT in the EU*, 2019 (ISBN 978-94-035-0861-0).

(64) Carla De Pietro (ed.), *New Perspectives on Fiscal State Aid: Legitimacy and Effectiveness of Fiscal State Aid Control*, 2019 (ISBN 978-94-035-1415-4).

(65) Giorgio Beretta, *European VAT and the Sharing Economy*, 2019 (ISBN 978-94-035-1435-2).

(66) Claudio Cipollini, *Special Tax Zones and EU Law: Theory, Implementations, and Future Challenges*, 2020 (ISBN 978-94-035-1885-5).

(67) Gianluigi Bizioli, Mario Grandinetti, Leopoldo Parada, Giuseppe Vanz & Alessandro Vicini Ronchetti (eds), *Corporate Taxation, Group Debt Funding and Base Erosion: New Perspectives on the EU Anti-Tax Avoidance Directive*, 2020 (ISBN 978-94-035-1170-2).

(68) Ronald Hein & Ronald Russo (eds), *Co-operative Compliance and the OECD's International Compliance Assurance Programme*, 2020 (ISBN 978-94-035-1951-7).

(69) Jeffrey Owens & Jonathan Leigh Pemberton, *Cooperative Compliance: A Multi-stakeholder and Sustainable Approach to Taxation*, 2021 (ISBN 978-94-035-3193-9).

(70) Christina Pollak, *Platforms in EU VAT Law: A Legal Analysis of the Supply of Goods*, 2022 (ISBN 978-94-035-1026-2).

(71) Shu-Chien Chen, *Towards a Neutral Formulary Apportionment System in Regional Integration*, 2023 (ISBN 978-94-035-3276-9).

www.ingramcontent.com/pod-product-compliance
Ingram Content Group UK Ltd.
Pitfield, Milton Keynes, MK11 3LW, UK
UKHW020225290926
15470UKWH00001B/386

9 789403 532769